Role of AI in Translation and Interpretation

Mohammed H. Al Aqad
University of Malaya, Malaysia

IGI Global
Scientific Publishing
Publishing Tomorrow's Research Today

Vice President of Editorial Melissa Wagner
Director of Acquisitions Mikaela Felty
Director of Book Development Jocelynn Hessler
Production Manager Mike Brehm
Cover Design Phillip Shickler

Published in the United States of America by
IGI Global Scientific Publishing
701 East Chocolate Avenue
Hershey, PA, 17033, USA
Tel: 717-533-8845
Fax: 717-533-7115
Website: https://www.igi-global.com E-mail: cust@igi-global.com

Library of Congress Cataloging-in-Publication Data

LCCN: 2025001344 (CIP Data Pending)
ISBN13: 979-8-3373-0060-3
Isbn13Softcover: 979-8-3373-0061-0
EISBN13: 979-8-3373-0062-7
British Cataloguing in Publication Data
A Cataloguing in Publication record for this book is available from the British Library.

Table of Contents

Detailed Table of Contents

This chapter examines the quality of machine translated texts of various genres with a view to finding out to what extent these texts/genres have been accurately translated by neural machine translation systems and LLMs. The chapter also examines the potential use of these technologies in editing and revisions to enhance both quality and productivity. A theoretical and conceptual framework that is based on text-typology linguistic models and Mossop's parameters of revising and editing in translation is used to assess the quality of transactions produced by Google Translate (GT) as a neural-based machine translation system and ChatGPT as a large language model (LLM). In particular, the chapter investigates the GT and ChatGPT translations of argumentation within journalistic texts, exposition within both promotional and philosophical genres, and instrumental texts within the legal genre. This emphasis on diverse text types allows for a comprehensive evaluation of the translation performance of neural-based systems and LLMs across different communicative purposes and stylistic demands.

With the ongoing advancement of artificial intelligence technology, large-scale language models have emerged as a significant breakthrough in the realm of interpreting intelligence. This evolution presents the interpreting profession with unprecedented technological changes. A review of the relevant research indicates that the rise of large models has introduced both new opportunities and challenges for the development of AI-driven interpreting technology. Firstly, the language generation capabilities of these large models are highly advanced, enabling them to produce more accurate and natural interpretation and translation outcomes. Secondly, these models possess strong learning abilities, allowing them to continuously enhance the performance of interpretation systems through extensive data training. Additionally, their rapid response characteristics facilitate efficient interpretation services in real-time scenarios.

Traditional methodologies have become real-time solutions thanks to AI in interpretation, improving cross-language communication. Traditional approaches like consecutive and simultaneous interpretation relied on human skill, which was effective but slow and inaccurate. Neural machine translation (NMT) and deep learning have made context-aware, scalable, and efficient language processing possible. AI interpreters now capture complex language, idioms, and cultural subtleties, enhancing translation quality. Managing cultural sensitivity and algorithmic bias requires a hybrid approach that blends AI and human control. This integration preserves human communication while using AI's speed and efficiency. As AI evolves, its interpretation role will be crucial to global communication and understanding.

The development of machine translation (MT) has profoundly reshaped the translation industry, which reignites debates about its relationship with human translation (HT). This chapter provides an exploration of the strengths and limitations inherent in MT and HT and emphasizes their complementary rather than competitive nature. First, the progression of MT is explored. Comparative analysis from multiple perspectives. MT excels in rapidly producing consistent translations of standardized content, yet it persistently struggles with complex, culturally embedded language, implicit meanings, and high-stakes specialized contexts. Human translation remains indispensable in scenarios demanding deep cultural insight, interpretive creativity, domain-specific precision, and ethical discernment. All of these underscores the continuing necessity for human translators. Acknowledging these complementary roles, the chapter further examines the rise of hybrid translation models. Lastly, this chapter concludes with the future tendencies within a collaborative framework.

The ubiquity of artificial intelligence (AI) has significantly influenced research and practice in translation studies. As an integral part of the globalized world, AI's impact continues to grow. But translation accuracy can be compromised if machine translations are not supported by post-editing. This study evaluates the accuracy of machine and human translation by comparing their outputs using a qualitative descriptive approach. Machine translation, while efficient, struggles with polysemous terms, historical references, and culturally embedded expressions, leading to semantic distortions and omissions. The indispensability of human expertise also has been highlighted in preserving the integrity of Arabic scholarly works in cross-cultural academic discourse. This study underscores the importance of hybrid approaches, combining machine translation's speed with human post-editing to enhance translation quality. Recommendations offered include improving machine translation systems through domain-specific training and contextual awareness algorithms.

Translation plays a critical role in bridging language barriers, and its evolution is closely tied to advancements in technology, particularly artificial intelligence (AI). AI has revolutionized translatio industry. These innovations have facilitated multilingual communication, offering cost-effective solutions while presenting challenges, such as ethical concerns and changing professional roles. Research highlights the need to adapt university translation programmes to prepare future translators for an AI-driven industry. Despite AI's growing role, human expertise remains vital, as dependency on AI poses risks in high-stakes multilingual communication. This study analyzes the integration of AI in university translation programmes by examining programme descriptions and institutional policies from publicly available sources. Employing content analysis, the research explores how AI is incorporated into undergraduate and postgraduate translation curricula, assessing its impact on the preparation of translators and interpreters for evolving industry demands.

This chapter explores the transformative impact of Natural Language Processing (NLP) on translation and interpretation. It provides a comprehensive overview of NLP methodologies, including Machine Translation (MT), Speech Recognition, Text-to-Speech (TTS), and Corpus-Based Translation. The chapter highlights the advancements in Neural Machine Translation (NMT) and the integration of NLP with augmented reality (AR) for immersive interpretation experiences. It also addresses the challenges and ethical considerations in NLP, such as data privacy, bias, and fairness. By examining recent research and case studies, the chapter underscores the importance of combining NLP technologies with human expertise to achieve accurate, efficient, and culturally sensitive translations.

Artificial intelligence (AI) has significantly transformed translation and interpretation through advancements in machine learning and natural language processing. AI tools, such as Google Translate and DeepL, offer rapid translations, enhancing usability and fostering cross-cultural communication. Despite these advancements, challenges persist regarding accuracy, context, and cultural nuances, leading to misunderstandings. A collaborative approach that integrates human expertise with AI is essential to improve translation quality and mitigate biases. This chapter critically assesses the relationship between human translators and AI, exploring collaborative models, ethical considerations, and strategies for future partnerships. By examining case studies, it emphasizes the need to balance technological efficiency with human insight to ensure cultural sensitivity and responsible AI integration in translation services. Ultimately, effective collaboration enhances the quality and efficiency of language services while addressing ethical concerns in cross-cultural communication.

This chapter presents the efficacy and obstacles associated with the quality of AI-generated translation, concentrating on instruments such as ChatGPT and Neural Machine Translation (NMT) technology. It emphasizes the superiority of NMT systems over traditional rule-based and statistical methodologies by employing deep learning techniques to understand language contextually, thereby yielding translations that are both more accurate, acceptable, and readable. Nonetheless, considerable challenges persist, particularly in navigating cultural subtleties, idiomatic phrases, and intricate linguistic frameworks. By using a Translation Quality Assessment (TQA), this chapter appraises ChatGPT's translation capabilities based on three criteria: accuracy, acceptability, and readability. Although ChatGPT exhibits commendable performance in terms of general linguistic accuracy and readability, it encounters difficulties regarding acceptability when confronted with culturally rich or highly contextualized texts, especially within specialized domains such as political communication discourses.

Artificial Intelligence has transformed the field of translation, yet concerns remain about its ability to handle culturally complex metaphors and nuances. This chapter addresses this issue and compares the capabilities of two AI models- ChatGPT 4o (free version) and Gemini 1.5 Flash (free version) in translating a culturally laden poem, "Subh-e-Azadi (The Dawn of Freedom)" by Faiz Ahmed Faiz, from Hindi to English. With an emphasis on accuracy and quality, this study compares the translations produced by ChatGPT and Gemini against a human translation of the poem. It explores how AI models handle linguistic subtleties, cultural adaptability, and emotional depth while also experimenting with prompting techniques to assess whether explicit instructions improve translation quality or not. The findings will provide an insight into the future of AI in translating literature with heavy contextual background.

Artificial Intelligence (AI) has been applied in translating various text types including literary texts. With the popularity of Chinese Internet (CIL) Literature, substantial translated novels have been automatically produced by machine translation systems. Idioms and expressions are integrated components of Chinese literature, with over ninety percent being four-character idioms. Translation of four-character idioms has always been challenging for human translators. Considering the contextual limitations of AI compared to human translators, the translation process becomes more challenging due to the unique structures and connotative meanings of four-character idioms. Based on Chan's categorization of four-character idioms, this study adopts a qualitative approach to identify translation techniques found in the English translation of Chinese four-character idioms by MT in Returning to '90s, She Became Famous in Major Surgical Fields, a popular CIL. Analysis confirms that established equivalents, reduction, and literal translation are the most frequently used techniques in translating these idioms.

The incorporation of artificial intelligence (AI) in translation has transformed global communication, providing swift and economical methods for overcoming language obstacles. This breakthrough presents considerable ethical difficulties, especially regarding accuracy, cultural sensitivity, and data privacy. AI translation systems frequently encounter difficulties with contextual subtleties, resulting in possible misinterpretations that may offend or mislead users. The management of sensitive user data presents significant privacy issues, requiring stringent security protocols and adherence to rules such as GDPR. A coordinated strategy including AI developers, enterprises, and expert translators is crucial to resolve these difficulties. By prioritizing ethical principles, stakeholders can improve the efficacy of AI translation while safeguarding cultural contexts and user privacy. This work underscores the necessity for ongoing surveillance and revisions of AI models, guided by cultural understanding, to preserve relevance and sensitivity in translations.

Preface

As we stand on the precipice of a revolution in language and communication, the role of technology in translation, interpretation, and linguistic analysis cannot be overstated. This reference book is a culmination of efforts to explore the diverse ways in which artificial intelligence (AI), particularly large language models (LLMs), is reshaping these fields. The chapters herein offer insights from a variety of perspectives—ranging from practical applications and technological advancements to ethical concerns and the intersection of human and machine capabilities. It is my privilege to introduce this volume, which examines how AI is advancing and, at times, challenging traditional approaches to translation and interpretation.

In particular, this book focuses on large-scale language models like ChatGPT and neural machine translation (NMT) systems such as Google Translate. These technologies are not just altering the way we think about translation, but are creating new opportunities for editing, revising, and refining texts across genres. As the editor, I have sought to provide a comprehensive overview of the current landscape, delving into both the strengths and limitations of AI-driven translation. The chapters explore everything from journalistic and promotional translations to the complexities of translating culturally rich literary works, all while considering the evolving role of human expertise in an increasingly automated world. Through a rigorous evaluation of both the technological and human factors at play, this volume invites readers to critically assess the future of translation and interpretation.

Each chapter presents unique contributions, drawing on real-world case studies, theoretical frameworks, and empirical research. Together, they form a holistic picture of where we stand today, where we are headed, and the implications of AI's integration into translation practices. As we navigate this technological shift, one thing becomes clear: the collaboration between human insight and AI efficiency will define the future of translation, and it is this partnership that we must learn to foster and refine. This book aims to guide both practitioners and scholars in understanding the complexities and potential of AI in translation, serving as both a critical resource and a catalyst for further research.

The integration of AI into translation and interpretation has far-reaching implications, not only for the technology itself but for the professional landscape that relies on it. Throughout this book, we have seen how neural machine translation and large language models can enhance efficiency, accuracy, and accessibility in translation processes. However, we have also encountered the challenges that accompany such advancements, particularly when dealing with nuanced cultural contexts, idiomatic expressions, and specialized subject matter. The diverse chapters in this volume highlight the need for a balanced approach that blends human expertise with AI's capabilities in order to overcome these hurdles.

Looking ahead, the role of AI in translation will continue to evolve, driven by the increasing sophistication of language models and the growing demand for multilingual communication. As such, the importance of integrating AI into translation curricula and professional training programs cannot be overstated. This book has made it clear that while AI has the potential to revolutionize the field, it is the continued development of hybrid approaches—where humans and machines work together—that will ensure the accuracy, cultural sensitivity, and ethical integrity of translations in the future. The contributions in this volume underscore the critical need for ongoing dialogue between technologists, translators, and educators to shape a future where AI serves as a tool for enhancing human creativity and understanding.

In conclusion, the future of translation is collaborative, and the partnership between humans and machines is not a competition but a complementary relationship. This book aims to be a stepping stone in understanding the dynamic interplay between human and machine translation and the ways in which this relationship will shape the future of global communication. As we continue to push the boundaries of AI's capabilities, it is essential that we remain mindful of its limitations and the invaluable role that human translators play in preserving the richness and diversity of language.

CHAPTER OVERVIEWS

Chapter 1: From Google Translate to ChatGPT: The Use of Large Language Models in Translating, Editing, and Revising

This chapter explores the effectiveness of machine translation and large language models (LLMs) in translating diverse text genres, evaluating their accuracy and performance. By assessing translations from Google Translate (GT) and ChatGPT, the chapter compares the handling of journalistic argumentation, philosophical exposition, and legal texts. Using a theoretical framework grounded in text-typology linguistic models and Mossop's editing parameters, the chapter highlights the strengths and weaknesses of these systems, particularly in terms of quality enhancement and productivity. The analysis emphasizes the role of LLMs in not just translating, but also in refining and editing texts across various communication contexts, offering valuable insights into the potential of these technologies for enhancing translation workflows.

Chapter 2: The Evolution and Development of Artificial Intelligence Interpretation Technology in the Era of Large-Scale Language Models

This chapter delves into the significant advances in AI-driven interpretation technologies, focusing on the impact of large-scale language models on the field. It outlines how these AI systems have improved language generation, accuracy, and naturalness in interpreting, enabling more efficient real-time services. Furthermore, it explores how these models learn from vast data sets, improving their performance over time. The chapter reviews the opportunities AI presents to the interpreting profession, as well as the challenges that come with relying on automated systems for high-stakes communication, ultimately highlighting the evolving role of AI in the future of interpreting.

Chapter 3: Evolution of AI in Interpretation: From Traditional Approaches to Real-Time Solutions

Focusing on the transition from traditional interpretation methods to AI-enhanced systems, this chapter explores how neural machine translation (NMT) and deep learning technologies have revolutionized interpretation. It discusses the limitations of human-based interpretation, including speed and accuracy, and highlights how AI interpreters are now able to process complex languages, idioms, and cultural nuances more efficiently. The chapter also addresses the critical need for a hybrid approach, combining AI's speed and scalability with human oversight to ensure both quality and cultural sensitivity in interpretation, ultimately redefining the role of AI in global communication.

Chapter 4: Strengths and Limitations of Machine Translation and Human Translation

This chapter examines the complementary relationship between machine translation (MT) and human translation (HT). It highlights the strengths of MT in providing fast, consistent translations of standardized content and its limitations when dealing with complex, context-heavy language. Conversely, HT is shown to excel in situations requiring cultural insight, creativity, and specialized knowledge.

The chapter stresses that the future of translation lies in hybrid models, where the advantages of both human and machine contributions are leveraged to optimize quality and efficiency.

Chapter 5: On Assessing the Accuracy of Arabic-English Translation by Machine and Human

Focusing on Arabic-English translation, this chapter compares the performance of machine translation (MT) and human translation (HT). It explores the challenges AI faces in handling polysemous terms, cultural references, and complex expressions, which often lead to semantic inaccuracies. The study emphasizes the importance of human post-editing to address these challenges, advocating for a hybrid approach that combines the speed of MT with the cultural and linguistic accuracy provided by human translators. Recommendations are made for improving MT systems through domain-specific training and enhanced contextual awareness.

Chapter 6: Aspects of AI Integration into University Translation Study Programmes

This chapter explores the growing role of AI in university translation programs, analyzing how institutions are adapting curricula to prepare future translators for an AI-driven industry. It examines the integration of AI into both undergraduate and postgraduate translation studies and addresses the challenges of balancing technological advancements with the need for human expertise. The chapter also highlights the ethical concerns and evolving professional roles that accompany AI's influence on the translation field, suggesting that the future of translator education will need to focus on human-AI collaboration.

Chapter 7: NLP in Action: Enhancing Translation and Interpretation

Focusing on the transformative power of Natural Language Processing (NLP), this chapter provides a comprehensive overview of how NLP technologies like machine translation (MT), speech recognition, and corpus-based translation have enhanced the fields of translation and interpretation. It also discusses the ethical concerns that arise with the use of NLP, such as data privacy, bias, and fairness. The chapter concludes by emphasizing the importance of combining human expertise with NLP technologies to ensure that translations are not only accurate but also culturally sensitive and contextually appropriate.

Chapter 8: The Collaborative Future of Translation Between Human-AI Partnerships

This chapter investigates the collaborative potential of AI and human translators in the future of translation and interpretation. It reviews the advancements in AI tools like Google Translate and DeepL and their impact on cross-cultural communication. While AI can produce rapid translations, challenges persist in terms of accuracy, context, and cultural nuances. The chapter argues that a collaborative approach—where AI handles speed and efficiency, while humans provide cultural insights and contextual understanding—will be key to improving translation quality and mitigating biases, ensuring ethical AI integration in language services.

Chapter 9: The Quality and Accuracy of AI-Generated Translation in Translating Communication-Based Topics: Bringing Translation Quality Assessments into Practices

This chapter evaluates the effectiveness of AI-generated translations, particularly focusing on tools like ChatGPT and Neural Machine Translation (NMT) systems. It highlights how deep learning technologies enable AI to produce more accurate and readable translations, but also identifies areas where challenges remain—especially with culturally rich texts or specialized topics. Using Translation Quality Assessment (TQA) criteria, the chapter assesses AI's performance in terms of accuracy, acceptability, and readability, offering insights into where AI excels and where further development is needed.

Chapter 10: Translating Subh-e-Azadi: ChatGPT, Gemini, and the Cultural Complexity of 1947 Partition Poetry

This chapter explores the complexities AI faces in translating culturally rich and emotionally charged texts, focusing on the Hindi poem "Subh-e-Azadi" by Faiz Ahmed Faiz. By comparing translations from ChatGPT and Gemini against a human translation, it investigates how well AI handles linguistic subtleties, cultural nuances, and emotional depth. The study also experiments with different prompting techniques to see if explicit instructions can improve translation quality, offering a glimpse into the future potential of AI in translating literature with heavy contextual background.

Chapter 11: Chinese Internet Literature in Translation Exploring Idioms Translated by AI

This chapter examines the translation of Chinese Internet Literature, specifically focusing on the challenges AI faces when translating idiomatic expressions, such as the four-character idioms that dominate Chinese literature. It analyzes the translation techniques used by machine translation systems and compares them with human translation strategies. By exploring how AI handles idioms in a popular Chinese Internet novel, the chapter demonstrates the complexities of AI translation in capturing the nuances and contextual meanings of these culturally significant expressions.

Chapter 12: Navigating Ethical Dilemmas in AI-Powered Translation: Challenges and Solutions

The final chapter addresses the ethical challenges that arise with the use of AI in translation, particularly regarding accuracy, cultural sensitivity, and data privacy. It explores how AI systems often struggle with context and may inadvertently lead to misinterpretations or cultural insensitivity. The chapter also tackles the ethical concerns surrounding the use of AI in translation, including issues related to data security and privacy regulations like GDPR. It calls for a coordinated effort among developers, translators, and policymakers to create ethical guidelines that ensure AI translation remains both effective and culturally responsible.

Mohammed Alaqad
University of Malaya, Malaysia

Chapter 1
From Google Translate to ChatGPT:
The Use of Large Language Models in Translating, Editing, and Revising

Tawffeek A. S. Mohammed
https://orcid.org/0000-0002-7314-9688
University of the Western Cape, South Africa

ABSTRACT

This chapter examines the quality of machine translated texts of various genres with a view to finding out to what extent these texts/genres have been accurately translated by neural machine translation systems and LLMs. The chapter also examines the potential use of these technologies in editing and revisions to enhance both quality and productivity. A theoretical and conceptual framework that is based on text-typology linguistic models and Mossop's parameters of revising and editing in translation is used to assess the quality of transactions produced by Google Translate (GT) as a neural-based machine translation system and ChatGPT as a large language model (LLM). In particular, the chapter investigates the GT and ChatGPT translations of argumentation within journalistic texts, exposition within both promotional and philosophical genres, and instrumental texts within the legal genre. This emphasis on diverse text types allows for a comprehensive evaluation of the translation performance of neural-based systems and LLMs across different communicative purposes and stylistic demands.

DOI: 10.4018/979-8-3373-0060-3.ch001

INTRODUCTION

Communication across languages and cultures has been one of the priorities of technology. With the advent of the Fourth Industrial Revolution (4IR), digital technologies, such as artificial intelligence (AI), automation, and the Internet of Things have become a reality and they have been integrated into various aspects of society (Alsulaimani & Islam, 2022; Park, 2018), and the field of translation and interpreting was no exception.

Early machine translation (MT) systems were based on rule-based approaches. That is, the generation of translation depends on a set of linguistic rules (Stein, 2018). Phrase-based statistical machine translation (PBSMT) systems have been introduced over the last decades (Lyons, 2020) and they have included more advanced features. While the role of these systems cannot be denied as they laid the foundation for advanced systems of machine translation (MT), the end translation product is poor in terms of fluency and accuracy (Jia et al., 2019). The problem is more complicated in the translation of complex linguistic structures and frozen and idiomatic expressions. In a post which gained immense traction on social media more than a decade ago, the frozen Arabic expressions *ḥill ʿan samāʾī* and *yastur ʿalā ʿirḍik* have been literally translated as "dilute my sky" and "cover your width". Undoubtedly, these translated expressions do not make any sense in the target language.

However, the introduction of neural machine translation (NMT) systems, powered by deep learning algorithms and trained on vast amounts of multilingual data (Bhadauria et al., 2023; Dabre et al., 2020), has made remarkable strides in producing more fluent and natural-sounding translations (Dwivedi et al., 2025). While they still have certain limitations, such as difficulties with low-resource languages or highly specialized domains, present-day machine translation systems have reached a level where they can provide usable translations for a wide range of texts. In addition, the advancements in artificial intelligence (AI) and the use of AI-driven machine translation (MT) systems have undoubtedly improved the accuracy and fluency of translations between various directionalities (Siu, 2024). The poor machine translations of some text types have become a matter of the past today. Google Translate (GT) among other systems have become so advanced that they can produce quality translations (Johnson et al., 2017) that can rival human capabilities. A recent report has revealed that a neural-based translation program similar to Google Translate (GT) can be used in the translation of Akkadian cuneiform into English (Krueger, 2023; Mair, 2023). It has successfully facilitated the decoding and translation of thousands of previously unread digitized tablets. The report has, however acknowledged that the accuracy of the translations remains a subject of debate (Mair, 2023). The fact that remains is that machine translation (MT) systems and large language models

(LLMs) have made the translation of some genres much easier and at the same time they are still underdeveloped and untrained to translate some other genres.

This chapter therefore investigates the quality of machine translated texts of various genres with a view to finding out to what extent these texts/genres have been accurately translated by neural machine translation (NMT) systems and large language models (LLMs). The chapter also examines the potential use of these technologies in post-translation tasks such as editing and revisions to enhance both quality and productivity.

LITERATURE REVIEW

Since AI-based translation is a relatively nascent discipline, with the field still in the process of formation and the establishment of its theoretical and applied foundations, it is beneficial to conduct a chronological survey of studies that have examined the use of artificial intelligence (AI) and large language models (LLMs) across various translation directions. Given that this field is grounded in big data applications for both high-resource and low-resource languages, each empirical study presents a distinct contribution. Accordingly, we will review these studies under various thematic headings, followed by a concise synthesis of the existing literature.

1. Large language models (LLMs) and their use in Arabic-English translation

The emergence of large language models (LLMs), such as ChatGPT, has added a new dimension to artificial intelligence (AI) translation. Unlike traditional machine translation (MT) systems, which prioritize direct word-for-word conversion, large language models (LLMs) leverage extensive training on vast datasets to grasp meaning, context, and stylistic nuances (Siu, 2024). This deeper understanding allows them to produce translations that are not only more fluent but also more stylistically accurate.

Several studies have compared LLM-based translations with neural-based machine translation (NMT) systems. For example, Alkhawaja (2024) investigates the use of ChatGPT for Arabic-English machine translation and the quality of its translations. The study has also compared the output against Google Translate (GT). The assessment includes a parallel corpus of 1000 English sentences and their machine Arabic translations which have been sourced from an open online platform called Tatoeba. The statistical metric BLEU (Bilingual Evaluation Understudy) was used to quantitatively evaluate and compare the quality of machine translation against a human reference translation. The findings of the study have shown that ChatGPT performs impressively well compared to Google Translate (GT). However, the quality of ChatGPT translation cannot be compared with human translation. In a similar vein, Khoshafah (2023) investigates the translation accuracy of ChatGPT 3.5 by comparing its outputs with professional translations of some texts from Arabic into English. The findings of the study have shown that even though ChatGPT can generally provide accurate translations, it may encounter some problems in the translation of some genres such as legal documents and medical reports. Similarly, Zayed and Nuirat (2024) assess the quality of the ChatGPT translations for some media texts that have been translated from Arabic into English. The study has also analysed the strategies used by professional translators during post-editing. The study has concluded that ChatGPT translations of media texts need to be post-edited by human translators. Addition or expansion, omission or semantic minimization and play over diction are three common strategies used by translators while post-editing outputs to enhance the quality and accuracy of translation.

2. Use of MT and AI translations in other languages

Literature abounds with a considerable number of studies on the use of various machine translation (MT) systems (rule-based, statistical, neural) and the recently generative AI-models such as ChatGPT in translation between various languages. Google Translate (GT) as a neural-based machine translation (NMT) system and ChatGPT as a large language model (LLM) have in particular received some attention in many empirical studies. Rao et al. (2024) evaluate the translation accuracy of ChatGPT-3.5 and Google Translate (GT) for medical documents in a number of languages including Spanish, Vietnamese, and Russian. The study has concluded that ChatGPT significantly outperformed Google Translate (GT) in Spanish translations, with fewer errors (3.8% vs. 18.1% incorrect sentences). In contrast, Google Translate (GT) provided better translations for Vietnamese (10.6% vs. 24.2% incorrect sentences). On the other hand, both tools struggled with Russian (35.6% vs. 41.6% incorrect sentences, respectively). ChatGPT introduced more severe errors in some cases, including fabricated content. The study concludes that while ChatGPT shows promise for Spanish translations, it remains unreliable for other languages and should not replace professional translators. Likewise, Jiang et al. (2024) explore the effectiveness of ChatGPT (versions 3.5 and 4.0) in evaluating Chinese-Portuguese translations. Using human and machine translations of political texts and classical Chinese poems, the study employed holistic scoring and comparative judgment methods to compare human and artificial intelligence (AI) evaluations. The findings reveal that ChatGPT 4.0 demonstrates high potential. It aligns closely with human assessments, especially in scoring accuracy and ranking consistency. However, challenges such as stability and occasional inconsistencies underscore the need for human oversight.

By the same token, Koh (2023) investigates the effectiveness of ChatGPT in translating Korean to English, using the film *Minari* as a case study. The study highlights the strengths and limitations of ChatGPT's translations, comparing them with human translations. While ChatGPT excels in speed and provides translations close to human-like fluency, it often struggles with cultural nuances, idiomatic expressions, and context-specific meanings.

3. Use of LLM in post-editing

The literature also includes many studies that tackle the vital role of large language models (LLMs) in enhancing the quality of machine translation (MT) and post-editing tasks. For example, Macken (2024) explores the use of ChatGPT in post-editing English-to-Dutch machine translations of literary texts. The study compared ChatGPT's post-edited outputs with those of professional literary translators. It concludes that ChatGPT makes more extensive edits than human editors. While such edits can enhance lexical richness, the programme often introduces errors and deviates from the source text's intended meaning. Thus, ChatGPT automatic post-editing is not yet a substitute for professional literary human translation despite its great potentials. Similarly, Ki and Carpuat (2024) explore the extent to which large language models (LLMs) can enhance machine translation (MT). The study underscores the significance of leveraging external feedback, specifically Multidimensional Quality Metric (MQM) annotations, to refine machine translation (MT) outputs. Using LLaMA-2 models, the study examines prompting strategies and fine-tuning techniques to improve translation quality. While prompting alone yields moderate improvements, fine-tuning significantly enhances machine translation (MT) accuracy by better integrating fine-grained feedback. Experiments conducted on Chinese-English, English-German, and English-Russian datasets demonstrate that this approach improves key translation quality metrics, such as TER, BLEU, and COMET scores. However, the study finds that while fine-grained feedback is beneficial, its effectiveness depends on how well large language models (LLMs) utilize it. The study recommends the combination of large language models (LLMs) with supervised machine translation (MT) to address quality inconsistencies across languages and translation directions.

4. Use of LLMs in translator training

In the context of translator training, Fan et al. (2023) explore how ChatGPT is reshaping translation education. It highlights the tool's potential in promoting personalized teaching, enhancing autonomous learning, and innovating teaching management. However, the study also addresses challenges, including ethical concerns, data security risks, and the potential weakening of teacher-student relationships. The study proposes strategies to harness ChatGPT's benefits while mitigating its risks, emphasizing the importance of teacher involvement, ethical education, and digital literacy. Furthermore, Sahari et al. (2023) compared the attitudes of both teachers and students of translation towards the use of Google Translate (GT) and ChatGPT while translating Arabic texts into English. The findings of the study revealed that while students preferred ChatGPT over Google Translate (GT), teachers favoured the latter.

5. Strengths and limitations of LLMs

Peng et al. (2023) explore the capabilities ChatGPT can bring to machine translation (MT) with special focus on temperature settings, task-specific prompts (TSP), and domain-specific prompts (DSP). The findings of the study show that a lower temperature improves translation performance, and in particular in complex or low-resource languages. task-specific prompts (TSP) and domain-specific prompts (DSP) enhance ChatGPT's translations as they provide more precise task and contextual domain instructions. In doing so, they may mitigate issues like hallucinations in non-English-centric tasks. The findings have also shown that advanced in-context learning strategies like few-shot learning can boost performance. However, the Chain-of-Thought (CoT) approach may degrade it by promoting word-by-word translations. Hence, prompt engineering plays a critical role in the optimization of ChatGPT in machine translation (MT).

Despite their capabilities, some limitations of large language models (LLMs) have been identified in some studies. Siu (2023) explores the capabilities and limitations of ChatGPT and GPT-4 in the translation industry. These two models and similar counterparts offer some advantages such as speed, versatility, and cost-effectiveness. However, their outputs often require human oversight to ensure quality. The study underscores the importance of integrating these tools into workflows. It also emphasizes the significance of human expertise in achieving high-quality translations. Contextual clarification, cultural explanation, and technical simplification might be necessary to maintain quality. In another study, Siu (2024) explores advancements in artificial intelligence (AI) translation technology, with special focus on neural-based machine translation (NMT) and large language models (LLMs). It discusses the technical foundations of these models, such as the transformer architecture, and evaluates their strengths and limitations in translation tasks. The study highlights large language models' potentials to support translators with contextual understanding and domain adaptation while cautioning about issues like hallucinations and domain-specific limitations. In a recent study on the pros and cons of large language models (LLMs), Lee (2024) examines the profound impact of advanced artificial intelligence (AI), particularly large language models (LLMs) like ChatGPT, on the field of translation. Despite not being specifically designed for translation, these models have achieved a level of technical sophistication that rivals or surpasses dedicated systems such as Google Translate (GT) and DeepL. This advancement challenges traditional translation practices and the professional identity of translators. Lee proposes a posthumanist perspective, suggesting that viewing artificial intelligence (AI) as an extension of the translator's cognitive abilities can broaden the scope of translation skills, modes, and media, thereby redefining the translator's role in the digital age.

Thus, the surveyed studies highlight the rapid advancements in machine translation (MT) and large language models (LLMs). They underscore the increasing role of these tools in translation across different language pairs. Research has confirmed that large language models (LLMs) and in particular ChatGPT has outperform neural-based machine translation (NMT) systems in terms of fluency and contextual accuracy. This is partially attributed to the vast datasets large language models (LLMs) utilize. However, large language models (LLMs) may fall short in the translation of some text types more than others. Empirical research has demonstrated that large language models (LLMs) have remarkable potential in the field of translation and at the same time they have many limitations and the encounter various challenges including hallucinations, inconsistencies in low-resource languages and difficulties in rendering culture-specific nuances. Moreover, research has raised some concerns regarding ethical considerations, translation fidelity, and the impact on professional translation workflows. Additionally, many studies seem in agreement that large language models (LLMs) improve productivity and accuracy in post-editing translation tasks. They also offer innovative applications to be used while training future translators and interpreters. A key takeaway from the above studies is that the outputs of these systems should not be accepted blindly. The intervention of human translators remains essential to ensure accuracy, coherence, and cultural appropriateness.

These limitations and concerns of large language models (LLMs) necessitate a balanced approach to the integration of AI-driven tools with human expertise. Undoubtedly, large language models (LLMs) have revolutionized the translation industry by enhancing productivity, efficiency and accessibility, but they should be used as supplementary tools, not a replacement for human translators and/or educator, especially in contexts requiring ethical, cultural and contextual sensitivity.

THEORETICAL AND METHODOLOGICAL CONSIDERATIONS

To evaluate the translation quality of machine and AI-based translations between Arabic and English, it seems beneficial to use a theoretical and conceptual framework that is based on text-typology linguistic models and Mossop's revising and editing approach (Mossop, 2001/2014). These theoretical underpinnings are described in the following sub-sections:

The text-typology model

The text-typology translation model focuses on key textual concepts such as structure, texture, and context (Mohammed, 2011). The term *texture* pertains to the organizational aspects of a text, namely, how various elements of discourse cohere to form a unified stretch of language and how texts respond to their respective contexts. Texture, as Halliday & Hasan (1976:2) explain, "distinguishes [a text] from something that is not a text... the texture is provided by cohesive relations."

Over time, various theories on text-typology have been proposed. With the advent of the pragmatic turn, functionalism has emerged as a critical criterion for text-typology. Reiss's (1971) typology (Reiss, 1971/2000) exemplifies a functionally oriented approach to text classification. This typology draws upon Bühler's (1979) assertion (Buhler, 1979) that "language serves simultaneously to represent (objectively), express (subjectively), and appeal (persuasively)" (Reiss, 1971:25). Accordingly, Reiss categorizes texts into distinct types based on these functions, as follows:

1. The content-focused (i.e., informative) type, which "would include press releases and comments, news reports, commercial and correspondence, inventories of merchandise, operating instructions, directions of use, patents specifications, treaties, official documents, educational works, non-fiction books of all sorts, essays, reports, theses, and specialized literature in the humanities, the natural sciences and other technical fields" (Reiss 1971:27).
2. The form-focused (i.e., expressive) type, which includes "literary prose (anecdotes, short stories, novellas, romances) and poetry in all its forms (from the didactic to balladry to the purely sentimental)" (Reiss 1971:35).
3. The appeal-focused or operative type, which includes "all texts in which the element of appeal is dominant, with advertising, publicity, preaching, propaganda, polemic, demagogy or satire providing either the purpose or linguistic means of expression" (Reiss 1971:39).

Although Reiss's model originates from the 1970s, it continues to be a highly relevant framework in translation studies, translation criticism, and translation pedagogy (Mohammed, 2011; Von, 2008). Her text-typology operates on the premise that each text type necessitates a corresponding and appropriate translation method. For example, when translating an informative text, priority should be given to achieving semantic equivalence, followed by attention to connotative meanings and aesthetic values. Conversely, in translating an expressive text, the emphasis must first be placed on its aesthetic elements, with the semantic content considered secondary. In the case of an operative text, the translator's primary objective is to achieve an extralinguistic equivalent effect such as persuasiveness while form and content serve as subordinate considerations (Hatim & Munday, 2004).

The text-typology model discussed above suggests that hybridization between text types may be unavoidable in some cases (Mohammed, 2011). Hatim (1984, 2001) and Hatim & Mason, (1990) address the issue of overlapping text types and propose an alternative text-typology model to account for these complexities. Their approach includes argumentation (i.e., counter-argumentation and through-argumentation), exposition (i.e., description, narration and conceptual) and instruction (e.g. contracts, resolutions, treaties) (Hatim, 2001:179).

A cursory look at many empirical studies that investigate the performance of machine translation or/and LLM models show that those studies do not give clear criteria of the texts selected for assessment and the selection is sometimes based on the preference of authors/researchers. Including various text types in assessments can provide a clearer picture of the performance of these systems/models across texts and genres.

In a similar vein, assessing the output of these systems/models should not undermine established theories/models of editing and revising in the filed such as Brian Mossop's revising and editing (Mossop, 2014). Mossop's key contribution is his book titled "Revising and Editing for Translators," (Mossop, 2001/2014) which is widely regarded as a valuable resource for translators and editors alike. In this book, Mossop provides practical guidelines and strategies for editing translations, addressing various aspects such as style, grammar, terminology, and cultural adaptation. Mossop emphasizes the importance of maintaining a balance between fidelity to the source text and readability in the target language. He emphasizes the importance of translations that are both clear and natural, ensuring they effectively capture the original meaning and intent while respecting the linguistic and cultural nuances of the target audience.

Mossop's approach elaborates 12 revision parameters, which categorize the common types of errors that revisers typically look for (Mossop, 2014, 134-149). These parameters are organized into four categories: meaning transfer, content, language and style, and physical presentation. Each parameter is thoroughly analyzed, with detailed explanations and practical suggestions on how to address and rectify specific issues. Table 1 below summarizes Mossop's approach including the various dimensions of the revision and editing process.

Table 1. Mossop's revision parameters (Mossop, 2014, 134-149)

	Group A	**Problems of meaning (Transfer)**
1	Accuracy	Does the translation reflect the message of the source text?
2	Completeness	Have any elements of the message been left out?
	Group B	Problems of content (Content)
3	Logic	Does the sequence of ideas make sense? Is there any nonsense or contradiction?
4	Facts	Are there any factual errors?
	Group C	Problems of language and style (Language)
5	Smoothness	Does the text flow: Are the connections between sentences clear? Are the relationships among the parts of each sentence clear? Are there any awkward, hard-to-read sentences?
6	Tailoring	Is the language adapted to the users of the translation and the use they will make of it?
7	Sub-language	Is the style suited to the genre, has correct terminology been used, and does the phraseology match that used in original target-language texts on the same subject?
8	Idiom	Are all the word combinations idiomatic? Does the translation observe the rhetorical preferences of the target language?
9	Mechanics	Have the rules of grammar, spelling, punctuation, house style, and correct usage been observed?
	Group D	Problems of physical presentation (Presentation)
10	Layout	Are there any problems in the way the text is arranged on the page: spacing, indentation, margins, etc.?
11	Typography	Are there any problems of text formatting: bolding, underlining, font type, font size, etc.?
12	Organization	Are there any problems in the way the document as a whole is organized: page numbering, headers, footnotes, table of contents, etc.?

Hence, this chapter qualitatively investigates the machine and LLM translations of some text types in the light of text-typology models and Mossop's approach to revising and editing. That is, the texts used in for assessment are carefully selected to represent various text types. The first text is an editorial of opinion piece. This critical commentary explores the experience of an Arab female activist who documented her participation in a 2011 march to Yemen's capital, Sana'a, demanding the regime's departure. As an expounding text-type, it presents a subjective, argumentative perspective. It critiques the activist's statements and actions, with special focus on sensitive religious and societal themes. The critical tone throughout the text aims to defame and demonize the activist and to persuade readers by highlighting perceived transgressions against societal norms and beliefs. Hence, it is content-focused (i.e., informative) text to a great extent.

The second is a promotional text (i.e., advert). The text is designed to promote a product, namely, 'Halal Chicken Fingers', by emphasizing its quality, compliance with religious standards, and suitability for specific dietary needs. It aims to inform and persuade potential customers. It belongs to Reiss's appeal-focused or operative type.

The third text to be analysed in this chapter is a philosophical and religious text. It narrates the life of Ahmad Bin Alwan (1208–1266 CE), a notable Islamic scholar, mystic, and poet. He is considered an influential figure in Sufism and Islamic theology, particularly in Yemen during the Ayyubid period. The text is not only informative or content-based but also expressive. Finally, the fourth text is a content-based instructional text in the form of a treaty between two tribes that have been at daggers for about a decade.

Table 2. provides some details about the texts selected for the study as well as some statistical details about the parallel corpus such as the tokens of the source texts, Google Translate (GT) and ChatGPT.

Text-Type	Genre	Source Text	GT	ChatGPT	Total Tokens
Argumentation	Journalistic	297	409	369	1075
Exposition	Promotional	72	77	79	228
Exposition	Philosophical	272	394	352	1018
Instrument	Legal	428	663	464	1555

Figure 1 visualizes these various aspects of the corpus.

Figure 1. Visualization of the parallel corpus

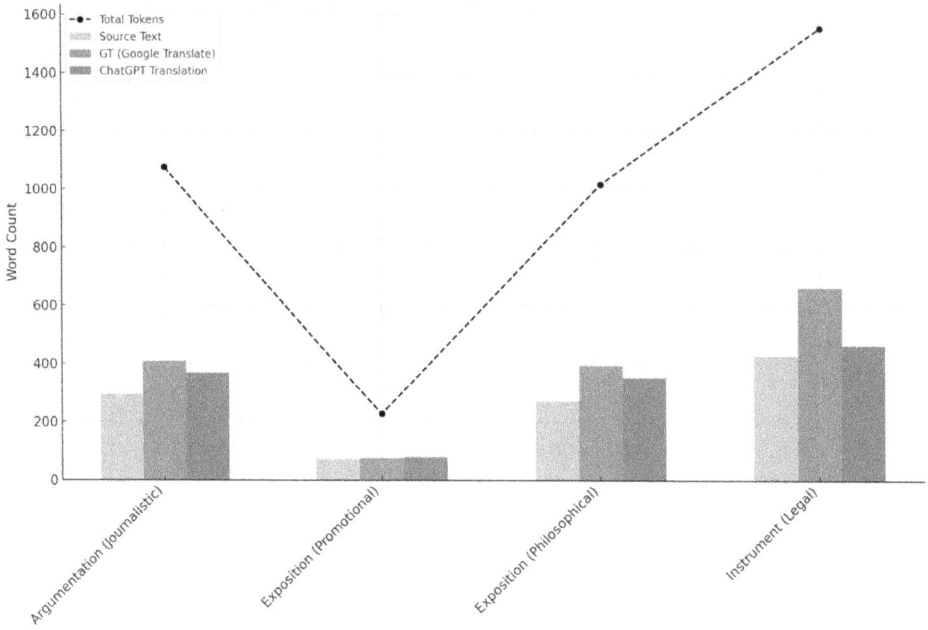

The parallel corpus used in the chapter can be found via the following link https://ske.li/6t4

ANALYSIS AND DISCUSSION

This section investigates the translation quality assessment of both Google Translate (GT) and ChatGPT for the above texts in the light of Mossop's revision parameters in Table 1.

1. Assessment of GT and ChatGPT of text 1.

As stated in the previous section, the first text is a content-focused (i.e., informative) text but it abounds with various expressive and literary features. A snapshot of the first text and its Google Translate (GT) and ChatGPT translations is given in Figure 2.

Figure 2. A snapshot of text 1 and its translations

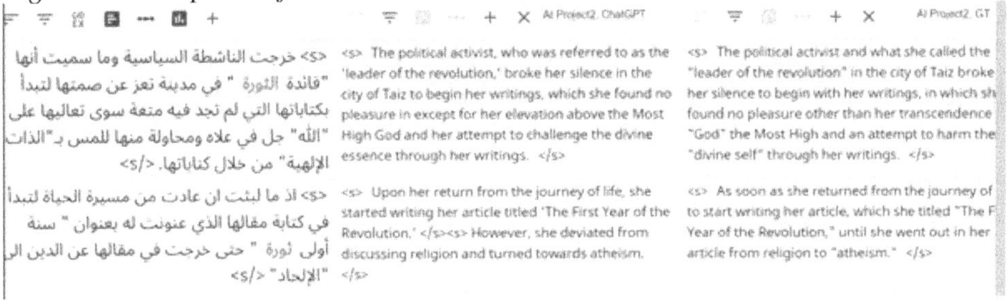

In terms of meaning (i.e., Accuracy and Completeness), the Google Translate (GT) generally conveys the meaning of the original text. However, there are some inaccuracies and omissions. There are instances where the translation doesn't capture the intended meaning accurately. For example, *ta ʿālīhā ʿalā Allāh* "transcendence to God" should be translated as "elevation above God," and *lil-mas bi-a-dhāt al-ilāhiyyah* "harm the divine self" should be translated as "challenging the divine essence". In addition, some details and nuances in the original text are not fully captured in the translation. For example, *li-yakhruj baʿdahā bi-ṭarīq an-naṣārā wa-yaʿtadhir lil-muslimīn min tilka al-kitābah* has been wrongly translated by Google Translate (GT) as "But he later took the path of the Christians and apologized to Muslims for that writing" and "He later apologized to Muslims for that writing" by ChatGPT. The expression *bi-ṭarīq an-naṣārā* which can be translated literally as 'The Patriarch of the Christians' has been wrongly translated as 'The path of Christians' in Google Translate (GT). In a similar vein, the identity of the sayer is not clearly articulated in ChatGPT as the pronoun 'he', which is used in the translation gives the impression that the Coptic student himself apologized rather than the Patriarch.

In terms of content (logic and facts), the translation maintains the logical flow of the original text. As for language and style (smoothness, idiom, tailoring, mechanics, and sub-language), the language used in the translation is generally clear and understandable. However, there are several grammatical errors, incorrect word choices, and awkward phrasings throughout the translation. The style of the translation could be improved to enhance readability and coherence. Some examples of grammatical errors include *wa-mā summiyat annahā qāʾidat ath-thawrah* "and what she called the leader of the revolution" which should be rather rendered as "and who was dubbed as a ' revolutionary leader'" to maintain grammatical consistency. Similarly, *lākina al-umūr lam taʿud ṭayyibah* "She is considered kind" should be "Conditions were no longer kind to us".

The translation also includes some instances of incorrect word choices, as we have stated in the rendition of *al-mas bi-dh-dhāt al-ilāhiyyah*, which has been translated as "harm the divine self" while "challenge the divine essence" is more appropriate in this context. Many awkward phrasings can be spotted as well. For instance, *wa-r-rabb ash-shakūr lam ya ʿud ḥāḍiran fī layl khidār* "The thankful Lord is no longer present in a cloaked night" is an awkward phrase. A more accurate and smooth translation would be "The grateful Lord is no longer present in the night of Khadar". Similarly, the translation of *lākina rabb as-sab ʿīn kāna maḥjūban bi-ʿabā ʾat as-safīr al-amrīkī* as "But the Lord of the seventies…" is unclear and needs clarification. The reference is clearly to the former president of Yemen, Ali Abdullah Saleh and his presidential palace in Al-Sabeen area in Sana'a.

Although Google Translate's translation attempts to capture the original text's meaning, it falls short in accuracy, completeness, language, and style. A revised version could help address these shortcomings and enhance overall quality. Meanwhile, ChatGPT's translation shows significant improvement in meaning, content, language, and style but still exhibits awkward phrasing and errors, particularly in handling culture-specific terms and expressions. See for instance, the rendition of *layl khidār, masīrat al-ḥayāh, sanat ūlā thawrah, rabb as-sab ʿīn* as well as the ironic use of some expression, and intertextuality. All these aspects are deeply rooted in the political context of the Yemeni uprising that took place in 2011, and they are lost in the ChatGPT translation.

2. Analysis of GT and ChatGPT of text 2

As indicated earlier, the second text is a promotional advertising text. A snapshot of the corpus is given in Figure 3.

Figure 3. A snapshot of text 2 and its translations

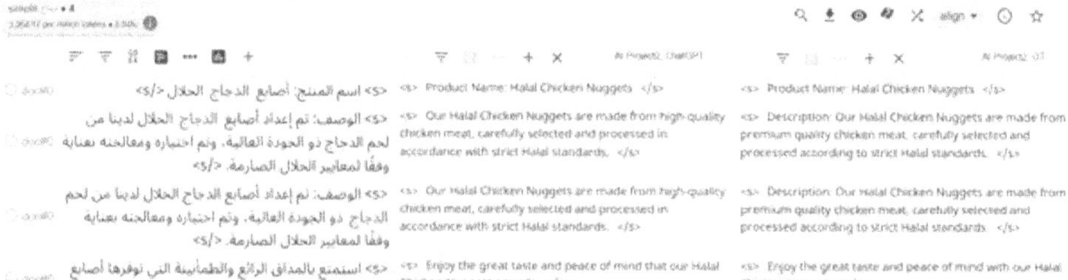

The parallel corpus above shows that both translations retain the force of the original text and its function. Examining the problems of meaning (transfer) shows that the translation accurately reflects the meaning of the source text. Key details such as the product being *dhū jawdah ʿāliyah* "carefully selected," *tamma ikhtiyāruhu wa-muʿālijatuhu bi-ʿināyah wifqan li-maʿāyīr al-ḥalāl aṣ-ṣārima* "processed under strict Halal standards," and *khāliyah min ayyi mukawwināt ghayr ḥalāl* "free from non-Halal ingredients" are preserved. In addition, no elements of the message have been left out. The translation covers all aspects, including the quality of the chicken, *halal* standards, absence of preservatives, and the texture of the product.

As for the problems of content, the sequence of ideas in the translation is logical and aligns with the original text. There are no contradictions or inconsistencies. Besides, there are no factual errors. The translation accurately conveys the product's *halal* certification and preparation details.

In terms of language and style, the text flows well. The connections between sentences are clear, and there are no awkward or hard-to-read sentences. The language is appropriately tailored for the target audience, which likely includes individuals looking for halal-certified products. It uses consumer-friendly terminology. The style suits the genre of food product descriptions. It uses terminology consistent with marketing texts for food products. Moreover, the translation uses idiomatic English appropriately. Phrases like *muqarmishah min al-khārij wa-ṭariyyah min al-dākhil* "crunchy on the outside and tender on the inside" are natural and effective in conveying the product's qualities.

Finally, grammar, spelling, and punctuation are correct throughout the text. The physical presentation is appropriate. The organization of the text is coherent, with a clear structure that introduces the product, highlights its qualities, and concludes with an encouraging statement for consumers to enjoy it.

3. Analysis of text 3

The third text to be analysed in this chapter is a philosophical and religious text. A snapshot of the text and its two translations is provided in Figure 4.

Figure 4. A snapshot of text 3 and its translations

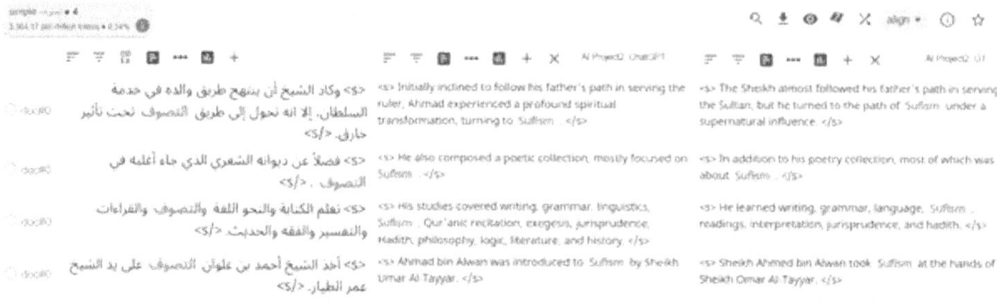

Investigating the problems of meaning (transfer) in the above parallel corpus shows that Google Translate (GT) captures the essence of the source text faithfully. However, some phrases could be refined for clearer expression, e.g., *nashaʾa fī aḥḍān ar-riʾāsah wa-al-ʿilm* "He grew up in the embrace of leadership and knowledge" feels less natural than the ChatGPT "He grew up in an environment of authority and scholarship". ChatGPT translation is slightly more idiomatic and fluid. For insatnce, "Ahmad experienced a profound spiritual transformation" conveys the idea of *taḥawwala ilā ṭarīq at-taṣawwuf* with more depth and nuance. However, referring to Ahmad Bin Alwan without an honorific title may seem less respectful, especially given his status as a knowledgeable and ascetic shaykh.

When it comes to completeness, Google Translate (GT) lacks informativity. Some cultural and contextual nuances, like the spiritual significance of the pilgrimage, could be expanded upon for non-native audiences. ChatGPT translation is generally complete and often provides a more culturally nuanced rendering, such as *ziyārah sanawiyyah* "an annual pilgrimage" instead of just "annual visit".

In so far as the content of both translations is concerned, logical sequence is preserved in Google Translate (GT), but some translations feel mechanical, e.g., *lazima al-khalwah wa-al-ʿibādah* "He remained in seclusion and worship" is straightforward but lacks fluidity in transitioning to the next sentence. ChatGPT translation shows stronger logical coherence, e.g., *lahu rasāʾil kathīrah wa-muʾallafāt jumiʿat fī mujalladāt* "Ahmad authored numerous letters and works, compiled in volumes" logically ties the volume content with specific works like *al-futūḥ al-maṣūnah wa-al-asrār al-makhzūnah* "Al-Futuh".

Furthermore, both translations maintain factual accuracy. However, ChatGPT occasionally provides more context, e.g., *al-Qādiriyyah* "Qadiriyya" is rendered with references to "Abdul Qadir Al-Jilani," providing historical depth.

In terms of language and style, the two translations meet the criteria to a great extent. The Google Translate (GT) translation flows well but has occasional awkward phrases. For instance, *hāḍa intiqāluk yā akhā al-ishfāq* "Your departure has come, O brother of compassion" is direct but lacks emotional smoothness. ChatGPT translation is generally smoother. For example, "Your departure, O brother of compassion, grieves me" flows more naturally and emotionally. While Google Translate's version is appropriate for a general audience, it lacks adaptation for readers with deeper cultural knowledge of Yemen or Sufism. ChatGPT translation, on the other hand, is more tailored for an informed audience, using terminology like "profound spiritual transformation". Google Translate (GT) uses general language, suitable for broad audiences but ChatGPT employs idiomatic expressions and specialized terminology. For instance, *faqad kāna yaskulu fī wa ʿẓihi ṭarīqat Ibn al-Jawzī* "His style mirrored that of Ibn al-Jawzi," shows a deeper engagement with the genre. While Idiomatic usage is present in Google Translate (GT), it is not consistent. The use of 'lamp' for *sirājunā*, for example, works but could be more culturally enriched. ChatGPT translation, on the other hand, displays better idiomatic expressions. For instance, the use of 'light' instead of 'lamp' conveys more abstract spiritual guidance. As for mechanics, both translations maintain correct grammar, spelling, and punctuation, with no notable issues detected.

The physical presentations of both translations are in order. In Google Translate (GT), information is organized logically but lacks certain contextual explanations that might enhance clarity. ChatGPT looks more reader-friendly, as it organizes content with clear transitions between historical, religious, and cultural elements.

4. Analysis of text 4

To examine the quality assessment of translation across text-types, this chapter examines Google Translate (GT) and ChatGPT translations of a content-based instructional text structured as a peace treaty between two tribes that have been in conflict for nearly a decade. A snapshot of the parallel corpus including the source legal text, its Google Translate (GT) and ChatGPT translations is given in Figure 5.

Figure 5. A snapshot of text 5 and its translations

	AI Project2, ChatGPT	AI Project2, GT
<s> كما قالت في نهاية نفس الفقرة: "وعيون لا ترحم تطل من بعيد. العسكر والقبائل والبيئة المعادية. والله الذي لا يرانا .. </s> " <s></s>. <s><s>	<s> She further commented, 'And merciless eyes loom from afar: the military, the tribes, the hostile environment, and God who no longer watches over us...' </s>	<s> She also said at the end of the same paragraph: "And merciless eyes loom from afar, the military, the tribes, the hostile environment, and God who does not see us..." </s>
<s> وبحضور جمع غفير من أبناء قبائل مضاربة لحج </s>	<s> and a large gathering of the tribes of Mudharaba, Lahj </s>	<s> and in the presence of a large gathering of the sons of the Mudarabah Lahj tribes. </s>
<s> التي أبت إلا أن تكون حاضرة في إبرام عهد بين كلا من قبيلة الكعللة وقبيلة الشبيقة </s>	<s> The covenant was established between the Ka'lala tribe and the Shubayqa tribe, represented by their respective sheikhs and elders. </s>	<s> who refused to be absent from concluding a covenant between both the Ka'lalah tribe and the Al-Shabiqa tribe. </s>
<s> قبيلة الكعللة ممثلة بمشايخها وعقالها </s>	<s> None </s>	<s> the Ka'lalah tribe represented by its sheikhs and notables. </s>
<s> وكذا قبيلة الشبيقة ممثلة بمشائخها وعقالها </s>	<s> None </s>	<s> as well as the tribe of Al-Shabiqa represented by its sheikhs and elders. </s>
<s> بين كلا القبيلتين المذكورتين على أن نحافظ على عدم سفك الدماء والاقتتال وعدم نهب الأموال والحقوق وغير ذلك </s>	<s> - Refrain from bloodshed and conflict. </s>	<s> between the two aforementioned tribes, on the condition that we maintain no bloodshed, no fighting, no looting of money and rights, etc. </s>
<s> ومن قبيلة الكعللة الشيخ راشد ضافر </s>	<s> - From the Ka'lala tribe: Sheikh Rashid Dhafir </s>	<s> from the Al-Ka'la tribe, Sheikh Rashid Dhafer. </s>
<s> ومن قبيلة الشبيقة الشيخ طالبي الشبيقي </s>	<s> - From the Shubayqa tribe: Sheikh Talbi Al-Shubayqi </s>	<s> and from the Al-Shabiqa tribe, Sheikh Talbi Al-Shabiqi </s>

Examining the issues of meaning (transfer) shows that the output of Google Translate (GT) is generally accurate, but it occasionally adheres too literally to the Arabic syntax, which could affect the naturalness in English. For instance, *idh ayyu fard yartakib ayya ḥadath jināʾī* "any individual who commits any criminal incident" could be rendered more smoothly as "any individual who commits a crime". The ChatGPT translation, on the other hand, tends to be more idiomatic and precise. For instance, "the perpetrator will be considered an enemy of their own tribe" provides a more fluid interpretation of *ʿaduww nafsihi* and seems more standard in English. With regard to completeness, both translations convey the key information without omitting significant details. However, the ChatGPT translation incorporates smoother explanations of context. For example, ChatGPT translates *al-ʿahd al-muqaddas li-llāhi taʿālā* as "a solemn and binding covenant" which seems more appropriate than Google Translate's "a sacred covenant".

As for content-oriented issues, logical sequencing is preserved in Google Translate (GT), but transitions between ideas are sometimes abrupt. For instance, the translation of *wayutammu taslīm al-jānī li-l-ʿadālah* as "and the perpetrator is handed over to justice" may require a conjunction or any additional connective expression to clarify its relationship to the preceding clause. ChatGPT translation seems stronger in logical flow. For instance, the translation of *wa-bimūjib hādhā al-ʿahd tumma tashkīl lujnah ḍammat kilā min* as "To ensure adherence and resolve any disputes, a committee was formed" better contextualizes the purpose of the committee than the Google Translate's "According to this covenant".

Both translations reflect factual accuracy. Key historical and procedural elements are preserved, such as the names of tribal leaders and the legal processes referenced.

The analysis of language and style of the two translations show that Google Translate (GT) occasionally feels stilted due to literal phrasing. For example, the translation of *murāqabatan li-llāhi taʿālā fīmā ʿahidnā wa-iltazamnā bih* as "observing God Almighty in what we pledged and committed to" could be more smoothly rendered. ChatGPT translation is generally smoother and more idiomatic. For example, wa-*llāhu al-muwaffiq* has been translated as "May Allah grant success", which flows more naturally than "And Allah is the Grantor of success". In a similar vein, while Google Translate (GT) is tailored for a formal and literal audience, it lacks the refined tone suitable for broader, non-Arabic-speaking audiences. ChatGPT translation, on the other hand, is better tailored to an English-speaking audience, providing clearer context for cultural and legal nuances. The sub-language of the two translations shows that both translations maintain formal and religious tones appropriate for the subject matter, but the ChatGPT version more effectively captures legal and cultural subtleties.

The use of idioms in the two translation is acceptable to a great extent. While Google Translate (GT) sometimes lacks natural idiomatic expression, as seen in its translation of *al-amn wa-al-amān wa-as-salām* as "security, safety, and peace", ChatGPT renders it more fluidly as "security, peace, and trust". In a similar vein, better use of idiomatic English is found in the ChatGPT version. For instance, *ʿahdan nihāʾiyyan mahdūman* has been translated as "final and irrevocable covenant", which is more apt than the Google Translate's "a final, destroyed, and fulfilled covenant".

As for mechanics, both translations adhere to grammatical rules. However, the ChatGPT translation displays superior punctuation and sentence structure.

No problems of physical presentation are detected. The two translations are good in terms of layout, typography and organization. However, ChatGPT version provides a more organized flow by contextualizing specific points. For instance, "The final clause of the covenant is crucial" introduces the key stipulations more effectively.

Hence, while ChatGPT translation is preferable for most audiences as it achieves better balance between literal accuracy and readability, the Google Translate (GT) could be more suitable if a strictly formal and literal tone is required.

It is worthwhile to mention that both Google Translate (GT), which represents neural-machine translation and large language models (LLMs) are progressively improving. The quality of translations may vary across different attempts due to ongoing enhancements in these systems. In the case of Google Translate (GT), improvements stem from translation memories and human feedback, whereas in large language models (LLMs), variations arise from their generative nature and dynamic interactions with users. The translation of the above texts can be enhanced by using proper prompts and training the large language models (LLM) to revise the translation accordingly. The translation of sensitive expression requires some care. Machine translation (MT) systems as well as large language models (LLM) will render the text based on the statistical or the training data available either through translation memories or knowledge systems but they may end up with a translation that does not consider the sensitivities of a particular community. Deletion, accommodation, acculturation are all translation strategies that can be employed by the translators when necessary. A large language models (LLM) needs to be trained on these strategies or prompted to use them to neutralize some aspects of the text. In Table 3, a fresh version of Google Translate (GT) and ChatGPT translations of the first text is provided. It is obvious that both show an improved quality translation.

Table 3. Google Translate (GT) and ChatGPT translations of Arabic

Arabic	Google Translate (GT)	ChatGPT
خرجت الناشطة السياسية وما سميت أنما "قائدة الثورة" في مدينة تعز عن صمتها لتبدأ بكتاباتها التي لم تجد فيها متعة سوى تعاليها على "الله" جل في علاه ومحاولة منها للمس بـ"الذات الإلهية" من خلال كتاباتها.	The political activist and so-called "leader of the revolution" in the city of Taiz broke her silence to begin her writings, in which she found no pleasure other than her arrogance towards "God" Almighty and her attempt to touch the "divine self" through her writings.	The political activist, who has been dubbed the "Leader of the Revolution" in the city of Taiz, has broken her silence, embarking on a series of writings that some have seen as an attempt to challenge the divine, specifically "God Almighty." Her writings have been interpreted as an attempt to undermine "the divine essence."
اذ ام تتشبث ان عادت من مسيرة الحياة لتبدأ في كتابة مقالها الذي عنونت له بعنوان " سنة أولى ثورة" حتى خرجت في مقالها عن الدين الى "الإلحاد"	As soon as she returned from the journey of life to begin writing her article, which she titled "The First Year of the Revolution," she went beyond religion to "atheism" in her article.	Shortly after returning from the "March of Life," she began writing an article titled "First Year of Revolution". In this piece, she seemed to transition from discussing religion to embracing "atheism."
فقالت في فقرتها الرابعة: "كانت الأمور كلها طيبة "بلدة طيبة ورب غفور" لكن الأمور لم تعد طيبة، والرب الشكور لم يعد حاضراً في ليل خادر .. تركنا الرب نتدبر أمورنا، ولم نستطع أن نفعل شيء أمام عجزنا البشري"	She said in her fourth paragraph: "Things were all good, 'a good town and a forgiving Lord,' but things were no longer good, and the grateful Lord was no longer present in the dark night... God left us to manage our affairs, and we were unable to do anything in the face of our human inability."	In the fourth paragraph of her article, she wrote: 'Everything was fine — 'a good land and a forgiving Lord' — but things are no longer fine. The grateful Lord is no longer present in the night of despair... The Lord left us to manage our own affairs, and we found ourselves powerless in the face of human frailty.'
كما قالت في نهاية نفس الفقرة: "وعيون لا ترحم تطل من بعيد، العسكر والقبائل والبيئة المعادية، والله الذي لا يرانا ..."	She also said at the end of the same paragraph: "And merciless eyes peered from afar, the military, the tribes, the hostile environment, and God who does not see us..."	Later in the same paragraph, she added: 'Unforgiving eyes watch from afar — the military, the tribes, the hostile environment, and God, who no longer sees us...'

continued on following page

Table 3. Continued

Arabic	Google Translate (GT)	ChatGPT
ةيادب يف تلاقو ةعباسلا اهترقف: "نيعبسلا بر نكل" ةءابعب اًبوجحم ناك يكيرمألا ريفسلا، تاحيرصتبو نييسايسلا نيدعترملا، ةداق تالاهتباو كرتشملا"	And she said at the beginning of her seventh paragraph: "But the Lord of the seventies was hidden by the cloak of the American ambassador, and by the statements of the trembling politicians, and by the supplications of the leaders of the Joint Parties."	In the seventh paragraph, she wrote: 'But the Lord of Seventy Square was veiled by the cloak of the American ambassador, by the trembling statements of politicians, and by the prayers of opposition leaders.'
سفن يف تلاق مث لبقو ةرقفلا كلت مل امنيحو" :اهتياهن مهمامأ يكبت نأ عطتست هللا نأل ،روهقم كنأل كلذخ"	Then she said in the same paragraph and before its end: "And when you could not cry in front of them because you were oppressed, because God let you down,"	Before concluding that paragraph, she remarked: 'And when you couldn't cry in front of them because you were oppressed, because God abandoned you...'
ةيادب يف تلاق امك ةعساتلا اهترقف: "هذه مغرو ينكل" رعشأ ةعئارلا ةريسملا مجحب ةريبك ةبيخب قوف عبرتت هللا يردص"	As she said at the beginning of her ninth paragraph: "But despite this wonderful journey, I feel a great disappointment as great as God sitting on my chest."	At the start of the ninth paragraph, she expressed: 'Despite this remarkable journey, I feel an overwhelming sense of disappointment, as vast as God, weighing heavily on my chest.'
يتلا ىرطقملا ىرشب ىوقلا ضعب تلواح يف ةحاسلا ةينميلا ةلطب اهنأب اهريوصت مل ةيروث ةدئاقو ةيموق مهنم دحا دعب قرطتي ام يتلا اهتديقع ىلا اناي ع اهرهظا نا ثتبل عيمجلل اًناي ب	Bushra Al-Maqtari, who tried Some forces in the Yemeni arena portrayed her as a national heroine and a revolutionary leader, and none of them have yet addressed her beliefs, which she has soon made clear to everyone,	Bushra al-Maqtari, who some forces in the Yemeni arena have tried to portray her as a national heroine and revolutionary leader, has openly revealed her beliefs.
شيعت اهنأ ةلهاجتم ملسم بعش طسو ىندا ضفري نيدتمو تاذلاب سملاب راكفأ تادقتعملا وا ةيهلإلا ةيمالسإلا.	Ignoring the fact that she lives among a Muslim and religious people who reject the slightest idea of harming the divine or Islamic beliefs.	She seems to disregard the fact that she lives in a deeply religious and Muslim society that vehemently rejects any affront to the divine or Islamic beliefs.
قرحَأ رصم يف نوملسملا تويب بلاط أرجتل طابقألا نم لينلا نم يطبق دمحم " ةيرشبلا لوسر ىلص هللا هيلع ملسو" لالخ نم ةباتك لاقم هل ىلع ناونع طئاح يف كوب سيفلا.	In Egypt, Muslims burned the homes of Copts because a Coptic student dared to attack the Messenger of Humanity, "Mohammed, peace be upon him," by writing an article on his Facebook wall.	In Egypt, Muslims burned Coptic homes after a Coptic student dared to insult the Prophet Muhammad (peace be upon him) by writing a post on his Facebook wall.

continued on following page

Table 3. Continued

Arabic	Google Translate (GT)	ChatGPT
ليخرج بعدها بطريق النصارى ويعتذر للمسلمين من تلك الكتابة ويحذر من المس بمعتقدات المسلمين.	He then came out in the Christian way and apologized to Muslims for that writing and warned against harming Muslims' beliefs.	He later issued a public apology to Muslims and warned against offending their beliefs.
لكن ما حدث هنا في اليمن هو العكس إذ لم تكن من النصارى او الأقباط، وانما مننا ومن أبناء جلدتنا لتقدح في معتقداتنا الإسلامية	But what happened here in Yemen is the opposite, as it was not from Christians or Copts, but from us and our own people to disparage our Islamic beliefs.	However, what happened in Yemen is quite the opposite: this affront did not come from a Christian or a Copt but from one of our own, someone from our community, who chose to attack our Islamic beliefs.

From our analysis of the translation quality of both Google Translate (GT) and ChatGPT so far, we can safely argue that the quality of translation of these systems has improved even though they still encounter some problems depending on text types. This finding is in line with those findings of other studies such as (Chaima, 2024; Shokoohifar, 2024). The translation complexity across the above text types may differ based on a number of criteria including accuracy (Öncü & Kutlu, 2024), cultural sensitivity (Mohammed et al., 2024; Mohammed, 2023), smoothness, idiomatic fluency (Hamood, 2024), and contextual adaptation (Tomenchuk & Popovych, 2024). Legal and technical texts, for instance, require strict adherence to specific terms and concepts to avoid any ambiguity. In addition, these texts rely on formal, structured language, which leaves little room for interpretative flexibility. Machine translations often struggle with maintaining exact phrasing while ensuring readability. Moreover, some terms have multiple meanings based on legal or technical contexts. This need for precision and lack of idiomatic flexibility make these texts difficult for machine translations, as even small inaccuracies can alter meaning significantly (Bajčić & Golenko, 2024; Moneus & Sahari, 2024). Religious and philosophical Texts pose several problems for both machine and human translators due to their cultural sensitivity, emotional tone and expressive language that abounds with ambiguity and symbolism. The translation of these text requires deep knowledge of religious traditions and historical context. The translation of the text about Ahmed Bin Alwan shows that preserving reverence, depth, and symbolic meaning is complex. The two translations fall short to balancing literal accuracy with idiomatic fluency (Ghozali et al., 2024; Swargiary, 2024). Commercial and marketing texts, on the other hand, pose less problems. That does not mean, however, that machine translation (MT) and large language models (LLMs) can render all aspects of a text. Marketing texts aim to be persuasive and engaging, which requires a creative translation approach to maintain appeal across cultures. Some terms like "crispy on the outside, tender on the inside" involve sensory and emotive language that machines often translate literally, losing their impact. In addition, the tone and style must be adapted to target audiences, which machines sometimes struggle with. Yet, these texts are less rigid in structure, allowing for more flexible translations, making them easier for machines compared to legal or religious texts (Tomenchuk & Popovych, 2024; Xiang, 2024). Narrative/Journalistic Texts range in their difficulty from moderate to high as these types of text require smooth transitions and logical progression, which machines occasionally render awkwardly (Guerberof-Arenas & Toral, 2022; Hadley et al., 2022; Hu & Li, 2023). For instance, the subtle implications, such as criticism embedded in the activist's remarks, require contextual awareness to translate effectively. Another challenge lies in maintaining the original tone, whether critical, neutral, or supportive. Hence, while journalistic and narrative texts are not as rigid as legal texts, they still require contextual and stylistic accuracy to convey the intended message properly.

In Figure 6, we attempt to compare the unique challenges of each text type on a complexity scale ranging from low to moderate to high and very high.

Figure 6. Complexity ranking of text types.

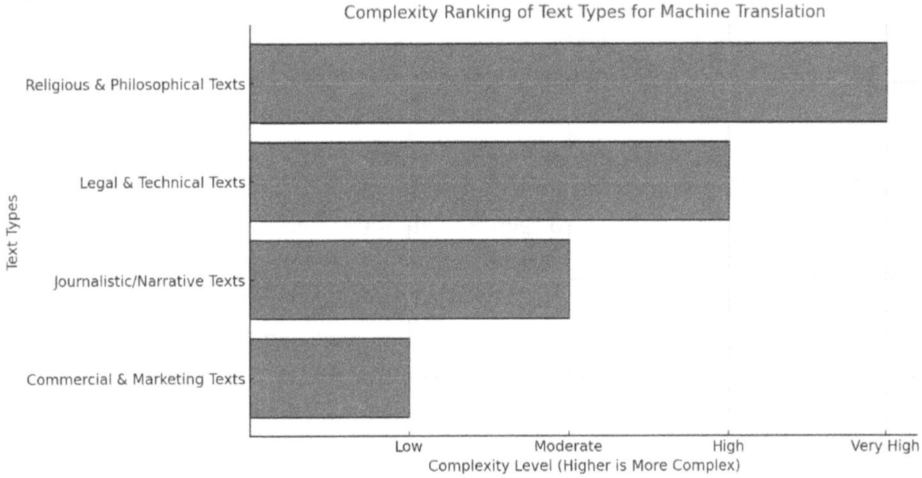

The bar chart above visualizes the complexity ranking of different text types used in this chapter for machine translation (MT) and large language models (LLMs). Religious and philosophical texts rank as the most complex, as they require high cultural sensitivity and nuanced interpretation. Legal and technical texts follow closely, because these texts require precision and formal structure. Journalistic/ narrative texts fall in the middle, because their translation needs to balance tone and logical flow. Commercial and marketing texts are the least complex, because they offer more flexibility and creative freedom.

Hence, despite the tremendous advancements in machine translation (MT) and large language models (LLMs), improving accuracy, fluency, and adaptability across diverse text types should be prioritized. Enhancing these systems requires a number of strategies including the incorporation of multiple domain-specific models (Gahoi, 2023; Zhang et al., 2021), the use of context-aware translation (Peng et al., 2024; Rauf & Yvon, 2020), the consideration of linguistic and cultural sensitivity (Dong, 2023; M Crisostomo et al., 2022), the enhancement of post-editing tools (Kim, 2024), the identification of errors by leveraging feedback loops and investment in Human-in-the-Loop Systems (Mosqueira-Rey et al., 2023; Wu et al., 2022), the use of data augmentation techniques and transfer learning in low-resource languages (Latief et al., 2024; Ranathunga et al., 2023), the development of multimodal translation (Sulubacak et al., 2020; Yao & Wan, 2020) among others.

CONCLUDING REMARKS

This chapter has examined the use of neural-based machine translation systems (NMT) and, in particular, Google Translate (GT) and large language models (LLMs) such as ChatGPT in Arabic-English translation. The chapter delimits itself to certain text types in line with text-typology models. In particular, the chapter investigates the Google Translate (GT) and ChatGPT translations of argumentation within journalistic texts, exposition within both promotional and philosophical genres, and instrumental texts within the legal genre. This focus on diverse text types allows for a comprehensive evaluation of the translation performance of these systems across different communicative purposes and stylistic demands. The translations from Google Translate (GT) and ChatGPT have been analysed on the basis of Mossop's parameters of revising and editing in translation. That is, the translation quality assessment of the outputs covered problems of meaning transfer, content, language and style as well as presentation. While some texts, such as journalistic or promotional ones, might appear easier to translate, this is not always true. The hybridity of genres can complicate the translation process. For instance, a narrative text about a scholar may present few challenges for tools like Google Translate (GT) or ChatGPT. However, when the text becomes more expressive, poetic, or rich in intertextuality and culture-specific concepts, it often exceeds the capabilities of machine translation, leading to significant inaccuracies. Our analysis has shown that some aspects of texts such as allusions and irony in journalistic text, visual aspects in a promotional text, culture-specific and religious concepts in a philosophical text as well as some presentation and structural aspects of the legal texts are lost in Google Translate (GT) and ChatGPT translations.

However, we need to acknowledge the fact that machine translation (MT) systems continue to improve with advancements in artificial intelligence and training data availability. Yet, human translators are still essential for handling text types that require cultural understanding, creative adaptations, and linguistic expertise to ensure accurate and nuanced translations.

REFERENCES

Alkhawaja, L. (2024). Unveiling the new frontier: ChatGPT-3 powered translation for Arabic-English language pairs. *Theory and Practice in Language Studies*, *14*(2), 347–357. DOI: 10.17507/tpls.1402.05

Alsulaimani, B., & Islam, A. (2022). Impact of 4IR technology and its impact on the current deployment. *International Journal of Computer Science and Information Technologies*, *14*(4), 53–67. DOI: 10.5121/ijcsit.2022.14405

Bajčić, M., & Golenko, D. (2024). Applying large language models in legal translation: The state-of-the-art. [JLL]. *International Journal of Language & Law*, *13*, 171–196. DOI: 10.14762/jll.2024.171

Bhadauria, A. S., Shukla, M., Kumar, P., & Dwivedi, N. (2023). Attention-based neural machine translation for multilingual communication. *International Conference on Trends in Computational and Cognitive Engineering*, 129–142.

Buhler, H. (1979). Supersentential semantics and translation. *Meta*, *24*(4), 451–458. DOI: 10.7202/002177ar

Chaima, H. (2024). *Prospecting the future of translator amid AI and machine practices and outputs* [PhD Thesis, Université Kasdi Merbah-Ouargla]. https://dspace.univ-ouargla.dz/jspui/handle/123456789/37029

M Crisostomo, M., P Bernarte, R., & C Ambag, S. (2022). Cross-Cultural Translation Studies in the Context of Artificial Intelligence: Challenges and Response. European Online Journal of Natural and Social Sciences: Proceedings, 11(4 (s)), pp-187.

Dabre, R., Chu, C., & Kunchukuttan, A. (2020). A survey of multilingual neural machine translation. *ACM Computing Surveys*, *53*(5), 1–38. DOI: 10.1145/3406095

Dong, J. (2023). Transfer learning-based neural machine translation for low-resource languages. *ACM Transactions on Asian and Low-Resource Language Information Processing*, *3618111*, 3618111. Advance online publication. DOI: 10.1145/3618111

Dwivedi, R. K., Nand, P., & Pal, O. (2025). Hybrid NMT model and comparison with existing machine translation approaches. *Multidisciplinary Science Journal*, *7*(4), 2025146–2025146. DOI: 10.31893/multiscience.2025146

Fan, P., Gong, H., & Gong, X. (2023). The application of ChatGPT in translation teaching: Changes, challenges, and responses. *International Journal of Education and Humanities*, *11*(2), 49–52. DOI: 10.54097/ijeh.v11i2.13530

Gahoi, A. (2023). *Using domain knowledge to improve machine translation in Indian languages* [PhD Thesis, International Institute of Information Technology Hyderabad].

Ghozali, N. I. M., Mansor, N. S., Awang, H., & Yusof, S. M. (2024). Automated translation tools for mualaf: Artificial intelligence solutions for accessing islamic texts and resources across languages. *International Journal of Islamic Theology & Civilization, 2*(3), 60–64. DOI: 10.5281/zenodo.13943174

Guerberof-Arenas, A., & Toral, A. (2022). Creativity in translation: Machine translation as a constraint for literary texts. *Translation Spaces, 11*(2), 184–212. DOI: 10.1075/ts.21025.gue

Hadley, J. L., Taivalkoski-Shilov, K., Teixeira, C. S., & Toral, A. (2022). *Using technologies for creative-text translation.* Taylor & Francis. DOI: 10.4324/9781003094159

Halliday Michael, A. K., & Hasan, R. (1976). *Cohesion in English.* Longman.

Hamood, M. I. (2024). The translation of English food idioms into Arabic through ChatGPT: Problems and solutions. *Midad Al-Adab Refereed Journal, 1*(Special issue of the Translation Department Conference), 55–76.

Hatim, B. (1984). A text typological approach to syllabus design in translator training. *The Incorporated Linguist, 22*(3), 146–149.

Hatim, B. (2001). *Teaching and researching translation.* Longman.

Hatim, B., & Mason, I. (1990). *Discourse and the translator.* Longman.

Hatim, B., & Munday, J. (2004). *Translation: An advanced resource book.* Routledge. DOI: 10.4324/9780203501887

Hu, K., & Li, X. (2023). The creativity and limitations of AI neural machine translation: A corpus-based study of DeepL's English-to-Chinese translation of Shakespeare's plays. *Babel. Revue Internationale de La Traduction / International Journal of Translation, 69*(4), 546–563. https://doi.org/DOI: 10.1075/babel.00331.hu

Jia, Y., Carl, M., & Wang, X. (2019). Post-editing neural machine translation versus phrase-based machine translation for English–Chinese. *Machine Translation, 33*(1-2), 9–29. DOI: 10.1007/s10590-019-09229-6

Jiang, L., Jiang, Y., & Han, L. (2024). The potential of ChatGPT in translation evaluation: A case study of the Chinese-Portuguese machine translation. *Cadernos de Tradução (Florianópolis), 44*(1), e98613. DOI: 10.5007/2175-7968.2024.e98613

Johnson, M., Schuster, M., Le, Q. V., Krikun, M., Wu, Y., Chen, Z., Thorat, N., Viégas, F., Wattenberg, M., Corrado, G., Hughes, M., & Dean, J. (2017). Google's multilingual neural machine translation system: Enabling zero-shot translation. *Transactions of the Association for Computational Linguistics, 5*, 339–351. DOI: 10.1162/tacl_a_00065

Khoshafah, F. (2023). ChatGPT for Arabic-English translation: Evaluating the accuracy. *Research Square*. https://doi.org/DOI: 10.21203/rs.3.rs-2814154/v2

Ki, D., & Carpuat, M. (2024). Guiding large language models to post-edit machine translation with error annotations. *arXiv Preprint, arXiv:2404.07851*. https://arxiv.org/abs/2404.07851 DOI: 10.18653/v1/2024.findings-naacl.265

Kim, Y. J. (2024). *The future of translation*. Jane Company.

Koh, S. (2023). An analysis of ChatGPT's language translation based on the Korean film Minari. *Journal of English Teaching through Movies and Media, 24*(4), 1–14. https://doi.org/DOI: 10.16875/stem.2023.24.4.1

Krueger, F. A. (2023, June). *I built the world's largest translated Cuneiform corpus using AI.* https://praeclarum.org/2023/06/09/cuneiform.html

Latief, A. D., Jarin, A., Yaniasih, Y., Afra, D. I. N., Nurfadhilah, E., Pebiana, S., Hidayati, N. N., & Fajri, R. (2024). Latest research in data augmentation for low resource language text translation: A review. *2024 International Conference on Computer, Control, Informatics and Its Applications (IC3INA)*, 185–190. https://ieeexplore.ieee.org/abstract/document/10732042/

Lee, T. (2024). Artificial intelligence and posthumanist translation: ChatGPT versus the translator. *Applied Linguistics Review, 15*(6), 2351–2372. DOI: 10.1515/applirev-2023-0122

Lyons, S. (2020). A review of Thai–English machine translation. *Machine Translation, 34*(2-3), 197–230. DOI: 10.1007/s10590-020-09248-8

Macken, L. (2024). Machine translation meets large language models: Evaluating ChatGPT's ability to automatically post-edit literary texts. *Proceedings of the 1st Workshop on Creative-Text Translation and Technology*, 65–81.

Mair, V. (2023, June). *AI for Akkadian.* https://languagelog.ldc.upenn.edu/nll/?p=59411

Mohammed, S. Y., Khalaf, A. S., & Aljanabi, M. (2024). Challenges and opportunities in translation studies: The evolving role. In Mansour, N., & Bujosa Vadell, L. M. (Eds.), *Sustainability and Financial Services in the Digital Age* (pp. 107–117). Springer., DOI: 10.1007/978-3-031-67511-9_7

Mohammed, T. A. (2023). Translating Islamic media discourse from Arabic into English: An analysis of translation process. In N. Bakrim (Ed.), *Translatology, Translation and Interpretation-Toward a New Scientific Endeavor*. IntechOpen. https://www.intechopen.com/chapters/1172609

Mohammed, T. A. S. (2011). *A taxonomy of problems in Arabic-English translation: A systematic functional grammar approach* [PhD thesis]. University of the Western Cape.

Moneus, A. M., & Sahari, Y. (2024). Artificial intelligence and human translation: A contrastive study based on legal texts. *Heliyon, 10*(6), e28106. Advance online publication. DOI: 10.1016/j.heliyon.2024.e28106 PMID: 38524597

Mosqueira-Rey, E., Hernández-Pereira, E., Alonso-Ríos, D., Bobes-Bascarán, J., & Fernández-Leal, Á. (2023). Human-in-the-loop machine learning: A state of the art. *Artificial Intelligence Review, 56*(4), 3005–3054. DOI: 10.1007/s10462-022-10246-w

Mossop, B. (2014). *Revising and editing for translators*. Routledge. DOI: 10.4324/9781315767130

Öncü, M. H., & Kutlu, Y. (2024). Performance comparison of known AI translation tools. *Tethys Env. Sci, 1*(3), 117–126. DOI: 10.5281/zenodo.13269233

Park, S. C. (2018). The Fourth Industrial Revolution and implications for innovative cluster policies. *AI & Society, 33*(3), 433–445. DOI: 10.1007/s00146-017-0777-5

Peng, K., Ding, L., Zhong, Q., Shen, L., Liu, X., Zhang, M., Ouyang, Y., & Tao, D. (2023). Towards making the most of ChatGPT for machine translation. *Findings of the Association for Computational Linguistics: EMNLP, 2023*, 5622–5633. DOI: 10.18653/v1/2023.findings-emnlp.373

Peng, Z., Bawden, R., & Yvon, F. (2024). *Handling very long contexts in neural machine translation: A survey* [PhD Thesis, Projet ANR MaTOS]. https://inria.hal.science/hal-04652584

Ranathunga, S., Lee, E.-S. A., Prifti Skenduli, M., Shekhar, R., Alam, M., & Kaur, R. (2023). Neural machine translation for low-resource languages: A survey. *ACM Computing Surveys, 55*(11), 1–37. DOI: 10.1145/3567592

Rao, P., McGee, L. M., & Seideman, C. A. (2024). A comparative assessment of ChatGPT vs. Google Translate for the translation of patient instructions. *Journal of Medical Artificial Intelligence*, *7*, 11. DOI: 10.21037/jmai-24-24

Rauf, S. A., & Yvon, F. (2020). *Document level contexts for neural machine translation* [PhD Thesis, LIMSI-CNRS]. https://hal.science/hal-03687190/document

Reiss, K. (2000). Type, kind and individuality of text: Decision making in translation. In Venuti, L. (Ed.), *The Translation Studies Reader* (pp. 168–179). Routledge.

Sahari, Y., Al-Kadi, A. M. T., & Ali, J. K. M. (2023). A cross sectional study of ChatGPT in translation: Magnitude of use, attitudes, and uncertainties. *Journal of Psycholinguistic Research*, *52*(6), 2937–2954. DOI: 10.1007/s10936-023-10031-y PMID: 37934302

Shokoohifar, M. (2024). *Artificial Intelligence-Assisted Translation: A Study of Cognitive Load and Time Through EEG* [PhD Thesis, Allameh Tabataba'i University].

Siu, S. C. (2023). *ChatGPT and GPT-4 for professional translators: Exploring the potential of large language models in translation*. Preprint., DOI: 10.2139/ssrn.4448091

Siu, S. C. (2024). Revolutionising translation with AI: Unravelling neural machine translation and generative pre-trained large language models. In Peng, Y., Huang, H., & Li, D. (Eds.), *New Advances in Translation Technology*. Springer., DOI: 10.1007/978-981-97-2958-6_3

Stein, D. (2018). Machine translation: Past, present and future. In Rehm, G., Stein, D., Sasaki, F., & Witt, A. (Eds.), *Language technologies for a multilingual Europe. (Translation and Multilingual Natural Language Processing 5)*. Language Science Press., DOI: 10.5281/zenodo.1291947

Sulubacak, U., Caglayan, O., Grönroos, S.-A., Rouhe, A., Elliott, D., Specia, L., & Tiedemann, J. (2020). Multimodal machine translation through visuals and speech. *Machine Translation*, *34*(2–3), 97–147. DOI: 10.1007/s10590-020-09250-0

Swargiary, K. (2024). *Sacred codes: Artificial intelligence and the creation of religious texts*. ERA.

Tomenchuk, M., & Popovych, K. (2024). *Large language models and machine translation*. https://dspace.uzhnu.edu.ua/jspui/handle/lib/68269

Von, V. (2008). *Towards an integrated translation approach: Proposal of a dynamic translation model (DTM)* [PhD dissertation]. der Universität Hamburg.

Wu, X., Xiao, L., Sun, Y., Zhang, J., Ma, T., & He, L. (2022). A survey of human-in-the-loop for machine learning. *Future Generation Computer Systems*, *135*, 364–381. DOI: 10.1016/j.future.2022.05.014

Xiang, C. (2024). Study on the effectiveness of ChatGPT in translating forestry sci-tech texts. *International Journal of Linguistics. Literature & Translation*, *7*(9), 88–94. DOI: 10.32996/ijllt.2024.7.9.11

Yao, S., & Wan, X. (2020). Multimodal transformer for multimodal machine translation. *Proceedings of the 58th Annual Meeting of the Association for Computational Linguistics*, 4346–4350. https://aclanthology.org/2020.acl-main.400/

Zayed, M. H. T., & Nuirat, W. (2024). Human touch in AI translation: Strategies employed by professional translators in post-editing Arabic-English AI generated translations of media texts. *Educational Administration: Theory And Practice*, *30*(4), 2055–2062. DOI: 10.53555/kuey.v30i4.1804

Zhang, S., Liu, Y., Xiong, D., Zhang, P., & Chen, B. (2021). Domain-aware self-attention for multi-domain neural machine translation. *Interspeech*, *2047–2051*, 2047–2051. Advance online publication. DOI: 10.21437/Interspeech.2021-1477

Chapter 2

The Evolution and Development of Artificial Intelligence Interpretation Technology in the Era of Large-Scale Language Models

Gurwinder Kaur Dua
https://orcid.org/0009-0003-3269-1969
Post Graduate Government College - 11, Chandigarh, India

ABSTRACT

With the ongoing advancement of artificial intelligence technology, large-scale language models have emerged as a significant breakthrough in the realm of interpreting intelligence. This evolution presents the interpreting profession with unprecedented technological changes. A review of the relevant research indicates that the rise of large models has introduced both new opportunities and challenges for the development of AI-driven interpreting technology. Firstly, the language generation capabilities of these large models are highly advanced, enabling them to produce more accurate and natural interpretation and translation outcomes. Secondly, these models possess strong learning abilities, allowing them to continuously enhance the performance of interpretation systems through extensive data training. Additionally, their rapid response characteristics facilitate efficient interpretation services in real-time scenarios.

DOI: 10.4018/979-8-3373-0060-3.ch002

INTRODUCTION

The rapid emergence of generative AI technologies, specifically Generative Pre-trained Transformers (GPT), has significantly reshaped industries worldwide. Companies, both international giants such as Google, Microsoft, and NVIDIA, and domestic powerhouses like Alibaba and Baidu, are intensively investing in the development of large-scale language models. These models are central to the ongoing journey of artificial intelligence (AI) towards achieving universal intelligence. Their potential to revolutionize various sectors, particularly information technology, has led many industry experts to predict that these innovations will transform the landscape of the global information industry. In the context of AI's evolution, the world is moving from an era dominated by data-driven internet technologies and cloud computing, towards a new era—an AI-driven world shaped by the power of large-scale language models like GPT (Seneff, 1992; Acosta et al. 2022; Krishnankutty et al. 2022; Tiwari et al. 2021; Bharti et al. 2022).

Chat GPT, a widely recognized example of such a language model, is designed to understand and generate human-like text by utilizing extensive training data. These models are incredibly versatile, capable of performing a wide array of tasks, including natural language processing, machine translation, sentiment analysis, and more. They rely on deep learning techniques, particularly transformer architectures, which have revolutionized the field of AI. By processing vast amounts of textual data and learning from diverse patterns, these models are able to generate text that mimics human thought and language with remarkable accuracy. As a result, they have become integral to advancing the frontiers of AI and unlocking its potential across industries (Huang et al. 2022).

Large-scale language models like Chat GPT are not only transforming AI research but also leading to profound changes in practical applications. One of the areas where these transformations are particularly noticeable is the field of interpretation and translation technology (Zingoni et al. 2021). AI has made inroads into nearly every aspect of modern society, and interpretation is no exception. The development of machine translation systems and AI-powered translation tools has revolutionized how languages are understood, communicated, and processed. These advancements are reshaping industries such as global communication, cross-cultural collaboration, and information exchange (Cellina et al. 2022; Nor et al. 2021).

The rise of AI in interpretation technology has sparked a significant transformation. The impact is felt across both the upstream and downstream segments of the industrial chain, which includes the development, deployment, and use of translation tools and systems (Ilkka, 2018; El-Meniawy et al. 2022). The applications of AI in interpretation technology are not just limited to translation services but extend to a wide range of related fields, such as real-time communication translation, content localization, and even the interpretation of complex texts. As AI-powered language models evolve, they continue to enhance their ability to understand nuanced meanings, cultural context, and specific terminologies, making them increasingly effective at handling the intricacies of translation and interpretation tasks (Kumar et al. 2023; Albulescu et al. 2021).

The rapid innovation in AI-driven translation systems has led to the creation of various translation machines and applications, which have become highly sought after by both the general public and professional sectors (Huang, 2021). Translation services, once limited to human translators, are now being augmented or even replaced by AI-based solutions. With the rise of machine translation, more people around the world can access information in different languages with greater ease (Heredia-Negron et al. 2023; Fernández et al. 2020). Whether it is in the form of personal translators, real-time language apps, or automatic translation features integrated into communication platforms, the demand for such tools is surging (Farahmand, 2021).

Both international and domestic translation technology providers see machine translation as a critical entry point for the broader adoption of AI technology. Recognizing the immense potential of large-scale language models, companies are working to refine their translation machines, aiming to offer increasingly accurate and context-aware translation services (Liang et al. 2021). This growing demand for AI-driven translation solutions is not just limited to the consumer market but is also expanding into more professional and specialized settings. Conferences, business meetings, and international summits are increasingly turning to AI tools to overcome language barriers, enabling more seamless global communication and collaboration (Udupa, 2022).

As the industry continues to embrace these emerging technologies, the applications of AI in interpretation and translation are evolving rapidly (Barriga et al. 2020). One notable trend is the integration of real-time translation capabilities into everyday devices and communication platforms (Laupichler et al. 2022; Salas-Pilco et al. 2022). Virtual assistants, messaging applications, and video conferencing tools are now offering real-time language translation, allowing individuals and businesses to communicate effortlessly across linguistic divides (Hwang et al. 2021). This is particularly important in a world that is becoming more interconnected and globalized, where effective communication between individuals who speak different languages is essential for success in various sectors (Jobin et al. 2019).

In addition to real-time translation, AI systems are being increasingly utilized to improve the accuracy and fluency of translations (Xing et al. 2023; Hamamoto et al. 2020). Machine learning techniques enable these systems to learn from vast amounts of multilingual data, improving their understanding of grammar, syntax, idiomatic expressions, and cultural subtleties (Xing et al. 2022). This, in turn, leads to more natural-sounding translations that are better suited to the specific needs of users (Ngwenya et al. 2022; Liu et al. 2022; Arsad et al. 2021). With advancements in neural machine translation (NMT) and deep learning, AI models can now translate not only individual words but also entire sentences, paragraphs, and even complex texts with a higher degree of contextual accuracy (Memon et al. 2022).

Moreover, the continuous evolution of AI-powered translation tools is also leading to greater customization (Chen et al. 2020; Gorze´n-Mitka et al. 2020). These tools can now be tailored to specific industries or domains, such as legal, medical, technical, or literary translation (Del Mondo et al. 2021; Lin et al. 2021). By training language models on specialized datasets, companies can develop translation tools that cater to the unique terminology and jargon of particular fields (Sun et al. 2022; Kuzior et al. 2022; Ribeiro et al. 2018; Barbosa et al. 2020). This is a significant advantage over traditional machine translation systems, which may struggle with specialized language or industry-specific terms (LeCun et al. 2015; Véstias et al. 2020; Wood et al. 2023).

The impact of AI on the interpretation and translation industry is not limited to improving the efficiency of translation processes (Touretzky et al. 2019; Hedderich et al. 2021; Pantelimon et al. 2021) It is also enabling new opportunities for cross-cultural exchange and collaboration. By breaking down language barriers, AI translation tools allow people from different linguistic and cultural backgrounds to interact and share ideas more effectively. This fosters greater understanding, cooperation, and innovation in fields such as international business, diplomacy, education, and research (Dai et al. 2020; Bañeres et al. 2020).

Despite the tremendous progress in AI-driven translation technologies, challenges remain. One of the key hurdles is the ongoing need to address issues of linguistic diversity and inclusivity (Chiu et al. 2020). AI models trained on large datasets may inadvertently introduce biases or fail to adequately represent minority languages or dialects. Ensuring that AI translation tools are capable of accurately handling a broad range of languages, especially underrepresented ones, is essential for their future success and widespread adoption (Povedano-Montero et al. 2020).

Furthermore, while AI systems are becoming increasingly sophisticated, they are still not perfect. Challenges such as handling idiomatic expressions, regional variations in language, and the emotional nuances of communication remain areas for improvement. Although AI-powered tools can produce highly accurate translations in many cases, there are still situations where human translators may be necessary to ensure the highest level of quality and precision (Gams et al. 2021; Erdil et al. 2019).

In conclusion, the emergence of large-scale language models like Chat GPT represents a pivotal moment in the development of AI technology. As these models continue to evolve, they will play an increasingly important role in transforming industries and reshaping how we communicate, share information, and collaborate across linguistic and cultural boundaries. The field of interpretation and translation is just one of many areas where AI is making a significant impact, and as the technology matures, we can expect to see even more exciting innovations that will shape the future of global communication and beyond.

II. THE RISE OF LARGE-SCALE LANGUAGE MODELS AND THE DEVELOPMENT OF INTERPRETATION TECHNOLOGY

The emergence of large-scale language models has positively influenced the evolution of interpretation technology. Firstly, the interpreting process primarily involves translating spoken expressions from one language to another. The advancements made by large-scale language models in natural language processing have significantly enhanced key tasks such as machine translation and speech recognition (Brown et al. 1993). By training extensive neural network models, these language models can acquire richer and more precise semantic information, thereby improving their ability to understand and convey meaning between source and target languages during interpretation (Dec et al. 2022).

Secondly, substantial advancements in language modeling, particularly with models like the GPT series, have enabled the generation of coherent and semantically consistent text. This capability provides valuable references and creative outputs for interpretation systems. By integrating the language generation strengths of large-scale language models with machine translation techniques, interpretation systems can execute oral translations more fluidly and adapt more effectively to various contexts and cultural nuances while preserving semantic accuracy (Pas´ko et al. 2022).

Moreover, large-scale language models can also be utilized in speech recognition and synthesis, offering a comprehensive solution for interpretation technology. When applied to speech recognition, these models enhance the system's ability to accurately recognize spoken input, thus providing more precise text for subsequent translation processes. Utilizing large-scale language models for speech synthesis can render the interpretation results generated by the system more natural and fluent, thereby enhancing user experience (Tedre et al.2021).

The rise of large-scale language models has significantly propelled the advancement of interpretation technology (Och et al. 1999). By leveraging the semantic understanding, generative capabilities, and speech processing technologies of these models, interpretation systems can achieve more accurate and fluent translations, facilitating cross-language communication. However, ongoing research and development of various technologies related to large-scale language models are essential to meet the practical needs of interpretation technology (Toivonen et al. 2020).

III. THE APPLICATION OF LARGE-SCALE LANGUAGE MODELS IN AI INTERPRETATION TECHNOLOGY

Large-scale language models, such as Chat GPT and Baidu's Wenxin, have substantial applications in AI interpretation technology. Key areas of application include:

A. Speech Recognition

Language models can significantly enhance speech recognition systems by improving their ability to accurately understand and transcribe spoken language. With their deep comprehension of grammar, context, and semantics, these models contribute to the development of more sophisticated and efficient speech recognition algorithms. Speech recognition is crucial in AI interpretation technology, with various applications where it plays a vital role.

Real-Time Transcription: Speech recognition technology enables the conversion of spoken language into written text instantly. This capability is particularly beneficial in contexts such as live events, lectures, conferences, or meetings, where immediate and precise transcriptions are essential.

- **Virtual Assistants**: At the heart of virtual assistant technologies like Siri, Google Assistant, and Amazon Alexa lies speech recognition. These assistants can comprehend and respond to voice commands, allowing users to interact with their devices and perform tasks without using their hands.
- **Voice Control**: Speech recognition facilitates the operation of various devices, appliances, or systems through voice commands. Whether controlling smart home devices, vehicles, or wearables, this technology offers a convenient and intuitive way to interact.
- **Dictation and Voice-to-Text**: Users can utilize speech recognition technology to dictate text rather than typing, simplifying the process of composing emails, writing documents, or entering text in messaging apps. This feature is especially advantageous for individuals with disabilities or those who find typing challenging.
- **Multilingual Voice Translation**: By combining speech recognition with machine translation, real-time translation between different languages becomes possible. Users can speak in their native language, and the system can transcribe and translate their speech into the target language, facilitating cross-language communication.
- **Call Center Automation**: In call centers, speech recognition technology automates customer support processes. By converting spoken customer inquiries into text, the system can analyze the queries and provide appropriate

responses or direct the call to the correct department, minimizing the need for manual intervention.

- **Accessibility and Assistive Technologies**: Speech recognition enhances the ability of individuals with disabilities to interact with digital devices and access information more easily. It supports hands-free operation, voice-controlled applications, and communication aids for those with speech impairments.
- **Voice Analytics**: This technology can analyze and extract insights from audio data, finding applications in sentiment analysis, market research, voice-based biometrics, and fraud detection (Miller et al. 1994).

Advancements in deep learning algorithms and large-scale language models have significantly enhanced the accuracy and speed of speech recognition capabilities, improving the reliability and real-time performance of interpretation technologies. Traditional speech recognition systems often rely on probability models and feature engineering, which can limit their accuracy and responsiveness. In contrast, large-scale language models can automatically learn abstract representations of speech signals through deep neural networks, leading to improved recognition accuracy.

These models leverage extensive training data and computational resources to learn richer and more precise speech features, capturing more nuances and variations in speech. They also exhibit stronger generalization capabilities, effectively handling speech input under complex conditions such as varying accents, speech rates, and background noise. Furthermore, the processing speed of large-scale language models has seen significant improvements. Unlike traditional systems that require lengthy processing times for large volumes of speech data, these models can achieve faster recognition speeds through parallel computing and optimization algorithms, enhancing the real-time responsiveness of interpretation technologies.

The integration of deep learning algorithms has led to substantial advancements in speech recognition, enhancing reliability and real-time performance, and providing improved experiences for both interpreters and users. As speech recognition technology continues to evolve, it benefits from developments in deep learning, natural language processing, and enhanced training datasets, leading to a broader range of applications and empowering users with more efficient and intuitive interactions with machines (Weerasekara et al. 2022).

Natural Language Processing (NLP) plays a vital role in AI interpretation technology. Here are some of its applications in this domain:

- **Speech Recognition**: NLP techniques are employed to convert spoken language into written text, enabling AI interpretation systems to accurately transcribe and comprehend human speech.

- **Language Translation**: NLP algorithms are utilized to translate languages, allowing AI interpretation technology to effectively bridge communication gaps.
  - **Sentiment Analysis:** Natural Language Processing (NLP) models are capable of analyzing the sentiment conveyed in both written texts and spoken language. In the context of AI interpretation, sentiment analysis enables the system to grasp the emotions and intentions behind users' expressions, allowing for appropriate responses.
  - **Contextual Understanding:** NLP empowers AI interpretation systems to understand the context of conversations. This capability aids in interpreting ambiguous statements and generating more accurate responses based on the overall context of the dialogue.
  - **Text Summarization:** NLP algorithms can condense lengthy texts into concise and coherent summaries. In AI interpretation, this feature can be utilized to extract essential information from conversations and present a summary to the user.
  - **Dialogue Management:** NLP techniques enhance the ability of AI interpretation systems to manage dialogues effectively. They allow the system to maintain context, handle interruptions, and engage in multi-turn conversations, resulting in a seamless and natural conversational experience.
  - **Named Entity Recognition:** NLP models can identify and extract named entities, such as names of individuals, organizations, locations, and dates, from texts or speech. This functionality helps AI interpretation systems accurately understand and process specific information mentioned by users.

The rise of large-scale language models has revolutionized natural language processing (NLP), significantly improving the quality of translation and addressing long-standing challenges faced by traditional machine translation systems. Traditional systems often rely on rule-based and statistical approaches, which are limited in their ability to capture the deep semantic meaning of text. These methods struggle with understanding context, relationships between words, and idiomatic expressions, often producing translations that lack fluency and naturalness. In contrast, large-scale language models, powered by deep learning algorithms, are trained on vast amounts of parallel corpus data, allowing them to learn rich semantic representations (Chen et al. 2022). This training enables them to understand the meaning of text more comprehensively, producing translations that are more accurate and contextually appropriate (Lis et al. 2020).

One of the key advantages of large-scale language models is their superior semantic understanding. Unlike traditional machine translation systems, which often rely on predefined rules and patterns, large-scale models learn from data, allowing them to grasp the intricate relationships between words, phrases, and sentences. This deeper understanding helps them interpret the intended meaning of input text with greater precision. For example, in translation tasks, these models can better handle nuances such as word order, context-specific meanings, and cultural differences, which are often challenging for traditional systems to manage. By recognizing the contextual relationships between elements in the text, large-scale models can generate translations that reflect a more accurate understanding of the source material.

Additionally, large-scale language models offer a more natural and fluent translation output. Traditional machine translation systems are often constrained by rigid patterns, leading to translations that sound mechanical or unnatural. These systems may struggle with idiomatic expressions, complex sentence structures, or culturally specific references, which results in translations that feel disconnected from the target language's natural flow. In contrast, large-scale language models can optimize the translation process through end-to-end learning, which directly transforms input text into output translations. This approach allows the models to generate expressions that are more in tune with the idioms, grammar, and habits of the target language, ensuring that the translation is not only accurate but also flows naturally and resonates with native speakers.

Another significant benefit of large-scale language models is their ability to continuously improve over time. Traditional machine translation systems often require manual updates and fine-tuning to account for new language trends, expressions, or emerging contexts. This can be time-consuming and may result in outdated translations. On the other hand, large-scale models can be retrained on new data, which enables them to adapt more quickly to language evolution and emerging linguistic patterns. As these models process more diverse data, they become increasingly proficient at handling a wide variety of language pairs, domains, and translation contexts, making them more versatile and effective across different translation tasks (Fan et al. 2022).

As NLP technology continues to advance, the impact of large-scale language models on AI interpretation systems is expected to grow even further. These models are poised to enhance the accuracy, contextual understanding, and naturalness of translations, making them increasingly effective in comprehending and responding to human language. In particular, advancements in AI interpretation systems will enable more fluid and dynamic communication across languages, whether in real-time conversations, conference settings, or multilingual content creation. As the technology matures, it will become even better at understanding the subtleties of human language, including tone, emotion, and intent, further bridging gaps in cross-cultural communication.

In conclusion, the development of large-scale language models marks a significant leap forward in natural language processing and translation technology. By leveraging deep learning algorithms and vast datasets, these models have overcome many of the limitations of traditional machine translation systems, offering more accurate, fluent, and context-aware translations. As AI interpretation systems continue to evolve, their ability to understand and generate human language with greater precision will transform the way we communicate, breaking down language barriers and facilitating more seamless global interactions.

Machine Translation: Machine translation is vital to AI interpretation technology, facilitating communication among individuals who speak different languages. Here are some key applications of machine translation in this field:

- **Real-time Interpretation:** Machine translation algorithms can instantly translate spoken language during conversations, enabling effective communication between individuals who do not share a common language.
- **Multilingual Virtual Assistants:** Virtual assistants equipped with machine translation capabilities can offer support in multiple languages, catering to a diverse global user base.
- **Language Learning:** Machine translation can aid language learners by providing accurate translations, helping them comprehend foreign texts and enhance their language skills.
- **Cross-Cultural Collaborations:** Machine translation allows individuals from different cultural and linguistic backgrounds to collaborate on projects, breaking down language barriers and promoting global cooperation.
- **Content Localization:** Machine translation can translate digital content, such as websites, applications, and video subtitles, making them accessible to users in various languages and regions.
- **Multilingual Customer Support:** Machine translation can enhance customer support services by automatically translating customer inquiries and responses in real-time, facilitating efficient communication between customers and support agents.
- **Conference Interpretation:** Machine translation can be integrated into conference interpretation systems, providing participants with real-time translations of speeches and discussions, thus overcoming language barriers at international events.

The advent of large-scale language models has ushered in significant advancements in machine translation, transforming intelligent interpreting technology to better address the challenges of translating multilingual and diverse texts. Traditional machine translation systems, though useful, often struggle with a range of issues when attempting to process these kinds of texts. One of the primary obstacles lies in handling the inherent variations in language structure, grammar rules, and specialized terminology across different fields. These issues can result in translations that lack accuracy, fluency, and relevance, which are common drawbacks in conventional systems. For instance, when dealing with complex or specialized content such as legal documents, medical texts, or technical manuals, traditional systems often fail to produce translations that truly capture the intended meaning and context.

In contrast, large-scale language models, particularly those built on deep learning neural networks, represent a profound leap forward in the field of machine translation. These models are trained on vast amounts of parallel corpus data, enabling them to acquire rich semantic and linguistic knowledge. By processing large datasets, they can recognize and interpret not just individual words but the relationships between words, phrases, and entire sentences, including nuances that traditional systems might miss. This ability to learn from large and varied datasets allows large-scale language models to tackle the challenges posed by diverse languages and text types, making them a significant improvement over earlier methods. Their ability to capture the subtleties and complexities of language—such as idiomatic expressions, varying sentence structures, and context-specific meanings—has greatly enhanced the quality of translations.

The application of large-scale language models has a transformative impact on intelligent interpreting technology. These models excel in processing and understanding multilingual content, adapting to various languages and their specific linguistic properties. As a result, they are capable of producing translations that are not only more accurate but also more fluent and natural. Traditional machine translation often resulted in mechanical translations that felt disconnected from the cultural and idiomatic norms of the target language. Large-scale models, however, excel in capturing the context of the original text and producing translations that read more naturally, aligning with the norms of the target language. This feature is particularly important when it comes to ensuring that the translation sounds authentic and resonates with native speakers, which is essential in professional contexts such as international business or diplomacy (Fan et al. 2022).

Another critical advantage of large-scale language models is their ability to adapt to the specific translation needs of different domains and text types. One of the major challenges in translation is the presence of specialized terminology and jargon that may not be easily understood or accurately translated by conventional systems. For example, a medical document requires the precise translation of technical terms that may differ significantly from terms used in general conversation. Traditional machine translation systems often struggle with such specialized language, leading to misinterpretations or loss of meaning. However, large-scale language models can be trained on domain-specific data, including industry-specific vocabulary and annotations, to improve their handling of specialized terms. By incorporating these specialized data sets into the training process, these models become proficient at translating highly technical or field-specific content accurately, which is crucial for professional settings like law, healthcare, and engineering.

This capability of adapting to various domains means that intelligent interpreting technology powered by large-scale language models can provide more accurate and professional translations across a wide range of fields. Whether the text is legal, technical, literary, or conversational, these models can generate translations that are not only linguistically sound but also contextually appropriate for the particular domain. As a result, large-scale language models are significantly improving the quality of machine translation in both general and specialized fields, making them valuable tools for businesses, governments, and organizations that require reliable and accurate multilingual communication (Wu et al. 2021).

Despite the considerable advancements brought about by large-scale language models, it is important to recognize that limitations still exist, particularly in capturing the full range of subtleties and context that human language entails. While these models have made great strides in understanding and processing linguistic data, they still face challenges when it comes to fully grasping the depth of human language, especially in complex or highly sensitive scenarios. For instance, in situations where cultural nuances, emotional undertones, or subtle contextual cues play a significant role, AI-driven translation systems may fall short. In these cases, human translators are still essential, as they can interpret these subtleties and provide the necessary nuance that AI models may miss.

Human translation is especially valuable in complex or sensitive scenarios, such as legal proceedings, diplomatic negotiations, or literary translations, where the precision of language and the understanding of cultural context are critical. In these situations, the human touch remains indispensable. While AI models have made impressive strides, they are still limited in their ability to account for all the non-verbal cues, cultural sensitivities, and emotional undertones that are often integral to human communication. Therefore, while large-scale language models can offer remarkable improvements in translation quality, human oversight is still necessary in certain contexts to ensure accuracy and appropriateness.

That said, the advancements made by large-scale language models have had a transformative impact on intelligent interpreting technology, making it much more effective in addressing the translation needs of multilingual and diverse texts. These advancements are not only improving translation quality but are also opening up new possibilities for cross-cultural communication, collaboration, and globalization. The ability of AI-driven systems to handle diverse linguistic and specialized content is enhancing the ability of organizations and individuals to communicate across language barriers, fostering greater international cooperation and understanding. As these technologies continue to evolve, it is likely that they will become even more adept at addressing the challenges of translation and interpretation, further bridging gaps in global communication.

In conclusion, large-scale language models have made substantial contributions to improving machine translation and intelligent interpreting technologies. Their ability to process vast amounts of data, understand complex linguistic relationships, and adapt to different domains has significantly enhanced the accuracy and fluency of translations. While there are still challenges to overcome, particularly in capturing the full depth of human language, the progress achieved so far has revolutionized the way multilingual and diverse texts are translated, promoting better communication and cooperation across languages and cultures. The future of intelligent interpreting technology looks promising, with continued advancements in AI-driven translation systems playing a key role in overcoming language barriers and facilitating global communication.

D. Real-time Interaction

Real-time interaction is pivotal in AI interpretation technology, as it enriches the user experience and ensures effective communication between humans and machines. Here are some key applications of real-time interaction in this field:

- **Language Translation**: Real-time interaction empowers AI interpretation systems to deliver instant translation services, allowing seamless communication across different languages. Users can input text or speech, and the AI system will promptly translate it into the desired language.
- **Voice Assistants**: Real-time interaction enables voice assistants like Siri, Alexa, and Google Assistant to quickly understand and respond to user inquiries. These assistants employ natural language processing algorithms to interpret voice commands and provide relevant information or perform tasks in real-time.
- **Customer Support**: Real-time interaction is extensively utilized in customer support chatbots, which assist users in resolving queries or issues. AI-powered chatbots can engage in real-time conversations, comprehending customer inquiries and offering immediate solutions.
- **Virtual Meetings and Conferences**: Real-time interpretation technology facilitates smooth communication in multilingual meetings and conferences. AI systems can translate speeches in real-time, allowing participants to understand and interact without language barriers.
- **Language Learning**: Real-time interaction enhances language learning experiences by providing instant feedback and corrections. AI-driven language

learning platforms can assess learners' speech or writing in real-time, offering suggestions and guidance to improve proficiency.

- **Speech Recognition**: Real-time interaction is crucial in speech recognition applications, such as transcription services or voice-controlled devices. AI systems can convert spoken words into text instantly, aiding tasks like note-taking, dictation, or hands-free device control.
- **Intelligent Personal Assistants**: Real-time interaction allows intelligent personal assistants to promptly understand and respond to user commands or requests. These assistants can perform tasks such as setting reminders, sending messages, playing music, or providing personalized recommendations in real-time.

The large-scale language model significantly enhances the accuracy and fluency of interpretation intelligence technology in real-time interactive scenarios through continuous learning and optimization algorithms, thereby improving the experience of cross-language communication.

This model has indeed advanced the precision and fluidity of interpretation technology in real-time interactions by employing real-time learning and optimization techniques, leading to a more seamless experience in multilingual communication.

Traditional machine translation technologies often struggle to meet user demands in real-time interactive contexts due to their limited understanding of context and inadequate real-time processing capabilities. For instance, during interpreting conversations, speakers require timely and accurate translations while also desiring that these translations are expressed smoothly and naturally.

The large-scale language model continuously enhances its translation quality and performance through real-time learning and optimization algorithms tailored for real-time interactions. Specifically, these models can provide immediate feedback and corrections based on user input, thus improving translation accuracy. Additionally, by incorporating more contextual information, the large-scale language model can produce translations that are smoother and more natural, thereby enriching the user experience of interpretation technology in real-time scenarios.

This capability to enhance both accuracy and fluency allows intelligent interpreting technology to better facilitate real-time dialogue and communication across languages. Whether in business meetings, international conferences, or everyday social interactions, advancements in large-scale language models have significantly improved cross-language communication, fostering globalization and collaboration among nations (Fan et al. 2022; Chen et al. 2022).

However, it is important to acknowledge that despite the substantial progress made by large-scale language models in enhancing the accuracy and fluency of interpretation technology, challenges remain. These include domain-specific translation needs, variations in accents and dialects, and the processing of long sentences. Future research and development efforts will continue to tackle these challenges and further improve the performance of interpretation technology in real-time interactions.

In summary, real-time interaction is crucial for AI interpretation technology, enabling instant communication, language translation, and personalized assistance. This enhances user experiences across various domains, making AI systems more versatile and accessible.

IV. CHALLENGES AND PROSPECTS OF AI INTERPRETATION TECHNOLOGY IN THE AGE OF LARGE-SCALE LANGUAGE MODELS

In the era of large-scale language models, AI interpretation technology encounters both challenges and opportunities.

A. Challenges

Data privacy and security are critical considerations for AI interpretation technology, particularly in the context of large-scale language models. These models require vast amounts of data for training, making data privacy and security issues pressing concerns in the ongoing development of interpretation technology. Additionally, several challenges must be addressed:

1. Data Quality and Diversity

Large-scale language models necessitate extensive high-quality data for training; however, the availability of interpretation data is relatively limited, posing challenges for training these models effectively. To address this issue, the following strategies can be implemented:

a) **Data Collection and Cleaning**

Efforts should be made to gather and cleanse as much data as possible within the interpretation field. Collaborating with professional translation agencies, language institutes, and foreign ministries can yield authentic and high-quality interpretation data. Furthermore, utilizing open text resources available online, such as news articles and speeches, can help expand the dataset in the interpretation domain.

b) **Data Enhancement**

In situations where data is scarce, Data Enhancement techniques can be employed to augment the dataset. These techniques can generate new virtual data by randomly replacing, rearranging, and inserting elements from existing data, thereby increasing data diversity and improving the translation model's generalization capabilities.

c) **Transfer Learning from Pre-trained Models**

Transfer learning can be utilized by leveraging large-scale language models trained in other related domains. By fine-tuning these pre-trained models for the interpretation domain, the interpretation model can benefit from extensive data from other fields, thereby reducing its reliance on interpretation-specific data.

d) Pre-treatment Technology

A variety of pre-processing techniques can enhance the diversity and richness of data in the interpretation domain. Techniques such as word segmentation, part-of-speech tagging, and named entity recognition can be applied to the source language text to extract additional linguistic features. Furthermore, cross-lingual alignment methods can align data in the interpretation domain with data from other domains, thereby enriching the training dataset.

In summary, through data collection, data augmentation, transfer learning, and preprocessing techniques, the challenge of limited data in the interpretation field can be addressed, leading to improved effectiveness and quality of translation models. However, it is crucial for users to remain cautious about sharing sensitive personal information or engaging in discussions that could jeopardize their privacy and security.

2) Domain-Specific Requirements

Interpretation spans various fields, each characterized by its own specialized terminology and language style. Large-scale language models may encounter difficulties when addressing translation needs in specific domains. This is primarily because these models learn language rules and patterns from extensive training data but may lack a comprehensive understanding of certain domain-specific terminology and industry knowledge. To enhance specificity, the following strategies can be employed:

a) **Domain Adaptation**

Targeted training of models for specific industries or fields can enhance their understanding and translation accuracy regarding terminology and language styles pertinent to that field. For instance, focused training in the medical sector can enable the model to better grasp medical terminology and texts.

b) **Professional Terminology Dictionary**

Creating a dictionary of professional terms relevant to the field and integrating it with the model can ensure accurate translation of specialized terms. This dictionary can be referenced during the translation process, thereby improving accuracy and consistency.

c) **Contextual Understanding**

To meet translation needs in specific fields, the model must possess a certain level of contextual understanding. Training on domain-specific data, academic papers, and related literature can enhance the model's ability to comprehend specific contexts.

d) **Manual Editing and Proofreading**

In certain interpreting tasks, incorporating manual editing and proofreading can significantly enhance translation quality. Professionals can review and revise AI-generated translations based on their expertise and knowledge.

In conclusion, by combining methods such as domain adaptation, professional terminology dictionaries, contextual understanding, and manual editing, the accuracy and professionalism of large-scale language models in specific domain translations can be significantly improved.

3) Real-Time and Fluency

Interpretation often occurs in real-time interactive settings, necessitating rapid responses and fluent expression. Large-scale language models face challenges in handling long sentences, complex contexts, and varying accents, requiring further optimization to deliver more accurate and fluent translations. The nature of interpreting demands quick responses and fluency, which can be difficult for large-scale language models when faced with interpretation tasks. Long sentences, intricate contexts, and accents can result in translations that are either inaccurate or lack fluency.

For long sentences and complex contexts, these models may struggle to understand and accurately translate due to the inherent flexibility and ambiguity of language. Current large-scale language models need further optimization to handle complex contexts effectively, ensuring more accurate and natural translation outcomes.

Accent variations across different regions and individuals also present challenges for interpretation tasks. Large-scale language models may not accurately comprehend or reproduce these accents.

To enhance interpretation services, it is essential to continuously refine and optimize the training methods of large-scale language models, incorporate more accent and context sample data, and improve the models' understanding of diverse accents and complex contexts.

4) Interpretability and Confidence

Large-scale language models exhibit strong generalization capabilities when addressing complex tasks, allowing them to apply learned knowledge to new and unprecedented situations. This ability stems from the extensive parameter space of these models, which enables them to capture intricate patterns and relationships within the data effectively.

The intricate structure of large-scale language models presents challenges in terms of interpretability and credibility, necessitating further research in these areas. The complexity inherent in these models, which often contain billions of parameters, complicates our ability to intuitively grasp how they arrive at predictions or decisions. Unlike traditional machine learning algorithms, large-scale language models function more like black boxes, making it challenging to elucidate their internal mechanisms.

Moreover, the vast number of parameters raises concerns about the models' credibility. Ensuring the accuracy and reliability of each parameter becomes increasingly difficult, and even after thorough training and validation, unpredictable issues may still arise, undermining confidence in the model's outputs.

To tackle these challenges, researchers are intensifying their efforts to enhance the interpretability and credibility of large-scale language models. For instance, some are investigating visualization techniques to clarify the decision-making processes of these models, thereby improving their interpretability. Concurrently, there is a focus on developing better evaluation metrics and validation methods to bolster the credibility of these models.

While the generalization capabilities of large-scale language models are impressive, their complexity poses significant hurdles for interpretability and credibility. Future research must delve deeper into these issues to enhance the practical application of these models.

Multimodal Fusion and Human-Computer Interaction

The advancement of large-scale language models (LLMs) has led to a growing integration of multimodal information into intelligent interpreting technologies, offering an enhanced and more holistic interpretation service experience. By incorporating various forms of input, such as speech signals, images, and visual data, these models can improve the accuracy, context, and fluency of interpretations, allowing for more effective communication across languages and cultures.

One of the key advancements brought by multimodal integration is the ability of LLMs to simultaneously process speech and visual information during the interpretation process. Traditional systems often focus primarily on one mode of communication, such as converting spoken language into text via speech recognition. However, with multimodal capabilities, LLMs can analyze both speech and images at the same time. This dual processing enables the model to gain a more complete understanding of the context and the meaning behind the words. For example, in a video conference, LLMs can not only transcribe the spoken words but also recognize visual cues, such as the speaker's gestures, facial expressions, and even background scenes. These additional elements provide context that can refine and enhance the translation, ensuring that it is both accurate and culturally appropriate.

In addition to improving accuracy, the fusion of multimodal information significantly enhances the quality of human-machine interaction. Traditional interpretation systems rely on text-based input and output, which can sometimes limit the depth of communication, especially in complex or dynamic environments. By integrating multimodal inputs—such as images, speech, and even emotional tone—LLMs enable more intuitive and natural communication between humans and machines. For example, interpreting results can be conveyed not only through text but also through images and audio, allowing for a richer, more engaging experience. This is particularly valuable in scenarios like remote conferences or virtual meetings, where visual and auditory cues play a crucial role in communication.

Moreover, this multimodal integration makes human-computer interaction more seamless and user-friendly. In situations where both visual and auditory elements are important, such as interpreting a live event, LLMs can provide translations in real-time that incorporate both spoken language and visual context. This level of integration allows for a more fluid and interactive experience, making it easier for users to understand and engage with the interpretation. It also supports more diverse use cases, such as providing real-time interpretation for multimedia content, like films, video conferences, and online lectures, where visual and audio elements are critical to the message (Toivonen et al. 2020; Dec et al. 2022).

In conclusion, the integration of multimodal information into large-scale language models is significantly advancing intelligent interpreting technologies, offering more accurate, context-aware, and engaging translations. By combining speech recognition, image analysis, and other sensory data, these models can provide a more comprehensive understanding of the content being interpreted. This, in turn, improves human-computer interaction by enabling more natural and intuitive communication. As multimodal capabilities continue to evolve, they will further enhance the efficiency and quality of interpretation services, making them more versatile and accessible in an increasingly globalized world. However, integrating multimodal information into intelligent interpreting technology presents challenges, such as effectively processing and merging different types of information while ensuring translation accuracy and real-time performance. Despite these challenges, they are not insurmountable, and ongoing research and development will likely drive innovation and application in interpretation technology. The fusion of multimodal information and enhanced human-computer interaction represents a promising avenue for future development.

Despite the various challenges facing AI interpretation technology, the outlook remains optimistic.

Prospects

1. **Language Accessibility**: AI interpretation technology enhances language accessibility by offering real-time translation and interpretation services, facilitating communication across diverse languages and cultures.
2. **Knowledge Discovery**: Large-scale language models can expedite knowledge discovery by efficiently processing vast amounts of information, helping users quickly find relevant answers, insights, and resources.
3. **Personalized Assistance**: AI interpretation technology has the potential to provide personalized assistance tailored to user preferences and needs, enhancing user experiences and addressing individual requirements.
4. **Automation and Efficiency**: AI interpretation can automate repetitive tasks such as summarization, information extraction, and content generation, saving time and improving overall efficiency and productivity.
5. **Creativity and Innovation**: Language models can act as creative assistants, generating ideas, aiding in content creation, and supporting creative endeavors across various fields.

While the potential of AI interpretation technology is encouraging, it is essential to tackle existing challenges to ensure its responsible and ethical implementation. Continuous research and development are vital to fully leverage the capabilities of large-scale language models for interpretation tasks.

CONCLUSIONS

Large language models (LLMs) have brought about significant advancements in the interpretation services sector, offering more accurate, fluent, and contextually appropriate translations. These models, powered by artificial intelligence (AI), are revolutionizing the way interpretation tasks are performed, making them more efficient, scalable, and accessible. With their ability to process and analyze vast amounts of data, LLMs can improve the quality of translations, handle a wider variety of languages, and respond more quickly to the demands of users. This transformation is opening up new growth opportunities within the interpretation industry, creating an environment where AI-driven solutions and human expertise can work together to elevate the quality of interpretation services. However, it is essential to acknowledge that despite the advancements in AI, human professional interpreters must still play a crucial role in ensuring the accuracy and professionalism of the translation process. The synergy between artificial intelligence and human expertise is key to achieving the true potential of intelligent interpretation technology.

One of the primary ways that large language models are enhancing interpretation services is by improving translation quality. Traditional machine translation systems were limited by rule-based approaches and statistical models, which often resulted in translations that lacked fluency, coherence, and accuracy. These systems struggled to handle the complexities and nuances of human language, especially when it came to idiomatic expressions, cultural references, and context-dependent meanings. In contrast, LLMs are trained on vast amounts of parallel corpus data, which enables them to understand the relationships between words and phrases more comprehensively. By leveraging deep learning techniques, LLMs learn to generate translations that are not only grammatically correct but also contextually appropriate, capturing the subtleties of the original language in a way that was previously difficult for machine systems to achieve.

Moreover, LLMs have the ability to produce translations that flow more naturally in the target language. Traditional machine translation systems often struggled with sentence structure and word order, producing translations that sounded awkward or unnatural. LLMs, however, are capable of optimizing their output through end-to-end learning processes. This means that they can translate entire sentences or paragraphs, accounting for the context and flow of the conversation. As a result, the translations produced by LLMs are more fluent and coherent, better aligning with the grammar and idiomatic expressions of the target language. This improvement in translation quality is especially valuable in professional and high-stakes settings, such as diplomatic negotiations, legal proceedings, and international business, where accuracy and naturalness are paramount.

In addition to enhancing translation quality, large language models also expand the language coverage of interpretation services. Traditional interpretation systems were often limited by the number of languages they could support, particularly for less widely spoken or regional languages. LLMs, however, can be trained on diverse and multilingual datasets, allowing them to handle a broader range of languages and dialects. This increased language coverage is especially beneficial for businesses, governments, and organizations that operate in global markets and require interpretation services across multiple languages. With the ability to translate a wider array of languages, LLMs help break down communication barriers, facilitating more seamless interactions between people from different linguistic and cultural backgrounds. This expanded language coverage also supports the globalization of services, enabling organizations to reach a broader audience and provide more inclusive and accessible services.

The integration of cutting-edge technologies further strengthens the capabilities of large language models in the interpretation industry. Beyond their ability to generate accurate and fluent translations, LLMs can also leverage other AI technologies, such as speech recognition and natural language understanding, to provide more comprehensive interpretation services. For instance, combining LLMs with speech recognition systems allows for real-time language translation during live conversations, conferences, or meetings. This integration enables businesses and organizations to hold multilingual discussions without the need for human interpreters to be physically present, offering a more efficient and cost-effective solution for communication in international settings. Furthermore, as LLMs continue to evolve and improve, they can incorporate advancements in areas like sentiment analysis and emotion detection, which would enable them to provide more nuanced translations that account for the emotional tone of the original speech. These cutting-edge technologies will play a critical role in the ongoing evolution of intelligent interpretation.

In addition to improving quality and expanding language coverage, large language models open up new application areas for interpretation services. Traditional translation services were often limited to written documents, but the capabilities of LLMs extend beyond text-based translation to include voice-to-text and real-time interpretation, further enhancing their versatility. For example, LLMs can be integrated into virtual assistants, chatbots, and automated customer service platforms, enabling businesses to offer multilingual support to their customers in real time. This is particularly valuable for companies operating in global markets, as it allows them to interact with customers in multiple languages without the need for a large team of human interpreters. Additionally, LLMs can be used to enhance the accessibility of content, such as providing real-time translation for online events, webinars, or live broadcasts. This expanded scope of applications demonstrates the growing potential of LLMs to revolutionize the interpretation industry, providing new opportunities for businesses to enhance customer experience, improve efficiency, and drive growth.

While the advancements brought by large language models have significantly improved the interpretation process, it is essential to recognize that these AI systems are not yet a complete replacement for human interpreters. Despite their impressive capabilities, LLMs still face limitations when it comes to handling complex or highly nuanced content. Language is inherently multifaceted and context-dependent, and while LLMs are effective at processing large datasets, they can struggle with understanding cultural references, emotional undertones, and other subtle aspects of human communication. In situations where accuracy and nuance are critical, such as in legal, medical, or diplomatic settings, human interpreters are still necessary to ensure that the translation captures the full meaning and context of the original message.

Therefore, the future of intelligent interpretation lies in the collaboration between AI and human experts. Large language models can provide valuable support in translating routine or straightforward content, improving efficiency and scalability. However, human interpreters bring an essential layer of expertise, experience, and cultural understanding that AI cannot replicate. By working together, AI and human interpreters can deliver translation services that are both highly accurate and culturally sensitive, providing clients with the best of both worlds.

In conclusion, the advent of large language models has transformed the interpretation industry by enhancing translation quality, expanding language coverage, integrating cutting-edge technologies, and creating new application opportunities. These models have the potential to significantly improve the efficiency and convenience of interpretation services, enabling more seamless communication across linguistic and cultural boundaries. However, despite the remarkable progress made by AI, human professional interpreters must still play an essential role in ensuring the accuracy and professionalism of the translation process. The true advancement of intelligent interpretation technology can only be realized through the collaboration of AI and human expertise, paving the way for a future where global communication is more accessible, efficient, and effective than ever before. With ongoing advancements in AI and deeper integration into interpretation services, large language models are poised to continue driving the evolution of interpretation intelligence technology, offering enhanced support and opening up new growth opportunities in the industry.

REFERENCES

Acosta, J. N., Falcone, G. J., Rajpurkar, P., & Topol, E. J. (2022). Multimodal biomedical AI. *Nature Medicine, 28*(9), 1773–1784. DOI: 10.1038/s41591-022-01981-2 PMID: 36109635

Albulescu, C. T., Tiwari, A. K., & Kyophilavong, P. (2021). Nonlinearities and chaos: A new analysis of CEE stock markets. *Mathematics, 9*(7), 707. DOI: 10.3390/math9070707

Arsad, A. Z., Sebastian, G., Hannan, M. A., Ker, P. J., Rahman, M. S. A., Mansor, M., & Lipu, M. S. H. (2021). Solid state switching control methods: A bibliometric analysis for future directions. *Electronics (Basel), 10*(16), 1944. DOI: 10.3390/electronics10161944

Bañeres, D., Rodríguez, M. E., Guerrero-Roldán, A. E., & Karadeniz, A. (2020). An early warning system to detect at-risk students in online higher education. *Applied Sciences (Basel, Switzerland), 10*(13), 4427. DOI: 10.3390/app10134427

Barbosa, A., Whiting, S., Simmonds, P., Scotini Moreno, R., Mendes, R., & Breda, J. (2020). Physical activity and academic achievement: An umbrella review. *International Journal of Environmental Research and Public Health, 17*(16), 5972. DOI: 10.3390/ijerph17165972 PMID: 32824593

Barriga, N. A., & Besoaín, F. (2020). Artificial intelligence and mobile programming courses for a video game development program in Chile. *Computing in Science & Engineering, 22*(4), 17–25. DOI: 10.1109/MCSE.2020.2986758

Bharti, T., Ojha, S. C., & Tiwari, A. K. (2022). Interplay of workplace sustainability, sustainable work performance, optimism, and resilience: The moderating role of green creativity in luxury hotels. *Sustainability (Basel), 14*(22), 15097. DOI: 10.3390/su142215097

Brown, P. F., Della Pietra, S. A., Della Pietra, V. J., & Mercer, R. L. (1993). The mathematics of statistical machine translation: Parameter estimation. *Computational Linguistics, 19*(2), 263–311.

Cellina, M., Cè, M., Irmici, G., Ascenti, V., Caloro, E., Bianchi, L., Pellegrino, G., D'Amico, N., Papa, S., & Carrafiello, G. (2022). Artificial intelligence in emergency radiology: Where are we going? *Diagnostics (Basel), 12*(12), 3223. DOI: 10.3390/diagnostics12123223 PMID: 36553230

Chen, Q., Wen, Y., Zhang, X., & Zhu, Z. (2022). Evolutionary overview of terrace research based on bibliometric analysis in web of science from 1991 to 2020. *International Journal of Environmental Research and Public Health, 19*(13), 7796. DOI: 10.3390/ijerph19137796 PMID: 35805456

Chen, S., Chen, Y., Yuan, F., & Chang, X. (2020). Establishment of herbal prescription vector space model based on word co-occurrence. *The Journal of Supercomputing, 76*(5), 3590–3601. DOI: 10.1007/s11227-018-2559-3

Chiu, T. K., & Chai, C. S. (2020). Sustainable curriculum planning for artificial intelligence education: A self-determination theory perspective. *Sustainability (Basel), 12*(14), 5568. DOI: 10.3390/su12145568

Dai, Y., Chai, C. S., Lin, P. Y., Jong, M. S. Y., Guo, Y., & Qin, J. (2020). Promoting students' well-being by developing their readiness for the artificial intelligence age. *Sustainability (Basel), 12*(16), 6597. DOI: 10.3390/su12166597

Dec, G., Stadnicka, D., Paśko, Ł., Mądziel, M., Figliè, R., Mazzei, D., Tyrovolas, M., Stylios, C., Navarro, J., & Solé-Beteta, X. (2022). Role of academics in transferring knowledge and skills on artificial intelligence, internet of things and edge computing. *Sensors (Basel), 22*(7), 2496. DOI: 10.3390/s22072496 PMID: 35408110

Del Mondo, G., Peng, P., Gensel, J., Claramunt, C., & Lu, F. (2021). Leveraging spatio-temporal graphs and knowledge graphs: Perspectives in the field of maritime transportation. *ISPRS International Journal of Geo-Information, 10*(8), 541. DOI: 10.3390/ijgi10080541

El-Meniawy, N., Rizk, M. R., Ahmed, M. A., & Saleh, M. (2022). An Authentication Protocol for the Medical Internet of Things. *Symmetry, 14*(7), 1483. DOI: 10.3390/sym14071483

Erdil, D. C., White, L., Foster, D., Adams, J., Arguelles Cruz, A. J., Hainey, B., & Stott, L. (2019, July). Toward developing a cloud computing model curriculum. In *Proceedings of the 2019 ACM Conference on Innovation and Technology in Computer Science Education* (pp. 255-256). DOI: 10.1145/3304221.3325536

Fan, X., & Zhong, X. (2022). Artificial intelligence-based creative thinking skill analysis model using human–computer interaction in art design teaching. *Computers & Electrical Engineering, 100*, 107957. DOI: 10.1016/j.compeleceng.2022.107957

Farahmand, F. (2021). Integrating cybersecurity and artificial intelligence research in engineering and computer science education. *IEEE Security and Privacy, 19*(6), 104–110. DOI: 10.1109/MSEC.2021.3103460

Fernández, C., Vicente, M. A., & Martínez-Rach, M. O. (2020). Implementation of a face recognition system as experimental practices in an artificial intelligence and pattern recognition course. *Computer Applications in Engineering Education, 28*(3), 497–511. DOI: 10.1002/cae.22218

Gams, M., & Kolenik, T. (2021). Relations between electronics, artificial intelligence and information society through information society rules. *Electronics (Basel), 10*(4), 514. DOI: 10.3390/electronics10040514

Gorzeń-Mitka, I., Bilska, B., Tomaszewska, M., & Kołożyn-Krajewska, D. (2020). Mapping the structure of food waste management research: A co-keyword analysis. *International Journal of Environmental Research and Public Health, 17*(13), 4798. DOI: 10.3390/ijerph17134798 PMID: 32635284

Hamamoto, R., Suvarna, K., Yamada, M., Kobayashi, K., Shinkai, N., Miyake, M., Takahashi, M., Jinnai, S., Shimoyama, R., Sakai, A., Takasawa, K., Bolatkan, A., Shozu, K., Dozen, A., Machino, H., Takahashi, S., Asada, K., Komatsu, M., Sese, J., & Kaneko, S. (2020). Application of artificial intelligence technology in oncology: Towards the establishment of precision medicine. *Cancers (Basel), 12*(12), 3532. DOI: 10.3390/cancers12123532 PMID: 33256107

Hedderich, D. M., Keicher, M., Wiestler, B., Gruber, M. J., Burwinkel, H., Hinterwimmer, F., & Navab, N. (2021, September). AI for doctors—A course to educate medical professionals in artificial intelligence for medical imaging. [). MDPI.]. *Health Care, 9*(10), 1278. PMID: 34682958

Heredia-Negron, F., Alamo-Rodriguez, N., Oyola-Velazquez, L., Nieves, B., Carrasquillo, K., Hochheiser, H., Fristensky, B., Daluz-Santana, I., Fernandez-Repollet, E., & Roche-Lima, A. (2023). Evaluation of AIML+ HDR—A Course to Enhance Data Science Workforce Capacity for Hispanic Biomedical Researchers. *International Journal of Environmental Research and Public Health, 20*(3), 2726. DOI: 10.3390/ijerph20032726 PMID: 36768092

Huang, X. (2021). Aims for cultivating students' key competencies based on artificial intelligence education in China. *Education and Information Technologies, 26*(5), 5127–5147. DOI: 10.1007/s10639-021-10530-2

Huang, X., & Qiao, C. (2024). Enhancing computational thinking skills through artificial intelligence education at a STEAM high school. *Science & Education, 33*(2), 383–403. DOI: 10.1007/s11191-022-00392-6

Hwang, G. J., & Tu, Y. F. (2021). Roles and research trends of artificial intelligence in mathematics education: A bibliometric mapping analysis and systematic review. *Mathematics, 9*(6), 584. DOI: 10.3390/math9060584

Ilkka, T. (2018). The impact of artificial intelligence on learning, teaching, and education. *European Union.*

Jobin, A., Ienca, M., & Vayena, E. (2019). The global landscape of AI ethics guidelines. *Nature Machine Intelligence*, *1*(9), 389–399. DOI: 10.1038/s42256-019-0088-2

Krishnankutty, R., Bharti, T., & Mishra, N. (2022). Herding behaviour and capital structure decision in BSE listed Indian firms. *International Journal of Managerial and Financial Accounting*, *14*(2), 118–137. DOI: 10.1504/IJMFA.2022.122226

Kumar, M. G. V., N, V., Čepová, L., Raja, M. A. M., Balaram, A., & Elangovan, M. (2023). Evaluation of the quality of practical teaching of agricultural higher vocational courses based on BP neural network. *Applied Sciences (Basel, Switzerland)*, *13*(2), 1180. DOI: 10.3390/app13021180

Kuzior, A., & Sira, M. (2022). A bibliometric analysis of blockchain technology research using VOSviewer. *Sustainability (Basel)*, *14*(13), 8206. DOI: 10.3390/su14138206

Laupichler, M. C., Hadizadeh, D. R., Wintergerst, M. W., Von Der Emde, L., Paech, D., Dick, E. A., & Raupach, T. (2022). Effect of a flipped classroom course to foster medical students' AI literacy with a focus on medical imaging: A single group pre-and post-test study. *BMC Medical Education*, *22*(1), 803. DOI: 10.1186/s12909-022-03866-x PMID: 36397110

LeCun, Y., Bengio, Y., & Hinton, G. (2015). Deep learning. *nature, 521*(7553), 436-444.

Liang, X., Haiping, L., Liu, J., & Lin, L. (2021). Reform of English interactive teaching mode based on cloud computing artificial intelligence–a practice analysis. *Journal of Intelligent & Fuzzy Systems*, *40*(2), 3617–3629. DOI: 10.3233/JIFS-189397

Lin, J., Zhao, Y., Huang, W., Liu, C., & Pu, H. (2021). Domain knowledge graph-based research progress of knowledge representation. *Neural Computing & Applications*, *33*(2), 681–690. DOI: 10.1007/s00521-020-05057-5

Lis, A., Sudolska, A., Pietryka, I., & Kozakiewicz, A. (2020). Cloud computing and energy efficiency: Mapping the thematic structure of research. *Energies*, *13*(16), 4117. DOI: 10.3390/en13164117

Liu, Z., Yang, Z., Xiao, C., Zhang, K., & Osmani, M. (2021). An investigation into art therapy aided health and well-being research: A 75-year bibliometric analysis. *International Journal of Environmental Research and Public Health*, *19*(1), 232. DOI: 10.3390/ijerph19010232 PMID: 35010491

Memon, A., Kilby, J., Breñosa, J., Espinosa, J. C. M., & Ashraf, I. (2022). Analysis and implementation of human mobility behavior using similarity analysis based on co-occurrence matrix. *Sensors (Basel), 22*(24), 9898. DOI: 10.3390/s22249898 PMID: 36560266

Miller, S., Bobrow, R., Ingria, R., & Schwartz, R. (1994, June). Hidden understanding models of natural language. In *32nd Annual Meeting of the Association for Computational Linguistics* (pp. 25-32). DOI: 10.3115/981732.981736

Ngwenya, S., & Boshoff, N. (2022). Different manifestations of 'context': Examples from a bibliometric study of research in Zimbabwe in Southern Africa. *Scientometrics, 127*(7), 3911–3933. DOI: 10.1007/s11192-022-04435-1

Nor, A. K. M., Pedapati, S. R., Muhammad, M., & Leiva, V. (2021). Overview of explainable artificial intelligence for prognostic and health management of industrial assets based on preferred reporting items for systematic reviews and meta-analyses. *Sensors (Basel), 21*(23), 8020. DOI: 10.3390/s21238020 PMID: 34884024

Och, F. J., & Ney, H. (2000). Statistical machine translation. In *5th EAMT Workshop: Harvesting Existing Resources.*

Pantelimon, F. V., Bologa, R., Toma, A., & Posedaru, B. S. (2021). The evolution of AI-driven educational systems during the COVID-19 pandemic. *Sustainability (Basel), 13*(23), 13501. DOI: 10.3390/su132313501

Paśko, Ł., Mądziel, M., Stadnicka, D., Dec, G., Carreras-Coch, A., Solé-Beteta, X., Pappa, L., Stylios, C., Mazzei, D., & Atzeni, D. (2022). Plan and develop advanced knowledge and skills for future industrial employees in the field of artificial intelligence, internet of things and edge computing. *Sustainability (Basel), 14*(6), 3312. DOI: 10.3390/su14063312

Povedano-Montero, F. J., Weinreb, R. N., Raga-Martínez, I., Romero, A., & López-Muñoz, F. (2020). Detection of neurological and ophthalmological pathologies with Optical Coherence Tomography using retinal thickness measurements: A bibliometric study. *Applied Sciences (Basel, Switzerland), 10*(16), 5477. DOI: 10.3390/app10165477

Ribeiro, A. P. D., Almeida, R. F., Medonca, J. G. A., & Leal, S. C. (2018). Oral health and its effect on the academic performance of children and adolescents. *Pediatric Dentistry, 40*(1), 12–17. PMID: 29482676

Salas-Pilco, S. Z., Xiao, K., & Oshima, J. (2022). Artificial intelligence and new technologies in inclusive education for minority students: A systematic review. *Sustainability (Basel), 14*(20), 13572. DOI: 10.3390/su142013572

Seneff, S. (1992). TINA: A natural language system for spoken language applications. *Computational Linguistics*, *18*(1), 61–86.

Sun, X., Li, T., Wang, P., Shang, L., Niu, M., Meng, X., & Shao, H. (2022). Nanomaterials and Advances in Tumor Immune-Related Therapy: A Bibliometric Analysis. *Journal of Biomedical Nanotechnology, 18*(9), 2154-2170.0

Tedre, M., Toivonen, T., Kahila, J., Vartiainen, H., Valtonen, T., Jormanainen, I., & Pears, A. (2021). Teaching machine learning in K–12 classroom: Pedagogical and technological trajectories for artificial intelligence education. *IEEE Access : Practical Innovations, Open Solutions*, *9*, 110558–110572. DOI: 10.1109/ACCESS.2021.3097962

Tiwari, A. K., Abakah, E. J. A., Gil-Alana, L. A., & Abakah, M. K. (2021). Inflation co-movement dynamics: A cross-country investigation using a continuous wavelet approach. *Journal of Risk and Financial Management*, *14*(12), 613. DOI: 10.3390/jrfm14120613

Toivonen, T., Jormanainen, I., Kahila, J., Tedre, M., Valtonen, T., & Vartiainen, H. (2020, July). Co-designing machine learning apps in K–12 with primary school children. In *2020 IEEE 20th International Conference on Advanced Learning Technologies (ICALT)* (pp. 308-310). IEEE. DOI: 10.1109/ICALT49669.2020.00099

Touretzky, D., Gardner-McCune, C., Martin, F., & Seehorn, D. (2019, July). Envisioning AI for K-12: What should every child know about AI? *Proceedings of the AAAI Conference on Artificial Intelligence*, *33*(01), 9795–9799. DOI: 10.1609/aaai.v33i01.33019795

Udupa, P. (2022). Application of artificial intelligence for university information system. *Engineering Applications of Artificial Intelligence*, *114*, 105038. DOI: 10.1016/j.engappai.2022.105038

Véstias, M. P., Duarte, R. P., de Sousa, J. T., & Neto, H. C. (2020). Moving deep learning to the edge. *Algorithms*, *13*(5), 125. DOI: 10.3390/a13050125

Weerasekara, S., Lu, Z., Ozek, B., Isaacs, J., & Kamarthi, S. (2022). Trends in adopting industry 4.0 for asset life cycle management for sustainability: A keyword co-occurrence network review and analysis. *Sustainability (Basel)*, *14*(19), 12233. DOI: 10.3390/su141912233

Wu, Y., Nouri, J., Li, X., Weegar, R., Afzaal, M., & Zia, A. (2021). Catching Group Criteria Semantic Information When Forming Collaborative Learning Groups. In *Technology-Enhanced Learning for a Free, Safe, and Sustainable World: 16th European Conference on Technology Enhanced Learning, EC-TEL 2021, Bolzano, Italy, September 20-24, 2021* [Springer International Publishing.]. *Proceedings, 16*, 16–27.

Xing, Z., Zhao, S., Guo, W., Guo, X., Wang, S., Li, M., Wang, Y., & He, H. (2023). Analyzing point cloud of coal mining process in much dust environment based on dynamic graph convolution neural network. *Environmental Science and Pollution Research International, 30*(2), 4044–4061. DOI: 10.1007/s11356-022-22490-2 PMID: 35963970

Xing, Z., Zhao, S., Guo, W., Guo, X., Wang, Y., Bai, Y., Zhu, S., & He, H. (2022). Identifying balls feature in a large-scale laser point cloud of a coal mining environment by a multiscale dynamic graph convolution neural network. *ACS Omega, 7*(6), 4892–4907. DOI: 10.1021/acsomega.1c05473 PMID: 35187309

Zingoni, A., Taborri, J., Panetti, V., Bonechi, S., Aparicio-Martínez, P., Pinzi, S., & Calabrò, G. (2021). Investigating issues and needs of dyslexic students at university: Proof of concept of an artificial intelligence and virtual reality-based supporting platform and preliminary results. *Applied Sciences (Basel, Switzerland), 11*(10), 4624. DOI: 10.3390/app11104624

Chapter 3
Evolution of AI in Interpretation:
From Traditional Approaches to Real-Time Solution

Andi Asrifan
https://orcid.org/0000-0002-9934-6129
Universitas Negeri Makassar, Indonesia

Mohammed H. Alaqad
https://orcid.org/0000-0002-9953-5763
University of Malaya, Malaysia

ABSTRACT

Traditional methodologies have become real-time solutions thanks to AI in interpretation, improving cross-language communication. Traditional approaches like consecutive and simultaneous interpretation relied on human skill, which was effective but slow and inaccurate. Neural machine translation (NMT) and deep learning have made context-aware, scalable, and efficient language processing possible. AI interpreters now capture complex language, idioms, and cultural subtleties, enhancing translation quality. Managing cultural sensitivity and algorithmic bias requires a hybrid approach that blends AI and human control. This integration preserves human communication while using AI's speed and efficiency. As AI evolves, its interpretation role will be crucial to global communication and understanding.

DOI: 10.4018/979-8-3373-0060-3.ch003

1. FOUNDATIONS OF INTERPRETATION TECHNOLOGY

1.1 Historical Overview of Interpretation Techniques

Human interpretation has developed over time to accommodate varied societies' complex communication needs (Zalasiewicz et al., 2021). Cross-linguistic communication relied on human-based translation, successive interpretation, and simultaneous interpretation before contemporary technology changed the picture. Each strategy had pros and cons in different situations.

Ancient civilizations used human-based translation. Aslanyan, 2021; Scorpo, 2023) renowned intellectuals and diplomats translated religious, literary, and legal materials to bridge civilizations. Their work promoted regional knowledge sharing, worldwide trade, and cultural exchange. Except for textual content or long-term contexts, human translation was time-consuming.

In the early 20th century, successive interpretation allowed interpreters to deliver spoken content in real time in diplomatic and legal settings (Pöchhacker, 2022; Tipà & Moratto, 2024). In successive interpretation, the speaker stops to let the interpreter deliver each message piece. The accuracy of this method makes it ideal for smaller settings that require fast involvement. It doubles communication time, making it unsuitable for fast-paced events.

Developed during World War II for the Nuremberg Trials, simultaneous interpretation was a major advance (Baigorri-Jalón et al., 2021). Interpreters immediately translate the speaker's message without interruptions. This method demands talent and concentration, typically requiring interpreter teams to avoid cognitive fatigue. Multilingual environments like the UN, where fast information flow is vital, adopted simultaneous interpretation. It works, but it requires specific equipment and trained staff.

These classical methods addressed accuracy, immediacy, and cultural sensitivity, laying the groundwork for modern interpretation technology (Zhao et al.2024; Lim, 2024). They also enabled the development of AI in interpretation, which tries to mimic and improve human talents. AI has transformed interpretation from human-dependent to real-time, automated solutions, from rule-based systems in the 20th century to machine learning and neural networks. This chapter describes AI's evolution from supporting existing approaches to pioneering instantaneous, scalable language interpretation.

1.2 Challenges in Traditional Interpretation

Traditional interpretation approaches are necessary for cross-linguistic communication, but they have drawbacks that affect efficiency, accuracy, and adaptability (Pan et al., 2023; Sun, 2025). Language complexity, cultural differences, and time limits can hinder information exchange for human interpreters, especially in high-stakes or fast-paced contexts.

A major issue is language difficulty. Human interpreters must accurately convey complex vocabulary, idioms, and specialised terms from medicine, law, and diplomacy (Pöchhacker, 2022; Tipà & Moratto, 2024). Japanese and Arabic, for example, have non-linear structures or contextual relationships, making interpretation more complex. Complex syntax and abstract phrases can cause misinterpretation, especially if the interpreter lacks subject understanding.

Cultural differences complicate matters. Interpretation involves linguistic and cultural transfers of meanings, values, and social cues (Lavrenteva & Orland-Barak, 2023; Rehfeldt et al., 2021). Cultural references, humor, and idioms that work in one language may offend in another. Direct communication may be impolite in one culture but normal in another. Thus, interpreters must carefully adjust tone and phrasing to retain the original message's intent while being culturally appropriate for the target audience. Misinterpreting cultural background can cause misunderstandings in critical situations like diplomatic negotiations or international business.

Speed limits complicate usual interpretation. Since speakers and interpreters take turns, consecutive interpretation doubles time (Hansen & Svennevig, 2021). While simultaneous interpretation reduces this latency by offering near-instantaneous translation, it also throws a huge cognitive burden on the interpreter. Stressing accuracy under pressure can cause mental fatigue and errors during sessions. Additionally, sequential and simultaneous interpretation require substantial training, which reduces interpreter availability and raises prices.

Traditional interpretation can be resource-intensive, sluggish, and imprecise due to these issues. AI aims to address these limitations. AI-driven interpretation systems automate language processing to manage complicated linguistic structures, cultural settings, and real-time findings (Zhao, 2024). This change from human dependency to AI-based interpretation allows for more accessibility, faster cross-cultural communication, and overcoming old limits.

Traditional interpretation methods were effective but time-consuming, cognitively demanding, and required specialized skill. Consecutive interpretation quadrupled communication time, whereas simultaneous interpretation needed expensive training and equipment. Limitations necessitated speedier, scalable solutions. AI-driven interpretation uses machine learning and neural networks to improve speed, accuracy, and accessibility. AI-powered technologies process massive linguistic data in real time, decreasing delays and interpreter fatigue. Moving from human-dependent to AI-driven solutions is a big step toward scalable, automated interpretation across languages.

1.3 Introduction to Technology in Interpretation

Digitization supported human interpreters and paved the way for AI-driven solutions (O'Brien, 2024; Gala et al., 2024). Initial goals were to improve efficiency, minimize interpreter effort, and improve accuracy in difficult or specialized circumstances. From basic reference tools to early machine-assisted translation, interpretation technology has steadily advanced, giving interpreters new skills in numerous disciplines. Late 20th-century computer-assisted translation (CAT) software was one of the first technology aids (Sin-wai, 2023). Interpreters used translation memory systems to manage enormous quantities of text and maintain terminology consistency. They saved translated phrases, sentences, and paragraphs for interpreters to use when comparable language patterns arose. This capability was especially useful for specialized or repetitious professions like legal and medical interpretation, where correct terminology is crucial. Terminology databases and glossaries were popular for real-time interpreters as technology evolved (Papatsimouli et al., 2023). These databases centralized terminology, idioms, and phrases, making it easy for interpreters to find precise jargon translations. In high-stakes contexts like multinational organizations, consistent terminology prevents misunderstandings, making such tools important. Interpreters working with engineering, financial, and international law vocabulary still need glossaries. Digital recording and playback systems helped interpreters analyze prior interpretations, improve their methods, and cross-check content in real time if pauses allowed (Park et al., 2024). Replaying recorded audio can assure accurate interpretation in court procedures. Recorded translations in healthcare reduce misunderstandings by verifying essential medical information. Automatic speech recognition (ASR) improved human interpretation. Early ASR technologies could transcribe spoken language into text, helping interpreters visualize material. Initial ASR systems used organized, predictable language inputs, but they improved and gained use in conferences, courtrooms, and corporate meetings. ASR, text-based reference aids, and glossary databases underpinned current AI-driven interpretation solutions. These early digital tools helped move from human-based interpretation to technology-supported procedures, preparing for AI integration. Early digital tools automated language management and data retrieval, simplifying interpretation and showing how technology may overcome traditional ways (Mhlongo et al., 2023). This progress led to AI-based interpretation platforms, which aspire to redefine cross-linguistic communication with real-time, scalable solutions across multiple languages and circumstances.

2. EMERGENCE OF AI IN LANGUAGE PROCESSING

2.1 Evolution of Artificial Intelligence in Language Technology

AI in language processing has evolved from simple text-based algorithms to large neural network-powered systems that can interpret and generate language like humans (Gruetzemacher & Whittlestone, 2022). Basic translation algorithms and subsequent improvements moved AI-driven interpretation closer to real-time, natural language communication, forging current language technology. Rule-based translation algorithms were the first AI language tools in the 1950s and 1960s (Gaspari, 2024). Expert-crafted linguistic rules stored within the software allowed basic translations between English and Russian during the Cold War. Due to subtleties, idioms, and flexible grammar structures, the rule-based method was limited. Translating unclear sentences produced stilted or incorrect output, demonstrating the rigidity of early AI algorithms. Rule-based translation was a crucial first step toward machine-driven language processing. Statistical machine translation (SMT) became increasingly flexible in the 1980s and 1990s (Wang et al., 2022). SMT used massive bilingual text datasets to find probabilistic word and phrase matching across languages without predefined rules. By letting the algorithm "learn" real-world language use patterns, this strategy boosted accuracy, especially in languages with large digital text archives like English and French. The government and large enterprises employed SYSTRAN for basic document translation as an early SMT application. SMT was more versatile than rule-based models but struggled with complicated language and context-specific semantics. The 2010s saw the breakthrough of neural machine translation (NMT) (Gaspari, 2024). NMT systems revolutionized language technology using neural networks, which mirror human cognition. Neural networks could analyse sentences rather than words or phrases, unlike previous models. This enabled more accurate, context-aware translations that captured natural flow and meaning. In 2016, Google's NMT algorithm made translations more accurate, faster, and less dependent on manually selected linguistic data. Deep learning breakthroughs led to transformer models like OpenAI's GPT and Google's BERT (Kampakis, 2024). Transformers developed the attention mechanism, which allowed AI models to focus on relevant phrases and ignore unnecessary information, improving understanding and generation accuracy. These developments expanded AI-driven interpretation to handle tone, idioms, and regional variances. AI in live interpretation became possible when real-time processing capabilities improved (Fadhel et al., 2024). This transition from rule-based to neural and transformer models improved translation accuracy and language dynamics management. Modern AI systems can interpret statements' direct meaning and implicit or cultural settings in real time (Gutierrez

Jr, 2024). This trip shows how AI has evolved rapidly from rule-based translations to models with human-like linguistic sensitivity and efficiency in real time.

2.2 Machine Learning and Natural Language Processing (NLP)

Machine learning (ML) and natural language processing (NLP) have revolutionised AI-driven interpretation, bringing language technology closer to human understanding and communication (Wang & Lin, 2023). These fields allow machines to learn from data and process language in sophisticated ways, allowing AI systems to understand linguistic nuances, infer context, and perform real-time language interpretation with high accuracy and fluency. Computers can learn from large datasets using machine learning techniques, a subset of AI (Sarker, 2021). Machine learning initially used statistical methods to find data patterns, allowing systems to anticipate outcomes, identify trends, and categorize simple data. Advanced ML models emerged as computer power and data access expanded. ML was powerful for language applications because supervised learning allowed systems to use labeled data to make more accurate predictions and unsupervised learning allowed them to find hidden patterns in large datasets. ML helped NLP systems analyse, understand, and generate human language (Naithani & Raiwani, 2023; Khurana et al., 2023). NLP includes tokenization, parsing, and semantic analysis. NLP helps AI-driven interpretation machines comprehend complicated language inputs and provide contextually suitable translations. Simple, rule-based NLP models were inflexible and struggled with language ambiguities. As NLP grew with ML, it learned to manage complicated structures, idioms, and language variances, which are necessary for accurate interpretation. Deep learning and neural networks revolutionized NLP (Lauriola et al., 2022; Dong, 2021). AI could process language more abstractly and nuancedly using neural networks inspired by the human brain. Deep learning let multi-layered neural networks handle larger datasets and learn words, relationships, tones, and contextual dependencies. The recurrent neural network (RNN), which could handle sequences, was a key architecture in early NLP tasks like speech recognition and translation. Transformer models emerged because RNNs struggled with long-term text dependencies. Transformers invented the attention mechanism, which allowed models to focus on relevant material, improving understanding and contextual awareness (Rahali & Akhloufi, 2023; Choi & Lee, 2023). Transformer-based models like Google's BERT and OpenAI's GPT were better at NLP because they could analyze texts simultaneously and capture context. AI models could rapidly understand and translate complex language dynamics after this accomplishment. These ML and NLP advances helped AI interpretation systems approach human skills. By evolving from rule-based models to sophisticated neural architectures, AI began to address not just the straight translation of words but also cultural, idiomatic, and contextual nuances required for successful interpretation. Today, NLP and ML constitute the backbone of AI-driven interpretation, providing real-time, scalable language solutions across numerous areas and circumstances. Initial AI-driven interpretation depended on rule-based systems, which faltered in addressing linguistic subtleties and contextual variability. The transition to machine learning (ML) and neural networks transformed language processing by facilitating data-driven models that examine patterns and enhance performance over time. Statistical machine translation (SMT) employed probabilistic methodologies, whereas neural machine translation (NMT) utilized deep learning to improve fluency and precision. Transformers, such BERT and GPT, enhanced AI comprehension by encapsulating intricate linguistic frameworks. The transition from inflexible, rule-based approaches to adaptable, machine learning-driven models has markedly enhanced AI's capacity for real-time interpretation with increased contextual awareness and accuracy.

2.3 From Rule-Based to Data-Driven Approaches

The transition from rule-based to data-driven methodologies in AI language processing signified a crucial evolution, facilitating significantly more precise, versatile, and adaptable systems for language interpretation (Sakshi et al., 2024). Rule-based models depended on manually encoded linguistic rules, but data-driven models, powered by machine learning, leveraged extensive language data to discern intricate patterns, context, and relationships. This transition enabled AI to manage language with unparalleled nuance, an essential ability for real-time interpretation. Rule-based models were the primary methodology for language processing in artificial intelligence (Xu & Cai, 2021). These systems, originating in the mid-20th century, depended on linguists and language specialists to develop extensive rule sets that encoded the grammatical, syntactical, and lexical frameworks of languages. For example, early translation systems such as SYSTRAN utilized established principles for sentence construction and word substitution to translate text. This method proved effective for uncomplicated and predictable sentence structures, especially among closely related languages with analogous syntax. Nonetheless, rule-based systems exhibited considerable constraints. They grappled with colloquial terminology, intricate sentence patterns, and contextual variances, frequently yielding inflexible or uncomfortable translations that inadequately conveyed content. The dependence on rigid rules rendered them inflexible and challenging to implement across several languages and dialects, especially in real-time interpretation contexts (Anderson et al., 2024).

The emergence of data-driven methodologies in the 1980s and 1990s substantially transformed AI's capacity for language processing (Shao et al., 2022; Samantray et al., 2024). Data-driven models, especially statistical machine translation (SMT), transitioned the emphasis from rules to probabilities, enabling AI systems to examine extensive multilingual corpora and discern trends in linguistic data. Statistical Machine Translation (SMT) can produce more natural translations than rule-based systems by calculating the probability of a specific word or phrase translating to another. Statistical Machine Translation (SMT) was prominently employed by Google Translate in its initial phase, showcasing the efficacy of data-driven methodologies for accessible, large-scale translation. Nevertheless, SMT exhibited inherent limits, frequently encountering difficulties with long-range dependencies and contextual significance, as it primarily concentrated on word-by-word or phrase-level probabilities.

The subsequent significant advancement occurred with neural network-based models, particularly with the advent of neural machine translation (NMT) in the 2010s (Gutierrez Jr, 2024). In contrast to SMT, NMT utilized deep learning methodologies to examine complete sentences as integrated entities, facilitating more contextually aware translations. Neural networks used data to train on languages holistically, handling complex syntax, idioms, and even stylistic nuances. Consequently, NMT models exhibited significantly greater accuracy and fluency, yielding translations that appeared more natural and aligned closely with human interpretation. Google's transition from Statistical Machine Translation (SMT) to Neural Machine Translation (NMT) in 2016 marked a significant milestone, demonstrating the substantial enhancement of translation quality through data-driven methodologies.

The most advanced evolution of data-driven language models emerged with transformer-based designs, including BERT, GPT, and T5 (Han et al., 2024; Sindhu et al., 2024; Rahali & Akhloufi, 2023). Transformers implemented an attention mechanism, enabling models to choose concentrate on pertinent segments of the input text during sentence processing. This method facilitated unparalleled contextual comprehension, as transformers could identify relationships between words and sentences over extended distances within a text. In real-time interpretation, this indicated that AI could more effectively discern nuances, adapt to diverse circumstances, and modify tone and intent.

3. AI-POWERED INTERPRETATION AND TRANSLATION SYSTEMS

3.1 Overview of AI Interpretation Systems

The advancement of AI-driven interpretation systems has drastically altered the domain of language translation, transitioning from conventional human-centric approaches to advanced automated solutions (Gutierrez Jr, 2024). Notable AI-powered tools like Google Translate and Microsoft Translator illustrate this transition, providing sophisticated features that improve communication across language barriers.

Google Translate, a prevalent translation service, utilizes neural machine translation (NMT) technology to deliver real-time translations of text and speech (Son & Kim, 2023; Gutierrez Jr, 2024). Through the analysis of extensive multilingual text data, Google Translate generates contextually aware translations that reflect the subtleties of language. Its intuitive design facilitates immediate translations in several languages, rendering it an essential tool for tourists, students, and professionals.

Microsoft Translator employs analogous ideas, incorporating neural machine translation and deep learning models to provide superior translations (Wang et al., 2022; Skadiņa et al., 2023). It provides distinctive functionalities, including conversation mode, which facilitates real-time verbal translations during multilingual dialogues. This feature is especially advantageous in business meetings and conferences, where effective communication is crucial.

Both platforms employ deep learning methodologies, allowing them to learn from user interactions and progressively enhance their translation precision. By analyzing complete sentences instead of individual words, these AI systems can more effectively comprehend context, idiomatic expressions, and cultural references, which are essential for proficient communication (Kasirzadeh & Gabriel, 2023).

Nonetheless, despite their advantages, AI interpretation systems encounter obstacles. A notable disadvantage is their difficulty with colloquial expressions and cultural subtleties that may not have straightforward translations (Moneus & Sahari, 2024). Expressions such as “kick the bucket” or “break the ice” may result in misinterpretations if not accurately understood. This underscores the necessity for human supervision in critical situations, where precision and cultural awareness are essential.

Furthermore, privacy issues emerge from the utilization of cloud-based computing, wherein sensitive data may be compromised during transmission. AI interpretation systems must emphasize user consent and transparency over data utilization to foster confidence and maintain adherence to privacy standards (Díaz-Rodríguez et al., 2023).

Although AI-driven interpretation systems improve accessibility and efficiency, ethical issues must be addressed promptly. AI-generated translations, while expedient, may lack the requisite complexity essential in legal and medical contexts, where accuracy is paramount. Excessive dependence on AI in judicial settings poses the possibility of misinterpretations that may influence verdicts, whilst in healthcare, erroneous translations of symptoms or dosages could jeopardize patient safety. Bias in training data may also harm marginalized languages and dialects. To alleviate these concerns, AI must be combined with human supervision, guaranteeing ethical protections and equity in real-time analysis. Proactively addressing these challenges enhances AI's function as a responsible linguistic instrument.

3.2 Neural Machine Translation and Deep Learning Models

Neural machine translation (NMT) and deep learning models have revolutionised AI interpretation by improving language translation accuracy, fluency, and context-awareness (Pym & Hao, 2024). NMT models use neural networks to assess phrases as cohesive pieces, allowing AI to translate with the source language's structure, tone, and intent. Before this innovation, rule-based and statistical machine translation systems struggled with sentence flow, colloquial idioms, and contextual nuance.

Neural networks are computational representations of the brain's interconnected neurons (Luo, 2021; Pavone & Plebe, 2021). These networks help AI grasp word-phrase associations in language translation, processing them as part of a sentence or paragraph. NMT systems train models to recognise linguistic patterns and context using massive volumes of bilingual text data (Han et al., 2024). This lets AI-powered systems "learn" language dynamically beyond rules and words. By switching from word-by-word translations to sentence-based, context-aware output, early NMT models like Google Translate's 2016 neural-based system improved translation fluency and readability.

Deep learning models improved NMT. Deep learning, a subtype of machine learning, uses multi-layered neural networks to analyze data hierarchically, allowing AI to capture complex language characteristics like idioms, tone, and formal versus informal register (Kumar, 2022). Translating these intricacies is essential for preserving meaning between languages, making this especially useful in interpretation. Fresh data improves deep learning models, making them adaptive to slang, cultural allusions, and changing terminology.

In 2017, Vaswani et al. introduced the transformer architecture, which revolutionised NMT (Bhadauria, 2023). Transformers can handle word sequences simultaneously, unlike prior neural networks. Transformers' attention system, which lets the model focus on sentence words and phrases that help it understand meaning, is their main breakthrough. This method helps AI preserve contextual coherence by capturing long-range word connections that prior models missed. Transformer-based models like OpenAI's GPT and Google's BERT handle complicated linguistic structures well, enhancing real-time translation accuracy and responsiveness.

One of the biggest benefits of deep learning for AI interpreters is context-awareness (Pradeep et al., 2021). Translations were sometimes uncomfortable or confusing since traditional methods ignored context. Instead, deep learning algorithms analyze text holistically, identifying how words operate in sentences and adapting translations. Depending on context, "bank" might mean a financial organization or a riverbank. AI interpreters with deep learning can recognize and apply the proper meaning based on surrounding words, minimizing misconceptions and improving reliability.

These accuracy and context-awareness advances have made NMT and deep learning models essential to real-time AI interpretation systems like Google Translate and Microsoft Translator. Transformer-based models provide fast, accurate translations that approximate human interpretation on these platforms. Deep learning allows real-time translation of spoken language, enabling multilingual discussions (Gutierrez Jr, 2024).

AI's interpretative abilities will certainly improve as deep learning advances (Taye, 2023; Oku et al.,2024). More complicated models trained on more diverse datasets should capture softer language features like emotional tone and regional dialects. AI interpretation will become more accurate as neural networks and deep learning learn from real-world usage, making it a feasible solution for complex, real-time cross-linguistic communication in professional, educational, and everyday settings.

4. REAL-TIME INTERPRETATION AND ITS APPLICATIONS

4.1 Real-Time Interpretation Capabilities

Recent breakthroughs in artificial intelligence and natural language processing have rendered real-time language interpretation more accessible, revolutionizing cross-linguistic communication (Papatsimouli et al., 2023). Essential technologies, such as neural machine translation (NMT), deep learning, and automated voice recognition (ASR), have facilitated real-time interpretation functionalities integrated into diverse devices and applications. These developments facilitate immediate translation and interpretation, reducing the challenges posed by language boundaries in professional, educational, and personal settings.

Automatic speech recognition (ASR) is a fundamental technology for real-time interpretation, converting spoken language into text by detecting and transcribing audio input (Parthasarathi et al., 2023; Parthasarathi et al., 2025). Advanced ASR systems, driven by deep learning models, analyze and interpret speech patterns in real time, becoming them essential for voice-based interpretation. ASR models trained on extensive multilingual audio datasets can identify various accents, dialects, and colloquial speech, which is essential for effectively capturing spoken language in real-time applications. Platforms such as Google Assistant and Amazon Alexa employ Automatic Speech Recognition (ASR) to provide real-time responses, whilst applications like Microsoft Translator and Google Translate incorporate ASR to provide immediate translation during live dialogues.

Neural machine translation (NMT) is a fundamental technology for real-time interpretation (Lankford et al., 2023). In contrast to earlier rule-based or statistical models, NMT analyzes complete sentences as unified entities, so more effectively capturing context, tone, and meaning. Neural Machine Translation (NMT) systems predominantly utilize transformer topologies, including BERT, GPT, and T5, which employ attention mechanisms to emphasize pertinent segments of a text. These models enable AI to process and provide translations that are natural-sounding and accurately convey the original message. NMT systems are optimized for real-time applications to provide translations within milliseconds, facilitating seamless, continuous interactions between languages. This functionality is essential in corporate meetings, international conferences, and travel applications, where delays might hinder communication flow.

These technologies have been incorporated into a diverse range of devices and applications. Smartphones and tablets have become indispensable instruments for real-time interpretation, with applications such as Google Translate and iTranslate offering mobile voice translation for travelers and business workers in diverse contexts. Wearable technology, like Google Pixel Buds, provide real-time interpretation via headphones, enabling users to engage in cross-linguistic conversations with hands-free ease. Furthermore, desktop and online programs, like as Zoom and Microsoft Teams, now include integrated real-time translation capabilities for virtual meetings (Hersh et al., 2023). This integration has proven particularly advantageous in the age of remote work, where global players must collaborate in real-time without linguistic obstacles.

Augmented reality (AR) and optical character recognition (OCR) have advanced real-time interpretation by broadening its uses beyond auditory and textual formats (Papatsimouli et al., 2023; Jain et al., 2023). Augmented reality-enabled technology, like smartphones and smart glasses, provide immediate translations of printed text in settings such as airports, restaurants, and foreign towns, enhancing navigation and information accessibility. OCR technology, which identifies and transforms printed or handwritten text in photos into digital format, facilitates real-time visual translation in applications such as Google Translate's camera feature, enabling users to instantaneously comprehend signs, menus, and documents by merely aiming their cameras.

The advent of real-time interpretation capabilities has enhanced the speed, accuracy, and accessibility of language translation, hence fostering significant exchanges across linguistic barriers. Nonetheless, technical obstacles persist. Interpretation models must consistently enhance their capabilities to address background noise, accents, idioms, and dialects in practical environments. Moreover, these systems necessitate considerable processing capacity, frequently depending on cloud-based servers to execute intricate computations, which may pose a constraint in regions with inadequate connectivity. Nevertheless, continuous progress in edge computing seeks to enhance processing capabilities in local devices, which may decrease latency and augment the reliability of real-time interpretation, even in offline contexts (Carvalho et al., 2021; Angel et al., 2021).

4.2 Applications in Different Industries

Real-time AI interpretation has created transformative opportunities across various sectors, where swift, precise, and accessible communication is essential. Industries including healthcare, legal, travel, and business are utilizing real-time interpretation to overcome language barriers, thereby improving service delivery, client engagement, and collaboration. Integrating advanced AI-driven translation tools enables these sectors to deliver more inclusive, efficient, and responsive services to a global, multilingual audience (Tian, 2024).

The healthcare sector has significantly profited from real-time AI interpretation (Shumba et al., 2022). In medical environments, effective communication between healthcare professionals and patients is essential for accurate diagnoses, informed consent, and appropriate treatment. AI-driven real-time interpretation tools, such as Microsoft Translator and Google Translate's healthcare-specific functionalities, assist medical personnel in communicating with non-English-speaking patients, frequently diminishing the necessity for on-site interpreters. Real-time translation systems can aid in emergencies where instant understanding is essential. While these technologies are beneficial, their deployment requires caution due to the critical nature of medical communication, necessitating continuous enhancements to appropriately manage intricate medical language and nuances.

The legal sector is undergoing substantial transformations due to real-time interpretation technology. In legal contexts, precision and subtlety are crucial to maintain equity and guarantee understanding of rights and obligations. AI-driven interpretation tools facilitate multilingual communication in courtrooms, police stations, and immigration services, aiding lawyers and clients who converse in different languages (Grey & Severin, 2022). Platforms such as Microsoft Translator provide real-time speech-to-text and text-to-speech capabilities for legal applications, facilitating instantaneous translation for both verbal and written communication. Nonetheless, ethical and confidentiality concerns are critical due to the sensitive nature of legal information. Technology continues to advance to fulfill these standards, improving accessibility while adhering to the legal sector's stringent privacy regulations.

In the travel and hospitality sector, real-time AI interpretation improves customer experience by facilitating effective communication across language barriers for travelers. Mobile apps, such as Google Translate and iTranslate, offer instant voice and text translation, helping tourists navigate foreign locations, interact with locals, and understand essential information like signage and directions. Augmented reality (AR) and optical character recognition (OCR) technologies enable travelers to point their cameras at signs, menus, or other written materials to receive instant translations (Sharma and Aggarwal, 2024). Hotels and tourism agencies are also incorporating AI-driven interpretation in their customer service channels to provide more personalized, accessible experiences for international guests.

The business sector has perhaps seen the most rapid adoption of real-time AI interpretation, especially with the rise of remote work and global teams. Multilingual companies are using real-time translation tools in virtual meetings and collaborative platforms, like Microsoft Teams and Zoom, to facilitate communication among diverse teams. AI interpretation allows team members to communicate seamlessly in their native languages, reducing misunderstandings and boosting productivity (Daramola et al.,2024). For international sales and client relations, real-time AI interpretation enables businesses to engage with clients and partners in their preferred languages, improving rapport and supporting a more inclusive business environment. Additionally, real-time interpretation assists businesses in localizing marketing materials, training sessions, and customer support, making their services more accessible to global markets.

While real-time AI interpretation offers considerable advantages in these sectors, challenges remain. High-stakes industries like healthcare and law require precise, context-aware translations, and even minor inaccuracies can have serious repercussions. Current AI systems are effective for broad communication but can still struggle with sophisticated terminology, dialects, and culturally particular expressions that require deep contextual knowledge (Mengesha et al.,2021). Moreover, privacy concerns persist, particularly when interpreting sensitive material, as AI interpretation generally relies on cloud-based processing, which may expose data to security dangers.

4.3 The Role of Cloud and Edge Computing in Real-Time AI

Cloud and edge computing have revolutionized real-time AI interpretation, making translation solutions faster, more accessible, and adaptable across devices (Guo, 2022). These technologies improve AI-powered interpretation tool speed, efficiency, and reliability by dispersing computational resources between cloud data centers and edge devices. This hybrid method lets real-time interpretation apps suit the needs of mobile, on-the-go users in corporate, travel, healthcare, and other situations.

AI-driven interpretation relies on cloud computing for processing power and storage to operate sophisticated neural networks and deep learning models (Devarajan, 2024). Cloud servers rapidly perform data-intensive models that require continuous training and real-time processing. Google and Microsoft can provide high-quality, scalable interpretation services without relying on local device capability by hosting models on the cloud. The cloud allows real-time interpretation model modifications and upgrades based on user feedback and fresh data. Thus, interpretation applications may accurately translate languages, dialects, and specialist vocabularies.

Mao & Chang (2023) say cloud computing is cross-device compatible. Smartphones, tablets, and computers with internet access can access cloud-based real-time interpretation programs, making them convenient and versatile. Google Translate and Microsoft Translator use cloud infrastructure to enable continuous translation across mobile, web, and desktop apps. This lets users start or join discussions from any device, which is useful for distant workers, vacationers, and multilingual people.

Edge computing computes data locally on the device or a nearby server rather than in a cloud. Processing linguistic data closer to the user minimizes latency, making this method ideal for real-time interpretation. Edge computing makes AI interpretation faster and more smooth by handling tasks locally (Mishra & Manda, 2024). Google's Pixel Buds use edge computing to provide real-time language interpretation without an internet connection. Cloud-based processing is less dependable in rural or vacation locales with low connectivity, therefore this is useful.

Scalability and responsiveness of real-time interpretation systems depend on cloud and edge computing integration. Cloud servers can handle data-intensive tasks like training huge language models and maintaining complicated speech-to-text conversions, while edge devices handle user-facing interpretation (Theodorakopoulos et al., 2024). In a live translation session on Microsoft Teams, the cloud processes complex linguistic data while edge computing on the user's device delivers real-time display and audio. Optimizing complex computations and user interactions with this division of work ensures seamless, continuous real-time interpretation.

Privacy and data security are crucial when interpreting cloud and edge computing (Ometov et al., 2022). Hybrid solutions reduce privacy risks by processing personal and sensitive data locally (edge) and general data in the cloud. Interpretation entails processing potentially sensitive interactions. In confidential domains like healthcare and legal interpretation, this balance is crucial.

Context-aware language processing will improve real-time interpretation applications as cloud and edge computing evolve (Ben Sada et al., 2023). Edge devices can optimize interpretations using real-time environmental data like location or context-specific terminology, while the cloud can update language models to follow linguistic trends.

5. ETHICAL AND CULTURAL CONSIDERATIONS IN AI INTERPRETATION

5.1 Accuracy and Reliability of AI in Sensitive Contexts

In legal and medical interpretation, where accuracy and sensitivity are crucial, AI-powered interpretation raises ethical concerns (Zafar, 2024). Precision is crucial in these circumstances since even tiny errors or misinterpretations can affect rights, health, and well-being. In high-stakes scenarios, using AI for interpretation poses ethical questions concerning its dependability and ability to manage complicated language dynamics, specialist terminology, and culturally sensitive material.

Legal misinterpretation can affect justice by misinterpreting legal rights, judicial proceedings, or case details. In a courtroom, an AI interpretation error could cause a defendant and lawyer to miscommunicate, influencing the case. It takes nuance to understand legal language's specialist vocabulary, idiomatic idioms, and complex sentence patterns (De and Gallage2024). AI models have improved, but they still make mistakes, especially with rare legal phrases or idioms that may not be in training data. These limitations highlight the ethical risk of using AI alone to understand legal language without human oversight, as AI may lack the contextual sensitivity to appropriately convey legal purpose and gravitas.

Medical interpretation is also risky. Patients need clear, precise communication to understand diagnoses, treatments, and care (Elendu et al.,2024). AI-driven medical interpretation errors can cause patients and healthcare practitioners to misinterpret symptoms, drug instructions, and procedural risks, compromising patient safety. Jargon, abbreviations, and vocabulary that differs by medical specialty make medical terminology complicated (Grossman et al.,2021). Even AI systems educated on enormous datasets may misread phrases, causing serious miscommunication. Misinterpreting a diagnosis or dose prescription could endanger a patient's health, creating ethical questions concerning AI interpretation in high-stakes healthcare interactions.

Inclusion and bigotry raise ethical difficulties. Training AI systems on huge datasets may introduce biases (Varsha, 2023). This is especially troublesome in sensitive professions that require cultural and linguistic inclusion. A Western medical terminology and patient interaction-trained AI model may struggle to understand cultural nuances or terminology from different locations or demographics, such as indigenous languages or dialects. This can lead to incomplete or biased interpretations and unfair treatment of disadvantaged linguistic or cultural groups.

In delicate domains where interpretation is crucial, reliability is another issue. AI interpretation is becoming more accurate for common use, but high-stakes scenarios may demand more reliability. Experience and adaptability help human interpreters understand dynamic talks (Kopp & Krämer, 2021). They can explain problematic words, ask for repetition, and adapt language according on the customer or patient's emotional or physical state, something existing AI cannot.

AI interpretation with human oversight in delicate situations is a realistic and ethical option. AI can provide real-time ideas or handle early tasks like document translation while human translators handle sophisticated exchanges that demand critical thinking and contextual judgment in healthcare and law (Pöchhacker, 2022). This hybrid paradigm uses AI's speed and accessibility while retaining human accuracy and empathy.

AI-driven interpretation enhances accessibility but also presents ethical dilemmas, particularly in legal and medical domains where misinterpretation may result in grave repercussions. In healthcare, AI misinterpretations of symptoms or prescriptions have resulted in erroneous treatments, jeopardizing patient safety. Likewise, legal contexts necessitate exact terminology; AI inaccuracies in judicial procedures or asylum matters can endanger justice. Bias in AI models, frequently originating from skewed training data, might exacerbate the disadvantages faced by underrepresented populations. To tackle this issue, developers are incorporating fairness-oriented algorithms and varied linguistic datasets to reduce biases. Ethical AI efforts prioritize human monitoring, guaranteeing that AI assists rather than supplants skilled interpreters in essential contexts.

5.2 Cultural Sensitivity and Bias in AI Algorithms

As AI interpretation becomes more incorporated into cross-cultural communication, the challenges of cultural sensitivity and algorithmic prejudice arise as major ethical issues (Ofosu-Asare, 2024). AI-driven interpretation models are trained on extensive datasets, frequently sourced from various origins; nonetheless, the intricate intricacies of cultural contexts and the potential for perpetuating biases pose significant challenges. Comprehending and mitigating these constraints is crucial for guaranteeing that AI interpretation promotes precise and respectful communication across diverse languages and cultures.

Cultural sensitivity is essential in interpretation, as language is intricately linked to cultural identity, values, and social standards. Effective interpretation needs not only language precision but also comprehension of cultural references, idioms, and etiquette. AI interpretation models are typically constrained to language patterns and may not grasp the cultural context that influences word selection, tone, or phrasing (Magee et al., 2023). Phrases deemed polite in one culture may be perceived as excessively direct or even disrespectful in another. AI systems may overlook these nuanced distinctions, leading to interpretations that fail to completely encapsulate the intended meaning or that unintentionally express insensitivity. Cultural misinterpretations can result in misunderstandings in professional environments, when respect and precision are crucial, such as in international corporate negotiations or diplomatic interactions.

Algorithmic bias is a significant concern in the understanding of AI. Bias in AI models frequently originates from the training data, which may mirror societal or cultural prejudices inherent in the sources utilized to construct these systems (Ferrara, 2023). If an AI model's training data is predominantly derived from a particular language variant, dialect, or demographic group, the resultant interpretations may exhibit inadvertent biases, privileging certain expressions, dialects, or linguistic structures over others. This may result in distorted or incomplete portrayals of specific languages or cultures, potentially marginalizing minority languages or perpetuating prejudices. AI interpretations may struggle to effectively represent languages with distinct cultural aspects, such as indigenous languages or dialects with minimal digital presence, which are frequently underrepresented in training datasets.

AI models not only mirror prejudices present in the data but also perpetuate preconceptions by linking specific words or phrases to distinct genders, roles, or social groups. A translation system may link particular professions or adjectives with specific genders due to biased patterns present in the training data. This misrepresents linguistic variety and reinforces detrimental stereotypes that might influence perceptions of individuals and groups in different circumstances.

Initiatives to mitigate bias and enhance cultural sensitivity in AI interpretation are currently progressing. One strategy is to augment and diversify training datasets to encompass a broader spectrum of languages, dialects, and cultural contexts, assuring comprehensive representation of underrepresented languages and variations (Zhang et al., 2023). Furthermore, integrating human supervision in the development process can assist in recognizing and alleviating any biases at an early stage. AI developers can implement approaches like bias detection and correction algorithms to identify and rectify biased outputs before to their delivery to users. This enhances the impartiality and fairness of interpretations, particularly in high-stakes environments such as legal, healthcare, and educational contexts.

Enhancing cultural sensitivity in AI interpretation necessitates refining algorithms to recognize and respond to contextual information. Certain advanced models integrate contextual learning, enabling AI to modify perceptions according to situational or cultural context. For example, comprehending the cultural context of a dialogue can assist AI in assessing the suitable degree of formality or identifying culturally relevant statements necessitating precise translations.

5.3 Data Privacy and Security in AI Interpretation

The utilization of AI-driven interpretation tools presents considerable data privacy and security issues, especially in real-time contexts where confidential information may be disclosed (Fontes et al., 2022). As AI interpretation proliferates in healthcare, legal, and economic sectors, safeguarding user data is essential to avert unwanted access, data breaches, and the exploitation of personal information. Implementing stringent data privacy and security protocols in AI interpretation is crucial for preserving user confidence, safeguarding individual rights, and complying with legal and ethical requirements.

Data Confidentiality Concerns regarding AI interpretation mostly arise from the characteristics of the linguistic data shared by users (Hasal et al., 2021). Discussions necessitating interpretation frequently encompass personal or sensitive information, including medical data, legal difficulties, or proprietary commercial issues. Real-time interpretation systems typically depend on cloud-based processing, wherein data is sent to remote servers for swift analysis and translation. This enhances the speed and precision of AI-driven interpretations, but it also heightens the risk of data exposure during transmission, as data is frequently stored, processed, or viewed by third-party service providers. If these technologies are inadequately safeguarded, they may be susceptible to interception or unlawful access, thus jeopardizing user privacy.

In critical sectors such as healthcare and legal services, privacy concerns are especially urgent. Legislation such as the Health Insurance Portability and Accountability Act (HIPAA) in the United States mandates stringent protocols for the confidentiality of patient data (Mulgund et al., 2021). AI interpretation systems employed in these areas must adhere to regulations to prevent infractions that could jeopardize patient privacy or compromise legal secrecy. In business contexts, real-time interpretation may encompass sensitive corporate information or client data, where breaches of privacy could result in significant financial and reputational repercussions.

Safety Challenges related to AI interpretation tools encompass threats of hacking, data breaches, and unauthorized access to stored or sent information. Cyberattacks aimed at AI platforms are increasing, as these systems frequently manage significant volumes of personal data, rendering them attractive targets for nefarious individuals (Bécue et al., 2021). The instantaneous functionality of interpretation tools results in a continuous exchange of data between devices and cloud servers, potentially exposing vulnerabilities. In the absence of rigorous security standards, hackers may get access to this data or disrupt the translation process, jeopardizing data integrity and user safety.

Data encryption is an essential security protocol that safeguards information during transmission, guaranteeing that data exchanged between users and AI servers is available just to authorized parties (Chen, 2021). End-to-end encryption is crucial for protecting real-time interpretation data, as it obstructs illegal access to or alteration of the content. Moreover, approaches for anonymization and data minimization—such as removing personal identifiers or limiting the volume of stored data—are beneficial in mitigating the danger of privacy infringements. By retaining just critical information and anonymizing sensitive data, AI platforms can mitigate the risk of personal detail exposure in the event of a data breach.

AI providers may also utilize edge computing to mitigate privacy issues. on edge computing, data processing transpires locally on the user's device instead of on the cloud, hence reducing the necessity to transfer critical information over potentially insecure networks (Alwakeel, 2021). This method improves privacy and security by ensuring that data remains under the user's control and is not dependent on outside servers, which may be vulnerable to external threats. Despite its limitations in processing capacity, edge computing serves as a significant alternative for privacy-sensitive applications in industries such as healthcare, legal, and government.

User consent and transparency are both essential in mitigating privacy and security issues. Providers of AI interpretation tools must exhibit transparency about data usage policies, clearly alerting users about the data acquired, its utilization, and potential access by third parties. Explicit consent protocols empower users to manage their information, enabling them to make informed choices regarding the balance between immediate convenience and data privacy. Privacy-by-design principles, which incorporate privacy into the AI system from the beginning, bolster ethical behaviors and conform to regulatory standards (Renuka et al., 2025).

6. CONCLUSION

The advancement of artificial intelligence (AI) in interpretation signifies a substantial transition from conventional techniques to instantaneous solutions, significantly altering our multilingual communication. Historically, human interpreters employed methods like consecutive and simultaneous interpretation, which, although successful, were frequently constrained by time limitations and the necessity for specialized expertise. These conventional approaches established the foundation for the incorporation of AI, which has brought forth unparalleled speed and efficiency in language processing.

AI-driven interpretation systems utilize sophisticated technology, such as machine learning and neural networks, to improve precision and responsiveness. The integration of cloud and edge computing has significantly transformed this domain, enabling real-time processing and minimizing latency. This hybrid method enhances user experience while mitigating privacy issues through local data processing, thereby protecting sensitive information.

Nonetheless, the emergence of AI in interpretation presents certain obstacles. Ethical considerations, especially in critical domains such as healthcare and legal contexts, highlight the significance of precision and cultural awareness. Misinterpretations may have significant repercussions, underscoring the necessity for human supervision in AI-driven operations.

As AI advances, its applications in several sectors are expected to improve communication and accessibility. The future of interpretation depends on the harmonious integration of human expertise with AI capabilities, effectively overcoming language barriers while preserving the subtleties of human contact. This continuous evolution will influence the realm of global communication, promoting enhanced understanding and cooperation in an increasingly interconnected globe.

The future of AI-driven interpretation is characterized by seamless collaboration between humans and AI, with AI augmenting speed and scalability while human interpreters maintain cultural and contextual precision. Progress in deep learning and real-time processing will enhance AI's capacity to comprehend tone, idioms, and regional dialects, hence rendering multilingual conversation more fluid. Ethical AI frameworks will be crucial in mitigating bias and ensuring equity. AI-driven wearables, augmented reality, and sentiment-sensitive translation algorithms will significantly transform interpretation in the forthcoming decade. Instead of supplanting human expertise, AI will function as an intelligent assistant, facilitating communication across languages while maintaining the subtleties of human contact.

REFERENCES

Alwakeel, A. M. (2021). An overview of fog computing and edge computing security and privacy issues. Sensors. https://doi.org/mdpi.comDOI: 10.3390/s21248226

Anderson, C., Vandenberg, B., Hauser, C., Johansson, A., & Galloway, N. (2024). Semantic coherence dynamics in large language models through layered syntax-aware memory retention mechanism. *authorea*.com DOI: 10.22541/au.173016320.04754825/v1

Angel, N. A., Ravindran, D., Vincent, P. D. R., Srinivasan, K., & Hu, Y. C. (2021). Recent advances in evolving computing paradigms: Cloud, edge, and fog technologies. Sensors, 22(1), 196. https://doi.org/ mdpi.comDOI: 10.3390/s22010196

Aslanyan, A. (2021). DANCING ON ROPES: Translators and the Balance of History. [HTML]

Baigorri-Jalón, J., Fernández-Sánchez, M. M., & Payàs, G. (2021, November). Historical developments in conference interpreting: An overview. In *The Routledge handbook of conference interpreting* (pp. 9–18). Routledge. [HTML], DOI: 10.4324/9780429297878-3

Bécue, A., Praça, I., & Gama, J. (2021). Artificial intelligence, cyber-threats and Industry 4.0: Challenges and opportunities. [HTML]. *Artificial Intelligence Review*, *54*(5), 3849–3886. Advance online publication. DOI: 10.1007/s10462-020-09942-2

Ben Sada, A., Naouri, A., Khelloufi, A., Dhelim, S., & Ning, H. (2023). A context-aware edge computing framework for smart internet of things. Future Internet. https://doi.org/mdpi.comDOI: 10.3390/fi15050154

Bhadauria, A. S., Shukla, M., Kumar, P., & Dwivedi, N. (2023, November). Attention-Based Neural Machine Translation for Multilingual Communication. In International Conference on Trends in Computational and Cognitive Engineering (pp. 129-142). Singapore: Springer Nature Singapore. https://doi.org/ [HTML]DOI: 10.1007/978-981-97-1923-5_10

Carvalho, G., Cabral, B., Pereira, V., & Bernardino, J. (2021). Edge computing: Current trends, research challenges and future directions. [HTML]. *Computing*, *103*(5), 993–1023. Advance online publication. DOI: 10.1007/s00607-020-00896-5

Chen, M. (2021). Accounting Data Encryption Processing Based on Data Encryption Standard Algorithm. Complexity. https://doi.org/wiley.comDOI: 10.1155/2023/9856582

Choi, S. R. & Lee, M. (2023). Transformer architecture and attention mechanisms in genome data analysis: a comprehensive review. Biology. https://doi.org/mdpi.comDOI: 10.3390/biology12071033

Daramola, G. O., Adewumi, A., Jacks, B. S., & Ajala, O. A. (2024). Navigating complexities: a review of communication barriers in multinational energy projects. International Journal of Applied Research in Social Sciences, 6(4), 685-697. DOI: fepbl.comDOI: 10.51594/ijarss.v6i4.1062

De Silva, D. I., & Gallage, I. S. (2024, November). The Role of Syntax and Semantics in Rule-Based Translation: A Comprehensive Review. In 2024 International Conference on Information and Communication Technology for Development for Africa (ICT4DA) (pp. 229-234). IEEE. https://doi.org/ [HTML]DOI: 10.1109/ICT4DA62874.2024.10777198

Devarajan, L. (2024). Innovations in Cloud Storage: Leveraging Generative AI for Enhanced Data Management. Generative AI and Implications for Ethics, Security, and Data Management, 322-349. DOI: [HTML]DOI: 10.4018/979-8-3693-8557-9.ch011

Díaz-Rodríguez, N., Del Ser, J., Coeckelbergh, M., de Prado, M. L., Herrera-Viedma, E., & Herrera, F. (2023). Connecting the dots in trustworthy Artificial Intelligence: From AI principles, ethics, and key requirements to responsible AI systems and regulation. Information Fusion, 99, 101896. https://doi.org/ sciencedirect.comDOI: 10.1016/j.inffus.2023.101896

Dong, S., Wang, P., & Abbas, K. (2021). A survey on deep learning and its applications. [HTML]. *Computer Science Review*, *40*, 100379. Advance online publication. DOI: 10.1016/j.cosrev.2021.100379

Elendu, C., Amaechi, D. C., Okatta, A. U., Amaechi, E. C., Elendu, T. C., Ezeh, C. P., & Elendu, I. D. (2024). The impact of simulation-based training in medical education: A review. Medicine, 103(27), e38813. *DOI:*lww.comDOI: 10.1097/MD.0000000000038813

Fadhel, M. A., Duhaim, A. M., Albahri, A. S., Al-Qaysi, Z. T., Aktham, M. A., Chyad, M. A., ... & Gu, Y. (2024). Navigating the metaverse: unraveling the impact of artificial intelligence—a comprehensive review and gap analysis. Artificial Intelligence Review, 57(10), 264. https://doi.org/ springer.comDOI: 10.1007/s10462-024-10881-5

Ferrara, E. (2023). Fairness and bias in artificial intelligence: A brief survey of sources, impacts, and mitigation strategies. Sci. https://doi.org/mdpi.comDOI: 10.3390/sci6010003

Fontes, C., Hohma, E., Corrigan, C. C., & Lütge, C. (2022). AI-powered public surveillance systems: why we (might) need them and how we want them. Technology in Society. https://doi.org/ sciencedirect.comDOI: 10.1016/j.techsoc.2022.102137

Gala, D., Behl, H., Shah, M., & Makaryus, A. N. (2024). The role of artificial intelligence in improving patient outcomes and future of healthcare delivery in cardiology: a narrative review of the literature. Healthcare. https://doi.org/mdpi .comDOI: 10.3390/healthcare12040481

Gaspari, F. (2024). The History of Translation Technologies. In *The Routledge Handbook of the History of Translation Studies* (pp. 324–338). Routledge. [HTML], DOI: 10.4324/9781032690056-22

Grey, A., & Severin, A. A. (2022). Building towards best practice for governments' public communications in languages other than English: A case study of New South Wales, Australia. [HTML]. *Griffith Law Review*, *31*(1), 25–56. Advance online publication. DOI: 10.1080/10383441.2022.2031526

Grossman Liu, L., Grossman, R. H., Mitchell, E. G., Weng, C., Natarajan, K., Hripcsak, G., & Vawdrey, D. K. (2021). A deep database of medical abbreviations and acronyms for natural language processing. Scientific Data, 8(1), 149. https:// doi.org/nature.comDOI: 10.1038/s41597-021-00929-4

Gruetzemacher, R. & Whittlestone, J. (2022). The transformative potential of artificial intelligence. Futures. https://doi.org/sciencedirect.comDOI: 10.1016/j. futures.2021.102884

Guo, S. (2022). Internet of things task migration algorithm under edge computing in the design of english translation theory and teaching practice courses. Computational Intelligence and Neuroscience. https://doi.org/wiley.comDOI: 10.1155/2022/9538917

Gutierrez, R.Jr. (2024). *Unifying linguistic landscapes: The potential of AI and nanotechnology in facilitating real-time translation.* Artificial Intelligence in the Age of Nanotechnology. [HTML], DOI: 10.4018/979-8-3693-0368-9.ch005

Han, L., Gladkoff, S., Erofeev, G., Sorokina, I., Galiano, B., & Nenadic, G. (2024). Neural machine translation of clinical text: an empirical investigation into multilingual pre-trained language models and transfer-learning. Frontiers in Digital Health, 6, 1211564. https://doi.org/frontiersin.orgDOI: 10.3389/fdgth.2024.1211564

Han, S., Wang, M., Zhang, J., Li, D., & Duan, J. (2024). A Review of Large Language Models: Fundamental Architectures, Key Technological Evolutions, Interdisciplinary Technologies Integration, Optimization and .... Electronics. https://doi.org/ mdpi. comDOI: 10.3390/electronics13245040

Hansen, J. P. B. & Svennevig, J. (2021). Creating space for interpreting within extended turns at talk. Journal of Pragmatics. https://doi.org/sciencedirect.comDOI: 10.1016/j.pragma.2021.06.009

Hasal, M., Nowaková, J., Ahmed Saghair, K., Abdulla, H., Snášel, V., & Ogiela, L. (2021). Chatbots: Security, privacy, data protection, and social aspects. Concurrency and Computation: Practice and Experience, 33(19), e6426. DOI: wiley.comDOI: 10.1002/cpe.6426

Hersh, M., Leporini, B., & Buzzi, M. (2023). A comparative study of disabled people's experiences with the video conferencing tools Zoom, MS Teams, Google Meet and Skype. Behaviour & Information Technology, 1-20. https://doi.org/ tandfonline.comDOI: 10.1080/0144929X.2023.2286533

Jain, P., Bhirud, N., Tatale, S., Kale, A., Bhale, M., Hajare, A., & Jain, N. K. (2023). Real-Time Interactive AR for Cognitive Learning. In *AI, IoT, Big Data and Cloud Computing for Industry 4.0* (pp. 219–239). Springer International Publishing. [HTML], DOI: 10.1007/978-3-031-29713-7_12

Kampakis, S. (2024). An introduction to AI. In The Decision Maker's Handbook to Data Science: AI and Data Science for Non-Technical Executives, Managers, and Founders (pp. 91-102). Berkeley, CA: Apress. https://doi.org/ [HTML]DOI: 10.1007/979-8-8688-0279-9_8

Kasirzadeh, A. & Gabriel, I. (2023). In conversation with artificial intelligence: aligning language models with human values. Philosophy & Technology. https://doi.org/springer.comDOI: 10.1007/s13347-023-00606-x

Khurana, D., Koli, A., Khatter, K., & Singh, S. (2023). Natural language processing: state of the art, current trends and challenges. Multimedia tools and applications. https://doi.org/springer.comDOI: 10.1007/s11042-022-13428-4

Kopp, S. & Krämer, N. (2021). Revisiting human-agent communication: The importance of joint co-construction and understanding mental states. Frontiers in Psychology. https://doi.org/ frontiersin.orgDOI: 10.3389/fpsyg.2021.580955

Kumar, C. R. (2022). Higher Level Abstraction of Deep Architecture. In Prediction and Analysis for Knowledge Representation and Machine Learning (pp. 143-161). Chapman and Hall/CRC. [HTML]

Lankford, S., Afli, H., & Way, A. (2023). adaptNMT: an open-source, language-agnostic development environment for neural machine translation. Language Resources and Evaluation. https://doi.org/ springer.comDOI: 10.1007/s10579-023-09671-2

Lauriola, I., Lavelli, A., & Aiolli, F. (2022). An introduction to deep learning in natural language processing: Models, techniques, and tools. [HTML]. *Neurocomputing*, *470*, 443–456. Advance online publication. DOI: 10.1016/j.neucom.2021.05.103

Lavrenteva, E. & Orland-Barak, L. (2023). Conceptual-analytical framework for exploring culture in EFL coursebooks: Analysis of teaching materials from a multimodal perspective. Social Sciences & Humanities Open. https://doi.org/ sciencedirect.comDOI: 10.1016/j.ssaho.2023.100441

Lim, W. M. (2024). What is qualitative research? An overview and guidelines. Australasian Marketing Journal. DOI: sagepub.comDOI: 10.1177/14413582241264619

Luo, L. (2021). Architectures of neuronal circuits. Science. https://doi.org/science .orgDOI: 10.1126/science.abg7285

Magee, L., Arora, V., & Munn, L. (2023). Structured like a language model: Analysing AI as an automated subject. Big Data & Society. DOI: sagepub.comDOI: 10.1177/20539517231210273

Mao, C., & Chang, D. (2023). Review of cross-device interaction for facilitating digital transformation in smart home context: A user-centric perspective. [HTML]. *Advanced Engineering Informatics*, *57*, 102087. Advance online publication. DOI: 10.1016/j.aei.2023.102087

Mengesha, Z., Heldreth, C., Lahav, M., Sublewski, J., & Tuennerman, E. (2021). "I don't think these devices are very culturally sensitive."—Impact of automated speech recognition errors on African Americans. Frontiers in Artificial Intelligence, 4, 725911. https://doi.org/frontiersin.orgDOI: 10.3389/frai.2021.725911

Mhlongo, S., Mbatha, K., Ramatsetse, B., & Dlamini, R. (2023). Challenges, opportunities, and prospects of adopting and using smart digital technologies in learning environments: An iterative review. Heliyon. https://doi.org/ cell.comDOI: 10.1016/j.heliyon.2023.e16348

Mishra, S., & Manda, J. (2024). Improving real-time analytics through the Internet of Things and data processing at the network edge. [scienceacadpress.com]. *Journal of AI-Assisted Scientific Discovery*, *4*(1), 184–206.

Moneus, A. M. & Sahari, Y. (2024). Artificial intelligence and human translation: A contrastive study based on legal texts. Heliyon. https://doi.org/cell.comDOI: 10.1016/j.heliyon.2024.e28106

Mulgund, P., Mulgund, B. P., Sharman, R., & Singh, R. (2021). The implications of the California Consumer Privacy Act (CCPA) on healthcare organizations: Lessons learned from early compliance experiences. [HTML]. *Health Policy and Technology, 10*(3), 100543. DOI: 10.1016/j.hlpt.2021.100543

Naithani, K., & Raiwani, Y. P. (2023). Realization of natural language processing and machine learning approaches for text-based sentiment analysis. [HTML]. *Expert Systems: International Journal of Knowledge Engineering and Neural Networks, 40*(5), e13114. Advance online publication. DOI: 10.1111/exsy.13114

O'Brien, S. (2024). Human-Centered augmented translation: against antagonistic dualisms. Perspectives. https://doi.org/tandfonline.comDOI: 10.1080/0907676X.2023.2247423

Ofosu-Asare, Y. (2024). Cognitive imperialism in artificial intelligence: counteracting bias with indigenous epistemologies. AI & society. https://doi.org/ springer.comDOI: 10.1007/s00146-024-02065-0

Oku, K., Samayamantri, L. S., Singhal, S., & Steffi, R. (2024). Decoding AI Decisions on Depth Map Analysis for Enhanced Interpretability. In Advancing Intelligent Networks Through Distributed Optimization (pp. 143-164). IGI Global. DOI: [HTML]DOI: 10.4018/979-8-3693-3739-4.ch008

Ometov, A., Molua, O. L., Komarov, M., & Nurmi, J. (2022). A survey of security in cloud, edge, and fog computing. Sensors. https://doi.org/mdpi.comDOI: 10.3390/s22030927

Pan, L., Sun, D., Zou, Y., Cao, Y., Zhang, J., & Li, F. (2023). Psycho-linguistic and educational challenges in Teaching Chinese (Mandarin) Language: voices from None-Chinese teachers of Mandarin language. BMC psychology. https://doi.org/springer.comDOI: 10.1186/s40359-023-01432-8

Papatsimouli, M., Sarigiannidis, P., & Fragulis, G. F. (2023). A survey of advancements in real-time sign language translators: integration with IoT technology. Technologies. https://doi.org/ mdpi.comDOI: 10.3390/technologies11040083

Park, C. S. Y., Kim, M. G., & Han, H. W. (2024). Transforming nursing practice through cutting-edge AI in healthcare: Opportunities, challenges, and ethical implications. Contemporary Nurse. https://doi.org/ tandfonline.comDOI: 10.1080/10376178.2024.2424787

Parthasarathi, A., Banu, A., & Joshi, A. (2023, December). Comprehensive Survey of Audio-to-Text Conversion. In International Symposium on Intelligent Informatics (pp. 129-145). Singapore: Springer Nature Singapore. https://doi.org/ [HTML]DOI: 10.1007/978-981-97-2147-4_10

Parthasarathi, A., Banu, A., & Joshi, A. (2025). Comprehensive Survey of Audio-to-Text. In Intelligent Informatics: Proceedings of Eighth International Symposium on Intelligent Informatics (ISI 2023) (Vol. 389, p. 129). Springer Nature. [HTML]

Pavone, A. & Plebe, A. (2021). How neurons in deep models relate with neurons in the brain. Algorithms. https://doi.org/mdpi.comDOI: 10.3390/a14090272

Pöchhacker, F. (2022). Interpreters and interpreting: shifting the balance?. The Translator. https://doi.org/ tandfonline.comDOI: 10.1080/13556509.2022.2133393

Pradeep, P., Krishnamoorthy, S., Pathinarupothi, R. K., & Vasilakos, A. V. (2021). Leveraging context-awareness for Internet of Things ecosystem: Representation, organization, and management of context. [HTML]. *Computer Communications*, *177*, 33–50. DOI: 10.1016/j.comcom.2021.06.004

Pym, A. & Hao, Y. (2024). How to Augment Language Skills: Generative AI and Machine Translation in Language Learning and Translator Training. [HTML]

Rahali, A. & Akhloufi, M. A. (2023). End-to-end transformer-based models in textual-based NLP. AI. https://doi.org/ mdpi.comDOI: 10.3390/ai4010004

Rehfeldt, R. A., Tyndall, I., & Belisle, J. (2021). Music as a cultural inheritance system: a contextual-behavioral model of symbolism, meaning, and the value of music. Behavior and Social Issues. https://doi.org/springer.comDOI: 10.1007/s42822-021-00084-w

Renuka, O., RadhaKrishnan, N., Priya, B. S., Jhansy, A., & Ezekiel, S. (2025). Data Privacy and Protection: Legal and Ethical Challenges. Emerging Threats and Countermeasures in Cybersecurity, 433-465. https://doi.org/ [HTML]DOI: 10.1002/9781394230600.ch19

Sakshi, T. M., Tyagi, P., & Jain, V. (2024). Emerging trends in hybrid information systems modeling in artificial intelligence. [HTML]. *Hybrid Information Systems: Non-Linear Optimization Strategies with Artificial Intelligence*, *115*, 115–152. Advance online publication. DOI: 10.1515/9783111331133-007

Samantray, K., İZGİ, F. D., Ocampo, M. B., Dehghan, M., Mohammadpour, S., Siriphaprapagon, Y., ... & Babu, S. D. (2024). The Power of Words in AI-Driven World: Exploring the Interplay of Language, Culture, and Communication. SKET-SAMEDIA.

Sarker, I. H. (2021). Deep learning: a comprehensive overview on techniques, taxonomy, applications and research directions. SN computer science. https://doi.org/springer.comDOI: 10.1007/s42979-021-00815-1

Scorpo, A. L. (2023). *Beyond Epistolary Standards? The Language of Entreaty in Political and Diplomatic Communications from Thirteenth-Century Iberia*. The Medieval Globe. [HTML]

Shao, Z., Zhao, R., Yuan, S., Ding, M., & Wang, Y. (2022). Tracing the evolution of AI in the past decade and forecasting the emerging trends. Expert Systems with Applications, 209, 118221. https://doi.org/sciencedirect.comDOI: 10.1016/j.eswa.2022.118221

Sharma, I., & Aggarwal, A. (2024). Revolutionizing Creative Tourism: Integrating AI in Marketing for Immersive Travel Experiences. Innovative Technologies for Increasing Service Productivity, 179-197. DOI: [HTML]DOI: 10.4018/979-8-3693-2019-8.ch011

Shumba, A. T., Montanaro, T., Sergi, I., Fachechi, L., De Vittorio, M., & Patrono, L. (2022). Leveraging IoT-aware technologies and AI techniques for real-time critical healthcare applications. Sensors, 22(19), 7675. https://doi.org/mdpi.comDOI: 10.3390/s22197675

Sin-wai, C. (2023). THE DEVELOPMENT OF TRANSLATION TECHNOLOGY 1967-2023. Routledge Encyclopedia of Translation Technology. [HTML]

Sindhu, B., Prathamesh, R. P., & Sameera, M. B., & KumaraSwamy, S. (2024, May). The evolution of large language model: Models, applications and challenges. In *2024 International Conference on Current Trends in Advanced Computing (ICCTAC)* (pp. 1-8). IEEE. https://doi.org/ [HTML]DOI: 10.1109/ICCTAC61556.2024.10581180

Skadiņa, I., Vasi jevs, A., Pinnis, M., Bērziņš, A., Aranberri, N., Bogaert, J. V. D., . . . Way, A. (2023). Deep Dive Machine Translation. In European Language Equality: A Strategic Agenda for Digital Language Equality (pp. 263-287). Cham: Springer International Publishing. https://doi.org/ springer.comDOI: 10.1007/978-3-031-28819-7_40

Son, J. & Kim, B. (2023). Translation performance from the user's perspective of large language models and neural machine translation systems. Information. https://doi.org/mdpi.comDOI: 10.3390/info14100574

Sun, S. (2025). Corpora and Assessment of Translator Expertise. In The Routledge Handbook of Corpus Translation Studies (pp. 582-599). Routledge. https://doi.org/[HTML]DOI: 10.4324/9781003184454

Taye, M. M. (2023). Understanding of machine learning with deep learning: architectures, workflow, applications and future directions. Computers. https://doi.org/mdpi.comDOI: 10.3390/computers12050091

Theodorakopoulos, L., Theodoropoulou, A., & Stamatiou, Y. (2024). A state-of-the-art review in big data management engineering: Real-life case studies, challenges, and future research directions. Eng. https://doi.org/ mdpi.comDOI: 10.3390/eng5030068

Tian, X. (2024). Personalized translator training in the era of digital intelligence: Opportunities, challenges, and prospects. Heliyon. https://doi.org/ cell.comDOI: 10.1016/j.heliyon.2024.e39354

Tipà, I. & Moratto, R. Chinese interpreting in Italy: An overview. The Routledge Handbook of Chinese Interpreting. [HTML]

Varsha, P. S. (2023). How can we manage biases in artificial intelligence systems–A systematic literature review. International Journal of Information Management Data Insights, 3(1), 100165. https://doi.org/sciencedirect.comDOI: 10.1016/j.jjimei.2023.100165

Wang, H., Wu, H., He, Z., Huang, L., & Church, K. W. (2022). Progress in machine translation. Engineering. https://doi.org/sciencedirect.comDOI: 10.1016/j.eng.2021.03.023

Wang, Y. H., & Lin, G. Y. (2023). Exploring AI-healthcare innovation: Natural language processing-based patents analysis for technology-driven roadmapping. [HTML]. *Kybernetes*, *52*(4), 1173–1189. Advance online publication. DOI: 10.1108/K-03-2021-0170

Xu, X., & Cai, H. (2021). Ontology and rule-based natural language processing approach for interpreting textual regulations on underground utility infrastructure. [HTML]. *Advanced Engineering Informatics*, *48*, 101288. Advance online publication. DOI: 10.1016/j.aei.2021.101288

Zafar, A. (2024). Balancing the scale: navigating ethical and practical challenges of artificial intelligence (AI) integration in legal practices. Discover Artificial Intelligence. https://doi.org/ springer.comDOI: 10.1007/s44163-024-00121-8

Zalasiewicz, J., Waters, C. N., Ellis, E. C., Head, M. J., Vidas, D., Steffen, W., ... & Zinke, J. (2021). The Anthropocene: Comparing its meaning in geology (chronostratigraphy) with conceptual approaches arising in other disciplines. https://doi.org/ wiley.comDOI: 10.1029/2020EF001896

Zhang, Y., Zhou, D., Hooi, B., Wang, K., & Feng, J. (2023). Expanding small-scale datasets with guided imagination. Advances in neural information processing systems, 36, 76558-76618. neurips.cc

Zhao, A. P., Li, S., Cao, Z., Hu, P. J. H., Wang, J., Xiang, Y., ... & Lu, X. (2024). AI for science: predicting infectious diseases. Journal of Safety Science and Resilience. https://doi.org/sciencedirect.comDOI: 10.1016/j.jnlssr.2024.02.002

Zhao, D. (2024). The impact of AI-enhanced natural language processing tools on writing proficiency: An analysis of language precision, content summarization, and creative writing…. [HTML]. *Education and Information Technologies.* Advance online publication. DOI: 10.1007/s10639-024-13145-5

Chapter 4
Strengths and Limitations of Machine Translation and Human Translation

Rui Fan
https://orcid.org/0000-0001-8768-932X
Guangdong University of Education, China

Yue Zhang
https://orcid.org/0000-0003-4109-2506
The Education University of Hong Kong, Hong Kong

ABSTRACT

The development of machine translation (MT) has profoundly reshaped the translation industry, which reignites debates about its relationship with human translation (HT). This chapter provides an exploration of the strengths and limitations inherent in MT and HT and emphasizes their complementary rather than competitive nature. First, the progression of MT is explored. Comparative analysis from multiple perspectives. MT excels in rapidly producing consistent translations of standardized content, yet it persistently struggles with complex, culturally embedded language, implicit meanings, and high-stakes specialized contexts. Human translation remains indispensable in scenarios demanding deep cultural insight, interpretive creativity, domain-specific precision, and ethical discernment. All of these underscores the continuing necessity for human translators. Acknowledging these complementary roles, the chapter further examines the rise of hybrid translation models. Lastly, this chapter concludes with the future tendencies within a collaborative framework.

DOI: 10.4018/979-8-3373-0060-3.ch004

1. INTRODUCTION

Translation serves as a crucial bridge across languages and cultures in the globalized world. The emergence of machine translation (MT) has changed the field, as it allows for rapid, large-scale text conversion at minimal cost. The discussion of the relationship between MT and human translation (HT) has been a heated topic as early as the beginning of the 21st century. Instead of competing with human translators, machine translation has been regarded as the complementary for quite a long time (Hutchins, 2001). With the introduction of neural machine translation (NMT) and artificial intelligence (AI)-driven models, MT has become more sophisticated. The landscape of translation has dramatically changed, since the generative AI-empowered MT offers greater fluency and coherence than earlier systems. Despite these developments, machine translation still faces numerous linguistic problems, especially when deep context understanding, cultural sensitivity, and pragmatic accuracy are required. These ongoing limitations have led scholars to reconsider the relationship between machine translation (MT) and human translation (HT) in the context of recent technological shifts (Calvo-Ferrer, 2024). In order to examine recent developments in the age of AI, this chapter revisits the relationship between MT and HT, particularly in terms of their strengths and limitations, as well as the future of translation.

The chapter first reviews how machine translation has evolved historically, from its earliest forms to recent advances driven by AI (Section 2). Next, it compares machine translation with human translation from four main angles (Section 3). Section 4 addresses the increasing adoption of hybrid translation methods and considers their potential future development. Finally, the chapter concludes by suggesting possible future directions and exploring their broader significance.

2. THE EVOLUTION OF MACHINE TRANSLATION

Although the initial endeavours in machine translation were marked by high expectations, the early results were limited in terms of both accuracy and practical application (Hutchins, 2001). MT has been largely improved after decades of development. The evolution through diverse methodologies illustrates advancements in linguistics, computer science, and artificial intelligence. The progression from rule-based machine translation (RBMT) to statistical machine translation (SMT), and subsequently to advanced neural machine translation (NMT) and Generative AI-powered machine translation, illustrates a series of incremental advancements and technological innovations (Koehn, 2010). This section mainly discusses the historical progression of MT, from its early conceptual stages to the sophisticated models of today.

2.1 The History of Machine Translation

In Translation Studies, using AI technology signals a clear shift from older machine translation (MT) methods. The traditional MT first appeared in the 1950s, when researchers began experimenting with language translations via computers (Hutchins, 2001). The earliest MT system, called rule-based machine translation (RBMT), remained the main method from the 1950s up to the 1980s. RBMT mainly depended on detailed bilingual dictionaries and carefully handcrafted grammar rules (Arnold et al., 1994). Such systems translated language by following explicit grammar and syntax guidelines, resulting in accurate translations within strictly defined language contexts. However, RBMT struggled with flexible, everyday language, idioms, and varied grammatical patterns. Furthermore, RBMT necessitated considerable labour and specialised linguistic expertise for the development and maintenance of these rules, rendering it impractical for scalable translation tasks (Hutchins & Somers, 1992).

In the late 1980s and early 1990s, research shifted towards statistical machine translation (SMT), driven largely by advances in computational power and the growing availability of parallel corpora. SMT systems, on the other hand, used statistical analyses of bilingual text corpora to come up with translations. These analyses relied heavily on probabilities from large datasets to guess the best possible translation (Brown et al., 1990). This data-driven approach allowed SMT to provide more fluent translations than RBMT, particularly for languages and domains with abundant parallel data (Och & Ney, 2003, 2004). Nevertheless, SMT had some limitations. Notably, it occasionally generated outputs that were grammatically incorrect or illogical due to its emphasis on surface-level phrase correspondences rather than deeper semantic coherence (Koehn, 2010). SMT did not implement deep learning, although it employed machine learning methodologies to analyse data and identify patterns. Compared with machine learning, deep learning is effective for using the neural network to effectively capture complex representations in datasets (Mohamed et al., 2024a).

A significant breakthrough occurred in the mid-2010s with the emergence of neural machine translation (NMT). This approach applied deep learning techniques, notably the encoder-decoder structure with attention mechanisms, significantly enhancing MT systems' ability to grasp nuanced contexts (Bahdanau et al., 2016). Introducing the transformer model (Vaswani et al., 2017) brings this field forward, as it substitutes traditional recurrent neural networks with self-attention mechanisms and considerably improves translation quality. Transformer-based models process entire sentences simultaneously, effectively capturing long-range dependencies and subtle contextual nuances. This leads to translations that are noticeably more fluent and coherent than those produced by previous systems (Vaswani et al., 2017; Wu et al., 2016).

2.2 Advances in AI-Driven Machine Translation

The recent developments in the field of AI have moved NMT further, facilitating AI-driven adaptive translation systems. These systems are designed to improve their translation performance through interactions with human users, containing corrections, adjustments and personalized linguistic preferences into translation models (Knowles et al., 2019; Knowles & Koehn, 2018a, 2018b). Such systems improve accuracy over time and also provide translation solutions tailored made for specific contexts and needs of users. Additionally, current research has explored into multimodal translation, integrating textual, audio, and visual data to enhance the context-awareness of machine translations. This multimodal approach addresses real-world scenarios such as interpreting sign language, live speech translation, and subtitling, highlighting the versatility and growing sophistication of contemporary MT systems (Sulubacak et al., 2020).

Large Language Models (LLMs) emerged from the year of 2020 and have since led a new era of AI-powered translation. Armed with their unique capabilities in dealing with multilingual and multimodal tasks, LLMs have changed translation by offering developments in dialogue, adaptability to users' needs, and enhanced contextual understanding. By making use of massive datasets and advanced architectures, LLMs have pushed the boundaries of translation, enabling more nuanced and human-like products. Empirical studies (Gao et al., 2023; Škobo & Petričević, 2023) also found that ChatGPT can achieve comparable or even better translation quality than commercial translation systems (e.g., Google Translate and DeepL) in high-resource language translations.

2.3 AI-Driven in Interpreting

AI technologies have also greatly impacted the interpretation market, in particular through developments in automated speech translation and computer-assisted interpreting tools (Horváth, 2022). Although the early attempts to develop automatic interpreting systems in the late 1980s and early 1990s were limited by language technology available at the time, modern AI-based devices have made considerable strides. Nowadays, these devices aim to fully automate the interpreting process in both consecutive and simultaneous modes, and are designed to handle commonly used phrases and expressions within well-defined contexts (Horváth, 2022).

Most speech-to-speech (S2S) interpretation devices operate via a cascade model, which involves multiple sequential steps: speech-to-text (STT) conversion through automatic speech recognition (ASR), the conversion of the source language text into target language text by MT, and text-to-speech (TTS) synthesis to produce spoken TL output. Some systems take a further step following ASR to filter live speech, removing disfluencies, restarts, and filler words such as "uhm" before the conversion. This approach can enable these devices to deliver more accurate and contextually appropriate translations, albeit within their predefined operational limits (Horváth, 2022). While it has been proven viable that the end-to-end (E2E) models are capable of direct translation from source language speech to MT (Jia & Weiss, 2019), the cascade architecture remains prevailing in commercial S2S translation systems, maintaining its position as the most sophisticated and widely implemented approach.

2.4 Emerging Challenges for Contemporary Machine Translation

Although there is significant progress, MT still has limitations. The failure of MT systems to consistently interpret implicit pragmatic meaning and context is a critical disadvantage. Contextual ambiguities, such as polysemy and anaphoric references, continue to cause significant problems (Hardmeier, 2012; Vieira et al., 2021). What is more, the ethical challenges in relation to MT are yet to be handled. Issues related to data privacy, confidentiality, intellectual property rights, and professional accountability emerge as significant barriers to the wider adoption of AI translation systems, particularly in sensitive domains such as medicine, law, and diplomacy (Bo, 2023). Thus, human translators are still vital for linguistic accuracy and also for maintaining ethical and professional standards. Therefore, the evolution of MT highlights remarkable technological advancements, yet persistent linguistic, contextual, and ethical challenges still remain. Recognizing these strengths and limitations is essential for assessing whether MT can operate independently or requires additional support from human translators.

3. COMPARATIVE ANALYSIS: MACHINE TRANSLATION VS. HUMAN TRANSLATION

The rapid development of MT has promoted research that compares the performance of MT to that of traditional human translation (HT). While MT increasingly demonstrates impressive fluency and scalability, critical assessments reveal that human translation continues to possess advantages, which are particularly evident in linguistic and cultural subtleties, accuracy in specialised domains, and ethical considerations. Although both MT and HT have distinct strengths and weaknesses that manifest differently across various translation contexts, the new progress made leads to ongoing debates about the capabilities and limitations of MT compared to traditional HT. Both MT and HT have distinct strengths and weaknesses that manifest differently across various translation contexts. Recent research (Calvo-Ferrer, 2024; Mohamed et al., 2024b; Rojo, 2018; Vieira et al., 2021) has helped us understand the differences better and has guided us to look at how professionals and regular people in different settings feel about machine-generated versus human-generated translations. This section provides a detailed comparative analysis of MT and HT from four perspectives: translation quality, efficiency and cost, cultural adaptability, and ethical implications.

3.1 Translation Quality

Several studies show that MT, especially generative AI-driven systems like ChatGPT, is very close to being as accurate as a human in areas like using the right words and grammar (Luo et al., 2024; Sebo & de Lucia, 2024). Sebo and de Lucia (2024) assessed the translation quality of medical abstracts, finding that the CUB-BITT system achieved 92% accuracy relative to human translations in specialized terminology. However, significant gaps remained in contextual expression, with a notably lower ROUGE-L score (by 9.3%), highlighting challenges in MT's ability to fully capture nuanced context. Similarly, Luo et al. (2024) observed that beam search algorithms employed by MT systems prioritize high-frequency collocations and reduce lexical diversity by approximately 18%–25% compared to human translations.

Human translation demonstrates irreplaceable strengths in complex contexts, such as literary translations (Hidalgo-Ternero, 2020; Yulianto & Supriatnaningsih, 2021) and high-risk contexts, such as translations in medical and law fields (Vieira et al., 2021).. Yulianto et al. (2021) analysed French-to-English drama translations, revealing that DeepL and Google Translate scored significantly lower than human translators—only 63% and 57%, respectively, in metaphor recognition and emotional conveyance. In the same way, Hidalgo-Ternero (2020) talks about how MT often fails to handle culturally specific idioms. For example, it has a 41% failure rate when translating Spanish proverbs correctly, which shows how important it is for human translators to step in and figure out what was meant. Vieira et al. (2021) conducted a systematic study on the societal impact of machine translation (MT) in high-risk contexts, specifically in the medical and legal fields. Using a critical literature review and qualitative meta-analysis, the authors examined official documents and relevant academic research to uncover the potential threats posed by the misuse of MT technology. Their findings indicate that existing studies in the medical and legal domains often overlook the complexity of language translation and as a result it leads to an inadequate understanding of the risks associated with MT. For instance, translation errors may exacerbate information inequality for patients with language barriers, exposing certain user groups to higher risks.

3.2 Efficiency and Cost

The advantage of MT in immediacy is particularly prominent when processing standardised texts (Kruger, 2022; Postigo, 2024; Rivera-Trigueros, 2022). Rivera-Trigueros (2022) illustrates this efficiency and he reports that NMT systems require approximately two minutes to translate a 10,000-word technical document, whereas human translators average about eight hours. However, the study emphasises that MT greatly speeds up the initial translation process, but the time required for post-editing is often underestimated. Human translators typically need to refine MT-generated content with additional effort amounting to roughly 30% of the original text's length. This extra step can considerably reduce the overall time savings and consequently raise questions about the efficiency of MT in real-world applications. Labarta Postigo (2024) further explores the impact of integrating ChatGPT with traditional NMT systems. What he finds is that the speed of producing an initial draft increases by 40%. Nevertheless, human intervention remains necessary for cultural adaptation and contextual accuracy, particularly in sensitive domains such as legal translation. In a specific case of contract translation, MT systems completed a single page in an average of 1.3 minutes, whereas human translators required approximately 25 minutes. On one hand, this shows the advantage of the efficiency of MT; on the other hand, this tells the need for expert review to ensure legal and cultural appropriateness.

MT demonstrates significant economic benefits, with translation costs substantially lower than human alternatives (Kruger, 2022; Postigo, 2024). Labarta Postigo (2024) provides a cost-benefit analysis, indicating that the per-unit translation cost of MT is just 12–15% of that of human translation. Nevertheless, the study highlights a "quality risk premium", where the cost gap narrows to a ratio of 1:3 for high-stakes, high-value content. Kruger (2022) further cautions against over-reliance on MT.

He argues that hidden costs, such as potential legal disputes and brand reputation damage, have yet to be adequately quantified.

Despite the rapid output of MT, Kruger (2022) identifies an "efficiency paradox" in professional translation workflows. While raw MT output can be over 200 times faster than human translation, post-editing corrections by professional translators account for 68% of the total project time in certain cases. This effect is especially evident in specific domains such as medical research report translations. In other words, the speed advantage of MT is often mitigated by the extensive effort required to refine and verify machine-generated text, particularly in fields where precision is paramount.

3.3 Cultural Adaptability

Cultural adaptability remains as another key challenge for machine translation (MT). While MT has shown improvements in handling general content, its ability to process culture-specific elements and adapt to different cultural contexts remains limited. Relevant studies have explored MT's performance from two key aspects: (1) adaptability to high- and low-context cultures and (2) processing culture-specific elements. When it comes to these aspects, there are significant distinctions between MT and HT. This holds especially true for literary and high-context writings, which are characterised by the presence of cultural references, metaphors, and hidden meanings that are essential to complete comprehension.

Research show that MT systems struggle to translate works rooted in high-context societies. Usually, this is marked by implicit social relationships and context-dependent interpretations (Asscher, 2023; Yulianto & Supriatnaningsih, 2021). Asscher (2023) claimed that MT systems failed with a failure rate above 40% for spotting latent social hierarchies and with an error rate as high as 38.7% for translating honorific systems. Conversely, human translators did rather well by deliberately using semantic rearranging and contextual reasoning. For instance, Yulianto and Supriatnaingsih (2021) found while translating culturally complex Japanese proverbs and honorific expressions that human translators achieved an accuracy rate of 92%, far greater than the outputs of robots.

MT demonstrates comparatively better performance within low-context cultures, which tend to express meanings explicitly. MT systems achieve around 91% accuracy in standardised terminological translations and have an error rate of only about 9.2% when distinguishing formal and informal registers in Germanic languages (Asscher, 2023). Nevertheless, HT remains superior in flexibly adjusting linguistic registers to context-specific requirements, such as precisely controlling formality in legal documentation. Human translators further show high proficiency (85%) in effectively replacing culturally loaded terms. Take a Japanese business correspondence as an example. The common Japanese expression " ," which MT translated literally as "Thank you for your support," loses the subtlety of continuing business connections that are a part of Japanese corporate culture (Asscher, 2023). Understanding the underlying cultural meaning, human translators will translate it as "We appreciate our ongoing collaboration," thereby preserving relational disparities.

MT often struggles with the slight differences of culture-specific proverbs and idioms, which produces translations that can feel overly literal and out of context (Hidalgo-Ternero, 2020; Vieira et al., 2021). For example, Hidalgo-Ternero (2020) found that the failure rate of MT in translating Spanish proverbs was as high as 41%. This statistic illustrates a notable lack of creative and interpretative abilities in the translation process. On the other hand, human translators employ various strategies, including cultural substitution and the use of explanatory footnotes. These approaches have led to an impressive explanatory note attachment rate of up to 62% (Vieira et al., 2021). Additionally, research exploring the capacity of machine translation to convey humour and wordplay reveals significant challenges (Postigo, 2024). According to Labarta Postigo (2024), machine translation systems manage to accurately recognise humorous intent only about one-third of the time. This limitation highlights their struggle to effectively adapt jokes and puns that are culturally specific. Conversely, human translators frequently employ creative rewriting and localisation strategies. They might replace English puns with humour that resonates in Chinese dialects, and sometimes even alter the meaning of sentences. This approach leads to approximately 78% success in effectively localising humour. It is worth noting that the update cycles for MT cultural databases typically average around six months. This means they are significantly behind the swift changes in culture that we see on social media, lagging by a factor of 3.2 (Luo et al., 2024).

3.4 Ethical and Societal Impacts

Ethical considerations can differentiate GenAI translation systems from traditional human translation. Although MT systems (including generative AI tools) provide fast translations at lower cost, questions have been raised in respect of biases inherent in their training data. Machine-generated translations often unintentionally reinforce gender or cultural stereotypes (Bianchi et al., 2023), thus raising concerns about fairness and social responsibility in AI translation deployment. The key responsibility of human translators is to protect confidentiality, cultural sensitivity and ethical integrity, especially in politically or socially sensitive contexts (Rojo, 2018). Human translators are uniquely trained and equipped to identify and rectify biased or inappropriate content. This is a task that generative AI systems are currently unable to complete due to their lack of genuine interpretive judgment and ethical awareness. Moreover, the MT have been discussed from an ethical perspective in sensitive fields (Calvo-Ferrer, 2024; Vieira et al., 2021). Vieira et al. (2021) found that the mistranslations in medical and legal discourses could seriously affect individual and social benefits. The increased reliance on GenAI translation tools thus calls for the necessity of firm ethical frameworks and reinforces the role of human translators to maintain responsible and reliable translation standards.

Second, MT also raises concerns about information equity and the evolving role of professional translators. These factors are the key differences between the two approaches, particularly in terms of accessibility and occupational sustainability. The widespread adoption of MT has exacerbated inequalities in the global distribution of linguistic resources (Ragni & Vieira, 2022). Ragni and Vieira (2022) recognize this important issue through noting that the quality of translation for low-resource languages, such as Swahili, falls significantly short compared to high-resource languages like French, with a gap of about 53%. The differences in access to information can really create larger divides in knowledge around the world, and as a result these differences make it even harder for communities with varying language resources to stay informed and connected. Further, the influence of MT is significantly reshaping the landscape of professional translation work (Lee, 2023; Salinas & Burbat, 2023). Lee (2023) highlighted important changes in the landscape of the translation industry, pointing out that around 52% of translation companies have begun to incorporate machine translation post-editing into their processes. However, this shift has contributed to "cognitive load transfer", transforming translators from creative language professionals into "quality supervisors", consequently reducing job satisfaction by an estimated 27%. Varela Salinas and Burbat (2023) also say that the rise of MT requires major changes in the way translation is taught, from teaching students how to convert languages to teaching them how to critically evaluate MT outputs.

3.5 Critical Debates and Future Directions

While there is agreement on several key aspects that differentiate MT from HT, substantial academic discussions continue regarding their practical application and assessment. There is ongoing debate regarding the adoption of differentiated evaluation standards and metrics to distinctly assess the outcomes of machine and human translation (Kruger, 2022). Researchers have pointed out that traditional assessment frameworks might not effectively capture the errors or strengths associated with MT. This limitation arises because these frameworks were originally designed for HT. As a result, developing evaluation metrics tailored specifically for machine translation systems could lead to a more accurate understanding of how well they perform.

Additionally, scholars remain divided on how best to position MT technologically within translation workflows, reflecting tensions between viewing MT as an autonomous translation solution or as a supportive tool requiring human oversight (Asscher, 2023; Postigo, 2024). Advocates of autonomous MT emphasize the efficiency, scalability, and cost reductions achieved by fully automated translation systems, while opponents emphasize the irreplaceable value of human oversight for ensuring linguistic accuracy, cultural appropriateness, and pragmatic coherence. This disagreement has important implications for the professional identity and skillset required of translators in a rapidly evolving technological landscape.

Finally, ethical considerations form another significant point of contention, particularly concerning MT use in sensitive domains such as legal and medical translations (Vieira et al., 2021). Scholars have pointed out potential risks associated with biases embedded in machine-generated translations and stress the urgent need for clearly defined ethical guidelines to regulate MT use. These discussions illustrate the continued necessity of human translators in contexts where translation errors can lead to serious real-world consequences, and they emphasize that clearly defined ethical boundaries and human oversight remain essential.

The ongoing discussions reveal that, despite the wealth of research examining the unique strengths and limitations of both machine and human translation, there are still important questions that linger without clear answers. The ongoing conversations about evaluation methodologies, the integration of technology, and the importance of ethical standards are not just academic; they touch on real-world implications and invite deeper investigation. Tackling these challenges will play a vital role in influencing the future landscape of translation practice and theory. Looking ahead, it is crucial that future research goes beyond just comparing quality assessments. Instead, we should focus on a thorough exploration of how to optimise collaboration between humans and machines, as well as understanding the wider impacts of these integrations within socio-technical translation systems.

4. HYBRID APPROACHES: THE FUTURE OF TRANSLATION

Considering the strengths and limitations that both machine and human translation bring to the table, an integration of these approaches has emerged as a practical solution. This hybrid method facilitates boosting efficiency while ensuring that accuracy and cultural relevance are maintained. The blend of AI-powered translation tools and the invaluable touch of human expertise, often referred to as computer-assisted translation (CAT), post-editing machine translation (PEMT), interactive translation systems, and human-in-the-loop (HITL) AI translation fosters a harmonious method that enhances productivity while ensuring exceptional quality standards are upheld.

4.1 Computer-Assisted Translation (CAT) Tools

Hybrid translation models use computer-assisted translation (CAT) tools that combine translation memory (TM), terminology management systems, and AI-driven translation modules into single platforms. These tools in the unified platforms can ensure terminological consistency, minimise duplicate translation chores, and help translators by providing suggestions based on previously translated content (Bowker & Fisher, 2010; Lagoudaki, 2006, 2008; O'Brien, 2007). CAT technologies increase translation output quality and terminology consistency, especially in specialized domains where accurate language is crucial (Bowker & Fisher, 2010). Some studies found that translators perceive CAT tools as beneficial for maintaining consistency and improving the overall quality of translations (Lagoudaki, 2006, 2008). The facilitation of CAT tools, on the other hand, is contingent upon the quality of the translation memories and the relevancy of the suggestions that are supplied. It is important to train professional translators regularly updating and maintaining translation memories to ensure the reliability of CAT tools (O'Brien, 2007).

4.2 Post-Editing of Machine Translation (PEMT)

Another hybrid method that is employed rather frequently is known as post-editing machine translation, or PEMT for short. The workflow is that MT systems provide translations first, and then human translators are responsible for improving and fixing those translations in the following steps. For the purpose of this collaboration, the goal is to combine the linguistic precision and cultural sensitivity that are ensured by human engagement with the speed and consistency of machine translation. PEMT has the potential to significantly enhance translation efficiency without compromising quality (Guerberof, 2009; Plitt & Masselot, 2010). One example is the research conducted by Guerberof Arenas in 2009. They discovered that post-editing MT results increased the production of translators while maintaining high standards, which ultimately led to an improvement in efficiency. In accordance with this, Plitt and Masselot (2010) found that PEMT might potentially save a significant amount of time when compared to traditional human translation. Their studies imply that this approach has great possibilities for the administration of big translation projects.

PEMT is particularly beneficial in technical, medical, and legal translation, where precise terminology is crucial. For example, in pharmaceutical translation, AI may translate a drug's instructions with minor errors that could lead to misinterpretation. For example, in medical contexts, a human post-editor can review the translation carefully in order to ensure that dosages, medical terms, and cautions are stated accurately. Such an approach helps reduce the risk of misunderstandings. On the other hand, PEMT comes with its set of challenges, particularly in terms of the cognitive demands it places on translators. The repeated nature of post-editing tasks causes translators to develop cognitive tiredness, which might affect their performance and motivation (Koponen, 2012). The degree of post-editing needed depends much on the quality of the machine translating output. Therefore, constant improvement of machine translation systems is quite essential to reduce the mental load translators must deal with. Therefore, PEMT still depends much on a balance between automation and human involvement.

4.3 Interactive and Adaptive Machine Translation

Another choice of hybrid translation models is the application of interactive and adaptive MT systems. Such systems can help translators to interactively affect the translation process, thus facilitating real-time cooperation between human translators and MT. Real-time human corrections enable adaptive MT systems to learn from them, hence gradually improving their performance and customizing translations to accommodate particular preferences of translators.

Some scholars have investigated into the benefits of interactive translation systems and have found that these systems can improve translation quality and reduce the time required for translation tasks (Green et al., 2013). More recent studies have also shown that adaptive machine translation systems can learn from post-editing and can enhance translation quality over time, which means that less post-editing work is required (Turchi et al., 2017). The findings from these studies are still meaningful to today's new context. Even with these benefits, though, adding interactive and adaptive MT systems to translation workflows means that translators need to be properly trained on how to use these tools.

In addition, considerations in respect of the user-friendliness of such systems are essential to ensure their successful adoption. For instance, tools such as Google Translate and DeepL Pro provide predictive typing, helping translators to receive AI-generated suggestions for immediate modification. Some adaptive MT systems also learn from human corrections, gradually improving translation quality based on user input (Koehn, 2020).

4.4 Human-in-the-Loop AI Translation

Human-in-the-Loop (HITL) translation systems explicitly position human translators within the translation loop, using human expertise not merely as a corrective measure but as integral input into the translation system's training and refinement processes. This iterative collaboration ensures continuous improvement of translation quality and responsiveness to user needs, promoting a dynamic feedback loop between human translators and AI systems. The potential of HITL systems to address biases and inaccuracies in MT outputs has been discussed and the role of human translators in refining AI models has been emphasized (Moorkens & O'Brien, 2017). This approach not only enhances the quality of translations but also aligns MT outputs with ethical considerations and cultural sensitivities. Unlike static NMT models, HITL systems incorporate human feedback to continuously improve translation accuracy and adaptability. For example, in multilingual customer support, AI chatbots can provide instant translations for customer queries, but human reviewers refine and correct the output to ensure clarity and cultural appropriateness. Over time, the system learns from human revisions, leading to more reliable automated translations.

Human-in-the Loop (HITL) translation technologies put human translators in the translation cycle. This method integrates human knowledge into the training and improvement mechanisms of the translating system, as a corrective action but also as essential input. This iterative cooperation improves translation quality and also enhance response to requests of users, thus building a dynamic feedback loop between human translators and AI systems. The possibility of HITL systems to solve biases and errors in MT outputs has been discussed as well as the need of human translators in improving artificial intelligence models (Moorkens & O'Brien, 2017). This method improves translators' quality and helps MT outputs to match ethical considerations and cultural sensitivity. Unlike NMT models, HITL systems can continuously increase translation accuracy and adaptability with human feedback. AI chatbots, for instance, can instantly translate consumer questions in multilingual customer service and human reviewers can polish and fix the output of AI chatbots to promote clarity and cultural appropriateness. The algorithm learns from human edits and produce increasingly accurate automated translations.

4.5 Challenges and Future Directions

Although hybrid translation models offer many advantages, they also bring up problems that need attention. Data privacy and intellectual property rights are two of the issues that need careful attention. First, as we mentioned in the previous section, one of the most significant problems that translators face is cognitive exhaustion when they are engaged in post-editing operations (Koponen, 2012; O'Brien & Ehrensberger-Dow, 2020). The exhaustion of human translators' cognition can cause decreased job satisfaction and increased cognitive strain due to the repetitive nature of post-editing. Second, ethical concerns pose significant challenges in hybrid translation methods. The danger that machine learning systems will reinforce preconceptions in training data is something that needs to be carefully considered

(Bender et al., 2021). It is important to note the openness and responsibility in artificial intelligence systems in order to assist in alleviating ethical concerns of this nature (Bender et al., 2021).

4.6 Future Prospects

Hybrid translation models are likely going to be at the forefront of the translation industry in the years to come as a result of the continuous improvements in artificial intelligence, natural language processing, and computational linguistics. This is because these fields are all undergoing significant advancements. There are a number of new technologies that have the potential to further increase collaborations between humans and artificial intelligence. Some examples of these technologies are explainable artificial intelligence (XAI), multimodal translation, and context-aware translating models. Consequently, translators will increasingly take on hybrid responsibilities, not just in the capacity of linguistic intermediates but also as adept operators at the intersection of language, culture, and technology.

The work of translators are evolving as a result of technological advancements, and new abilities, such as the ability to make ethical decisions and computer literacy, are required (Pym, 2013). Because of the increasing sophistication of the instruments used for artificial intelligence, translators will need to adapt to the changing times in order to make the most of the opportunities available to them. At the end of the day, hybrid translation systems are not just a practical compromise; rather, they are a strategic alignment between the computational efficiency of technology and the cognitive capacity of humans. Several literary works provide the impression that human translation and machine translation (MT) are more comparable to each other than they are to competitors. Every one of them provides something that is one of a kind, which is necessary for accurate, nuanced, and appropriate translations in a variety of settings. The ongoing development of hybrid approaches highlights the fact that interactions between human translators and technology driven by artificial intelligence will be characterised by cooperative rather than competitive interactions in the future.

5. FUTURE DIRECTIONS AND IMPLICATIONS

The rapid development of translating technologies has brought about significant changes to the translation industry and the methods that it employs. These changes have been primarily driven by advancements in artificial intelligence. The ongoing growth of translation has resulted in significant repercussions for the practice of translation, the education of translation, and on ethics. Recent research envisages that these two approaches can strategically complement one other, leading to the improvement on translation outputs. This is different to the traditional approach of viewing MT and HT as competitors. Over the course of this section, we will analyse the repercussions of this shifting connection, with a specific emphasis on the future directions of professional practice and translation studies.

5.1 The Evolving Relationship Between Human and Machine Translation

The respective strengths of human and machine translation indicate their complementary nature rather than competitive one. Human translations are necessary for translation tasks requiring great cultural insights, creative interpretation, and nuanced contextual accuracy, particularly in fields such as literary, diplomatic, and legal translation. On the other hand, machine translation, notably neural machine translation (NMT), is more suitable for handling high-volume, routine texts efficiently and cost-effectively. Consequently, translation strategies will emphasize more on leveraging both human and machine strengths to promote an integrated, hybrid workflow.

5.2 Toward Enhanced Hybrid Translation Models

The growing popularity of hybrid models signals a future characterized by close collaboration between human translators and AI technologies. A particularly influential approach is post-editing machine translation (PEMT), where human translators improve and validate AI-generated translations, significantly enhancing efficiency without sacrificing accuracy. The continued evolution of PEMT systems promises greater integration of human judgment within AI-powered workflows, allowing translators to concentrate on culturally nuanced and cognitively demanding translation tasks. Moreover, interactive and adaptive MT technologies represent a notable future direction. Adaptive systems, which incorporate translator input in real-time, progressively refine translation accuracy, demonstrating substantial potential for continuous learning and improvement. By embracing these interactive MT systems, human translators become active participants, directly influencing the quality and reliability of machine outputs.

5.3 The Expanding Role of Computer-Assisted Translation (CAT) Tools

The translation industry will work with advanced computer-assisted translation (CAT) tools more, integrating translation memory (TM), terminology databases, and AI-driven predictive features. CAT tools improve productivity of translators by keeping consistency in terminology and minimizing unnecessary translation efforts via translation memory technology. With continuous developments, CAT tools will provide increasingly context-aware, domain-specific translation suggestions, further simplifying translation processes and reducing cognitive burdens on translators. Future CAT tools will likely incorporate sophisticated artificial intelligence capabilities, including adaptive machine translation, real-time terminology management, and personalised translation memories, fostering highly customised translation environments. Consequently, translators will need to acquire new technological skills to effectively utilise these increasingly intelligent systems, marking a significant shift in professional training and translation skillsets.

5.4 Emerging Ethical and Societal Considerations

Despite the promising potential of AI-driven translation tools, there are serious ethical and societal implications that yet to be fully addressed. A problem with bias still exists in AI translation systems. This is because AI models are trained on large datasets and may naturally reflect biases present in source texts, leading to translations which are offensive or harmful to certain cultures or communities. Ensuring fairness, inclusivity, and cultural appropriateness in AI-generated content will require human oversight, transparent algorithmic design, and ethical governance frameworks. Additionally, data privacy and authorship attribution present ethical challenges. Confidentiality and data security have become critical, particularly in fields such as medicine, law, diplomacy, and finance, where sensitive information must remain protected from unauthorised access or misuse. Protocols for data handling, user privacy, and intellectual property rights will be necessary for responsible hybrid translation practices.

The translators must adapt to the changing technological landscape by redefining the role of human translators as not just linguistic experts but also as ethical gatekeepers and intercultural mediators. Translators must develop new skills in computational literacy, ethical decision-making, and AI governance. These skills enable them to critically evaluate AI-generated content and keep professional standards of accuracy, accountability, and ethical translation practice. Translators will thus serve better as quality gatekeepers of translation, ensuring that translation outputs maintain cultural integrity and respect societal norms.

5.4. Implications for Translator Education and Training

The integration of MT and HT into cohesive workflows indicates a necessary transformation in translator education and training. Future education and training programmes must stress computational literacy, corpus linguistics, postediting abilities, and ethical AI usage. Teachers should assist translators in effectively managing hybrid systems and in grasping the technical features of AI-driven translating tools as well as the complexity of linguistic and cultural aspects. This change calls for including computational linguistics, machine translation literacy, and data ethics into translation education and training thereby enabling future professionals to acquire the tools to properly interact with developing technology.

6. CONCLUSION: TOWARD COLLABORATIVE TRANSLATION PRACTICES

Future directions for the translation studies show cooperative, hybrid translating approaches instead of competition between machine and human translators. While AI-driven translation continues to develop, human translators remain indispensable for tasks demanding cultural sensitivity, inventiveness, and ethical discernment. Hybrid models, combining human expertise with technological efficiencies, promise the optimal balance, enabling the translation profession to respond to the complexities of multilingual communication effectively. The successful integration of these approaches will depend heavily on continued innovation, ethical vigilance, and education tailored to equip human translators with new technological competencies, ultimately fostering translation practices that are both efficient and deeply human-centered.

Translation is not merely a technical process of substituting words between languages. It is an act of cultural mediation and knowledge transmission. While AI-driven translation is becoming more sophisticated, it remains a tool rather than a replacement for human expertise. The future of translation lies in striking a balance between technological efficiency and human linguistic intuition, ensuring that translations remain both accurate and meaningful. As AI continues to shape the translation industry, translators and researchers must actively engage with technological advancements, fostering a synergistic relationship between human and machine translation to uphold quality, accessibility, and ethical standards in cross-linguistic communication.

Acknowledgment of AI Assistance

This study acknowledges the use of ChatGPT, an AI language model developed by OpenAI, as a supplementary tool for refining language expression and improving readability. The authors take full responsibility for the conceptualization, analysis, and argumentation presented in this work. Any AI-generated suggestions were critically evaluated and revised to align with the academic rigor and scholarly standards of this research.

REFERENCES

Arnold, D., Balkan, L., Meijer, S., Humphreys, R. L., & Sadler, L. (1994). *Machine translation: An introductory guide.*

Asscher, O. (2023). The position of machine translation in translation studies a definitional perspective. *Translation Spaces*, *12*(1), 1–20. DOI: 10.1075/ts.22035.ass

Bahdanau, D., Cho, K., & Bengio, Y. (2016). Neural machine translation by jointly learning to align and translate. *Arxiv.Org*. https://www.proquest.com/publiccontent/docview/2079082715?pq-origsite=primo&accountid=10134

Bender, E. M., Gebru, T., McMillan-Major, A., & Shmitchell, S. (2021). On the dangers of stochastic parrots: Can language models Be too big? . *Proceedings of the 2021 ACM Conference on Fairness, Accountability, and Transparency*, 610–623. DOI: 10.1145/3442188.3445922

Bianchi, F., Fornaciari, T., Hovy, D., & Nozza, D. (2023). Gender and age bias in commercial machine translation. In Moniz, H., & Parra Escartín, C. (Eds.), *Towards Responsible Machine Translation: Ethical and Legal Considerations in Machine Translation* (pp. 159–184). Springer International Publishing., DOI: 10.1007/978-3-031-14689-3_9

Bo, L. (2023). *Ethical issues for literary translation in the era of artificial intelligence.* Babel-Revue Internationale De La Traduction-International Journal of Translation., DOI: 10.1075/babel.00334.li

Bowker, L., & Fisher, D. (2010). Computer-aided translation. In Y. Gambier & L. Van Doorslaer (Eds.), *Handbook of Translation Studies* (Vol. 1, pp. 60–65). John Benjamins Publishing Company. DOI: 10.1075/hts.1.comp2

Brown, P. F., Cocke, J., Pietra, S. A. D., Della Pietra, V. J., Jelinek, F., Lafferty, J. D., Mercer, R. L., & Roossin, P. S. (1990). A statistical approach to machine translation. *Computational Linguistics - Association for Computational Linguistics, 16*(2), 79–85.

Calvo-Ferrer, J. R. (2024). Can you tell the difference? A study of human vs machine-translated subtitles. *Perspectives-Studies in Translation Theory and Practice*, *32*(6), 1115–1132. DOI: 10.1080/0907676X.2023.2268149

Gao, Y., Wang, R., & Hou, F. (2023). Unleashing the power of ChatGPT for translation: An empirical study. *Arxiv Preprint Arxiv:2304.02182*. https://arxiv.org/pdf/2304.02182v1/1000

Green, S., Heer, J., & Manning, C. D. (2013). The efficacy of human post-editing for language translation. *Proceedings of the Sigchi Conference on Human Factors in Computing Systems*, 439–448. DOI: 10.1145/2470654.2470718

Guerberof, A. (2009). Productivity and quality in MT post-editing. *Beyond Translation Memories: New Tools for Translators Workshop.* https://aclanthology.org/2009.mtsummit-btm.7.pdf

Hardmeier, C. (2012). Discourse in statistical machine translation. A survey and a case study. *Discours. Revue De Linguistique, Psycholinguistique Et Informatique. a Journal of Linguistics, Psycholinguistics and Computational Linguistics, 11.* https://journals.openedition.org/discours/8726

Hidalgo-Ternero, C. M. (2020). Google translate vs. DeepL: Analysing neural machine translation performance under the challenge of phraseological variation. *Monti. Monographs in Translation and Interpreting*, 154–177. DOI: 10.6035/MonTI.2020.ne6.5

Horváth, I. (2022). AI in interpreting: Ethical considerations. *Across Languages and Cultures, 23*(1), 1–13. DOI: 10.1556/084.2022.00108

Hutchins, J. (2001). Machine translation and human translation: In competition or in complementation. *International Journal of Translation, 13*(1–2), 5–20.

Hutchins, J., & Somers, H. L. (1992). *An introduction to machine translation.* Academic Press.

Jia, Y., & Weiss, R. (2019, May 15). *Introducing Translatotron: An End-to-End Speech-to-Speech Translation Model.* https://research.google/blog/introducing-translatotron-an-end-to-end-speech-to-speech-translation-model/

Knowles, R., & Koehn, P. (2018a). Context and copying in neural machine translation. *2018 Conference on Empirical Methods in Natural Language Processing*, 3034–3041. https://www.research.ed.ac.uk/en/publications/context-and-copying-in-neural-machine-translation

Knowles, R., & Koehn, P. (2018b). Lightweight word-level confidence estimation for neural interactive translation prediction. *Workshop on Translation Quality Estimation and Automatic Post-Editing*, 35–40. https://www.research.ed.ac.uk/en/publications/lightweight-word-level-confidence-estimation-for-neural-interacti

Knowles, R., Sanchez-Torron, M., & Koehn, P. (2019). A user study of neural interactive translation prediction. *Machine Translation, 33*(1–2), 135–154. DOI: 10.1007/s10590-019-09235-8

Koehn, P. (2010). *Statistical machine translation*. Cambridge University Press.

Koehn, P. (2020). *Neural machine translation*. University Press. DOI: 10.1017/9781108608480

Koponen, M. (2012). Comparing human perceptions of post-editing effort with post-editing operations. *Proceedings of the Seventh Workshop on Statistical Machine Translation*, 181–190. https://aclanthology.org/W12-3123.pdf

Kruger, R. (2022). Some translation studies informed suggestions for further balancing methodologies for machine translation quality evaluation. *Translation Spaces, 11*(2), 213–233. DOI: 10.1075/ts.21026.kru

Lagoudaki, E. (2006). Translation memories survey 2006: User's perceptions around TM usage. *Proceedings of Translating and the Computer 28*. https://aclanthology.org/2006.tc-1.2.pdf

Lagoudaki, E. (2008). The value of machine translation for the professional translator. *Proceedings of the 8th Conference of the Association for Machine Translation in the Americas: Student Research Workshop*, 262–269. https://aclanthology.org/2008.amta-srw.4/

Lee, S.-M. (2023). The effectiveness of machine translation in foreign language education: A systematic review and meta-analysis. *Computer Assisted Language Learning, 36*(1–2), 103–125. DOI: 10.1080/09588221.2021.1901745

Luo, J., Cherry, C., & Foster, G. (2024). To diverge or not to diverge: A morphosyntactic perspective on machine translation vs human translation. *Transactions of the Association for Computational Linguistics, 12*, 355–371. DOI: 10.1162/tacl_a_00645

Mohamed, Y. A., Khanan, A., Bashir, M., Mohamed, A. H. H. M., Adiel, M. A. E., & Elsadig, M. A. (2024a). The Impact of Artificial Intelligence on Language Translation: A Review. *IEEE Access, 12*, 25553–25579. IEEE Access. DOI: 10.1109/ACCESS.2024.3366802

Mohamed, Y. A., Khanan, A., Bashir, M., Mohamed, A. H. H. M., Adiel, M. A. E., & Elsadig, M. A. (2024b). The impact of artificial intelligence on language translation: A review. *IEEE Access : Practical Innovations, Open Solutions, 12*, 25553–25579. DOI: 10.1109/ACCESS.2024.3366802

Moorkens, J., & O'Brien, S. (2017). Assessing user interface needs of post-editors of machine translation. In *Human Issues in Translation Technology* (pp. 127–148). Routledge., https://www.taylorfrancis.com/chapters/edit/10.4324/9781315648934-17/assessing-user-interface-needs-post-editors-machine-translation-joss-moorkens-sharon-brien

O'Brien, S. (2007). An empirical investigation of temporal and technical post-editing effort. *Translation and Interpreting Studies*, *2*(1), 83–136. DOI: 10.1075/tis.2.1.03ob

O'Brien, S., & Ehrensberger-Dow, M. (2020). MT literacy—A cognitive view. *Translation. Cognition & Behavior*, *3*(2), 145–164. DOI: 10.1075/tcb.00038.obr

Och, F. J., & Ney, H. (2003). A systematic comparison of various statistical alignment models. *Computational Linguistics*, *29*(1), 19–51. DOI: 10.1162/089120103321337421

Och, F. J., & Ney, H. (2004). The alignment template approach to statistical machine translation. *Computational Linguistics*, *30*(4), 417–449. DOI: 10.1162/0891201042544884

Plitt, M., & Masselot, F. (2010). A productivity test of statistical machine translation post-editing in a typical localisation context. *Prague Bull. Math. Linguistics*, *93*(1), 7–16. DOI: 10.2478/v10108-010-0010-x

Postigo, M. L. (2024). ChatGPT and MT-systems: Advantages and limitations when translating english to spanish and portuguese. *Lengua Y Habla*, *28*, 369–390.

Pym, A. (2013). Translation skill-sets in a machine-translation age. *Meta*, *58*(3), 487–503. DOI: 10.7202/1025047ar

Ragni, V., & Vieira, L. N. (2022). What has changed with neural machine translation? A critical review of human factors. *Perspectives-Studies in Translation Theory and Practice*, *30*(1), 137–158. DOI: 10.1080/0907676X.2021.1889005

Rivera-Trigueros, I. (2022). Machine translation systems and quality assessment: A systematic review. *Language Resources and Evaluation*, *56*(2), 593–619. DOI: 10.1007/s10579-021-09537-5

Rojo, J. J. L. (2018). Aspects of human translation: The current situation and an emerging trend. *Hermeneus: Revista De La Facultad De Traducción E Interpretación De Soria, 20*, 257–294.

Salinas, M.-J. V., & Burbat, R. (2023). Google translate and DeepL: Breaking taboos in translator training. Observational study and analysis. *Ibérica (New York, N.Y.)*, *45*(45), 243–266. DOI: 10.17398/2340-2784.45.243

Sebo, P., & de Lucia, S. (2024). Performance of machine translators in translating french medical research abstracts to english: A comparative study of DeepL, google translate, and CUBBITT. *PLoS One*, *19*(2), e0297183. DOI: 10.1371/journal.pone.0297183 PMID: 38300946

Škobo, M., & Petričević, V. (2023). Navigating the Challenges and Opportunities of Literary Translation in the Age of AI: Striking a Balance Between Human Expertise and Machine Power. *Društvene i Humanističke Studije, 8*(2(23)). *Article, 2*(23). Advance online publication. DOI: 10.51558/2490-3647.2023.8.2.317

Sulubacak, U., Caglayan, O., Grönroos, S.-A., Rouhe, A., Elliott, D., Specia, L., & Tiedemann, J. (2020). Multimodal machine translation through visuals and speech. *Machine Translation, 34*(2–3), 97–147. DOI: 10.1007/s10590-020-09250-0

Turchi, M., Negri, M., Farajian, M., & Federico, M. (2017). Continuous learning from human post-edits for neural machine translation. *The Prague Bulletin of Mathematical Linguistics, 108*(1), 233–244. DOI: 10.1515/pralin-2017-0023

Vaswani, A., Shazeer, N., Parmar, N., Uszkoreit, J., Jones, L., Gomez, A. N., Kaiser, Ł., & Polosukhin, I. (2017). Attention is all you need. *Advances in Neural Information Processing Systems, 30*. https://proceedings.neurips.cc/paper/2017/hash/3f5ee243547dee91fbd053c1c4a845aa-Abstract.html

Vieira, L. N., O'Hagan, M., & O'Sullivan, C. (2021). Understanding the societal impacts of machine translation: A critical review of the literature on medical and legal use cases. *Information Communication and Society, 24*(11), 1515–1532. DOI: 10.1080/1369118X.2020.1776370

Wu, Y., Schuster, M., Chen, Z., Le, Q. V., Norouzi, M., Macherey, W., Krikun, M., Cao, Y., Gao, Q., Macherey, K., Klingner, J., Shah, A., Johnson, M., Liu, X., Kaiser, Ł., Gouws, S., Kato, Y., Kudo, T., Kazawa, H., . . . Dean, J. (2016). *Google's neural machine translation system: Bridging the gap between human and machine translation* (No. arXiv:1609.08144). arXiv. http://arxiv.org/abs/1609.08144

Yulianto, A., & Supriatnaningsih, R. (2021). Google translate vs. DeepL: A quantitative evaluation of close-language pair translation (french to english). *Ajelp: Asian Journal of English Language and Pedagogy, 9*(2), 2. Advance online publication. DOI: 10.37134/ajelp.vol9.2.9.2021

Chapter 5
On Assessing the Accuracy of Arabic–English Translation by Machine and Human

Syazwan Naim Ibrahim
https://orcid.org/0000-0003-2457-3615
Universiti Malaya, Malaysia

ABSTRACT

The ubiquity of artificial intelligence (AI) has significantly influenced research and practice in translation studies. As an integral part of the globalized world, AI's impact continues to grow. But translation accuracy can be compromised if machine translations are not supported by post-editing. This study evaluates the accuracy of machine and human translation by comparing their outputs using a qualitative descriptive approach. Machine translation, while efficient, struggles with polysemous terms, historical references, and culturally embedded expressions, leading to semantic distortions and omissions. The indispensability of human expertise also has been highlighted in preserving the integrity of Arabic scholarly works in cross-cultural academic discourse. This study underscores the importance of hybrid approaches, combining machine translation's speed with human post-editing to enhance translation quality. Recommendations offered include improving machine translation systems through domain-specific training and contextual awareness algorithms.

DOI: 10.4018/979-8-3373-0060-3.ch005

INTRODUCTION

The omnipresence of artificial intelligence (AI) considerably affected and is affecting a plethora of scientific fields including translation studies in terms of its research and practice and the effects it brings will continue to be propagated as it has indeed become an integral part of this globalized world. Such effects include both positive effect as translation works, be they in a small or great scale, can be done in no time and without prior onerous cognitive efforts in identifying equivalents just as in traditional way of translating, satisfying customers' demands. However, this also poses negative effect which is often overlooked by translators themselves as the most fundamental and critical aspect of measuring a translation quality; accuracy is sometimes questionable if and only if the translation is not followed up by post-editing or humans supervision, shifting their roles from translators to editors of machine-generated content as the machine system continues to advance (Muftah, 2024). When translating, machine translation (MT) as one of the artificial intelligence products only depends on access to available online corpora by means of neural networks and computational algorithms (Obeidat & Jaradat, 2024) while humans make full use of their skills and creativity, heavily relying on repository of 'mental corpora' previously encountered and gained through training and experience in specific languages.

While translation is regarded as one of the oldest human activities since the dawn of time, it has never been thought of that technological advancement achieved by humans in this day and age will impact translational activities where the pervasive influence the technology brings on translation could not be denied. A few critical questions are still being discussed by both translation teachers and practitioners themselves; Does technology work hand in hand with humans, complementing their translation? Or will the machine agency totally replace the human agency in such a way that they will be relying on it, compromising translation quality? The first being the perk of having a machine-assisted translation and the other being the pitfall of leveraging technology. Whether technology represents a treat or a threat to human translators depends solely on how it is applied and contextualized. It is a double-edged sword.

The extent to which MT can preserve accuracy, particularly in such a high-context language as Arabic, remains under scrutiny. Arabic, characterised by its rich morphology, cultural and contextual nuances, poses significant challenges for MT systems which often struggle to capture the intricate grammatical and morphological relationships of the language (Farghaly & Shaalan, 2009; Habash & Sadat 2006). It is due to the MT's limited ability to account for historical, cultural, and linguistic intricacies that its use for translating Arabic academic texts, for instance, often results in outputs that distort meaning, misinterpret cultural concepts, or omit key information. Arabic language heavily relies on implicit meaning, contextual cues, and cultural references, which MT algorithms, particularly those trained primarily on Western or Indo-European language data, are ill-equipped to handle (Alqudsi et al., 2014). This is problematic that the translation of academic texts which rely on precision, clarity, and cultural sensitivity suffer disproportionately when processed by the machine without human oversight or post-editing benefit (Koponen, 2016).

Additionally, Arabic's morphological richness poses unique linguistic hurdles for current MT models including neural machine translation (NMT) which usually performs better with morphologically simpler languages as investigated by Belinkov and Glass (2019) and Habash and Sadat (2006). Such factors hindering the accessibility of Arabic academic scholarship to non-Arabic audiences and contributing to the marginalisation of knowledge produced in Arabic within global academic discourse as inaccurate translations, terminological inconsistencies, and culturally inappropriate renderings should therefore be overcome. It becomes imperative, then, given the increasing reliance on MT within academic and professional settings, to critically access the suitability and limitations of the MT for Arabic academic texts. Not only does such scrutiny is essential to improve the technological performance of the MT but also to safeguard the Arabic knowledge production integrity and cross-cultural academic communication. Thus, this inspires the following objectives this study aims to achieve:

1. To identify the linguistic and cultural challenges faced by human and machine translation when translating Arabic academic texts into English.
2. To compare the accuracy of human and machine translation in translating Arabic academic texts into English.
3. To explore the potential for improving machine translation accuracy in Arabic-English academic context.

To achieve these objectives, three questions are addressed:

1. What are the linguistic and cultural challenges faced by human and machine translation when translating Arabic academic texts into English?
2. How does the accuracy of machine translation compare to human translation when translating Arabic academic texts into English?
3. What strategies or approaches could enhance the accuracy of machine translation in Arabic-English academic context?

As can be seen, this study sets out to investigate several aspects related to the translation of Arabic academic texts (a paragraph from the book *Muqaddimah Ibn Khaldūn* (Ibn Khaldūn's Prolegomenon)) into English, particularly focusing on the performance of such machine translation tool as Google Translate. Firstly, it seeks to identify linguistic and cultural difficulties encountered by the machine translation tool in translating Arabic academic texts into English, guided by Newmark's (1988) Semantic and Communicative Translation Theory which emphasizes the importance of balancing communicative and semantic translation approaches when addressing cultural nuances and language-specific challenges. Next, it compares the accuracy of translations produced by both human and machine translator, informed by Nababan's (2004) Translation Accuracy Level which evaluates translations based on accuracy. Finally, it explores ways to enhance the quality of machine-generated translations within academic contexts, underpinned by Vermeer's (1978) *Skopos* Theory which highlights the importance of translation purpose (*skopos*) and target audience needs in shaping translation strategies and improving outcomes. As the overall undertaking revolves around comparing the human and machine translation, this study thus adapted Sjahrony and Ahmad (2013)'s proposed analytical framework on comparing these two types of translators' outputs.

This study is significant as it theoretically contributes to the evolving discourse on the role of AI in translation studies, particularly in the Arabic-English language pair. It also practically provides valuable insights for translation teachers and practitioners as well as AI developers to highlight areas where MT struggles and where human expertise remains indispensable. While in terms of its societal significance, this study ensures accurate representation of Arabic academic thought in global academic discourse.

LITERATURE REVIEW

Machine vs Human Translation

Although such machine-assisted translation as Neural Machine Translation (NMT) has made significant strides in translation technology, but to help improve translation quality and ensure greater precision and cultural sensitivity when translating Arabic Islamic terms into English, several key recommendations could be worked on (Alharazi et al., 2024). First is to develop specialized corpora that include such Islamic texts as the Quran, prophetic traditions and theological writings in order to provide the NMT systems with contextually relevant data. Second is to integrate the NMT with other such translation methods as rule-based and statistical approaches to better manage idiomatic expressions and contextual interpretation. Third is to employ post-editing where human translators refine machine-generated text to ensure contextual and cultural accuracy and finally to have greater collaboration among researchers, developers, and translators from all walks of life to enhance the effectiveness and accuracy of the NMT systems. It is believed that by executing the recommendations offered, translation technology could be advanced and interdisciplinary cooperation in the field of machine translation could be fostered to tackle the issues of limited availability of large corpora, NMT's difficulty handling specific linguistic features, and its lack of cultural and contextual understanding in accurately translating complex Arabic and Islamic texts. Sakhr, ATA software, Cimos, SYSTRAN, Babylon, and Bing Translator are examples for web-based machine translation systems that support Arabic language whether as a source or target language (Muftah, 2024).

Contrary to the fact that MT helps expedite translation process and is cost-effective as stated in the abovementioned studies, several other studies (Al-Kaabi et al., 2024; Obeidat & Jaradat, 2024; Adiel et al., 2023; Alowedi & Al-Ahdal, 2023, Toral & Way, 2018) also have shown that MT often fails to grasp meanings conveyed by linguistic systems, cultural conventions, and aesthetic nuances when it comes to translating literary works. As the meanings are served in implicit manners and are not straightforward, this indicates that extensive efforts are required to post-edit the translation where a significant number of errors were detected as well as to improve readability. For instance, translating culture-specific terms in the Arabic-English translation of Naguib Mahfouz's *Zuqāq al-Midaqq* has proven to pose a significant challenge for professional translators, requiring deep knowledge of both linguistic and cultural aspects (Al-Kaabi et al., 2024). Although recent technological advancements have improved machine translation quality, yet challenges persist with regards to the translatability of the cultural connotations. By employing a descriptive qualitative research design and qualitative content analysis, the study analysed human translations alongside outputs from Google Translate (GT) and ChatGPT and evaluated the translations for their ability to accurately convey the cultural connotations embedded in the Arabic source text. It is found that the human translations demonstrated greater naturalness and precision in capturing cultural nuances, concluding that human expertise remains indispensable for producing high-quality translations of literary works, ensuring the preservation of cultural significance. The machine translations, however, struggled with rhetorical devices, idiomatic expressions, and cultural subtleties. But among the AI translation tools used to translate the literary text, ChatGPT performed better than GT in preserving cultural elements.

In line with the effort in comparing both the AI translation tools and human translation, challenges of translating resistance literature based on short story *Until We Return* by using GT and ChatGPT through the lens of Berman's 12 tendencies framework have also been investigated, focusing exclusively on Arabic-English direction as well (Obeidat & Jaradat, 2024). The machine translations lack cultural and contextual sensitivity, risk diluting the core essence of the resistance literature where there occurred significant alterations in the original text by both GT and ChatGPT.

Key tendencies include rationalization (36% for both), qualitative impoverishment (32% for GT and 26% for ChatGPT), and the destruction of rhythms (10% for GT and 11% for ChatGPT). Both platforms exhibit quantitative impoverishment and the destruction of linguistic patterns (7% each) as well as expansion (5% for GT and 8% for ChatGPT). Minimal distortions are noted in clarification (2% for both), while GT shows null destruction of underlying networks of signification, and ChatGPT records a 3% occurrence. Ennoblement is rare, appearing at 0% for GT and 1% for ChatGPT. Therefore, the need for alternative translation approaches is emphasized here to preserve the authenticity of resistance literature as maintaining fidelity to the original text is critical for honoring the voices of the oppressed and marginalized, ensuring accurate representation amidst leveraging technology. Other critical challenges when rendering Arabic text to English include word sense disambiguation, Arabic named entity, rich and complex morphology and low resource (Almaaytah and Alzobidy, 2023).

Interestingly, Adiel et al. (2023) combined linguistic analysis and mathematical equation the latter by which they employed word error rate (WER) metric to measure translation accuracy of MT compared to HT from Arabic into English of the two technically and linguistically distant languages in the context of distinct subject areas: medical (Health Awareness Texts) representing publicly available scientific translations, sourced from translation projects at King Fahad Hospital of Imam Abdulrahman Bin Faisal University and literary (Ancient Arabic Poetry Stanzas) representing unpublished literary translations, drawn from a previously unpublished article by the first author. They conducted their experiments and compared the results with previous research in the field. While machine translation offers certain privileges, it cannot fully replace human translators, as the output still requires substantial editing from them. Another critical linguistic analysis of Arabic poems, *Nothing of Note* and *One Day* translated into English by both machine and human translator has also been conducted (Alowedi & Al-Ahdal, 2023). For example, in *Nothing of Note*, the protagonist's salary is inaccurately translated to "pounds" and the use of varying adjectives alters the poem's meaning. Thus, this study confirms that MT struggles to capture cultural nuances and that the human translation preserves the lyrical quality of adjectival antonyms through conjunctive pairs. Contextual elements were also lost in MT such as the phrase "the dust-dunned street" which was simplified to "dusty street". Additionally, MT erroneously introduces two protagonists whereas the HT maintains the original narrative's singular focus. MT therefore fails to grasp the nuances of such beyond-linguistic contexts as figurative language, historical references, and poetic genre crucial in literary work and is incapable of extending meaning beyond its database or understanding the cultural framework of the poetry, making it an inappropriate tool for translating Arabic poetry into English. While on examining the performance of the NMT on literary texts, Toral and Way (2018) built an English-to-Catalan NMT system adapted for literary translation and compared it to a statistical phrase-based machine translation (PMSMT) system. Both systems were trained on over 100 million words of literary text and evaluated on twelve renowned novels from the 1920s to the present. According to BLEU scores, the NMT significantly outperformed the PBSMT across all novels. A human evaluation on those novels showed that 17% to 34% of NMT translations were perceived to be of equivalent quality to professional human translations compared to only 8% to 20% for PBSMT.

Newmark's Semantic and Communicative Translation Theory

Peter Newmark's (1988) Semantic and Communicative Translation Theory offers a practical approach to understanding the balance between accuracy and readability in translation. Newmark asserts that **semantic translation** focuses on preserving the precise meaning, cultural nuances, and stylistic features of the source text, making it suitable for texts where fidelity to the original is paramount. In contrast, **communicative translation** prioritises conveying the intended message clearly and naturally for the target audience, often requiring adaptation to the target culture and linguistic norms.

Several studies which have applied the theory include Molina and Hurtado Albir (2002) who explored the use of semantic and communicative approaches in translating cultural elements. They found that communicative translation was more effective for texts requiring natural readability and semantic preserved cultural nuances more accurately. Similarly, Xiao's (2023) case study conducted to explore the theory within tourism setting emphasizes the impact of the communicative translation strategy on target readers offering valuable guidance for translating tourism texts from English to Chinese.

Thus, this dual framework highlights the inherent tension between staying faithful to the source and ensuring the translation is accessible to the target audience, making it particularly useful in analysing the linguistic and cultural challenges faced when translating between languages with significant structural and cultural differences such as Arabic and English. Thus, it is due to the framework's technicality that it deemed suitable to be used in this study in identifying linguistic and cultural gaps faced by both human and machine translation when translating Arabic academic texts into English.

Nababan's Translation Accuracy Level

Mangatur Nababan's (2004, as cited in Silalahi, 2009: 99) Translation Accuracy Level provides a framework for evaluating the quality and accuracy of translations, particularly on how well a target text reflects meaning, style, and intent of a source text. It acknowledges that accuracy is not merely a matter of word-for-word substitution, but rather a multi-layered process influenced by linguistic accuracy and communication effectiveness.

As meaning is the main element when translating and that failure to transfer meaning from source text to target text will result in a translation being labelled a maltranslation, this measuring instrument focuses on linguistic elements ranging from words, phrases, clauses and sentences, arguing that these elements encode shades of meaning and therefore need to be properly addressed by a translator. While Scale 3 concludes that a translation is **accurate** when meaning of all the elements have been transferred without distorting it into a TT, Scale 2 indicates **less accuracy** when there exists distortion, ambiguity or omission of meaning and Scale 1 signals an **inaccurate** translation caused by meaning being inaccurately transferred or omitted. The instrument is as follows (translated by the author of the current study himself from Indonesian to English):

Table 1. Translation Accuracy Level Measuring Instrument by Nababan (2004, as cited in Silalahi, 2009: 99)

SCALE	DEFINITION	CONCLUSION
3	The meaning of words, phrases, clauses and sentences from source language is transferred accurately into target language; without any distortion of meaning at all.	Accurate
2	Most of the meaning of words, phrases, clauses and sentences from source language have been transferred accurately into target language. But there are still distortions of meaning or double-meaning translations (ambiguity) or omissions of meaning, which disrupt overall message.	Less accurate
1	The meaning of words, phrases, clauses and sentences from source language is transferred inaccurately into target language or omitted.	Not accurate

Therefore, viewed from this perspective, this instrument provides a holistic view in assessing translation accuracy of human and machine translation when translating Arabic academic texts into English after taking into consideration the transference of structural and cultural elements.

Vermeer's *Skopos* Theory: Translation as Purpose-Driven Action

Skopos Theory, introduced by Hans J. Vermeer as a general theory of translation in a lecture course held at the University of Mainz, Germany during the academic year 1976-1977 (de León, 2019) represents a significant shift in translation studies from source-text oriented approaches to a more functionalist perspective. This theory emphasizes that the primary determinant of translation strategies and decisions is the purpose (*skopos*) of the target text within its specific communicative context (Du, 2012). Unlike traditional equivalence-based models, which prioritize fidelity to the source text, Schäffner (2009) states that *Skopos* Theory underscores the importance of the translator's role as a cultural mediator, adapting the translation to suit the needs, expectations, and cultural norms of the target audience. It has been widely discussed and furthered by other such functionalist scholars as Katharina Reiß (book coauthored with her) and Christine Nord (English translation in 2014), whose contributions further clarified the practical application of *skopos* principles in professional translation contexts.

Vermeer (1978: 100, as cited in Schäffner, 2009) puts that the core idea of this functional approach can be summarized as follows: the translation process is not primarily guided by the source text itself, its impact on the original audience, or the purpose intended by the author – as emphasized in equivalence-based translation theories. Instead, it is driven by the intended purpose, or *skopos*, of the target text, which is determined by the client's requirements. Therefore, the *skopos* is heavily influenced by the target audience, their context, and cultural background. Vermeer further adds that there are two important general principles apply: the **coherence rule** and the **fidelity rule**. The former requires that the target text must be clear and understandable to the intended audience, taking into account their background knowledge and the specific situation in which they will encounter the text. The translation process starts with a source text that exists within its own cultural and situational context. The goal is to produce a target text that fits into the target audience's world in a way that they can understand as coherent within their own cultural and situational framework. While the latter refers to maintaining a connection between the translation (translatum) and the original source text. It simply requires that there must be some form of relationship between the two, but only after ensuring that the primary focus on the *skopos* and the internal coherence of the target text have been fulfilled. Xinfei (2024), for instance, has conducted a case study for an in-depth analysis of English film subtitle translation through the lens of *Skopos* Theory. It is found that this theory serves as an effective approach in subtitle translation that audience could better appreciate the film with minimal cognitive effort.

In a word, after having considered the technical and holistic perspective of translation of Arabic academic texts into English, the *Skopos* Theory assesses the functional perspective of the translation and will eventually be employed to enhance the accuracy of machine translation in Arabic-English academic context.

METHODOLOGY

Data in this qualitative form of study were descriptively analyzed using comparative textual analysis method as this qualitative form of analysis fits the exploration of both linguistic and cultural nuances in any textual data (Creswell and Guetterman, 2021). Data for this study were drawn from the selected corpus taken from the academic book *Muqaddimah Ibn Khaldūn* (Ibn Khaldūn's Prolegomenon) which was originally written in Arabic by a renowned Muslim social scientist; Ibn Khaldūn. The selected corpus, with its rich linguistic and cultural references as well as syntactic and lexical complexities, is a paragraph on explaining the science of lexicography (Page 500, Section 46: The sciences concerned with the Arabic language, Chapter 6: The various kinds of sciences. The methods of instruction. The conditions that obtain in these connections) was selected to be the subject of comparison between the translation of Google Translate (machine translation service) – due its widespread use and accessibility despite its limited contextual understanding, inadequacy of Arabic academic domain training, and tendency towards surface-level translations – and Franz Rosenthal who was an eminent scholar of Arabic literature and Islam (human; page 632-633), revealing to readers translation quality of each translator. These translations were then scrutinized to assess each translation's accuracy. To systematically conduct the overall analysis of this study, an analytical framework proposed by Sjahrony and Ahmad (2013) is adopted due to its conceptual clarity which facilitates coherent, consistent and transparent analytical processes. The summary of the procedures taken is as follows:

Figure 1. Procedures to Compare Machine and Human Translation

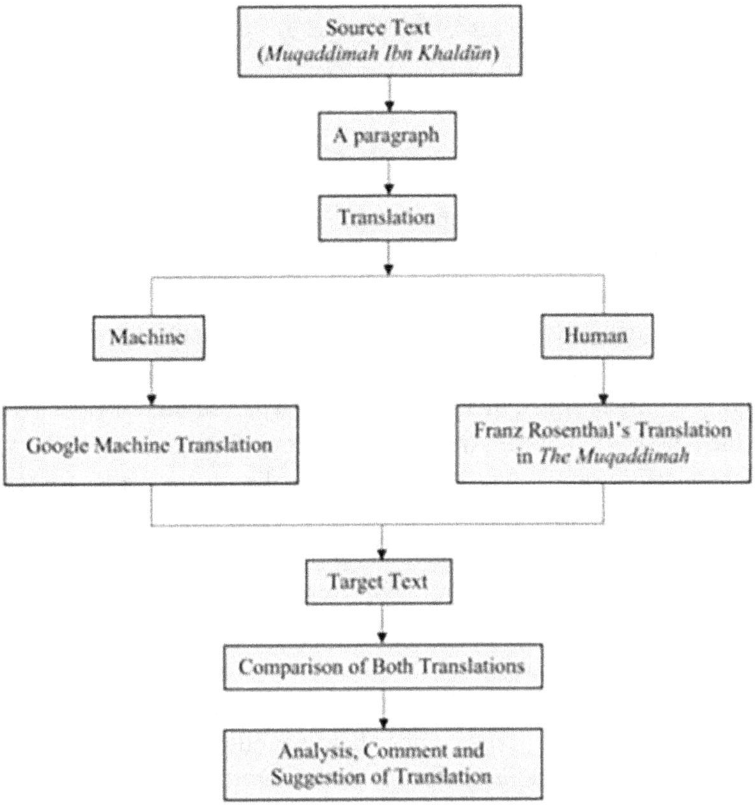

Adapted from Sjahrony and Ahmad (2013)

Adapted from Sjahrony and Ahmad (2013)

As stated earlier in the introduction, Newmark's (1988) Semantic and Communicative Translation Theory will guide this study in identifying linguistic and cultural challenges faced by both translators in translating the Arabic academic texts into English. Next, to measure the level of accuracy of the translations, a measuring instrument on a three-point (1-3) accuracy scale form introduced by Nababan (2004, as cited in Silalahi, 2009: 99) is adopted. Vermeer's (1978) *Skopos* Theory will then be used to explore what potentials could be made to enhance the accuracy of the machine translation.

Below is the ST of the paragraph divided into 10 sections, as the author (Ibn Khaldūn) himself had indicated by the commas:

هذا العلم هو بيان الموضوعات اللغوية[1]/، وذلك أنه لما فسدت ملكة اللسان العربي
في الحركات المسماة عند أهل النحو والإعراب[2]/، واستنبطت القوانين لحفظها كما
قلناه[3]/، ثم استمر ذلك الفساد بملابسة العجم ومخالطتهم[4]/، حتى تأدى الفساد
إلى موضوعات الألفاظ[5]/، فاستعمل كثير من كلام العرب في غير موضوعه عندهم[6]/،
ميلا مع هجنة المتعربين في اصطلاحاتهم المخالفة لصريح العربية[7]/، فاحتيج
إلى حفظ الموضوعات اللغوية بالكتاب والتدوين[8]/، خشية الدروس وما ينشأ عنه من
الجهل بالقرآن والحديث[9]/، فشمر كثير من أئمة اللسان لذلك وأملوا فيه الدواوين[10]/.

Google Translation as of 25 November 2024:

This science is the clarification of linguistic subjects[1]/, and that is when the faculty of the Arabic tongue became corrupted in the so-called vowels among the grammarians and parsers[2]/, and the laws were devised to memorize them as we said[3]/, then that corruption continued with the exposure of the non-Arabs and mixing with them[4]/, until the corruption led to the subjects of words[5]/, so many of them were used. The Arabs speak in a way that is not appropriate for them[6]/, inclining towards the Arabization of the Arabs in their terminology that contradicts the clear Arabic language[7]/, so there is a need to preserve linguistic topics. By writing and writing[8]/, fearing the lessons and the resulting ignorance of the Qur'an and the Hadith[9]/, many imams frowned upon this and wrote collections about it[10].

And below is the English translation by Franz Rosenthal of the Arabic academic text which is also divided into the same amount of sections, showing the corresponding translation of each section:

This science is concerned with explaining the (conventional) meanings of the (words of the) language[1]/. This comes about as follows. The habit of the Arabic language became corrupted[2]/. Rules for protecting the (vowel endings) were developed[3]/. However, the (process of) corruption continued on account of the close contact (of the Muslims) with non-Arabs[4]/. Eventually, it affected the conventional meanings of words[5]/. Many Arabic words were no longer used in their proper meaning[6]/. This was the result of indulgence shown to the incorrect language used by non-Arab speakers of Arabic in their terminologies, in contradiction to the pure Arabic language[7]/. It was, therefore, necessary to protect the conventional meanings of the words of the language with the help of writing and systematic works[8]/, because it was to be feared that they might be wiped out and that ignorance of the Qur'ân and the traditions would result[9]/. Many leading philologists set out eagerly on this task and dictated systematic works on the subject[10].

RESULTS AND DISCUSSION

Data 1

Table 2. 1st Sample that Compares between Machine and Human Translation

Google Translation	Franz Rosenthal's Translation
This science is the clarification of linguistic subjects,	This science is concerned with explaining the (conventional) meanings of the (words of the) language.

As knowledge on lexicography is being touched on by Ibn Khaldūn in this paragraph and the following paragraphs in the book that he narrates the first lexicographer in the Arab world and his dictionary, Franz Rosenthal has therefore aptly referred the overall sentence to the science of lexicography. Though the word "الموضوعات" can be translated as "subjects" as one of its meanings, the intended meaning here by adhering to the context is Arabic words meanings that are firstly introduced and agreed upon by native speakers of the language. The word is derived from the verb "وضع" which means "to put", as if the meanings of Arabic words are first put by Arabs themselves during earlier times and therefore regarded as conventional.

As Ibn Khaldūn introduces to readers a stand-on-its-own science known as lexicography, the word "بيان" should be translated as something which signifies what the science is about. According to Newmark, Franz Rosenthal uses a communicative approach to clarify the cultural and disciplinary context (the science of lexicography) while Google's output leans more toward word-for-word semantic translation, missing the broader communicative intent.

Thus, based on Nababan's level of translation equivalence, the human translation has accurately (Scale 3) translated the word with the introductory phrase "concerned with explaining" rather than "clarification" as translated by the machine which, despite the correct meaning, does not fit the context of the source language as it fails to represent the contextual sense required in academic discourse on lexicography. This scales the machine output a not accurate (Scale 1) translation.

From the perspective of Vermeer's *Skopos* Theory, ensuring that machine translation processes are informed by the intended function and readership of the translation, in this case, academic researchers, would help MT systems prioritise accuracy and cultural-contextual over simplistic word-for-word rendering. In addition, adopting hybrid approaches where machine outputs are post-edited by human translators who understand the *skopos* (purpose) of the text could significantly enhance the final product's communicative and semantic accuracy.

Data 2

وذلك أنه لما فسدت ملكة اللسان العربي في الحركات المسماة عند أهل النحو بالإعراب،

Table 3. 2nd Sample that Compares between Machine and Human Translation

Google Translation	Franz Rosenthal's Translation
and that is when the faculty of the Arabic tongue became corrupted in the so-called vowels among the grammarians and parsers,	This comes about as follows. The habit of the Arabic language became corrupted.

Here in this section, the machine translation outperformed the human one by appropriately recognizing the preceding sentence and faithfully translating all the linguistic elements. As shown in the Google Translation, the accuracy of the machine in translating the phrase "ملكة اللسان العربي" into the target language as "the faculty of the Arabic tongue" is witnessed. However, this is not the case as in the human translation where the phrase is translated as "The habit of the Arabic language". The word "ملكة" means an innate propensity of human and the word "tongue" was chosen to translate "اللسان". It is an accurate translation as tongue is an organ used by human to communicate and connect with each other by means of a language. Thus, tongue also means language but in a rather metaphorical sense. With a closer look at the overall human translation, it is found that omission of meanings took place where the considerable length of the phrase "في الحركات المسماة عند أهل النحو والإعراب" left untranslated. This leads to scaling the human translation, according to Nababan, not accurate (Scale 1) one due to the omission of significant technical content despite maintaining grammatical fluency. Thus, the long phrase should be translated as the machine did. The two phrases "في الحركات المسماة" (in the so-called vowels) and "عند أهل النحو والإعراب")among the grammarians and parsers) have been translated accurately (Scale 3) by the machine, conveying the full meaning with proper attention to linguistic details.

By addressing the context in which Ibn Khaldūn talks about a uniqueness facet of the Arabic language that sets it different from other languages in the world, the machine has aptly captured the meaning of "الحركات" by translating it as "vowels". Arabic language has three fundamental vowels (namely *ḍammah*, *fatḥah*, *kasrah*) through which a subject, predicate, agent, object, and other syntactic elements could be well identified. Rules of all these are systematically discussed and studied under the science of grammar termed in Arabic as "النحو". The Arabic grammar is crucial in understanding Arabic oral and written discourse and therefore each of the named vowels are then specifically studied under a topic called "parsing" subsumed under النحو termed in Arabic as "الإعراب", giving rise to other such terms as *marfū'* (nominative), *manṣūb* (accusative), and *majrūr* (genitive) which correspond to the vowels. So, the possessive phrase "أهل النحو والإعراب' which has been translated by the machine as "the grammarians and parsers" is accurate. Another translation of vowels into the target language could also be suggested here that is "diacritics".

Thus, Newmark's semantic translation is reflected in the machine translation's faithful rendering of technical terms while the human translation leans toward communicative which prioritises fluency but at the cost of omitting crucial content. While the machine translation performs relatively well in this data, ensuring the machine process is aware that its intended *skopos* is to serve academic audiences in linguistics and translation studies would encourage more consistent treatment of technical terms and historical references. Hybrid workflows would also enhance functional accuracy in line with the *skopos* where machines generate drafts that are then post-edited by experts in Arabic grammar and linguistics.

Data 3

واستنبطت القوانين لحفظها كما قلناه،

Table 4. 3rd Sample that Compares between Machine and Human Translation

Google Translation	Franz Rosenthal's Translation
and the laws were devised to memorize them as we said,	Rules for protecting the (vowel endings) were developed.

Both the outputs from the machine and human translator are accurate (Scale 3) in general but the former possesses better accuracy as all linguistic elements are fully presented in this section. Whether to translate the third-person feminine singular pronoun "ـها" in the phrase "حفظها" as "them" by also using third-person pronoun but in a plural form as non-human plurals in Arabic are treated as singular feminine or "the vowel endings" by iterating the antecedent "الحركات" are still acceptable. Franz Rosenthal, however, did not fully translate the section, leaving the few last elements "كما قلناه" untranslated. This makes the human translation falls under the category of less accurate (Scale 2) due to the omission. It is imperative to have these few elements translated too although the absence of their translation did not disrupt or negatively affect the overall message intended by Ibn Khaldūn himself. Thus, it is best for the human translator to translate them as "as we said" like the machine did.

The machine translation, according to Newmark, employs a more semantic approach faithfully rendering every element including the final phrase "كما قلناه" (as we said) and ensuring completeness at the expense of some fluency. This is not the case for the human translator who applies a more communicative approach, simplifying some elements (the omission) in favor of producing a smoother, target-oriented text. However, this omission risks reducing accuracy, which becomes critical in academic translations where precision and completeness are valued.

While the machine performs well in this section, future improvements could focus on increasing the contextual awareness of antecedents especially in cases where pronouns refer to previously mentioned terms (الحركات). Machine systems could benefit from enhanced co-reference resolution algorithms that can dynamically assess whether to repeat the antecedent (vowel endings) or replace it with a pronoun (them) depending on the register and *skopos* of the translation. According to Vermeer, ensuring that the purpose of the translation (serving academic audience) is embedded into the translation process would guide machines to prioritise complete, culturally embedded, and technically precise translations even if this results in slightly longer outputs.

Data 4

ثم استمر ذلك الفساد بملابسة العجم ومخالطتهم،

Table 5. 4th Sample that Compares between Machine and Human Translation

Google Translation	Franz Rosenthal's Translation
then that corruption continued with the exposure of the non-Arabs and mixing with them,	However, the (process of) corruption continued on account of the close contact (of the Muslims) with non-Arabs.

Regarding the translation of the Arabic connector "ثم" as "then" or "However", each of these two are deemed correct and accurate (Scale 3). This is because, viewed from the Newmark's theory, the machine takes a semantic approach, staying close to the literal sense of the Arabic connector by translating it as "then" while the human opts for a communicative approach using "However", signaling the contradiction of the preceding section on the rules developed to preserve the purity of Arabic language where undesirable occasion corrupting yet tarnishing the purity has occurred as indicated by the causal statement "بملابسة العجم ومخالطتهم". Hence, the human translator has better accuracy in translating the connector. Despite the slight difference in translating the words "ملابسة" and "مخالطة" as "exposure", "mixing with", and "close contact" in the causal statement by both translators, they are in fact referring to the same condition of mingling of the Arabs with races other than them that eventually corrupts the prescriptive proper use of Arabic language amongst its natives. This is due to the inability of most of the non-Arabs coming to the Middle East for trading, religious, and other purposes to converse with the inhabitants in the language. Thus, according to Nababan, such slight stylistic differences as the handling of "ثم" and the terms for contact (mixing, exposure, close contact) does not impede the accurate transmission of meaning preserving both linguistic content and cultural context.

Albeit the machine performs well, it could be further improved by incorporating context-sensitive strategies that detect and interpret discourse markers in historical or academic Arabic texts. Tools drawing on discourse analysis techniques could help machines distinguish whether "ثم" functions as a simple sequential connector (then) or a contrastive device (however) based on preceding and following content. Informed by the *Skopos* Theory, the *skopos* of translating Ibn Khaldūn's work for academic audiences would justify such enhancements as readers expect explicit logical coherence between sections in scholarly writing.

Data 5

حتى تأدى الفساد إلى موضوعات الألفاظ،

Table 6. 5th Sample that Compares between Machine and Human Translation

Google Translation	Franz Rosenthal's Translation
until the corruption led to the subjects of words,	Eventually, it affected the conventional meanings of words.

The Google Translation is not accurate (Scale 1) in this section compared to Franz Rosenthal's (Scale 3). There seems to have been a distortion of meaning in the GT that it failed to translate the phrase "موضوعات الألفاظ" as Nababan puts it. This completely disrupts the overall meaning which is not intended by the author. Hence, this kind of translation is not acceptable. Returning to section 1 that the word "موضوعات" has accurately been translated by Franz Rosenthal as "conventional meanings", the same word also has an accurate translation in this section, producing an overall intended meaning as the word requires semantic precision especially when such word reflects established linguistic concepts in Arabic philology. And surprisingly, Google also has the same translation for the word encountered in section 1. As "subjects" is not an accurate English equivalent according to the context in section 1, this is also the case for this fifth section. The GT's literal translation fails to communicate this conventional linguistic meaning while Rosenthal's communicative translation successfully bridges the cultural and scholarly gap for English readers according to Newmark. Another observation here is that both the translators have well translated the word "الفساد" where the machine reiterated the antecedent "corruption" and the human opted to use anaphoric element "it", summarizing and avoiding the reiteration of the word.

To improve the machine translation in this section, it could be trained on domain-specific corpora including annotated glossaries of Arabic linguistic and philological terms. It could adopt context-aware processing where preceding and following segments are considered to determine the correct translation of such polysemous term as "موضوعات" thereby ensuring functional adequacy that meets the expectations of academic readers.

Data 6

فاستعمل كثير من كلام العرب في غير موضوعه عندهم،

Table 7. 6th Sample that Compares between Machine and Human Translation

Google Translation	Franz Rosenthal's Translation
so many of them were used. The Arabs speak in a way that is not appropriate for them,	Many Arabic words were no longer used in their proper meaning.

There exist totally maltranslations of the whole sentence in this section by the machine unlike the human's accurate (Scale 3) translation. Hence, the machine translation is not accurate (Scale 1) at all as it misunderstood the focus of the sentence resulting in a semantic shift that is neither faithful nor appropriate considering Nababan's scale. As the section in the source language comprises only a sentence, so should its translation in the target language be in a sentence. But the machine translated it into two separate sentences that did not address the author's intended meaning, giving a peculiar yet unnatural-sounding translations. The core focus of the sentence is a huge number of misused Arabic words based on their conventional meanings, not the Arabs themselves who did not speak the way they should. Also, the sentence touches on the usage issue conveyed by the passive verb "استعمل" in a general sense, not specifying it to only speaking as the machine understood. Thus, as the machine has erroneously translated the word, it has then shifted the overall focus of the sentence into what is semantically and contextually unaccepted. Although the sentence syntactically negates the conventional meaning of many Arabic words wrongly used by the Arabs, but Franz Rosenthal's translation still holds true based on the context even the negation was placed on the many Arabic words that were no longer used according to their conventional meaning in his translation. Following Newmark's theory on semantic and communicative translation, there is not any distortion of meaning performed by the human and by this, he has preserved both the linguistic and cultural essence unlike the machine that failed to communicate the cultural context appropriately as evident in its literal breakdown into two unnatural sentences.

To revisit, the *skopos* (purpose) of translating the text here is to make observations on the corruption of the Arabic language accessible and understandable to academics. To achieve this, machine translation could be improved by incorporating domain-specific training data including classical Arabic texts, linguistic treatises as well as glossaries of historical linguistic terms. The accuracy and cultural appropriateness of translations in Arabic academic contexts could also be enhanced by adopting context-aware translation mechanisms where the machine considers preceding and following paragraphs.

Data 7

الميل مع هجنة المتعربين في اصطلاحاتهم المخالفة لصريح العربية،

Table 8. 7th Sample that Compares between Machine and Human Translation

Google Translation	**Franz Rosenthal's Translation**
inclining towards the Arabization of the Arabs in their terminology that contradicts the clear Arabic language,	This was the result of indulgence shown to the incorrect language used by non-Arab speakers of Arabic in their terminologies, in contradiction to the pure Arabic language.

As for the first word "الميل" in the sentence, the machine has better translated it as "inclining towards", addressing both syntactic and semantic features of it compared to the human translation "This was the result". Next, it is obvious that in this section, the machine failed to capture the meaning of the core phrase "هجنة المتعربين" that it was translated as "Arabization of the Arabs" which is a complete semantic distortion. The exact meaning of the word "هجنة" in this context is like the one translated by the human translator as "incorrect language". However, both the translators inaccurately translated "المتعربين" as it is not really referring to Arabs and to translate it as "non-Arab speakers of Arabic" is also somewhat inaccurate as it still omits the ethnic and genealogical nuance. Instead, it refers to Arabs whose descendant is not purely from the Arab roots but a mix of both Arab and non-Arab. Thus, the translation should also be in Arabic word "*muwallad*" for both translators and by appending necessary footnote or parenthetical clarification as the word has not yet been lexicalized (does not have a direct equivalent) in the English language. This aligns with Newmark's semantic translation approach which aims at retaining cultural meaning at the expense of fluency. To scale the accuracy of translation according to Nababan, the human's is low (Scale 2) while the machine's is the lowest (Scale 1).

As Vermeer stresses that a translation should always be tailored to its *skopos* (purpose), which in this case is an academic analysis, then retaining the culturally embedded term "المتعربين" is essential. The accuracy of the machine could be improved by incorporating specialized glossaries for classical Arabic sociocultural terms, training on bilingual corpora containing annotated historical texts to ensure the machine recognizes historical and genealogical contexts, and allowing for footnote or annotation generation where such complex cultural term as "المتعربين" is retained in its transliteration (*muwallad*) and supplemented with an automatically generated cultural note.

Data 8

فاحتيج إلى حفظ الموضوعات اللغوية بالكتاب والتدوين،

Table 9. 8th Sample that Compares between Machine and Human Translation

Google Translation	**Franz Rosenthal's Translation**
so there is a need to preserve linguistic topics. By writing and writing,	It was, therefore, necessary to protect the conventional meanings of the words of the language with the help of writing and systematic works,

Understanding all the meanings of the linguistic elements in the whole sentence, Franz Rosenthal has accurately transferred them into English where there is no any errors detected, causing his translation to be an exemplary model for this section. As can be seen from the Google Translation, there are two sentences produced which are illogical and unconnected to each other, failing to accurately (Scale 2) capture the intended meaning. While the human translation had demonstrated again an accurate (Scale 3) translation for the word "الموضوعات" reiterated in the source text, the machine had nevertheless demonstrated again a faulty translation but this time with the word's synonym "topics". The machine therefore reflects a literal and fragmented approach while the human aligns with Newmark's communicative approach. As it is clear from the source text that the sentence is single, the machine however produced two sentences as its outputs. There has been an iteration of the word "writing" in the machine translation of the phrase "بالكتاب والتدوين" that it did not successfully differentiate between "الكتاب" and "التدوين". Although these two words have to do with the activity of writing where the former firstly takes place to produce written works and the latter is a proper preservation and compilation of the written works in large volumes after the influx of non-Arabs into the Islamic society, but their translation should be different. Thus, the ideal translation of the words are "writing" and "systematic works" as performed by the human translator. "Anthology" can also be the translation of "التدوين". No translation issue for the particle "بـ" attached to the words as both are acceptable based on the context.

Since the *skopos* (purpose) is to provide an accessible translation for academics, the machine translation should incorporate glossaries for classical Arabic linguistic terminology, recognize common collocations in historical Arabic texts (بالكتاب والتدوين) and apply phrase-level translation strategies instead of word-by-word approaches, improve handling of complex sentence structures especially in classical Arabic texts where long sentences are common and logical flow is key. Automatic checking for parallel concepts in classical Arabic historiography and generating a side annotation or footnote to explain the historical practice of "التدوين" linking it to the development of linguistic and legal canons in Islamic civilization could also be devised.

Data 9

خشية الدروس وما ينشأ عنه من الجهل بالقرآن والحديث،

Table 10. 9th Sample that Compares between Machine and Human Translation

Google Translation	Franz Rosenthal's Translation
fearing the lessons and the resulting ignorance of the Qur'an and the Hadith,	because it was to be feared that they might be wiped out and that ignorance of the Qur'ân and the traditions would result.

In general, Google has inaccurately (Scale 1) translated the sentence as a whole and has rather adopted a word-for-word translation, disregarding the context and breaking the logical flow as put by Newmark. It is not the lessons which are to be feared of in this section. The polysemous word "الدروس" in Arabic is generally understood as lessons (plural of "الدرس") and this meaning will be first appeared in one's mind. Hence, the confusion of the machine caused by the rich and intricate Arabic morphology, differing greatly from other languages (Almaaytah and Alzobidy, 2023). But context as a very fundamental element while translating needs to be factored in and deeply recognized before searching for the nearest equivalent. The sentence speaks about the state of worry about repercussions of not having proper yet systematic writings that preserve all that pertains to the Arabic language system and any ignorance of the Quran and prophetic traditions stemming from the undesirable state. Therefore, as seen from Franz Rosenthal's accurate (Scale 3) translation, the third-person plural pronoun "they" is used to refer to the conventional meanings of Arabic words previously mentioned. This reflects his understanding of the context by not promptly choosing what is commonly translated maintaining full equivalence by preserving meaning, flow, and coherence of the previous discussion. The machine however only depends on any available corpora for the word and it chooses translation that is widely used regardless of the context.

With regards to the overall *skopos* (purpose) that it translates classical linguistic historiography for academic researchers, the machine needs a specialised lexicon for classical Arabic linguistics and Islamic scholarship, algorithms of historical sense disambiguation that can identify whether such word as "الدروس" should be translated as "lessons" or "being wiped out" according to context, and better cohesion tracking.

Data 10

فشمر كثير من أئمة اللسان لذلك وأملوا فيه الدواوين.

Table 11. 10th Sample that Compares between Machine and Human Translation

Google Translation	Franz Rosenthal's Translation
many imams frowned upon this and wrote collections about it.	Many leading philologists set out eagerly on this task and dictated systematic works on the subject.

The last section witnesses the accuracy (Scale 3) of the translation by the human translator; Franz Rosenthal as compared to the machine (Scale 2). The translation of the past tense verb "شمّر" by Google Translate as "frowned upon" which is a modern, yet unrelated sense of the verb is a clear semantic distortion that disrupts the intended meaning. "Set out eagerly" as translated by the human is the perfect English equivalent instead as the verb implies that an undertaking will be performed by someone thoughtfully and with a strong desire. This aligns with Newmark's communicative translation approach in transferring intended meaning and tone rather than literal forms. Hence, the adverb "eagerly". Similar error also occurs with, the literal yet inaccurate translation for the broken plural "أئمة" of singular noun "إمام" as "imams" by the machine that confuses readers; they will swiftly think of "imams" as in the mosque who lead the Muslims' prayers. As the context of the first section concerns the science of Arabic lexicography and sets the scene for all the sections, thus the human translation has accurately translated the phrase "أئمة اللسان" as "leading philologists" who study languages history, by firstly adding the adjective "leading" as "أئمة" specifically means scholars in a field who are at the forefront and being referred to. To be able to produce contextually accurate and relevant translations, any contextual information must be stored in machine readable representation (Salam and Kadir, 2017). Another accurate and precise translation performed by the human translator is the other past tense verb "أملوا". The verb does not implicitly mean "wrote" erasing the critical pedagogical process as inaccurately translated by Google Translate. Rather, it means there is someone (a guru) who reads aloud (dictates) so that hearers (students) can write down details being said (transcribe). It is a classical practice of oral transmission in Islamic scholarly settings. Thus, "dictated" is the best translation for the verb which restores the intended meaning.

To provide accurate translations of historical Arabic texts for academic researchers aligned with the skopos (*purpose*), the machine translation should be trained on classical Arabic philology corpora. This includes pre-modern lexicons and early linguistic scholarship. The machine should also use contextual tagging to distinguish between, for instance, religious and scholarly uses of "أئمة" and incorporate cultural glossaries in handling such verb as "أملوا" which is anchored in Islamic and Arabic academic traditions.

Tying back the overall synthesis of findings to the objectives listed at the outset, this comparative analysis has thus far provided valuable insights into the performance differentials between Google Translate (machine translation) and Franz Rosenthal (human translation) covering all the ten representative data samples extracted from Ibn Khaldūn's *Muqaddimah*. A consistent pattern has emerged across the data through the lens of the three objectives; identifying linguistic and cultural challenges, comparing accuracy, and exploring enhancement strategies.

Objective 1: Identifying the linguistic and cultural challenges faced by human and machine translation when translating Arabic academic texts into English.

The machine translation, exemplified by Google Translate, demonstrated notable weaknesses in dealing with context-sensitive lexemes, culturally embedded terms, and historical references. Due to the Google's overreliance on common or contemporary meanings, such polysemous words as "الدروس" (Data 9) and "رمش" (Data 10) were often mistranslated disregarding historical and thematic contexts. Next, such phrases as "حجة المتعربين" (Data 7) and "أئمة اللسان" (Data 10) revealed the Google's inability to map culturally and historically nuanced terminology to appropriate English equivalents. On the other hand, Rosenthal representing the human translation consistently demonstrated higher semantic precision and better pragmatic adaptation yet sensitivity to both source and target cultural expectations making his translation aligns with Newmark's communicative translation approach.

Objective 2: Comparing the accuracy of human and machine translation in translating Arabic academic texts into English.

According to Nababan (2004, as cited in Silalahi, 2009: 99), a translation will be scaled 3 (accurate) if a translator has accurately transferred ST meaning conveyed by words, phrases, clauses and sentences to TT, avoiding any potential distortion of the meaning. Thus, drawing on the above findings, accurate translations produced by Google Translate are 30% and by Franz Rosenthal 80% with a very higher degree of accuracy. This seems to confirm AlSaleem's (2024) study arguing that, although machine translation has significantly advanced, human translation always outperformed it especially in fields requiring deep understanding, linguistic precision, and specialized knowledge. The machine-generated translation always requires human oversight to help improve translation quality especially for highly-difficult texts (Alharazi et al., 2024). This, the role of a human expert is always paramount despite the assistance offered by technology in translation process (Salam & Kadir, 2017). A translation is scaled less accurate (Scale 2) on the other hand when:

Most of the meaning of words, phrases, clauses and sentences from source language have been transferred accurately into target language. But there are still distortions of meaning or double-meaning translations (ambiguity) or omissions of meaning, which disrupt overall message. (Nababan (2004, as cited in Silalahi, 2009: 99)).

Thus, there are only 10% of less accurate translations by the human translator and 20% by the machine translator. A translation is then deemed the least accurate one (Scale 1) if the transference of meaning conveyed by words, phrases, clauses and sentences into TT by a translator is inaccurate in accordance with ST or there has been an omission of the meaning (Nababan (2004, as cited in Silalahi, 2009: 99)). Thus, the machine records a higher percentage (50%) translations which are not accurate while the human only records 10%. This proves that the machine lacks finesse of human translator (Al-Kaabi et al., 2024). The less and no accuracy found in the human translation perhaps signify that human still needs to improve from time to time as he or she only acquired mastery of certain fields of knowledge, heavily relying on previous limited learning, training, and experience. Or to put it laconically, human translation is not without errors. The below table summarizes the percentage of accuracy level achieved by each translator:

Table 12. Accuracy Percentage of Both Machine and Human Translation

SCALE	GOOGLE TRANSLATE	FRANZ ROSENTHAL	%
3 (ACCURATE)	2, 3, 4	1, 3, 4, 5, 6, 8, 9, 10	30/80
2 (LESS ACCURATE)	8, 10	7	20/10
1 (NOT ACCURATE)	1, 5, 6, 7, 9	2	50/10

Objective 3: Exploring the potential for improving machine translation accuracy in Arabic-English academic context.

By basing on the Vermeer's *Skopos* Theory to serve the academic audience, the machine translation appeared to be consistently failed to align with the *skopos* due to its literalism rendering, failure to detect thematic cohesion across sentences and sections, and inability to preserve historical terminology. Thus, several *skopos*-driven improvements to tackle such issues are incorporation of domain-specific translation memory and terminological databases, algorithms of context propagation to track referents across larger text segments, models of polysemy disambiguation trained on particularly classical Arabic corpora, and integration of cultural-historical metadata.

CONCLUSION

Although both machine and human translation have their respective strengths and shortfalls, the study found that the translation produced by human is more perfect, accurate and quality compared to machine for the Arabic academic text under scrutiny. Human translation remains significantly superior for translating Arabic academic texts. Human translators excel in contextual adaptation, cultural sensitivity, and semantic precision. However, MT offers speed and scalability. While machine translation undeniably processed simple syntactic structures and modern lexical items with increasing accuracy, it is still in the adequacy of the ability to decode and appropriately translate culturally embedded expressions and historically bounded terminologies.

But instead of favoring and relying on either translator, it is suggested that both translators be married (hybrid approach), when confronted with texts requiring deep historical, cultural, and domain-specific knowledge, to tackle any inaccuracy issues of both translators, yielding linguistically accurate outputs and ensuring that machine translator remains a treat rather than a threat to human. It is unfruitful to leverage machine-assisted translation due to its unparallelled convenience and accessibility in finding equivalents of either small or large volume of source texts but at the meantime suffers from translation issues, misinterpretations, and poor language quality in the target text that eventually compromise translation quality. It goes without saying that saving the accuracy and language in translation are a lot more important than saving time.

Ultimately, this study, due to its limitations in terms of small corpus size, single machine tool, and absence of statistical validation, recommends several future research to be conducted which include comparing Google Translate, DeepL, and ChatGPT for Arabic-English academic translation, expanding corpus to include legal, scientific, and literary texts, exploring machine translation's handling of culturally loaded terms, and investigating hybrid models (machine basic drafting and human post-editing) and their effectiveness particularly in the context of classical Arabic and other high-context languages. It is hoped that the above recommendations could be materialized in translation pedagogy, machine translation system development, and translator training modules.

REFERENCES

Adiel, M. A. E., Elsadig, M. A., Altigani, A., Mohamed, Y. A., Ahmed, B. E. S., & Elhassan, S. M. O. (2023). Accuracy and problems of machine-based translation in contrast to human-based translation when rendering health awareness texts versus poetry texts. *Academic Journal of Interdisciplinary Studies, 12*(4), 223–231. DOI: 10.36941/ajis-2023-0108

Al-Kaabi, M. H., AlQbailat, N. M., Badah, A., Ismail, I. A., & Hicham, K. B. (2024). Examining the Cultural Connotations in Human and Machine Translations: A Corpus Study of Naguib Mahfouz's Zuqāq al-Midaqq. *Journal of Language Teaching and Research, 15*(3), 707–718. DOI: 10.17507/jltr.1503.03

Alharazi, A. F. A., Alhebshi, S. H. S., & Taleb, N. R. M. (2024). Leveraging AI-Powered Neural Machine Translation to Bridge the Gap: Translating Arabic Islamic Terminology into English. *Pakistan Journal of Life and Social Sciences, 22*(2), 7150–7164. DOI: 10.57239/PJLSS-2024-22.2.00541

Almaaytah, S. A., & Alzobidy, S. A. (2023). Challenges in Rendering Arabic text to English using Machine Translation: A Systematic Literature Review. *IEEE Access : Practical Innovations, Open Solutions, 11*, 94772–94779. DOI: 10.1109/ACCESS.2023.3309642

Alowedi, N. A., & Al-Ahdal, A. A. M. H. (2023). Artificial Intelligence based Arabic-to-English machine versus human translation of poetry: An analytical study of outcomes. *Journal of Namibian Studies: History Politics Culture, 33*, 1523–1538.

Alqudsi, A., Omar, N., & Shaker, K. (2014). Arabic machine translation: A survey. *Artificial Intelligence Review, 42*(4), 549–572. DOI: 10.1007/s10462-012-9351-1

AlSaleem, B. I. (2024). Evaluating the Role of Machine Translation in Enhancing the Quality of Scientific Publishing in Arabic: A Comparative Study with Human Translation.

Belinkov, Y., & Glass, J. (2019). Analysis methods in neural language processing: A survey. *Transactions of the Association for Computational Linguistics, 7*, 49–72. DOI: 10.1162/tacl_a_00254

Creswell, J. W., & Guetterman, T. C. (2021). *Educational Research: Planning, Conducting, and Evaluating Quantitative and Qualitative Research* (6th ed.). Pearson.

de León, C. M. (2019). Functionalism. In Baker, M., & Saldanha, G. (Eds.), *Routledge encyclopedia of translation studies* (3rd ed., pp. 199–203). Routledge. DOI: 10.4324/9781315678627-43

Du, X. (2012). A brief introduction of Skopos theory. *Theory and Practice in Language Studies*, *2*(10), 2189–2193. DOI: 10.4304/tpls.2.10.2189-2193

Farghaly, A., & Shaalan, K. (2009). Arabic natural language processing: Challenges and solutions. [TALIP]. *ACM Transactions on Asian Language Information Processing*, *8*(4), 1–22. DOI: 10.1145/1644879.1644881

Habash, N., & Sadat, F. (2006, June). Arabic preprocessing schemes for statistical machine translation. In *Proceedings of the human language technology conference of the naacl, companion volume: Short papers* (pp. 49-52). DOI: 10.3115/1614049.1614062

Ibn Khaldūn, A. (2010). *Muqaddimah Ibn Khaldūn* (1st ed.). Dār Ibn al-Jawziy.

Koponen, M. (2016). Is machine translation post-editing worth the effort? A survey of research into post-editing and effort. *The Journal of Specialised Translation*, *25*(2), 131–148.

Molina, L., & Hurtado Albir, A. (2002). Translation techniques revisited: A dynamic and functionalist approach. *Meta*, *47*(4), 498–512. DOI: 10.7202/008033ar

Muftah, M. (2024). Machine vs human translation: A new reality or a threat to professional Arabic–English translators. *PSU Research Review*, *8*(2), 484–497. DOI: 10.1108/PRR-02-2022-0024

Newmark, P. (1988). *A textbook of translation* (Vol. 66). Prentice hall.

Obeidat, M. M., & Jaradat, M. A. (2024). Artificial intelligence accuracy in translating resistance literature from Arabic into English: Google Translate and ChatGPT as a model. *Research Journal in Advanced Humanities*, *5*(2), 45–62.

Rosenthal, F. (1958). *The Muqaddimah: An Introduction to History*. Princeton University Press.

Salam, Z. A. A., & Kadir, R. A. (2017). A Study of Context Influences in Arabic-English Language Translation Technologies. *Jurnal Teknologi Maklumat dan Multimedia Asia-Pasifik*, *6*(2), 43-52.

Schäffner, C. (2009). Functionalist approaches. In Baker, M., & Saldanha, G. (Eds.), *Routledge encyclopedia of translation studies* (2nd ed., pp. 115–121). Routledge.

Silalahi, R. (2009). *Dampak teknik, metode, dan ideologi penerjemahan pada kualitas terjemahan teks medical surgical nursing dalam Bahasa Indonesia (The Impact of the Translation Techniques, Methods, and Ideologies on the Quality of the Translated Text Medical-Surgical Nursing in Bahasa Indonesia)*. Tesis Kedoktoran, Universitas Sumatera Utara.

Sjahrony, K., & Ahmad, M. (2013). Penterjemahan Frasa Al-Idafah Arab-Melayu Menggunakan Google Translate (*Translating Phrases of Al-Idafah of Arab-Malay Using Google Translate*). *Islāmiyyāt: International Journal of Islamic Studies, 35*(2), 101–108.

Toral, A., & Way, A. (2018). What level of quality can neural machine translation attain on literary text?. *Translation quality assessment: From principles to practice*, 263-287.

Xiao, L. (2023). The Use of Translation Strategy and Translation Methods in Tourism Texts under the Guidance of Peter Newmark's Translation Theory: A Case Study of Everglades National Park, Florida. *Educalitra: English Education, Linguistics, and Literature Journal, 2*(2), 52–63.

Xinfei, L. (2024). A study on film subtitle translation from the perspective of skopos theory: A casestudy of kung fu panda. *Lecture Notes on Language and Literature, 7*(1), 168–176.

Chapter 6
Aspects of AI Integration Into University Translation Study Programmes

Jolita Horbacauskiene
https://orcid.org/0000-0002-5982-9329
Kaunas University of Technology, Lithuania

Milda Ratkeviciene
https://orcid.org/0000-0003-3924-7281
Kaunas University of Technology, Lithuania

ABSTRACT

Translation plays a critical role in bridging language barriers, and its evolution is closely tied to advancements in technology, particularly artificial intelligence (AI). AI has revolutionized translatio industry. These innovations have facilitated multilingual communication, offering cost-effective solutions while presenting challenges, such as ethical concerns and changing professional roles. Research highlights the need to adapt university translation programmes to prepare future translators for an AI-driven industry. Despite AI's growing role, human expertise remains vital, as dependency on AI poses risks in high-stakes multilingual communication. This study analyzes the integration of AI in university translation programmes by examining programme descriptions and institutional policies from publicly available sources. Employing content analysis, the research explores how AI is incorporated into undergraduate and postgraduate translation curricula, assessing its impact on the preparation of translators and interpreters for evolving industry demands.

DOI: 10.4018/979-8-3373-0060-3.ch006

INTRODUCTION

Translation is crucial for breaking down language barriers in different scenarios and environments. However, as with any human activity, translation is influenced by various external factors, such as technological progress. Artificial intelligence (AI) is perhaps one of the most relevant technological developments in our society today. AI has greatly impacted many industries including language usage, translation, and interpretation. However, the rapid development of AI also poses a number of challenges that are being addressed by the development of legal frameworks both nationally and internationally. For example, the correct and ethical use of AI is being promoted at the European Union level and is regulated by legislation such as the Artificial Intelligence for Europe (European Commission, 2018), the Digital Decade Policy Programme 2030 (European Parliament, 2022), the EU Artificial Intelligence Act (2024).

Advances in AI-assisted language technologies have transformed how society handles multilingual communication. As argued by Annoni et al. (2018), from machine translation to image recognition to music production, many AI tools have been introduced into everyday life and are increasingly used in industry, government, and commerce. The language industry has been one of the most affected industries by AI. The advancements of such innovations as machine translation tools, AI-assisted interpreting technologies, and natural language processing (NLP) algorithms help to overcome intercultural barriers while also posing some challenges. These tools are now widely used in both personal and high-stakes situations, offering quick solutions to language challenges at minimal cost (Vieira, 2020). The integration of AI into university translation study programmes became an inevitable aspect due to the changing role of translators and interpreters (Kanglang & Afzaal, 2021). Thus, as Bernardini (2020) argues, with rapid changes and advances in artificial intelligence, it is necessary for the translation discipline to consider how the competence requirements of the translator will change and what the translator of the future will have to do.

The impact of AI-assisted language technologies on translation has been analysed from a number of aspects in recent years (Vieira et al., 2022; Mehandru et al., 2022; Heath et al., 2023; Groves & Mundt, 2015; Buden et al., 2009; Gambier, 2016; Kanglang & Afzaal, 2021). Recent research shows that to prepare translators to work effectively in an AI-driven translation industry, translation curricula need to be regularly reviewed in collaboration with leaders in the translation industry and AI experts (Zaghlool & Khasawneh, 2024). Therefore, it is crucial to analyse how translation study programmes are constructed and the emphasis they place on AI. However, despite the fact that AI and machine translation are becoming a natural part of translation studies, the results of the study conducted by Kanglang

& Afzaal (2021) reveal that there is still a lack of research on the application of AI in translation studies: how to integrate, what are the threats, benefits, etc. However, the growing dependency on AI-assisted technologies might pose a risk while using these innovations in everyday life; therefore, the expertise and skills of a human translator become vitally important in multilingual communication. Our study aims to present an overview of the impact and role of AI in university translation study programmes and how AI is integrated into study programmes that prepare translators and interpreters in universities. The chapter is organised in the following manner: the theoretical background discusses the overall picture of current research on how AI influences translation, its processes, and possible outcomes, and the empirical study on AI integration in university translation study programmes.

To shed light on the situation of integration of AI into university translation study programmes, the study presents data from an analysis of translation-oriented undergraduate and postgraduate study programmes. The analysis is constructed on the overview of publicly available programme descriptions on the websites of universities running translation study programmes for manifestations of AI, that is, whether AI is integrated into the studies and, if so, how. Furthermore, websites of universities with translation-oriented degree programmes were analysed to see if the institution has a declared policy on the use of AI in the study process. To analyse the data collected during the study, a content analysis approach was chosen which, according to Azizan, Smith, Cooper & Bakar (2018), allows the annotation and interpretation of textual data.

THEORETICAL STANCE OF THE STUDY

The influence of AI-powered language technologies on translation has been examined from various perspectives in recent years (Vieira et al., 2022; Mehandru et al., 2022; Heath et al., 2023; Kasperė et al., 2024). Multimodal translation models with integrated text, speech, and images are becoming central in bridging linguistic gaps (Barrault et al., 2023). AI technology is driving a paradigm shift in translation studies, reshaping its theoretical frameworks, research methodologies, and practical applications. Although these developments offer unprecedented opportunities, careful attention should be paid to ethical, methodological, and disciplinary challenges to ensure a balanced and comprehensive approach to translation research (Yu & Liu, 2024). Soysal (2023) explores the synergies, challenges, and potential advancements in translation studies and AI. Aini et al. (2024) argue that AI has significantly transformed translation studies by improving efficiency and accessibility while raising ethical, cultural, and professional challenges.

Sze Ming & Sin-Wai (2024) note that integration of neural machine translation and large language models like ChatGPT has enhanced translation accuracy and efficiency. Although these technologies excel in processing vast linguistic data and enable more precise translations, however, challenges persist in accurately translating idiomatic and culturally sensitive expressions, and here human translators often outperform AI (Rothwell et al., 2023). Reevaluation of translation pedagogy is becoming necessary as educators are integrating AI tools into curricula to prepare students for a technology-rich translation landscape where students are provided with training and feedback and offered practical experiences with AI-assisted translation (Bowker, 2020). Nevertheless, as noted by Koponen et al. (2020), collaboration between AI and human expertise remains essential when combining AI's efficiency with human nuanced understanding, particularly in complex translation tasks.

Lee (2023) argues that AI initiated a paradigm shift in translation studies by significantly improving translation efficiency and quality, especially in applied fields like business, law, and medicine. At the same time, emphasis is placed on the importance of human-computer collaboration to address specific challenges such as domain-specific terminology and cultural nuances (Geng & Hu, 2023). The role of translators is changing toward quality control and post-editing, as the main theoretical constructs are being redefined as data-driven and collaborative translation models are becoming more popular. Reconstruction of the traditional approach to translation studies is happening due to AI inclusion, as the integration of AI-driven tools has expanded the scope of translation studies by enabling multilingual and cross-cultural research using large datasets and advanced analytics (Song, 2024). Moreover, Soysal (2024), while exploring the intersection between translation studies and AI, argues that collaboration between AI and translators is needed to improve translation quality and accessibility. Such collaboration will ensure that AI serves as a complementary tool rather than a replacement for human translators and transforms translation practices, improving efficiency, overcoming language barriers, broadening access to information, and improving productivity and consistency in translation tasks (Zhao & Jin, 2022; O'Hagan, 2016). Although AI excels at data processing and pattern recognition, it struggles with empathy and cultural interpretation, areas where human translators excel (Low et al., 2022; Vaswani et al., 2018). This gap is crucial to achieving translations that are both technically accurate and culturally appropriate.

Nanomi Arachchige et al. (2022) argue that AI systems often fail to grasp idiomatic expressions, cultural nuances, and contextual subtleties, necessitating human oversight to ensure translation quality and cultural appropriateness, so the promotion of interdisciplinary projects between AI developers and translation scholars to address challenges such as bias, contextual understanding, and cultural sensitivity is of increasing importance (Yang & Kyun, 2022; Kenny, 2018). Many studies highlight the opportunities for interdisciplinary collaboration between translation studies and computer science, psychology, sociology (Cai et al., 2023; Chetouani et al., 2023; Costa-Jussa & Fonollosa, 2015; Ghosh & Caliskan, 2023). AI has significantly transformed translation studies by improving efficiency and accessibility, while raising some challenges as well (Amini et al., 2024). More attention should be paid to hybrid approaches, multimodal capabilities, and ethical safeguards to maximise the benefits of AI while mitigating its limitations.

One more challenge raised by AI concerns ethical issues and the usage of AI-assisted translation. As Drugan & Tipton (2017) note, it is very important to establish robust ethical practices to address biases and ensure transparency in AI-assisted translation. In addition, Wu and Chen (2023) highlight the need to critically assess the implications of AI while maintaining the theoretical and cultural depth of translation studies. Jiménez-Crespo (2020) argue that AI technologies are transforming translation studies into a more interdisciplinary and data-driven field. However, addressing ethical and methodological challenges is vital to ensure that the discipline retains its depth, diversity, and cultural relevance in this new setting.

From the perspective of ethics while using AI in translation, several concerns have emerged such as confidentiality, transparency, cultural sensitivity, and employment issues. AI-driven translation systems rely on large datasets for training, so if these datasets contain biases or lack linguistic diversity, AI-generated translations may continue to use stereotypes or inaccuracies (Castilho & Knowles, 2023). Another aspect that raises ethical issues is translation of cultural details that may produce translations that are technically accurate, but culturally inappropriate or insensitive (Venuti & Venuti, 2021). This limitation highlights the importance of integrating cultural awareness into AI models and maintaining human oversight in sensitive translation contexts. One more aspect to mention is translator employment, as the widespread adoption of AI in translation has raised concerns about job displacement. Although AI can efficiently handle routine translations, human expertise remains critical for complex, literary, and creative translation tasks (Hao & Pym, 2023). Many experts argue that rather than replacing translators, AI will shift their role toward post-editing and quality control (Bowker, 2022). The goal of eliminating the various ethical issues that arise poses challenges to both AI experts and developers, and the translation community. It is therefore natural that translator training processes must take this into account.

As for the ethical considerations of AI in university translation study programmes, attention should be paid to the fact that such integration presents several ethical issues that educators must address to prepare students for the evolving professional career. Universities must educate students about responsible AI usage, particularly with respect to sensitive content translation, ensuring that students understand the ethical implications of handling confidential materials (Bowker, 2023). Educators should train students to critically assess AI-generated translations and understand their limitations, as AI still lacks clear responsibility, making error tracing difficult. AI translation systems may fail to grasp cultural details, resulting in technically correct but culturally inappropriate translations. Integrating cultural competence training into university curricula can help students navigate these challenges effectively (Bowker, 2022). To address these challenges, translation study programmes should incorporate AI ethics into the curriculum, including specialised courses on ethical AI usage, interdisciplinary collaboration, and discussions on the societal impacts of AI on the translation profession (Slator, 2024). By proactively integrating these ethical considerations, university translation programmes can equip students with the necessary awareness and skills to navigate the complexities introduced by artificial intelligence in their profession.

Furthermore, the integration of AI into translation programmes has been analysed from various perspectives. Kanglang and Afzaal (2021) analysed the integration of AI into pedagogical practices, highlighting benefits and limitations. According to the authors, while AI significantly aids translation teaching by introducing cost-effective and rapid translation solutions, its current limitations require human interaction. The study emphasises the need for balanced integration of AI in educational practices to improve learning without undermining the human element of translation. Wang (2023) argue that AI technologies play a transformative role in translation education, enhancing efficiency and competency development. However, a hybrid approach that combines AI tools and human expertise is essential to address cultural and semantic complexities. Hu and Li (2023) argue that AI is reshaping translation pedagogy by introducing tools for personalised learning and real-time feedback, and such innovations require curriculum redesign to equip future translators with skills in AI-assisted translation environments. This idea is in line with the remark of Kanglang and Afzaal (2021) that AI offers innovative teaching methodologies, enabling self-learning and helping students in complex translation tasks. However, there is still a gap in critical reflection and instructional principles for AI integration. They also note that translation teaching has currently evolved into specialised courses where artificial intelligence is becoming a core component. Such applications as Google Translate, SDL Trados, MemoQ, or Neural Machine Translation tools have been incorporated into translation teaching across universities as they facilitate rapid translation, reducing costs and time, but are prone to errors in less common languages or context-specific usages. Furthermore, there is still a lack of standardisation in teaching approaches. AI lacks the ability to fully replicate human cognition, leading to issues in understanding semantics and cultural contexts, that is why human translators remain essential for refining and correcting AI-generated translations to ensure accuracy. As Kanglang and Afzaal (2021) note, AI-driven translation has potential, but its accuracy in translating complex texts is still limited. Wang (2023) argues that further research is needed to optimise AI integration in translation pedagogy while preserving human creativity and cultural sensitivity. The balance of technology use with the cultivation of creativity, ethical judgment, and critical thinking should be essential in teaching translation (Urlaub & Dessein, 2022; Hubscher-Davidson & Devaux, 2021). The extremely rapid pace of change in AI and the challenges posed by researchers highlight key gaps that translator training institutions and their staff should fill.

Translator training curriculums should be redesigned by integrating AI with a focus on critical thinking and problem-solving skills, and awareness of understanding limitations of AI tools should be constantly raised while training translators. Geng and Hu (2023) note that translators are shifting from traditional roles to acting as editors or quality controllers in human-AI translation. To sum up, it can be noted that the integration of AI into the curriculum of translation studies programmes curriculum represents both a transformative opportunity and a significant challenge. Its integration into education has the potential to enhance learning experiences and efficiency, but also risks reinforcing inequities and biases. As Bahroun et al. (2023) note, addressing these challenges requires a multifaceted approach, combining equitable access, ethical regulation, and comprehensive digital literacy initiatives.

METHODOLOGICAL IMPLICATIONS

Taking into account the complexity of the topic and the research questions, the present empirical research is focused on the analysis of documents in three stages: (1) policy documents regulating the use of artificial intelligence in translation and in the study process; (2) documents defining the policy of the Baltic universities, where the translation study programmes are conducted, on the use of artificial intelligence in the study process; (3) undergraduate and postgraduate study programmes in translation and their descriptions conducted in the universities of the Baltic countries.

In the empirical research phases (1) and (2), universities in the Baltic states, Lithuania, Latvia, and Estonia, were selected to conduct undergraduate and postgraduate programmes in translation studies. By analysing publicly available data, six universities (three in Lithuania, two in Latvia and one in Estonia) were selected for this analysis, which offer five undergraduate (Bachelor's) and six postgraduate (Master's) degree programmes in translation. Undergraduate programmes range from 180 ICTS (3 years) to 240 ICTS (4 years), while postgraduate programmes range from 90 ICTS (1.5 years) to 120 ICTS (2 years). It is also important to note that this study analysed information that is publicly available: in some cases this is just the programme description, but in most cases it is both the programme description and the grid or detailed descriptions of the courses themselves.

Data analysis. Given the large number of texts of various types selected for the empirical study, a qualitative approach to document analysis was chosen. According to Shava et al. (2021), it is pertinent to note that qualitative research methods are particularly relevant when analysing educational practice, because, unlike quantitative research, qualitative research takes into account the different interactions that take place in the social environment, allows us to delve into the different facets of the situation being analysed and can help to solve problems, validate existing theories, or generate new knowledge and models. Content analysis was chosen for the study because, first of all, as Azizan et al. (2018) argue, it is designed to analyse qualitative data: verbal, textual. It allows researchers to have access to large amounts of information. Furthermore, according to Čepienė and Vaitiekienė (2019), content analysis allows the researcher to summarise large amounts of information and to group the research data into subcategories and categories according to content and meaning.

RESEARCH RESULTS

Analysis of policy documents. With the rapid development of artificial intelligence, it is only natural that in the political context there is also an effort to declare and define the ethics, possibilities, and similar issues of its application and use. This is particularly true in the context of studies, as studies are one of the areas where the challenges related to AI and its application remain quite numerous. This is particularly true in the field of translation studies because, as Moneus and Sahari (2024) point out, the field of translation is highly influenced by artificial intelligence. Therefore, translation study programmes have to deal with artificial intelligence in terms of both competences and the study process. As studies and their implementation are not primarily defined at the institutional level but at a higher level – national or international – it is important to look at what key documents on the application of AI in study programmes in general and on translation policy in particular can potentially influence the design and implementation of programmes in translation studies.

Some of the most important documents currently defining the organisation of studies on artificial intelligence are the Guidance for generative AI in education and research adopted by UNESCO in 2023, Artificial Intelligence for Europe adopted by the European Commission in 2018, the Digital Decade Policy Programme 2030 adopted by the European Parliament in 2022, the EU Artificial Intelligence Act adopted in 2024, and the European Commission's Ethical Guidelines on the use of artificial intelligence (AI) and data in teaching and learning for educators adopted in

2022. All of these documents emphasise the importance of artificial intelligence in education. However, they also declare fundamental ethical norms on how artificial intelligence should be incorporated into studies and what steps educators should take to ensure the inevitable but fair and safe use of artificial intelligence in educational processes. It is therefore natural that the norms set out in these documents also apply to study programmes in translation.

With specific reference to translation and its quality requirements, some of the most important documents are ISO standards, that is, ISO Standard No. 17100:2015, ISO Standard No. 18587: 2017 and ISO Standard No. 11669: 2024 (International Organisation for Standardisation, 2015, 2017, 2024).).).).). In all these ISO standards, machine translation is important in the context of artificial intelligence. However, in the ISO standard Translation Projects General guidance, adopted in 2024, a specific focus on AI already appears. As stated in the aforementioned standard, the recent very rapid change and globalization of the translation industry is also increasing the demand for translation, and technological innovations such as artificial intelligence or machine translation are making it possible to develop solutions to meet such needs (International Organization for Standardization, 2024).). As already mentioned, until then ISO standards defined only machine evaluation, but the adoption of ISO Standard No. 11669:2024 and its focus on artificial intelligence shows that translation and its industry are responding to technological change. Thus, according to the ISO standard (International Organization for Standardization, 2024), while technological change increases the choice of translation for consumers, it also poses a challenge to ensure that translation output meets the requirements. This creates another component of professional competence for existing and future translators, focussing on the reliable application of artificial intelligence in translation processes.

Another important policy aspect in the context of translation studies is the European Master's in Translation (EMT) offered by the European Commission's Directorate-General for Translation (DG Translation). It represents a quality label for MA university programmes in translation studies. This label indicates that the study programme meets the European Commission's requirements and defined standards for the translation profession. It is also important to note that according to the European Commission Map (n. d.) of EMT members, three of the study programmes presented in this chapter analysis – one study programme per country in Lithuania, Latvia, and Estonia – have this label. The approved European Master's in Translation Competence Framework 2022 again emphasises the importance of machine translation, which is an increasing part of the translation workflow, and machine translation skills are therefore seen as an integral part of professional translation competence (European Commission, 2022b).). However, the European Master's in Translation Competence Annual Report 2023 highlights that "the rapid development of artificial intelligence (AI) calls for an update of translation skills, which should be handled in conjunction with other working groups and interested parties, without becoming too frequent" (European Commission, 2024, p. 13). This shows that the field of translation is not only heavily influenced by technological change, but is also able to respond in a timely and appropriate manner.

As the analysis of the documents shows, there have been a number of recent policy developments that focus on artificial intelligence, both in studies in general and in the field of translation. Therefore, it is natural and expected that in the future more and more of this transformation will be integrated into the study process as a result of the rapid changes in artificial intelligence. However, such changes are also likely to be taking place in studies and in translation study programmes in particular. Therefore, it is relevant to look at the current situation in Baltic universities offering undergraduate and postgraduate translation study programmes.

Analysis of university documents on the use of artificial intelligence in the study process. In order to reveal how artificial intelligence and its application are reflected in undergraduate and postgraduate translation study programmes in the Baltic states, it is appropriate to look at the policies of universities offering these programmes in the region of the analysis. For this purpose, it was chosen to analyse the guidelines for the use of artificial intelligence in the study process adopted by universities. Of the six universities that offer study programmes in translation studies in the Baltic states, the guidelines of five universities are publicly available, which define the basic principles of the use of artificial intelligence in the study process.

Despite the fact that, as Wang and Li (2024) argue, the integration of AI into university processes is inevitable and has not been new for quite some time, it can be noted that policy making in this regard has only been active in universities in the last couple of years. The analysis showed that, in general, the most common guidelines of all universities focus on the nuances of the use of AI, such as potential opportunities, existing risks, risks of plagiarism and ways to identify it, possibilities for educational practices using AI, citation guidelines, etc. It is also very important to understand that "since the world and our understanding of it are evolving rapidly, these guidelines serve as a preliminary agreement that may be influenced, for example, by national restrictions arising from data protection" (University of Tartu, 2023), that is, artificial intelligence and its regulation are as fluid as ever in the daily life of universities and therefore require constant monitoring and revision.

All universities take the perspective that AI and its integration into the study process are inevitable (eg, "As with calculators, spell checkers, language editing tools, search engines, and other similar tools, there is generally no point in prohibiting AI chatbots. *Instead, one should consider how to learn to use them purposefully, ethically, and critically" (University of Tartu, 2023), but there is a positive and a negative side.* When analysing guidelines on the use of AI in the study process, it has been observed that these documents are generally focused on two strands: ethical issues covering plagiarism, academic integrity, etc., and the potential of using AI. Therefore, it is appropriate to look in more detail at policies on the use of artificial intelligence in terms of ethics and potential application in studies.

The interaction between AI and ethics is an important area of research (Memarian & Doleck, 2023; Sam & Olbrich, 2023; Castelló-Sirvent, et al., 2024). Regarding the question of ethics of the application of AI in studies, it is appropriate to point out that, in general, the guidelines of all universities start with a declaration of a value framework: responsibilities, principles, values (e.g., "The values, ethical principles, and norms that are binding to students, academic, scientific, and general staff" (University of Latvia, 2024), 'When using AI tools, the student must appreciate that the responsibility for the content generated by these tools lies with the user, i.e., the student. *The student is responsible for checking the content of the text produced by the AI tool and must be able to explain every aspect of the content generated by the AI tool*" (Mykolas Romeris University, 2024). This essentially also refers to the position of universities themselves to organise their studies using artificial intelligence only on the basis of transparency and the responsibility of each member of the community.

It can also be noted that the most commonly defined need is to meet the challenges arising from person-centered approaches (e.g. "The most significant ethical risks associated with the use of AI in the teaching process: misleading content <...>; erroneous and unfair assessment of academic work – <...>; conflicts due to misunderstandings – <...>; decrease in trust <...>; decrease in solidarity <...>; discriminatory content <... >*; decrease in equal opportunities and inclusivity* <...>*; violations of rights* <...>*" (University of Latvia, 2024); "Personal data must not be entered into an AI tool without the person's consent" (University of Tartu, 2023) and in the results of studies (e.g., "In the case of a written work, the use of a generative AI application must be appropriately described and referenced. Submitting a text created by AI under one's name is academic fraud*" (University of Tartu, 2023) ethical issues. Ensuring and managing these ethical issues in the application of AI in the study process is crucial. In translation study programmes, the ethical issue is also important. As Wang and Li (2024) argue, despite the rapid advances in various AI tools focused on translation, there are still a number of errors in AI-based translation. Therefore, integrity and ethical standards in all of their various aspects also have an impact on the quality of work.

As Wang and Li (2024) argue, the integration of artificial intelligence into translation study programmes is inevitable. Therefore, a targeted policy on the integration of AI into the study process is also essential not only to address the ethical issues that arise, but also to provide the necessary opportunities for specific AI-based study practices. As the analysis of the guidelines for the application of artificial intelligence in the study process of universities offering translation study programmes shows, it is generally acknowledged that artificial intelligence "as it currently enters the study process, it can be considered a tool used to achieve certain goals" (University of Latvia, 2024) and that it "can be used to complement the teaching process, to facilitate interpretation and understanding of existing teaching content, <. ...> *be used as a complementary resource and only used in conjunction with other reliable sources" (Kaunas University of Technology, 2024); also, AI "generative models can be useful for learning and teaching at the university. They can help lecturers save time when preparing teaching activities <...>. For students, they can help them learn better <...> and complete tasks better and faster <...>" (Vilnius University, 2024).* Therefore, it can be assumed that the integration of AI in the institutions of higher education analysed is a natural and timely process.

Universities have established certain guidelines for integrating artificial intelligence into study programmes and processes. First, it is necessary to "rethink the study and assessment methods used in the module, taking into account the opportunities and risks of using generative AI <...>, the effective achievement of learning outcomes and academic integrity, and to develop students' digital competences" (Kaunas University of Technology, 2024). It is also important to acknowledge that AI should be used for "1) personalising teaching <...>; 2) interactive assignments and simulations <...>" (Vilnius University, 2024), as AI "can help identify students' strengths and weaknesses by providing personalised assignments and offering additional resources in areas of the curriculum that need support" (University of Latvia, 2024). Finally, it is important to empower students to use AI tools "*to complete an assignment only when the course instructor specifies this possibility in the wording of the assignment*" (Mykolas Romeris University, 2024) and "*these instructions must be included in the course information in the Study Information System or clearly stated in the instructions for the specific assignment*" (University of Tartu, 2023). As can be seen, the roles of the teacher in the construction of the content and the student in working with that content are both important in the use of AI.

However, it is also very important to consider that the use of AI in the study process should be purposeful and beneficial, i.e. "the use of AI tools should promote active, continuous, and responsible student participation, critical thinking, cooperation, and problem-solving skills in the student-centered study process" (University of Latvia, 2024).). In this regard, AI tools "*should not be used in cases where the student has the task of developing and proving one's ability to create a structurally and grammatically correct text, to conduct independent research to strengthen one's understanding, which is necessary to be able to work with the acquired knowledge and skills further*" (University of Latvia, 2024). This means that although AI is inevitable and its integration into the study process is a natural phenomenon, it requires critical thinking on the part of everyone – both teacher and student – when using it.

However, it is also very important that university policies reflect some of the characteristics of the application of artificial intelligence focused on linguistic competences. For example, the use of AI is acceptable when it is used for "*revising the language of the manuscript content using spell and grammar checkers; for predictive writing* <...> *using widely used tools that suggest template words or phrases; and for natural language processing* <...>" (Kaunas University of Technology, 2024), as well as "*to overcome writer's block or the so-called fear of the blank page;* <...> *to assist with editing and translating* <...>" (University of Tartu, 2023). While AI tools focused on these activities can simplify the performance of some tasks, it is important to note that they can be used in cases where the student does not have to perform these activities independently.

As can be seen, universities offering translation study programmes in the Baltic states have a clear and well-reasoned position on the use of AI in the study process. In this context, it is appropriate to look at how artificial intelligence and its application are reflected in specific undergraduate and postgraduate translation programmes.

Analysis of translation study programmes. As already mentioned, the Baltic region was chosen for this study. Analysis of translation study programmes was carried out in 11 undergraduate and postgraduate translation study programmes at universities in Lithuania, Latvia, and Estonia. When performing the analysis, we searched for the term artificial intelligence or its abbreviation AI. It is worth noting that only in four – two undergraduate programmes (in Lithuania and Latvia) and two postgraduate programmes (in Lithuania and Latvia) – the searched terms were found. It is also important to note that both postgraduate programmes have the European Master's in Translation quality label.

First of all, it should be noted that during the analysis of the programme descriptions, which are accessible on university websites and serve to inform the public or promote the study programmes, it was noticed that only one postgraduate study programme in the field of translation, which is conducted at the Lithuanian university, also focusses on artificial intelligence. The description states that the study programme will focus on content-generating artificial intelligence tools and therefore one of the skills to be developed during the study process is the management of artificial intelligence technologies. It can be assumed that programme promoters are interested in integrating the latest technologies that are rapidly changing the translation market into the study process, thus ensuring the competitiveness and adaptability of trained professionals in the labour market.

However, when analysing the descriptions of the study programmes in the field of translation available on the web pages of universities, it was noted that although, as mentioned above, only one programme description specifically mentions artificial intelligence, the importance of new translation technologies is also recorded in the descriptions of the other study programmes. The study programmes in the field of translation emphasise the aim to "*implement an open and flexible study process that ensures the integration of state-of-the-art information technologies* <...>" (postgraduate studies, Latvia) and to develop "*modern skills of translators and the latest information technologies*" (undergraduate studies, Latvia), and the graduates are "*proficient in the latest information and translation technologies* <...>" (postgraduate studies, Lithuania). However, it should be noted that the importance of new technologies and their integration in translation studies is highlighted in the curricula of translation studies at universities with a technological orientation. This could also be linked to the profile of the universities themselves, which obliges higher education institutions to base their studies on the latest technologies and to familiarise students with them. It is also worth mentioning that the descriptions of almost all universities' translation study programmes highlight the competitiveness of future graduates and their ability to adapt to the labour market, which means that the integration of artificial intelligence into translation study programmes is likely to become a natural development in the future.

The analysis also shows that separate topics related to artificial intelligence and its applications are being integrated into study courses. For example, in some cases, topics related to AI are integrated into general courses such as *Philosophy of Media* (undergraduate studies, Lithuania). In this course, artificial intelligence is included as an element of the continuous progress of society ("*to learn about the principles of the functioning and effects of different media, from writing to artificial intelligence*"), which each student has to understand from different perspectives, including philosophical ones. In other cases, when AI is included as a separate topic in the course, it is usually related to the construction of knowledge focused on specific elements of the translation process. For example, in the Modern Methods of Text Analysis course (postgraduate programme, Latvia), the topic is Natural language processing as a subfield of artificial intelligence and linguistics; in the *Technical Language Translation, Post-editing and Project Management* course (postgraduate programme, Lithuania), the topic is *Machine Learning and Artificial Intelligence Influence on the Technologisation of the Translator's Profession* and the *Career of a Translation Project Manager; Technical Language Translation, Post-editing and Professional Ethics* in the course (postgraduate programme, Lithuania) on *Ethical Aspects of the Use of Artificial Intelligence, Translation Technologies and Post-editing*. As can be seen, artificial intelligence and the integration of related knowledge emerge as a complementary subtheme to the broader themes. This shows that artificial intelligence is becoming an integral part in the study programmes of translation studies.

However, there is also a tendency to include a separate course on artificial intelligence in the study programme in translation studies. For example, the undergraduate study programme in the field of translation at the Lithuanian university includes a course "*Translation Technologies and Artificial Intelligence*" (6 ECTS). The course covers topics such as automated translation tools and artificial intelligence, artificial intelligence and machine translation, speech recognition systems, etc., and one of the main competencies to be developed in this course is the ability to describe the specific features of translation technologies and the impact of artificial intelligence in translation. The postgraduate programme in translation at the same university includes the course "AI Query Engineering for the Humanities" (6 ECTS), which provides students with an understanding of the key principles of the design, formulation and use of AI queries and the evaluation of the quality of the results received. This focus on AI in translation in both undergraduate and postgraduate studies reflects the University's consistent approach to the need to integrate the most up-to-date and relevant topics into the study process, thus enabling the development of timely and competitive student competences and rapid adaptation to global labour market changes.

A separate course "*Artificial Intelligence in Humanities*" (3 ECTS) is also integrated into the postgraduate programme in translation studies at a Latvian university. As with the artificial intelligence-orientated courses discussed above, this course aims to develop students' understanding of artificial intelligence and basic skills in applying artificial intelligence methods to real-world problems in the social sciences and humanities. As can be seen, the development of students' critical thinking towards AI is of great importance to the programme. Universities are aware of the need to integrate AI into their studies in a way that enables students to take advantage of its good potential in a responsible way.

An analysis of the curricula shows that some higher education institutions are focused on transferring new and relevant knowledge to students. Therefore, the integration of elements of artificial intelligence into the study process is also observed. This suggests that universities are able to adapt to the changes and needs of society, technology, and the labour market, and they are able to adjust the content of their studies to reflect these changes and needs.

FUTURE RESEARCH DIRECTIONS

AI technologies are transforming translation studies into a more interdisciplinary and data-driven field. However, addressing ethical and methodological challenges is vital to ensure that the discipline retains its depth, diversity, and cultural relevance in this new era (Jiménez-Crespo, 2020; Kenny, 2022). The introduction of innovative tools, the expansion of methodological perspectives, and the redefining of traditional roles are shaping translation studies. However, it remains critical to address ethical concerns and cultural sensitivity challenges. By fostering interdisciplinary collaboration and developing sustainable ethical frameworks, the field can harness the potential of AI while preserving the cultural depth and essence of translation.

The ethical issue is also relevant for future research on the integration of artificial intelligence into translation study programmes from the perspective of lecturers and students (Soysal, 2023). In this respect, it is relevant to develop research that helps reveal the challenges faced by lecturers when AI becomes not only a tool to improve their studies but also an opportunity for unethical behaviour. However, it is also important to analyse the students' perspective on how to transform the educational process so that AI is seen and treated by students themselves as a tool to develop competences, promote learning, etc.

Despite the considerable development of AI in the field of translation, researchers (Kanglang & Afzaal, 2021; Moneus & Sahari, 2024) note that AI still has many shortcomings and cannot ensure a smooth translation process without human intervention. Nuances such as cultural features of a language are also a crucial element of the translation process (Kanglang & Afzaal, 2021). Therefore, it seems appropriate not to talk about AI replacing humans in translation, but about how to create a synergy between human subjectivity and AI's objectivity. In this context, various studies focused on artificial intelligence in translation are very important and should be encouraged.

However, it is worth noting that when analysing AI in the context of translation studies, the career prospects of future translators are also very important. There are already studies (e.g., Vaughn, 2023) that raise concerns about whether translators as a professional group will still be needed in the future and what the future holds for professional translators as AI advances so rapidly. However, as Alharbi (2024) points out, in addition to concerns about whether the profession of translator will disappear, it is also important to analyse how translators can adapt in the age of artificial intelligence and what competencies they need to develop to avoid being displaced by artificial intelligence from the labour market. According to Shahmerdanova (2025), Mohamed et al. (2024), it can be observed that AI in translation, like any other phenomenon, has its strengths and weaknesses. Shahmerdanova (2025) observes that the human factor remains important when it comes to cultural and inclusive aspects. Therefore, according to Alharbi (2024), here we can see the need to analyse and study how to bridge the gap between academic training and industry expectations, i.e., to look for tools that allow translators to maintain their demand as qualified professionals in the labour market, even in the presence of a strong competitor such as artificial intelligence.

However, it is appropriate to view AI not only as a practical tool but also as a dynamic and not always predictable future with which everyone must learn to work and live. In this context, research focussing on how artificial intelligence should be integrated into translation study programmes is essential to ensure that this integration is coherent and sustainable. This means that research must help institutions of higher education to make decisions on how to integrate AI into translation study programmes in order to make it effective in the long term: which roles of AI and human beings to focus on, which competences to develop, etc.

CONCLUSION

Recent rapid developments in artificial intelligence and its underlying technologies have touched many areas of human life. One of the areas that has been most affected is translation. Therefore, it is natural that translation study programmes are also affected by artificial intelligence. As the analysis has shown, AI technologies are transforming translation studies into a more interdisciplinary and data-driven field, changing established theoretical frameworks, research methodologies, and practical applications. Despite the unprecedented opportunities that AI has brought to the field of translation, ethical and methodological challenges need to be addressed to ensure that the discipline of translation retains its depth, diversity, and cultural relevance in this new era (Jiménez-Crespo, 2020; Kenny, 2022). The introduction of innovative tools, the broadening of methodological perspectives, and the redefinition of traditional roles of translators are transforming translation studies. However, the challenge of addressing ethical issues and cultural sensitivity remains crucial. Therefore, the integration of artificial intelligence into translation studies is seen both as a transformative opportunity for learning experiences and performance, but also as a challenge that leads to gaps in the enforcement of ethical norms such as equality and objectivity. By fostering interdisciplinary collaboration and creating sustainable ethical frameworks, translation studies can harness the potential of artificial intelligence while preserving the cultural depth and essence of translation.

Overall, looking at both the policy framework at the European level and the position of universities in relation to the application of AI in study programmes and processes, it is clear that the greatest need so far is to define the application of AI in studies in general from an ethical and teacher/student perspective. Meanwhile, from the perspective of translation study programmes, AI is becoming for the developers of these programmes not only an auxiliary tool for facilitating general study-related processes, but also an important tool for skilled work, the mastery of which is also an element of their modern competences.

The empirical study has shown that a policy framework orientated toward AI and its ethical use has been actively developed at European level over the past few years, both in studies in general and in translation study programmes. The analysis of Baltic universities' policies on the application of AI in curricula and processes has shown that, in general, AI and its integration into the study process are seen as an elusive reality. However, it is evident that universities have so far focused on defining the application of AI in studies in general from an ethical and lecturer/ student perspective. It is also noticeable that university policies reflect some features of AI applications that focus on linguistic competences in the context of task performance. Specifically, with regard to the translation study programmes in the universities selected for this study, it is observed that for the developers of translation study programmes, artificial intelligence is not only a tool to facilitate general study-related processes, but also an important tool for skilled work, the mastery of which is also an element of modern competences of translator. An analysis of study programmes shows that translation programmes at universities with a technological profile focus more on the latest technologies, including artificial intelligence. The analysis shows that translation study programmes are integrating separate topics related to artificial intelligence and its applications, as well as a tendency to include a whole separate course dedicated to artificial intelligence in translation studies. This suggests that universities are able to adapt to the changes and needs of society, technology, and the labour market and, in this context, are able to adjust the content of their study programmes in order to respond to the intense changes that are taking place, including those resulting from AI.

To sum up, it could be argued that the swift advancement of artificial intelligence is reshaping translation studies into a more data-driven and interdisciplinary discipline, influencing theoretical approaches, research methods, and practical applications while offering new opportunities and ethical dilemmas, as universities progressively incorporate AI into their curricula to align with shifting technological and societal demands.

ACKNOWLEDGEMENT

This research received no specific grant from any funding agency in the public, commercial, or not-for-profit sectors.

REFERENCES

Aini, R. P., Yuliati, Y., Febriyanto, B., & Safira, R. F. (2024, November). Meretas Paradigma Baru: Artificial Intelligence (AI) Dalam Pembelajaran IPA Di Sekolah Dasar. In *Prosiding Seminar Nasional Pendidikan* (Vol. 6, pp. 91-104).

Alharbi, W. (2024). Future Translators' Linguistic and Non-linguistic Competencies and Skills in The Age of Neural Machine Translation and Artificial Intelligence: A Content Analysis. *International Journal of Linguistics. Literature and Translation*, *7*(4), 124–143. DOI: 10.32996/ijllt.2024.7.4.16

Amini, M., Ravindran, L., & Lee, K.-F. (2024). Implications of using AI in translation studies: Trends, challenges, and future direction. *Asian Journal of Research in Education and Social Sciences*, *6*(1), 740–754.

. Annoni, A., Benczur, P., Bertoldi, P., Delipetrev, B., De Prato, G., Feijoo, C., ... & Junklewitz, H. (2018). Artificial intelligence: A European perspective.

Arachchige, I. A. N., Suraweera, S., & Herath, D. (2022). Transformer-based Language models for the Identification of Idiomatic Expressions. In *Proceedings of the International Conference EUROPHRAS* 2022 (short papers, posters and MUMTTT workshop contributions) (ss. 119-127). Incoma Ltd. Shoumen, Bulgaria. https://doi .org/DOI: 10.26615/978-954-452-080-9_015

Azizan, N., Smith, R., Cooper, V., & Abu Bakar, N. (2018). Qualitative Content Analysis: A Case Study of a Malaysian Government Education Website. *Malaysian Journal of Science Health & Technology*, *1*(1). Advance online publication. DOI: 10.33102/mjosht.v1i1.14

Bahroun, Z., Anane, C., Ahmed, V., & Zacca, A. (2023). Transforming education: A comprehensive review of generative artificial intelligence in educational settings through bibliometric and content analysis. *Sustainability (Basel)*, *15*(17), 12983. DOI: 10.3390/su151712983

Barrault, L., Chung, Y. A., Meglioli, M. C., Dale, D., Dong, N., Duquenne, P. A., . . . Wang, S. (2023). SeamlessM4T-Massively Multilingual & Multimodal Machine Translation. https://arxiv.org/pdf/2308.11596

Bernardini, S. (Ed.). (2020). *Language service provision in the 21st century: challenges, opportunities and educational perspectives for translation studies*. Bologna: Bologna University Press (BUP).

Bowker, L. (2020). Machine Translation and the Future of Language Professions. pp. 262-278. In Koskinen, K., & Pokorn, N.K. (Eds.). (2020). *The Routledge Handbook of Translation and Ethics*. Routledge. DOI: 10.4324/9781003127970

Buden, B., Nowotny, S., Simon, S., Bery, A., & Cronin, M. (2009). Cultural translation: An introduction to the problem, and Responses. *Translation Studies*, *2*(2), 196–219. DOI: 10.1080/14781700902937730

Cai, Z., Haslett, D. A., Duan, X., Wang, S., & Pickering, M. J. (2023). Does ChatGPT resemble humans in language use? *arXiv Preprint.*https://doi.org//arXiv.2303.08014 .DOI: 10.48550

Castelló-Sirvent, F., Roger-Monzó, V., & Gouveia-Rodrigues, R. (2024). Quo Vadis, University? A Roadmap for AI and Ethics in Higher Education. *Electronic Journal of e-Learning*, *22*(6), 35–51. DOI: 10.34190/ejel.22.6.3267

. Castilho, S., & Knowles, R. (2024). A survey of context in neural machine translation and its evaluation. *Natural Language Processing*, 1–31. .DOI: 10.1017/nlp.2024.7

Čepienė, A., & Vaitiekienė, N. (2019). Studentų profesinės praktikos organizavimo proceso kolegijoje analizė. *Mokslo Taikomieji Tyrimai Lietuvos Kolegijose*, (14), 53-62. Retrieved from https://ojs.kaunokolegija.lt/index.php/mttlk/article/view/256

Chetouani, M., Dignum, V., Lukowicz, P., & Sierra, C. (2023). Lecture notes in computer science: Vol. 13500. *Human-centered artificial intelligence: Advanced lectures*. Springer., DOI: 10.1007/978-3-031-24349-3

Costa-Jussa, M. R., & Fonollosa, J. A. (2015). Latest trends in hybrid machine translation and its applications. *Computer Speech & Language*, *32*(1), 3–10. DOI: 10.1016/j.csl.2014.11.001

. Drugan, J., & Tipton, R. (2017). Translation, ethics and social responsibility. *The translator, 23*(2), 119-125. https://doi.org/.DOI: 10.1080/13556509.2017.1327008

European Commision. (n. d.). EMT members 2024-29. Retrieved from: https://commission.europa.eu/education/skills-and-qualifications/develop-your-language-skills/european-masters-translation-emt/emt-members-2024-29_en

European Commission. (2018). Artificial Intelligence for Europe. Retrieved from: https://eur-lex.europa.eu/legal-content/EN/TXT/HTML/?uri=CELEX:52018DC0237

European Commission. (2022a). Ethical guidelines on the use of artificial intelligence (AI) and data in teaching and learning for educators. Retrieved from: https://op.europa.eu/en/publication-detail/-/publication/d81a0d54-5348-11ed-92ed-01aa75ed71a1/language-en

European Commission. (2022b). European Master's in Translation Competence Framework 2022. Retrieved from: chrome-extension://efaidnbmnnnibpcajpcglclefindmkaj/https://commission.europa.eu/system/files/2022-11/emt_competence_fwk_2022_en.pdf

European Commission. (2024). European Master's in Translation Competence Annual Report 2023. Retrieved from: chrome-extension://efaidnbmnnnibpcajpcglclefindmkaj/https://commission.europa.eu/document/download/b0884886-305d-49f8-b2ba-a9a9ddcd66e5_en?filename=EMT_Annual_Report_2023.pdf

European Parliament. (2022). Digital Decade Policy Programme 2030. Retrieved from: https://commission.europa.eu/strategy-and-policy/priorities-2019-2024/europe-fit-digital-age/europes-digital-decade-digital-targets-2030_en

Gambier, Y. (2016). Translationsl Rapid and Radical Changes in Translation and Translation Studies. *International Journal of Communication*, *10*, 887–906. https://ijoc.org/index.php/ijoc/article/view/3824

Geng, F., & Hu, J. (2023). New direction of artificial intelligence-assisted post-translation editing: A case study of ChatGPT-based translation. *Chinese Foreign Language*, *3*, 41–47.

Ghosh, S., & Caliskan, A. (2023). ChatGPT perpetuates gender bias in machine translation and ignores non-gendered pronouns: Findings across Bengali and five other low-resource languages. *arXiv Preprint.*https://doi.org//arXiv.2305.10510 .DOI: 10.1145/3600211.3604672

Groves, M., & Mundt, K. (2015).Friend or foe? Google Translate in language for academic purposes, *English for Specific Purposes*, Volume 37, p. 112-121, ISSN 0889-4906, https://doi.org/DOI: 10.1016/j.esp.2014.09.001

Hao, Y., & Pym, A. (2023). Where Do Translation Students Go? A Study of the Employment and Mobility of Master Graduates. *The Interpreter and Translator Trainer*, *17*(2), 211–229. DOI: 10.1080/1750399X.2022.2084595

Heath, M., Hvass, A. M. F., & Wejse, C. M. (2023). Interpreter services and effect on healthcare - a systematic review of the impact of different types of interpreters on patient outcome. *Journal of Migration and Health*, *7*, 100162. DOI: 10.1016/j.jmh.2023.100162 PMID: 36816444

Holmes, W., & Miao, F. (2023). *Guidance for generative AI in education and research.* UNESCO Publishing. Retrieved from: https://unesdoc.unesco.org/ark:/48223/pf0000386693

Hu, K., & Li, X. (2023). Development of Translation Research in the Context of Large Language Modeling: Problems and Prospects. *China Translation*, (6), 65–74.

Hubscher-Davidson, S., & Devaux, J. (2021). Teaching translation and interpreting in virtual environments. *The Journal of Specialised Translation, 36*, 184–192.

International Organization for Standardization. (2015). *Translation services – Requirements for translation services* (ISO Standard No. 17100:2015). https://www.iso.org/obp/ui/en/#iso:std:iso:17100:ed-1:v1:en

International Organization for Standardization. (2017). *Translation services – Post-editing of machine translation output – Requirements* (ISO Standard No. 18587:2017). https://www.iso.org/obp/ui/en/#iso:std:iso:18587:ed-1:v1:en

International Organization for Standardization. (2024). *Translation projects – General guidance* (ISO Standard No. 11669:2024). https://www.iso.org/obp/ui/en/#iso:std:iso:11669:ed-1:v1:en

Jiménez-Crespo, M. A. (2020). The "technological turn" in translation studies: Are we there yet? A transversal cross-disciplinary approach. *Translation Spaces, 9*(2), 314–341. DOI: 10.1075/ts.19012.jim

Kanglang, L., & Afzaal, M. (2021). Artificial Intelligence (AI) and Translation Teaching: A Critical Perspective on the Transformation of Education. *International Journal of Educational Sciences, 33*(1-3). Advance online publication. DOI: 10.31901/24566322.2021/33.1-3.1159

Kasperė, R., Horbačauskienė, J., Liubinienė, V., Motiejūnienė, J., Patašienė, I., & Patašius, M. (2024). *Machine translation and society: The case of Lithuania*. Kaunas University of Technology Press., DOI: 10.5755/e01.9786090218808

. Kaunas University of Technology (2024). Generatyvinio dirbtinio intelekto etiško naudojimo Kauno technologijos universiteto studijų procese politika.

Kenny, D. (2018). Machine translation. In Rawling, P., & Wilson, P. (Eds.), *The Routledge Handbook of Translation and Philosophy* (pp. 428–445). Routledge. DOI: 10.4324/9781315678481-27

Kenny, D. (2022). *Machine translation for everyone: Empowering users in the age of artificial intelligence*. Language Science Press.

Koponen, M., Mossop, B., & Robert, S. I., & Scocchera, G. (Eds.). (2020). *Translation Revision and Post-editing: Industry Practices and Cognitive Processes*. Routledge. DOI: 10.4324/9781003096962

Lee, T. K. (2023). Artificial intelligence and posthumanist translation: ChatGPT versus the translator. *Applied Linguistics Review*. Advance online publication. DOI: 10.1515/applirev-2023-0122

Low, D. S., Liew, C. J., & Ng, R. W. (2022). Endangered languages: A sociocognitive approach to language death, identity loss, and preservation in the age of artificial intelligence. *Journal of Language and Social Psychology, 41*(1), 45–60. DOI: 10.1177/0261927X21100001

Mehandru, N., Robertson, S., & Salehi, N. (2022). Reliable and Safe Use of Machine Translation in Medical Settings. *FAccT '22: 2022 ACM Conference on Fairness, Accountability, and Transparency*, Seoul, Republic of Korea. https://doi.org/DOI: 10.1145/3531146.3533244

Memarian, B., & Doleck, T. (2023). Fairness, Accountability, Transparency, and Ethics (FATE) in Artificial Intelligence (AI) and higher education: A systematic review,Computers and Education. *Artificial Intelligence, 5*, 100152. Advance online publication. DOI: 10.1016/j.caeai.2023.100152

Mohamed, Y. A., Khanan, A., Bashir, M., Mohamed, A. H. H., Adiel, M. A., & Elsadig, M. A. (2024). The impact of artificial intelligence on language translation: a review. *Ieee Access, 12*, 25553-25579. . .DOI: 10.1109/ACCESS.2024.3366802

Moneus, A. M., & Sahari, Y. (2024). Artificial intelligence and human translation: A contrastive study based on legal texts. *Heliyon, 10*(6), e28106. DOI: 10.1016/j.heliyon.2024.e28106 PMID: 38524597

Mykolas Romeris University. (2024). Generatyvinio dirbtinio intelekto įrankių naudojimo Mykolo Romerio universiteto studijų procese tvarka. Retrieved from: chrome-extension://efaidnbmnnnibpcajpcglclefindmkaj/https://www.mruni.eu/wp-content/uploads/2024/04/GDI-irankiu-naudojimo-MRU-studijose-tvarka_viesinimui.pdf

O'Hagan, M. (2016). Massively Open Translation: Unpacking the relationship between technology and translation in the 21st century. *International Journal of Communication, 10*, 929–946. https://ijoc.org/index.php/ijoc/article/view/3507/1572

Rothwell, A., Moorkens, J., Fernández-Parra, M., Drugan, J., & Austermuehl, F. (2023). *Translation Tools and Technologies*. Routledge., DOI: 10.4324/9781003160793-1

Sam, A. K., & Olbrich, P. (2023). The need for AI ethics in higher education. In *AI ethics in higher education: Insights from Africa and beyond* (pp. 3–10). Springer International Publishing. DOI: 10.1007/978-3-031-23035-6_1

Shahmerdanova, R. (2025). Artificial Intelligence in Translation: Challenges and Opportunities. *Acta Globalis Humanitatis et Linguarum*, *2*(1), 62–70. DOI: 10.69760/aghel.02500108

Shava, G. N., Hleza, S., Tlou, F., Shonhiwa, S., & Mathonsi, E. (2021). Qualitative Content Analysis, Utility, Usability and Processes in Educational Research. *International Journal of Research and Innovation in Social Science*, *5*(07), 553–558.

Slator (2024). *Language AI Briefing August 2024.*https://slator.com/language-ai-briefing-august-2024/

Song, B. (2024). What is translation cultural studies in the context of new technology? *Foreign Languages*, *47*(1), 11–14.

Soysal, F. (2023). Enhancing translation studies with artificial intelligence (AI): Challenges, opportunities, and proposals. *Karamanoğlu Mehmetbey University International Journal of Philology and Translation Studies*, *5*(2), 177–191. DOI: 10.55036/ufced.1402649

Sze Ming, L., & Sin-Wai, C. (Eds.). (2024). *Applying Technology to Language and Translation.* Routledge., DOI: 10.4324/9781003399261

University of Latvia. (2024). Guidelines for the use of artificial intelligence in the University of Ltavia. Retrieved from: chrome-extension://efaidnbmnnnibpcajpcgl-clefindmkaj/https://www.lu.lv/fileadmin/user_upload/LU.LV/www.lu.lv/Studijas/Guidelines_for_the_use_of_AI_in_the_UL_11.04.2024.v.0.1.pdf

University of Tartu. (2024). University of Tartu guidelines for using AI applications for teaching and studies. Retrieved from: https://ut.ee/en/node/151731

Urlaub, P., & Dessein, E. (2022). Machine translation and foreign language education. *Frontiers in Artificial Intelligence*, *5*, 936111. DOI: 10.3389/frai.2022.936111 PMID: 35937139

Vaswani, A., Bengio, S., Brevdo, E., Chollet, F., Gomez, A., Gouws, S., & Uszkoreit, J. (2018, March). Tensor2Tensor for Neural Machine Translation. In *Proceedings of the 13th Conference of the Association for Machine Translation in the Americas,* pp. 193-199.

Vaughn, F. C. (2023). Viability of a career in the interpretation and translation industry with the advancements of artificial intelligence. Retrieved from: chrome-extension://efaidnbmnnnibpcajpcglclefindmkaj/https://www.theseus.fi/bitstream/handle/10024/806809/Vaughn_Fernando.pdf?sequence=2

Venuti, L., & Venuti, L. (Eds.). (2021). *The Translation Studies Reader* (4th ed.). Routledge., DOI: 10.4324/9780429280641

Vieira, L. N. (2020). Machine translation in the news: A framing analysis of the written press. *Translation Spaces*, *9*(1), 98–122. DOI: 10.1075/ts.00023.nun

Vieira, L. N., O'Sullivan, C., Zhang, X., & O'Hagan, M. (2022). Machine translation in society: Insights from UK users. *Language Resources and Evaluation*. Advance online publication. DOI: 10.1007/s10579-022-09589-1

Vilnius University. (2024). Dirbtinio intelekto naudojimo Vilniaus universitete gairės. Retrieved from: chrome-extension://efaidnbmnnnibpcajpcglclefindmkaj/https://www.vu.lt/site_files/SPN-54_2024_priedas.pdf

Wang, N., & Li, M. (2024). Teachers' perceptions of the risks and benefits of AI in higher education: A case study of ERNIE Bot. *Innovations in Education and Teaching International*, •••, 1–13. DOI: 10.1080/14703297.2024.2432429

Wang, Y. (2023). Artificial Intelligence Technologies in College English Translation Teaching. *Journal of Psycholinguistic Research*, *52*(5), 1525–1544. DOI: 10.1007/s10936-023-09960-5 PMID: 37100967

Wu, M. X., & Chen, H. J. (2023). Ethical issues of machine translation in the age of artificial intelligence. *Waiguoyu*, *7*(4), 80–89.

Yang, H., & Kyun, S. (2022). The current research trend of artificial intelligence in language learning: A systematic empirical literature review from an activity theory perspective. *Australasian Journal of Educational Technology*, •••, 180–210. DOI: 10.14742/ajet.7492

Yu, J., & Liu, K. (2024). Reshaping Translation Studies: Paradigm Shifts and Future Directions in the Age of AI Technology. *Waiguoyu*, *47*(4), 72–81.

Zaghlool, Z. D. M., & Khasawneh, M. A. S. (2024). Aligning translation curricula with technological advancements; Insights from artificial intelligence researchers and language educators. *Studies in Media and Communication*, *12*(1), 58–70. DOI: 10.11114/smc.v12i1.6378

Zhao, X., & Jin, X. (2022). A comparative study of text genres in English-Chinese translation effects based on deep learning LSTM. *Journal of Chinese Linguistics, 50*(3), 287–304. DOI: 10.1177/00754242221100001 PMID: 35693269

ADDITIONAL READING

Amaro, V., & João Pires, M. (2024). Found in translation, lost in education: Artificial intelligence's impacts on translation tertiary education in Macao. *Asian Education and Development Studies, 13*(4), 269–281. DOI: 10.1108/AEDS-01-2024-0012

Arias, A. M., Fedyukovskaya, M., & Fedyukovsky, A. (2022). Challenges in Professional Translation: Implications for Linguistic Education and the Modern Digital Economy. In: Rumyantseva, A., Plotnikov, V., Minin, A., Anyigba, H. (eds) *Challenges and Solutions in the Digital Economy and Finance.* Springer Proceedings in Business and Economics. Springer, Cham. https://doi.org/DOI: 10.1007/978-3-031-14410-3_9

Chen, M. (2024). Trust, understanding, and machine translation: The task of translation and the responsibility of the translator. *AI & Society, 39*(5), 2307–2319. DOI: 10.1007/s00146-023-01681-6

Su, W. (2021). Integrating Blended Learning in Computer-Assisted Translation Course in Light of the New Liberal Arts Initiative. In Jia, W. (Eds.), Lecture Notes in Computer Science: Vol. 13089. *Emerging Technologies for Education. SETE 2021.* Springer., DOI: 10.1007/978-3-030-92836-0_37

Sun, L. (2025). Transforming business interpretation education with AI: Perspectives from instructors and learners. *Education and Information Technologies.* Advance online publication. DOI: 10.1007/s10639-024-13270-1

Trojszczak, M. (2022). Translator Training Meets Machine Translation—Selected Challenges. In Lewandowska-Tomaszczyk, B., & Trojszczak, M. (Eds.), *Language Use, Education, and Professional Contexts. Second Language Learning and Teaching*. Springer., DOI: 10.1007/978-3-030-96095-7_11

Xujun Tian, X. (2024). Personalized translator training in the era of digital intelligence: Opportunities, challenges, and prospects. *Heliyon, 10*(20), e39354. Advance online publication. DOI: 10.1016/j.heliyon.2024.e39354 PMID: 39502214

KEY TERMS AND DEFINITIONS

Translation Studies: is a multidisciplinary academic field dedicated to exploring the theory, practice, and analysis of translation. It investigates the process of conveying written or spoken content from one language (the source language) to another (the target language) while maintaining the original meaning, context, and cultural aspects.

Artificial Intelligence: (AI) refers to the branch of computer science and technology that focuses on creating systems or machines capable of performing tasks that typically require human intelligence.

Artificial Intelligence in Translation: refers to the application of AI technologies to automate, enhance, and optimize the process of translating text or speech from one language to another. It involves the use of machine learning algorithms, natural language processing, and neural networks to produce accurate and contextually appropriate translations.

Translator training: refers to the education and preparation provided to individuals to develop the skills, knowledge, and expertise necessary for professional translation. It combines theoretical knowledge of language and translation studies with practical exercises to enhance linguistic, cultural, and technical abilities.

Ethics in Translation Studies: refers to the principles and guidelines that govern the behavior, decisions, and responsibilities of translators and researchers in the field of translation. It addresses the moral and professional standards required to ensure integrity, fairness, and respect in the practice of translation and its study.

Transformative Translator Skills: refer to the advanced abilities and competencies that enable translators to not only convey meaning across languages but also add value through creativity, cultural adaptation, and critical thinking. These skills allow translators to go beyond a literal transfer of words to create impactful, culturally resonant, and contextually appropriate translations.

Curriculum: is a structured framework that outlines the educational content, learning objectives, and instructional strategies for a course, program, or field of study. It serves as a guide for educators and students, detailing what is to be taught, how it will be delivered, and the outcomes to be achieved.

Chapter 7
NLP in Action:
Enhancing Translation and Interpretation

Mohammad Ali Al-Saggaf
https://orcid.org/0000-0001-7401-0509
Xiamen University Malaysia, Malaysia

ABSTRACT

This chapter explores the transformative impact of Natural Language Processing (NLP) on translation and interpretation. It provides a comprehensive overview of NLP methodologies, including Machine Translation (MT), Speech Recognition, Text-to-Speech (TTS), and Corpus-Based Translation. The chapter highlights the advancements in Neural Machine Translation (NMT) and the integration of NLP with augmented reality (AR) for immersive interpretation experiences. It also addresses the challenges and ethical considerations in NLP, such as data privacy, bias, and fairness. By examining recent research and case studies, the chapter underscores the importance of combining NLP technologies with human expertise to achieve accurate, efficient, and culturally sensitive translations.

1. INTRODUCTION

Now, Natural Language Processing (NLP) would revolutionize translation and interpretation activities by machines understanding human language, processing, and generating it. This chapter focuses on the role of NLP in translation and interpretation and analyses these with respect to that future vision: its impact, methods employed, and future possibilities. By offering a holistic overview of how NLP technologies can improve translation in terms of accuracy, efficiency, and availability, this chapter attempts to cover the difficulties as well as ethical concerns surrounding the use

DOI: 10.4018/979-8-3373-0060-3.ch007

of NLP in such fields. NLP stands for those subparts of AI dealing with the way computers interact with the language of humans. Computational linguistics with machine learning and deep learning is, therefore, the mix that enables machines to understand and generate the natural language. Under translation and interpretation, the core functions of NLP technologies will primarily focus on machine translation (MT), speech recognition, and text-to-speech (TTS) systems.

2. BACKGROUND

2.1 Natural Language Processing (NLP)

Natural Language Processing (NLP) is a branch of artificial intelligence (AI), focusing on enabling computers to understand, interpret, and generate human language. It combines computational linguistics with machine learning and deep learning to obtain information from and analyze massive amounts of natural language data. The diverse applications of NLP include language translation, sentiment analysis, speech recognition, and text generation (IBM, 2023). NLP has undergone a lot of changes since its inception, with deep learning and neural network architectures being the prominent factors in its advancement. Recent studies show that grasping the intricacy of human language and dealing with ambiguity and contextuality will enhance NLP systems' functioning (Khurana, Koli, Khatter, & Singh, 2023).

2.2 Definition and Scope of NLP

NLP is an area of artificial intelligence (AI) that allows computers to understand, interpret, and generate human language. It combines computational linguistics with machine learning and deep learning to process and analyze huge amounts of natural language data. NLP is used in several applications, including language translation, sentiment analysis, speech recognition, and text generation (IBM, 2023). NLP encompasses a wide spectrum of tasks and applications, such as NLP techniques used in Text Processing to pre-process and analyze text data, like tokenization, stemming, lemmatization, and part-of-speech tagging (OpenGenus, 2023); in Machine Translation, NLP automatically translates text from one language into another while preserving meaning and context (Wu et al., 2016); NLP-based Speech Recognition systems transcribe spoken language in text, providing real-time interpretation and transcription (Dalayli, 2023); Text-to-Speech (TTS) NLP generates spoken language from text in support of multilingual communication and accessibility (IBM, 2023). NLP techniques in Sentiment Analysis serve to analyze text to perceive sentiment or opinion expressed, often used for social media monitoring and customer feedback analysis (Khurana et al., 2023); NLP systems in Named Entity Recognition (NER) identify and classify named entities in text such as names of individuals, locations, and organizations (OpenGenus, 2023).

3. NLP METHODOLOGIES USED IN TRANSLATION

This section will delve into the major three NLP methodologies used in translation and interpretation, namely Machine Translation (MT), Speech Recognition and Synthesis, and Corpus Linguistics. The core approaches and mechanisms for each of these three methodologies are thoroughly explored and discussed with examples and representative case studies. Analytical comparisons are drawn cross approaches and against human translator to examine their impact on the field of translation and interpretation.

3.1 Machine Translation (MT)

Machine Translation (MT) systems, such as Google Translate and DeepL, deploy statistical, rule-based, and neural approaches to synthesize one language into another. Specifically, the use of Neural Machine Translation (NMT) technology has greatly improved translation with the help of deep learning techniques (Language Science Press, 2023). Machine Translation (MT) systems such as Google Translate and DeepL rely on statistical, rule-based, and neural approaches to translate text from one language to another. Significant improvements in translation quality have been shown by Neural Machine Translation (NMT) systems through the application of deep learning techniques (Language Science Press, 2023). The use of deep learning algorithms by NMT systems creates a more holistic understanding of language. These models are trained with massive data sets that consist of bilingual text corpus for learning to recognize and predict patterns in language data. Layering and recurrent connections constitute the training process, whereby these models develop a more nuanced representation of the source and target languages. As a result, the contemporary NMT systems can produce translations that bear good naturalness, coherence, and contextual appropriateness (BeTranslated, 2023).

Recent advances in NMT research mainly include Transformer networks, which significantly improve accuracy and fluency in translation (Vaswani et al., 2017). Self-attention mechanisms in the Transformer model allow for an improvement of relations in the input and output sequences, hence leading to accurate translations (Wu et al., 2016). In a study conducted by Keles, Gunay, and Caglar (2024), they demonstrated that tailored models of NMT proved to be effective for medical translation. Since they fine-tuned small NMT models on domain-specific data, they achieved better translation quality than general purpose models and large language models: an important finding to emphasize training for domain specificity and opened the opportunity of NMT in specialized fields. Another such study was done by Wan et al. (2022), which takes into consideration the issues related to NMT for short texts, exposing problems such as over-translation and mistranslation. Some suggestions made in the study to improve translation quality for short sequences include balancing data distribution and adding contextual information (Wan et al., 2022).

3.1.1 Statistical Machine Translation (SMT)

Statistical machine translation relies on a statistical model whose parameters are estimated from the analyses of bilingual textual corpora. The probability that a string in the target language constitutes the translation of a string in the source language is the mantra of SMT (Ahammad et al., 2024). Recent studies have supported SMT, as Shaik (2025) used curriculum learning and semi-supervised training to improve SMT performance by giving rise to more accurate translation (Shaik, 2025). On the other end of the spectrum, Marie et al. (2021) carried out work to ameliorate SMT performance of low-resource languages through transfer learning and data augmentation methods, improving translation quality decidedly (Marie et al., 2021). Assessing the meta-evaluation performed by Marie et al. (2021) on 769 papers about MT, the importance of rigorous evaluation practice and the immediate necessity of standardized metrics to bring credibility to SMT studies were underlined (Marie et al., 2021).

Statistical machine translation can be fully understood by going through its two major concept models: the language model, which deals with the target language and assesses the probabilities of strings made up of sequences of words, ensuring that grammatically correct and fluent translations are generated, and the translation model, which deals with the source language and assesses the probability that a sequence of words in the source language translates itself into a sequence of words in the target language at the level of phrases. To better show the workings of this model, some examples from other languages will be presented.

French to English Translation: Consider translating the French sentence “Le chat mange une pomme” to English. The SMT system would use a language model to ensure the English sentence is grammatically correct and a translation model to align the French words with their English counterparts. The system might generate the translation “The cat eats an apple” based on the highest probability distribution (Koehn, 2020). *Chinese to English Translation*: Translating the Chinese sentence “ ” to English, an SMT system would analyze the sentence structure and word probabilities to generate the translation “He likes to eat apples” (Wu et al., 2016). *Spanish to German Translation*: For the Spanish sentence “Ella está leyendo un libro," an SMT system would use phrase-based translation to produce the German sentence "Sie liest ein Buch," ensuring grammatical correctness and contextual accuracy (Ahammad et al., 2024). *Arabic to English Translation*: For the Arabic sentence " ," an SMT system would analyze the sentence structure and word probabilities to generate the translation "The child is playing in the garden" (Reverso Context, 2023).

As we can see from the above discussion and examples, SMT can handle large vocabularies and produce fluent translations by leveraging extensive bilingual corpora. It is also adaptable to new language pairs and domains with sufficient training data. However, SMT struggles with rare words and out-of-vocabulary terms. It may also produce translations that lack coherence and context, especially for longer sentences (Ahammad et al., 2024).

These advantages and limitations of SMT can be further illustrated when referring to some case studies like the case study on sign language SMT explored the methodologies and technologies involved in translating sign languages to and from spoken languages, highlighting the challenges and successes in this niche area (SpringerLink, 2023). Hardmeier (2012) conducted a detailed investigation on the translation of anaphoric pronouns in SMT, providing insights into the discourse-related challenges and solutions in statistical translation (Hardmeier, 2012). Another case study by Sreelekha (2017) compared SMT and RBMT systems for English-Indian language translation, revealing the strengths and weaknesses of both approaches in handling linguistic nuances and cultural context (Sreelekha, 2017).

3.1.2 Rule-Based Machine Translation (RBMT)

Rule-Based Machine Translation (RBMT) is a traditional method that employs linguistic knowledge of both source and target languages into machine translation. The RBMT systems depend on dictionaries, grammars, and rules candidates to represent semantically, morphologically, and syntactically the structure both languages. (Coleman et al., 2024).

Meanwhile, recent studies focused on the packing and evaluation of RBMT. Coleman et al. (2024) introduced LLM-Assisted RBMT for low-resource languages with details on significant improvement in the translation quality of languages with reasonably low amounts of data (Coleman et al., 2024). Another related exploration on RBMT is Paul (2023), who reviewed the impacts of such a mechanism upon technical domains, emphasizing its rule-based benefits in the translation of highly technical documents with high accuracy (Paul, 2023). Binu Paul, in a review in 2023, also described the developments in machine translation from being rule-based to being neural, laying emphasis on the aspect of its relevance within multilingual contexts and its gradual fusion with contemporary techniques (Paul, 2023).

The key concepts to RBMT are Direct Translation, Transfer-Based, and Interlingual Translation, the three major approaches to RBMT. The Direct Translation approach entails word-to-word mapping using bilingual dictionaries and uncomplicated rules from the source language into the target form. Hence, the Transfer-Based translates in three stages: analysis of the source language, transfer of the source language syntactic structure to the target language, and generation of the sentence in the target language. Whereas, from the source language, he translates into an intermediate representation called 'interlingua'; this representation is converted into the target language.

These approaches can be illustrated by referring to some examples from different languages. *English to German Translation*: Consider translating the English sentence "A girl eats an apple" to German. An RBMT system would use dictionaries to map each English word to its German counterpart and apply grammatical rules to generate the German sentence "Ein Mädchen isst einen Apfel" (FlowGent AI, 2023). *Japanese to English Translation*: Translating the Japanese sentence " " to English, an RBMT system would analyze the sentence structure and apply rules to produce the translation "He is reading a book" (Reverie Inc., 2024). *French to Spanish Translation*: For the French sentence "Elle aime les fleurs," an RBMT system would use linguistic rules to generate the Spanish sentence "Ella ama las flores," ensuring grammatical accuracy and semantic consistency (Summa Linguae, 2024). *Arabic to English Translation*: For the Arabic sentence " ," an RBMT system would use dictionaries and grammatical rules to produce the English sentence "The child is playing in the garden" (Reverso Context, 2023).

3.1.3 Hybrid Machine Translation (HMT)

Hybrid Machine Translation (HMT) combines multiple machine translation approaches within a single system to improve translation accuracy and fluency. The motivation for developing hybrid systems stems from the limitations of individual techniques in achieving satisfactory translation quality (Omniscien Technologies, 2023).

To embark on HMT, the key approaches need to be addressed first. *Multi-Engine* approach involves running multiple machine translation systems in parallel and combining their outputs. For example, a system might use both SMT and RBMT subsystems to generate translations and then select the best output based on predefined criteria (Omniscien Technologies, 2023). *Statistical Rule Generation* is another approach uses statistical data to generate lexical and syntactic rules, which are then applied as if they were part of an RBMT system. This method attempts to avoid the labor-intensive process of manually creating linguistic rules (Omniscien Technologies, 2023). *Multi-Pass* approach involves serially processing the input multiple times. For example, an RBMT system might preprocess the input, and the output is then refined by an SMT system. This technique reduces the complexity of the translation task and improves overall quality (Omniscien Technologies, 2023).

These approaches are further illustrated in the following examples. *English to Spanish Translation:* A hybrid system might first use an RBMT approach to translate a legal document, ensuring high precision and consistency. The output is then refined using SMT to improve fluency and handle idiomatic expressions, resulting in the Spanish sentence "Un documento legal traducido con precisión" (Omniscien Technologies, 2023). *Chinese to French Translation:* For the Chinese sentence " ," a hybrid system might use SMT to generate an initial translation and then apply RBMT rules to refine the output, producing the French sentence "Il aime manger des pommes" (Wikipedia, 2023). *German to Japanese Translation*: Translating the German sentence "Sie liest ein Buch," a hybrid system might use RBMT for initial translation and SMT for refinement, resulting in the Japanese sentence " " (Omniscien Technologies, 2023). *Arabic to English Translation*: For the Arabic sentence " ," a hybrid system might use SMT to generate an initial translation and then apply RBMT rules to refine the output, producing the English sentence "The child is playing in the garden" (Reverso Context, 2023).

It is very evident that hybrid systems would produce better translations by harnessing the strengths of various approaches. They are also flexible and adaptable to meet various domain and language pair requirements. However, hybrid systems may be rather complex in concept and implementation, with careful integration of the various components involved. These systems are likely to be more resource-intensive than single-approach systems (Omniscien Technologies, 2023).

3.1.4 Neural Machine Translation (NMT)

Neural Machine Translation (NMT) is an approach to machine translation that uses artificial neural networks to predict the likelihood of a sequence of words, typically modeling entire sentences in a single integrated model. NMT has become the dominant approach in machine translation due to its ability to produce high-quality translations that rival human translations under certain conditions (Vaswani et al., 2017).

Likewise, NMT has key concepts that need to be highlighted. *Encoder-Decoder Architecture* NMT models typically use an encoder-decoder architecture. The encoder processes the input sentence and converts it into a fixed-length vector representation. The decoder then generates the output sentence word by word, using the encoded representation and the previously generated words (Sutskever et al., 2014). *Attention Mechanism*: The attention mechanism allows the model to focus on different parts of the input sentence while generating each word of the output sentence. This helps the model handle long sentences and improves translation quality (Bahdanau et al., 2015). *Transformer Model:* The Transformer model, introduced by Vaswani et al. (2017), replaces the recurrent layers in traditional NMT models with self-attention mechanisms. This allows for more parallelization and improves the efficiency and accuracy of the translation process (Vaswani et al., 2017).

These approaches are further illustrated in the following examples. *English to French Translation*: Consider translating the English sentence "The cat is on the mat" to French. An NMT system using the Transformer model would encode the input sentence into a vector representation and then decode it to generate the French sentence "Le chat est sur le tapis" (Vaswani et al., 2017). *Spanish to English Translation*: Translating the Spanish sentence "Ella está leyendo un libro" to English, an NMT system would use the attention mechanism to focus on relevant parts of the input sentence and generate the translation "She is reading a book" (Wu et al., 2016). *Chinese to English Translation*: For the Chinese sentence " ," an NMT system would encode the input sentence and use the decoder to generate the English sentence "He likes to eat apples" (Wu et al., 2016). *Arabic to English Translation*: For the Arabic sentence " ," an NMT system would use the encoder-decoder architecture to produce the English sentence "The child is playing in the garden" (Reverso Context, 2023).

Evaluative of SMT, RBMT, HMT, NMT & Human Translators

Statistical Machine Translation (SMT), Rule-Based Machine Translation (RBMT), Hybrid Machine Translation (HMT), and Neural Machine Translation (NMT) collectively define an individual methodology with various strengths and limitations in machine translation. SMT can map a general model learning based on analysis of large bilingual corpora, the identification of statistical patterns and their probabilities to translate. However, this is a paradigm that works for languages much rich in data because it faces a frequently serious deficit in performance for rare words and idiomatic expressions (Lopez, 2008). On the other hand, the RBMT uses lexical, syntactic, and semantic predefined grammatical rules and dictionaries into which the words are roped to translate a text. This leads to high accuracy for some specified language pairs and domains. Its major limitation is the labor cost involved in defining and maintaining these rules, which makes it less scalable and adaptable to new languages or domains (Torregrosa et al., 2019).

HMT is a machine translation (MT) approach that combines the advantages of both SMT and RBMT in that there is a statistical method applied to a massive number of data but grammar-wise and consistency-wise it will be a rule-based approach to the translation part of it. Providing such an excellent solution is not free from complexity in implementation and maintenance (Costa-jussà & Rapp, 2016). The more recent form is Neural Machine Translation (NMT), which uses deep learning models trained with high performance to capture the context and nuance of a language, producing generally fluent and natural translations. Though NMT exceeds at handling idiomatic expressions and long-range dependencies, it also needs heavy computational resources and huge training datasets (Bahdanau, Cho, & Bengio, 2016). Indeed, even while RBMT and SMT have built the foundation for modern machine translation, it is HMT and NMT that have taken the field leaps and bounds ahead in terms of pretty accurate and contextually sensitive translations. In my opinion, NMT is likely the most hopeful type, simply because it produces its translation on the model of humanly quality translations but requires vast resources and great dependence on data.

Machine translation technologies, such as SMT, RBMT, HMT, or NMT, have advanced tremendously in the quest for improved translation accuracies and efficiencies; however, they have not been able to match human translators in certain other respects. Human translators know very well how to recreate cultural subtleties, idiomatic meanings, and those context-dependent motivations that machines have a difficult time capturing. Where machines fail, humans can interpret the subtleties of tone, humor, and emotion so that a translated piece hits the right chord with the audience. Human translators also provide individualized and creative translations that tailor fit a client's specifics when appropriate; this is a level of personalization that MT finds very hard to match. No doubt, human translators shall continue playing a vital role in those communications or documents that demand a higher level of accuracy, cultural sensitivity, and context-related understanding. The combination of those strengths from both MT and professional human translators would derive the most effective and interesting translations.

3.2 Speech Recognition and Synthesis

NLP (natural language processing) is a technology that helps speech recognition systems convert spoken language into text in real-time. Speech recognition systems utilize sophisticated algorithms to extract audio signals and recognize speech patterns. TTS, on the other hand, converts text into spoken language to aid communication among various languages. Such TTS systems are critical in automated customer service, language teaching projects, or accessibility tools for users suffering from blindness (IBM, 2023).

The development of speech recognition obviously emerged in tandem with NLP techniques. Today, our speech recognition systems can accurately transcribe spoken language in almost real-time; hence, they are particularly useful in live interpretation and transcription services. TTS systems identify the text and conversationally transform it into intelligible speech in potentially multiple languages, thereby contributing positively to increasing the accessibility and usability of digital content (Dalayli, 2023)

Recent research has shown that the currently developed systems are in dire need of contextual awareness and idiomatic understanding (Thompson, 2024). In addition, it became possible to construct a more advanced TTS system that can create speech with a high degree of naturalness and expressiveness due to a range of recent advances in deep learning (Devlin et al., 2019).

3.2.1 Text-to-Speech (TTS):

TTS systems convert written text into spoken language with the use of techniques from speech synthesis. They find an important place in applications necessitating auditory output, for instance, screen readers, language learning tools, and voice-enabled devices (BeTranslated, 2023). Like any model, TTS has several important concepts that need to be understood, such as Concatenative TTS. This technique is the most widely used TTS method, making complete utterances by concatenating pre-recorded speech segments (phonemes, syllables, words). It produces highly natural speech but requires a large database (Chowdhury & Hussan, 2023). The other coinage is Formant Synthesis. It generates speech through a simulation of the human vocal tract. It possesses great flexibility with respect to possible voice generations but tends to sound artificial (Chowdhury & Hussan, 2023). Another one is Statistical Parametric TTS. With this technique, statistical models generate parameters describing the speech, and the parameters are then converted to speech waveforms. This method is good at balancing the level of naturalness and flexibility in TTS (Chowdhury & Hussan, 2023). Neural TTS refers to deep learning approaches that produce high-quality natural speech with expressive variations. Models like WaveNet and Tacotron are some of the advanced systems in TTS (Xie et al., 2024).

From those concepts and outlines, you can realize this application to translate languages on many online platforms. For the English voice, Google's WaveNet provides TTS voices that sound highly natural, and are exploited by Google Assistant, Google Maps (Google Cloud, 2025). For Mandarin Chinese, iFlytek's TTS system is widely used in educational tools and smart devices in China (iFlytek, 2025). For TTS voices in Spanish, Amazon Polly is the TTS engine for use in Alexa applications (Amazon Web Services, 2025). And of course, this is true with respect to Japanese: NTT Docomo's TTS system is employed in multiple Japanese navigation systems and customer service solutions (NTT Docomo, 2025).

TTS presents an array of advantages, and of course, it bears some disadvantages, just like any other NLP translation route. Benefits include: Accessibility: TTS enables digital content accessibility for the visually impaired and those with reading difficulties. Convenience: It allows for hands-free content consumption while driving or multitasking (PrimeGroupUSA, 2023) as a big plus. TTS affords language learners opportunities to practice pronunciation and listening comprehension (RF

Wireless World, 2023). On the flip side, disadvantages for TTS go on to include: Lesser Comprehension: TTS listeners might not comprehend as much information as when reading. Limited Application: Many complex diagrams or graphics just cannot be conveyed well using TTS (PrimeGroupUSA, 2023). Naturalness: Some of the synthesized speech, regardless of improvements, still lacks the naturalness of human speech (RF Wireless World, 2023). In several case studies and recent research findings, the advantages and disadvantages of TTS are highlighted. Research has shown that one of the breakthroughs that revolutionized TTS is Google WaveNet, which generates output in a manner sufficiently resembling human voices using deep neural networks to synthesize the input. This is utilized in Google Assistant and Google Maps, for interaction with natural and engaging voice proposals (Google Cloud, 2025). The Chinese educational tools are those furthered with the application of iFlytek TTS systems in helping students in pronunciation and listening. With its capability to generate accurate and natural-sounding Mandarin speech, the system has become a must-have in any language-learning toolkit (iFlytek, 2025). Supporting Alexa with TTS technology to converse naturally in many languages has made user experience better and reach wider with Amazon Polly (Amazon Web Services, 2025). And last, NTT Docomo's TTS is utilized by Japanese navigation to effectively give by voice clear and precise spoken instructions, thus enhancing Japanese navigation devices' usability (NTT Docomo, 2025).

3.2.2 Automatic Speech Recognition (ASR)

Automatic Speech Recognition (ASR) systems use language models, pronunciation dictionaries, and acoustic models to transcribe spoken language into text. Some typical applications of ASR technology are virtual assistants, transcription services, and real-time interpretation (BeTranslated, 2023).

The following are the key models for ASR. 1. Hidden Markov Models (HMMs): HMMs are statistical models that represent the probabilities of sequences of observed events, for example phonemes in speech. They are widely used in ASR and usually in the decades (Rabiner, 2023). 2. Deep Neural Networks (DNNs): Deep neural networks such as convolutional neural networks and recurrent neural networks have significantly improved the ASR quality concerning their capability to learn very complex audio patterns for data (Hinton et al., 2023). 3. Transformer Models: Transformative models, that is, BERT and GPT, have transformed language modeling through their facilitation of parallel processing and by capturing long-range dependency across text input (Vaswani et al., 2023). 4. End-to-End ASR: End-to-end models, including Deep Speech and Whisper, simplify the ASR pipeline by directly mapping audio features with text, which is performed through a single neural network (Hannun et al., 2024).

Many of the applications of ASRs are focused applications that are of much relevance to diverse businesses and firms. These applications take on several types which may include 1. Voice Assistants: ASR is put into action in voice assistants such as Amazon Alexa, Google Assistant, and Apple's Siri so that the user command is understood and acted upon (Shaip, 2024). 2. Transcription Services: This refers to by ASR, which transforms what has been spoken during meetings, interviews, or lectures into written text (Simon Says AI, 2023). 3. Customer Support: ASR is used by automated customer service systems to manage inquiries and provide information (Shaip, 2024). 4. Healthcare: ASR helps with medical record-keeping activities by documenting the notes from doctors and patient conversations (Shaip, 2024).

The same goes for ASR. The advantages of ASR surely have their fast lane, but what also comes alongside these advantages are limitations. ASR encompasses some of the key advantages: 1. Efficiency: ASR provides fast speech-to-text conversion process making transcription and voice commands efficient and timely ways of doing things (Shaip, 2024). 2. Accessibility: ASR technology makes digital content accessible to persons with disabilities, such as people with hearing impairment (Simon Says AI, 2023), and 3. Multitasking: ASR frees the hands of users, and as such, it is useful in driving or cooking (Shaip, 2024). But it still remains a bucketful of concerns, along some of the limitations such as speech disfluency, accuracy in a noisy environment, and multilingual issues are always associated with ASR. It takes a great deal of training data and even more elaborate models to deal with several languages and dialects (Katkov et.al,2025). Generally, ASR engines have problems with background noise and other types of acoustic interference, which in turn result in errors in transcription (Katkov et.al,2025). In addition, natural speech is characterized by the presence of disfluencies such as pauses and fillers that can mislead ASR systems (Southwell et al., 2024).

TTS, ASR & Human Translators

Text-to-Speech (TTS) and Automatic Speech Recognition (ASR) are technologies that are complementary to each other and play important roles in human computer interaction. TTS systems convert written text to spoken language using different techniques such as concatenative synthesis, formant synthesis, and synthesis based on neural networks for producing a more natural sounding speech (Kumar, Koul, & Singh, 2023). An ASR system analyzes an audio signal as the input, while the output is a textual transcription, accomplished using acoustic and language models for recognizing speech patterns (Hinton et al., 2023). The main agenda behind the TTS process is from text to speech; the opposite is the case for the ASR process. Both technologies, however, have advanced by leaps and bound with the advent of deep learning in the areas of accuracy and naturalness. Yet, challenges are still persistent in such things as the diversity of accents, background noise, and data sparsity where huge amounts of data are required for training systems.

If these were compared with a human translator, both speed and efficiency would be the core advantages of TTS and ASR systems, which contribute to their use for real-time applications such as virtual assistants or automated customer service (Shaip, 2024). On the contrary, human translators are much more able than machines in understanding context and cultural nuances or idioms (Berman & Tyyskä, 2011). They can adapt the translation according to different specific needs and preferences an individual may have, bringing personalization and creativity in the area beyond TTS and ASR. Although these two technologies - TTS and ASR - continue to advance, best output and success in translation remains when human translators are used to finally refine the work.

3.3. Corpus Linguistics

Analysing and modelling language patterns is achieved by using large corpora in NLP to enhance the translation and interpretation of languages for the systems. When studying language through large collections of texts, called corpora, corpus linguistics can analyze this corpus and help gain from the linguistic rules and patterns that improve NLP's performance in translating or interpreting (Language Science Press, 2023).

Corpus linguistics enables improved understanding of the structure and use of languages. This way, NLP can tackle various linguistic phenomena. The use of big data ensures that NLP models can identify and learn from the patterns of use in a language, resulting in more accurate and contextually appropriate translations. Such use takes care of idiomatic expressions, cultural references, and other difficult aspects of language (Khurana et al., 2023). Recent research has pointed out the importance of training NLP models with varied and representative corpora so that they would generalize accurately across linguistic variation and context (Thompson, 2024). Furthermore, data augmentation has led to more powerful and generalizable NLP models (Luong, Pham, and Manning, 2015).

3.3.1 Corpus-Based Translation (CBT)

NLP systems contribute to the enhancement of translation accuracy by analyzing patterns and correlations between the two languages by processing large bilingual corpora. Domain-specific translations benefit significantly from this, where specialized terminology abounds (Khurana et al., 2023). Corpus-based translation does exactly this by employing large bilingual corpora to identify patterns and correlations between the languages, hence improving the translation accuracy.

The Corpus-Based Translation contains important concepts and methods relevant to say about. For instance, 1. Translation Universals: Linguistics features that will find a place in any translated text, irrespective of the language pair across which the translation is being carried out are the translation universals. The translation universals spoke of include simplification, explicitation, and normalization (Baker, 1993); 2. Translator Style: The translator's unique style should be visible through corpus-based research, such as his or her choice of words or perception of syntactic structure (Gao & Zhou, 2024). 3. Translation Norms: Conventions and expectations informing the translation practice and why corpus analysis would be of aid in discerning these norms and how they validated themselves through their translation (Laviosa, 2021). 4. Parallel Corpora: Texts aligned at the sentence or paragraph level in two or more languages and important for the training and evaluation of translation models (Vasheghani Farahani & Dastjerdi, 2021).

There are now visible applications of Corpus-Based Translation across a wide array of domains ranging from medicine to law to even literary translation. For Medical Translation-The medical translations act to ensure terminology and regulatory assurance applied in translating medical documents using specialized medical corpora (Laviosa, 2021); while in Legal Translation- Legal translation has helped in ensuring legal documents maintain accuracy and consistency of interpretation (Vasheghani Farahani & Dastjerdi, 2021). A technical manual-Furnishing corpus-based translation offers adherence to the subject (-Laviosa, 2021). In the literary style-By way of literary corpus studies, they put to good use the exercise of capturing salient stylistic features of the original in the translation, thus guaranteeing its lasting literary worth (Gao & Zhou, 2024).

CBT is used for becoming more accurate, consistent, and efficient. Corpus-based models focus on large datasets and subsequently enhance accuracy during translations. These models help maintain terminology and style consistent, which is essential in domain-specific translations (Vasheghani Farahani & Dastjerdi, 2021). In addition, automated translation applying corpora is quick relative to that done on the manual side; hence suitable for large-scale projects (Laviosa, 2021). However, there are limitations; Translation quality relies on that and size of corpus that would be employed in the training live (Laviosa, 2021). Corpus-based models will face challenges in understanding texts within domains poorly represented in training data (Vasheghani Farahani & Dastjerdi, 2021). Context and the cultural factors of the meaning of the source text are sometimes difficult to capture, especially where source text idiomatic expressions and culturally specific references are concerned (Gao & Zhou, 2024).

CBT has a wide scope of application such as in the major project European Union Translation Services. Parallel huge corpuses with the EU serve to translate the legislative documents into different languages, thus ensuring consistency and accuracy across the member states (Laviosa, 2021). Another project is that of a multilingual corpus provided by UNESCO in the form of a multilingual corpus that would accommodate translation for educational and cultural materials. This corpus ensures the quality and consistency of translated content across languages (Vasheghani Farahani & Dastjerdi, 2021). The most preferred among free online translation platforms Google Translate; uses massive parallel corpora to train its neural machine translation models. By so doing, high-quality translation can be done in many languages and domains (Laviosa, 2021). Even Literary Translation of Mencius is corpus-based study English translations of Mencius substantiated different stylistic choices exercised by various translators, stressing importance of translator's style in literary translation (Gao & Zhou, 2024).

3.3.2 Language Modeling

The language models trained on huge amounts of data can also predict the possible word sequences. Hence, they serve as significant help in processing translation, speech recognition, and text generation (Khurana et al., 2023). By training models on large corpora to predict sequences of words, it is possible to model language. Language modeling is an essential aspect of learning key concepts and approaches. N-grams, however, are contiguous sequences of n items from a sample text. They predict the next item within a sequence based on the previous n-1 items (Jurafsky & Martin, 2023).

Recurrent Neural Networks are neura l networks that are designed to think in terms of a sequence of data. It maintains a hidden state that recalls prior tokens in the sequence (Hochreiter & Schmidhuber, 1997). Long Short-Term Memory is an RNN that learns a long-term dependency in data. It has gates to control the information passing through which represents it as one of the effective models for language modeling (Hochreiter & Schmidhuber, 1997). These self-attention Transformers are models like BERT and GPT. They allow parallel processing and are capable of understanding long-range dependencies, thus revolutionizing language modeling (Vaswani et al., 2023).

It also has excellent examples of applications of Language Modeling such as Machine Translation. For instance, machine translation language models predict the most likely translation of any given text by taking into consideration the context and structure of both the source and target languages (Brown et al., 2020). Language models also transfer spoken language into text through transcription by predicting the most probable word sequences from audio input in speech recognition (Hinton et al., 2023). Regarding Text Generation, language models can indeed generate text coherently and relevantly based on the given context, hence their application in chatbots, content production, and automated writing (Brown et al., 2020).

The contextual awareness, flexibility, and scalability characteristic of language modeling are highly cherished. Language models can observe context and meaning concerning a word sequence to be able to make better predictions (Vaswani et al., 2023). The arsenal of NLP tasks on which such models can be deployed includes translation and text generation (Brown et al., 2020). The modern language models are made used with a great chunk of conflicting datasets and are therefore flexible in that they suit numerous applications (Vaswani et al., 2023).

However, there come some severe limitations with it as well. This includes Data Dependency, Computational Resources, and Bias and Fairness. Language models dearly rely on the size and quality of their training dataset for good performance (Jurafsky & Martin, 2023). In the training of large language models, a hefty computational cost and input of resources must be invested (Brown et al., 2020). Language models can absorb and manifest biases introduced in the training data, resulting in bias_predictions and outputs (Jurafsky & Martin, 2023).

Yet the language-modelling concept is still regarded as one that has yielded a lot of good output through mega-scale digital projects such as The OpenAI GPT-3, which is the state-of-the-art language model developed by OpenAI. The model has gained astronomical recognition and applications, including chatbots and content and code generation. Its ability to produce human text has made it widely used in major industries (Brown et al., 2020). Another such project is Google BERT. BERT (Bidirectional Encoder Representations from Transformers) is a language model distinctively engineered by Google. It has scored better in many NLP tasks-from question answering to sentiment analysis-by analyzing the context of words in a sentence (Devlin et al., 2019). Another similar case is that of Facebook's RoBERTa. RoBERTa (Robustly optimized BERT approach) is an optimized version of the BERT model developed by Facebook. RoBERTa has been used to achieve state-of-the-art results on various NLP benchmarks by training on larger datasets and employing more robust training methods (Liu et al., 2019). Microsoft Turing-NLG is also a language model from Microsoft. This has been utilized for tasks like summarization, translation, and text generation. With its capability to do large-scale language tasks, this model has been an effective tool for several applications (Rosset et al., 2020).

CBT, Language Modeling & Human Translators

Language Modeling and Corpus-Based Translation form two of the most significant pillars in natural language processing. Language Modeling trains models on large corpora to predict the likelihood of word sequences and supports such applications as machine translation, speech recognition, and text generation (Jurafsky & Martin, 2023). To model the statistical properties of language and predict the next word in a sequence, n-grams, Recurrent Neural Networks (RNNs), Long Short-Term Memory networks (LSTM), and Transformer models are used (Vaswani et al., 2023). Conversely, Corpus-Based Translation uses large bilingual corpora to identify patterns and relationships across languages to enhance the translations' accuracy. This is especially true in cases like domain-focused translations, wherein translation involves specific terminologies in large amounts (Laviosa, 2021). Translation models can thus be trained from corpus analysis to predict the most probable translation of a given input, thereby ensuring an accurate and contextually appropriate rendered text (Vasheghani Farahani & Dastjerdi, 2021).

On one hand, Language Modeling and Corpus-Based Translation offer speed and effectiveness in comparison to human translators, which makes them beneficial for real-time applications or large-scale translation (Calvo-Ferrer, 2023). Human translators, on the other hand, manifest a degree of supremacy when discussing cultural nuances, idiomatic expressions, or contextual knowledge; understanding which is a challenge to machines (Berman & Tyyskä, 2011). A deep understanding of human translators concerning the shades of tone, humor, and emotions concerned with the audience will be bearing this extra advantage. Hence, they will be able to modify translations in accordance with particular requirements or preferences rather than simply providing one or two existing standard options. With this consideration of extra personalization and creativity-in-flexibility, any machine model finds it hard to imitate. Therefore, for practical good translations of the highest quality and contextually appropriate translation, Language Modeling and Corpus-Based Translation remain to improve when used together along with a human translator.

4. IMPACT AND APPLICATIONS

Natural Language Processing (NLP) has significantly impacted the translation and interpretation industry by improving accuracy, enhancing efficiency, and facilitating multilingual communication. This section delves into these impacts and explores various applications of NLP technologies.

4.1 Improving Accuracy

Accuracy, in fact, has been one of the major benefits of the application of NLP into translation and interpretation. More advanced algorithms associated with NLP minimize errors in translation and ensure fidelity, thus making the translated output on the source language meanings and nuances (Wu et al., 2016). Neural Machine Translation (NMT) systems, for example, have been quite impressive in rendering complex sentences and idiomatic expressions. NMT models have captured very deep linguistic patterns using deep learning paradigms so that they understand and translate much more naturally within contexts (Vaswani et al., 2017). Recent research indicates that context and the polysemy issue are of utmost importance in achieving greater accuracy in translation (Koehn, 2020). Also, considerable advances in transfer learning as well as pre-trained language models such as BERT and GPT have elevated the accuracy of NLP systems for translation tasks (Devlin et al., 2019). Google's NMT has transformed the quality of translations greatly through its deep neural network that makes the context of sentences understood before translating into accurate correspondence (Wu et al., 2016). DeepL's translation service is also said to deliver translations of remarkable quality that may exceed many other MT systems (BeTranslated, 2023).

4.2 Enhancing Efficiency

In recent years, NLP technologies have largely improved processes of translation and interpretation. Automation thereby saves time and resources while making translation and interpretation services more accessible and affordable. It works, for example, by Machine Translation (MT) systems, which can translate vast amounts of text in no time, participating in the reduction of the time involvement of human translation (BeTranslated, 2023).

The blend of speech recognition and synthesis leads to real-time interpretation, with instantaneous two-way communication on the other side of the language barrier. Such systems find themselves particularly helpful in situations like international conferences, customer service, and emergency response contexts when accurate and timely interpretation is fundamental (Dalayli, 2023). A specific example is the application of NLP to customer service chatbots that allow businesses to deliver instant support to customers in different languages, thus enhancing customer satisfaction and reducing operational costs (Thompson, 2024). In the medical field, NLP systems can assist by translating medical documents and interpreting interactions with patients to ensure that non-native speakers are accurately informed in a timely manner on medical matters (Khurana et al., 2023)..

4.3 Facilitating Multilingual Communication

NLP technologies bridge language barriers, enabling effective communication in diverse linguistic contexts. By providing accurate and efficient translation and interpretation services, NLP systems facilitate multilingual communication in various domains, including business, education, healthcare, and government (Khurana et al., 2023).

For instance, NLP-powered chatbots and virtual assistants can interact with users in multiple languages, providing personalized and contextually relevant responses. These applications enhance user experience and accessibility, particularly for non-native speakers (Thompson, 2024). In the education sector, language learning apps like Duolingo use NLP to provide personalized feedback and practice exercises, helping users learn new languages more effectively. These apps analyze user input to identify areas for improvement and adapt the learning experience accordingly (Devlin et al., 2019).

5. CHALLENGES AND ETHICAL CONSIDERATIONS

Despite its advancements, NLP in translation and interpretation faces several challenges, including data privacy, bias and fairness, and ethical use. Each of these areas presents unique issues that must be addressed to ensure the responsible development and deployment of NLP technologies.

5.1 Data Privacy

Personal data has so many serious concerns when used for training in an NLP model. This is mainly because, for proper functioning of any NLP system, it needs to process so much data which involves very sensitive nature personal information - such as private communications, medical records, or financial data, making it imperative to keep this information private from unauthorized access or misuse. Various approaches have recently emerged from research in privacy-preserving techniques, for example, differential privacy which introduces random noise into a particular data set to hide the identities of individuals while still being useful for overall dataset usage (Liu et al., 2024). Differential privacy has shown high success in striking a balance between data utility and privacy as it has proved to be superior to conventional methods like data anonymization and homomorphic encryption as far as computational efficiency and scalability are concerned (Liu et al., 2024).

A prominent case study with respect to this field is the research work by Yermilov et al. (2023) that explores the extent to which pseudonymization methods can deter privacy breaches while still offering NLP model applicability. Such techniques were a part of the investigation into various pseudonymization options, from rule-based substitutions to fully piggybacking on pre-trained large language learning models (LLMs) over other tasks such as text classification and summarization. The study provided information regarding the balance between protection of data and performance of the model so that it concludes that there is a need for high-quality anonymization techniques to ensure privacy and utility (Yermilov et al., 2023).

5.2 Bias and Fairness

Translation into a different language may be unfair or inaccurate according to the bias manifested by the training data behind such NLP systems. Sources of bias include data selection, algorithm design, and result interpretation, among many others. Forms of biases due to these factors range from gender bias, racial bias, and then cultural bias, which could carry significant social ramifications. Some of the recent works done in this regard include analysis of coming up with detection, mitigation, and fairness evaluation techniques to address and answer the observed biases in NLP (Gallegos et al., 2024). For instance, use of counterfactual data augmentation and adversarial training has made it possible to reduce gender bias in the machine translation models (Savoldi et al., 2021).

A comprehensive case study was undertaken by Savoldi et al. (2021), which analyzed the gender bias of machine translation systems. The findings of the researching indicated that such systems tend to reinforce gender stereotypes by translating gender-neutral sentences into gendered ones, in accordance with the underlying social biases in the training data. To this effect, counterfactual data augmentation was employed, wherein synthetic examples were created that question the biases of the model, while adversarial training secures the model against biased inputs within the training corpus. Results confirmed a significant reduction in gender bias, thus serving as very promising proof techniques for fairness in NLP (Savold)..

5.3 Ethical Use

Ensuring the ethical use of NLP technologies in sensitive contexts, such as legal or medical interpretation, is paramount. NLP systems deployed in these areas must adhere to strict ethical standards to avoid potential harm. This includes ensuring accuracy, transparency, and accountability in the system's outputs. Ethical considerations also involve respecting user autonomy and obtaining informed consent when processing personal data. Recent research has emphasized the importance of integrating ethical principles into the design and deployment of NLP systems, advocating for frameworks that prioritize user rights and societal well-being (Vida et al., 2023).

Ethical issues in health care applications of NLP are paramount and will concern valuable privacy concerns of patients, that of issues such as patient privacy-database security. Some techniques such as differential privacy and federated learning would provide security for patient data while developing adequate NLP models, as shown in Liu et al. (2024). Additionally, training NLP models on uneven and biased data exposes each individual to possible bias and unequal health care outcomes. Very specifically, there is a need to ensure that trained or pretrained systems would have equal and diverse datasets for accurate processing, given above (Gallegos et al., 2024). Another example of privacy-preserving NLP in healthcare is federated learning being applicable to medical NLP applications. Federated learning allows models to be trained from decentralized data sources in the absence of a transfer of sensitive data to a central server. This approach has been deployed successfully among various healthcare platforms while taking care of patient privacy but increasing accuracy in the medical NLP models (Liu et al., 2024).

Accuracy and fairness are essentials in NLP when it comes to legal interpretation. Misreading or misinterpretation can have grave legal consequences. Transparency and explainability of the NLP models using can also amplify its tenor of trust in these systems, eliminating potential rejection by the end-user. Eliminating bias in these legal NLP applications is necessary towards equal treatment across the demographic divides (Savoldi et al., 2021). Bias Mitigation in Legal NLP, a study by Savoldi et al. (2021) concerning the gender bias in legal NLP systems and implemented counterfactual data augmentation and adversarial training to reduce bias brought significant results in bias reduction thus highlighting the importance of these techniques in promoting fairness in legal NLP applications.

6. LATEST TRENDS IN NLP

Other NLP trends flooding the arena in the present day for shape and reshape the future are Pretrained Language Models; the likes of GPT-3, BERT, and RoBERTa, which have literally changed the face of NLP by providing powerful, general-purpose language understanding capabilities (Devlin et al., 2019); with Multilingual NLP, where certain attempts target designing models towards the capability of handling various languages so as to eliminate language barriers and offer a better workflow in translation (Wu et al., 2016). Trendy in NLP are the Virtual Assistants, which involve enhancements for virtual assistants that now are more likely to give accurate and context-aware responses toward improved user experience (Thompson, 2024). Moreover, Sentiment Analysis is on the brink of more evolved sentiment analysis models that are capable of comprehending and interpreting emotional subtleties of text data (Khurana et al., 2023). Reinforcement Learning sits at the top of NLP trends, especially regarding the use of reinforcement learning to involve the improvement of the performance of NLP models through learning via interaction with the environment (Thompson, 2024). As always, and due to upscaling concern, Ethical

NLP is standing at a hot spot as the need arises to address bias and fairness issues in NLP models for ethical and responsible use of AI technology (Khurana et al., 2023).

Likewise, the trend is also emerging into integration of the NLP with the AR and VR systems. Through these technologies, bulk interpretation communication immersion will be enhanced (Skaria et al., 2024) with multilingual scenarios. A Case Study on AR-based Interpretation in Tourism: The study by Skaria et al. (2024) focused on using AR-enhanced interpretation in tourism. The researchers created an AR application that enabled real-time translation of the speeches of tour guides and informational signs into multiple languages. The application was based on natural language processing for understanding and translating spoken language, and the AR component superimposed the translations with the view of the user through smart glasses. The study found that this method greatly enhanced the travel experience by offering instant and contextually appropriate translations (Skaria et al., 2024). Language Teaching through VR Another case is in Language learning through VR. The VR environments simulate the situation of the real world so that students can undergo added immersion in learning a language. It is also possible to bring NLP technologies into these VR environments for real-time feedback and translation, thereby making language learning more interesting and efficient-Al-Ansi et al. (2023).

7. FUTURE DIRECTIONS

The future of Natural Language Processing (NLP) in translation and interpretation is poised for exciting advancements, driven by emerging trends such as zero-shot translation and the integration of NLP with augmented reality (AR) for immersive interpretation experiences. These innovations promise to enhance the capabilities of NLP systems, making them more versatile and effective in various applications.

7.1 Zero-Shot Translation

Zero-shot translation is one of the new and interesting things in NLP, which makes the system translate between a pair of languages without any actual training data. It is done through the training of multilingual models in several different languages and then using the relation the trained languages have with one another to infer a translation from an unseen pair of languages (Wu et al., 2024). Recently, research has shown that zero-shot translation can be significantly improved when multilingual models are fine-tuned with a small quantity of data, say, for example, a very small amount of multiparallel data-it increases the translation quality significantly (Wu et al., 2024). Oh, what a joy of this method! It might be very useful for languages with little resources because they cannot generate good parallel corpora sufficiently.

A famous case study from Wu et al. (2024) proved that even a little amount of multilingual parallel data could improve zero-shot translation. From India, it improved the fine-tuning of an Indian-centered model using just 100 samples of multiparallel, which resulted in a drop of +21.7 ChrF in non-English translation directions. This approach preserved the performance of the model in English-centric directions while greatly improving its zero-shot capabilities, thus showcasing the potential of fine-tuning with a limited amount of data to produce high-quality translations (Wu et al., 2024).

8.2 Integration of NLP with Augmented Reality (AR)

Another exciting path for the future in both translation and interpretation is actually the fusion of NLP with augmented reality (AR). The interpretation can be augmented in an immersive mode where the translations of what the presenters say are overlaid over users' field of view. All this translates to a better experience in communication when it is necessary in environments where multiple languages exist. The technology is not limited to only international conferences but becomes hugely relevant for tourism and cross-culture meetings where a participant sometimes attends a real-time session and needs translation awareness of the context (Skaria et al., 2024).

A case study was conducted by Skaria et al. (2024), which focused on how augmented reality-enhanced interpretation was supposed to work in tourism. They developed an AR app that gives tourists real-time translations of what their tour guides say and signs on tourist destinations in different languages. NLP was employed for the processing of language input, conducting translations, and projecting the corresponding translation through smart glasses to what the user sees, all through the AR technology. According to the author's study of this use, it has brought significant improvement to the experience of tourists, giving seamless and contextually appropriate translations - pointing out the possibilities of integrating AR-NLP tech for improved multilingual communication (Skaria et al., 2024).

8.3 Comparison with Human Translators

No matter how advanced these systems in natural language processing become, they cannot replace the human translator in most respects. From knowledge of cultural aspects, idiomatic terms, and connotation of specific meaning per context, machines have much to learn before they can come close to the understanding and exactitude exhibited by humans (Berman & Tyyskä, 2011). They also specialize in tone, humor, and emotional interpretation through which most readers interpret their reading and thus the possibility of maintaining a smooth flow throughout the text is ensured. In addition, human translators can bend the translation towards a particular purpose or preference regarding the personalizations one might wish to have, whereas the machine could not. Today human translators are still necessary for those tasks that require a greater measure of cultural understanding, contextualization, and accuracy despite the advancements in zero-shot translation and augmented reality.

8. CONCLUSION AND RECOMMENDATIONS

In conclusion, the advancements in Natural Language Processing (NLP) have significantly enhanced the fields of translation and interpretation, offering innovative solutions such as Text-to-Speech (TTS), Automatic Speech Recognition (ASR), Language Modeling, and Corpus-Based Translation. These technologies have improved the accuracy, efficiency, and accessibility of translation services, making it possible to handle a wide range of languages and contexts. However, challenges such as data privacy, bias and fairness, and ethical use remain critical areas that need ongoing attention. Addressing these challenges through privacy-preserving techniques, bias mitigation strategies, and ethical frameworks is essential to ensure the responsible development and deployment of NLP technologies.

The future of NLP in translation and interpretation looks promising with emerging trends like zero-shot translation and the integration of NLP with augmented reality (AR) for immersive interpretation experiences. Zero-shot translation enables systems to translate between language pairs without direct training data, making it particularly valuable for low-resource languages. The integration of NLP with AR can provide real-time, context-aware translations, enhancing communication in multilingual environments. These innovations hold the potential to further advance the capabilities of NLP systems, making them more versatile and effective in various applications.

Despite these technological advancements, human translators remain indispensable for tasks that require high levels of accuracy, cultural sensitivity, and contextual understanding. Human translators bring a deep understanding of cultural nuances, idiomatic expressions, and context-specific meanings that machines often struggle to capture. Therefore, it is recommended to combine the strengths of both NLP technologies and human translators to achieve the highest quality and most contextually appropriate translations. By leveraging the speed and efficiency of NLP systems alongside the expertise and insight of human translators, we can ensure that translation and interpretation services are both effective and culturally resonant.

REFERENCES

Ahammad, T., Rahman, M. M., & Islam, M. S. (2024). Advances in Statistical Machine Translation: Techniques and Applications. *Journal of Computational Linguistics.*

Bahdanau, D., Cho, K., & Bengio, Y. (2015). Neural Machine Translation by Jointly Learning to Align and Translate. *Proceedings of the 3rd International Conference on Learning Representations (ICLR 2015).*

Bahdanau, D., Cho, K., & Bengio, Y. (2016). Neural machine translation by jointly learning to align and translate. *arXiv preprint arXiv:1409.0473.*

Berman, R. C., & Tyyskä, V. (2011). A critical reflection on the use of translators/ interpreters in a qualitative cross-language research project. *International Journal of Qualitative Methods, 10*(2), 178–190. DOI: 10.1177/160940691101000206

BeTranslated. (2023). Machine Translation with Natural Language Processing.

Brown, T. B., Mann, B., Ryder, N., Subbiah, M., Kaplan, J., Dhariwal, P., & Amodei, D. (2020). Language models are few-shot learners. *arXiv*. Retrieved from https:// arxiv.org/abs/2005.14165

Calvo-Ferrer, J. R. (2023). Can you tell the difference? A study of human vs machine-translated subtitles. *Perspectives*. Advance online publication. DOI: 10.1080/0907676X.2023.2268149

Chowdhury, A., & Hussan, M. (2023). A review-based study on different Text-to-Speech technologies. *arXiv*. Retrieved from https://arxiv.org/abs/2312.11563

Coleman, J., Krishnamachari, B., Rosales, R., & Iskarous, K. (2024). LLM-Assisted Rule-Based Machine Translation for Low/No-Resource Languages. *Proceedings of the 4th Workshop on Natural Language Processing for Indigenous Languages of the Americas (AmericasNLP 2024)*, 67-87. DOI: 10.18653/v1/2024.americasnlp-1.9

. Reverso Context. (2023). Arabic to English Translation.

Costa-jussà, M. R., & Rapp, R. (2016). *Hybrid approaches to machine translation.* Springer. DOI: 10.1007/978-3-319-21311-8

Dalayli, F. (2023). *Use of NLP Techniques in Translation by ChatGPT: Case Study.* ACL Anthology.

Devlin, J., Chang, M. W., Lee, K., & Toutanova, K. (2019). BERT: Pre-training of deep bidirectional transformers for language understanding. *Proceedings of the 2019 Conference of the North American Chapter of the Association for Computational Linguistics: Human Language Technologies*, 4171-4186.

Docomo, N. T. T. (2025). TTS system for Japanese navigation. *NTT Docomo*. Retrieved from https://nttdocomo.com

FlowGent AI. (2023). *What is a Rules-based Machine Translation*. RBMT.

Gallegos, I. O., Rossi, R. A., Barrow, J., Tanjim, M. M., Kim, S., Dernoncourt, F., Yu, T., Zhang, R., & Ahmed, N. K. (2024). Bias and fairness in large language models: A survey. *Computational Linguistics*, *50*(3), 1097–1179. DOI: 10.1162/coli_a_00524

Gao, Y., & Zhou, G. (2024). Revealing the translator's style: A corpus-based study of English translations of Mencius. *PLoS One*, *19*(7), e0305894. Advance online publication. DOI: 10.1371/journal.pone.0305894 PMID: 39012898

Hannun, A., Case, C., Casper, J., Catanzaro, B., Diamos, G., Elsen, E., & Prenger, R. (2024). Deep Speech: Scaling up end-to-end speech recognition. *arXiv*. Retrieved from https://arxiv.org/abs/1412.5567

Hardmeier, C. (2012). Discourse in Statistical Machine Translation: A Survey and a Case Study. *Discours*, *11*(11), 1–23. DOI: 10.4000/discours.8726

Hinton, G., Deng, L., Yu, D., Dahl, G. E., Mohamed, A. r., Jaitly, N., . . . Kingsbury, B. (2023). Deep neural networks for acoustic modeling in speech recognition: The shared views of four research groups. *IEEE Signal Processing Magazine*. Retrieved from https://ieeexplore.ieee.org/document/6296526

Hochreiter, S., & Schmidhuber, J. (1997). Long short-term memory. *Neural Computation*. Retrieved from https://www.mitpressjournals.org/doi/abs/10.1162/neco.1997.9.8.1735

IBM. (2023). *What is NLP*. Natural Language Processing.

iFlytek. (2025). iFlytek TTS system for Mandarin Chinese. *iFlytek*. Retrieved from https://iflytek.com

Jurafsky, D., & Martin, J. H. (2023). Speech and language processing. *Pearson*. Retrieved from https://web.stanford.edu/~jurafsky/slp3/

Katkov, S., Liotta, A., & Vietti, A. (2025). ASR systems under acoustic challenges: A multilingual study. In *AIxIA 2024 – Advances in Artificial Intelligence* (pp. 200–213). Springer., Retrieved from https://link.springer.com/chapter/10.1007/978-3-031-80607-0_16 DOI: 10.1007/978-3-031-80607-0_16

. Keles, H., Gunay, E., & Caglar, M. (2024). Tailored Neural Machine Translation Models for Medical Translation. *Journal of Medical Informatics*.

Khurana, D., Koli, A., Khatter, K., & Singh, S. (2023). Natural language processing: State of the art, current trends and challenges. *Multimedia Tools and Applications*, *82*(3), 3713–3744. DOI: 10.1007/s11042-022-13428-4 PMID: 35855771

Khurana, D., Koli, A., Khatter, K., & Singh, S. (2023). Natural language processing: State of the art, current trends, and challenges. *Journal of Artificial Intelligence Research*, *56*(1), 1–42. PMID: 35855771

Koehn, P. (2020). *Neural machine translation*. Cambridge University Press. DOI: 10.1017/9781108608480

Kumar, Y., Koul, A., & Singh, C. (2023). A deep learning approach in text-to-speech systems: A systematic review and recent research perspective. *Multimedia Tools and Applications*. Retrieved from https://link.springer.com/article/10.1007/s11042-022-13943-4

Language Science Press. (2023). Translation and Multilingual Natural Language Processing.

Laviosa, S. (2021). Corpus-based translation studies: Theory, findings, applications. *Cambridge Scholars Publishing*. Retrieved from https://www.cambridgescholars.com/resources/pdfs/978-1-5275-7244-7-sample.pdf

Liu, S., Liu, G., Zhu, B., Luo, Y., Wu, L., & Wang, R. (2024). Balancing innovation and privacy: Data security strategies in natural language processing applications. *arXiv preprint arXiv:2410.08553*. DOI: 10.1109/ICMLCA63499.2024.10754062

Liu, Y., Ott, M., Goyal, N., Du, J., Joshi, M., Chen, D., & Stoyanov, V. (2019). RoBERTa: A robustly optimized BERT pretraining approach. *arXiv*. Retrieved from https://arxiv.org/abs/1907.11692

Lopez, A. (2008). Statistical machine translation. *ACM Computing Surveys*, *40*(3), 1–49. DOI: 10.1145/1380584.1380586

. Luong, M. T., Pham, H., & Manning, C. D. (2015). Effective approaches to attention-based neural machine translation.

Marie, B., Foster, G., & Kuhn, R. (2021). Improving SMT for Low-Resource Languages. *Journal of Machine Translation, 35*(2), 123–145.

Marie, B., Fujita, A., & Rubino, R. (2021). Scientific Credibility of Machine Translation Research: A Meta-Evaluation of 769 Papers. *Proceedings of the 59th Annual Meeting of the Association for Computational Linguistics and the 11th International Joint Conference on Natural Language Processing(*Volume 1*: Long Papers)*, 7297-7306. DOI: 10.18653/v1/2021.acl-long.566

OpenGenus. (2023). *Key Terms/ Topics in Natural Language Processing*. NLP.

Paul, B. (2023). Advancements and Perspectives in Machine Translation: A Comprehensive Review. *1st International Conference on Recent Innovations in Computing, Science & Technology*, 6 Pages. DOI: 10.2139/ssrn.4562254

PrimeGroupUSA. (2023). Advantages and limitations of Text-to-Speech technology. *PrimeGroupUSA*. Retrieved from https://primegroupusa.com

Rabiner, L. R. (2023). A tutorial on hidden Markov models and selected applications in speech recognition. *Proceedings of the IEEE*. Retrieved from https://ieeexplore .ieee.org/document/18626

Rosset, C., Cheng, J., Saleh, M., & Dolan, B. (2020). Turing-NLG: A 17-billion-parameter language model by Microsoft. *Microsoft Research Blog*. Retrieved from [https://www.microsoft.com/en-us/research/blog/turing-nlg-a-17-billion-parameter-language-model-by-microsoft/](https://www.microsoft.com/en-us/research)

Savoldi, B., Gaido, M., Bentivogli, L., Negri, M., & Turchi, M. (2021). Gender bias in machine translation. *Proceedings of the 2021 Conference on Empirical Methods in Natural Language Processing (EMNLP 2021).*

Shaik, R. (2025). Enhancing text generation in joint Nlg/Nlu learning through curriculum learning, semi-supervised training, and advanced optimization techniques. *Multimedia Tools and Applications*. Advance online publication. DOI: 10.1007/s11042-025-20665-w

Shaip. (2024). ASR (Automatic Speech Recognition) - Definition, use cases, example. *Shaip*. Retrieved from https://www.shaip.com/blog/automatic-speech-recognitiona-complete-overview/

Simon Says, A. I. (2023). What is ASR? How does it work? Our in-depth 2023 guide. *Simon Says AI*. Retrieved from https://www.simonsaysai.com/blog/automatic-speech-recognition

Skaria, S., Kumar, A., & Singh, R. (2024). AR-enhanced interpretation in tourism: A case study. *Journal of Tourism Studies*, *12*(2), 145–160.

Southwell, R., Pugh, S., Perkoff, E. M., Clevenger, C., Bush, J. B., Lieber, R., . . . D'Mello, S. (2024). Challenges and feasibility of automatic speech recognition for modeling student collaborative discourse in classrooms. *Institute of Cognitive Science, University of Colorado Boulder*. Retrieved from [https://www.colorado.edu/research/ai-institute/sites/default/files/attached-files/challengesfeasibility.pdf] (https://www.colorado.edu/research/ai-institute/sites

SpringerLink. (2023). Sign Language Statistical. *Machine Translation.*

Sreelekha, M. (2017). Comparing RBMT and SMT for English-Indian Language Translation. *Journal of Computational Linguistics*, *23*(4), 567–589.

Sutskever, I., Vinyals, O., & Le, Q. V. (2014). Sequence to Sequence Learning with Neural Networks. *Advances in Neural Information Processing Systems*, *27*, 3104–3112.

Technologies, O. (2023). What is Hybrid. *Machine Translation.*

Thompson, O. (2024). Advancements in Natural Language Processing: AI's Impact on Language Translation and Interpretation. *International Journal of Sustainable Development in Computing Science.*

Torregrosa, D., Pasricha, N., Masoud, M., Chakravarthi, B. R., Alonso, J., & Casas, N. (2019). Leveraging rule-based machine translation knowledge for under-resourced neural machine translation models. In *Proceedings of Machine Translation Summit XVII: Translator, Project and User Tracks* (pp. 125-133). European Association for Machine Translation.

Vasheghani Farahani, M., & Dastjerdi, H. V. (2021). Corpora and translation studies: Implications and applications. *Journal of Language and Translation.* Retrieved from https://www.researchgate.net/publication/361950371*Corpora*and*Translation-*Studies*Implications*and_Applications

Vaswani, A., Shazeer, N., Parmar, N., Uszkoreit, J., Jones, L., Gomez, A. N., Kaiser, Ł., & Polosukhin, I. (2017). Attention is all you need. *Advances in Neural Information Processing Systems*, *30*, 5998–6008.

Vida, K., Simon, J., & Lauscher, A. (2023). Values, ethics, morals? On the use of moral concepts in NLP research. *Findings of the Association for Computational Linguistics: EMNLP, 2023*, 5534–5554. DOI: 10.18653/v1/2023.findings-emnlp.368

Wan, X., Zhang, Y., & Liu, J. (2022). Challenges and Solutions in Neural Machine Translation for Short Texts. *Computational Linguistics*, *48*(2), 321–342. DOI: 10.1162/coli_a_00435

Wireless World, R. F. (2023). Text-to-Speech technology in language learning. *RF Wireless World*. Retrieved from https://rfwirelessworld.com

Wu, Y., Schuster, M., Chen, Z., Le, Q. V., Norouzi, M., Macherey, W., Krikun, M., Cao, Y., Gao, Q., Macherey, K., Klingner, J., Shah, A., Johnson, M., & Liu, X. Łukasz Kaiser, Gouws, S., Kato, Y., Kudo, T., Kazawa, H., … & Dean, J. (2016). Google's neural machine translation system: Bridging the gap between human and machine translation. *arXiv preprint arXiv:1609.08144*.

Xie, T., Rong, Y., Zhang, P., & Liu, L. (2024). Towards controllable speech synthesis in the era of large language models: A survey. *arXiv*. Retrieved from https://arxiv.org/abs/2412.06602

Yermilov, O., Raheja, V., & Chernodub, A. (2023). Privacy- and utility-preserving NLP with anonymized data: A case study of pseudonymization. *Proceedings of the 3rd Workshop on Trustworthy Natural Language Processing (TrustNLP 2023)*. DOI: 10.18653/v1/2023.trustnlp-1.20

Chapter 8
The Collaborative Future of Translation Between Human–AI Partnerships

Raed Awashreh
https://orcid.org/0000-0002-2252-0299
A'Sharqiyah University, Oman

Ahmed Aboeisheh
University of Buraimi, Oman

ABSTRACT

Artificial intelligence (AI) has significantly transformed translation and interpretation through advancements in machine learning and natural language processing. AI tools, such as Google Translate and DeepL, offer rapid translations, enhancing usability and fostering cross-cultural communication. Despite these advancements, challenges persist regarding accuracy, context, and cultural nuances, leading to misunderstandings. A collaborative approach that integrates human expertise with AI is essential to improve translation quality and mitigate biases. This chapter critically assesses the relationship between human translators and AI, exploring collaborative models, ethical considerations, and strategies for future partnerships. By examining case studies, it emphasizes the need to balance technological efficiency with human insight to ensure cultural sensitivity and responsible AI integration in translation services. Ultimately, effective collaboration enhances the quality and efficiency of language services while addressing ethical concerns in cross-cultural communication.

DOI: 10.4018/979-8-3373-0060-3.ch008

INTRODUCTION

In recent years, artificial intelligence (AI) has significantly transformed the fields of translation and interpretation, driven by advancements in machine learning, natural language processing (NLP), and the growing demand for multilingual communication in an increasingly globalized world. AI-powered tools, such as Google Translate and DeepL, have gained widespread popularity, providing quick translations across multiple languages. While these tools have made substantial progress in quality and usability, they still face challenges in accurately capturing the richness of human expression, particularly in complex contexts requiring cultural sensitivity and nuanced understanding (De la Vall & Raya, 2023).

As AI evolves, its influence extends beyond written translation into the realm of interpretation. AI-assisted tools now enable real-time translation during conferences, meetings, and personal interactions, significantly enhancing cross-cultural communication. Virtual assistants and chatbots are also increasingly used to bridge language barriers in customer service interactions, streamlining processes and improving user experiences (Marzuki et al., 2023). However, concerns persist about the potential for misunderstandings due to AI's limited ability to fully grasp context, idiomatic expressions, or cultural nuances, raising critical questions about the future role of human translators and interpreters. Human expertise has traditionally ensured effective communication and cultural understanding (Alkanaani, 2024).

While AI excels at processing vast amounts of data and identifying patterns, human translators bring essential qualities such as contextual understanding, cultural sensitivity (Lau et al., 2024), and the ability to convey emotions, humor, and cultural references that AI may overlook. For example, AI might provide a literal translation of a culturally specific idiom, such as "breaking the ice," which could fail to convey the intended meaning. In such cases, human translators are vital in interpreting not just the words, but the emotions and context behind them, highlighting the importance of combining AI's efficiency with human expertise to preserve the subtleties of language and culture (Al Saadi & Awashreh, 2024).

To maximize the strengths of both AI and human translators, a collaborative approach is essential. AI can handle repetitive tasks and large datasets with ease, while human translators ensure that translations remain culturally accurate and contextually appropriate (Al Saadi & Awashreh, 2025). For instance, AI may expedite the translation of legal documents, but human translators provide critical oversight, ensuring legal terminology is correctly applied and cultural considerations are respected (Khasawneh, 2023). Furthermore, collaboration can help address significant challenges, such as bias in AI-generated translations. Without human intervention, AI may perpetuate stereotypes or misrepresent certain groups, especially when trained on biased data sets. Human involvement ensures that translations remain culturally inclusive and free of bias (Awashreh, 2024b).

Ethical concerns also play a critical role in integrating AI into translation. As AI systems become more autonomous, issues of transparency, accountability, and cultural sensitivity are increasingly important (Awashreh & Ramachandran, 2025). For instance, if an AI system is trained primarily on data from one region or culture, it may fail to account for the diverse ways certain phrases or concepts are understood in other cultures. This raises an ethical dilemma: how can we ensure that AI-powered translations do not marginalize certain communities or misrepresent their voices? Human translators, deeply aware of these cultural dynamics, can correct such errors and safeguard against these risks (Schwartz et al., 2021).

The relationship between AI and human translators is enriched by key theoretical perspectives in translation studies, which emphasize the complexities of collaboration and the role of context in translation (Amaro & Pires, 2024). Skopos theory stresses the importance of the translation's purpose within the target culture, suggesting that AI, despite its efficiency, cannot replace human sensitivity to cultural norms and communicative goals. Similarly, post-editing theory highlights the need for human intervention in refining AI-generated translations to meet standards of accuracy, fluency, and cultural relevance (Ali, 2023). Additionally, sociolinguistic perspectives emphasize how AI systems, shaped by societal biases, can introduce ethical concerns such as gender and racial biases, underscoring the need for human oversight to ensure culturally sensitive translations (Awashreh, 2025).

As AI systems continue to evolve, the collaboration between human translators and AI has become a critical area of study. Early research has emphasized the importance of human post-editing in improving AI translations, while more recent studies explore how AI can support human expertise, especially in repetitive or technical translations (Al Sharairi, 2025). In real-time translation settings, such as conferences, AI systems show promise, but human oversight remains necessary to ensure accuracy and relevance. Despite advancements, neural machine translation (NMT) still faces challenges, particularly with low-resource languages and specialized domains, which highlight the ongoing need for human involvement to maintain translation quality. The evolution of AI in translation, informed by theoretical perspectives and ongoing studies, reveals the intricate dynamics of human-AI collaboration, which will continue to develop as AI technology advances (Naveen & Trojovský, 2024).

Machine translation (MT) has evolved significantly since its inception. Early systems, such as those in the Georgetown-IBM experiment in the 1950s, were rule-based, relying on linguistic rules and lexicons. These systems struggled with idiomatic expressions and nuances. In the 1980s, statistical machine translation (SMT) emerged, using large bilingual corpora to improve translation quality (Mirela, 2024), though it still had issues with fluency and semantic accuracy, especially for complex texts. The breakthrough came with neural machine translation (NMT), built on deep learning algorithms. NMT, as seen in systems like Google Translate, uses large neural networks to learn contextual meanings, significantly improving fluency and accuracy. Recent transformer-based models have further enhanced translation quality, making translations more human-like (Stahlberg, 2020).

This chapter critically assesses the collaborative relationship between human translators and AI technologies in translation and interpretation, examining how these partnerships will shape the future of language services. The chapter's multifaceted purpose includes analyzing existing collaborative models, identifying best practices and challenges, evaluating the capabilities and limitations of AI-powered translation tools, addressing obstacles arising from human-AI collaboration, exploring ethical implications, and providing insights and strategies for future human-AI collaboration in translation. It emphasizes the importance of balancing AI technologies with human expertise to ensure effective, culturally sensitive communication in an increasingly globalized world.

To achieve its objectives, the chapter first examines collaborative models that illustrate how AI and human translators interact, highlighting best practices and real-world challenges. It then evaluates AI-powered translation technologies, assessing how well they complement human skills while identifying their limitations. The chapter further addresses challenges such as trust, quality control, and bias in AI-generated translations, using real-world examples like AI misinterpreting complex cultural references in diplomatic negotiations. It also explores the ethical considerations of integrating AI into translation, stressing the need for transparency, accountability, and cultural sensitivity. Finally, it offers future perspectives, proposing strategies to foster effective human-AI collaboration that empowers human translators in an AI-driven world.

By exploring the potential for AI and human translators to work together to enhance the quality and efficiency of language services, this chapter addresses both practical and ethical concerns, ensuring that cultural nuances are preserved. Drawing on case studies and expert insights, it illuminates strategies for effective collaboration and outlines the future of translation and interpretation in a world increasingly influenced by AI. This collaborative approach not only enhances the overall quality of translation services but also paves the way for a more nuanced, culturally aware communication landscape.

OVERVIEW OF INCREASING INTEGRATION OF AI TRANSLATION AND INTERPRETATION

In recent years, the integration of artificial intelligence (AI) into the fields of translation and interpretation has accelerated dramatically. This transformation is driven by advancements in machine learning, natural language processing (NLP), and the increasing demand for multilingual communication in our globalized world. AI technologies, particularly machine translation systems such as Google Translate and DeepL, have become household names, offering users instantaneous translation of text across multiple languages. These tools leverage vast datasets and sophisticated algorithms to generate translations that, while not perfect, have significantly improved in quality and usability (Benmansour & Hdouch, 2023).

Beyond text translation, AI is also making strides in the realm of interpretation. AI-assisted interpretation tools can now provide real-time translation services during conferences, meetings, and even in personal conversations. This has opened up new possibilities for cross-cultural communication, making it easier for individuals and organizations to engage in international dialogue. Moreover, the rise of chatbots and virtual assistants has introduced AI into customer service scenarios, where effective communication across language barriers is crucial (Benmansour & Hdouch, 2023). However, the increasing reliance on AI in translation and interpretation does not come without challenges. While these technologies can enhance speed and efficiency, concerns about accuracy, context, and cultural nuances persist. AI systems can sometimes produce translations that lack the subtleties of human expression, leading to misunderstandings or the loss of important cultural references. Furthermore, the reliance on AI raises questions about the future role of human translators and interpreters, who have traditionally been seen as essential to the process of effective communication (Moneus & Sahari, 2024)

The Significance and Complexity of Collaborative Approaches

The complexity of integrating AI into translation and interpretation necessitates a collaborative approach that leverages the strengths of both human expertise and AI capabilities. This synergy is significant for several reasons (Bekouche, 2024). First, collaboration can enhance the quality of translations. While AI can process vast amounts of data and recognize patterns, human translators bring contextual understanding, cultural sensitivity, and the ability to convey nuances that machines may overlook. By working together, human professionals can utilize AI as a tool to streamline their workflows, allowing them to focus on the more nuanced aspects of translation that require human intuition and creativity (Moneus & Sahari, 2024) Second, collaborative approaches can address the challenges associated with AI in translation. For instance, human oversight can help mitigate issues of bias that may arise from AI algorithms trained on biased datasets. By incorporating diverse perspectives, human translators can ensure that AI-generated translations reflect a broader range of cultural contexts and meanings. This collaboration also allows for ongoing feedback, enabling AI systems to learn and improve over time based on human insights (Albaroudi, Mansouri & Alameer, 2024).

Moreover, the significance of collaboration extends beyond mere efficiency; it fosters a more ethical framework for the use of AI in translation and interpretation. As language professionals navigate the ethical implications of AI integration, a collaborative model emphasizes transparency and accountability. By ensuring that human translators remain integral to the process, we can preserve the human touch essential for effective communication (Garcia Valencia et al., 2023). This is particularly important in sensitive contexts, where cultural nuances and emotional resonance are paramount. In conclusion, the increasing integration of AI in translation and interpretation presents both opportunities and challenges. Collaborative approaches that combine the strengths of human translators with AI technologies can enhance the quality and efficiency of language services while addressing ethical concerns and maintaining cultural sensitivity. As we move forward in this evolving landscape, fostering effective collaboration will be key to harnessing the full potential of AI in the realm of translation and interpretation (Mirzayev, 2024).

METHODOLOGY

This study employs qualitative methods to explore the dynamics of human-AI collaboration in translation and interpretation. By utilizing secondary data, including case studies from existing literature, academic studies, and online sources, the research seeks to gain insights into both the effectiveness and challenges of these collaborative approaches as suggested Smith (2008). Through the examination of a diverse range of materials, the study aims to construct a comprehensive understanding of how AI technologies are reshaping the translation landscape and what implications this has for human translators.

The secondary data sources for this research are varied and include several key components. First, academic literature, such as peer-reviewed journal articles, conference papers, and dissertations, discusses the intersection of AI technologies and translation practices. These sources provide empirical data, theoretical frameworks, and critical analyses of existing collaborative models. Second, case studies offer detailed examinations of real-world applications of AI in translation and interpretation, providing practical insights into both successful and problematic human-AI collaborations while highlighting the nuances of implementation and the outcomes of different strategies. Third, online resources, including reports, white papers, and industry publications, analyze current trends in AI-assisted translation. These sources often include statistics, expert opinions, and case examples that illustrate the evolving role of AI in language services. Lastly, media articles and blogs from reputable outlets contribute contemporary perspectives on the challenges and opportunities associated with integrating AI into translation workflows (Chen, Wu & Wang, 2023; Wagner, Lukyanenko, & Paré, 2022).

The data collection process involves systematically reviewing and synthesizing information from the identified secondary sources. A comprehensive literature review will be conducted to identify key themes, methodologies, and findings related to AI in translation. This review will inform the study's understanding of the current state of research and highlight areas requiring further exploration. Selected case studies will be analyzed to understand the practical implications of human-AI collaboration, with each case being examined for its context, methodologies employed, outcomes, and lessons learned regarding the interaction between human translators and AI technologies. Furthermore, the gathered data will undergo thematic analysis to identify recurring themes and patterns related to human-AI collaboration, involving coding the data, grouping similar findings, and drawing connections between different sources to construct a cohesive narrative (Maeda et al., 2022; Chen, Wu& Wang, 2023).

The qualitative data analysis will follow a structured approach (Awashreh & AlGhunaimi, 2024). Initial coding will categorize the data into key themes such as collaboration models, challenges, ethical considerations, and future directions in human-AI translation. This coding process will facilitate a systematic analysis of the data. Based on the coded information, themes will be developed that capture the essence of the findings, articulated in relation to existing literature and case studies. The final analysis will synthesize insights gained from the literature, case studies, and online resources, presenting a nuanced understanding of human-AI collaboration in translation. This synthesis will inform discussions about best practices, challenges, and future considerations for practitioners in the field.

While this methodology provides a structured approach to exploring human-AI collaboration in translation, it is essential to acknowledge inherent limitations. The reliance on secondary data may restrict the study's ability to capture the full range of experiences and insights from human translators actively engaged with AI technologies. Additionally, the quality and scope of the available literature and case studies may vary, which could influence the robustness of the findings (Dengel, 2023). This qualitative methodology, grounded in secondary data and case studies, aims to provide a comprehensive understanding of the collaborative dynamics between human translators and AI technologies. By examining existing literature and real-world applications, the study seeks to contribute valuable insights into the future of translation and interpretation in an increasingly AI-driven world (Cheong et al., 2023)

CURRENT AI TECHNOLOGY IN TRANSELATION

The integration of artificial intelligence (AI) into translation and interpretation has significantly transformed how we communicate across languages. Advancements in machine learning, natural language processing (NLP), and other AI technologies have remarkably improved the efficiency and accessibility of language services. This section provides an in-depth examination of current AI technologies in translation, focusing on three key areas: machine translation, AI-assisted interpretation, and NLP tools. These technologies not only accelerate the speed of language translation but also introduce innovative solutions to the challenges of cross-cultural communication (Benmansour & Hdouch, 2023)

Machine Translation

Machine translation stands out as one of the most prominent applications of AI in language services. It refers to the automated process of translating text from one language to another using AI algorithms. Tools such as Google Translate, DeepL, and Microsoft Translator have gained widespread recognition, enabling users to translate text across multiple languages in real time. These systems leverage extensive datasets of multilingual content and sophisticated machine learning models to generate translations that, while not perfect, have become increasingly accurate and contextually relevant over time (Doherty, 2016). At the core of modern machine translation systems is deep learning, particularly neural machine translation (NMT). Unlike earlier models that relied on rule-based or statistical approaches, NMT employs neural networks to learn language patterns from large datasets. This allows the system to "understand" the context of a sentence rather than simply translating word for word. NMT models are trained on bilingual corpora, and through repeated exposure to extensive data, they learn to generate translations that are more natural and coherent. For instance, Google Translate now supports over 100 languages, demonstrating improved fluency and contextual accuracy due to its NMT system (Ashraf, 2024).

Despite these advancements, machine translation has its limitations. While AI systems have become proficient at handling simple and structured texts, they often struggle with idiomatic expressions, humor, and complex cultural references. A phrase that carries specific cultural or emotional significance in one language may be mistranslated or lose its impact when processed by an AI system. Furthermore, machine translation tools can produce errors when confronted with ambiguous language, where the same word or phrase may have multiple meanings depending on the context (Naveen & Trojovský, 2024). To address these challenges, an emerging solution is the use of domain-specific machine translation models. By training AI systems on specialized datasets, such as legal, medical, or technical texts, developers aim to enhance translation accuracy in specific fields. This approach helps mitigate some contextual issues that arise in general-purpose translation tools, ensuring that translations in critical domains are more reliable and accurate. Nonetheless, the role of human translators remains essential, as they provide oversight and address nuanced or culturally sensitive aspects of translation that machines may overlook (Kimera, Kim & Choi, 2024).

AI-Assisted Interpretation

In addition to text translation, AI technologies have made significant strides in real-time interpretation. AI-assisted interpretation tools are increasingly being used to facilitate live conversations, whether in business meetings, conferences, or informal settings. These tools aim to break down language barriers, enabling participants who speak different languages to communicate seamlessly. AI-powered interpretation systems use a combination of speech recognition, machine translation, and speech synthesis to provide real-time translation of spoken language. A prime example is the use of AI in conference settings, where interpretation services allow multilingual participants to follow discussions in their own languages. Tech giants like Google, Microsoft, and Skype have incorporated AI-assisted interpretation into their platforms, making these services widely accessible (Moneus & Sahari, 2024)

One notable example is Google's "Interpreter Mode," available on Google Assistant. This tool enables users to hold conversations in different languages by providing real-time translations of spoken words. Similarly, Skype Translator offers live audio translation during voice or video calls, allowing users to communicate across language barriers instantly. These innovations have the potential to revolutionize international communication, particularly in business and diplomatic contexts, where accurate and timely interpretation is crucial (Barman, 2024). However, AI-assisted interpretation faces its own set of challenges. The technology is highly dependent on the quality of speech recognition, which can be affected by accents, speech speed, background noise, or technical jargon. Additionally, real-time interpretation requires the system to process spoken language instantaneously, which increases the risk of errors, especially when dealing with complex or fast-paced conversations. Like machine translation, AI-assisted interpretation can struggle with cultural references or idiomatic expressions, potentially leading to misunderstandings (Basak et al., 2022).

Another critical issue with AI-assisted interpretation is the potential loss of the human touch. Professional interpreters bring not only linguistic expertise but also an understanding of the tone, emotion, and cultural context, all of which are essential for effective communication, particularly in sensitive situations such as legal or diplomatic discussions. While AI systems can offer speed and accessibility, they lack the emotional intelligence and cultural awareness that human interpreters provide. Thus, the future of AI-assisted interpretation will likely involve hybrid models where AI handles simpler, more routine tasks, while human interpreters focus on more complex and nuanced communication needs (Singh, Saxena & Saxena, 2024).

NLP Tools in Translation

Natural language processing (NLP) is a branch of AI that focuses on the interaction between computers and human language. NLP tools are crucial in advancing the capabilities of both machine translation and AI-assisted interpretation. These tools allow machines to understand, interpret, and generate human language in a way that is meaningful and contextually appropriate (Shi, 2021). NLP involves several subfields, including syntax, semantics, and sentiment analysis, all of which play a role in improving translation quality. For example, syntactic analysis helps AI systems understand sentence structure, while semantic analysis ensures that the meaning of words and phrases is preserved in translation. Sentiment analysis allows the system to detect the tone or emotion behind a statement, ensuring that the emotional intent of the speaker or writer is not lost in translation (Jim et al., 2024). One of the key contributions of NLP to translation is the development of context-aware systems. Traditional machine translation systems often struggled with homonyms (words that have the same spelling but different meanings) or polysemous words (words with multiple meanings). NLP tools, however, enable AI systems to analyze the surrounding text or speech and determine the correct meaning based on context. This results in more accurate translations, particularly for complex sentences or phrases with multiple interpretations (Naveen & Trojovský, 2024).

Furthermore, NLP tools have expanded the use of AI beyond just translation, enabling applications such as text summarization, sentiment analysis, and language generation. These tools can be particularly useful in fields such as journalism, customer service, and legal documentation, where understanding the emotional tone and summarizing large volumes of text are essential tasks. In translation, NLP tools are being used to create more refined and contextually accurate outputs, addressing some of the limitations that earlier translation models faced (Khurana, Koli, Khatter & et al., 2023). Despite these advancements, NLP still faces challenges in cross-linguistic understanding. For example, languages with rich morphological structures, such as Arabic or Finnish, present difficulties for NLP models due to the complexity of their word formations. Moreover, cultural nuances and regional dialects continue to pose obstacles for NLP-based translation systems, as AI often lacks the deep cultural knowledge necessary to capture the full meaning of certain expressions or terms (Shaalan et al., 2024)

The Future of AI Technologies in Translation and Interpretation

The current landscape of AI in translation and interpretation is marked by rapid innovation, with machine translation, AI-assisted interpretation, and NLP tools playing central roles. As these technologies continue to evolve, we are likely to see even more sophisticated systems that are better at handling cultural nuances, contextual meaning, and emotional tones. Hybrid models, where AI and human professionals work together, may become the norm, allowing for the efficiency of AI with the accuracy and cultural sensitivity of human expertise (Eszenyi, Bednarova-Gibova, & Robin, 2023). In the future, the integration of AI technologies in language services may extend beyond text and speech translation to include more advanced applications, such as multilingual chatbots, virtual assistants, and immersive interpretation experiences using augmented reality (AR) or virtual reality (VR). These innovations hold the potential to further enhance communication across languages and cultures, bridging gaps that have historically hindered global collaboration (Betal, 2023).

However, the ongoing development of AI in translation and interpretation must address key ethical concerns, particularly regarding bias, privacy, and the potential marginalization of human translators. As AI technologies become more pervasive, it is crucial to maintain a balanced approach that values the expertise and insight of human professionals while leveraging the power of AI to expand the reach and efficiency of language services (Moneus & Sahari, 2024). In short, AI technologies are reshaping the landscape of translation and interpretation, offering new possibilities for cross-cultural communication while also presenting unique challenges. Machine translation, AI-assisted interpretation, and NLP tools have already made significant impacts, but the full potential of these technologies will be realized when they work in tandem with human professionals to deliver language services that are not only efficient but also culturally sensitive and ethically sound (Moneus & Sahari, 2024).

A detailed examination of AI technologies in translation highlights three key areas: machine translation, AI-assisted interpretation, and natural language processing (NLP) tools. Machine translation, exemplified by platforms like Google Translate and DeepL, uses neural machine translation (NMT) models to produce more accurate and context-aware translations, although it still struggles with idiomatic expressions and cultural nuances (Kenny, 2024). AI-assisted interpretation, used in tools like Skype Translator, offers real-time speech translation but faces challenges with accents, speech speed, and cultural references. NLP tools enhance these systems by enabling deeper language understanding, improving context sensitivity, and facilitating tasks like sentiment analysis, but they still face limitations with complex languages and regional dialects. Together, these technologies are transforming language services, though human oversight remains essential to address nuances and ethical concerns (Moneus & Sahari, 2024)

CASE STUDIES OF SUCCESSFUL AND PROBLEMATIC AI COLLABORATIONS

The integration of AI in translation processes has transformed the field, highlighting both successful collaborations, such as IBM Watson in healthcare, and challenges like Google Translate in complex legal contexts.

Successful and Problematic Collaborations in Human-AI Translation

The integration of artificial intelligence (AI) in translation processes has revolutionized the field, leading to both successful outcomes and significant challenges. Various case studies illustrate these dynamics, showcasing how the interaction between human translators and AI technologies can produce varying results (Moneus & Sahari, 2024). However, current discussions often lack concrete real-world examples that highlight both the advantages and limitations of human-AI collaboration. By examining specific case studies, we can better understand the factors that contribute to success or failure in AI-assisted translation (Jiang et al., 2024).

One notable example of a successful collaboration is the European Parliament's use of machine translation (MT) in managing multilingual communication. With 24 official languages, the institution relies on AI-powered translation tools to handle vast amounts of legislative documents and correspondence efficiently (Mendez et al., 2024). These AI tools function within a hybrid model, where human translators post-edit AI-generated translations to ensure linguistic accuracy and contextual appropriateness. This collaboration enhances efficiency, allowing translators to focus on refining complex legal and policy-related language rather than translating from scratch. As a result, the European Parliament maintains high translation quality while benefiting from the speed and scalability that AI provides (Wang, 2024).

Conversely, problematic human-AI collaborations highlight the limitations of AI translation, particularly when dealing with context-heavy or nuanced language. A striking example is Netflix's use of AI-generated subtitles, which has faced criticism for inaccuracies and cultural insensitivity. Automated translation tools often struggle with humor, idiomatic expressions, and culturally specific references, leading to misleading or awkward subtitles. In some cases, AI-generated subtitles failed to convey the intended meaning, affecting audience comprehension and reception. This example underscores the necessity of human oversight, as professional translators play a crucial role in refining AI outputs to preserve accuracy and cultural relevance (Marzuki et al., 2023). Another case study that highlights the importance of human intervention is Google Translate's use in legal translations. While Google Translate is widely used for everyday communication, it has demonstrated significant limitations in legal contexts. Legal language requires precision, and AI-generated translations can misinterpret technical terms, leading to serious consequences in contracts and legal proceedings. By contrast, the European Commission employs a hybrid approach, combining AI with human translators to ensure clarity and accuracy in legal documents. This method minimizes errors and ensures compliance with legal standards, demonstrating the importance of structured human-AI collaboration in high-stakes translation scenarios (Tatineni, 2019).

Beyond technical challenges, ethical concerns also shape the discourse on human-AI collaboration in translation. AI algorithms can inherit biases from the datasets they are trained on, leading to skewed translations that misrepresent certain languages or cultures. Addressing these biases requires ongoing evaluation and improvements in AI training methodologies to ensure fairness and inclusivity. Organizations using AI in translation must implement robust quality control mechanisms and ethical guidelines to prevent biased or misleading outputs (Moneus & Sahari, 2024).

Ultimately, the analysis of successful and problematic case studies underscores the necessity of a balanced approach in human-AI translation. AI excels in speed, scalability, and consistency, but human expertise remains indispensable in refining accuracy, cultural sensitivity, and contextual understanding. The most effective translation models are those that integrate AI as an assistive tool rather than a replacement, ensuring that human translators guide the process to achieve high-quality outcomes. By embracing this collaborative approach, the translation industry can harness the strengths of AI while mitigating its limitations, leading to more effective and inclusive multilingual communication (Bekouche, 2024).

Successful Human-AI Collaboration: Microsoft Translator at the United Nations

One notable instance of successful human-AI collaboration took place during a significant United Nations conference, where Microsoft Translator was utilized for real-time translation services. In this scenario, the AI-powered tool efficiently managed straightforward translations, effectively addressing the immediate need for clear communication among delegates speaking different languages (Taylor, 2025). However, the system faced limitations in handling legal and highly specialized terminology, leading to instances where human intervention was crucial to maintain accuracy and contextual appropriateness. This automation allowed human interpreters to concentrate on more intricate aspects of language, such as complex syntax, idiomatic expressions, and culturally sensitive content that requires a nuanced understanding of context and meaning (Al-Wasy, Alkodimi & Alqahtani, 2024).

The partnership between AI and human interpreters proved to be highly beneficial, as it not only enhanced the overall speed of translation but also minimized the potential for errors. If either humans or AI had operated independently, the likelihood of misunderstandings and inaccuracies would have increased, particularly in a high-stakes environment like the UN, where precise communication is crucial (Taylor, 2025). A comparable case was observed in the European Parliament's use of AI-powered machine translation (MT), where initial reliance on AI alone resulted in inaccuracies, prompting a shift to a hybrid model incorporating human post-editing. This adjustment significantly improved the final translations, particularly for legal and policy-related texts that demand a high degree of precision (Tavares et al., 2023). By harnessing the rapid processing capabilities of AI, which can quickly translate simple phrases and sentences, alongside the accuracy and cultural insights provided by experienced human interpreters, this collaboration illustrated a model for effective communication that capitalizes on the strengths of both technologies.

Further illustrating the complexities of human-AI collaboration, Google Translate's limitations in legal translation have demonstrated the risks of over-reliance on AI. In contrast, the European Commission employs a hybrid AI-human approach, ensuring that legally binding documents undergo thorough human review to prevent misinterpretations. The comparison between these approaches highlights the necessity of balancing AI efficiency with human expertise, particularly in contexts where precision is paramount (Bekouche, 2024). The successful outcome of this collaboration serves as a compelling case study for other organizations seeking to improve their communication strategies, showcasing the potential for AI to enhance, rather than hinder, human efforts in complex and sensitive tasks (Al-Wasy, Alkodimi & Alqahtani, 2024).

Problematic Collaboration: Google Translate in Legal Document Translation

A significant challenge arose during a corporate merger between U.S. and Japanese companies, where Google Translate was utilized to translate essential legal documents. While Google Translate provided a rudimentary translation, it struggled with accurately conveying intricate legal terminology and the contextual nuances crucial in cross-border agreements. Legal jargon, particularly in international transactions, is notoriously complex, and the AI failed to differentiate between legal terms that carried distinct implications in U.S. and Japanese contexts (Al-Romany & Kadhim, 2024). This issue was further compounded by the substantial differences in the two countries' legal systems and frameworks, including their approaches to contract law, corporate governance, and regulatory compliance (Rahim, 2024).

The AI's failure to account for these distinctions led to multiple translation errors, ranging from minor inaccuracies to substantial misinterpretations of key legal concepts. For example, a clause related to corporate liability was mistranslated in a way that shifted financial responsibility between parties, creating legal ambiguity that required immediate rectification (Li, 2024). These mistakes had serious implications, as even small errors in legal documents can create ambiguities that may lead to misinterpretations, potential legal disputes, or financial liabilities. Human translators were tasked with correcting these mistakes, but the extent of the errors was so pervasive that over 60% of the translated content required significant revisions, with some sections needing complete retranslation. This reworking process consumed considerable time and resources, causing significant delays in the merger process and inflating the overall costs (Boulanger, 2024). Moreover, the errors in translation revealed the limitations of AI when it comes to capturing the cultural and contextual subtleties embedded in legal language. Legal frameworks are deeply intertwined with a country's culture, history, and societal values. In this case, Google Translate was unable to bridge the cultural divide between U.S. and Japanese legal principles, further underscoring the importance of human expertise in navigating these intricacies (Al Saadi & Awashreh, 2024).

In contrast, the European Commission's hybrid AI-human translation model for legal documents has demonstrated greater success, where AI-generated drafts are systematically refined by human experts to ensure legal and cultural accuracy. This approach has significantly improved the reliability of legal translations, reducing errors by over 40% compared to AI-only models (Tavares et al., 2023). This case highlights the significant risks associated with over-reliance on AI, particularly in specialized fields such as legal translation, where precision, cultural sensitivity, and a deep understanding of legal context are critical. While AI can be a valuable tool for basic translations or initial drafts, its inability to interpret legal intricacies necessitates human oversight. In high-stakes environments like corporate mergers, the costs of such inaccuracies can be substantial, leading to delays, increased legal fees, and even the potential derailment of critical business deals. Comparing this scenario with successful hybrid translation models emphasizes the necessity of integrating AI with human expertise to optimize both efficiency and accuracy. The incident serves as a cautionary example of the importance of combining AI with human expertise, particularly in areas where accuracy and attention to detail are paramount (Rahim, 2024).

Successful Collaboration: IBM Watson in Medical Translation

On the other hand, IBM Watson showcased notable success in the field of medical translation, particularly in translating patient records between hospitals in the U.S. and Spain. Leveraging its advanced AI capabilities, Watson was able to process and analyze vast amounts of complex medical terminology, significantly improving both the speed and accuracy of the translation process (IBM, 2020). Unlike conventional machine translation tools, Watson's sophisticated algorithms were specifically trained to recognize and interpret the nuances of medical language, including intricate terms related to diagnoses, treatments, and procedures. A key advantage was its ability to integrate real-time updates from medical databases, ensuring that newly emerging terminology, such as advancements in treatment protocols or novel diseases, was accurately reflected in translations. This capability allowed it to deliver translations that were not only fast but also highly precise (IBM, 2020).

Importantly, Watson did not operate in isolation. Human medical translators collaborated closely with the AI system, validating its outputs and ensuring that critical medical terms and procedures were conveyed with the utmost accuracy (Dolfing, 2024). For example, when Watson translated a rare disease diagnosis, human experts cross-checked the AI's output to verify that regional medical guidelines were appropriately reflected in the translation. This human-AI partnership was essential in addressing any potential ambiguities or errors, especially when dealing with life-or-death medical details. By working together, Watson and the human translators were able to maintain the integrity of vital medical information, ensuring that patient care was not compromised during the translation process (Xu et al., 2023).

Comparatively, a study on AI-driven medical translations in non-English-speaking regions, such as Japan and Germany, found that AI-only translation models introduced critical errors in 18% of cases, necessitating substantial human intervention. This reinforces the effectiveness of IBM Watson's hybrid approach, which systematically reduces translation errors while maintaining linguistic and contextual accuracy in sensitive medical documentation (Karalis, 2024).

This successful integration of AI in medical translation highlighted the potential of advanced technologies like Watson to revolutionize specialized fields. When paired with human expertise, AI systems can enhance the efficiency and reliability of services, ensuring that complex, domain-specific content is accurately translated without sacrificing the nuanced understanding that human professionals bring to the table (Davenport & Kalakota, 2019). The success of Watson's implementation has set a benchmark for AI-human collaboration in healthcare, with similar models now being explored in pharmaceutical research and telemedicine translation services. The IBM Watson case underscores the transformative role AI can play in specialized translation services, particularly when its capabilities are complemented and fine-tuned by human oversight (IBM, 2024; Karalis, 2024).

Problematic Collaboration: AI in Customer Service Translation

However, not all applications of AI in translation have been successful. A multinational retail company deployed AI chatbots in its customer service department to manage multilingual queries. Unfortunately, these bots often struggled to comprehend nuanced customer complaints and culturally specific questions, particularly in non-Western languages. For instance, in interactions with Arabic- and Japanese-speaking customers, the AI frequently misinterpreted idiomatic expressions, leading to responses that were irrelevant or even offensive (Ahmed, et al., 2024). Misunderstandings frequently arose, resulting in frustrated customers and necessitating human agents to intervene and resolve issues. One notable failure involved an AI-generated response to a refund request that incorrectly translated a policy term, misleading customers about their eligibility for reimbursement. This over-reliance on AI, without adequate human intervention, compromised the quality of customer service and underscored the limitations of AI in managing complex, context-dependent communications (Ghosh, Ness & Salunkhe, 2024).

Comparatively, companies that implemented a hybrid AI-human model—where AI handles routine queries and escalates ambiguous cases to human agents—saw improved customer satisfaction scores. Research on AI-driven customer service in multinational corporations revealed that fully automated AI responses resulted in a 25% increase in customer complaints, whereas hybrid models reduced miscommunication errors by 40% (Yazdi et al., 2024). These case studies collectively underscore the critical importance of balancing AI's capabilities with human expertise. While AI can significantly enhance efficiency and streamline workflows, human oversight remains essential for navigating complex, specialized, or sensitive content where cultural nuances, precision, and context are vital. By adopting a structured collaboration model—such as AI-assisted initial processing followed by human validation—businesses can optimize AI's strengths while mitigating its weaknesses. The successful integration of AI in translation processes hinges on a collaborative approach that harnesses the strengths of both human translators and AI technologies (Yazdi et al., 2024).

MODELS OF COLLABORATION

This section explores different models of collaboration between human translators and AI technologies in the translation process. It examines the advantages and challenges of post-editing and interactive translation models, emphasizing the need for effective integration of AI tools while maintaining human expertise.

Models of Collaboration in Human-AI Translation

In the post-editing model, AI-generated translations serve as the first draft, and human translators are responsible for reviewing and correcting the output. This model has gained popularity due to its efficiency, as AI can quickly generate translations that humans can refine. The key advantage of this approach is that it saves time while ensuring that the final product meets quality standards. For example, in technical and repetitive content such as user manuals, AI systems can produce translations with minimal errors, allowing human translators to focus on improving clarity and addressing contextual issues (Omar & Salih, 2024) However, this model also presents challenges. AI-generated translations often struggle with more complex texts that involve idiomatic expressions, metaphors, or cultural references. Translators may find that correcting AI mistakes can be as time-consuming as translating from scratch, particularly when the AI produces awkward or misleading content. Moreover, some translators might experience reduced job satisfaction, as they spend more time fixing errors rather than applying their linguistic creativity and expertise (Moneus & Sahari, 2024) On the other hand, the interactive translation model emphasizes real-time collaboration between human translators and AI. In this setup, AI assists by offering translation suggestions, providing context, or flagging potential errors as the translator works. This model leverages AI's speed and pattern recognition capabilities while maintaining human control over the final output. The interactive model proves particularly effective in specialized fields such as legal or medical translation, where precision is critical. Translators can reject AI suggestions that do not fit the specific context and guide the AI to improve its understanding over time. This dynamic foster a more engaged process, allowing human translators to combine their linguistic knowledge with AI-generated input for optimal results. However, this approach requires a high level of technological literacy and adaptability from human translators. Learning to manage the back-and-forth interaction with AI suggestions can be challenging, and some translators might find the constant AI interaction disruptive, potentially slowing their workflow, especially when the AI frequently suggests incorrect or irrelevant translations (UK Government, 2024)

Key Factors Contributing to or Hindering Successful Collaboration

Several key factors influence the success or failure of human-AI collaboration in translation. One of the most critical factors is the **quality of the AI output**. High-quality AI-generated translations can significantly reduce the amount of post-editing required, making the process smoother for human translators. However, if the quality of the AI's translation is poor, the burden on human translators increases, reducing the overall efficiency of the collaboration. The **complexity of the source text** also plays a significant role. AI excels at translating straightforward, technical texts but struggles with more complex, creative, or culturally nuanced content. In these cases, human translators must intervene more frequently, reducing the effectiveness of AI assistance (Al-Wasy et al., 2024).

Another essential factor is the **degree of human control**. Successful collaboration hinges on maintaining human oversight of the final output. Models that allow human translators to retain authority over critical translation decisions—such as word choice, tone, and cultural appropriateness—are more effective. When AI tools are viewed as supporting rather than replacing human expertise, the partnership becomes more seamless. **Training and adaptability** are also crucial for successful human-AI collaboration. Translators must be adequately trained to use AI tools effectively (AlSaadi & Awashreh, 2025). The success of interactive models, in particular, depends on the translator's ability to manage AI suggestions and navigate the technology efficiently. Furthermore, AI systems improve when they are fine-tuned based on feedback from human translators, creating a learning loop that enhances future performance. Finally, **trust and transparency** between human translators and AI systems are essential. Translators need to feel confident in the AI's ability to contribute positively to the translation process. Transparency regarding how AI-generated translations are produced—such as which data the AI was trained on and how it handles ambiguous language—can build trust and encourage more effective collaboration (Hamed, 2023; Al-Wasy, et al., 2024). By critically analyzing these models and understanding the factors that contribute to or hinder success, it becomes evident that human-AI collaboration in translation is most effective when it strikes a balance between leveraging AI's speed and pattern recognition and preserving human expertise in handling linguistic subtleties and cultural nuances.

Challenges in Human-AI Collaboration

Human-AI collaboration in translation faces several challenges, with accuracy, bias, and quality assurance being among the most prominent. While AI-powered translation tools have advanced significantly, they still struggle to achieve the nuanced accuracy that human translators bring to the table. AI systems can misinterpret idiomatic expressions, cultural references, or contextual subtleties, resulting in translations that lack precision or convey unintended meanings. This challenge is particularly evident in complex or creative texts where meaning is shaped by context and cultural nuance (Benmansour & Hdouch, 2023). Bias is another critical issue in human-AI collaboration. AI systems are trained on vast datasets that may contain inherent biases from the language and sources they are exposed to. These biases can influence the AI's translation choices, leading to outputs that reflect stereotypes or skewed perspectives. For instance, gender biases in certain languages might result in translations that assign gendered roles inappropriately. Addressing bias is essential to ensuring that AI-generated translations are inclusive and culturally sensitive (Benmansour & Hdouch, 2023).

Quality assurance is an ongoing challenge, as AI-generated translations often require human intervention to meet professional standards. While AI can process large volumes of text quickly, it can also introduce errors that undermine the overall quality of the translation. Human translators must review and correct these errors, which can be time-consuming, especially when the AI struggles with more sophisticated content. Balancing the speed of AI with the need for high-quality output requires careful management and quality control mechanisms. To mitigate these challenges and enhance collaboration, several strategies can be implemented. One effective approach is improving the training data for AI systems. By exposing AI to more diverse and high-quality datasets, it can better learn to handle complex language structures and reduce biases in its translations. Additionally, human translators can play a vital role in fine-tuning AI systems by providing feedback on errors and areas for improvement, creating a continuous learning loop that enhances the AI's performance over time (Dwivedi et al., 2023).

Another strategy involves refining the collaborative models themselves. In the post-editing and interactive models, ensuring that human translators maintain control over the final output is crucial. Human oversight helps catch inaccuracies and biases, allowing translators to correct and refine the AI's suggestions. Moreover, fostering technological literacy among translators can improve their ability to navigate AI tools efficiently, making the collaboration more seamless. Finally, transparency in AI processes is key to building trust and enhancing the partnership between humans and AI. Understanding how AI systems make decisions and which data they are trained on allows translators to better assess the reliability of AI-generated outputs. This transparency, combined with robust quality assurance practices, ensures that human-AI collaborations produce accurate, culturally sensitive, and high-quality translations (Briva-Iglesias, 2024).

ETHICAL CONSIDERATIONS IN HUMAN-AI IN TRANSLATION

The integration of AI into translation raises significant ethical concerns that demand careful examination, particularly regarding the necessity of human oversight and cultural sensitivity. As AI technologies become more prevalent in language services, the potential for ethical dilemmas increases, especially in contexts where accuracy and cultural nuance are essential. One primary concern is that while AI can efficiently process information, it lacks the ability to fully grasp the complexities of human communication, including the subtleties of culture, emotion, and context. This limitation can result in translations that may be technically correct but miss the deeper, intended meaning or convey unintended biases (Awashreh, 2024).

Human oversight is crucial in mitigating these issues. Although AI can analyze vast amounts of data quickly, it requires human translators to ensure that the translations are not only accurate but also culturally appropriate. Without human involvement, AI-generated outputs risk perpetuating stereotypes or misrepresenting cultural values, particularly when dealing with sensitive topics or multilingual communication in diverse contexts. Human translators play an essential role in interpreting the cultural and contextual nuances that AI systems often struggle to detect. Another key ethical consideration is accountability in AI-generated translations (Amini et al., 2024). When errors or cultural insensitivities occur in an AI-produced translation, questions arise regarding responsibility—should it lie with the technology or the human user? Establishing clear guidelines for accountability is essential to ensure that AI is viewed as a tool supporting human expertise rather than a replacement for it. To maintain the ethical integrity of the work, human translators must retain the final say in translation outputs. This accountability extends to the developers of AI systems, who must ensure their tools are trained on diverse, unbiased datasets and designed with transparency in mind (Enqvist, 2023).

Transparency in how AI systems operate, including the data they rely on and their methods for handling ambiguous language, is critical for fostering trust between human translators and AI. When translators understand the limitations and strengths of the AI tools they use, they can better ensure that the final translation upholds ethical standards, respects cultural diversity, and accurately reflects the intended message. In short, the ethical considerations surrounding AI in translation highlight the ongoing need for human oversight and cultural sensitivity. By ensuring that AI systems are used responsibly and that human professionals remain central to the translation process, the industry can maintain the integrity and quality of language services in an increasingly AI-driven world (Díaz-Rodríguez et al., 2023).

FUTURE DIRECTIONS IN AI- DRIVEN TRANSELATIOSN AND INTERPRETATION

As artificial intelligence continues to evolve, the landscape of translation and interpretation is poised for significant transformation. Predictions for the future suggest that AI will increasingly become an integral part of the translation process, enhancing efficiency, accuracy, and accessibility. However, this evolution must be approached with caution to ensure that the essential qualities of human expertise and cultural nuance remain at the forefront of the field. One potential direction is the development of more sophisticated AI tools that better understand context, cultural references, and emotional subtleties in language. As machine learning algorithms advance, we may see AI systems capable of producing translations that are not only accurate but also resonate with the intended cultural and emotional undertones. This would enable more effective communication across languages, making interactions smoother and more meaningful. Additionally, the rise of collaborative platforms could facilitate real-time cooperation between human translators and AI, allowing for a dynamic exchange of ideas and corrections that enhance the overall translation process (Way with Words, 2024).

To effectively integrate AI while maintaining professional integrity and human agency, practitioners should consider several key recommendations. First, ongoing education and training are crucial. Translators and interpreters must familiarize themselves with emerging AI technologies to leverage their strengths and understand their limitations. This knowledge will empower professionals to make informed decisions about when and how to utilize AI in their work. Second, maintaining a focus on human oversight is essential. AI should be viewed as a supportive tool rather than a replacement for human translators. Professionals should ensure they retain control over the final output, using AI-generated translations as a starting point for their expertise. This balance will help safeguard the quality and cultural appropriateness of translations, reinforcing the value of human insight in the process (Muñoz-Basols et al., 2023).

Moreover, fostering an ethical framework around AI usage in translation is paramount. Practitioners should advocate for transparency in AI algorithms and demand accountability for any biases present in AI-generated outputs. Engaging with developers to create tools that prioritize ethical considerations can further enhance the collaboration between human professionals and AI systems. Finally, practitioners should actively participate in discussions about the future of translation and interpretation in an AI-driven world. By engaging with peers, researchers, and technologists, they can contribute to shaping the direction of the field, ensuring that the integration of AI enhances rather than undermines the core values of translation: accuracy, cultural sensitivity, and human connection. In short, the future of translation and interpretation in an AI-driven world holds great promise, but it requires a thoughtful and proactive approach from practitioners. By embracing technological advancements while prioritizing professional integrity and human agency, translators and interpreters can navigate the complexities of this evolving landscape and continue to provide high-quality language services that respect the nuances of human communication (Mensah, 2023)

CONCLUSION

This chapter has critically examined the evolving collaboration between human translators and AI technologies, emphasizing the importance of fostering these partnerships to ensure a sustainable future for translation and interpretation. The discussion highlighted the development of collaborative models, such as post-editing and interactive translation, which demonstrate both the efficiency gains and challenges of integrating AI into language services. While AI offers considerable potential to boost productivity, the complexities of language—especially in nuanced contexts—underscore the need for human expertise and oversight.

The chapter also identified key challenges in human-AI collaboration, including issues of accuracy, bias, and quality assurance, which can compromise the effectiveness of translations if not properly addressed. To overcome these obstacles, strategies like continuous training, fostering ethical AI practices, and ensuring human control over translation outputs were recommended. Ethical considerations are crucial in preserving cultural sensitivity and accountability, ensuring AI systems are designed to respect these values.

Furthermore, as AI technologies evolve, it is essential for practitioners to remain vigilant about the ethical implications of their use, maintaining human agency in the translation process. The collaborative relationship between humans and AI is central to reshaping the future of translation, where AI can handle routine tasks and humans provide critical judgment on complex linguistic and cultural nuances.

To enhance the success of human-AI collaboration, the following recommendations are proposed:

1. **Invest in Collaborative Models**: Refine models that allow human translators to maintain control over final outputs while leveraging AI's efficiency for routine tasks.
2. **Enhance AI Training**: Ensure AI systems are trained on diverse, high-quality datasets to minimize biases and improve accuracy.
3. **Prioritize Ethical Frameworks**: Design AI systems with cultural sensitivity, transparency, and accountability at the forefront.

4. **Encourage Ongoing Professional Development**: Provide translators with continuous education to stay updated on AI advancements and best practices.

By implementing these strategies, organizations and translators can foster a more effective, ethical, and culturally sensitive translation environment. The future of translation lies in the seamless integration of AI's speed and efficiency with the irreplaceable insights of human expertise, ensuring high-quality, accurate, and culturally relevant translations in an increasingly AI-driven world.

Limitations

This study acknowledges several limitations. Firstly, the focus on human-AI collaboration in translation is based primarily on existing case studies and theoretical frameworks, which may not fully reflect the real-time, evolving dynamics of AI integration in diverse translation environments. Additionally, the research is limited by the available data on AI translation systems, particularly in non-Western languages and culturally unique contexts, where AI tools may face distinct challenges. These limitations restrict the generalizability of the findings across all languages and translation scenarios.

Directions for Further Research

Future research could explore more diverse linguistic and cultural contexts to better understand the challenges and opportunities AI presents in non-Western translation environments. Additionally, there is a need for empirical studies that evaluate the long-term impact of human-AI collaboration on translation quality, particularly in professional settings. Investigating the development of AI systems that adapt more seamlessly to human judgment and cultural nuances, as well as exploring the ethical implications of AI-generated translations, would further enrich the understanding of this evolving field.

REFERENCES

Abdedaim, K. (2023). Cultural implications of AI-powered language translation: In Proceedings of the 3rd International Conference on Translation and Technological Developments. Elwahrani Academy for Scientific Studies and Cultural Interaction. https://www.researchgate.net/publication/374700791

Ahmed, N., Saha, A. K., Al Noman, M. A., Jim, J. R., Mridha, M. F., & Kabir, M. M. (2024). Deep learning-based natural language processing in human–agent interaction: Applications, advancements, and challenges. *Natural Language Processing Journal*, *9*, 100112. DOI: 10.1016/j.nlp.2024.100112

Albaroudi, E., Mansouri, T., & Alameer, A. (2024). A comprehensive review of AI techniques for addressing algorithmic bias in job hiring. *AI*, *5*(1), 383–404. DOI: 10.3390/ai5010019

Alkanaani, M. (2024). Navigating ethics in AI-driven translation for a human-centric future. *Academia Open*, *9*(2), 13. DOI: 10.21070/acopen.9.2024.9407

Ali, N. (2023). Translating cultural identity: Skopos theory in the translation of Abdullah Al Faisal's Revolution of Doubts. *International Journal of English Literature and Social Sciences*, *8*(5), 1–9. DOI: 10.22161/ijels.85.26

Al-Romany, T. A. H., & Kadhim, M. J. (2024). Artificial intelligence impact on human translation: Legal texts as a case study. *International Journal of Linguistics Literature & Translation*, *7*(5), 89–95. DOI: 10.32996/ijllt.2024.7.5.11

Alsaadi, A., & Awashreh, R. (2025). Practical university training impact on job performance of translation graduates in Oman. *Forum for Linguistic Studies*, *7*(2), 786–796. DOI: 10.30564/fls.v7i2.8306

Al Saadi, A., & Awashreh, R. (2024). Enhancing the performance of translation graduates through training: A proposed practical model. In N. Mansour & L. M. Bujosa Vadell (Eds.), Finance and law in the metaverse world (pp. 295–308). Contributions to Finance and Accounting. Springer. DOI: 10.1007/978-3-031-67547-8_19

Al Sharairi, R. (2025). Review paper on the evolving role of human translators in the age of AI. *Pakistan Journal of Life and Social Sciences*, *23*(1), 2672–2679. DOI: 10.57239/PJLSS-2025-23.1.00210

Al-Wasy, B. Q., Alkodimi, K., & Alqahtani, O. O. A. (2024). Human-AI collaboration in translation and back translation of literary texts. *The Journal of Social Studies*, *30*(2), 2024. DOI: 10.20428/jss.v30i2.2404

Amini, M., Ravindran, L., & Lee, K.-F. (2024). Implications of using AI in translation studies: Trends, challenges, and future directions. *Asian Journal of Research in Education and Social Sciences*, *6*(1), 740–754. DOI: 10.55057/ajress.2024.6.1.67

Amaro, V., & Pires, M. J. (2024). Found in translation, lost in education: Artificial intelligence's impacts on translation tertiary education in Macao. *Asian Education and Development Studies*, *13*(4), 269–281. DOI: 10.1108/AEDS-01-2024-0012

Ashraf, M. (2024). Innovations and challenges in neural machine translation: A review. [IJSR]. *International Journal of Science and Research (Raipur, India)*, *13*(10), 656–662. DOI: 10.21275/SR241008113336

Awashreh, R. (2025). AI in higher education: AI ethics, quality assurance, and academic integrity. In *Optimizing leadership and governance in higher education* (pp. 203–232). IGI Global., DOI: 10.4018/979-8-3693-3534-5.ch006

Awashreh, R. (2024). Be Aware: Navigating Challenges in AI-Driven Higher Education. *The International Journal of Interdisciplinary Educational Studies*, *20*(1), 203–218. DOI: 10.18848/2327-011X/CGP/v20i01/203-218

Awashreh, R., & AlGhunaimi, H. (2024). Navigating burnout in the public sector: Strategies for enhancing employee well-being and organizational performance. *Evolutionary Studies in Imaginative Culture*, *211*, 211–225. https://esiculture.com/index.php/esiculture/article/view/1855. DOI: 10.70082/esiculture.vi.1855

Awashreh, R., & Ramachandran, B. (2025). A study on ethical implementation of AI in collegiate studies using fuzzy implication. *Pakistan Journal of Life and Social Sciences*, *23*(1), 3998–4013. DOI: 10.57239/PJLSS-2025-23.1.00317

Awashreh, R. (2024b). Omani private universities: Debates between progress in human development but weak education quality. *The International Journal of Educational Organization and Leadership*, *32*(1), 1–15. DOI: 10.18848/2329-1656/CGP/v32i01/1-15

Barman, S. (2024). Digital diplomacy: The influence of digital platforms on global diplomacy and foreign policy. VIDYA - A Journal of Gujarat University, 3(1), 61-75. DOI: 10.47413/vidya.v3i1.304

Basak, S., Agrawal, H., Jena, S., Gite, S., Bachute, M., Pradhan, B., & Assiri, M. (2022). Challenges and limitations in speech recognition technology: A critical review of speech signal processing algorithms, tools and systems. *Computer Modeling in Engineering & Sciences*, *135*(2), 1–37. DOI: 10.32604/cmes.2022.021755

Bekouche, M. F. (2024, November). Integrating artificial intelligence in translation: Analyzing technologies, ethical implications, and the future of human-AI collaboration. DOI: 10.13140/RG.2.2.28826.66242

Benmansour, M., & Hdouch, Y. (2023). The role of the latest technologies in the translation industry. Emirati Journal of Education and Literatures, 1(2), 31–36. https://www.emiratesscholar.com/system/publish/061223101243907.pdf

Betal, A. K. (2023). Enhancing second language acquisition through artificial intelligence (AI): Current insights and future directions. *Journal for Research Scholars and Professionals of English Language Teaching*, *7*(39). Advance online publication. DOI: 10.54850/jrspelt.7.39.003

Boulanger, A. (2024). The pros and cons of machine translation and AI in legal translation. McGill University, School of Continuing Studies. https://www.mcgill.ca/continuingstudies/article/pros-and-cons-machine-translation-and-ai-legal-translation

Briva-Iglesias, V. (2024). Fostering human-centered, augmented machine translation: Analysing interactive post-editing (Doctoral dissertation, Dublin City University). Advisor: S.

Cheong, H. I., Lyons, A., Houghton, R., & Majumdar, A. (2023). Secondary qualitative research methodology using online data within the context of social sciences. *International Journal of Qualitative Methods*, *22*, 16094069231180160. DOI: 10.1177/16094069231180160

Chen, P., Wu, L., & Wang, L. (2023). AI fairness in data management and analytics: A review on challenges, methodologies, and applications. *Applied Sciences (Basel, Switzerland)*, *13*(18), 10258. DOI: 10.3390/app131810258

Davenport, T., & Kalakota, R. (2019). The potential for artificial intelligence in healthcare. *Future Healthcare Journal*, *6*(2), 94–98. DOI: 10.7861/futurehosp.6-2-94 PMID: 31363513

Dengel, A., Gehrlein, R., Fernes, D., Görlich, S., Maurer, J., Pham, H. H., Großmann, G., & Eisermann, N. D. (2023). Qualitative research methods for large language models: Conducting semi-structured interviews with ChatGPT and BARD on computer science education. *Informatics (MDPI)*, *10*(4), 78. DOI: 10.3390/informatics10040078

Díaz-Rodríguez, N., Del Ser, J., Coeckelbergh, M., López de Prado, M., Herrera-Viedma, E., & Herrera, F. (2023). Connecting the dots in trustworthy artificial intelligence: From AI principles, ethics, and key requirements to responsible AI systems and regulation. *Information Fusion*, *99*, 101896. DOI: 10.1016/j.inffus.2023.101896

Doherty, S. (2016). The impact of translation technologies on the process and product of translation. [The University of New South Wales, Australia.]. *International Journal of Communication*, *10*, 947–969.

Dolfing, H. (2024,). Case study 20: The $4 billion AI failure of IBM Watson for Oncology. Henricodolfing. https://www.henricodolfing.com/2024/12/case-study-ibm- watson-for-oncology-failure.html

Dwivedi, Y. K., Kshetri, N., Hughes, L., Slade, E. L., Jeyaraj, A., Kar, A. K., Baabdullah, A. M., Koohang, A., Raghavan, V., Ahuja, M., Albanna, H., Albashrawi, M. A., Al-Busaidi, A. S., Balakrishnan, J., Barlette, Y., Basu, S., Bose, I., Brooks, L., Buhalis, D., & Wright, R. (2023). "So what if ChatGPT wrote it?" Multidisciplinary perspectives on opportunities, challenges and implications of generative conversational AI for research, practice and policy. *International Journal of Information Management*, *71*, 102642. Advance online publication. DOI: 10.1016/j.ijinfomgt.2023.102642

Enqvist, L. (2023). 'Human oversight' in the EU artificial intelligence act: What, when and by whom? *Law, Innovation and Technology*, *15*(2), 508–535. DOI: 10.1080/17579961.2023.2245683

Eszenyi, R., Bednarova-Gibova, K., & Robin, E. (2023). Artificial intelligence, machine translation & cyborg translators: A clash of utopian and dystopian visions. Orbis Linguarum, 21(2). DOI: 10.37708/ezs.swu.bg.v21i2.13

Garcia Valencia, O. A., Suppadungsuk, S., Thongprayoon, C., Miao, J., Tangpanithandee, S., Craici, I. M., & Cheungpasitporn, W. (2023). Ethical implications of chatbot utilization in nephrology. *Journal of Personalized Medicine*, *13*(9), 1363. DOI: 10.3390/jpm13091363 PMID: 37763131

Ghosh, S., Ness, S., & Salunkhe, S. (2024). The role of AI enabled chatbots in omnichannel customer service. *Journal of Engineering Research and Reports*, *26*(6), 327–345. DOI: 10.9734/jerr/2024/v26i61184

Hamed, H. M. (2023). Exploring translation approaches for popularized scientific texts: Human- machine collaboration in the Arabic context. *Migration Letters : An International Journal of Migration Studies*, *20*(S11), 1301–1318. https://www.migrationletters.com

IBM. (2020). IBM Watson Health recognizes top-performing U.S. hospitals and health systems. https://newsroom.ibm.com/2020-06-30-IBM-Watson-Health-Recognizes-Top-Performing-U-S-Hospitals-and-Health-Systems

IBM. (2024). Getting ready for artificial general intelligence with examples. https://www.ibm.com/think/topics/artificial-general-intelligence-examples

Jiang, T., Sun, Z., Fu, S., & Lv, Y. (2024). Human-AI interaction research agenda: A user- centered perspective. *Data and Information Management*, *8*(4), 100078. DOI: 10.1016/j.dim.2024.100078

Jim, J. R., Talukder, M. A. R., Malakar, P., Kabir, M. M., Nur, K., & Mridha, M. F. (2024). Recent advancements and challenges of NLP-based sentiment analysis: A state-of-the-art review. *Natural Language Processing Journal*, *6*, 100059. DOI: 10.1016/j.nlp.2024.100059

Karalis, V. D. (2024). The integration of artificial intelligence into clinical practice. *Applied Biosciences*, *3*(1), 14–44. DOI: 10.3390/applbiosci3010002

Khasawneh, M. A. S. (2023). The potential of AI in facilitating cross-cultural communication through translation. King Khalid University. https://orcid.org/0000-0002-1390-3765

Kenny, D. (Ed.). (2024). Machine translation for everyone: Empowering users in the age of artificial intelligence (Translation and Multilingual Natural Language Processing 18). https://library.oapen.org/bitstream/id/2bf04510-1edf-4f35-be06-662f1632ae8e/external_content.pdf

Khurana, D., Koli, A., Khatter, K., & Singh, S. (2023). Natural language processing: State of the art, current trends and challenges. *Multimedia Tools and Applications*, *82*(3), 3713–3744. DOI: 10.1007/s11042-022-13428-4 PMID: 35855771

Kimera, R., Kim, Y.-S., & Choi, H. (2024). Advancing AI with integrity: Ethical challenges and solutions in neural machine translation. https://arxiv.org/pdf/2404.01070

Lau, Y. L., Chee, S. P., Chua, R. H. H., Yong, Z. H., Yong, I. K., Tan, J. C., Yong, H. W., & Bakar, A. L. A. (2024). The datasets of human and AI translation. *Journal of Open Humanities Data*, *10*(45), 1–10. DOI: 10.5334/johd.212

Li, T. (2024, August). Exploring failures and possible remedies in AI and human translation of English idioms. DOI: 10.62051/199nqb23

Maeda, Y., Caskurlu, S., Kenney, R. H., Kozan, K., & Richardson, J. C. (2022). Moving qualitative synthesis research forward in education: A methodological systematic review. *Educational Research Review*, *35*, 100424. DOI: 10.1016/j.edurev.2021.100424

Marzuki, , Widiati, U., Rusdin, D., Darwin, , & Indrawati, I. (2023). The impact of AI writing tools on the content and organization of students' writing: EFL teachers' perspective. *Cogent Education*, *10*(2), 2236469. Advance online publication. DOI: 10.1080/2331186X.2023.2236469

Mendez, C., Gazzola, M., Clement-Wilz, L., Bachtler, J. F., Charamboulos, A., Djouvas, C., Mendez, F., & Triga, V. (2024). The European Union's approach to multilingualism in its own communications policy. ResearchGate. https://www.researchgate.net/publication/365777293

Mensah, G. B. (2023). Artificial intelligence and ethics: A comprehensive review of bias mitigation, transparency, and accountability in AI systems. DOI: 10.13140/RG.2.2.23381.19685/1

Moneus, A., & Sahari, Y. (2024). Artificial intelligence and human translation: A contrastive study based on legal texts. *Heliyon*, *10*(10), e28106. DOI: 10.1016/j.heliyon.2024.e28106 PMID: 38524597

Mirzayev, E. (2024). Machine translation vs. human translation: A comparative analysis. *Journal of Foreign Language Teaching and Applied Linguistics*, *10*(1), 31–38.

Muñoz-Basols, J., Neville, C., Lafford, B. A., & Godev, C. (2023). Potentialities of applied translation for language learning in the era of artificial intelligence. Hispania, 106(2). Johns Hopkins University Press. https://muse.jhu.edu/article/899427

Naveen, P., & Trojovský, P. (2024). Overview and challenges of machine translation for contextually appropriate translations. *iScience*, *27*(10), 110878. DOI: 10.1016/j.isci.2024.110878 PMID: 39391737

Omar, L. I., & Salih, A. A. (2024). Systematic review of English/Arabic machine translation postediting: Implications for AI application in translation research and pedagogy. *Informatics (MDPI)*, *11*(2), 23. DOI: 10.3390/informatics11020023

Rahim, N. R. (2024). Google and legal translation: The case study of contracts. *Arab World English Journal for Translation & Literary Studies*, *8*(2), 196–210. DOI: 10.24093/awejtls/vol8no2.14

Rebolledo Font de la Vall, R., & Gonzalez Araya, F. (2023). Exploring the benefits and challenges of AI-language learning tools. *The International Journal of Social Sciences and Humanities Invention*, *10*(01), 7569–7576. DOI: 10.18535/ijsshi/v10i01.02

Schwartz, R., Vassilev, A., Greene, K., Perine, L., Burt, A., & Hall, P. (2021). Towards a standard for identifying and managing bias in artificial intelligence (NIST Special Publication 1270). National Institute of Standards and Technology. DOI: 10.6028/NIST.SP.1270

Shaalan, K., Siddiqui, S., Alkhatib, M., & Abdel Monem, A. (2018). Challenges in Arabic natural language processing. In Computational linguistics, speech and image processing for Arabic language (pp. 59-83). DOI: 10.1142/9789813229396_0003

Shi, Z. (2021). Brain-like intelligence. In Intelligence Science (pp. 537-593). DOI: 10.1016/B978-0-323-85380-4.00014-2

Singh, A. P., Saxena, R., & Saxena, S. (2024). The human touch in the age of artificial intelligence: A literature review on the interplay of emotional intelligence and AI. *Asian Journal of Current Research, 9*(4), 36–50. DOI: 10.56557/ajocr/2024/v9i48860

Smith, E. (2008). Pitfalls and promises: The use of secondary data analysis in educational research. *British Journal of Educational Studies, 56*(3), 323–339. DOI: 10.1111/j.1467-8527.2008.00405.x

Stahlberg, F. (2020). Neural machine translation: A review. *Journal of Artificial Intelligence Research, 69*, 343–418. DOI: 10.1613/jair.1.12007

Taylor, A. (2025, February 5). How real-world businesses are transforming with AI – with 50 new stories. Microsoft Blog. https://blogs.microsoft.com/blog/2025/02/05/https-blogs-microsoft-com-blog-2024-11-12-how-real-world-businesses-are-transforming-with-ai/

Tatineni, S. (2019). Ethical considerations in AI and data science: Bias, fairness, and accountability. *International Journal of Information Technology and Management Information Systems, 10*(1), 11–20. https://iaeme.com/Home/issue/IJITMIS?Volume=10&Issue=1

Tavares, C., Oliveira, L., Duarte, P., & Moreira da Silva, M. (2023). Artificial intelligence: A blessing or a threat for language service providers in Portugal. *Informatics (MDPI), 10*(4), 81. DOI: 10.3390/informatics10040081

UK Government. (2024). Generative AI framework for HMG. https://www.gov.uk/government/publications/generative-ai-framework-for-hmg/generative-ai-framework-for-hmg-html

Wang, Y. (2024). The impact of technology on human translators and translation quality: A study on machine translation and computer-assisted translation tools. *English Linguistics Research, 13*(1), 19. DOI: 10.5430/elr.v13n1p19

Wagner, G., Lukyanenko, R., & Paré, G. (2022). Artificial intelligence and the conduct of literature reviews. *Journal of Information Technology*, *37*(2), 209–226. DOI: 10.1177/02683962211048201

Way With Words. (2024). What is the future of AI translation? The future of AI in language translation and interpretation explained. https://waywithwords.net/resource/future-ai-translation-and-interpretation/

Xu, Y., Zheng, X., Li, Y., Ye, X., Cheng, H., Wang, H., & Lyu, J. (2023). Exploring patient medication adherence and data mining methods in clinical big data: A contemporary review. *Journal of Evidence-Based Medicine*, *16*(3), 342–375. Advance online publication. DOI: 10.1111/jebm.12548 PMID: 37718729

Yazdi, M., Zarei, E., Adumene, S., & Beheshti, A. (2024). Navigating the power of artificial intelligence in risk management: A comparative analysis. *Safety (Basel, Switzerland)*, *10*(2), 42. DOI: 10.3390/safety10020042

Chapter 9
The Quality and Accuracy of AI-Generated Translation in Translating Communication-Based Topics:
Bringing Translation Quality Assessments Into Practices

Andang Saehu
https://orcid.org/0000-0002-9264-9645
Sunan Gunung Djati State Islamic University, Bandung, Indonesia

Mahi M Hkikmat
https://orcid.org/0000-0002-5037-2190
Sunan Gunung Djati State Islamic University, Bandung, Indonesia

ABSTRACT

This chapter presents the efficacy and obstacles associated with the quality of AI-generated translation, concentrating on instruments such as ChatGPT and Neural Machine Translation (NMT) technology. It emphasizes the superiority of NMT systems over traditional rule-based and statistical methodologies by employing deep learning techniques to understand language contextually, thereby yielding translations that are both more accurate, acceptable, and readable. Nonetheless, considerable challenges persist, particularly in navigating cultural subtleties, idiomatic phrases, and intricate linguistic frameworks. By using a Translation Quality Assessment (TQA), this chapter appraises ChatGPT's translation capabilities based on three criteria:

DOI: 10.4018/979-8-3373-0060-3.ch009

accuracy, acceptability, and readability. Although ChatGPT exhibits commendable performance in terms of general linguistic accuracy and readability, it encounters difficulties regarding acceptability when confronted with culturally rich or highly contextualized texts, especially within specialized domains such as political communication discourses.

INTRODUCTION

AI-generated translation is an automatic rapid message translation processed from a source language into a target language using Artificial Intelligence technology, such as Google Translate, DeepL, ChatGpt, Microsoft Translator, Amazon Translate, IBM Watson Language Translator, SYSTRAN, Reverso, Papago, iTranslate, Amazon Translate, Microsoft Translator, and Translate.com. These applications are the best in their field, with the ability to translate various languages and fields with a level of accuracy that is getting closer to human translation (Gupta, 2020). The translation process differs significantly from Rule-Based Machine Translation (RBM) and Statistical Machine Translation (SMT). The former is processing the message while considering the naturalness of language norms. Costa-Jussà and Fonollosa (2015) stated that the first step of machine translation development bases the transfer system on the linguistic rules such as semantics, morphology, and syntaxes of the language pairs. In line with this, Tao (2023) pointed out that it minimises grammatical errors in the translation process. These two approaches (RBM and SMT) are then commonly knows as traditional approaches. Meanwhile, the latter transfers the message by considering idiomatic expressions and language ambiguity (Bojar et al., 2016). It is more dynamic than the former because the corpus system has been developed inside. It is successfully used in language pairs with similar linguistic rules. It was initially used by Google Translate prior to developing Google Neural Machine Translation technology.

The AI-generated translation process makes use of Neural Machine Translation (NMT), which allows the system to be organised from the bottom up as the algorithm has deep learning capabilities. It processes human language and learns language patterns for better contextual understanding. In comparison to SMT, NMT has three main advantages. First, NMT understands how words co-occur. Second, the NMT system takes the whole sentence into account in its translation process. Third, NMT systems can learn complex linguistic relations (Agarwal et al., 2024). NMTs are typically 60% better at translating than SMTs (Ernst et al., 2019). The system can also reduce word order errors by 50%, grammatical mistakes by 19%, and lexical errors by 17% compared to SMT systems (Pestov, 2018). To clarify the ways the

NMT works, Table 1 shows the rule-based, statistics approach, and AI-Generated translation results in the following sentence about Billateral Communication.

Table 1. The comparison of translation results.

The ambassador emphasized the importance of maintaining open channels of communication between the two countries to avoid misunderstandings.	
Rule-based translation	*Duta besar menekankan pentingnya menjaga saluran komunikasi terbuka antara dua negara untuk menghindari kesalahpahaman.*
Statistics Approach translation	*Duta besar menggarisbawahi pentingnya menjaga jalur komunikasi terbuka antara kedua negara untuk mencegah kesalahpahaman*
AI-Generated translation: ChatGpt	*Duta besar menekankan pentingnya menjaga jalur komunikasi tetap terbuka antara kedua negara untuk mencegah kesalahpahaman.*

Table 1 shows that the result of rule-based translation strongly preserves the original sentence structure or grammar without considering language style and cultural context. For example, the use of "*Duta besar menekankan pentingnya...*" already meets the regular subject and predicate according to the rules. However, using the word "*saluran komunikasi*" is considered less natural. It also indicates that the result of the statistical approach seeks to use words that are more common in the context of diplomacy, such as the words "*menggarisbawahi*," "*jalur*," and "*mencegah*."

With the difference in the results of the traditional approaches, the author tried to translate the above sentence using ChatGpt (AI-generated translator). The results are surprising, as AI combines rule-based translation with a statistical approach. NMT tries to retain the sentence structure and language style appropriate to the bilateral communication context (Liang et al., 2021). The phrase "*menghindari kesalahpahaman*," translated as "*mencegah kesalahpahaman*," seems more subtle than "*menghindari kesalahpahaman*." Although the translation appears to be a combination of rule-based and statistical translation, the AI shows that the sentence structure is more flexible and natural because the AI, especially the NMT, understands the context of the whole sentence. Buch et al. (2022) stated that AI can adopt a language style more appropriate to a particular context, such as the language of diplomacy, which requires subtlety and precise word choice.

From the above example, the role of NMT in the AI-generated translation process is crucial. Koehn (2020) mentioned that NMT can learn translation patterns between languages and understand the whole context of a sentence, not just word by word. Reinforcing Koehn's opinion, Wu et al. (2016), in their research on Google Translate showed how NMT reduces the gap between the quality of machine translation and human translation through continuous learning. AI-generated translation, particularly through the Neural Machine Translation (NMT) approach, has significantly revolutionised automatic translation. Experts such as Bahdanau et al. (2014), Vaswani et al. (2017), and Bai (2024) have highlighted that NMT utilises deep learning to capture complex linguistic patterns and ensure translation coherence. However, AI-generated translation still has limitations, particularly in understanding cultural nuances, language style, and highly contextualised idioms. Wilkens (2020) has identified this as an area for improvement.

Being compared to traditional approaches, AI-generated translation offers flexible solutions and significant gains in accuracy and efficiency. The technology is not without its challenges, such as the handling of idioms, cultural nuances, languages with complex structures and other challenges that must be addressed for future improvements in the quality of machine translation. Hence, this study reports not only the quality and accuracy of AI-generated translations, particularly focusing on ChatGPT in translating communication-based topics, especially in political communication, but also the challenges in AI-generated translation.

LITERATURE REVIEW

Translation Quality and Accuracy of AI-Generated Translation

In the field of translation, the aspect of quality is of paramount importance, particularly when addressing high-stakes subjects such as interpersonal communication, mass media dissemination, public proclamations, political communication, and healthcare-related content. Erroneous translations can result in dire misconceptions, exemplified by the translation of health-related documents during the COVID-19 pandemic, where inaccuracies could propagate disinformation or ambiguity in the communication of essential medical guidance (Newell, et al., 2022). Moreover, another instance illustrates a significant miscommunication between nations in the Middle East, specifically involving Iran and Saudi Arabia. According to Indonesian Times, in mid-2024, drone strikes purportedly executed by Iran-backed militias targeted the oil infrastructure of Saudi Arabia. This incident prompted Saudi Arabia to intensify its military operations in Yemen, exacerbating regional tensions and adversely impacting global oil market stability.

Given the importance of translation in political communication contexts, this article explores how quality and accuracy can be assessed to evaluate translation quality in political communication. By focusing on these key criteria, we can determine whether a translation meets the specific needs of diplomatic communication. The translation of political texts requires a high level of accuracy, sensitivity to nuances, and an understanding of the political context. The term accuracy refers to the degree to which the translated text preserves the meaning, tone, and intent of the source text. It is the core quality of translation alongside acceptability and readability. The translation experts like Larson (1984), Nida and Taber (1969), House (1977, 1997), Newmark (1988), Baker (1992), Hatim and Mason (1997), Pym (2014), Nord (2005), and Nababan (2012) have the same wavelength that the quality instrument is required to evaluate the translation quality. It consists of quality parameter (High Accuracy, Moderate Accuracy, and Low Accuracy), score (3, 2, and 1), and Description (an explanation of the quality parameter).

Accuracy in translation is essential for balancing subjectivity, as it offers an objective framework for assessing the quality of a translation. By balancing the subjectivity of accuracy, the evaluation process becomes more structured and based on measurable criteria, which helps minimize the influence of personal biases (Jiamei & Zhang, 2024). There are some key concepts for balancing the subjectivity of accuracy in translation: 1) Anchor to the source text by ensuring that the meaning, intent, and nuances of the original text are accurately conveyed; 2) Maintain consistency among evaluators to reduce disagreements that may arise from different cultural or linguistic interpretations; and 3) Minimize the focus on style, as the primary goal of translation is to communicate the meaning of the source text, rather than to produce an aesthetically pleasing but inaccurate version.

Translation is not merely about converting words from one language to another. It involves preserving the meaning, tone, and intent of the original message while ensuring that the translated version resonates with the target audience (Kizi & Saporbayevich, 2024). This process requires a careful balance between quality and accuracy. While the former ensures that the translation fits within the cultural, social, and linguistic norms of the target audience, preserving both the tone and context of the original, the latter ensures that the message is faithfully conveyed without distortion. Wu et al. (2022) proposed several approaches to achieve the quality and accuracy of the translation, including: 1) Aligning with High-Stakes Texts that carry significant consequences, such as political communications, legal documents, and medical reports; 2) Adapting to Audience Needs to ensure that the translation resonates with and is fully understandable for the target audience; and 3) Balancing Flexibility and Fidelity to ensure that the translation is both accurate and culturally appropriate while preserving the original intent of the source text.

ChatGpt as an AI-generated Machine Translation

In light of the remarkable capacity demonstrated by ChatGPT to produce written content that is not only coherent but also well-structured, several educational districts have taken proactive measures to limit its accessibility within their academic institutions. On December 12, 2022, the Los Angeles Unified School District determined to restrict access to OpenAI's ChatGPT across all its network infrastructures and school-owned devices, referencing considerable apprehensions about the possible detrimental impacts this technology might impose on the integrity of academic endeavors and the capacity of students to participate in autonomous learning activities. Based on the information retrieved from https://www.edweek.org, this particular initiative was promptly followed by the New York City Department of Education, which enacted a comparable ban towards the decision of December 2022, thereby indicating a growing trend among educational authorities to scrutinize the implications of advanced AI tools in academic settings.

These strategic decisions indicate more extensive issues within the educational domain concerning the integration of AI. Hading et al. (2024) stated that some teachers worry that dependence on such technological resources may inhibit the development of critical thinking skills and impede students' comprehensive academic development. In contrast, others argue that these tools might function as beneficial auxiliary resources, augmenting pedagogical assistance and promoting innovation within the curriculum. In order to tackle these intricate challenges, multiple educational organizations, such as the California School Boards Association, are establishing task forces to investigate the incorporation of AI, taking into account both its pedagogical advantages and possible hazards. This endeavor encompasses the formulation of protocols for suitable AI application and the enhancement of digital literacy curricula to equip students for environments influenced by AI technologies (California School Boards Association, 2023).

The implementation of AI-generated translation tools such as ChatGPT provides notable benefits in terms of speed and operational efficiency in language translation (Mohan et al., 2023). However, it also introduces challenges regarding accuracy and contextual comprehension. ChatGPT, underpinned by sophisticated models like GPT-4, is capable of producing responses that resemble human interaction and streamlining translation processes, yet it often encounters difficulties in capturing intricate cultural and literary subtleties, which are essential for producing high-quality translations. This underscores the need for a harmonious strategy that integrates AI capabilities with human proficiency to guarantee translations that are both accurate, contextually acceptable, and easily understandable (Hading et al., 2024).

ChatGPT has emerged as a significant tool in the realm of machine translation, particularly for translating political communication discoueses and other types of texts into Indonesian. Its capabilities are highlighted by its ability to accelerate the translation process and enhance the quality of expressions used in the translated text (Ferreira, 2024). This is particularly evident in its application to political communication texts, where the richness of language and context is crucial (Mingazheva & Propova, 2024). The following sections provide examples and insights into how ChatGPT effectively translates text into Indonesian.

A frequently utilized prompt for AI-ChatGpt when seeking translation support is "Hi, ChatGpt! Kindly translate the subsequent text into Indonesian, ensuring that the intricacies of political discourse and cultural contexts are preserved. Additionally, please take into account the accuracy, acceptability, and readability!"

Table 2. Sample of ChatGpt Translation

Political communication	*Komunikasi Politik*
Source Language	**Target Language**
Political communication is the study of political messaging that is communicated, usually to the public e.g. political campaigns, speeches and political advertising, often concerning the mass media. It is an interdisciplinary field that draws from communication and political science. Political communication is concerned with ideas such as information flow, politicalinfluence, policy making, news, and their effects on citizens. The field also focuses on the study of political social media, propaganda, political economy of communication and non-profit organisations that communicate to affect political processes. Modern societal changes that have affected the field include the digitization of media, polarization and a movement towards a post-truth media environment. Political communication has existed since antiquity. During this era it was common for rulers to use symbols and monuments to communicate power and authority to the masses. In ancient Greece, public speeches such as those delivered by Pericles in Athens, played a crucial role in shaping political discourse and rallying public support for war efforts. During the era of the Roman Empire, political communication took on a more sophisticated form with the use of propaganda, rhetoric, and public spectacles in order to try and influence public opinion. Figures famed for their political communication skills include Cicero.	*Komunikasi politik adalah studi mengenai penyampaian pesan-pesan politik yang ditujukan kepada publik, seperti dalam kampanye politik, pidato, dan iklan politik, yang sering melibatkan peran media massa. Sebagai bidang yang bersifat interdisipliner, komunikasi politik memadukan ilmu komunikasi dan ilmu politik. Fokus utamanya meliputi aliran informasi, pengaruh politik, proses pembuatan kebijakan, pemberitaan, serta dampaknya terhadap masyarakat.* *Komunikasi politik juga mencakup kajian tentang penggunaan media sosial dalam politik, propaganda, ekonomi politik komunikasi, serta organisasi nirlaba yang berupaya memengaruhi proses politik. Perkembangan teknologi dan sosial, seperti digitalisasi media, polarisasi politik, serta munculnya era media pasca-kebenaran, telah membawa tantangan dan peluang baru dalam komunikasi politik.* *Komunikasi politik telah berlangsung sejak zaman kuno. Pada masa itu, simbol dan monumen sering digunakan oleh penguasa untuk menunjukkan kekuasaan dan otoritas kepada masyarakat. Di Yunani kuno, pidato-pidato publik, seperti yang disampaikan oleh Pericles di Athena, memainkan peran penting dalam membentuk wacana politik dan menggalang dukungan masyarakat, termasuk dalam persiapan perang.* *Di era Kekaisaran Romawi, komunikasi politik menjadi lebih terstruktur melalui penggunaan propaganda, retorika, dan pertunjukan publik untuk memengaruhi opini masyarakat. Tokoh-tokoh seperti Cicero dikenal karena keahlian mereka dalam menyampaikan pesan politik dengan retorika yang kuat dan strategis.*

The text is taken from https://en.wikipedia.org/wiki/Political_communication

METHODOLOGY

This study employed qualitative research approach with content analysis to documentation analysis (communication-based text). Qualitative research method was chosen as the data require in depth exploration of the sentence complexities and political nuances involved in assessing AI-generated translation and in depth explanation of the challenges in AI-generated translation, particularly in translating the text of political communication. The content analysis was selected for this study as it is designed to analyse textual data. The use of documentation analysis as the research instrument was to gather and assess the existing political communication text and its AI-generated translation. The source of text was taken from Wikipedia official website about poitical communication and the target text was taken from the ChatGPT.

In working with the content analysis to document, the Translation Quality Assessment (TQA) parameters proposed by Nababan et al. (2012), consisting of accuracy, acceptability, and readability, was applied to assesss the quality of AI-generated translation, particularly ChatGPT. After the text was generated, the TQA process was carried out sentence by sentence to explore the accuracy, acceptability, and readability levels with a scale of 1 to 3 indicating low, moderate and high levels. Each parameter uses weighting system to reflect the priority level, to balance the subjectivity, and to tailor the evaluation. The weighting is sequentially 3 for accuracy, 2 for acceptability, and 1 for readability. Detailed descriptions about the scale and weighting can be seen in Tables 4, 5, and 6.

The content analysis was also used to access large amounts of data as pointed out by Madugu & Ibrahim (2025) that content analysis allows the researcher to summarize and group large amounts of information. To cater the data relating to challenges in AI-generated translation, the researcher synthesized and categorized the information taken from previous research such as research by Baziotis et al. (2022), Dewayanti & Margana (2024), and Mohammed (2022).

RESULTS

The Translation Quality Assessments of Communication-Based Text

This section presents the source text and target text presented in Table 2 into assessment practices. Translation plays a crucial role in facilitating communication across linguistic and cultural boundaries. In political communication, the messages exchanged between countries or political entities often carry significant implications—diplomatic, economic, and even security-related. As global relations become more interconnected, accurate and culturally appropriate translations of political messages are indispensable (Silu, 2024). Misunderstandings caused by inaccurate translations can lead to diplomatic conflicts, economic repercussions, or misinformed policy decisions. Therefore, ensuring the quality of translations in these sensitive contexts is essential.

The role of Translation Quality Assessment (TQA) becomes even more crucial in political communication. When political leaders communicate internationally, their words can shape public opinion, influence bilateral relationships, and dictate future policy decisions. Missteps in translation—whether through errors in factual details or the misinterpretation of tone—can have far-reaching consequences. Therefore, a systematic and structured approach to evaluating translations ensures that the messages are not only linguistically accurate but also culturally and contextually appropriate. A comprehensive approach to TQA helps maintain the integrity of the original message, supports effective communication, and minimizes the risks associated with translation errors in high-stakes situations (Lee et al., 2022). Therefore, assessing translation quality in such a domain is not just a matter of linguistic correctness but also involves a deep understanding of cultural, political, and diplomatic factors.

To bring the TQA into practices, the source and target texts provided in Table 3 are then evaluated based on the parameter of accuracy, acceptability, and readability as displayed in Table 3.

Table 3. The Translation Quality Assessment of Political Communication Text

No	Source Language	Target Language	Accuracy Level	Acceptability Level	Readability Level
Paragraph 1					
1	Political communication is the study of political messaging that is communicated, usually to the public e.g. political campaigns, speeches and political advertising, often concerning the mass media.	*Komunikasi politik adalah studi mengenai penyampaian pesan-pesan politik yang ditujukan kepada publik, seperti dalam kampanye politik, pidato, dan iklan politik, yang sering melibatkan peran media massa.*	3	3	3
2	It is an interdisciplinary field that draws from communication and political science.	*Sebagai bidang yang bersifat interdisipliner, komunikasi politik memadukan ilmu komunikasi dan ilmu politik.*	3	3	3

continued on following page

Table 3. Continued

No	Source Language	Target Language	Accuracy Level	Acceptability Level	Readability Level
3	Political communication is concerned with ideas such as information flow, politicalinfluence, policy making, news, and their effects on citizens.	*Fokus utamanya meliputi aliran informasi, pengaruh politik, proses pembuatan kebijakan, pemberitaan, serta dampaknya terhadap masyarakat.*	2	2	2
Total			8	8	8
Average Score			2.67	2.67	2.67
Paragraph 2					
1	The field also focuses on the study of political social media, propaganda, political economy of communication and non-profit organisations that communicate to affect political processes.	*Komunikasi politik juga mencakup kajian tentang penggunaan media sosial dalam politik, propaganda, ekonomi politik komunikasi, serta organisasi nirlaba yang berupaya memengaruhi proses politik.*	2	3	3
2	Modern societal changes that have affected the field include the digitization of media, polarization and a movement towards a post-truth media environment.	*Perkembangan teknologi dan sosial, seperti digitalisasi media, polarisasi politik, serta munculnya era media pasca-kebenaran, telah membawa tantangan dan peluang baru dalam komunikasi politik.*	2	2	3
Total			4	6	6
Average Score			1.3	2	2
Paragraph 3					
1	Political communication has existed since antiquity.	*Komunikasi politik telah berlangsung sejak zaman kuno.*	3	3	3
2	During this era it was common for rulers to use symbols and monuments to communicate power and authority to the masses.	*Pada masa itu, simbol dan monumen sering digunakan oleh penguasa untuk menunjukkan kekuasaan dan otoritas kepada masyarakat.*	3	2	3

continued on following page

Table 3. Continued

No	Source Language	Target Language	Accuracy Level	Acceptability Level	Readability Level
3	In ancient Greece, public speeches such as those delivered by Pericles in Athens, played a crucial role in shaping political discourse and rallying public support for war efforts.	*Di Yunani kuno, pidato-pidato publik, seperti yang disampaikan oleh Pericles di Athena, memainkan peran penting dalam membentuk wacana politik dan menggalang dukungan masyarakat, termasuk dalam persiapan perang.*	3	2	3
Total			9	7	9
Average Score			3	2.3	3
Paragraph 4					
1	During the era of the Roman Empire, political communication took on a more sophisticated form with the use of propaganda, rhetoric, and public spectacles in order to try and influence public opinion.	*Di era Kekaisaran Romawi, komunikasi politik menjadi lebih terstruktur melalui penggunaan propaganda, retorika, dan pertunjukan publik untuk memengaruhi opini masyarakat.*	2	2	3
2	Figures famed for their political communication skills include Cicero.	*Tokoh-tokoh seperti Cicero dikenal karena keahlian mereka dalam menyampaikan pesan politik dengan retorika yang kuat dan strategis.*	3	3	3
Total			5	5	6
Average Score			1.6	1.6	2

Measuring Accuracy

Accuracy refers to how faithfully the meaning, facts, and nuances of the original text are transferred into the target language. It is the core quality of translation alongside acceptability and readability. To see the degree of to which the translated text preserves the meaning, tone and intent of the source text, take a look at the following table 4.

Table 4. Accuracy Translation Parameter

Quality Parameter	Weighting	Score	Description
High Accuracy	3	3	Accuracy ensures that the core message of the source text is delivered without distortion, omission, or addition.
Moderate Accuracy		2	The translation is mostly accurate, but minor errors in terminology or nuances are present.
Low Accuracy		1	The translation contains significant errors that affect the meaning or accuracy of the political message.

Table 4 shows that accuracy parameter consists of High Accuracy, Moderate Accuracy, and Low Accuracy with their score (3, 2, and 1). Each of which has different Description (an explanation of the quality parameter). The quality instrument also requires the weighted scoring system to reflect the priorities, to balance the subjectivity, and to tailor the evaluation. Song (2024) stated that subjectivity can emerge from various factors, such as differing interpretations, stylistic preferences, or cultural nuances.

Of the three quality parameters, the translation accuracy is the priority of the translation quality. The weighting system for the accuracy is the highest one—scored 3. There are some considerations of becoming the priority: 1) inaccurate translations can lead to misinterpretations, which may cause confusion, misinformation, or even serious consequences; 2) no matter how acceptable or readable a translation is, if it fails to accurately reflect the source text, it cannot fulfil its purpose; and 3) the accurate transfer of meaning is non-negotiable; and 4) accurate translations build trust between the source text author and the target audience. Another important reason for weighting the scoring system towards accuracy is to tailor the evaluation process. By customizing the translation evaluation, the accuracy should be ensured to align with the specific needs and purposes of the text being translated (Wu et al., 2022).

In the context of political communication, accuracy is paramount because even minor errors or distortions in translation can lead to significant misunderstandings. A politically incorrect translation could jeopardize negotiations, inflame tensions, or lead to diplomatic fallout. To evaluate the accuracy of a translation, it is essential to juxtapose the source and target text messages, meticulously verify structure and consistency, identify cultural and political communication subtleties, and assess the language style (Mahale, et al., 2023). In Table 6, the scores assigned to each sentence differ (3 and 2). Within the target language column, every sentence preserves the original meaning of the source language without any alteration in context or meaning. The assessment proceeded to assess the suitability of the structure, which revealed that the translated sentences adhered to the proper grammatical conventions in Indonesian.

While the translation results demonstrate a high level of accuracy in preserving the fundamental meaning, it is essential to consider various aspects concerning the nuances of political discourse, cultural background, and langauge style. When examining the nuances of political discourse, it is crucial to ensure that particular concepts or terminology pertinent to politics are rendered with their intended meaning, free from distortion. For instance, analyzing the translation of the phrase "Political communication is concerned with ideas such as information flow, political influence, policy making, news, and their effects on citizens," into "*Fokus utamanya meliputi aliran informasi, pengaruh politik, proses pembuatan kebijakan, pemberitaan, serta dampaknya terhadap masyarakat*" highlights the challenges faced by AI-Generated Translation. The expression "*dampaknya terhadap masyarakat*" could be enhanced to "*dampaknya terhadap opini publik atau partisipasi politik masyarakat*" to more accurately encapsulate the essence of political communication.

Assessing the cultural framework, the level of accuracy in translating the statement "Modern societal changes that have affected the field include the digitization of media, polarization, and a movement towards a post-truth media environment" to "*Perkembangan teknologi dan sosial, seperti digitalisasi media, polarisasi politik, serta munculnya era media pasca-kebenaran, telah membawa tantangan dan peluang baru dalam komunikasi politik*" can be regarded as moderate. This assessment stems from the fact that the phrase "*era media pasca-kebenaran*" might lack clarity without supplementary context for Indonesian audiences. For instance, instances of disinformation on social media platforms in Indonesia could be illustrated to enhance cultural pertinence.

In relation to language style, certain sentences indicate that the translation employs a formal and scholarly language style that is fitting for the context of political communication. For instance, the expression "It is an interdisciplinary field that draws from communication and political science," translated as "*Sebagai bidang yang bersifat interdisipliner, komunikasi politik memadukan ilmu komunikasi dan ilmu politik*," exhibits a succinct sentence structure and a language style that is appropriate for academic discourse. Nevertheless, in the statement "During the Roman Empire, political communication took a *more structured* form with the use of propaganda, rhetoric and public spectacles to try to influence public opinion," the translation reveals a minor inconsistency in linguistic style. The term "*lebih terstruktur*" could be substituted with "*lebih canggih dan strategis*" to better convey the level of complexity in question.

Measuring Acceptability

Translation acceptability refers to the degree to which a translated text conforms to the linguistic, cultural, and stylistic norms of the target language (Burazer, 2013). In political communication texts, acceptability goes beyond literal translation and addresses how well the translation adheres to the norms, expectations, and political sensitivities of the target country. It focuses on whether the translation is acceptable in the cultural and social context of the target audience (Kizi & Saporbayevich, 2024). To see the level of acceptability, Table 5 is presented below.

Table 5. Acceptability Translation Parameter

Qualtiy Parameter	Weighting	Score	Description
High Acceptable		3	The translation uses culturally appropriate terms and maintains the intended tone and sensitivity.
Moderate Acceptable	2	2	The translation includes phrases in the target text generally sounds natural, but there are one or two word that are inappropriate in the target language linguistic principle.
Low Acceptable		1	The translation includes phrases that may offend or cause misunderstandings due to cultural or political differences.

Table 5 shows that acceptability, while important, generally has a slightly lower weight (e.g., 2 out of 3). Some consideration can be taken for granted that the weighting is because it focuses on cultural and linguistic adaptation, ensuring that the translation is natural and conforms to the norms of the target audience. It complements accuracy but does not replace its core function of preserving meaning. Another reason is it is due to the fact that acceptability is more subjective. It depends on cultural nuances, audience expectations, and the evaluator's perception of how "natural" and "appropriate" the translation feels. This subjectivity makes acceptability difficult to standardize, as it can vary widely among evaluators. In relation to this, Sanesi (2024) stated that cultural differences significantly influence what is deemed acceptable, requiring translators to adapt idioms, metaphors, humor, and social references to resonate with the target audience.

In working with how acceptability works, the evaluation result has been presented in Table 3, which illustrates that the degree of acceptability of translations exhibits considerable variability. This variation is significantly affected by the nuances of political communication, the cultural context, and the tone employed. In the initial sentence of paragraph 1, the translation already encompasses acceptable nuances of political communication, such as the conveyance of political messages, which include essential concepts (campaigne, speeches, political advertisements) that are rendered in an acceptable and relevant manner within the political communication framework. However, in the third sentence, there exists a need for the AI to enhance its proficiency in addressing cultural context issues, even though the political nuance and tone have been successfully interpreted. The translation of the third sentence in paragraph 1 indicates that terms like "information flow"' and "political influence" could benefit from a deeper contextualization. For instance, it would be advantageous to acknowledge the significant role of local media or public opinion by articulating "*penyebaran berita melalui media massa atau media social*." Additionally, the phrase " *proses pembuatan kebijakan* " could be elucidated further by providing context for those readers who may be unfamiliar with formal terminology.

In the second sentence of paragraph two, the challenge faced by the AI in addressing cultural context is exemplified by the term 'post-truth media environment,' which is translated as '*era media pasca-kebenaran*.' Nevertheless, this nomenclature fails to resonate with Indonesian audiences. An elucidation or a pertinent local instance, such as the phenomenon of hoax news proliferating on social media, could enhance its relevance. Additionally, another issue that emerges in the second sentence pertains to tone. Although a formal style is preserved, the phrase '*era media pasca-kebenaran*' appears somewhat strange. To enhance its acceptability, the translation should be modified for relevance; for instance, for an academic audience, employing terms such as '*era dominasi opini*' or '*zaman distorsi informasi*' would be more fitting and acceptable. Conversely, for a general readership, '*era kaburnya fakta*' presents a simpler and more palatable alternative.

A high level of acceptability in terms of political communication nuance, cultural context, and tone can be seen in the second sentence of paragraph four. The capability of Cicero political communication is explained appropriately and relevant. The cultural contextual of the sentence is not needed anymore because the context is global and relevant. Seen from the tone, the formality of the source language is maintained with the addition of appropriate details without inviting emotional or speculative interpretations (Hyman, 2014).

Measuring Readability

In translation, readability refers to how easily a translated text can be read and understood by the target audience. It ensures that the message of the source text is delivered in a clear, fluent, and engaging manner (Lines, 2022 & Matricciani, 2023). The acceptability of a translation is crucial, but it must be balanced with its accuracy (Köprülü, 2023). Maintaining the integrity of the original message in the translated text while ensuring it is comprehensible for the intended audience presents a significant challenge (Lines, 2022). To evaluate the degree to which the translated texts in readable, take a look at the Table 6 below.

Table 6. Readability Translation Parameter

Qualtiy Parameter	Weighting	Score	Description
High Readable	1	3	The translation employs terminology, specialized language, expressions, clauses, statements, or written content that can be readily comprehended by the audience.
Moderate Readable		2	The translation is generally comprehensible to the intended audience; however, certain sections of the material may require multiple readings for full comprehension by the readers.
Low Readable		1	The translation can often pose challenges for the reader's comprehension.

In Table 6, the weighting of readability in translation quality is typically lower than accuracy and acceptability. The consideration of a low weighting score one (1) for readability is based on the specific context and priorities of the translation project (Shakirovna & Fries, 2023). While readability is essential, its significance varies across specific contexts depending on the purpose of the text, the target audience, and the balance with other translation criteria such as accuracy and acceptability. Zuo (2024) stated that the readability of literary work translation is different from political communication translation. In some cases, maintaining the stylistic complexity of the literary works and political communication texts might outweigh the need for smooth readability.

Political communication often involves complex sentences, legal terminology, and dense jargon, which can affect the readability of the text. A readable translation is one that conveys the message clearly and is easily digestible, even by those with no specialized knowledge. The readability of translated texts, particularly within the political communication, is crucial for ensuring that the messages delivered are comprehensible and pertinent to the intended audience. Nonetheless, there are obstacles encountered in the translation of texts that encompass: political communication nunaces, cultural context, and language style. To evaluate the readability of a translation, the grading scale as displayed in Table 3 is applied.

The initial statement in paragraph 1 indicates that translations imbued with political nuances can be rendered accurately, exemplified by terms such as 'political campaigns' and 'mass media.' Considering their pertinence to the Indonesian cultural context, the phrases '*kampanye politik*' and '*media massa*' align with widely recognized terminology within Indonesia. Furthermore, in light of the langauge style employed, the resultant translations exhibit a level of formality that aligns with the intended purpose of the text. Thus, in summary, the translation of the initial sentence is notably readable.

While a significant portion of the translated sentences exhibit a commendable level of readability, there exists one sentence within paragraph 1 that presents a moderate readability level. The sentence 'Political communication encompasses concepts such as information dissemination, political influence, policy formulation, news, and their implications for citizens' is rendered into Bahasa Indonesia as '*Fokus utamanya meliputi aliran informasi, pengaruh politik, proses pembuatan kebijakan, pemberitaan, serta dampaknya terhadap masyarakat*,' which reveals a challenge in addressing the subtleties of political communication. Indeed, the term 'news,' translated as '*pemberitaan*,' is relatively commonplace. However, it fails to encapsulate the complexities of contemporary media or specific political dynamics that more critical readers may seek.

Another issue that arises when translating the third sentence of paragraph 1 pertains to the cultural dimension that must be made explicit in the phrase '*dampaknya terhadap masyarakat*.' This phrase is somewhat vague and could benefit from a more precise delineation of particular outcomes, such as public opibion or political participation, which hold significance within the Indonesian milieu. Moreover, the formal register employed could be enhanced by incorporating illustrations or terminologies that mirror the local political landscape, such as the influence of mass media or the process of digitalization in policy formulation. To augment clarity, the term '*pemberitaan*' should be refined to expressions like '*media berita*' or '*konten berita politik*' to better convey its political significance. Additionally, it is crucial to provide a detailed context for '*dampaknya terhadap masyarakat*,' for instance, '*serta pengaruhnya terhadap pembentukan opini publik dan partisipasi warga negara*.'

The results derived from the assessment of translations quality related to political communication utilizing AI-generated methodologies, focusing on accuracy, acceptability, and readability, indicate a spectrum of outcomes. Consequently, it is imperative to assess the final evaluation—determining the quality of the AI translation—specifically whether the translation achieves standards of accuracy, acceptability, and readability.

Table 7. Recapitulation of Translation Quality Assessment

Paragraph	**Sentence**	**Score**			**Level of Quality**
		Accuracy	**Acceptability**	**Readability**	
1	1 – 3	8	8	8	Moderate
Average Score		2.67	2.67	2.67	
2	1 – 2	4	6	6	Low
Average Score		1.3	2	2	

continued on following page

Table 7. Continued

Paragraph	Sentence	Score			Level of Quality
		Accuracy	Acceptability	Readability	
3	1 – 3	9	7	9	Moderate
Average Score		3	2.3	3	
4	1 – 2	5	5	6	Low
Average Score		1.6	1.6	2	

Table 7 presents a synthesis of the assessment of translation quality for ten sentences extracted from political communication texts. Each sentence is evaluated according to the parameters of accuracy, acceptability, and readability. To elucidate the overall quality, the results of the assessments are calculated for each paragraph, thereby providing a comprehensive overview. The average score for the accuracy of the translations for sentences 1 to 3 in the first paragraph is calculated at 2.67, derived from the ratio of total accuracy to the number of TQA parameters (8: 3). This score is subsequently multiplied by the accuracy weight, yielding 2.67 x 3 = 8. In the same paragraph, the average acceptability score mirrors that of accuracy, also standing at 2.67. However, given its weight is positioned at 2, the resultant score becomes 2.67 x 2 = 5.3. A comparable average score is attained for the readability quality of the translation, which is 2.6 with a weight of 1, thus maintaining a score of 2.67. Following the determination of the average score for each TQA parameter, the quality level can be ascertained as accurate, acceptable, readable, or otherwise. To establish the overall quality level, the total of all averages is computed and divided by the sum of the weights. The resulting calculation is 8 + 5.3 + 2.6 = 15.9: 6 = 2.65. This average score indicates that, in general, the translation is characterized by moderate levels of accuracy, acceptability, and comprehensibility for the intended audience.

The mean score regarding the acceptability and readability of the translation of the two sentences in the second paragraph is recorded as 2. Conversely, the mean score for accuracy is determined to be 1.3. When these scores are adjusted according to the respective weightings of each parameter, the resultant scores are as follows: 1.4 x 3 = 4.2 for accuracy, 2 x 2 = 4 for acceptability, and an additional score of 2 for readability. The cumulative average score is calculated to be 1.7, derived from the total of 4.2 + 4 + 2 = 10.2, which is then divided by 6. This average score indicates that the translation of the two sentences in the second paragraph is characterized by inaccuracies, unacceptability, and a lack of readability for the intended audience. In the third paragraph, the computed average score amounts to 9 + 4.6 + 3 = 16.6, which when divided by 6 yields an average of 2.8. This average score suggests that the translation quality of the sentences in the third paragraph is assessed as moderate. This implies that the translation exhibits moderate accuracy, acceptability, and comprehensibility for the target audience (Kizi & Saporbayevich, 2024). The lowest average score is observed in the translation of sentences within paragraph 4, culminating in an overall score of 1.6. This average score is classified as indicative of low-level translation quality. In essence, it highlights that certain terms have been translated inaccurately, rendered unacceptable, and remain challenging for the target audience to comprehend.

Challenges in AI-Generated Translation

The challenges of AI-generated translation include several vital aspects that various studies in automatic translation and machine learning have identified. One of them is Nord (2005), who outlines four translation problems, namely pragmatic translation problems, convention-related translation problems, linguistic translation problems, and text-specific translation problems. Each of which will be described below.

Pragmatic Translation Problems

The limitation of AI in understanding the full context of a sentence or paragraph is a considered pragmatic problem in AI-generated translation. AI has a tendency to translate simple words or phrases and is often clumsy at understanding the context of complex sentences that have contextual, idiomatic meanings or different grammatical structures (Baziotis, et al., 2022). The meaning of a word can change depending on other words in the sentence in a contextual sentence. Koehn & Knowles (2017) point out that NMT tends to lose context when translating long sentences. This is because according to Zhu (2022), NMT models usually work on a sentence-by-sentence basis, without considering the relationship between sentences in a paragraph.

A common example used to render the meaning of diplomatic phrases with cultural nuances is the phrase "peace talks". It is literally transferred into Bahasa "*pembicaraan damai*." Take a look at the complete sentence below.

"The peace talks between the two nations were stalled due to disagreements over border control."

The sentence seems to be simple, but it has a comples phrase inside. Pay attention to the AI-generated translation below.

"Pembicaraan damai antara kedua negara terhenti karena ketidaksepakatan tentang kontrol perbatasan."

Although the literal translation seems accurate, AI-generated translation is failed to grasp the complexity behind the phrase "peace talks" in the field of diplomatic or political communication. In the conflict between Israel and Palestine, the phase "peace talks" is not enough transferred literally into "*pembicaraan damai*," it should show the complexity issue which refers to the set of sensitive and formal negotiation such as international mediation, temporary agreement, and segmented process to reach out the peaces. It should also indicate the involvement of United Nation, which is vital in this context to strengthen its meaning. The failure of AI in generating the meaning of the phrase "peace talks" shows that AI-generated translation is restricted to render the contexts. This coincides with the statement by Castilho et al. (2018) and Silu (2024) that AI-generated translation is frequently inaccurate because the NMT doesn't have any capabilities to render the cultural, historical, and political contexts of the sentences.

Another problem showing pragmatic translation can be seen in a study conducted by Voita, et al. (2019) who found that NMT requires improvement in translating anaphoric sentences. They further found that NMT has a problem with the reference for pronouns. They added that when NMT translates the pronouns, it refers to the part of words or terms in the previous sentences incorrectly. The following examples will provide you clear understanding:

1. The chairman of the Executive Board met with the President of Republic of Indonesia. He said that the visit was an opportunate moment to strengthen bilateral relations between the two countries.
2. The peace talks have resumed in Egypt after mediation. They failed to reach a negotiation.

The first anaphoric sentence shows that the use of pronoun "he" is confusing whether "he" refers to the chairman of the Executive Board or the President of Republic of Indonesia. The use of "They" in the second sentence also not clear whether "they" refer to "The peace talks or people" involved in the sentence. Therefore, using an explicit noun rather than "he" and "they" will be obvious. The sentence 1 should be "The chairman of the Executive Board met with the President of Republic of Indonesia. The president said that the visit was an opportunate moment to strengthen bilateral relations between the two countries." Meanwhile, the sentence 2 should use "The mediators" rather than "They". In line with this, Naveen & Trojovsky (2024) showed that AI-generated translation is limited to understand the broader and complex contexts, especially in the reference of culture, history, and idiomatic expression.

In summary, the inability of AI to fully grasp the broader context of text remains a major limitation, affecting the quality and accuracy of translations, especially for complex or culturally sensitive material.

Convention-Related Translation Problems

The subsequent challenge encountered in the employment of artificial intelligence for the translation of texts, particularly those pertaining to Communication thems, is its frequent deficiency in accuracy when translating idiomatic expressions or culturally specific phrases (Dewayanti & Margana, 2024). AI models commonly engage in literal translations, failing to grasp the intricate cultural context or the metaphorical significance embedded within these expressions. As articulated by Castilho et al. (2018), the translation of idiomatic phrases continues to represent one of the most formidable obstacles in AI-driven translation, given that such expressions do not invariably possess a direct equivalent in the target language. "Translation of idiomatic expressions remains one of the most significant challenges in machine translation, as such phrases often lack direct equivalents in the target language" (Castilho et al., 2018, p. 14).

Idioms are intricately embedded within cultural frameworks, frequently expressing significances that diverge from their straightforward literal interpretations. This intricacy is further exacerbated by the constraints of contemporary artificial intelligence models, which predominantly emphasize literal translations while failing to comprehensively apprehend the cultural subtleties and metaphorical implications (Knowles, 2016; Mishra, 2024). When an idiomatic expression is rendered in a literal manner, the outcome frequently appears nonsensical or may even create confusion among native speakers of the target language. Here is the example with idiomatic expression:

"The new policy aims to cut through the red tape to make foreign investment easier."

An English phrase like "Cut through the red tape," which literally means "*memotong jalur birokrasi*," would pose significant challenges for comprehension if rendered literally into Indonesian as "*Kebijakan baru ini bertujuan untuk memotong jalur birokrasi agar investasi asing lebih mudah dilakukan*." Rather than being interpreted as "*menyederhanakan prosedur birokrasi*," AI may opt to translate it literally, failing to accurately encapsulate the true circumstances. This phenomenon arises from the AI model's inability to recognize that "Cut through the red tape" functions as an idiomatic expression denoting excessive bureaucratic hurdles or regulatory constraints. This is consistent with Prabhakaran et al's (2022) view that "AI lacks the capacity for cultural intuition needed to interpret idiomatic language correctly, leading to literal translations" (p. 3).

Another illustrative instance is the Indonesian idiom "*buah bibir*," as exemplified in the statement, "*Tindakan pemerintah dalam menangani isu lingkungan menjadi buah bibir di kalangan aktivis dan media, menciptakan berbagai opini di masyarakat*." The connotation of this idiom signifies a topic of widespread discussion. A direct translation into English would likely render it as "*the fruit of lips*," which could perplex native English speakers. The accurate interpretation would be "*the talk of the town*," as demonstrated in the ensuing sentence, "*The government's actions on environmental issues have become the talk of the town among activists and the media, sparking various public opinions*."

The limitation of AI in comprehending cultural nuances indicates that such technology continues to encounter a significant obstacle in realizing genuinely natural and contextually suitable translation (Kim, 2022). Various strategies aimed at mitigating this challenge encompass the incorporation of an augmented volume of contextual and culturally-informed training datasets, in addition to the implementation of specialized training designed to accurately identify and translate idiomatic expressions in accordance with their original connotations (Costa-jussà & Fonollosa, 2015; Mounadil, 2023).

Linguistic Translation Problems

As the name implies, linguistic translation problems pertain to variances in lexical choice and syntactic constructions between two distinct languages (Nord, 2005; Mohammed, 2022). At the lexical dimension, AI frequently encounters obstacles in accurately translating sentences that include words possessing multiple interpretations or exhibiting polysemy. Lample et al. (2019) & Mohammed (2022) observed that "AI encounters difficulties in disambiguating polysemous terms, particularly in instances where meanings intersect and contextual indicators are insufficient" (p. 153). Conversely, AI commonly opts for the most generalized interpretation when the contextual information is not sufficiently precise. Nonetheless, the resultant translation harbors the potential to engender misunderstandings.

For instance, within the nuance of political communication, terminology such as "party," "campaign," and "representative" possesses diverse interpretations across the political, social, and colloquial domains. The term "party" may denote either a political organization or a festive occasion. In a political context, as exemplified by the statement, "The party's strategy will determine the outcome of the election," an AI system might erroneously select an incongruous meaning (festive occasion—*acara perayaan*) if it fails to recognize that "party" is utilized here to signify a political entity. The term "campaign," within the framework of political discourse, refers to a political campaign or initiatives aimed at advocating for a candidate or a specific policy. However, in a marketing or business context, "campaign" may signify an advertising campaign or the promotion of a product. A statement such as "The president launched a new campaign to gather public support" could be rendered inaccurately if the AI fails to comprehend the political context and interprets "campaign" in the commercial promotion sense.

The term "representative" denotes an individual who has been elected to serve as an advocate for a collective of individuals within a legislative or governing institution. Nevertheless, in colloquial discourse, this term is commonly understood to signify an individual who acts on behalf of persons or groups across a variety of contexts, including commercial enterprises, organizations, or particular events. In the ensuing political communication example, "The representative from our district addressed the assembly about local issues," a misinterpretation may occur if AI fails to consider the contextual framework of the statement. According to Kim (2022), the limitations of AI in comprehending contextual nuances frequently result in its selection of the most prevalent interpretation found within the training dataset, which may not be suitable. "The reliance on frequency over context creates substantial risks in domains like political communication, where terms are deeply contextualized" (Naveen et al., 2024, p. 7). Supporting Kim, Naveen et al. (2024) pointed out that the dependence on frequency rather than context engenders significant dangers in areas such as political communication, wherein terminology is profoundly contextualized. Within the nunace of political communication, these inaccuracies in translation can yield severe ramifications, culminating in misinterpretations or biases towards particular statements or policies.

AI-generated translation systems encounter a multitude of significant challenges when confronted with the intricacies associated with complex sentence structures, particularly in languages that exhibit variable word arrangements and a diverse array of grammatical particles. These particular challenges are prominently observable in languages such as German, Japanese, and Indonesian, wherein the inherent flexibility of sentence structures can frequently result in translations that lack precision and accuracy (Reinig & Markert, 2023). The inherent complexity of these multifaceted structures often necessitates the application of advanced syntactic analysis and subsequent restructuring processes, capabilities that current AI models find exceedingly difficult to execute with a consistent degree of reliability. Bella et al. (2022) pointed out that the intersection of linguistic diversity and technological advancement thus poses a compelling area for future research and development, necessitating a more nuanced understanding of both language mechanics and AI capabilities. As the field continues to evolve, a concerted effort will be essential in addressing these profound challenges to enhance the overall efficacy of AI-generated translation systems in handling complex syntactic structures across a variety of languages.

In sum, these challenges illustrate that although AI-generated translation has achieved notable advancements, numerous domains still necessitate additional exploration and refinement, particularly in the realms of contextual comprehension, bias mitigation, and the assurance of accuracy and consistency in translation.

CONCLUSION

Results from ChatGPT translations show conflicting outcomes in three crucial areas: accuracy, readability, and acceptability. While ChatGPT is quite good at maintaining grammar and producing translations that make sense, it sometimes misses the source text's intended meaning or cultural significance. The TQA study shows gaps in acceptability, particularly when translating idiomatic or culturally dense information, but it also shows considerable success in accuracy and readability. This implies that although ChatGPT is capable of handling broad translations with ease, more contextual and cultural alignment is required for specialist domains like political discourse in order to guarantee improved translation quality.

ChatGPT exhibits considerable promise as a translation tool, but faces some challenges, particularly in overcoming pragmatic issues, convention-related issues, and linguistic issues. It requires supplementary human engagement to achieve optimal results. Its capacity to deliver rapid and easily accessible translations renders it beneficial for initial drafts or low-stakes contexts. However, for high-stakes translations, such as those in political communication, legal, or diplomatic contexts, the involvement of human expertise is crucial. The integration of AI's efficiency with the contextual acumen of human translators guarantees that translations are not only accurate and comprehensible but also culturally and contextually acceptable.

REFERENCES

Agarwal, U., Gupta, R., & Saranya, G. (2024, May). Advancing Multilingual Communication NLP based Translational Speech to Speech Dialogue System for Indian Languages. In *2024 International Conference on Electronics, Computing, Communication and Control Technology (ICECCC)* (pp. 1-6). IEEE.

Bahdanau, D., Cho, K., & Bengio, Y. (2014). Neural machine translation by jointly learning to align and translate. *arXiv preprint arXiv:1409.0473*. https://arxiv.org/abs/1409.0473

Bai, W. (2024). Advancements and challenges in AI-driven creative translation: A comprehensive analysis. *Applied and Computational Engineering*, *82*(1), 82–87. DOI: 10.54254/2755-2721/82/20240937

Baker, M. (1992). *In other words: A coursebook on translation*. Routledge.

Baziotis, C., Mathur, P., & Hasler, E. (2022). Automatic evaluation and analysis of idioms in neural machine translation. arXiv preprint arXiv:2210.04545.

Bella, G., Byambadorj, E., Chandrashekar, Y., Batsuren, K., Cheema, D. A., & Giunchiglia, F. (2022). Language diversity: Visible to humans, exploitable by machines. arXiv preprint arXiv:2203.04723.

Bojar, O., Chatterjee, R., Federmann, C., Graham, Y., Haddow, B., Huck, M., & Zampieri, M. (2016). *Proceedings of the First Conference on Machine Translation (WMT)*. Berlin: Association for Computational Linguistics.

Buch, A., Eagleman, D., & Grosenick, L. (2022). Engineering diplomacy: How AI and human augmentation could remake the art of foreign relations. *Perspective*, *2*, 25.

Burazer, L. (2013). Examining the Differences in Assessing Quality of Translations and Acceptability of Texts. *ELOPE, 10*(2), 127–137. DOI: 10.4312/elope.10.2.127-137

California School Boards Association. (2023).AI has arrived: Task force will guide how artificial intelligence can be used in schools (Publication). Retrieved from https://publications.csba.org.) *Lardieri*, A. (2023, January 4).

Castilho, S., Gaspari, F., Moorkens, J., & Way, A. (2018). A comparative quality evaluation of PBSMT and NMT using professional translators. *Machine Translation*, *32*(1-2), 97–110.

Costa-Jussà, M. R., & Fonollosa, J. A. R. (2015). Latest trends in hybrid machine translation and its applications. [checked]. *Computer Speech & Language*, *32*(1), 3–10. DOI: 10.1016/j.csl.2014.11.001

Dewayanti, D., & Putu, S. (2024). The impact of contextual understanding on neural machine translation accuracy: A case study of Indonesian cultural idioms in English translation. *Englisia: Journal of Language. Education and Humanities, 12*(1), 223–223. DOI: 10.22373/ej.v12i1.24433

Ernst, C., Schröter, J., & Sudmann, A. (2019). AI and the imagination to overcome difference. Spheres: Journal for Digital Culture. Retrieved from https://mediarep.org/bitstream/handle/doc/14423/spheres_5_0301_Ernst_ea_AI-Imagination-Difference .pdf

Gupta, R. (2020). Microsoft Translator: Integrating translation with business platforms. *Journal of Business Language Solutions*, 15(2), 45-59. **checked**

Hading, E., Rustan, D. R. H. P., & Ruing, F. H. (2024). EFL Students' Perceptions on the Integration of AI in Fostering Critical Thinking Skills. *Global English Insights Journal, 2*(1), 1–10. DOI: 10.61220/glens.v2i1.466

Hatim, B., & Mason, I. (1997). *The Translator as Communicator*. Routledge.

House, J. (1977). *A model for translation quality assessment.* Gunter Narr Verlag.

House, J. (1997). *Translation quality assessment: A model revisited.* Gunter Narr Verlag.

Hyman, Larry, M. (2014). How to Study a Tone Language, with Exemplification from Oku (Grassfields Bantu, Cameroon). *Language Documentation and Conservation, 8*(3), 525–562.

Kim, H. (2022). Cultural nuances in Asian languages and translation tools: A focus on Papago. *Asian Language Studies, 14*(1), 102–118.

Kizi, T. G. A., & Saporbayevich, A. O. (2024). Pragmatic Strategies in Artistic Translation: Balancing Creativity and Cultural Adaptation. *International Journal of Language Learning and Applied Linguistics, 3*(3), 51–57. DOI: 10.51699/ijllal.v3i3.77

Knowles, L. (2016). *Artificial Intelligence and Language: Bridging the Cultural Gap*. University of Massachusetts Press.

Koehn, P. (2020). *Neural machine translation.* Cambridge University Press. DOI: 10.1017/9781108608480

Koehn, P., & Knowles, R. (2017). Six challenges for neural machine translation. *Proceedings of the First Workshop on Neural Machine Translation*, 28-39. DOI: 10.18653/v1/W17-3204

Köprülü, S. G. (2023). Comprehensibility in translation of medical texts. *RumeliDe Dil ve Edebiyat Arastirmalari Dergisi*, (35), 1487–1504.

Lample, G., Conneau, A., Ranzato, M., Denoyer, L., & Jégou, H. (2019). Unsupervised Machine Translation Using Monolingual Corpora Only. *International Journal of Machine Learning*, *38*(1), 141–164.

Larson, M. A. (1984). *Meaning-Based Translation.* University Press.

Liang, Y., Meng, F., Chen, Y., Xu, J., & Zhou, J. (2021). Modeling bilingual conversational characteristics for neural chat translation. arXiv preprint arXiv:2107.11164.

Maciel, T. (2024). Strategies for Professors on How to Mitigate the Negative Effects of ChatGPT in Higher Education.

Madugu, U., & Ibrahim, F. (2025). Six Questions for Every Content Analysis: Revisiting the Stemler's Overview. *International Journal of Research and Innovation in Social Science*, *VIII*(XII), 2788–2794. DOI: 10.47772/IJRISS.2024.8120233

Mahale, A., Desmukh, A.S., Mahajan, R., Vidyadharan, A., Hegde, V.S., & Vijayaraghavan, K. (2023). Data Validation using Sentence Transformers. 1504-1508. DOI: 10.1109/ICOEI56765.2023.10125780

Matricciani, E. (2023). Readability across Time and Languages: The Case of Matthew's Gospel Translations. *AppliedMath*, *3*(2), 497–509. DOI: 10.3390/appliedmath3020026

Mishra, S. K. (2024). Translation Strategies and challenges for translating Maithili Idioms and Proverbs into English. *RESEARCH REVIEW International Journal of Multidisciplinary*, *9*(4), 79–88.

Mohammed, A. (2022). Linguistic and Cultural Problems in Translation and Solutions. *Govarî Qeła*, *7*(2). Advance online publication. DOI: 10.25212/lfu.qzj.7.2.37

Mohan, G. (2023). *Vekariya., L., Natrayan., Amit, Barve* (Vol. K). G., Satish., Harshal, Patil. AI-Powered Chatbot for Bridging Language Barriers with Translation., DOI: 10.1109/ICIMIA60377.2023.10426216

Mounadil, T. (2023). Strategies for translating idioms and proverbs from English into Arabic. British Journal of Translation, Linguistics and Literature, 3(2), 02-09.

Nababan, M., Nuraeni, A., & Sumardiono. (2012). Pengembangan Model Penilaian Kualitas Terjemahan. Kajian Linguistik dan Sastra, 24(1), 39-57.

Naveen, P., & Trojovský, P. (2024). Overview and Challenges of Machine Translation for Contextually Appropriate Translations. *iScience, 27*(10), 110878–110878. DOI: 10.1016/j.isci.2024.110878 PMID: 39391737

Newell, R., George, S., Patel, M., Dawe, H., Roelas, M., Wedmore, F., & Morris, M. (2022). Improving the quality of translation for patients with language barriers. *European Journal of Public Health, 32*(Supplement_3), ckac129.639. Advance online publication. DOI: 10.1093/eurpub/ckac129.639

Newmark, P. (1988). *A textbook of translation*. Prentice Hall.

Nida, E. A., & Taber, C. R. (1969). *The theory and practice of translation*. Brill.

Nord, C. (2005). *Text analysis in translation: Theory, methodology, and didactic application of a model for translation-oriented text analysis*. Routledge.

Pestov, I. (2018). A History of Machine Translation from the Cold War to Deep Learning. Freecodecamp.org. 12 Maret 2018. https://www.freecodecamp.org/news/a-history-of-machine- translation-from-the-cold-war-to-deep-learning-f1d335ce8b5/

Prabhakaran, V., Qadri, R., & Hutchinson, B. (2022). Cultural incongruencies in artificial intelligence. arXiv preprint arXiv:2211.13069.

Pym, A. (2014). *Exploring translation theories* (2nd ed.). Routledge.

Reinig, I., & Markert, K. (2023). Can current NLI systems handle German word order? Investigating language model performance on a new German challenge set of minimal pairs. doi: /arxiv.2306.04523DOI: 10.48550

Sanesi, M. (2024). Enhancing translation pedagogy through culture-specific terms. Педагогика. Вопросы теории и практики, 9(4), 287-294.

Scannell, C., Lambkin, K., O'Brien, E., Nolan, P., Holloway, P., Ryan, P., . . . Delmar, J. (2023). TRANSLATE: Providing Standardised National Climate Services for Ireland (No. EMS2023-296). Copernicus Meetings.

Silu, P. (2024). *Issues in Machine Translation with reference to the Story "Thakur ka kuan" by Munshi Premchand*. International Journal For Multidisciplinary Research., DOI: 10.36948/ijfmr.2024.v06i05.28130

Song, Z. (2024). A Comparative Study of Two Translated Versions of Walden in Chinese from the Perspective of the Translator's Subjectivity. *Journal of Social Sciences and Humanities*, *6*(8), 122–127. DOI: 10.53469/jssh.2024.06(08).24

Tao, G. (2023). A Study on Error Feature Analysis and Error Correction in English Translation Through Machine Translatio. [lithuanian Academy of Sciences]. *Informatica (Vilnius), 47*(8). Advance online publication. DOI: 10.31449/inf.v47i8.4862

Vaswani, A., Shazeer, N., Parmar, N., Uszkoreit, J., Jones, L., Gomez, A. N., Kaiser, Ł., & Polosukhin, I. (2017). Attention is all you need. In *Advances in Neural Information Processing Systems* (pp. 5998-6008). https://arxiv.org/abs/1706.03762

Voita, E., Serdyukov, P., Sennrich, R., & Titov, I. (2019). Context-aware neural machine translation learns anaphora resolution. *Proceedings of the 57th Annual Meeting of the Association for Computational Linguistics*, 1264-1274.

Wilkens, K. (2020). DeepL's role in revolutionizing the translation industry. *Translation Journal.* https://translationjournal.net/DeepL_revolution_translation

Wu, D., Wang, M., & Li, X. (2022). Automatic Scoring for Translations Based on Language Models. *Computational Intelligence and Neuroscience, 2022*, 1–10. DOI: 10.1155/2022/2171206 PMID: 35800703

Wu, Y., Schuster, M., Chen, Z., Le, Q. V., Norouzi, M., Macherey, W., . . . Dean, J. (2016). Google's neural machine translation system: Bridging the gap between human and machine translation. *arXiv preprint arXiv:1609.08144.* https://arxiv.org/abs/1609.08144

Zhu, G. (2022, January). Fast translation method of complex English sentences based on artificial intelligence technology. In 2022 14th International Conference on Measuring Technology and Mechatronics Automation (ICMTMA) (pp. 638-642). IEEE.

Zuo, C. (2024). The Influence of Literary Translation in Drama and Film Works. *Scientific and social research*, 6(6):66-72. DOI: 10.26689/ssr.v6i6.7172

Chapter 10
Translating Subh-e-Azadi:
ChatGPT, Gemini, and the Cultural Complexity of 1947 Partition Poetry

Priyanka Bisht
https://orcid.org/0000-0002-3408-0454
Christ University, India

Jyoti Prakash Pujari
Christ University, India

ABSTRACT

Artificial Intelligence has transformed the field of translation, yet concerns remain about its ability to handle culturally complex metaphors and nuances. This chapter addresses this issue and compares the capabilities of two AI models- ChatGPT 4o (free version) and Gemini 1.5 Flash (free version) in translating a culturally laden poem, "Subh-e-Azadi (The Dawn of Freedom)" by Faiz Ahmed Faiz, from Hindi to English. With an emphasis on accuracy and quality, this study compares the translations produced by ChatGPT and Gemini against a human translation of the poem. It explores how AI models handle linguistic subtleties, cultural adaptability, and emotional depth while also experimenting with prompting techniques to assess whether explicit instructions improve translation quality or not. The findings will provide an insight into the future of AI in translating literature with heavy contextual background.

DOI: 10.4018/979-8-3373-0060-3.ch010

INTRODUCTION

"So, in the first part of the word "translation", "trans" means "across". The other part of the word – "lation" – comes from the Latin verb that means "to carry". So, if we put the two elements together, we can see that "translation" essentially means "to carry across"." (Bowker, 2023, p. 9).

The meaning of translation, as given by Lynee Bowker in her book *De- mystifying Translation Introducing Translation to Non- translators* (2023) makes it an act of carrying across the words from one language to another. However, this is not synonymous to merely replacing or substituting the word as it is, rather it also involves the pragmatic task of preserving the meaning, intent, and cultural nuances within specific contexts. This is so because, in the process of translation it is not just the words that are 'being carried' but along with that, the original context, nature and culture.

In this sense, a fair and accurate translation is the one which honors the thoughts, sentiments and intent of the original text along with its precise meaning. Translation, therefore, is a profoundly creative and intellectual undertaking rather than just a language exercise (Muñoz-Basols et al.). That is why, traditionally, human translators, equipped with cultural and intellectual expertise, have undertaken this task (Lee, 2023). However, globalization has driven demand for rapid and cost-effective translation, leading to the rise of AI-powered tools. This shift raises a crucial question: Can AI-driven translation tools effectively carry forward the cultural and emotional depth along with the translated words?

These automated machine translations began as complimentary to human translators but gradually started eliminating them. Though they were "...best suited for translating instruction manuals" (Khoshafah, 2023, p.1), the development of AI powered by machine learning, deep learning, and natural language processing (NLP), has further altered the field (Gupta et al., 2021; Bhargava & Sharma, 2021). Tools like Microsoft Translator, DeepL, and Google Translate now provide real-time translation services. Beyond text translation, AI enhances accessibility, facilitates global communication, and supports speech-to-text and automatic subtitling (Sayers et al.). However, issues remain, including quality inconsistencies and biases stemming from training data, particularly for low-resource languages (Ousidhoum et al.). These restrictions, while important, remind one of the intricacies of the translation process itself and operate more as reflections than as restraints.

Building on these discussions this chapter compares the translating abilities of two cutting-edge AI models, ChatGPT 4o (free version) and Gemini 1.5 Flash (free version). It is done via the prism of a particular translation task: translating the Partition poem "Subh-e-Azadi (The Dawn of Freedom)" by Faiz Ahmed Faiz from Hindi, a low resource language to English, a high resource language. The study also investigates if prompting techniques affect the caliber of AI translations or produce the same result. The complex interaction of content, emotion, and cultural background in poetry poses special difficulties that push the limits of AI translation systems. This study looks at how each model handles these difficulties, in an effort to better understand AI's capabilities and constraints when it comes to translating creative and cultural texts.

LITERATURE REVIEW

The field of artificial intelligence has seen a dramatic change in the last few years, starting with the emergence of Generative LLM ChatGPT in November 2022 to the arrival of its rival AI models in a whirlwind such as Google DeepMind's Gemini in March 2023. These models, equipped with sophisticated neural networks, exhibit remarkable proficiency in content generation, interpretation, and translation. These various AI tools are also frequently studied in comparison to each other, to determine their relative strengths and weaknesses, with particular attention given to ChatGPT and Gemini as leading contenders in the field.

Although both ChatGPT and Gemini make use of sophisticated neural networks, there are minor but significant differences between them (McIntosh et al.). For example, while ChatGPT prioritizes a user-centered strategy refined through "RLHF" (Liu, 2024, p. 06), Gemini leverages Google's extensive neural network infrastructure for multilingual and creative tasks (Mazur & Thimmesch). Rane et al.'s (2024) study, "Gemini versus ChatGPT: Applications, Performance, Architecture, Capabilities, and Implementation", highlights how ChatGPT's adaptability contrasts with Gemini's multimodal capabilities, concluding that "Gemini's multimodal versatility and enhanced language understanding represent significant strengths, while ChatGPT's widespread adoption and ongoing development underscore its potential for further progress" (Rane et al., 2024, p. 90). However, both models require further optimization for improved scalability and contextual comprehension.

While these studies offer insights into AI capabilities, their effectiveness in translating literary and cultural texts, particularly poetry, remains an evolving field of research. Comparative studies in this domain have explored how AI-driven translation navigates linguistic intricacies, poetic structures, and cultural contexts, shedding light on both the potential and limitations of these technologies. This section reviews recent studies in this area, situating the chapter within broader challenges AI encounters in cultural and literary translation, and highlighting the gaps that this study aims to address.

Farghal and Haider (2024) investigate the translation of classical Arabic poetry to English, comparing human translations with AI-generated outputs from ChatGPT and Gemini. Their study reveals that while AI models demonstrate competency in thematic clarity and creativity, they struggle with prosody, an essential element in poetry translation. Notably, "because of its generative characteristics, which are intended to tackle creative language tasks, GPT is more capable of navigating through these complications…in comparison, GeM's methodology might be more inflexible, resulting in translations that overlook subtle prosodic elements crucial to poetry" (p.12). This highlights the ongoing challenge of ensuring that AI translations maintain poetic fidelity and raises questions about the models' ability to adapt to culturally rich literary texts.

This assessment is consistent with Alsajri et al. (2024), "Generative Models in Natural Language Processing: A Comparative Study of ChatGPT and Gemini". The study states that, "ChatGPT demonstrates proficiency in generating original and human-like prose, rendering it appropriate for jobs necessitating fluency and creative composition. In contrast, Gemini exhibits greater variation and adaptability in intricate activities, highlighting its proficiency in contextual comprehension and problem-solving" (p. 144). While both studies highlight the strengths of ChatGPT and Gemini in different aspects of language generation, they also underscore the limitations of AI in preserving the nuanced aesthetic and cultural dimensions of literary texts.

Doudou and Faizi (2024) further contribute to this discourse by examining ChatGPT 3.5's ability to translate Arabic poetry while preserving its formal qualities. Their research finds that AI-assisted translations can preserve meter and rhyme but often need human refinement to capture metaphorical depth and cultural authenticity. The study therefore, suggests a hybrid approach, wherein human translators refine AI-generated drafts, ensuring that the emotional and artistic essence of poetry is not lost. Building upon this, Resende and Hadley (2024) explore the use of LLMs in poetry translation, emphasizing the models' ability to enhance human translation through lexical variety and density. Their findings suggest that while AI-generated translations may offer novel linguistic solutions, their outputs require significant post-editing to achieve quality comparable to human translations. This underscores the ongoing debate regarding AI's role as an assistive tool rather than a replacement for human translators, particularly in the nuanced domain of literary texts.

Wei (2024) extends this discussion by evaluating the translation of Buddhist texts from Classical Chinese to Modern English using ChatGPT, ERNIE Bot, and Gemini. The study finds that while AI tools can recognize and translate specialized terminology, they often struggle with grammatical structures unique to classical texts. As stated in the article that, "although they can generally produce a translation of a 400–500-word passage of Buddhist classical Chinese, accurately translating classical Chinese remains a daunting task, especially in the subtle context of Buddhist literature" (p. 31-32). These findings highlight the importance of contextual and semantic accuracy in translation, a challenge that extends beyond religious texts to poetry and culturally embedded narratives.

Taghian (2024) examines AI-assisted translation of prophetic hadiths, highlighting challenges such as, "...their limitations in word sense disambiguation (WSD), handling out-of-vocabulary (OOV) terms, part-of-speech (POS) tagging, morphological segmentation, lexicosemantic, and comprehending the contextual, cultural, and pragmatic dimensions became evident" (p.255). The study's findings reinforce the importance of human intervention in ensuring accurate and culturally sensitive translations, further demonstrating the necessity of integrating AI translation tools with expert oversight.

Almaktary (2025) extends this argument by analyzing ChatGPT's translation of poetry across Arabic, English, and French. His study identifies AI's limitations in preserving poetic devices, emotional undertones, and cultural context. Elements such as metaphor and alliteration, deeply embedded in linguistic traditions, remain challenging for AI to translate accurately. The findings support the notion that while LLMs can assist in translation, human expertise remains crucial for achieving artistic and cultural fidelity.

Collectively, these studies illustrate the evolving role of AI in literary translation and suggest that AI is best utilized as an assistive tool rather than a replacement for human expertise. These works highlight the key areas where AI translation still falls short, framing the need for further exploration into AI's ability to preserve cultural authenticity in literary settings. However, most of these works are concentrated on high-resource languages like Arabic, French and English.

For the low-resource languages, the ability of ChatGPT and Gemini to translate has been examined in only very limited experiments such as K. S. Kishore and R. Shaik's 2024 study, "Evaluating Telugu Proficiency in Large Language Models- A Comparative Analysis of ChatGPT and Gemini". Their results showed that,

While both models demonstrate a base level of understanding, their performance diverges significantly. Gemini's superior ability to provide comprehensive answers, engage in natural language generation tasks, and demonstrate cultural awareness positions it as the more proficient LLM in handling the intricacies of Telugu. Conversely, ChatGPT's strength lies in factual knowledge retrieval, suggesting a need for broader training data and development in areas requiring creative expression and reasoning within the Telugu language (Kishore & Shaik, 2024).

Similar to this, Hasan et al. (2024) investigated how well several LLMs performed when processing low-resource languages like Bangla, Hindi, and Urdu in their work. They found notable differences in translation accuracy and underlined the necessity of additional model enhancements to bring these models up to par in terms of their

English-language capabilities. Consequently, it can be said that comparative studies between ChatGPT and Gemini regarding their translation abilities have largely focused on high-resource languages rather than low-resource languages. This highlights a critical research gap, which will be further explored in the next section.

RESEARCH GAP

Despite its widespread use in India, Hindi remains classified as a low-resource language (Dey et al., 2024). While there is a growing body of research comparing ChatGPT and Gemini across various domains, there is a notable lack of studies evaluating their translation capabilities with respect to literary texts in Hindi. Although research such as Doshi (2024) has highlighted the limitations of AI models in translating Jain texts from Hindi to English, particularly in conveying the religious and cultural nuances of the source material, there remains a significant gap in addressing the specific challenges of translating Hindi poetry.

This chapter aims to fill up these voids by concentrating on how ChatGPT and Gemini manage Faiz Ahmed Faiz's poem, "Subh-e-Azadi" (1971) Hindi to English translation. In contrast to previous research, this study looks at how these models manage context-specific, evocative, and cultural subtleties. In addition to pointing out areas that require development, this framework will advance knowledge of AI's function in translation research and its consequences for intercultural communication. For the same, the chapter has the following research questions.

Research Questions

These research questions that serve as the foundation for this chapter are:

1. How do AI models, specifically ChatGPT and Gemini, handle the translation of complex cultural and historical nuances in Faiz Ahmed Faiz's "Subh-e-Azadi" (1971) from Hindi to English?
2. How accurate are AI-generated translations compared to an established human translation in terms of quality, accuracy, and cultural adaptation?
3. What specific biases or misinterpretations emerge in AI translations of "Subh-e-Azadi" (Faiz, 1971), and how might these effect readers' interpretations of the poem?
4. Does the amount of prompting, minimal versus detailed, affect the precision and lyrical appeal of AI translations?

5. Which AI model provides a more effective translation of "Subh-e-Azadi" (Faiz, 1971), and what implications does this have for AI's role in translating culturally embedded texts?

METHODOLOGY

The chapter employs a qualitative research methodology to examine how well the AI models-ChatGPT and Gemini translate culturally complicated Partition poetry, "Subh-e-Azadi" (1971) by Faiz Ahmed Faiz. By comparing AI-generated translations with a recognized human translation, the analysis aims to assess the quality, precision, and cultural adaptability of these translations. The research intends to determine the advantages and disadvantages of AI models in processing culturally complex texts by performing a line-by-line comparison.

For the same, the chapter uses the English translation of "Subh-e-Azadi" (Penguin Random House, 2020) by Baran Farooqui, which is available on the official Penguin Random House India page, and the Hindi version translated by Mahmood Jamal as posted on the Rekhta website, as a standard for assessing AI translations. The translation by Farooqui was chosen due to its critical praise and faithfulness to the source material, providing a sophisticated interpretation that maintains the poem's emotional and cultural core. Mahmood Jamal's Hindi version has been chosen, as it is freely and readily accessible online, and hence, frequently used and favored by the readers and academics. Thus, making both of these as the suitable resource for evaluating the advantages and disadvantages of translations produced by artificial intelligence.

The data will be collected from the translation generated by ChatGPT and Gemini. Two scenarios will be considered with *User 1* and *User 2*. The first user (*User-1*) will provide no additional prompts to the AI models and simply command to "translate this to English" (ChatGPT; Gemini - Chat to Supercharge Your Ideas, n.d.). *User 2*, is slightly more advanced and will request a "structured line-by-line translation" (ChatGPT; Gemini - Chat to Supercharge Your Ideas, n.d.) of the poem.

The AI-generated translations will be analyzed in comparison to Farooqui's English translation of the poem, with particular emphasis on factors such as translation quality, the adaptability of contextual metaphors, and linguistic precision. The accuracy of AI-generated outputs will be assessed by examining their syntax, cohesiveness, and overall fluency in relation to the established English translation. Additionally, cultural adaptation will be evaluated based on the extent to which the AI models preserve the poem's historical and cultural context, effectively convey cultural allusions and colloquialisms, and retain its emotional depth. A comprehensive analysis will be conducted to identify both accurate and inaccurate interpretations, as well as the handling of cultural nuances within the AI translations.

Case Study Selection

The 1947 Indian Partition remains one of the most significant and painful moments in South Asian history. As Mushirul Hasan writes in his article, "Partition Narratives" (2002), the Partition is, "…the defining moment in South Asian history, and, in the words of Intizar Husain, 'the great human event which changed the history of India'" (52). The Radcliffe Line, drawn by the British in 1947, ignored the subcontinent's intricate socioeconomic structure and divided India into two separate nations-India and Pakistan.

Beyond being a political act, the Partition was a profound psychological and cultural upheaval. It led to widespread confusion, unprecedented intercommunal violence, and ingrained trauma that continues to shape the sociopolitical climate of both nations. The resulting human misery gave rise to the Partition literature, which aims to depict the impact of the Partition on individuals and communities. It "delineates the stings of partition with empathy as well as sympathy" (Sobti & Kumar, 2022, p. 731).

The Partition literature spans genres like memoirs, oral histories, poems, short stories, and novels. Authors such as Saadat Hasan Manto, Khushwant Singh, Bhisham Sahni, and Bapsi Sidhwa have vividly portrayed intercommunal violence, identity loss, and the struggle for survival, in their works. By creating a space for grieving and remembering, this literature ensures that the voices of victims and survivors are heard, and the pain of Partition is not overshadowed by the celebration of independence.

The poem "Subh-e-Azadi (The Dawn of Freedom)" by Faiz Ahmed Faiz stands out as a powerful indictment of the realities of freedom. In lines like, "□□ □□□□ □□□□ □□□□□ □□ □□-□□□□□□ □□□; □□ □□□□□□□□ □□ □□□ □□ □□ □□ □□□ □□ □□□□; □□ □□ □□□ □□ □□□□ □□□ □□ □□□□□ □□ □□…" ("□□□□□ □□□□ □□□□□ - □□□□□"), the poem questions whether the newly gained freedom was truly what citizens had fought for. The 1947 Partition brought sorrow, brutality, and displacement instead of the hoped-for progress and harmony. Faiz's vivid metaphors and artistic beauty demonstrate his mastery of the Urdu language. Through symbolism and metaphor, he conveys the people's suffering and hopelessness, and his poetry often "...poses a notorious problem of interpretation" (Mufti, 2004, p. 246). These qualities make "Subh-e-Azadi" an ideal case for evaluating the cultural translation capabilities of ChatGPT and Gemini.

FINDINGS AND ANALYSIS

This section looks at the findings gathered from the English translation generated by ChatGPT and Gemini of the Hindi version of "Subh-e-Azadi" (□□□□□ □□□□ □□□□□ - □□□□□, n.d.) under two different prompting scenarios: a simple translation prompt by *User 1* and a more comprehensive, line-by-line translation command by *User 2*. Although there were no major variations in the general standard of translation across the two scenarios, minor enhancements were observed when the AI models were given more specificity. These improvements were particularly noticeable in areas such as the translation of cultural metaphors and the use of punctuation to better capture the evocativeness of the original poem. The next subsections offer a thorough examination of the translations generated under each scenario, highlighting important advantages, and drawbacks in the AI generated translation.

User-1: Straightforward prompt

In the first scenario, *User-1* submitted the entire poem in the Devanagari script to ChatGPT and Gemini with a straightforward prompt to "translate the poem to English" (ChatGPT; Gemini - Chat to Supercharge Your Ideas, n.d.). There was no further context, guidance or instructions given to both the AI's (see *Figure 1*).

Figure 1. ChatGPT and Gemini generated translation.

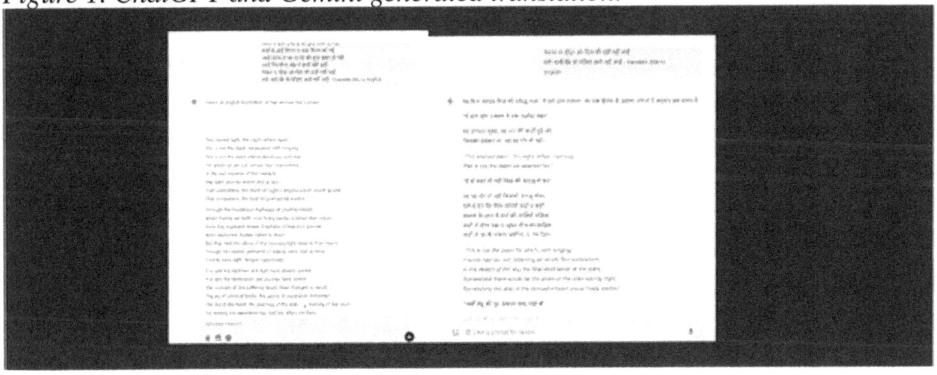

The above figure illustrates that the AI-generated translations differ significantly from the original poetry in terms of structure. Both the AI models have generated translations with more stanzas than the source material, which is structured into a predetermined number of two stanzas. This reorganization implies that AI models apply their own structural norms to the original content in an effort to improve readability and logical consistency.

It is possible that the AI-generated divisions are the result of their computational processing, which puts readability and grammatical consistency ahead of the source's artistic quality. In light of this structural inquiry, the chapter will now assess the standard and precision of the translations produced by AI.

Preserving Meaning but Losing Poetic Magic

One of the key findings that came forward during the comparison of the translated version by both the AI models is the extent to which these technologies attempt to maintain the source verses' accuracy. For the same, they even employ identical phrasing, as also demonstrated in the following lines where the AI models' use same wording as the source text:

Table 1. Same phrasing given by ChatGPT and Gemini

Human Translation	**This light, smeared and spotted, this night-bitten dawn**
ChatGPT Translation	This stained light, this night-bitten dawn
Gemini Translation	This stained dawn, this night-bitten morning

But even with these same phrases, the AI translations lack the poetic resonance and nuance. For example, in the above lines, the light of the freedom is defined as "smeared and spotted" (Penguin Random House, 2020). This refers to the horrifying bloodshed that accompanied the independence of India because of the Partition. When ChatGPT, translates the phrase and combines it as "stained light" (ChatGPT) it expresses a similar sense but without the lyrical appeal of the human version. However, Gemini chooses "stained dawn" (Gemini - Chat to Supercharge Your Ideas, n.d.) which, while introducing a metaphorical dimension, alters the structural balance of the original imagery. It leads to a corresponding change in the latter half of the sentence, rendering "night-bitten dawn" as "night-bitten morning" (Gemini - Chat to Supercharge Your Ideas, n.d.) and simplifies the complexity of the original metaphor in that part. This simplification pattern is also repeated in the other lines as well such as,

Table 2. Simplification of Imagery and Symbolisms by ChatGPT and Gemini

Human Translation	When, from the mysterious paths of youth's hot blood
ChatGPT Translation	Through the mysterious highways of youthful blood
Gemini Translation	From the mysterious highways of young blood

The human translated version uses the phrases "youth's hot blood" (Penguin Random House, 2020) where the adjective 'hot' is very important to describe the noun "blood" (Penguin Random House, 2020) as it intensifies the tone of the poem and creates a vivid imagery of an angry youth. However, this adjective is omitted from both AI versions, making the sentence simpler and a little more neutral. This also lessens the emotional urgency that was originally expressed. These modifications reflect a larger pattern in which AI translations give priority to readability and clarity above the complex levels of content included in the source text.

The diminution of the emotional depth is further exhibited in the translation of the following lines where the human translator deliberately chooses words to improve symbolic significance but not the AI,

Table 3. The lack of emotional depth in the ChatGPT and Gemini's translated version

Human Translation	Open arms called, bodies entreated From the impatient bedchambers of beauty—
ChatGPT Translation	From the impatient dream chambers of beauty's domain, Arms beckoned, bodies called to them.
Gemini Translation	From the impatient dream-chambers of the land of beauty, Arms kept calling, bodies kept beckoning,

The human translation uses "impatient bedchambers" (Penguin Random House, 2020), which conveys a sense of urgency and ache, suggesting an unsatisfied want that is consistent with the main theme of Partition literature's pining and grief. However, this term is substituted with "dream chambers" (ChatGPT; Gemini - Chat to Supercharge Your Ideas, n.d.) in AI translations, which slightly changes the overall mood from one of haste to one of passivity and reflection.

The original metaphor's profundity is diminished by this alteration, which removes the line's emotional and sensual tension. The romantic tone is maintained by ChatGPT's usage of "beckoned" (ChatGPT) while the Gemini's use of "kept calling, kept beckoning" (Gemini - Chat to Supercharge Your Ideas, n.d.) provides a sense of continuity. With the word "entreated" (Penguin Random House, 2020) the human translation expresses greater emotional intensity, whilst the AI translations have a more neutral tone. This lack of lyrical rhythm and concentration on directness is also demonstrated in the following lines,

Table 4. The Simplification of poetic lines by ChatGPT and Gemini

Human Translation	**From where did the beloved, the morning breeze come?** **Where did it go?** **The street-lamp at the edge of the road has no notion yet**
ChatGPT Translation	From where did the morning breeze arise, and where has it gone? There is still no news of the path's guiding lamp
Gemini Translation	Where did the image of the morning breeze come from, where did it go? The lamp at the crossroads still knows nothing,

In these lines, "Beloved," (Penguin Random House, 2020), which is added by the human translator, offers more profound emotive and mystical meaning that the AI translations lack. Although ChatGPT's rendition is simple, it is devoid of the poetic cadence and the translation of Gemini as "image of the morning breeze" (Gemini - Chat to Supercharge Your Ideas, n.d.) provide a new visual metaphor which Faiz Ahmed Faiz has not even mentioned. In the next line, the phrase "no notion" (Penguin Random House, 2020) adds a poetic quality by personifying the lamp. While Gemini effectively conveys the metaphor with "crossroads" (Gemini - Chat to Supercharge Your Ideas, n.d.) which keeps the sense of bewilderment and change, ChatGPT emphasizes utility with "guiding lamp" (ChatGPT) losing lyrical nuance.

Syntactical Changes and Their Impact

This minimization of lyrical qualities in AI translations goes beyond the selection of words and encompasses the translated text's syntactic framework. AI models frequently reword lines and restructure phrases to make poems seem more understandable and plainer. But this structural change detracts from the complex rhythm and multi-layered meanings that were there in Faiz Ahmed Faiz's original work. For instance, consider the lines below,

Table 5. The syntactical changes by ChatGPT and Gemini

Human Translation	**The boat of the afflicted heart's grieving will drop anchor somewhere,**
ChatGPT Translation	That somewhere, the boat of grief would anchor.
Gemini Translation	Somewhere the ship of the sorrowful heart would finally anchor.

In the above table, through the preservation of the subject, emotion, and action's sequential development, the human translation preserves the original framework. By highlighting the heart's suffering before reaching the conclusion of releasing anchor, the expression "afflicted heart's grieving" (Penguin Random House, 2020) deepens its emotional effect.

On the other hand, ChatGPT rewords the sentence by starting it with "somewhere" (ChatGPT) which moves the focus from the mourning heart's burden of emotion to the action of anchoring. The line feels more strong than reflective due to the syntactical inversion, which produces a more straightforward but less lyrical impression. The framework is further simplified in Gemini's translation by changing "boat" to "ship" and inserting "finally" (Gemini - Chat to Supercharge Your Ideas, n.d.) which adds a sense of completion that might not be as ambiguous or depressing as Faiz had meant.

The poet's flow and cadence are meticulously preserved in the human-translated version, but AI-generated translations typically put clarity first, breaking the syntax and transforming difficult lines into less complex ones. In these lines, for example:

Table 6. Change in the syntax by ChatGPT and Gemini

Human Translation	**But the yearning for the dawn's face was too dear**
ChatGPT Translation	But they held the allure of the morning light close to their hearts,
Gemini Translation	But dear was the longing for the face of dawn

Sensitivity and conceptualization are delicately balanced in the human translation, where "yearning" and "dawn's face" (Penguin Random House, 2020) elicit strong psychological reactions while highlighting both absence and longing for the dawn of freedom. The word "too dear" (Penguin Random House, 2020) evokes a sense of bitter- sweetness, implying a strong desire that has a price. Conversely, the translation provided by ChatGPT presents a more casual and tangible framing. This reformulation simplifies the complex meaning contained in the original by moving the emphasis from an abstract desire to a concrete act of holding, even if it is still successful in expressing emotional attachment. In contrast, the translation by Gemini follows the original framework more faithfully, but also adds a traditional poetic flavor with a minor inversion. But by rearranging the structure, the reader's attention is slightly diverted from the object of desire, the face of the dawn, to the longing itself.

These kinds of syntactical modifications by the AI models, highlight the conflict between maintaining poetic complexity and making the poem an easy read. These structural adjustments unintentionally compress the original poem's complex meanings and emotional impact, even while they make it easier for a larger audience to understand. See another example, in the following lines:

Table 7. Changes in the syntactical structure and emotional tone

Human Translation	The protocols of those who held the pain in their hearts have changed now Joy of union-yes; agony of separation— forbidden!
ChatGPT Translation	The customs of the suffering hearts have changed so much, The joy of union is lawful, the agony of separation forbidden.
Gemini Translation	The custom of the people of pain has greatly changed, The joy of union is lawful, and the torment of separation forbidden,

In order to highlight the sharp contrast between happiness and suffering, the human translation uses punctuation in a fragmented, nearly declarative form. The reader can absorb the words' emotional impact because of the pause created by the semicolons and dashes used. Both AI-generated versions, however, reword the statement to be more basic and rely on standard grammatical structures, which eliminates the reflective sense of the lines.

The terms "lawful" and "forbidden" (ChatGPT) which are used by ChatGPT, provide a strict, legalistic tone that might not adequately convey the original's emotional and cultural elements. Similar to this, Gemini's version, which is more syntactically fluid, is smoother to read but does not have the dramatic pause that adds to the human translation's emotional gravitas. Identical patterns can be seen in:

Table 8. Syntactic changes by ChatGPT and Gemini

Human Translation	It's said the darkness has been cleft from light already
ChatGPT Translation	It is said the darkness and light have already parted,
Gemini Translation	We have heard that the separation of darkness and light has already happened,

The usage of "cleft" (Penguin Random House, 2020) in the human translation in this case conveys an understanding of rupture and everlasting change by implying a strong, nearly violent split, the Partition. This is replaced by softer, more neutral terms like "parted" and "separation" (ChatGPT; Gemini - Chat to Supercharge Your Ideas, n.d.) in the AI translations, which do not have the same emotional or symbolic weight.

By adding "We have heard" (Gemini - Chat to Supercharge Your Ideas, n.d.), Gemini further alters the sentence structure and turns the emphasis from the incident to the act of hearing, which lessens the overall feeling of intensity that Faiz's poetry evokes. These illustrations show how alterations to the poem's sentence structure can result in unexpected changes to its emphasis and meaning while simultaneously making it easier for modern readers to understand.

The Weight of Words: Cultural Connotations and Lost Symbolism

In addition to the linguistic modifications in translation, the problem of cultural connotations makes translating Faiz's poetry even more difficult. Translation, as the introductory section explains, is never a straightforward word-for-word replacement, particularly when the text has significant cultural, historical, and emotional significance. Regarding Faiz's work, the original lines are infused with cultural subtleties that have their roots in the sociopolitical setting of Partition and the trauma that lingered in its wake. Removing these cultural allusions from their original linguistic and cultural context frequently causes them to lose their full meaning.

Despite being able to parse meaning, AI models find it difficult to grasp these nuances, which results in translations that could seem appropriate at first glance but fail to reflect the underlying emotional and cultural resonance. The following line can be used to demonstrate how cultural connotations affect translation:

Table 9. Changes in the cultural metaphors by ChatGPT and Gemini

Human Translation	**This light, smeared and spotted, this night-bitten dawn**
ChatGPT Translation	This stained light, this night-bitten dawn
Gemini Translation	This stained dawn, this night-bitten morning

The human translation of "dawn" (Penguin Random House, 2020) alludes to "sehar" *(□□□□□ □□□□ □□□□□ - □□□□□, n.d.)* from the original version, a certain moment before sunrise that has profound poetic meaning in Faiz's writing. "Sehar" *(□□□□□ □□□□ □□□□□ - □□□□□, n.d.)* is not merely a marker of time; it symbolizes hope and fresh starts by standing at the intersection of darkness and light, night and day. Here, it is symbolic of the midnight of India's independence, when the country gained its freedom from colonial domination.

This is emphasized by the expression "night-bitten dawn" (Penguin Random House, 2020) which conjures up a vision of a tough and agonizing new day that is marred by the gloom of the Partition. Both the AI translations, however, miss some of these subtleties of culture. Even though ChatGPT keeps the phrase "night-bitten dawn" (ChatGPT), Gemini's version changes it to "night-bitten morning" (Gemini - Chat to Supercharge Your Ideas, n.d.) which further lessens its cultural importance. The alteration from "dawn" (Penguin Random House, 2020) to "morning" (Gemini - Chat to Supercharge Your Ideas, n.d.) alters the time period and makes the translation less consistent with the historical meaning of "sehar" *(□□□□□ □□□□ □□□□□ - □□□□□, n.d.)* than it is in the human translation. The following is another example of the difficulties caused by cultural implications in the translation:

Table 10. Change in the cultural metaphors by ChatGPT and Gemini

Human Translation	**The hem of the radiant beauty's garment was very close**
ChatGPT Translation	Though the radiant garments of beauty were near at hand.
Gemini Translation	When friends set out, how many hands tugged at their sleeves,

In this context, "the hem" (Penguin Random House, 2020) is the translation of the word "daaman" *(□□□□□ □□□□ □□□□□ - □□□□□, n.d.)* which has profound cultural and historical connotations. It expresses a sense of desperation from the cherished or the loved ones of the freedom warriors, asking the young fighters to think again, before they march into danger. Given that people left behind cling frantically to the hem of the clothing in an effort to prevent or postpone the departure, it can be viewed as the last thread of attachment in this instance.

When the specific "daaman" *(□□□□□ □□□□ □□□□□ - □□□□□, n.d.)* is replaced with a more general word like "garments of beauty" (ChatGPT) in the translation offered by ChatGPT, the personal touch and intensity of the source are lost. The translation provided by Gemini deviates considerably more from its original imagery and traditional significance. While "tugging at sleeves" (Gemini - Chat to Supercharge Your Ideas, n.d.) conveys a sense of estrangement on a collective or general level, it lacks the intimate, nearly selfless connection that comes with clutching onto the "daaman" *(□□□□□ □□□□ □□□□□ - □□□□□, n.d.)*. Here, there is an intense emotional loss. Another noteworthy illustration of cultural sensitivity can be found in the translation of the lines,

Table 11. Cultural metaphors as translated by ChatGPT and Gemini

Human Translation	**It's said the journeying feet have found union with the destination**
ChatGPT Translation	It is said the destination and journey have united.
Gemini Translation	We have heard that the union of destination and journey has already taken place,

The statement captures the difficult path of the Partition refugees, which was emotionally charged and characterized by displacement and a need for stability. The idea of a long journey coming to a conclusion is maintained in the human translation. The version provided by ChatGPT loses the moving imagery of a striving migrants achieving their objective in favor of a more abstract and impersonal interpretation. At the same time, Gemini's version substitutes a more passive composition that lessens the emotional impact for the original line's sincerity and individual suffering. These instances demonstrate how, despite their skill at language conversion, AI translations can fall short in capturing the complex cultural and historical nuances that are essential to comprehending poetry.

Scenario 2: Guided Line-by-Line Translation

In the second case, *User-2* gave the AI instructions to "translate the poem line by line to English" (ChatGPT; Gemini - Chat to Supercharge Your Ideas, n.d.), offering a more methodical approach. The purpose of this approach was to determine whether dividing the task of translating into manageable chunks would enhance quality and preserve poetical characteristics. In contrast to the first scenario, which gave the AI models complete control of the translation procedure, the guided method allowed for a deeper understanding of the structure and meaning of the poetry. But there were still certain difficulties and discrepancies in translation, which will be covered in this section.

The Structural Arrangement

In the first place, the *User 1* translation structurally rearranged the poem by breaking it up into more paragraphs than the original text. In contrast, the *User 2* translation proceeded line-by-line, making it easier to maintain the poem's emotional depth and tempo.

Figure 2. The line by line translated text by ChatGPT and Gemini

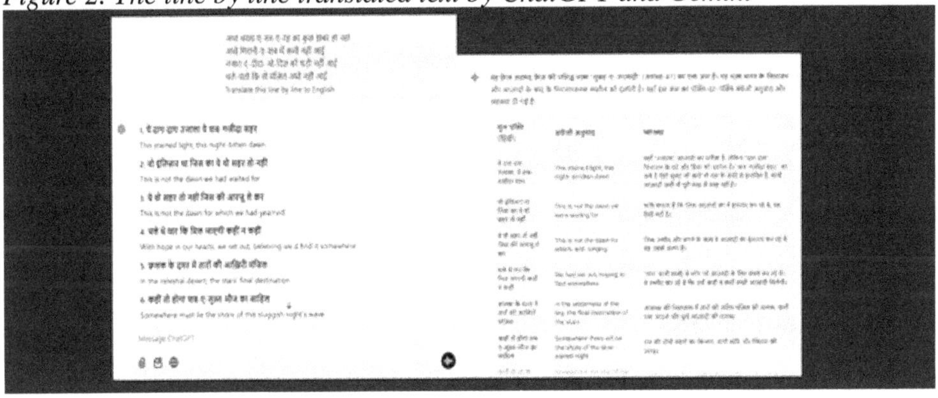

Thus, the result generated in the case of *User-2* outperforms the outcome of *User-1* in terms of structural alignment with the human translation. Building on this structural analysis, this section will now proceed to evaluate the quality and accuracy of the AI-generated translations for *User-2*.

Oversimplification and Loss of Poetic Complexity

In terms of poetic impact and complexity the translation received by the *User-1* demonstrates oversimplified phrases (see tables- 1,2,3, and 4) lacking the emotive significance of the human translation. The second scenario continues this trend, in the line-by-line translations, which frequently demonstrate a narrowing of the original's subtle phrasing and a diminution in semantic depth. *Table 1*, for example, shows that the AI models frequently employ the word "stained light" (ChatGPT; Gemini - Chat to Supercharge Your Ideas, n.d.) in place of more poetic terms like "smeared" or "spotted" (Penguin Random House, 2020) an arrangement that continues in the line-by-line translations. This indicates that the models have a restricted vocabulary and a propensity to use general or simplistic phrases.

When it comes to using adjectives to emphasize the poem's meaning, *User-2's* translations are constantly deficient in the use of descriptive language, which is similar to the issues with *User-1's* outputs as shown in the table below,

Table 12. Lack of adjectives in the translation by ChatGPT and Gemini

Human Translation	**When, from the mysterious paths of youth's hot blood**
ChatGPT Translation	Through the mysterious highways of young blood
Gemini Translation	From the mysterious highways of young blood

Although ChatGPT shows some improvement by substituting "young" for "youthful" (ChatGPT) in its *User-2* translation, it still does not fully employ the range of adjectives that are available to express the desired emotional weight and profundity. This shortcoming suggests the AI models' lack of knowledge about the complex adjectives and its influence on the overall impact and tone of the poem.

Syntactic Limitations

Beyond the problem of adjective usage, a rigorous examination of the AI-generated translations identifies serious syntactic problems. The human translation follows a simple subject-verb-object framework, illustrated in *Table 5*, providing a clear and succinct syntactic grounding. On the other hand, there is a tendency for notable syntactic variances in the AI models even in this scenario,

Table 13. Syntactic changes by ChatGPT and Gemini for User-2

Human Translation	**The boat of the afflicted heart's grieving will drop anchor somewhere,**
ChatGPT Translation	Somewhere, this ship of sorrow—the heart—must come to rest,
Gemini Translation	Somewhere the ship of the sorrowful heart will finally anchor

In the above table, though Gemini reproduces the same translation output as in the *User-1* scenario, ChatGPT drastically changes the translation but still displays syntactic mistakes. Even though they may seem insignificant, these grammatical changes have important ramifications. They somewhat change the metaphor's emphasis, tone, and overall meaning, which may have an impact on the reader's emotional reaction and comprehension of the underlying meaning. This emphasizes how crucial it is, to closely examine syntactic decisions when assessing the precision and caliber of translations produced by AI, particularly when it comes to poetry and other literary genres.

Metaphorical Accuracy

Alongside grammatical factors, determining how accurately and faithfully the underlying metaphors are represented is a critical component of judging translation quality. While metaphorical depth is still not accurately found in the translations of *User-2* but there is still better translation which is closer to the metaphors used by Faiz, as shown below,

Table 14. The cultural metaphors in User-2's outcome

Human Translation	**This light, smeared and spotted, this night-bitten dawn**
ChatGPT Translation	This stained light, this night-bitten dawn
Gemini Translation	This stained light, this night-stricken dawn

Human Translation	**Numerous were the hands that rose to clutch the hems of their garments,**
ChatGPT Translation	When the friends set forth, so many hands pulled at their hems
Gemini Translation	When the friends set out, how many hands tugged at their sleeves

According to the examination, while ChatGPT and Gemini both show improvements in some cases such as, Gemini changing "morning" to "dawn" ((Gemini - Chat to Supercharge Your Ideas, n.d.) and ChatGPT changing "garments" to "hems" (ChatGPT), these improvements are not always present. For instance, in both cases, Gemini reproduces the identical translation of the line "Numerous were the hands that rose to clutch the hems of their garments" (Penguin Random House, 2020), indicating that it may not be able to provide as varied and nuanced of outputs. According to this study, while AI models are capable of translating some textual elements precisely, it is still very difficult to capture and communicate the subtleties and cultural meanings that are incorporated into metaphors.

The investigation concludes that utilizing AI models to translate the poetry of Faiz Ahmed Faiz presents serious difficulties. Although ChatGPT and Gemini both did a fair job of translating the material into English, their translations were always unable to capture the subtleties of the source language. These drawbacks include the presence of syntactic faults, a reduction of cultural overtones and profundity of emotion, and a simplified form of poetic language.

Although *User-2's* line-by-line method demonstrated some progress in preserving the poem's structure, these difficulties were not entirely resolved. These findings demonstrate how difficult it is for existing AI models to translate intricate literary works, especially those with a lot of emotional and cultural meaning. The significance of these findings will be covered in more detail in the part that follows, along with the shortcomings of the AI translation systems available today and possible directions for further study and advancement in this field.

DISCUSSION AND IMPLICATIONS

This section examines the findings' broader implications and how they relate to academics, teachers, and students who utilize artificial intelligence (AI) to study, and translate literary works. Additionally, it examines the necessity for a more critical and contextual approach when incorporating these techniques into the analysis of the Partition texts.

The first finding of variations in AI-generated translations according to the specificity of user prompts emphasizes the complex function of prompting in translation quality. The generated translations can be improved by employing strategic prompting techniques, such as "give line by line" (ChatGPT; Gemini - Chat to Supercharge Your Ideas, n.d.) translation or outlining the poem's context, which guarantees that the complex meanings and emotional depth are more precisely expressed. These results thus, urges academics, instructors, and students to carefully examine the part prompting plays in producing more accurate and useful translations.

Secondly, the structural changes in the translations produced by ChatGPT and Gemini without any explicit guidance implies that the models put readability and grammatical consistency ahead of the original creative intention. This reorganization runs the risk of warping the poem's original tempo, rhythm, and emotional impact, all of which are essential in literary works that address historical trauma like Partition.

The unintentional inclusion of additional stanzas could lead to an artificial division of concepts and themes, which might break the poem's overall coherence and significance. The structural changes could cause misunderstandings for researchers and educators who depend on AI-generated translations. This reorganization could affect the reader's understanding, making it difficult for them to completely understand the poet's tone, historical significance, and intended message.

Additionally, ChatGPT and Gemini both have a tendency to use simple language, which inadvertently deprives the content of its artistic significance and nuanced meanings, two things that are crucial for interpreting the emotional and psychological effects of the Partition. The poetry may appear more literal and simpler to readers interacting with AI translations, resulting in ignoring the deeper allegorical and metaphorical layers of Faiz Ahmed Faiz's writing.

The fact that AI models frequently employ the same wording reveals a trend of language homogeneity. This suggests that rather than generating original or complex interpretations, AI prefers to mimic frequently used language and depends on a corpus of previously translated content. Because of this standardization, translations may become homogenized and lose the variety of interpretations that human translators provide. This predilection for repetition and reduction suggests that AI-generated translations may be more appropriate for broad understanding than literary analysis, where nuances are crucial.

Reading can become less engaging and evocative as a result of AI models' propensity to neutralize or change emotionally laden language. The poem may not have the same overall impact if readers are unable to empathize with the poet's suffering and the historical significance of the words. Additionally, it suggests that translation systems lack cultural and historical understanding, which leads to ambiguities or a weakening of the poem's content. This can result in a distorted portrayal of the Partition literature for audiences around the world who are not familiar with its background. This emphasizes the necessity for more context-driven translation frameworks and culturally sensitive training datasets to be included by AI developers.

The findings, analysis and its implication in this chapter suggest that, if applied carelessly, AI translations could weaken the intricacy of Partition literature and turn it into a textual record rather than an emotional and experiential artifact. Thus, for complex literary works, AI translations may not yet be trustworthy enough. To guarantee correctness and faithfulness to the source material, academics and translators must keep evaluating AI results rigorously. A balanced strategy is thus required, in which AI supports human translation and interpretation rather than replaces it.

CONCLUSION

In conclusion, this study shows that although ChatGPT and Gemini provide helpful assistance in deciphering intricate literary works like "Subh-e-Azadi (The Dawn of Freedom)" by Faiz Ahmed Faiz, they also present important issues that demand careful consideration. Although human translations are still the best way to convey the richness, nuanced cultural aspects, and emotional impact of Partition poetry, the results indicate that both AI models, ChatGPT and Gemini, perform almost as well, but with different advantages and disadvantages.

ChatGPT exhibits a greater understanding of cultural meanings, frequently producing translations that closely match the original text's metaphorical and symbolic components. However, Gemini is particularly good at providing notes in addition to translations, which can help with understanding but can include interpretive biases that change the poem's intended meaning. Both AI approaches, however, have serious shortcomings that are impossible to ignore, including simplifying, syntactical restructuring, and the loss of lyrical depth, all of which can obstruct an effective reading experience. Hence, it can be concluded that ChatGPT is a better option for the tasks that involve translating culturally embedded texts and Gemini can be more useful for tasks that require understanding and analyzing, providing additional comments that facilitate interpretation.

Despite the insightful information this comparison analysis provided, it is important to recognize a number of limitations. User prompt specificity and detail have a significant impact on the quality of AI translations. It can be difficult to generalize findings across many use cases since varied prompting strategies and contextual information may produce different outcomes. The main subjects of this study are Gemini and ChatGPT. A more thorough grasp of AI translation skills might be obtained by conducting a more extensive comparison analysis across various platforms, as other AI translation tools might exhibit distinct performance.

The original poetry is subjectively interpreted in the human translation that is utilized for comparison. Diverse translators may present different viewpoints, which may affect how accurately and sympathetically AI is assessed. The results of this study may not apply to later iterations of AI models since they are always being updated and improved. Over time, AI's literary text translation skills might advance, possibly resolving some of the present issues and therefore continuous research on this subject is a necessity in today's world.

REFERENCES

□□□□□ □□□□ □□□□□ - □□□□□. (n.d.). Rekhta. https://www.rekhta.org/nazms/subh-e-aazaadii-august-47-ye-daag-daag-ujaalaa-ye-shab-gaziida-sahar-faiz-ahmad-faiz-nazms?lang=hi

Almaktary, H. (2025). Reflections on Translating Poetry through ChatGPT: Insights from Arabic, English, and French. *Journal of English Studies in Arabia Felix*, *4*(1), 1–12. DOI: 10.56540/jesaf.v4i1.108

Alsajri, A., Salman, H. A., & Steiti, A. (2024). Generative Models in Natural Language Processing: A Comparative Study of ChatGPT and Gemini. *Deleted Journal*, *2024*, 134–145. DOI: 10.58496/BJAI/2024/015

Bhargava, C., & Sharma, P. K. (2021). *Artificial intelligence: Fundamentals and Applications*. CRC Press. DOI: 10.1201/9781003095910

Bowker, L. (2023). *De-mystifying translation: Introducing Translation to Non-translators*. Taylor & Francis. DOI: 10.4324/9781003217718

Dey, K., Tarannum, P., Hasan, M. A., Razzak, I., & Naseem, U. (2024). Better to Ask in English: Evaluation of Large Language Models on English, Low-resource and Cross-Lingual Settings. *arXiv (Cornell University)*. https://doi.org//arxiv.2410.13153DOI: 10.48550

Doshi, A. V. (2024). The Loss in AI Translation. *ResearchGate*. https://www.researchgate.net/publication/383037053_The_Loss_in_AI_Translation

Doudou, W., & Faizi, H. (2024). *Enhancing Poetry Translation via ChatGPT 3.5: A Comparative Contrastive Study on Translated versions Qabbani's Poem Belqees & Fortune Teller by Kevin Moore* [MA Dissertation, Kasdi Merbah Ouargla University]. https://dspace.univ-ouargla.dz/jspui/bitstream/123456789/36859/1/Enhancing%20Poetry%20Translation%20Via%20ChatGPT%203.5.pdf

Farghal, M., & Haider, A. S. (2024). Translating classical Arabic verse: Human translation vs. AI large language models (Gemini and ChatGPT). *Cogent Social Sciences*, *10*(1), 2410998. Advance online publication. DOI: 10.1080/23311886.2024.2410998

Gemini - chat to supercharge your ideas. (n.d.). Gemini. https://gemini.google.com/app?utm_source=google&utm_medium=cpc&utm_campaign=2024enIN_gemfeb&gad_source=1&gclid=Cj0KCQjwzby1BhCQARIsAJ_0t5PGHpF7rjUJug9QyXooWyoepqcoaVfpBOh9oMbRx-bQr-QhZylAMi4aAlloEALw_wcB

Gupta, R., Srivastava, D., Sahu, M., Tiwari, S., Ambasta, R. K., & Kumar, P. (2021). Artificial intelligence to deep learning: Machine intelligence approach for drug discovery. *Molecular Diversity, 25*(3), 1315–1360. DOI: 10.1007/s11030-021-10217-3 PMID: 33844136

Hasan, M. (2002). Partition narratives. *Social Scientist (New Delhi), 30*(7/8), 24. DOI: 10.2307/3518150

Hasan, M. A., Tarannum, P., Dey, K., Razzak, I., & Naseem, U. (2024). Do Large Language Models Speak All Languages Equally? A Comparative Study in Low-Resource Settings. *arXiv (Cornell University)*. https://doi.org//arxiv.2408.02237DOI: 10.48550

Khoshafah, F. (2023). ChatGPT for Arabic-English translation: Evaluating the accuracy. *Research Square(Research Square)*. DOI: 10.21203/rs.3.rs-2814154/v2

Kishore, K. S., & Shaik, R. (2024). *Evaluating Telugu Proficiency in Large Language Models_ A Comparative Analysis of ChatGPT and Gemini*. https://www.semanticscholar.org/paper/Evaluating-Telugu-Proficiency-in-Large-Language-A-Kishore-Shaik/a0dc190626901a6e06db47a0fbe802b5226bb4a2

Lee, T. K. (2023). Artificial intelligence and posthumanist translation: ChatGPT versus the translator. *Applied Linguistics Review, 15*(6), 2351–2372. DOI: 10.1515/applirev-2023-0122

Liu, J. (2024). ChatGPT: Perspectives from human–computer interaction and psychology. *Frontiers in Artificial Intelligence, 7*, 1418869. Advance online publication. DOI: 10.3389/frai.2024.1418869 PMID: 38957452

Mazur, O., & Thimmesch, A. B. (2024, May 28). *Beyond ChatGPT: Transforming Government with Augmented LLMs*. https://papers.ssrn.com/sol3/papers.cfm?abstract_id=4846472

McIntosh, T. R., Susnjak, T., Liu, T., Watters, P., & Halgamuge, M. N. (2023). From Google Gemini to OpenAI Q* (Q-Star): A Survey of Reshaping the Generative Artificial Intelligence (AI) Research Landscape. *arXiv (Cornell University)*. https://doi.org//arxiv.2312.10868DOI: 10.48550

Mufti, A. R. (2004). Towards a lyric history of India. *Boundary 2, 31*(2), 245–274. DOI: 10.1215/01903659-31-2-245

Muñoz-Basols, J., Neville, C., Lafford, B. A., & Godev, C. (2023). Potentialities of Applied Translation for Language Learning in the Era of Artificial Intelligence. *Hispania, 106*(2), 171–194. DOI: 10.1353/hpn.2023.a899427

Ousidhoum, N., Beloucif, M., & Mohammad, S. M. (2024). Building Better: Avoiding Pitfalls in Developing Language Resources when Data is Scarce. *arXiv (Cornell University).* https://doi.org//arxiv.2410.12691DOI: 10.48550

Penguin Random House. (2020, February 23). Subh-e-Azadi (B. Farooqui, Trans.). *Penguin Random House India.* https://www.penguin.co.in/subh-e-azadi-an-anguished-evocation-of-the-pain-of-partition/

Rane, N., Choudhary, S., & Rane, J. (2024). Gemini Versus ChatGPT: Applications, Performance, Architecture, Capabilities, and Implementation. SSRN *Electronic Journal.* DOI: 10.2139/ssrn.4723687

Resende, N., & Hadley, J. (2024). The Translator's Canvas: Using LLMs to enhance Poetry translation. In *Proceedings of the 16th Conference of the Association for Machine Translation in the Americas* (Vol. 1). https://aclanthology.org/2024.amta-research.16.pdf

Sayers, D., Sousa-Silva, R., Höhn, S., Ahmedi, L., Allkivi-Metsoja, K., Anastasiou, D., Beňuš, Š., Bowker, L., Bytyçi, E., Catala, A., Çepani, A., Chacón-Beltrán, R., Dadi, S., Dalipi, F., Despotovic, V., Doczekalska, A., Drude, S., Fort, K., Fuchs, R., . . . Yayilgan, S. Y. (2021, May 19). *The Dawn of the Human-Machine Era: A forecast of new and emerging language technologies.* https://hal.science/hal-03230287/

Sobti, P., & Kumar, D. (2022). Partition as Memory: Construing Women Narratives. *Journal of Positive School Psychology*, *6*(9), 731–738.

Taghian, M. A. (2024). Assessing the Accuracy Criteria of AI Tools-aided Translation: A Case Study of Two-word Prophetic Hadiths. *CDELT Occasional Papers in the Development of English Education, 87*(1), 217–262. DOI: 10.21608/opde.2024.384369

Wei, X. (2024). The Use of Large Language Models for Translating Buddhist Texts from Classical Chinese to Modern English: An Analysis and Evaluation with ChatGPT 4, ERNIE Bot 4, and Gemini Advanced. *Religions*, *15*(12), 1559. DOI: 10.3390/rel15121559

Chapter 11
Exploring the Translation of Idioms by AI in Chinese Internet Literature

Luyan Guo
https://orcid.org/0009-0005-3964-2910
Universiti Malaya, Malaysia

Amin Amirdabbaghian
https://orcid.org/0000-0001-6503-8446
Universiti Malaya, Malaysia

ABSTRACT

Artificial Intelligence (AI) has been applied in translating various text types including literary texts. With the popularity of Chinese Internet (CIL) Literature, substantial translated novels have been automatically produced by machine translation systems. Idioms and expressions are integrated components of Chinese literature, with over ninety percent being four-character idioms. Translation of four-character idioms has always been challenging for human translators. Considering the contextual limitations of AI compared to human translators, the translation process becomes more challenging due to the unique structures and connotative meanings of four-character idioms. Based on Chan's categorization of four-character idioms, this study adopts a qualitative approach to identify translation techniques found in the English translation of Chinese four-character idioms by MT in Returning to '90s, She Became Famous in Major Surgical Fields, a popular CIL. Analysis confirms that established equivalents, reduction, and literal translation are the most frequently used techniques in translating these idioms.

DOI: 10.4018/979-8-3373-0060-3.ch011

INTRODUCTION

Translation is a cross-cultural and cross-language communication activity. Translators are required to be proficient in both source and target languages and have knowledge of both cultures. Cultural awareness of translators also influences the dissemination and impact of translations in foreign markets (Zong, 2024). CIL has recently been developing promisingly in China in the wake of the rise of the Internet in the 1990s. At the beginning of the 21st century, Chinese contemporary literature demonstrated the feature of diversification in the progress of moving towards the world. With the assistance of the Internet, CIL has received numerous readers locally and abroad (Wu & Gu, 2019). The emerging type of Chinese literature, CIL, which has been considered lower tier by readers in China, has become a popular category overseas and has drawn a substantial international readership (Wang, D., 2017). It enables authors to publish their works with great potential for a wider audience beyond China's physical borders (Yang, Y., 2021). Compared with traditional literature, internet literature is more readable for its various themes, winding plots, and room for imagination. CIL has appeared overseas since 2010, taking 盗墓笔记 (daomubiji) (*The Grave Robbers' Chronicles*) as an example. With the rise of internet literature, a batch of literature translation websites and forum communities with Wuxia-world, Gravity Tales, and Novel Updates as representatives have also made their way to the digital world (Wu & Gu, 2019).

MT is a field of research and development in which one natural language is translated into another natural language with the instrument of computer software. Accompanied by a series of experiments in MT that commenced after the Second World War, various MT systems have been trained based on different texts. The newest MT systems, such as Neural MT, can produce a much higher quality rendition more efficiently (Koehn, 2020). However, when it comes to literary translation, the problem is evident as the writing conventions differ between authors, genres, and the like.

Vocabulary, as an integral component in a language, plays an essential role in cross-cultural communication. Chinese idioms are often culture-embedded and can indicate the proficiency level of individuals in the Chinese language by manipulating them (Jia, 2023). Chinese idioms are frequently used in Chinese literature and speech, which makes sentences more concise and vivid, enriching colloquial expressions and leaving a deep impression on readers and listeners. They can function grammatically as predicates, attributives, adverbials, subjects, or objects in sentences. The meaning of an idiom is more than the sum of the meanings of the components (Chan, 2016).

The translation of four-character idioms in Chinese literary works poses challenges for human translators due to their implicit meanings, diverse structures, and rich cultural images (Wang, 2024). It might be more challenging for MT systems to recognize and convey their intended meanings without losing their cultural nuances. MTL Novel is a RAW Novel translator using automatic MT, which attracts countless readers overseas for its efficient translation. This study focuses on the translation techniques used by MT systems to translate Chinese four-character idioms into English and identifies the translation errors in the novel *Returning to '90s, She Became Famous in Major Surgical Fields* on the MTL Novel website. This novel revolves around the female protagonist who, after traveling back to the 1990s, uses her modern medical knowledge and exceptional surgical skills to achieve remarkable success in the medical field of that time, gradually becoming a leading figure in surgery. Chinese four-character idioms and their English translations are collected using simple random sampling from this novel. Based on Molina and Albir's (2002) model, translation techniques are identified using contrastive analysis. Established equivalent, reduction and literal translation are primarily employed. Literal and partially literal translations are identified as major obstacles to sentence intelligibility. This study will shed light on the translation of CIL with a particular focus on the Chinese four-character idioms within context.

Research Gap

Many studies have examined translation strategies for idioms or idiomatic expressions by human translators. Several studies (Ali et al., 2023; Floranti & Mubarok, 2020) have been conducted on Indonesian idiomatic expressions in English. Valizadeh and Vazifehkhah (2021) and Sharahil et al. (2022) explored strategies for translating English idioms into Persian and Arabic, respectively. Many studies (Kong, 2014; Liu, D., 2012; Wang, L., & Wang, S., 2013; Yang, C., 2010) have explored translation strategies between Chinese and English idioms from the cultural perspective. On the other hand, Chen, L. (2009, 2020) discussed literal and free translations of English idioms in Chinese. In the context of translation strategies for Chinese idioms into English, Hu (2021), drawing on George Steiner's Fourfold Hermeneutic Motion Theory, contrasts with that of Zhang and Wang (2010), who adopted Nida's functional equivalence theory. Many studies (Deng & Abdullah, 2024; Duan, et al., 2014; Liu, J., 2019) examined translation strategies for English and Chinese idioms relating to animals through comparative analysis. Several studies (Idami et al., 2022; Kayed, 2023) also looked into problems while translating idiomatic expressions through a qualitative content analysis approach, whereas Sipayung et al. (2024) adopted a mixed method implementing House's (2014, as cited in Sipayung et al., 2024) theory of non-dimensional mismatch. However, few studies (Kang & Yang, 2022) probe into translation by MT systems in the context of Chinese four-character idioms. This study probes into translation techniques and problems in translating Chinese four-character idioms encountered by MT systems.

Research Aim

This study aims to categorize the four-character idioms and analyze their translation techniques in the CIL *Returning to '90s, She Became Famous in Major Surgical Fields*.

The research objectives are as follows:

1. To identify and categorize the four-character idioms found in *Returning to '90s, She Became Famous in Major Surgical Fields* based on Chan (2016).
2. To identify and discuss the translation techniques employed by MT on Chinese four-character idioms in *Returning to '90s, She Became Famous in Major Surgical Fields*.

The research questions are as follows:

1. What is the distribution of four-character idioms across different categories in *Returning to '90s, She Became Famous in Major Surgical Fields* based on Chan's (2016) classification?
2. What translation techniques are frequently employed by machine translation when translating four-character idioms in *Returning to '90s, She Became Famous in Major Surgical Fields*?

LITERATURE REVIEW

The development of MT

MT systems occurred along with the emergence of computers. Warren Weaver first proposed the concept of MT in 1947, and it was then regarded as one of the trickiest tasks for natural language processing (Wang et al., 2021). Natural language is inherently ambiguous from word level to text level (Koehn, 2020). A batch of commercial translation systems has been developed since the late 1960s. In the 1980s and 1990s, researchers focused on developing systems that use interlingua to represent meaning without relying on any particular language (Koehn, 2020). Statistical MT emerged in the late 1980s and was widely applied around the turn of the millennium (Koehn, 2020). Approaches to MT can be classified into rule-based methods which remained dominant until the 1990s, and corpus-based methods (Wang et al., 2021). Hybrid methods are usually adopted in practical systems to improve the performance of MT (Wang et al., 2021). MT is widely used in various communication forms including Skype translators, chat translators, travel translators, lecturer translators, and sign language translators (Naveen & Trojovský, 2024). It is also adopted in text translation as automated MT translates the source text into the target language in an efficient way (Naveen & Trojovský, 2024). Moreover, it is used for cross-lingual information retrieval and extraction. It can access cross-lingual information on the internet (Koehn, 2020). Multimodal MT, as a branch of MT, can process information in multi-modal forms that has been gaining attention (Koehn, 2020). With the assistance of MT, human translators become more efficient. However, applying MT in the translation industry is still controversial in fields such as literature and poetry. Achieving accurate renditions in specific domains requires MT systems to be trained with domain-specific knowledge (Naveen & Trojovský, 2024). Take idiomatic expressions, for example; their meanings are not the sum of the meanings of each word. Producing accurate renditions for culture-specific texts poses a problem for MT systems.

The advantages of MT systems lie in four aspects as Tekwa (2023) explains. Firstly, the MT system exceeds human translators in speed since it can process substantial information in minutes. Secondly, MT systems cost much less than human translators. Thirdly, they are adaptable in that they can be trained with unknown vocabulary in different fields. Fourthly, they can cope with myriads of languages (Tekwa, 2023, p. 32). MT is significant in the context of globalization. It is conducive to overcoming language barriers, fostering multicultural awareness, and enabling global collaboration (Naveen & Trojovský, 2024). The application of MT in Chinese literature translation made diverse Chinese cultures available to foreign readers. However, generating translations that are contextually relevant and accurate remains challenging for MT. It is difficult for MT systems to capture and utilize contextual information from original texts and maintain grammatical correctness and syntactic coherence. Jargon, idiomatic expressions, and cultural nuances impede achieving contextually appropriate translations (Naveen & Trojovský, 2024).

The application of MT has been developed in various domains, such as business, diplomacy, education, personal communication, research, and travel (Naveen & Trojovský, 2024). Jeffrey (2024) synthesized developments of MT in the legal field from legal translators' viewpoint. Hatano (2024) investigated the application of consecutive speech MT technology in a face-to-face exchange. Boulanger (2024) summarized the advantages and disadvantages of applying neural MT and generative AI tools in medical translation. Alhaj (2024) explored the application of MT technology in tourism translation from the perspectives of translators and translation specialists in Saudi Arabia. Wang, Y. (2024) probed into automated MT in the field of online video education.

Some researchers delved into the translation of culture-related contexts by MT. They compared the performance of human translators with machine translation systems on identical contents. Mehawesh (2023) and Al-Kaabi et al. (2024) compared two English renditions of the same Arabic content made by human translators and MT systems. Mehawesh (2023) probed into a culture-abound novel *Palace Walk*. The results revealed that human translators are more versatile and effective in translation than MT systems. Al-Kaabi et al. (2024) focused on translating Arabic cultural connotations. It concluded that human translation exhibited higher accuracy and depth in conveying core cultural connotations and performed better in capturing cultural metaphors. While translating cultural expressions, MT failed to express their allegorical meanings. Human translation proved better than MT in maintaining cultural connotations. Aldelaa and Malkawi (2024) and Shao et al. (2017) identified literal translation as the most frequent problem in MT. Aldelaa and Malkawi (2024) also noted other difficulties encountered by MT such as unjustified omission, culture-loaded expressions, incorrect lexical prediction, in-cohesion, ambiguity caused by homonymy and polysemy, incorrect word choice, and colloquial idiomatic expressions in translating Arabic idiomatic expressions into English. Shao et al. (2017) evaluated the quality of MT in translating Chinese idioms. The results implied that idiom translation remains challenging for MT systems. Liang et al. (2024) conducted an error analysis of the translated text of subtitles from Chinese to English made by Google neural MT based on Petersen's FAR model. The distribution of errors according to functional equivalence, acceptability, and readability are 53%, 33%, and 14% respectively. Recommendations on post-editing were proposed to address these errors. Subtitlers were recommended to focus on errors in semantics, idiomaticity, grammar, and line length due to the mistranslation of incomplete sentences, culture-bound terms, and proper nouns. Several studies propose new learning models to address the challenges in translating culture-embedded terms. Chia et al. (2024) constructed manually and automatically translated datasets of irony and sarcasm from English to Chinese and assessed the quality of MT renditions of irony and sarcasm using a novel evaluation metric. After the problems that occurred while translating them by MT were investigated, they explored optimal translation settings and the most suitable model for irony. Zhang and Xia (2024) proposed a deep semantic learning model for MT in translating Chinese tea-cultured terms into English. They constructed a Chinese-English parallel corpus on tea culture for model training. Tea-cultured expressions are challenging for MT to capture their cultural connotation accurately. MT systems can effectively convey cultural information about these expressions with the deep semantic learning model trained in tea culture-loaded vocabulary. This learning model proved successful for MT in tackling tea-cultured expressions.

The definition of four-character idioms

Idioms have become an essential component in the Chinese language and have received considerable attention in the wake of the new culture movement in the 1910s when classical Chinese was gradually replaced by vernacular Chinese (Chan, 2016). Chinese idioms become fixed phrases after being shaped and refined for a long time. Typically, the meaning of idioms is not equal to the combination of the meaning of each part. They usually convey richer meanings than the combined meanings of individual words (Chan, 2016). As phrases, Chinese idioms primarily function grammatically as predicates, attributives, or adverbials and rarely serve as objects, complements, or subjects. They can form clauses or even stand alone as complete sentences contingent on the surrounding context (Chen, X., 2009). Chinese idioms, along with collocations, two-part allegorical sayings, and proverbs are four types of idiomatic expressions (Chan, 2016). 成语 (chengyu) is conventionally translated as "idiom", "set phrase", or "four-character expression". Four-character idioms can be divided into two groups when recited at normal speed. They account for over 90% of Chinese idioms. Chinese four-character idioms can be categorized into five categories and 15 types (Chan, 2016). The incorporation of Chinese idioms in written or spoken language can enhance the conciseness and vividness of expressions.

The challenges encountered by MT systems while translating Chinese idioms

Idioms are a tricky area for human translators. Idiomatic expressions often have figurative or metaphorical meanings deeply rooted in culture. To generate accurate translations, translators must not only understand the underlying cultural and linguistic subtlety but also identify the equivalent expressions in the target language. Baker (2018) states four main difficulties in the translation of idioms and fixed expressions: a. Unable to find equivalents in the target language. b. Have a similar counterpart with a different connotation in the target language. c. An idiom is used in both its literal and idiomatic meanings simultaneously. d. Differences in contexts and frequency of the idioms' usage between source texts and target texts. The first difficulty in interpreting idioms is to recognize them (Baker, 2018, p. 71). The same applies to Chinese four-character idioms. Human translators can easily recognize them for their unique structures, but this might be challenging for MT systems without relevant training. Secondly, MT systems are challenged to translate idiomatic expressions without missing their subtle meanings. Many Chinese four-character idioms have literal and idiomatic meanings. MT systems may translate them literally and overlook the intended meanings. Thirdly, MT systems face challenges in dealing with cultural references that usually require adaptation due to the lack of direct equivalents in the target language. An idiom can be misleading if it has a close matching that is lexically similar but semantically different in the target language (Baker, 2018, p. 72).

Studies on idiom translation into other languages

Many scholars have extensively researched translation strategies for idiomatic expressions. According to Mona Baker (1992, pp. 72-77), idioms can be translated using the following strategies. The first strategy is to use an idiom conveying a similar meaning and form in the target language as the source language. The second strategy is to use a similar meaning to the source language in a different lexical form. The third strategy is paraphrasing. It is the most common translation strategy for idioms. The fourth strategy is omission. It is employed when an idiom has no close equivalent in the target language. The fifth strategy is compensation. A feature within the source text that is downplayed or omitted in the original position but occurs elsewhere in the target language. Based on Baker's framework (1992), Floranti and Mubarok (2020) and Ali et al. (2023) examined strategies for translating idiomatic expressions from Indonesia to English, whereas Idami et al. (2022) focused on Arabic idioms into English. Floranti and Mubarok (2020) also investigated the accuracy of the renditions. Ali et al. (2023) uncovered the cultural nuances of these idioms and the effectiveness of employed strategies. Baker (2011) modified her model of translation strategies for idiomatic expressions, expanding to six strategies. This revision incorporates borrowing and omission of a play on idiomatic expression and excludes compensation. Based on Baker's (2011) model, using a similar meaning but different forms was most frequently used while omitting the whole idiomatic expression was least employed in translating English idioms into Persian (Valizadeh & Vazifehkhah, 2021). Based on Baker's (2018) taxonomy of translation strategies, Sharahil et al. (2022) identified that paraphrasing, literal translation, total equivalence, and partial equivalence are the main strategies adopted in translating English idiomatic expressions into Arabic. They also detected instances of inaccurate translation and loss of meaning. Studies on translation strategies for idiomatic expressions showed that paraphrasing is the most frequently employed translation strategy (Ali et al., 2023; Floranti & Mubarok, 2020; Sharahil et al, 2022). Several investigators (Idami et al., 2022; Kayed, 2023) also investigated problems while translating Indonesian idiomatic expressions into English, particularly for students. Idami et al. (2022) found that differences in cultural and stylistic aspects are the main obstacles for students. Kayed (2023) identified the following problems encountered by students: lack of adequate knowledge, insufficient linguistic or pragmatic competence, preference for literal translation, and cultural differences. This study also noted that total equivalence and literal translation are frequently used strategies by students. Based on Baker's (2018) model of common problems of non-equivalence and House's (2014, as cited in Sipayung et al., 2024) taxonomy of errors, Sipayung et al. (2024) identified common problems and overt errors in translating English idioms into Indonesian. They found that semantically complex words in the source language are the dominant problem. Failure to translate and violations of the language system were identified as the most frequent overt errors.

Studies on idioms translation between Chinese and English

Studies on translation strategies for Chinese idioms have been conducted from different perspectives. In the context of translation strategies for English idioms into Chinese. Chen, L. (2009) elaborated on literal translation with representative examples. Chen, L. (2020) discussed the explanation strategy according to Nida's perspective of translation and culture. Several researchers (Liu, D., 2012; Wang, L., & Wang, S., 2013) have explored idiom translation between English and Chinese. Liu, D. (2012) examined translation methods in English-Chinese parallel translation of idioms from a cultural perspective. Literal translation, literal translation with footnotes or explanation, and equivalent were identified. Wang, L. and Wang, S. (2013) put forward strategies such as literal translation, free translation, abridged translation, and borrowing translation. Researchers (Hu, 2021; Zhang & Wang, 2010) have explored translation strategies for Chinese idioms into English. From the perspective of George Steiner's Fourfold Hermeneutic Motion Theory, Hu (2021) elaborated on literal translation, free translation, and combined strategies found in Bonsall's English version of the Chinese masterpiece, *The Red Chamber*. Adopting Nida's functional equivalence theory, Zhang and Wang (2010) discussed nine translation methods that include literal translation, literal translation supplemented with annotation, borrowing, integration, combination, omission, amplification, transposition, and free translation. Few researchers (Deng & Abdullah, 2024; Duan, et al., 2014; Liu, J., 2019) explored translation strategies for English and Chinese animal-related idioms. Duan, et al. (2014) discussed direct translation, direct translation with annotation, and free translation. Liu, J. (2019) identified equivalent translation (reserving image), corresponding translation (changing image), and compromising translation (abandoning image). Deng and Abdullah (2024) found that literal translation, the shift of animal category, and omission were frequently used strategies. Kong (2014) explored the translation of Chinese and English numerical idioms. Yang, C. (2010) investigated the translation of Chinese and English diet-related idioms. Using the same structure, accompanied by substituting the improper words, and literal translation with annotations were identified while translating Chinese diet-related idioms into English. Kang and Yang (2022) analyzed translation strategies and problems while translating Chinese four-character idioms into English. Literal translation, free translation, and combined translation are the main translation strategies. They also highlighted common challenges such as poor acceptance by foreigners, loss of cultural elements, and unbalanced cultural status.

Description of the chosen novel *Returning to'90s, She Became Famous in Major Surgical Fields*

Female network literature occupies half of the territory of Chinese network literature (Ai, 2020). Literature is under the influence of the surrounding environment. After the awakening of female consciousness, contemporary female web literature demonstrates the characteristics of female consciousness (Ai, 2020). The portrayal of women has gradually evolved from a traditional image that is weak and dependent to a modern woman who is more independent and even features some male-specific characteristics (Ai, 2020). In recent years, online women's literature has gained widespread popularity among female readers. It also provides numerous coming-of-age stories in which women achieve self-worth and transform their destinies through knowledge or technology. (Ma, 2022) 回到九零,她在外科大佬圈火爆了 (huidaojiuling, tazaiwaikedalaoquanhuobaole) *Returning to '90s, She Became Famous in Major Surgical Fields* reflects the characteristics of contemporary female network literature. It is a wish-fulfillment novel featuring time travel written by 肥猫向善 (a kind-hearted fat cat) who has over 112 thousand followers on Chuangshi Chinese Network, one of the well-known online literature platforms in China ([Description of the author], n.d.). It is a novella published as a serialized work on women's literature websites like 红袖添香 (hongxiutianxiang),起点 (qidian),潇湘书院 (xiaoxiangshuyuan) and completed in Feb 2024. It revolves around a female protagonist who experiences time travel or reincarnation, returning to the 1990s. The heroine is an experienced and excellent surgeon in the modern world. In an accident, she is reborn back to the 1990s when many technologies and concepts in the medical field were underdeveloped and fell far behind modern times in China. With her advanced medical knowledge and professional skills, she became prominent in the medical field. Although there existed social prejudice against female doctors and young doctors, the heroine gradually gained recognition from her peers through her efforts. She cured many patients with dubious or hard-to-treat cases and proposed many novel treatment methods, which successfully renewed certain old concepts in medical science. She also endured oppression from society, family, and even her male superiors and faced incomprehension from her family. However, she eventually broke through limitations and became a leader in the field of surgery using her modern medical knowledge and skills. Her medical skills have caused a sensation in the male-dominated field and even attracted the attention of many medical bigwigs.

METHODOLOGY

In this study, Chinese four-character idioms in the novel *Returning to '90s, She Became Famous in Major Surgical Fields* are classified based on Chan's (2016) categorization of Chinese four-character idioms.

Figure 1.

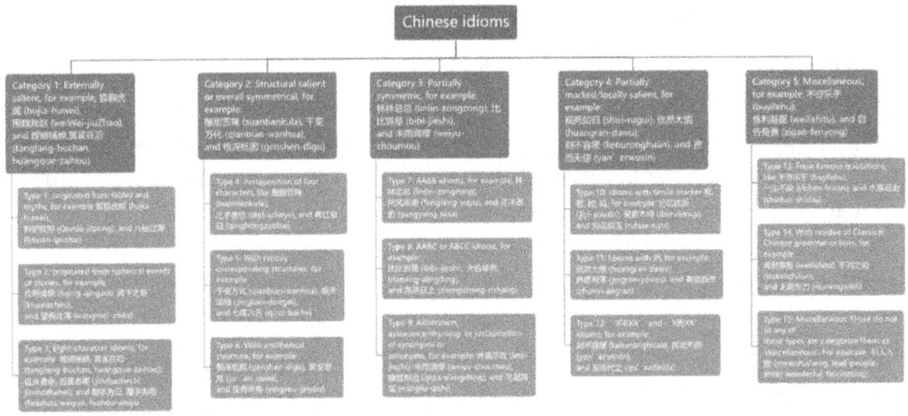

Adapted from Chan, 2016, pp. 71-79

Translation Techniques

This study adopts the translation techniques model developed by Molina and Albir (2002). According to Molina and Albir (2002), literal translation is to translate a word or its meaning word by word according to its function and meaning in the sentence. Calque means translating a word or phrase concerning its lexical or structural form. Transposition involves changing an expression's grammatical category. Furthermore, it is categorized into four types: 1. Compulsory or automatic shifts 2. Grammatical structural shift. 3. Transposing due to reasonable expressions because the source language equivalents are reasonable or not natural in the target language. 4. Transposing language units, for example, words into phrases (Hartono, 2020). Reduction means to reduce partial information in the target language that exists or is more stressed in the source language. Linguistic compression refers to condensing or synthesizing linguistic elements in the target language. Discursive creation is a method of establishing a temporary equivalence that is unpredictable without context considered. An established equivalent seeks to employ a familiar term or phrase from the source language as an equivalent in the target text. This approach utilizes a term or expression recognized by dictionaries as a corresponding word or phrase in the recipient language.

Research Design

This study adopts a qualitative method using contrastive analysis. Charts are employed to present the distribution of different types of Chinese four-character idioms and the frequency of translation techniques. Translation techniques are identified by comparing Chinese four-character idioms with their machine-translated renditions with context considered where necessary. Translation techniques are discussed elaborately and profoundly with representative examples from different types of idioms. Simple random sampling is an efficient method that allows researchers to use smaller resources to achieve similar results as the larger one. Due to limited time, simple random sampling is adopted in this study.

Data Collection

This study collects Chinese four-character idioms in an online novel *Returning to '90s, She Became Famous in Major Surgical Fields*. The English version of this novel is available at the website MTL Novel[1]. MTL Novel is a RAW Novel translator using automatic MT, which attracts myriads of readers overseas for its efficient translation. It provides renditions in English, Español, Bahasa Indonesia, Français, Portuguese, and Russian. This novel has received over 18.4 million views on this website. Both the Chinese and English versions of this novel are open access. This study applies the random sampling method since it will be time-consuming to deal with the whole online novel having 4464 chapters and 4,934,880 Chinese words. Four-character phrases in Chinese are collected from the initial 450 chapters of the novel manually. To select four-character idioms, all of them are checked on 成语大词典 (在线)[2] (online chengyu dictionary) is a comprehensive online idiom dictionary that stores over 60,000 idioms and constantly revises and expands its resources. Four-character phrases with no record in the dictionary are excluded. Chinese four-character idioms, their English definitions, and machine-translated versions are compiled with one-to-one correspondence in an Excel sheet. The total number of four-character idioms is 520. Including those idioms that occur repeatedly but have different translations, the total count rises to 622.

Data analysis

Based on Chan's (2016) categorization of Chinese idioms, the distribution of four-character idioms is presented below:

Figure 2. Distribution of Each Category Graph

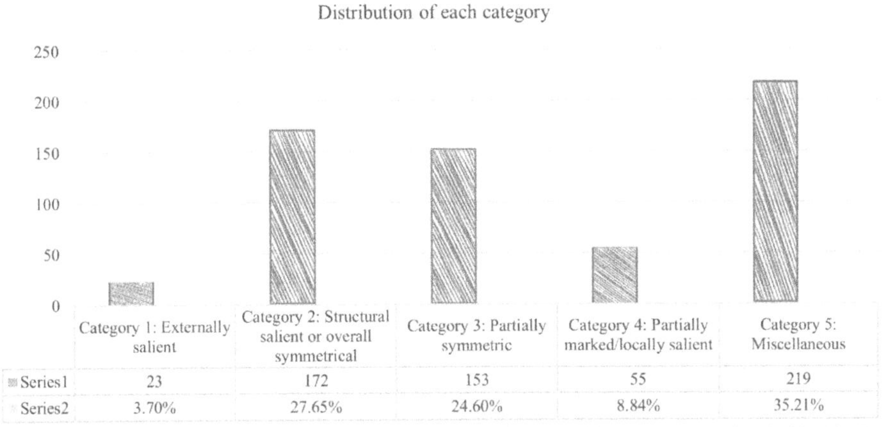

Category 5 accounts for the largest proportion while Category 1 shares the smallest proportion.

Figure 3. Distribution of Each Type Graph

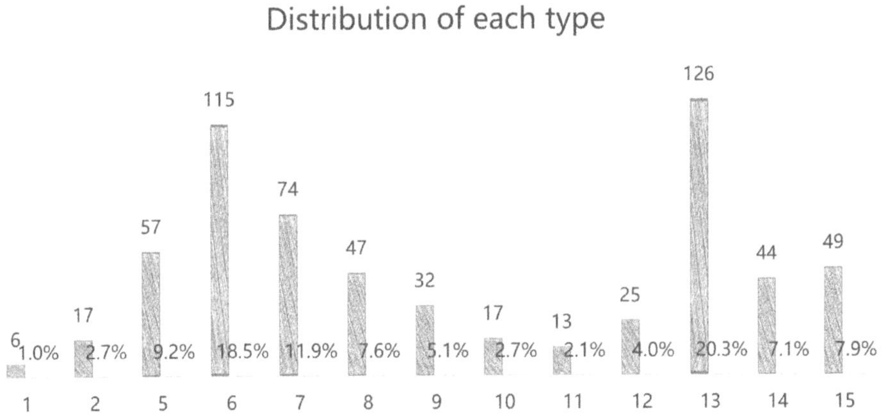

Thirteen out of 15 types of Chinese idioms are identified, with types 3 and 4 missing. Additionally, types 6 and 13 occupy the largest proportion.

By dividing the number of idioms with multiple renditions by the total number of the categories they belong to, the tendency for each category to be translated differently is shown below:

Figure 4. Tendencies for each category to be translated differently

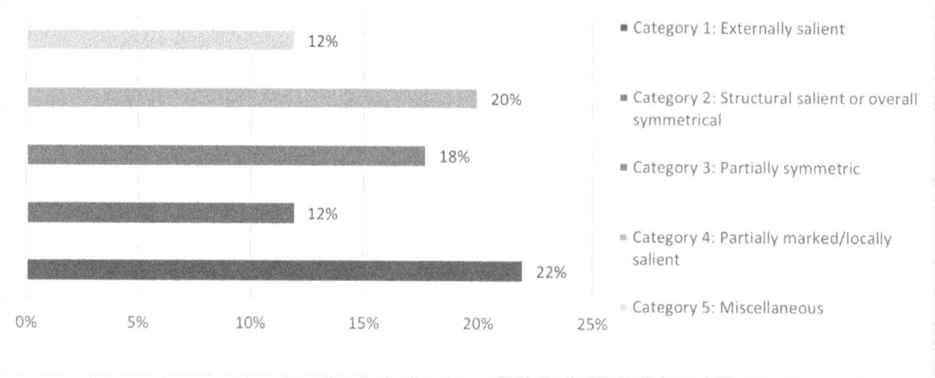

Idioms from Category 1 are most likely to be translated differently while idioms from Category 5 and Category 2 are least likely to be translated differently.

The translation techniques for Chinese four-character idioms in *Returning to '90s, She Became Famous in Major Surgical Fields* are identified, and the distribution of each strategy is illustrated below:

Figure 5. Distribution of translation techniques for four-character idioms

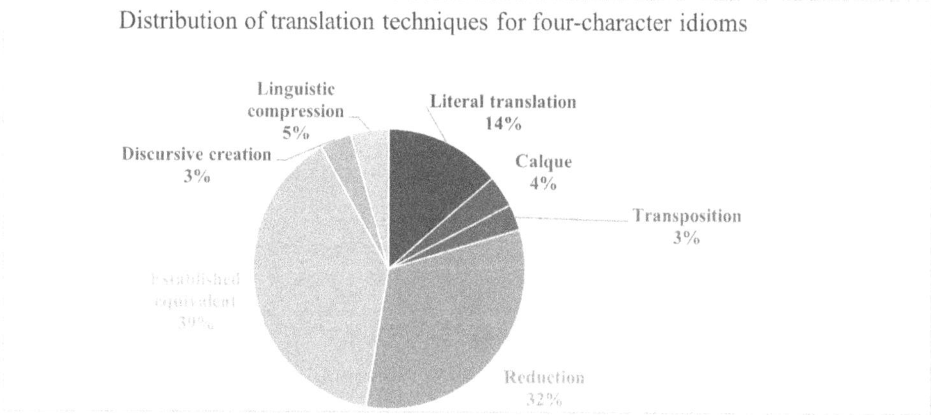

The representatives for each type of four-character idiom are selected based on the following criteria: first, covering all the identified translation techniques; second, they are culture-specific; third, possessing multiple interpretations; and fourth, they are ubiquitously employed in everyday discourse. The excerpts are presented below for further clarification.

Category 1: Externally salient

Type 1: Idioms from this type are derived from fables that are recognizable by both professionals and ordinary people.

Example 1: 亡羊补牢 (wangyangbulao) means that it is not too late to mend the sheep's pen after the sheep have escaped and metaphorically means "trying to remedy a problem after it has arisen, to avoid further losses" (*Learn Chinese Words: wáng yáng b□ láo*, 2023). AI translated it differently in different contexts, one was translated as "making up for a dead sheep" which is a literal translation. "亡羊补牢能做到吕主任这样程度的,也没有几个人" (There are not many people who can remedy this situation successfully as Director Lu did). The rendition by MT: There are not many people who can make up for a dead sheep to the level of Director Lu. Translating this idiom literally may affect readers' understanding of the whole sentence. It can be replaced by a close equivalent "closing the stable door after the horse has bolted". The other two renditions: "make amends" is through established equivalent, while "be repaired" is through reduction that overlooks the deeper meaning of taking responsibility for past actions.

Example 2: 狐假虎威 (hujia-huwei) means "the fox assuming the majesty of the tiger or borrowing power to do evil" ([Explanation of Chinese idioms], n.d.). It was omitted in the sentence using reduction: 王老师连拿着教务处身份狐假虎威都不敢了 (Teacher Wang did not dare to exploit his identity as an Academic Affairs Officer to do evil). The rendition by MT: Teacher Wang didn't even dare to hold the identity of the Academic Affairs Office. This idiom functions as a predicate and its omission leads to an incomplete interpretation.

Example 3: 狡兔三窟 (jiaotu-sanku) It literally means "a wily rabbit has more than one burrow" and metaphorically means "a sly individual has more than one plan to fall back on" ([Explanation of jiaotu-sanku], n.d.). It was translated as "a cunning rabbit" using reduction.

Type 2: Idioms that originate from historical events or stories.

Example 1: 名列前茅 (minglie-qianmao) means "to rank among the best" ([Explanation of minglie-qianmao], n.d.). It was translated as "among the best" using an established equivalent. This idiom is sourced from *Zuo Zhuan* (a commentary on the ancient Chinese chronicles the Spring and Autumn Annals) describing a historical event during this period of war and instability. One year, upon being invaded by the state of Chu, the state of Zheng resisted resolutely while asking the state of Jin for help but was defeated before the arrival of the reinforcements. The triumph of the state of Chu was attributed to its well-trained and organized soldiers. "茅" (mao), as a specialty of the state of Chu, was often used as a signaling flag by its spearhead when they detected any movement of the enemy. "前茅" (qianmap) means "in the leading position" while "名列" (minglie) is the ranking.

Example 2: 班门弄斧 (banmen-nongfu) means "to display one's slight skill before an expert" ([Explanation of banmen-nongfu], n.d.) and its equivalent in English is "teach your grandmother to suck eggs". However, it was translated using literal translation and reduction in this sentence: 谢婉莹心头有点点打鼓了,因为她好像在一群技术大佬老师面前班门弄斧了? (Xie Wanying felt a little nervous, as it seemed like she had shown off her skills in front of a group of experts.), only part of the phrase "弄斧" (nongfu) was translated literally as "get an axe" ignoring the words "班门" (banmen). The rendition by MT: Xie Wanying felt a little bit of a drum in her heart, because she seemed to be getting an axe in front of a group of technical master teachers? "Getting an axe" in this sentence does not align with the original meaning of the idiom and makes this sentence confusing. "班" (ban) refers to Lu Ban, a famous carpenter in the Spring and Autumn Period. "班门" (banmen) means the gate of Lu Ban's or Shi's. Shi is also a carpenter whose skill is comparable to Lu Ban's at that time. It was said that Shi often delivered performances together with his friend. In the performances, Shi held his axe to sweep the thin layer of white ash on the tip of his nose without rubbing off the skin of his friend's nose. Both Lu Ban and Shi are unsurpassable in the field of craftsmanship. People who have self-knowledge dare not play in front of the gate of Lu Ban's or Shi's otherwise they will be seen as being overconfident.

Example 3: 金蝉脱壳 (jinchan-tuoqiao) means that the cicada sheds its carapace and metaphorically means a crafty escape plan ([Explanation of jinchan-tuoqiao], n.d.). The MT system translated this idiom using literal translation as "escape the shell of Jin Chan" in which "Jin Chan" is directly borrowed from Chinese words. However, using this translation strategy might create difficulties for readers' comprehension.

Example 4: 先见之明 (xianjianzhiming) means "foresight" [Explanation of xianjianzhiming], n.d.). It was translated differently: "foresight" is an established equivalent translation, while the other one "presciently" was converted from a noun to an adverb using transposition.

Category 2: Structural salient or overall symmetrical

Type 5: With crossly corresponding structures

Example 1: 冷嘲热讽 (lengchao-refeng) means making sarcastic remarks against someone, with 冷 (cold) and 热 (hot) being contradictory antonyms. This idiom underwent a conversion using transposition from the verb phrase "make sarcastic remarks against someone" to the noun "sneers" in the sentence: 班上没一个同学主动站出来为谢婉莹说话,冷嘲热讽的却很多. The rendition by MT: None of the students in the class took the initiative to speak up for Xie Wanying, but there were many sneers.

Example 2: 夫唱妇随 (fuchangfusui), which is composed of a crossly corresponding structure, means "the husband to sing and the wife to follow" and metaphorically means the wife follows the husband's lead or decisions without protest. However, it was translated using literal translation as "sing along" with 夫妇(husband and wife) neglected in the following sentence. 谢家不能没有孙子不能没有男丁不能没有了香火,这是她爸爸和整个谢家的态度,她妈妈只能夫唱妇随。(The Xie family cannot survive without grandsons, without male heirs, without the continuation of the family line. This is the attitude of her father and the entire Xie family. Her mother can only go along with it.) The rendition by MT: The Xie family can't live without grandsons, can't live without men, can't live without incense, this is the attitude of her father and the entire Xie family, her mother can only sing along. "Sing along" refers to singing in unison or following a leader in a musical context. It is incongruous in this context and fails to convey the intended meaning of the wife's compliance or submission.

Example 3: 阴差阳错 (yincha-yangcuo) metaphorically means "an accident arising from many cause" ([Explanation of yincha-yangcuo], n.d.), with 阴 (Yin) and 阳 (Yang) constituting a pair of dialectical antonyms. It was translated as "something wrong" using reduction by AI ignoring the role of unexpected events or fate in the outcome. Chinese numerology developed at a very early time and became part of traditional Chinese culture. 阴差阳错 (yincha-yangcuo) is a numerology term that means "too much and not enough" and discordance between men and women. People whose destiny is involved with阴差阳错 (yincha-yangcuo) usually have illegitimate children or adopted children and do not get along with their relatives. They lack the opportunity or failure to achieve success.

Example 4: 七倒八歪 (qidao-bawai) means "in disarray", with 七 (seven) and 八 (eight) being related words. Idioms with this structure of七X八X have the connotation of chaos. This idiom was omitted using reduction when translating the following sentence without leading to difficulties in understanding the context. 几个组内的老师笑得七倒八歪,想着一个女孩子主动说要负责吃,几乎没见过的。女孩子大都生怕吃胖了。(The teachers in the group couldn't stop laughing, imagining a girl voluntarily saying she'd take responsibility for eating, something they had rarely seen. Most girls are usually too worried about gaining weight.) The rendition by MT: The teachers in several groups laughed, thinking that a girl took the initiative to say that she was responsible for eating, which was almost never seen.

Example 5: 五湖四海 (wuhu-sihai) means "all over the world" ([Explanation of wuhu-sihai], n.d.), with 湖 (lake) and 海 (sea) being related words. It was translated as "all over the world" applying established equivalent. This idiom refers to five lakes and four seas in China including Poyang Lake, Dongting Lake, Tai Lake, Hongze Lake, Chaohu Lake, the Bohai Sea, the Yellow Sea, the East Sea, and the South Sea.

Type 6: With antithetical structure

Example 1: 荣华富贵 (ronghua-fugui), which is an antithetical structure, means "high position and great wealth". The MT system respected its coordinated structure and directly translated it as "rich and rich", which results in an unnatural formulation in English.

Example 2: 凤毛麟角 (fengmao-linjiao) meaning "rare and precious" was translated as "very few", which is a reduction translation. "凤" (feng) is the acronym for 凤凰 (Chinese phoenix). Unlike the Western phoenix, it was seen as the king of all birds in ancient Chinese legend and has the same status as the dragon in Chinese culture. "凤毛" (Chinese phoenix's feather) are very rare. Similarly, "麟" (lin) is the acronym for 麒麟 (qi lin) with qi for male and lin for female. It is a mythical beast in ancient Chinese mythology. It was said to have a gentle temperament and the ability to live for 2,000 years. Although it has a long horn that can be used as a weapon, it does not harm human beings or animals, even insects or plants. According to legend, it only appears when the times are peaceful and prosperous or when there is a saint in the world, so it is also called the Rui Beast which is a symbol of auspiciousness. 凤毛 (Chinese phoenix feather) and 麟角 (qilin's horn) constitute an antithetical structure with two parts expressing the same meaning of preciousness and rarity. As a whole, it is often used to describe an extremely rare object.

Example 3: 初来乍到 (chulaizhadao) meaning "newly arrived" ([Explanation of chulaizhadao], n.d.) is a verb phrase and was converted into a noun phrase "a newcomer" using transposition.

Example 4: 崇洋媚外 (chongyang-meiwai) means "worship and have blind faith in foreign things" ([Explanation of chongyang-meiwai], n.d.), in which崇洋 (chongyang) shares a similar meaning with媚外 (meiwai) forming an antithetical structure. It was translated as "admiring foreigners" using literal translation and reduction, which fails to convey its critical or disapproving connotation that someone is excessively admiring or trying to please foreign (often Western) cultures, possibly at the expense of their culture or identity.

Example 5: 眉飞色舞 (meifei-sewu) literally means "eyebrows were raised" and metaphorically means "radiant with delight" ([Explanation of meifei-sewu], n.d.). The rendition "with a beaming expression" fails to capture the vivid imagery of this idiom and thus is a reduced expression. 眉飞 (eyebrows were raised) and 色舞 (face glows with joy) are facial expressions that appear when someone is excited and complacent.

Example 6: 怜香惜玉 (lianxiang-xiyu) literally means "be so sympathetic and cherishing jade" and metaphorically means "have compassion for womanhood". This idiom was translated literally in the following sentence without conveying its intended meaning and might confuse the target audience. The MT rendition of this sentence "你这么的怜香惜玉了" ("When did you become so compassionate for womanhood?"): Are you so sympathetic and cherishing jade?

Example 7: 焦头烂额 (jiaotou-lane) means extremely overwhelmed. It was translated as "the extreme" using discursive creation in this sentence: 听着这人这话,谢婉莹不免回想起以前的自己,那会儿她年纪大了一样被催婚,被催到焦头烂额。The rendition by MT: Listening to this person's words, Xie Wanying couldn't help but recall her past self, when she was urged to get married at an old age, and she was pushed to the extreme.

Some idioms whose characters A and C or B and D are the same.

Example 1: 全心全意 (quanxin-quanyi) means "wholehearted". It was translated as "wholehearted" which is an established equivalent.

Example 2: 无拘无束 (quanxin-quanyi) means "free". It was translated as "free" using established equivalent.

Example 3: 大手大脚 (dashou-dajiao) functions as an adverb in the collocation "花钱" (spend money) meaning extravagantly in the context. However, "花钱大手大脚" was translated as "spend a lot of money" through transposition, in which the grammatical function of this idiom shifted from an adverb (extravagantly) to a determiner (a lot of).

Category 3: Partially symmetric

Idioms that consist of AABB / AABC / ABCC, structures such as 熙熙攘攘 (bustling), 洋洋得意 (Proud and pleased),

Type 7: AABB idioms

Example 1: 热热闹闹 (rerenaonao) which is a repetitive structure means "bustling" and was translated as "lively and lively" which follows its original repetitive structure using calque. However, this expression is uncommon in English and may make readers feel strange.

Example 2: 口口声声(koukoushengsheng) means "to keep on saying" ([Explanation of koukoushengsheng], n.d.). It was omitted through reduction in the sentence: 一直口口声声说 (repeated keep on saying). This idiom functions as the adjunct and its meaning is equivalent to the meaning of the rest of the sentence. Reduction is an appropriate translation strategy for this idiom since it overlaps the meaning of other parts in the same sentence.

Example 3: 吵吵闹闹 (chaochaonaonao) means noisy. It was translated as "a lot of noise" through transposition in this sentence: 这里吵吵闹闹 (It was noisy here). Its grammatical function was transposed from the predicate adjective into the subject in the machine-translated version: There is a lot of noise here. It was also translated as "noisy" in another sentence using linguistic compression with the redundancy be deleted.

Example 4: 干干净净 (ganganjingjing) means “a state of absolute cleanliness” and metaphorically means “there is no trace left at all”. It was translated as “cleanly” using linguistic compression in the following sentence. However, it was mistranslated since the idiom conveys its metaphorical sense of “leaving no trace at all” in this sentence: 眼里那抹冰融化的干干净净,只剩下一抹春意盎然的池水了。The rendition by MT: The ice in his eyes melted cleanly, leaving only a touch of spring water. “融化的干干净净” means fully melted away which indicates there is no trace left.

Type 8: AABC or ABCC idiom

Example 1: 众目睽睽 (zhongmukuikui) means “in full view of everybody” ([Explanation of zhongmukuikui], n.d.). It was translated as “in full view of everybody” through established equivalent.

Example 2: 虎视眈眈 (hushidandan) means “to glare like a tiger watching his prey” ([Explanation of hushidandan], n.d.). It was omitted in the context using reduction leading to meaning loss.

Type 9: Alliteration, assonance/rhyming, or juxtaposition of synonyms or antonyms

Example for alliteration: 淋漓尽致 (linli-jinzhi) means “performing vividly and thoroughly” in which 淋漓 (lin li) are alliterative. It was translated as “vividly” using reduction with the characteristics of thoroughness neglected.

Example for assonance: 途无 (tuwu) are assonant in前途无量 (qiantu-wuliang). This idiom means “having a promising future” and was translated as “a promising future” applying established equivalent.

Examples for the juxtaposition of synonyms:

Example 1: 耳目一新 (ermu-yixin) means “refreshing” ([Explanation of ermu-yixin], n.d.) in which 耳 (ears) and目 (eyes) are hyponyms of facial features was translated as refreshing using established equivalent.

Example 2: 鸦雀无声 (yaque-wusheng) means “absolute silence” ([Explanation of yaque-wusheng], n.d.) in which 鸦 (crows) and 雀 (sparrows) are hyponyms of birds. It was simplified to “silent” using reduction, losing the vividness of original phrase. 鸦雀 (crows and sparrows) are regarded as rather noisy creatures in China. The surrounding environment is extremely quiet, with even crows and sparrows falling silent.

Example 3: 青黄不接 (qinghuangbujie), in which 青 (green) and 黄 (yellow) are hyponyms of the broader category color, means “yellow does not reach green”, (yellow means the autumn crop and green means the green spring crop) and metaphorically means “a temporary deficit in manpower or resources” (Explanation of qinghuangbujie], n.d.). AI translated part of this idiom, 不接 (bujie), as “is not answering” through literal translation: 造成的后果可想而知,后面的医生青黄不接。不行的,医生的技术是需要给机会练出来的 (The consequences are predictable: the subsequent shortage of experienced doctors. This is not acceptable; doctors need opportunities to practice their medical skills.) The MT rendition: The consequences can be imagined, the doctor behind is not answering. No, the doctor's skills need to be given the opportunity to practice. "Not answering" in this rendition which bears no similarity to the original meaning poses a challenge to readers' comprehension.

Example of the juxtaposition of antonyms:

Example 1: 哭笑不得 (kuxiao-bude) means "not to know whether to laugh or cry" ([Explanation of kuxiao-bude], n.d.), in which哭 (cry) 笑 (smile) are antonyms. It was translated as "dumbfounded" using discursive creation considering the context. 小孙老师这个夸,让她哭笑不得,摇摇头否认:"孙老师你不用夸我。(The compliment from Teacher Sun left her unsure whether to laugh or cry, and she shook her head in denial: "Teacher Sun, you don't need to praise me".) The rendition by MT: Mr. Sun's praise made her dumbfounded, shaking her head in denial: "Mr. Sun, you don't need to praise me. "dumbfounded" seems to have no connection to the idiom and it is understandable in this sentence.

Example 2: 公私分明 (gongsi-fenming), in which 公 (public) 私 (private) are antonyms, means "be scrupulous in separating public from private interests" [Explanation of gongsi-fenming], n.d.). It was translated as "a clear distinction between public and private" through literal translation. However, this rendition sounds awkward and ambiguous in the machine-translated sentence: His evaluation of her is definitely a clear distinction between public and private. (他对她的评价绝对是公私分明-His judgment of her is definitely clear-cut between the public and private spheres) This idiom, along with this sentence, was omitted: 爱她最好是公私分明,记得自己的身份. (If you love her, you had better remember your own identity and distinguish between public and private matters) However, this omission does not hinder understanding, as the same idea was already conveyed in the previous text.

Category 4: Partially marked/locally salient

Type 10: Idioms with simile marker 犹, 若, 如, 似

Example 1: 惜字如金 (xizirujin) means "a person of very few words". It was translated as "cherish words like gold" through literal translation which corresponds to the same structure as the original one.

Example 2: 沉默是金 (chenmoshijin) means "silence is golden". The structure of this idiom is preserved through calque. The rendition "silence is golden" corresponds to the structure of the idiom. "Silence" corresponds to the first two words, "is" to the third, and "golden" to the fourth, making it a calque translation.

Example 3: 暴跳如雷 (baotiaorulei) literally meaning "jumping violently like thunder" and metaphorically meaning "to fly into a rage" ([Explanation of baotiaorulei], n.d.) was translated using reduction as "was furious" with its metaphorical richness omitted. This idiom consists of a verb-object structure and was transposed into a linking verb+subject complement structure.

Example 4: 如虎添翼 (ruhutianyi) means "like a tiger with added wings", and metaphorically means "with redoubled power" ([Explanation of ruhutianyi], n.d.). It was translated as "more powerful" using reduction and fails to reflect the metaphorical characteristic of the original phrase.

Type 11: Idioms with 然 which indicate the condition of affairs

Example 1: 勃然大怒 (boran-danu) means to become very angry suddenly. It was translated as "furious" through transposition, a process in which its adverb-verb phrase structure was transposed into the adjective "furious." However, it was also a reduction translation, failing to convey the sudden, explosive outburst characteristic of this idiom.

Example 2: 理所当然 (lisuodangran) means "as it should be by rights" ([Explanation of lisuodangran], n.d.). It was translated as "of course" using established equivalent.

Example 3: 截然不同 (jieran-butong) meaning "entirely different" was translated as "completely different" which is a literal translation.

Type 12: Idioms with the discordance of 不or 而: X不XX; X而XX; 不X而X

Example 1: 不言而喻 (buyaneryu) means "it goes without saying". It was translated as "self-evident" using established equivalent.

Example 2: 互不相让 (hubuxiangrang) means "neither giving way to the other". MT system translated it as "refuse to give in to each other" through literal translation.

Category 5: Miscellaneous

Type 13: From famous quotations, like 不亦乐乎 (buyilehu)

This type of idiom has notable origins which helped them gain fixed form and popularity.

Idioms that originate from famous writers or famous works of literature.

Example 1: 孤陋寡闻 (gulou-guawen) means "being ignorant due to limited exposure or experience" and can be translated as "ill-informed ignorant". AI simplified it to "ignorant" using reduction, neglecting the implied reason behind the term. This idiom is sourced from *The Book of Rites* is a humble expression and consists of a causal relationship.

Example 2: 狗血淋头 (gouxie-lintou) means "to scold in a very humiliating fashion" ([Explanation of gouxie-lintou], n.d.), which originates from *The Water Margin*. It was omitted in MT through reduction without affecting the comprehension of this sentence. It functions as the adjunct in the sentence: 孙爷爷对女婿的话火冒三丈,骂个狗血淋头 (Grandpa Sun was furious at his son-in-law's words, scolding him.)

Example 3: 捧腹大笑 (pengfu-daxiao) means "double up with laughter" ([Explanation of pengfu-daxiao], n.d.), which is sourced from *Records of the Grand Historian*. It was translated as "burst into laughter" using reduction without conveying the intensity and physicality of the laughter in the source text.

Idioms that originate from Buddhist works. Buddhism is a highly influential religion in China and has significantly shaped Chinese vocabulary.

Example 1: 三头六臂 (santou-liubi) means "to have three heads and six arms" and metaphorically means "possess remarkable abilities". It was translated as "three heads and six arms" through literal translation. However, this translation may confuse foreign readers since this expression does not exist in Western culture. This supernatural power originally referred to the phantom of a dharma-protecting deity in Buddhism. It later refers to a preternatural power possessed by Ne Zha in Chinese mythology. Ne Zha was portrayed in many classic novels like *Journey to the West*. He welds six weapons to attack enemies in the three-headed and six-armed form, which enables him to fight them one against six. His magical abilities and strength in battle are remarkable.

Example 2: 醍醐灌顶 (tihu-guanding) is a Buddhist term. Its literal meaning is to anoint your head with the purest cream and its metaphorical meaning is "to enlighten people with perfect wisdom" ([Explanation of tihu-guanding], n.d.). Its rendition "enlightening" serves as a reduced transl ation, missing the richness and cultural depth of the idiom. "醍醐" (tihu) is the essence of milk produced after a complex procedure and originally refers to an outstanding person. It was also often used to explain doctrines in the dissemination of Buddhism. The production of "tihu" indicates that all human beings can develop their Buddhahood. "灌顶" (guanding) is the most important ritual of Buddhism and originated in India allegedly. It was said that the head of the succeeding king or crown prince would be poured on with seawater from four different directions during his ceremony of enthronement. This process evolved into sprinkling special water (Buddhist water of great compassion) or "tihu" on the head of the disciple during the conversion to Buddhism. With the process completed, this person is imbued with wisdom and becomes enlightened metaphorically.

Example 3: 贻笑大方 (yixiaodafang) means "being a laughingstock before experts". The MT system mistook its structure for coordinated structure and translated it as "be laughable and generous" using literal translation in this sentence: 不是什么情况下都可以认师兄师妹的。随便给认能得了,让猪狗羊等都叫师兄师姐等于贻笑大方了。 (Under no circumstances should one casually recognize someone as a senior brother or sister. It will be a laughingstock before experts to have pigs, dogs, sheep, and others address you as senior brothers and sisters.) The rendition by MT: It is not always possible to recognize brothers and sisters. If you can recognize it casually, it would be laughable and generous to let the pigs, dogs, sheep, etc. call you brothers and sisters. "Be laughable and generous" is somewhat contradictory, making this sentence confusing.

Type 14: With the residue of Classical Chinese grammar or lexis

Example 1:独占鳌头 (duzhan-aotou) means "come out first" ([Explanation of duzhan-aotou], n.d.). It was translated as "rank first among" using established equivalent. "鳌头" (aotou) is the arowana-shaped relief carved on the doorstep leading to the palace. The top scorer in the imperial examination often has to stand on this relief to receive the emperor's designation. Later, it generally referred to someone who ranks in first place in a competition. The imperial examination system, as an important political system to select officials in ancient China, played a significant role in shaping Chinese society and culture. It lasted over 1300 years ranging from 587 to 1905 and has evolved into the civil service selection system in modern China.

Example 2: 平心而论 (pingxinerlun) means "to give the devil his due" ([Explanation of pingxinerlun], n.d.). It was translated as "in all fairness" using established equivalent.

Example 3: 无话可说 (wuhuakeshuo) is "to have nothing to say". It was translated as "said nothing" which is a literal translation.

Example4: 火冒三丈 (huomao-sanzhuang) literally means the flames rise to about ten meters. MT omitted this figurative characteristic and translated it as "furious" through reduction. 丈 (zhang) refers to Chinese unit of length, equal to 3.3 meters This idiom evokes the image of high-rising flames, symbolizing intense anger. Its grammatical category changes from a verb phrase to an adjective in this sentence through transposition: "你说什么?"李启安听见他这话一下子火冒三丈 "What did you say?" Li Qi'an was furious when he heard what he said.

Type 15: Miscellaneous

Idioms that do not fit previous types are "miscellaneous".

Example 1: 鸡同鸭讲 (jitongyajiang) means "chicken speaking with duck" and metaphorically means "talking without communicating" ([Explanation of jitongyajiang], n.d.). It was omitted through reduction in the sentence "给学生讲两句发现学生听不懂肯定不再讲了,讲了等于是废话,鸡同鸭讲". (They won't continue talking the topic if they found students do not understand it. If they continue talking, it is tantamount to talking nonsense. They are unable to understand one another). Although this idiom was omitted in MT, it does not affect the understanding of the whole sentence.

Example 2: 徇私枉法 (xunsiwangfa) means "to bend the law to favor one's relatives or associates" ([Explanation of xunsiwangfa], n.d.). It was translated as "favoritism" using reduction, failing to convey its specific connotation of being used in illegal or unethical contexts.

Example 3:自作主张 (zizuozhuzhang) means "act on her initiative" ([Explanation of zizuozhuzhang], n.d.). It was translated as "make her own decision" through reduction which omits the potentially negative connotations of acting independently or without considering others.

Example 4: 通俗易懂 (tongsu-yidong) means "easy-to-understand". AI translated this idiom as "plain" through literal translation, simplifying its meaning. It neglects the meaning of understandability or universal accessibility emphasized in the original word. However, since plain is collocated with language within the context, "plain language" fully conveys the meaning of being easy to understand.

Example 5: 蜂拥而至 means to come in great numbers ([Explanation of fengyongerzhi], n.d.) and was translated as "swarms of" through transposition, a process in which it underwent a conversion from a verb phrase to a noun phrase.

Example 6: 坦白从宽 (tanbai-congkuan) means "to tell the truth for leniency" ([Explanation of tanbai-congkuan], n.d.) and can be translated as "cop a plea." It is a juxtaposition of two verb constructions linked by the word "从" (cong) forming a causal relationship. The MT system confused this structure with the coordinated structure and translated it as "be frank and lenient" through literal translation.

Figure 6. Distribution of translation techniques for Category 1

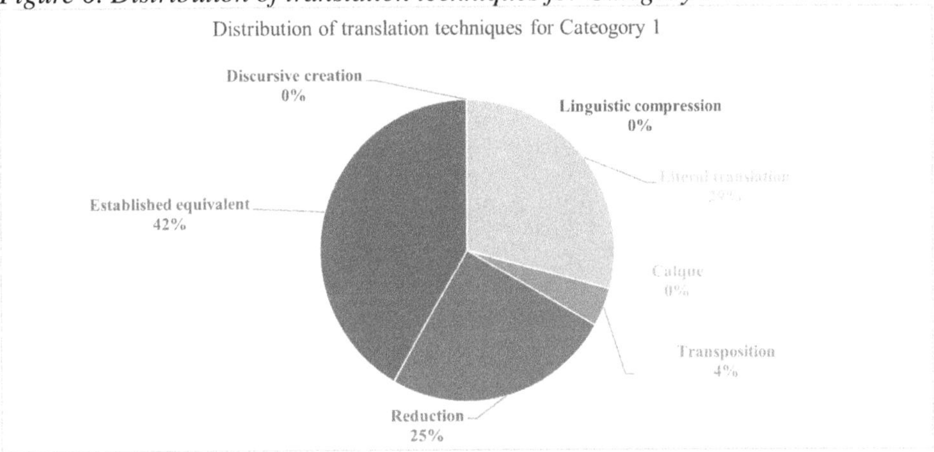

As for Category 1, established equivalent accounts for the largest proportion at 42%, followed by reduction, literal translation, and transposition.

Figure 7. Distribution of translation techniques for Category 2

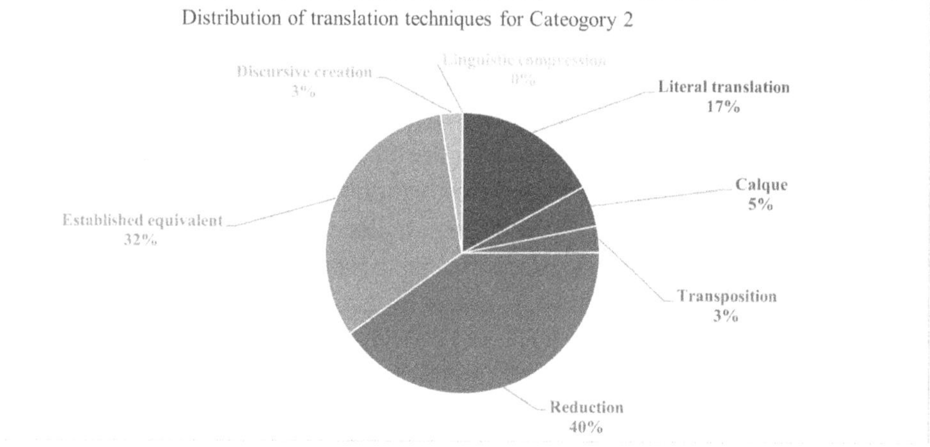

As for Category 2, the reduction is most frequently employed accounting for 40%, followed by established equivalent at 32%, literal translation at 17%, calque at 5%, discursive creation at 3%, and transposition at 3%.

Figure 8. Distribution of translation techniques for Category 3

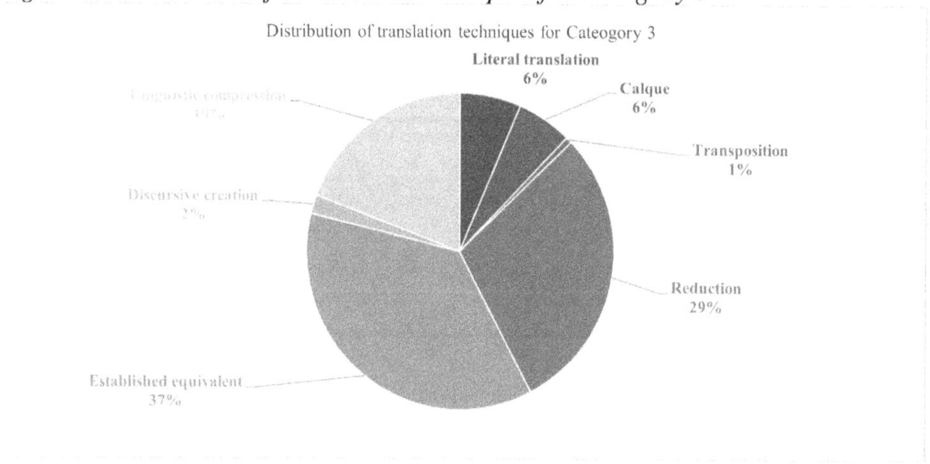

In translating idioms from Category 3, established equivalent constitutes 37%, followed by reduction at 29%, linguistic compression 19%, literal translation at 6%, calque at 6%, discursive creation 2% and transposition at 1%.

Figure 9. Distribution of translation techniques for Category 4

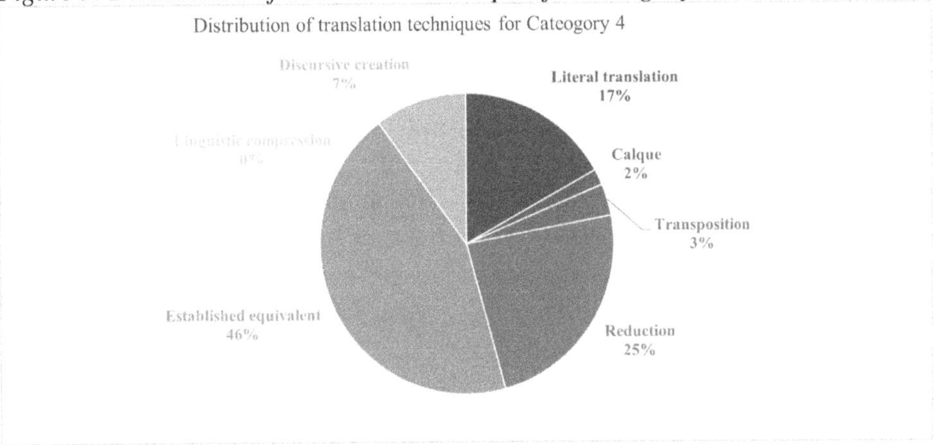

As for Category 4, Established equivalent accounts for 46%, followed by reduction at 25%, literal translation at 17%, discursive creation 7%, transposition at 3%, and calque at 2%.

Figure 10. Distribution of translation techniques for Category 5

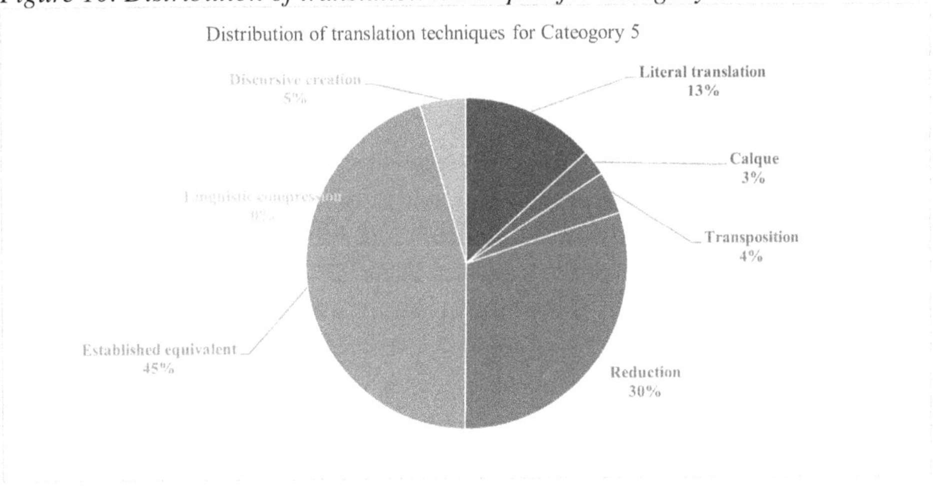

In translating idioms from Category 5, 45% were rendered using established equivalents, 30% through reduction, 13% through literal translation, 5% through discursive creation, 4% through transposition and 3% through calque.

As shown in the pie charts above, established equivalent is most frequently applied in translating these four-character idioms, with the highest rate of 46% for translating idioms from Category 4. Many idioms from Category 3 that are composed of repetitive structure are translated as a single word in English using linguistic compression. Literal translation is used more frequently in translating Category 1 than in other categories. However, it is not an appropriate strategy for idioms from Category 1 which usually have metaphorical meanings. Reduction is employed more often for Category 2 than other categories. Idioms from Category 2 are structurally salient. Reduction is an appropriate translation strategy for idioms of crossly corresponding structures expressing repetitive meaning. Discursive creation, transposition and calque are the least applied techniques for translating all categories.

DISCUSSION

Reviewing previous studies on the translation strategies for idiomatic expressions based on Baker's (1992, 2011, 2018) models, paraphrasing and using similar meanings but different forms are the most frequently used methods (Ali et al., 2023; Floranti & Mubarok, 2020; Sharahil et al, 2022). Distinct from previous studies, this study identified established equivalent as the most frequently used technique for Chinese four-character idioms in MT based on Molina and Albir's (2002) model. In translating Chinese idioms, the main strategies discussed in previous studies are direct translation including literal translation and borrowing, indirect translation including transposition, reduction, and abridged translation, and combined strategies using free translation and literal translation or literal translation combined with other strategies like explanation. This study discusses established equivalent, reduction, literal translation, linguistic compression, discursive creation, calque, and transposition in translating Chinese four-character idioms. Previous research has identified literal translation as the primary cause of translation errors in idiomatic expressions for the MT systems (Aldelaa & Malkawi, 2024; Shao et al., 2017). This study also identifies literal translation as a primary problem in the context of Chinese four-character idioms. The results confirm that translation of idioms is still challenging for MT systems. This study not only sheds light on the limitations of current MT systems but also raises human beings' awareness of improving MT systems to produce more accurate and culturally sensitive renditions.

CONCLUSION

This study first introduces the definition of Chinese four-character idioms, Chan's (2016) taxonomy of these idioms, and the development of MT. A review of previous studies on idiom translation reveals that translation strategies for Chinese four-character idioms by MT remain unexplored. According to Chan (2016), 13 types of four-character idioms in the internet novel *Returning to '90s, She Became Famous in Major Surgical Fields* are identified. The distributions of categories and translation techniques are depicted in charts. The primary translation techniques for Chinese four-character idioms from each type are discussed in detail. The findings reveal that Chinese idioms are still challenging for MT systems. MT systems still have great potential for improvement. This study contributes to the growing body of literature on MT within the context of Chinese four-character idioms.

Based on Chan's (2016) taxonomy of Chinese four-character idioms, the distribution of each category is calculated as follows: Category 1 constitutes 3.70%, Category 2 constitutes 27.65%, Category 3 constitutes 24.60%, Category 4 constitutes 8.84%, and Category 5 constitutes 35.21%. Categories 2, 3, and 5 comprise the majority of these idioms. The techniques employed by MT in translating four-character idioms include literal translation, calque, reduction, transposition, and established equivalent. The distribution of these translation strategies is as follows: established equivalent for 39%, reduction for 32%, literal translation accounts for 14%, linguistic compression for 5%, calque for 4%, discursive creation for 3%, and transposition for 3%. Established equivalent, reduction and literal translation are most frequently employed. Some idioms were translated correctly using literal translation because they were used in their literal meanings in the context. However, literal translation is not an appropriate technique for idioms used in their metaphorical meanings. As for transposition, some Chinese four-character idioms were transposed into nouns or other forms to obey the English grammatical rules. Reduction involves partial reduction and total reduction. Partial reduction conveys the core meaning of some idioms with the cultural nuances neglected. Four-character idioms can be omitted without affecting the target audience's understanding of the whole sentence if they function as adverbials. It is worth noting that many four-character idioms were translated as single words in English.

The significance of this study lies in several aspects. Firstly, it addresses the research gap regarding translation strategies for Chinese four-character idioms by MT. This study contributes to the growing body of literature on MT, particularly in the context of culturally rich and linguistically complex expressions like Chinese four-character idioms. Secondly, this study contributes to refining MT systems and improving their translation accuracy. Some four-character idioms can be translated as equivalent idioms in English culture instead of being translated literally. Analyzing

REFERENCES

Ai, J. (2020). 网络文学中的女性写作流行演变 [Popular evolution of female writing in network literature]. *Writing*, (4), 61–65. DOI: 10.19867/j.cnki.writing.2020.04.007

Al-Kaabi, M. H., AlQbailat, N. M., Badah, A., Ismail, I. A., & Hicham, K. B. (2024). Examining the cultural connotations in human and machine translations: A corpus study of Naguib Mahfouz's Zuqāq Al-Midaqq. *Journal of Language Teaching and Research*, *15*(3), 707–718. DOI: 10.17507/jltr.1503.03

Albir, A. H., & Molina, L. (2002). Translation techniques revisited: A dynamic and Functionalist approach: A dynamic and functionalist approach. *Meta: Journal Des Traducteurs = Translators'. Journal*, *47*(4), 498–512. https://dialnet.unirioja.es/servlet/articulo?codigo=2809718

Aldelaa, A. S., & Malkawi, M. K. M. (2024). Investigating problems related to the translation of idiomatic expressions in the Arabic novels using neural machine translation. *Theory and Practice in Language Studies*, *14*(1), 71–78. DOI: 10.17507/tpls.1401.08

Alhaj, A. M. (2024). The impact of machine translation on the development of tourism translation from the perspectives of translators and experts in Saudi Arabia. *Theory and Practice in Language Studies*, *14*(4), 1274–1283. DOI: 10.17507/tpls.1404.35

Ali, K., Ambreen, S., Begum, R., & Sadiq, S., ul Haq, T., & Sahar, N. (2023). Exploring Translation Strategies For Idiomatic Expressions: A Study Of Sadat Hassan Manto's Short Stories "Khol Do" And "License". *Journal of Positive School Psychology*, *7*(6), 708–715.

Baker, M. (1992). *Other Words: A Coursebook on Translation*. Routledge.

Baker, M. (2011). *In Other Words: A Coursebook on Translation* (2nd ed.). Routledge. DOI: 10.4324/9780203832929

Baker, M. (2018). *In Other Words: A Coursebook on Translation* (3rd ed.). Routledge. DOI: 10.4324/9781315619187

Boulanger, A. M. (2024). The use of machine translation and AI in medical translation: Pros and cons. *Medical Writing*, *33*(1), 62–65. DOI: 10.56012/fcbh4324

Chan, S.-W. (Ed.). (2016). *The Routledge Encyclopedia of the Chinese Language*. Routledge., DOI: 10.4324/9781315675541

Chen, L. (2009). On literal translation of English idioms. *English Language Teaching*, *2*(2). Advance online publication. DOI: 10.5539/elt.v2n2p164

Chen, L. (2020). Application of Explanational Translation approach to English idioms. *Theory and Practice in Language Studies*, *10*(11), 1462. DOI: 10.17507/tpls.1011.17

Chen, X. (2009). 成语的语法、修辞及角色扮演 [The Grammar, Rhetoric, and Role-play of Chinese Idioms]. *Showwe Information Co., Ltd.*

Chia, Z. L., Ptaszynski, M., Karpinska, M., Eronen, J., & Masui, F. (2024). Initial exploration into sarcasm and irony through machine translation. *Natural Language Processing Journal*, *9*, 100106. DOI: 10.1016/j.nlp.2024.100106

Deng, L., & Abdullah, M. R. (2024). Category shifts in the Chinese–English translation of animal idioms in Journey to the West. *Journal of Language Teaching and Research*, *15*(3), 953–959. DOI: 10.17507/jltr.1503.29

Duan, H., Cui, W. W., & Gao, Y. D. (2014). Cultural Metaphor and translation Strategies in English and Chinese animal idioms. *Journal of Language Teaching and Research*, *5*(6). Advance online publication. DOI: 10.4304/jltr.5.6.1292-1300

Floranti, A. D., & Mubarok, Y. (2020). Indonesia–English translation of idiomatic expressions in the novel This Earth of Mankind. *Buletin Al-Turas*, *26*(2), 207–220. DOI: 10.15408/bat.v26i2.13834

Hartono, R. (2020). *Translation techniques & methods*. LPPM UNNES Press.

Hatano, K. (2024). The characteristics of Face-to-Face communication using consecutive speech machine translation technology. *Journal of Business Communication & Technology*, 44–53. https://doi.org/DOI: 10.56632/bct.2024.3104

Idami, Z., Wati, S., & Balqis, R. (2022). An Analysis of Students' Difficulties in Translating Idiomatic Expressions: What and Why? *ACITYA Journal of Teaching & Education*, *4*(1), 175–188. DOI: 10.30650/ajte.v4i1.3208

Jia, F. (2023). Promoting the international dissemination of Chinese culture through international Chinese language education: A case study of Chinese-English idiomatic equivalence. 当代社会科学 [*Contemporary Social Sciences*], 2023(6). https://doi.org/DOI: 10.19873/j.cnki.2096-0212.2023.06.007

Kang, H., & Yang, Y. (2022). A study on English translation of Chinese four-characteridioms: Strategies and problems. *Linguistics and Culture Review*, *6*(1), 200–213. DOI: 10.21744/lingcure.v6n1.2185

Kayed, M. M. A. (2023). The Challenges Facing Translation Students in Translating Sports Idiomatic Expressions from Arabic into English. *International Journal of Arabic-English Studies*. https://doi.org/DOI: 10.33806/ijaes.v24i1.568

Koehn, P. (2020). *Neural MT*. Cambridge University Press.

Kong, Y. (2014). The study of English and Chinese Numerical Idioms and their translation. *Journal of Language Teaching and Research*, *5*(2). Advance online publication. DOI: 10.4304/jltr.5.2.446-451

Learn Chinese Words: wáng yáng b□ láo. (2023, November 8). ChineseLearning. https://www.chineselearning.com/chinese-words/learn-chinese-words-wang-yang-bu-lao

Liang, C., Ghassemiazghandi, M., & Jamal, M. (2024). Post-editing challenges in Chinese-to-English neural machine translation of movie subtitles. *Social Sciences & Humanities Open*, *10*, 100949. DOI: 10.1016/j.ssaho.2024.100949

Liu, D. (2012). Translation and Culture: Translating Idioms between English and Chinese from a Cultural Perspective. *Theory and Practice in Language Studies*, *2*(11). Advance online publication. DOI: 10.4304/tpls.2.11.2357-2362

Liu, J. (2019). A comparative study on Chinese and English Animals Idioms and translation Strategies. *Theory and Practice in Language Studies*, *9*(2), 231. DOI: 10.17507/tpls.0902.14

Ma, J. (2022). 社会代际视域中的网络女性文学精神图谱及话语表达 [Online Women's Literature from Social Generational Perspective: Spiritual World and Discourse Expression]. *Journal of Shenzhen University (Humanities & Social Sciences)*, *39*(6)

Mehawesh, M. I. (2023). Human Translation vs. Machine Translation in the Naguib Mahfouz's Novel Palace Walk: A Case Study. *Mutah Journal of Humanities and Social Sciences*, *38*(2). Advance online publication. DOI: 10.35682/mjhsc.v38i2.631

Naveen, P., & Trojovský, P. (2024). Overview and challenges of MT for contextually appropriate translations. *iScience*, *27*(10), 110878. DOI: 10.1016/j.isci.2024.110878 PMID: 39391737

Nida, E. A. (1993). *Language, culture, and translating*. Shanghai Foreign Language Education Press. https://ci.nii.ac.jp/ncid/BA71847354

Shao, Y., Sennrich, R., Webber, B. L., & Fancellu, F. (2017). Evaluating Machine Translation Performance on Chinese Idioms with a Blacklist Method. *ArXiv, abs/1711.07646*. https://doi.org//arxiv.1711.07646DOI: 10.48550

Sharahil, F. B., Lin, D. T. A., & Abbaspour, B. N. (2022). TRANSLATING IDIOMATIC EXPRESSIONS IN LITERARY PROSE: THE CASE OF HARPER LEE'S TO KILL A MOCKINGBIRD. *Deleted Journal, 19*(2). Advance online publication. DOI: 10.17576/ebangi.2022.1902.14

Sipayung, K. T., Pasaribu, A. N., & Sinaga, N. T. (2024). Common Problems and Overt Errors in Translating Idioms in The Film Maleficent. *Eurasian Journal of Applied Linguistics, 9*(2), 23–31. DOI: 10.32601/ejal.10203

Tekwa, K. (2023). *Machine translation and foreign language learning*. Springer., DOI: 10.1007/978-981-99-8602-6

Valizadeh, M., & Vazifehkhah, A. E. (2021). Applied strategies in translating idiomatic expressions: Cultural-bound analysis in Brida novel by Paulo Coelho. *RumeliDe Dil ve Edebiyat Arastirmalari Dergisi, 23*(23), 1058–1066. DOI: 10.29000/rumelide.950001

Wang, D. (2017, April,22).World Book Day: China's online fantasy novels earn fans abroad. *CGTN*.https://news.cgtn.com/news/3d456a4d33557a4d/index.html

Wang, H., Wu, H., He, Z., Huang, L., & Church, K. W. (2021). Progress in machine translation. *Engineering (Beijing), 18*, 143–153. DOI: 10.1016/j.eng.2021.03.023

Wang, L. (2023). Applying automated machine translation to educational video courses. *Education and Information Technologies, 29*(9), 10377–10390. DOI: 10.1007/s10639-023-12219-0

Wang, L., & Wang, S. (2013). A Study of Idiom Translation Strategies between English and Chinese. *Theory and Practice in Language Studies, 3*(9). Advance online publication. DOI: 10.4304/tpls.3.9.1691-1697

Wang, Y. (2024). Translating Four-Character Structures in Chinese Literary Works on Traditional Architecture—A Case Analysis of Canal Towns South of the Yangtze and Folk Houses South of the Yangtze. *Theory and Practice in Language Studies, 14*(10), 3221–3229. DOI: 10.17507/tpls.1410.25

Wu, Y., & Gu, Y. q. (2019). 中国网络文学在英语世界的译介:内涵、路径与影响 [Chinese Internet literature in the English-speaking world: Web-based writing, translation and dissemination]. *Comparative Literature in China*, (03), 66–79.

Yang, C. (2010). Cultural differences on Chinese and English idioms of diet and the translation. *English Language Teaching, 3*(1). Advance online publication. DOI: 10.5539/elt.v3n1p148

Yang, Y. (2021, March,12). Chinese web novels and their TV spinoffs find welcoming audience abroad. *CGTN*.https://news.cgtn.com/news/2021-03-12/Chinese-web-novels-and-their-TV-spinoffs-find-audience-abroad-YzzUghnsB2/index.html

Yun, H. (2021). A Study of Idiom Translation in Bonsall's The Red Chamber Dream. *Contemporary Social Science*, *2021*(6), 114–123. DOI: 10.19873/j.cnki.2096-0212.2021.06.008

Zhang, Q., & Wang, J. (2010). Application of Functional Equivalence Theory in English translation of Chinese idioms. *Journal of Language Teaching and Research*, *1*(6). Advance online publication. DOI: 10.4304/jltr.1.6.880-888

Zhang, W., & Xia, Y. (2024). A deep semantic learning framework based on cultural features for English machine translation: Taking tea culture as an example. *Pakistan Journal of Agricultural Sciences*, *61*(3), 971–981. DOI: 10.21162/PAKJAS/24.327

Zong, J. H. (2024). 网络玄幻小说对外传播现状与路径探索 —— 以《斗破苍穹》为例 [Internet Fantasy Fiction External Communication Status and Path Exploration-- Take "Fighting To Break The Sky" as an Example]. *ETR*, *2*(10), 41–43. DOI: 10.61369/ETR.7403

Chapter 12
Navigating Ethical Dilemmas in AI-Powered Translation:
Challenges and Solutions

Andi Asrifan
https://orcid.org/0000-0002-9934-6129
Universitas Negeri Makassar, Indonesia

ABSTRACT

The incorporation of artificial intelligence (AI) in translation has transformed global communication, providing swift and economical methods for overcoming language obstacles. This breakthrough presents considerable ethical difficulties, especially regarding accuracy, cultural sensitivity, and data privacy. AI translation systems frequently encounter difficulties with contextual subtleties, resulting in possible misinterpretations that may offend or mislead users. The management of sensitive user data presents significant privacy issues, requiring stringent security protocols and adherence to rules such as GDPR. A coordinated strategy including AI developers, enterprises, and expert translators is crucial to resolve these difficulties. By prioritizing ethical principles, stakeholders can improve the efficacy of AI translation while safeguarding cultural contexts and user privacy. This work underscores the necessity for ongoing surveillance and revisions of AI models, guided by cultural understanding, to preserve relevance and sensitivity in translations.

DOI: 10.4018/979-8-3373-0060-3.ch012

INTRODUCTION TO AI IN TRANSLATION AND ITS ETHICAL LANDSCAPE

1.1 The Rise of AI in Language Translation

The integration of artificial intelligence (AI) in language translation has dramatically reshaped global communication (Wang, 2023; Kuddus, 2022). AI-powered tools, especially powerful neural machine translation (NMT) systems, have made it feasible to quickly and economically translate content across several languages, opening up new paths for accessibility and worldwide participation. Platforms like Google Translate and DeepL enable users to bridge language gaps instantly, helping organizations, governments, and individuals communicate seamlessly with diverse audiences worldwide (Pym & Hao, 2024).

AI's quick growth in translation has given tremendous benefits, particularly in expanding accessibility to information (Currie, 2023). For individuals who don't speak the primary language of material, AI-powered translation enables access to resources in education, healthcare, business, and beyond, offering increased opportunities for non-native speakers to connect with global information. This democratization of knowledge, traditionally limited by the time and cost of human translation, has helped empower communities and has been important in disaster settings where rapid translation may enhance emergency response and aid distribution.

However, the increasing reliance on AI for translation creates ethical problems, notably regarding accuracy and cultural sensitivity. Unlike human translators, who can interpret context, emotions, and cultural nuances, AI systems may mistake or overlook these subtleties (Mughal et al., 2024). This can lead to translations that, while legally correct, may lack the intended meaning or unwittingly offend owing to cultural insensitivity. The difficulties of AI to completely comprehend idioms, regional dialects, and context-specific expressions underline the significance of addressing the ethical consequences of depending only on AI for correct, respectful translations.

Data privacy is another key ethical consideration, as many translation technologies require access to user-generated content that may contain sensitive or private information. The potential for misuse of this data, whether through insecure storage techniques or illegal sharing, highlights the necessity for stringent data protection rules in AI translation systems (Nadji)(Nanayakkara et al., 2024). Ensuring that these technologies adhere to privacy rules is vital to maintaining user trust and ensuring individuals' rights to information security.

Additionally, AI-driven translation offers socio-economic issues, particularly for human translators. As AI technology continues to advance, there may be a reduced demand for human translators, impacting employment opportunities, especially for those specialized in less commonly spoken languages (Moneus & Sahari, 2024; Vieira et al., 2021). This move could ultimately harm linguistic variety, as AI technologies tend to emphasize frequently used languages, thereby contributing to the marginalization of minority languages.

1.2 Understanding Ethical Dilemmas in AI Translation

As AI-driven translation systems become more important to global communication, ethical issues arise. AI systems interpret language using massive datasets and strong algorithms, but without human intuition or understanding (Asrifan et al., 2025). The ethical issues of bias, accuracy, and data privacy affect how successfully and ethically these tools can be utilized.

AI translation bias is a major ethical issue (Moneus & Sahari, 2024; Tiribelli et al.,2024). Translations can reflect and even amplify data biases because AI programs learn from data. If a training dataset incorporates gender preconceptions, the AI may distort or offend particular groups with its translations. The AI may use gendered terminology when translating languages with differing grammatical structures, which is problematic. These difficulties require data curation and bias-detecting systems.

Another issue in AI-powered translation is accuracy. Translation algorithms are improving, but they can still mistake words with idioms, cultural references, or context-specific nuances. In professional or sensitive settings, inaccurate translations can cause misunderstandings and negative repercussions (Vieira et al., 2021). Mistranslations in legal or medical papers could hurt or misinform. AI systems cannot adjust to situational context, hence they may produce literal translations that lack subtlety, emphasizing the necessity for oversight in high-stakes situations.

AI translation technologies routinely access user-generated content, which may contain sensitive data (Khatiwada et al., 2024; Ghiurău & Popescu, 2024). Data privacy is also important. Translation users risk having their data saved, shared, or used to train the model without their agreement. Protecting user trust and privacy requires stringent data protection policies and data usage openness. This includes clear opt-out alternatives and strong encryption to protect private data.

1.3 The Role of Stakeholders in Ethical AI Translation

As AI-powered translation becomes a worldwide communication standard, AI developers, corporations, professional translators, and end-users must ensure its ethical use (Tian, 2024). From eliminating biases to ensuring data privacy and accuracy, each organization must handle AI translation ethics. Encouraging safe AI use that maximizes benefits and minimizes risks requires collaboration.

AI developers pioneer fair, transparent, and inclusive systems (Xivuri & Twinomurinzi, 2023). Train AI systems using unbiased and representative data to avoid skewed or incorrect translations. To avoid literal or insensitive translations, developers must construct algorithms that recognize and respond to cultural and contextual variances. Ethical AI translation needs audits, bias prevention, and model limitation transparency.

AI translation companies also promote ethics. Customer service and localization companies serving worldwide markets must respect cultural variations and avoid stereotyping. Businesses should prioritize accuracy and contextual relevance in high-stakes areas like healthcare and legal services (Petro anu et al., 2023; Vieira, 2021). Mistranslations can have catastrophic consequences. They choose translation suppliers with robust privacy practices, clarify data usage regulations, and advocate for AI user rights to protect user data.

AI's efficiency may harm professional translators, yet ethical AI translation need them. Their language and culture skills can help AI systems translate more accurately and politely. Translators assist engineers find and repair automated translation problems, enhancing AI tool ethics and quality (Chen, 2024). Nuanced feedback from translators helps AI developers build systems that respect linguistic and cultural diversity. End-users can support ethical AI translation by learning how AI systems manage data and using these tools with understanding of their limitations (Hartmann et al., 2024; Leikas, 2022). Convenient AI translation may omit context or cultural nuances in complex or sensitive topics. Encourage feedback mechanisms that help developers and businesses improve by reporting bias or errors.

GDPR, HIPAA, and the EU AI Act set data privacy and compliance standards for ethical AI translation. To avoid prejudice, developers must use fairness-aware algorithms and diverse training datasets. AI translation companies must stress user permission, secure data storage, and transparent data usage practices. To improve system precision and cultural awareness, ethical AI development requires continual audits, human oversight, and linguist collaboration (Campino, 2024; Woo & Choi, 2021). Protocols ensure AI translation is responsible and inclusive in varied global contexts.

The ethical use of AI translation requires many stakeholders, each with a significant role. By post-editing AI-generated content, translators ensure accuracy and cultural nuance. By reducing bias and improving contextual understanding, developers promote ethical AI design. Governments create laws like GDPR and the AI Act to ensure compliance, equity, and transparency. These stakeholders collaborate to translate AI ethically and efficiently. Interdisciplinary collaboration can boost AI's credibility by ensuring accurate, culturally relevant, and legal and ethical translations.

BIAS IN AI-POWERED TRANSLATION SYSTEMS

2.1 Identifying Bias in AI Translation Models

Bias in AI translation systems comes from training data, developer opinions, and societal influences, making it an ethical issue (Tomalin et al., 2021; Al-kfairy, 2024). It is crucial to understand how these biases arise to reduce their influence. The training data utilized to construct AI translation algorithms leads to bias. Machine learning algorithms use massive datasets from the internet and other public sources (Sarker, 2021). These sources represent societal biases and assumptions, which can accidentally implant gender, racial, and cultural biases into AI systems. Translating gender-unmarked languages like English into gender-marked ones leads to gender-based assumptions. Some languages use masculine gender markers for "The doctor examined the patient" due to gender and professional role biases (Dobreva et al., 2023).

With languages with diverse structures and contexts, the model may default to cultural norms in the data, reinforcing prejudices rather than giving unbiased translations.

Developers who build and improve these systems also introduce bias (Ray, 2023). Developers' conscious or unconscious beliefs might affect model outcomes, especially when choosing data and labeling or processing ambiguous language. A developer's cultural awareness or linguistic expertise may influence regional dialects, idiomatic phrases, or local vernacular, marginalizing less common or underrepresented languages. These perspectives can lead to restricted translation systems that alienate users from other cultures and languages without diverse teams and inclusive model creation (Hoang et al., 2022; Mor et al., 2022).

Societal factors also influence AI translation bias (Curto et al., 2024; Belenguer, 2022). Social biases like ethnic or gender prejudices can influence training dataset language. The AI model may adopt these biases when exposed to massive amounts of biased data. Translating terms about professions, family duties, or culture might lead to biases that align with traditional or dominant societal perspectives, neglecting more inclusive representations. This bias reinforces inequalities and shapes individuals' views of specific groups or roles.

2.2 Case Studies on Bias in Translation Outputs

AI translation systems can be powerful but can also produce biased or insulting translations with serious repercussions (Nemani et al., 2024). Real-world biases in translation outputs reveal their sorts and social effects.

AI translations often show gender prejudice. Google Translate assigns genders based on stereotypical roles when translating gender-neutral languages like Turkish into gender-specific languages like English or Spanish. According to Google Translate, "o bir doktor" means "he is a doctor" in Turkish, whereas "o bir hemşire" means "she is a nurse." These translations reinforce workplace stereotypes by associating certain professions with certain genders. Beyond verbal errors, such biases promote outdated beliefs that can influence gender roles (Marinucci et al., 2023).

Another Google Translate case showed cultural and racial bias in translations (Tomalin et al., 2021). For instance, translating "Black" from certain languages into English has generated problems. If the word is connected with negative connotations or rendered in a way that perpetuates racial biases, it may be offensive or insensitive. This has caused criticism, especially when AI-generated translations appear in public spaces like social media posts or official papers, where they might promote misunderstandings and harmful stereotypes.

AI-powered translations exhibit religious and political biases (Alkhouri, 2024; Moneus & Sahari, 2024). One Arabic-to-English translation of religious terminology had disparaging connotations. Translations of Arabic language on religion or politics can be derogatory or inaccurate due to training data biases. When employed in sensitive circumstances like media reporting or government communications, mistranslations can disrupt intercultural relations and disseminate disinformation.

AI translation bias was also seen in Facebook's translation service. In a high-profile incident, Facebook's AI mistranslated an Arabic post with a normal "good morning" expression as a lethal threat. Due to this mistake, authorities temporarily detained the poster, demonstrating the seriousness of mistranslations. The scenario showed that AI translation in important applications might unintentionally worsen circumstances or misrepresent messages, requiring careful management (Sun et al., 2024).

These cases show how biased or incorrect AI translations affect people and communities. It can lead to professional issues, social misunderstandings, and possibly legal action (Galderisi et al., 2024; Muldoon, 2022). Addressing these biases needs constant AI training dataset upgrades, oversight, and understanding of translation cultural sensitivity. As AI translation becomes increasingly common, eliminating such biases is crucial for inclusive, courteous, and accurate cross-cultural communication.

Practical AI translation applications underscore both achievements and obstacles. In healthcare, AI-assisted translation facilitates patient communication but poses risks of medical errors due to contextual misinterpretations (Kelly et al., 2019; Sharma et al., 2023). The legal sector depends on AI for contract management; yet, mistakes may result in liability concerns. Global enterprises utilize systems such as DeepL and Google Translate, which enhance efficiency however falter in addressing cultural subtleties. Hybrid models that integrate AI with human oversight improve accuracy (Liang, 2023; Zou et al., 2022). Organizations employ bias detection algorithms and post-editing processes to reduce inaccuracies. These case studies underscore the necessity for ongoing enhancement, adherence to regulations, and ethical issues in the implementation of AI translation.

2.3 Strategies for Minimizing Bias

Limiting bias in AI-powered translation systems is difficult, but several methods can improve accuracy and inclusivity. Developers and stakeholders can eliminate biases and enhance translation quality via different training datasets, ongoing testing, and manual oversight (González-Gonzalo et al., 2022). AI translation tools should produce fair, respectful, and contextually relevant translations across languages and cultures.

Multiple and representative training datasets are an excellent way to reduce bias (Van Giffen et al., 2022). Data obtained from the internet can influence AI translation algorithms. Including data from several sources, languages, and cultures can help produce a balanced model that better represents global variety. Curating datasets to avoid over-representing stereotyped associations—such as associating certain professions to specific genders—can also help the model avoid propagating societal biases. Develop datasets with diverse gender representations in roles throughout medical, engineering, and education to combat gender stereotyping. Identifying and correcting bias requires ongoing testing and review. Developers can identify and fix issues early by comparing AI translation outputs against bias and accuracy benchmarks. AI bias-detection algorithms can identify instances when the AI may make assumptions, such as choosing gendered pronouns based on occupational preconceptions (Ding, 2024). Testing translations in diverse cultures and dialects might uncover subtle biases that a single-language or monocultural assessment may miss. Developers can mimic real-world settings with different test cases to evaluate the AI's handling of subtle words, idioms, and culturally sensitive terms.

Manual monitoring is also essential for AI translation bias reduction. Human reviewers, especially linguists and culturally sensitive ones, can notice difficulties automatic methods miss. Translation professionals can identify instances where AI misinterprets context or nuances, providing useful input on incorrect translations

(Naveen & Trojovský, 2024; Aziza, 2024). When training data is scarce, languages and dialects that are more prone to errors and biases need manual inspection. Feedback loops involving human translators can improve AI systems.

Bias-mitigation algorithms can help AIs uncover and correct biases in real time. For instance, algorithms that remove stereotyped assumptions or allow users to alter gender markers in translations might improve flexibility and accuracy. Transparency approaches include disclosing datasets, sources, and model restrictions help users and developers understand and enhance the system (Balasubramaniam et al., 2023).

ACCURACY AND RELIABILITY IN AI TRANSLATION

3.1 Challenges in Maintaining Translation Accuracy

AI-powered translation is difficult to keep accurate due to its inability to understand context, idioms, and subtle meanings (Abdelali & Bennoudi, 2023). Google Translate and DeepL have improved at translating simple texts, but they struggle with human language's nuances and subtleties. In situations that require exact meaning and cultural awareness, these shortcomings might cause miscommunication.

The system's inability to understand context hinders AI translation accuracy. AI systems focus largely on patterns and probabilities, overlooking the intended nuances (Mitchell, 2021; Park et al., 2024). Human translators understand that words and phrases get meaning from context. The word "bank" can mean a financial institution or a riverbank, depending on context. AI models may mistake such words without contextual signals, especially in languages with many word meanings. In complex or specialized writings like legal or medical records, inaccurate translations might cause major misunderstandings or judgment errors.

AI translation systems also struggle with idiomatic idioms and figurative language, which rarely translate across languages (Chuanmao & Juntao, 2024). Culturally particular idioms like "it's raining cats and dogs" or "a blessing in disguise" might be perplexing if translated literally. AI models trained on huge datasets can recognize common idioms, but they may translate less familiar or region-specific terms literally, resulting in meaningless outputs. This constraint impairs the readability of the translated content and might lead to misunderstandings because idioms typically have important meanings or connotations.

In languages with subtle distinctions that AI cannot imitate, nuanced meanings are another challenge (Kallens & Christiansen, 2024; Samantray et al., 2024). Japanese has numerous words for "I" and "you," reflecting formality, intimacy, and humility. AI systems may translate to formal, colloquial, or even hostile language due to their inability to select the right terms. Tonal languages like Mandarin Chinese might challenge AI since various tones change word meanings. Such misinterpretations might have unforeseen social or professional consequences, especially in formal situations.

Cultural context complicates AI translation accuracy. AI systems may struggle to understand cultural references, humor, and terminology that are distinctive to certain communities (Abu-Rayyash, 2024). AI algorithms lack the cultural knowledge to translate jokes or cultural references. Without this knowledge, the AI may produce mechanical or unintelligible translations.

3.2 Ethical Implications of Translation Errors

AI-powered translation errors can have serious ethical consequences, especially in high-stakes domains like healthcare, law, and diplomacy (Swiatek et al., 2023; Varela, 2024). AI translation techniques make multilingual communication fast, but blunders in sensitive areas can have catastrophic, often permanent repercussions. Understanding the potential harms emphasizes the ethical obligation of accurate and dependable AI translation systems.

Small translation errors can compromise patient safety in healthcare. Misinterpretation of medical jargon, symptoms, and treatment instructions can lead to inaccurate diagnoses, prescription errors, and improper treatment regimens (Nagappa & Naik, 2022; Gala and Makaryus, 2023). If an AI translation system mistranslates a patient's symptoms, a doctor may administer the wrong treatment or miss a serious ailment. Healthcare terminology is complex and varies by language and locale, making AI systems untrained in medical language difficult. Mistranslating patient instructions, especially dose or food restrictions, can be fatal. Mistranslations impair care and the patient's access to informed decision-making, presenting serious ethical concerns with AI in healthcare contexts.

Translation errors also impede justice and fair representation in the legal sector (Angermeyer, 2021; Matulewska & Wagner, 2021). Legal documents require accurate interpretation of technical terms, phrases, and phrasing. Contract, court transcript, and legal declaration translations that misrepresent an individual's comments or change agreement meanings may result in false convictions or unjust outcomes. For instance, misinterpreting a document's legal rights may cause someone to unknowingly waive protections or entitlements. AI systems also struggle to understand legal jargon and distinguish between similar-sounding legal terminology with differing meanings in different languages (Sinclair-Palm & Chokly, 2023). Such inaccuracies have legal consequences and pose ethical problems concerning justice system equality and fairness, especially for non-native speakers or those who need translations.

Translation errors can strain international ties and cause severe political or diplomatic crises in diplomacy. AI systems may misread diplomatic language due to its careful phrasing, culturally particular idioms, and inferred meanings (Naveen & Trojovský, 2024; Malyuga, 2024). A slight translation error in a political speech or negotiating document could change its tone or intent, causing diplomatic difficulties or misunderstandings between countries. Mistranslations of official announcements or agreements can damage trust, cooperation, and conflict. Diplomatic translation ethics require accuracy and contextual sensitivity because errors might affect international relations and peacekeeping.

The ethical consequences of translation failures underline the necessity for accountability in the deployment of AI in crucial areas (Manning et al., 2022). Errors in healthcare, law, and diplomacy are not only technical failures; they can cause injury, violate rights, and exacerbate injustices. With human oversight, AI translation systems can provide accurate, contextually relevant, and ethical translations, especially in high-stakes applications. Focusing on translation accuracy ethics can help responsible AI use promote human welfare, justice, and global harmony.

3.3 Improving Accuracy through Hybrid Models

Hybrid models that mix AI and human experience may improve translation accuracy (Sarker, 2022). These hybrid approaches combine AI's efficiency and human translators' contextual and cultural awareness to produce more accurate and dependable translations, especially in high-stakes situations. Hybrid models can avoid contextual errors, linguistic misinterpretations, and subtleties that AI misses by include human oversight.

Hybrid translation approaches sometimes use AI to draft a translation that human translators revise. AI can handle repeated or simple translation tasks, speeding up the process and decreasing human workload. Human translators correct errors, provide cultural context, and maintain communication tone and intent (Naveen & Trojovský, 2024). In high-precision fields like healthcare, legal services, and diplomatic communications, a single mistake can cause serious harm.

Hybrid models are essential in healthcare, since precise translation affects patient safety (Bates et al., 2021). An AI system may quickly translate a patient's symptoms or medical history, and a skilled medical interpreter can validate and adjust it. This two-tiered method helps interpret complex medical terminology and avoid life-threatening misunderstandings. Hybrid systems can also identify terms or phrases for human evaluation, focusing translators on accuracy-critical regions.

Legal translation also benefits from hybrid methods. Legal documents use technical language that requires clarity and knowledge of local laws. After AI quickly produces a draft translation, a legal expert checks and corrects it to ensure contextual accuracy and legal intent (Moneus & Sahari, 2024). Compared to human translation, this method improves accuracy and saves time, making legal resources more accessible to more people while maintaining quality and reliability.

Hybrid models prevent misinterpretations in diplomatic interactions, where context and nuance are crucial. AI can quickly translate, but diplomats and linguists must examine sensitive language's tone and connotations to ensure diplomatic finesse (Zhou, 2022). Hybrid models prevent trivial translation errors from becoming diplomatic issues, improving communication and international understanding.

By employing human-reviewed translations to retrain the AI system, hybrid models can improve over time at handling certain language pairs or terminologies (Landa Oregi, 2023). AI learns from human modifications in this cyclical feedback loop, improving its accuracy and capacity to handle complicated language patterns and cultural nuances.

Hybrid models combine AI efficiency and human intuition to generate a powerful solution that outperforms either alone. Hybrid models combine AI's speed and scalability with human translators' judgment and contextual awareness to provide accurate, ethical translations (Moneus & Sahari, 2024; Gutierrez Jr, 2024). As hybrid techniques mature, they could set new norms for translation accuracy and reliability across varied sectors, assuring precise, nuanced, and culturally appropriate global communication.

PRIVACY AND DATA SECURITY IN AI TRANSLATION

4.1 Data Privacy Concerns in AI Translation Services

Given the large amount of user data collected by AI-powered translation services, data privacy and security are major concerns (Alhitmi et al., 2024). AI translation solutions handle everything from conversational text to sensitive medical, legal, and personal data. Safe and ethical AI translation services need understanding data kinds and privacy risks.

Users submit text to AI translation systems, which may contain personal information, corporate secrets, and confidential communications. People may use translation tools to translate medical records, legal contracts, or private letters without knowing that their text may be saved, evaluated, or used to improve the system's learning model. Mishandled or poorly protected text data can lead to data breaches and illegal dissemination of sensitive information. Some services collect metadata like the user's location, language preferences, and usage patterns in addition to the text, which can create a privacy-sensitive profile when combined with other personal data (Komljenovic, 2022; Pandey et al., 2023).

Data breaches, where unauthorized parties access sensitive AI translation system data, are a major concern (Saeed et al., 2024). Businesses and individuals handling confidential information like corporate agreements, patient data, and classified government communications should be concerned about translation service breaches. If breached, this data could cost individuals and businesses money, identity, or reputation. To protect user data, AI translation businesses must utilize encryption, secure storage, and access limits.

Unauthorized usage of user data to train AI models is also possible. AI translation companies may analyze or store user inputs to improve their algorithms (Haleem et al., 2022). This improves system performance but raises ethical problems about user consent and data control. Privacy regulations are sometimes unclear, so consumers may not realize their data is being stored. To let users know how their data is being used and opt out, policies must be transparent.

AI systems may accidentally share sensitive data due to poor anonymization (Williamson & Prybutok, 2024). Translations used to refine the model may reveal sensitive data in unrelated situations. The system's memory may accidentally save confidential content, which could leak in future translations.

The ethical use of AI in translation requires addressing data privacy problems. Strong encryption, privacy regulations, and data usage transparency may reduce risks and create user trust. Localized processing or data deletion can improve privacy in sensitive applications. Through data security and user consent, AI translation services can provide seamless communication without compromising personal or organisational privacy (Williamson & Prybutok, 2024).

4.2 Regulations and Compliance in AI Translation

AI translation services manage increasingly sensitive user data, making data protection compliance essential (Farhad, 2024; Hasal et al., 2021). The General Data Protection Regulation (GDPR) in the EU and the Health Insurance Portability and Accountability Act (HIPAA) in the US require AI translation providers to manage and protect user data. Organizations building and using translation technology must understand these standards to build user trust and avoid legal issues.

The GDPR sets strict data protection and transparency criteria for EU companies and those processing EU data. GDPR requires AI translation providers to protect user data, limit data retention, and obtain user consent before collecting data (Meszaros & Ho, 2021; Lorè et al., 2023). Users must know how translation services will use, store, and share their data. GDPR requires "data minimization," or gathering only data needed for a specific purpose. AI translation services must manage only the text of the translation and avoid unnecessary data collection, especially when sensitive information is at stake. In order to comply with the GDPR, AI translation services must remove users' data from the system.

HIPAA regulates healthcare AI translation systems in the US. Translation technology that handle medical records, diagnoses, or other sensitive health data must comply with HIPAA (Keshta & Odeh, 2021). HIPAA requires healthcare providers and their affiliates, including AI translation businesses, to secure PHI. AI translation services working with healthcare providers must implement encryption, access controls, and audit trails to prevent PHI theft (Wang et al., 2022). Healthcare practitioners and AI companies may face severe fines for HIPAA violations.

Other regional and sector-specific laws affect AI translation alongside GDPR and HIPAA (Kaduskar et al., 2024). Data collection must be transparent and users have control over their personal data under the California Consumer Privacy Act (CCPA), similar to the GDPR. AI translation organizations in several regions must comply with a complicated set of data protection laws, requiring uniform and strict data management policies and adaptive solutions to meet various regulatory needs.

These regulatory frameworks are not only legal requirements, but they also give companies a competitive edge as customers and organizations prefer data-protected and ethical services. Many AI translation companies use privacy-by-design methodologies to ensure data safety from the start (Santos & Radanliev, 2024). This strategy reduces data breaches and meets GDPR and HIPAA transparency and user autonomy requirements.

The GDPR protects data privacy and the EU AI Act imposes risk-based constraints on AI translation (Schmitt & Koutroumpis, 2025). Conversely, the U.S. AI Bill of Rights promotes ethical AI without comprehensive federal regulation (Hine & Floridi, 2023; Schmitt & Koutroumpis, 2025). These differences highlight regulatory shortcomings, including bias management and accountability. Europe regulates transparency, whereas the U.S. uses sector-specific rules. A common norm could reduce these discrepancies and ensure ethical AI translation. Improved data security, user consent, and bias reduction regulations would strengthen AI governance and promote equitable and responsible translation technology worldwide (BaHammam, 2023).

4.3 Best Practices for Ensuring Data Security

In AI translation systems, safeguarding user data is crucial for preserving trust and adhering to privacy requirements (Wang et al., 2022; Williamson & Prybutok, 2024). Given that these tools frequently manage sensitive information, including personal correspondence, legal papers, and health records, it is imperative to adopt stringent security measures such as encryption, data anonymization, and secure data storage. These policies protect user privacy, mitigate the danger of data breaches, and assure compliance with legal norms by AI translation providers.

Encryption is a fundamental method for safeguarding data in AI translation services (Gupta et al. 2024). By encrypting data during transmission and storage, providers guarantee that any information conveyed over the system stays inaccessible to unauthorized individuals. For example, when a user submits text for translation, encryption transforms the text into an unreadable format during transmission to the translation server. Only authorized systems possessing the appropriate decryption key can convert the encrypted data into intelligible text. This method greatly diminishes the probability of data being intercepted or accessed during transmission. At-rest encryption, implemented on stored data, provides an additional layer of security, especially effective in mitigating data loss or exposure during a security incident (Kalra et al., 2025). Collectively, these encryption methods safeguard user data from external threats and unlawful internal access.

Data anonymization is an essential strategy, particularly when translation providers utilize textual data to enhance their AI models (Patsakis & Lykousas, 2023). Anonymization eliminates personally identifiable information (PII) from user data, guaranteeing that any preserved data cannot be linked to the specific user. For instance, if an AI translation service preserves parts of translated text for quality enhancement, anonymization techniques can be utilized to eliminate any identifiable information, like names, addresses, or contact details. This procedure enables providers to utilize the data for enhancing translation precision while safeguarding customer privacy. Advanced methodologies such as differential privacy, which introduces statistical noise to anonymized data, enhance the safeguarding of user identities while maintaining the data's utility for model training.

Access control techniques are crucial for safeguarding data. Restricting access to sensitive data guarantees that only authorized individuals can access or handle user information. Role-based access control (RBAC) limits data access according to the user's job function, thereby mitigating the danger of inadvertent or intentional exposure. Access control systems in AI translation services can inhibit unauthorized individuals from accessing sensitive text entries or information, thereby safeguarding against internal data misuse (Alkaeed et al., 2024). Furthermore, recording and scrutinizing data access activities might facilitate the identification of anomalous access patterns, serving as a proactive alert system for possible breaches.

Regular audits and security evaluations are essential for preserving data security in AI translation systems. Providers can discover and remedy weaknesses by performing regular assessments of encryption standards, anonymization methods, and access control protocols before data breaches occur (Kulkarni & Girish, 2024). Penetration testing, which emulates cyberattacks, can identify vulnerabilities in the system, whereas third-party audits provide an impartial evaluation of security protocols. These proactive procedures ensure that AI translation services comply with data protection rules and adapt to emerging security threats.

CULTURAL SENSITIVITY AND ETHICAL RESPONSIBILITY

5.1 The Role of Cultural Context in Translation

In language translation, comprehending and effectively expressing cultural context is as essential as attaining linguistic precision. AI-driven translation systems necessitate cultural sensitivity that beyond mere word replacement, demanding comprehension of nuances, idioms, and the extensive social and historical connotations associated with language (Khasawneh, 2023). Neglecting these factors might result in translations that, although technically precise, may be perceived as offensive or improper, so eroding confidence and causing misunderstandings. Highlighting cultural context in AI translation systems is crucial for respectful and effective cross-cultural communication (Zhai et al., 2024).

Cultural context affects language interpretation, with statements that are neutral in one language potentially possessing significantly different implications in another (Dobrovol'skij & Piirainen, 2021; Malyuga, 2024). The expression "breaking bread" may convey a sense of communal sharing in English, however direct translations may lack equivalent significance in cultures where bread is not a dietary essential. Color symbolism differs significantly among civilizations; whilst white typically represents purity in Western societies, it may denote grief in certain East Asian traditions. AI translation systems that neglect these distinctions may provide translations that misread or misrepresent the intent of the source language, thus leading to confusion or offense.

Idiomatic expressions represent another domain in which cultural context is essential (Dobrovol'skij & Piirainen, 2021; Wang & Luo, 2021). Expressions such as "kick the bucket" or "spill the beans" are widely recognized as idioms in English, however they would appear absurd if translated literally into other languages. Human translators inherently interpret these phrases by replacing them with equivalent idioms or modifying the language to convey the intended meaning. Conversely, AI models frequently depend on pattern recognition, rendering them susceptible to producing literal translations that overlook colloquial connotations. The absence of cultural understanding is especially detrimental in sensitive domains, such as journalism, marketing, or diplomacy, where accurately transmitting the intended tone is crucial.

Another cultural factor is the evasion of terminology that may be perceived as offensive or disrespectful. AI translation systems, developed using extensive internet data, are susceptible to integrating biased or improper language found within their datasets (Ray, 2023). If these systems do not effectively filter or modify such terminology, they may generate outputs that unintentionally reinforce stereotypes or employ pejorative phrases, mirroring biases inherent in the training data. The risk is particularly elevated when translating text pertaining to ethnicity, religion, gender, or other sensitive subjects. Developers must integrate bias-detection systems and cultural filters to avert the unintended generation of offensive language by AI and to preserve cross-cultural comprehension.

Enhancing cultural sensitivity in AI translation necessitates several solutions. Diverse and representative training datasets facilitate systems in acquiring language usage across many cultural contexts, hence preventing excessive dependence on data from a singular region or demographic. Furthermore, AI models can gain from post-translation human evaluation, especially for high-stakes material where cultural subtleties are essential. Human translators and cultural specialists can recognize and rectify language that may be misconstrued, ensuring that AI-generated translations correspond with the original text's intended meaning and cultural nuances (Abdelali & Bennoudi, 2023).

Ultimately, user feedback from varied backgrounds can yield immediate insights into possible cultural inaccuracies in AI translations, enabling systems to learn and adjust accordingly. This feedback enhances the AI's performance and aids in developing models that are more aligned with diverse cultural perspectives, resulting in translations that are polite, precise, and considerate to all audiences (Gough, 2024).

5.2 Ethical Responsibilities of AI Developers in Cultural Sensitivity

In the domain of AI translation, developers bear substantial ethical obligations to guarantee cultural sensitivity, as the language produced by AI significantly influences cross-cultural communication (Weber-Lewerenz, 2021). Efficient and respectful translation necessitates systems that comprehend not only words but also the cultural subtleties and social significances associated with them. Accomplishing this necessitates not only technical accuracy but also culturally informed AI models, developed and enhanced by diverse teams and representative datasets. For AI engineers, cultivating cultural sensitivity is a fundamental aspect of their ethical obligation to promote inclusive and respectful communication across diverse languages and cultures.

Developers can significantly improve cultural sensitivity in AI translation systems by assembling diverse teams (Lu et al., 2023). Teams consisting of persons from diverse cultural, linguistic, and ethnic backgrounds contribute a multitude of perspectives to the development process, enhancing the AI's comprehension of cultural context. A multicultural team can recognize potential biases, detect culturally insensitive outputs, and enhance the model's capacity to comprehend idioms, regional dialects, and expressions with distinct implications across several languages (Hackett et al., 2023). For example, team members from diverse locations can identify terms that may possess unwanted connotations in translation, a difficulty that engineers from a singular cultural background could neglect. This diversity in thought and experience improves the ethical design of AI, enabling it to generate translations that are precise, nuanced, and culturally sensitive.

Alongside diverse teams, employing representative training data is essential for fostering cultural sensitivity in AI models (Timmons et al., 2023). AI systems acquire linguistic patterns via their training data; thus, biased or unrepresentative data may result in translations that embody stereotypes, insensitivities, or geographical biases. If a model is predominantly trained on Western data sources, it may struggle to comprehend terms or customs unique to other cultural contexts. By assembling datasets that encompass voices, languages, and cultural expressions from a wide range of societies, developers can create models that are more aligned with global variety. Diverse datasets allow AI to comprehend linguistic variances and diminish dependence on default patterns that may not be globally applicable, yielding translations that honor and mirror the diversity of global language usage (Yu et al., 2024).

Developers hold the ethical obligation to implement bias mitigation measures to safeguard against culturally inappropriate outcomes. AI translation systems are susceptible to acquiring and perpetuating biases inherent in training data, including gender stereotypes and culturally charged terminology (Bella et al., 2024; Liyanage and Ranaweera, 2023). Developers can rectify this by employing bias-detection algorithms and conducting regular audits of translations for precision and propriety. Algorithms can be designed to identify the unnecessary introduction of gendered language or to indicate idiomatic expressions that may carry bad connotations in specific cultures. By diligently overseeing the system's output, developers can decrease the probability of dangerous words being overlooked.

Ethically responsible AI development necessitates transparency with users (Bogina et al., 2022). When constraints in cultural sensitivity are present within a model, developers must inform users, establishing realistic expectations regarding the system's capabilities. This transparency develops trust and helps users to use the AI with more knowledge, particularly when engaging with complex or sensitive topics. Comprehensive and comprehensible documentation elucidating the AI's development process, encompassing the diversity of training data and implemented bias mitigation strategies, aids users in grasping the measures taken to maintain cultural sensitivity.

5.3 Mitigating Cultural Risks through Continuous Monitoring

In AI-driven translation systems, maintaining cultural sensitivity necessitates continuous monitoring and updating, as language and cultural nuances are ever developing (Tian, 2024). Ongoing surveillance is crucial for identifying and rectifying potential cultural insensitivities or biases in translations, enabling developers to modify AI models in accordance with emerging linguistic trends, societal shifts, or user input. By using mechanisms for continuous assessment and enhancement, AI developers can more effectively fulfill their ethical obligation to promote courteous and accurate cross-cultural communication.

A proficient approach for ongoing assessment is the implementation of real-time feedback loops from users (Jelsch et al., 2021). User feedback serves as a primary source of insight regarding cultural errors, biases, or misunderstandings that occur in translations. Users can utilize built-in reporting tools to indicate translations that are erroneous, offensive, or inappropriate, allowing developers to swiftly examine and rectify these concerns. This method enables developers to rectify flaws in specific translations and to discern patterns of persistent mistakes that may reveal underlying problems inside the model. If users repeatedly indicate issues with gender assumptions or abusive language in specific settings, developers can analyze the model's training data and algorithms to pinpoint and address the origin of the bias.

Consistent evaluation of translation products is an essential technique (Mökander et al., 2023). Periodic audits, involving the examination of a representative sample of translations for accuracy and cultural relevance, assist developers in identifying biases that may be overlooked in routine operations. Audits may be performed by teams of linguists and cultural specialists who comprehend the nuances of both source and target languages (Biswas et al., 2024). These specialists can discern when translations fail to convey intended subtleties or when culturally significant terminology are inaccurately rendered. Audits must concentrate on critical or sensitive areas, like legal, healthcare, and diplomatic translations, where cultural precision is essential. By proactively evaluating translations, developers can modify the model before minor flaws turn into substantial cultural errors.

Automated bias identification serves as an additional instrument to sustain cultural sensitivity (Mengesha et al., 2021). Machine learning algorithms can be trained to identify biased or insensitive language patterns, highlighting problematic phrases for evaluation. An algorithm may, for instance, identify instances of gendered language in translations that ought to be neutral or recognize phrases that are frequently misconstrued across cultures. This procedure can identify instances of bias promptly, allowing the team to adjust the model or refine data sources to avert recurrence of the issue. Although automated systems are not infallible, they serve as an effective initial line of defense that enhances human supervision.

Modifying AI models in accordance with these monitoring insights is essential for maintaining cultural sensitivity over time. Language is dynamic, with new idioms, phrases, and cultural references continually evolving (Siregar, 2023). Frequent model upgrades, guided by continuous monitoring and user feedback, ensure that AI translation systems maintain accuracy and relevance. These upgrades may entail retraining the model on more current, representative data or enhancing algorithms to better manage intricate cultural expressions. Integrating perspectives from cultural and linguistic specialists guarantees that the model adapts to cultural transformations, enhancing its capacity to accurately perceive and communicate meaning across diverse contexts (Brown & Vacca, 2024).

CONCLUSION

Addressing the ethical implications of AI-driven translation necessitates an acknowledgment of the complex challenges posed by biases, cultural sensitivities, and data privacy issues. AI translation systems, despite their considerable progress in communication, frequently exhibit biases inherent in their training data, thereby resulting in misinterpretations and the reinforcement of cultural preconceptions. This highlights the necessity of utilizing broad and representative datasets, together with ongoing testing and supervision, to reduce biases and improve translation accuracy.

Furthermore, cultural context is essential for successful translation. AI systems must transcend basic linguistic precision to encompass the nuances and intricacies of other cultures. This necessitates continuous cooperation with cultural and language specialists to guarantee that translations are both accurate and contextually suitable and courteous. Frequent modifications to AI models, guided by user feedback and cultural changes, are crucial for ensuring relevance and sensitivity in translations.

Data privacy is an essential element that must not be disregarded. Given that AI translation systems manage sensitive information, it is essential to incorporate stringent security measures, including encryption and data anonymization, to safeguard user privacy and adhere to legal requirements. By emphasizing ethical norms in AI translation, stakeholders may cultivate trust and guarantee that these technologies function as effective instruments for cross-cultural communication, ultimately promoting a more inclusive and understanding global community.

REFERENCES

Abdelali, Z. A. I. D., & Bennoudi, H. (2023). AI vs. Human Translators: Navigating the Complex World of Religious Texts and Cultural Sensitivity. International Journal of Linguistics, Literature and Translation, 6(11), 173-182. DOI: al-kindipublisher.comDOI: 10.32996/ijllt

Abu-Rayyash, H. (2024). AI meets comedy: Viewers' reactions to GPT-4 generated humor translation. Ampersand. https://doi.org/ sciencedirect.comDOI: 10.1016/j.amper.2023.100162

Al-kfairy, M., Mustafa, D., Kshetri, N., Insiew, M., & Alfandi, O. (2024). Ethical challenges and solutions of generative AI: An interdisciplinary perspective. Informatics. https://doi.org/ mdpi.comDOI: 10.3390/informatics11030058

Alhitmi, H. K., Mardiah, A., Al-Sulaiti, K. I., & Abbas, J. (2024). Data security and privacy concerns of AI-driven marketing in the context of economics and business field: an exploration into possible solutions. Cogent Business & Management, 11(1), 2393743. https://doi.org/ tandfonline.comDOI: 10.1080/23311975.2024.2393743

Alkaeed, M., Qayyum, A., & Qadir, J. (2024). Privacy preservation in Artificial Intelligence and Extended Reality (AI-XR) metaverses: A survey. [PDF]. *Journal of Network and Computer Applications*, *231*, 103989. DOI: 10.1016/j.jnca.2024.103989

Alkhouri, K. I. (2024). The role of artificial intelligence in the study of the psychology of religion. Religions. https://doi.org/mdpi.comDOI: 10.3390/rel15030290

Angermeyer, P. S. (2021). Beyond translation equivalence: Advocating pragmatic equality before the law. Journal of Pragmatics. https://doi.org/ sciencedirect.comDOI: 10.1016/j.pragma.2020.12.022

Asrifan, A., Rusmayadi, R., Hasmawaty, H., Nirwana, N., Sivaraja, S., & Dewi, A. C. (2025). Synergizing Human and Machine: Innovations in Knowledge Discovery and Management. In AI and Green Technology Applications in Society (pp. 249-282). IGI Global Scientific Publishing. DOI: [HTML]DOI: 10.4018/979-8-3693-9879-1.ch010

Aziza, S. (2024). Artificial Intelligence in Translation: Benefits and Drawbacks. International Journal of Scientific Trends. scientifictrends.org

BaHammam, A. S. (2023). Balancing innovation and integrity: The role of AI in research and scientific writing. *Nature and Science of Sleep*, •••, 1153–1156.

Balasubramaniam, N., Kauppinen, M., Rannisto, A., Hiekkanen, K., & Kujala, S. (2023). Transparency and explainability of AI systems: From ethical guidelines to requirements. Information and Software Technology, 159, 107197. https://doi.org/ sciencedirect.comDOI: 10.1016/j.infsof.2023.107197

Bates, D. W., Levine, D., Syrowatka, A., Kuznetsova, M., Craig, K. J. T., Rui, A., ... & Rhee, K. (2021). The potential of artificial intelligence to improve patient safety: a scoping review. NPJ digital medicine, 4(1), 54. https://doi.org/nature.comDOI: 10.1038/s41746-021-00423-6

Belenguer, L. (2022). AI bias: exploring discriminatory algorithmic decision-making models and the application of possible machine-centric solutions adapted from the pharmaceutical .... AI and Ethics. https://doi.org/ springer.comDOI: 10.1007/ s43681-022-00138-8

Bella, G., Helm, P., Koch, G., & Giunchiglia, F. (2024, June). Tackling Language Modelling Bias in Support of Linguistic Diversity. In The 2024 ACM Conference on Fairness, Accountability, and Transparency (pp. 562-572). hal.science DOI: 10.1145/3630106.3658925

Biswas, P., Neogi, S. G., Arockiam, D., & Mitra, A. (2024, March). The Importance of Multi-Lingual Sentiment Analysis in Digital Marketing. In 2024 11th International Conference on Reliability, Infocom Technologies and Optimization (Trends and Future Directions)(ICRITO) (pp. 1-8). IEEE. https://doi.org/ [HTML]DOI: 10.1109/ICRITO61523.2024.10522115

Bogina, V., Hartman, A., Kuflik, T., & Shulner-Tal, A. (2022). Educating software and AI stakeholders about algorithmic fairness, accountability, transparency and ethics. International Journal of Artificial Intelligence in Education, 1-26. https:// doi.org/springer.comDOI: 10.1007/s40593-021-00248-0

Brown, S., & Vacca, F. (2022). Cultural sustainability in fashion: reflections on craft and sustainable development models. Sustainability: Science. *Practice and Policy*, *18*(1), 590–600.

Campino, J. (2024). Unleashing the transformers: NLP models detect AI writing in education. In Journal of Computers in Education. Springer Science+Business Media. https://doi.org/DOI: 10.1007/s40692-024-00325-y

Chen, M. (2024). Trust, understanding, and machine translation: the task of translation and the responsibility of the translator. AI & SOCIETY. https://doi.org/ springer. comDOI: 10.1007/s00146-023-01681-6

Chuanmao, T. & Juntao, D. (2024). Translating the Future: Exploring the Impact of Technology and AI on Modern Translation Studies. [HTML]

Currie, G. M. (2023). Academic integrity and artificial intelligence: Is ChatGPT hype, hero or heresy? [HTML]. *Seminars in Nuclear Medicine*, *53*(5), 719–730. Advance online publication. DOI: 10.1053/j.semnuclmed.2023.04.008 PMID: 37225599

Curto, G., Jojoa Acosta, M. F., Comim, F., & Garcia-Zapirain, B. (2024). Are AI systems biased against the poor? A machine learning analysis using Word2Vec and GloVe embeddings. AI & society. https://doi.org/ springer.comDOI: 10.1007/s00146-022-01494-z

Ding, L. (2024). Assessing and Mitigating Social Bias in Text and Natural Language Processing Systems. ualberta.ca

Dobreva, M., Rukavina, T., Stamou, V., Vidaki, A. N., & Zacharopoulou, L. (2023, July). A Multimodal Installation Exploring Gender Bias in Artificial Intelligence. In International Conference on Human-Computer Interaction (pp. 27-46). Cham: Springer Nature Switzerland. https://doi.org/ [HTML]DOI: 10.1007/978-3-031-35681-0_2

Dobrovol'skij, D. & Piirainen, E. (2021). Figurative language: Cross-cultural and cross-linguistic perspectives. [HTML]

Farhad, M. A. (2024). Consumer data protection laws and their impact on business models in the tech industry. [HTML]. *Telecommunications Policy*, *48*(9), 102836. Advance online publication. DOI: 10.1016/j.telpol.2024.102836

Gala, D., & Makaryus, A. N. (2023). The utility of language models in cardiology: a narrative review of the benefits and concerns of ChatGPT-4. International Journal of Environmental Research and Public Health, 20(15), 6438. https://doi.org/mdpi.comDOI: 10.3390/ijerph20156438

Galderisi, S., Appelbaum, P. S., Gill, N., Gooding, P., Herrman, H., Melillo, A., Myrick, K., Pathare, S., Savage, M., Szmukler, G., & Torous, J. (2024). Ethical challenges in contemporary psychiatry: An overview and an appraisal of possible strategies and research needs. [wiley.com]. *World Psychiatry; Official Journal of the World Psychiatric Association (WPA)*, *23*(3), 364–386. DOI: 10.1002/wps.21230 PMID: 39279422

Ghiurău, D. & Popescu, D. E. (2024). Distinguishing Reality from AI: Approaches for Detecting Synthetic Content. Computers. https://doi.org/ mdpi.comDOI: 10.3390/computers14010001

González-Gonzalo, C., Thee, E. F., Klaver, C. C., Lee, A. Y., Schlingemann, R. O., Tufail, A., ... & Sánchez, C. I. (2022). Trustworthy AI: closing the gap between development and integration of AI systems in ophthalmic practice. Progress in retinal and eye research, 90, 101034. https://doi.org/sciencedirect.comDOI: 10.1016/j.preteyeres.2021.101034

Gough, J. (2024). Individual variations in information behaviour of professional translators: towards a classification of translation-oriented research styles. Translation studies. https://doi.org/ tandfonline.comDOI: 10.1080/14781700.2023.2231933

Gupta, B. B., Gaurav, A., Arya, V., Alhalabi, W., Alsalman, D., & Vijayakumar, P. (2024). Enhancing user prompt confidentiality in Large Language Models through advanced differential encryption. [HTML]. *Computers & Electrical Engineering*, *116*, 109215. DOI: 10.1016/j.compeleceng.2024.109215

Gutierrez, R.Jr. (2024). *Unifying linguistic landscapes: The potential of AI and nanotechnology in facilitating real-time translation.* Artificial Intelligence in the Age of Nanotechnology. [HTML], DOI: 10.4018/979-8-3693-0368-9.ch005

Hackett, S., Janssen, J., Beach, P., Perreault, M., Beelen, J., & Van Tartwijk, J. (2023). The effectiveness of Collaborative Online International Learning (COIL) on intercultural competence development in higher education. International Journal of Educational Technology in Higher Education, 20(1), 5. https://doi.org/ springer.comDOI: 10.1186/s41239-022-00373-3

Haleem, A., Javaid, M., Qadri, M. A., Singh, R. P., & Suman, R. (2022). Artificial intelligence (AI) applications for marketing: A literature-based study. International Journal of Intelligent Networks, 3, 119-132. https://doi.org/ sciencedirect.comDOI: 10.1016/j.ijin.2022.08.005

Hartmann, K. V., Primc, N., & Rubeis, G. (2023). Lost in translation? Conceptions of privacy and independence in the technical development of AI-based AAL. *Medicine, Health Care, and Philosophy*, *26*(1), 99–110.

Hasal, M., Nowaková, J., Ahmed Saghair, K., Abdulla, H., Snášel, V., & Ogiela, L. (2021). Chatbots: Security, privacy, data protection, and social aspects. Concurrency and Computation: Practice and Experience, 33(19), e6426. DOI: wiley.comDOI: 10.1002/cpe.6426

Hine, E., & Floridi, L. (2023). The Blueprint for an AI Bill of Rights: In Search of Enaction, at Risk of Inaction. In Minds and Machines (Vol. 33, Issue 2, p. 285). Springer Science+Business Media. https://doi.org/DOI: 10.1007/s11023-023-09625-1

Hoang, T., Suh, J., & Sabharwal, M. (2022). Beyond a numbers game? Impact of diversity and inclusion on the perception of organizational justice. [HTML]. *Public Administration Review*, *82*(3), 537–555. Advance online publication. DOI: 10.1111/puar.13463

Jelsch, M., Roggo, Y., Kleinebudde, P., & Krumme, M. (2021). Model predictive control in pharmaceutical continuous manufacturing: A review from a user's perspective. [HTML]. *European Journal of Pharmaceutics and Biopharmaceutics*, *159*, 137–142. DOI: 10.1016/j.ejpb.2021.01.003 PMID: 33429008

Kaduskar, V. P., Mhetre, H. V., Khatavkar, S. M., Chougule, P. A., Patil, M. V., Moje, R. J., & Naik, N. (2024). Navigating the Frontier of Generative AI Integration in Healthcare: Adoption, Governance, and Legal Compliance. In AI Healthcare Applications and Security, Ethical, and Legal Considerations (pp. 261-289). IGI Global. DOI: [HTML]DOI: 10.4018/979-8-3693-7452-8.ch016

Kallens, P. C., & Christiansen, M. H. (2024). Distributional Semantics: Meaning Through Culture and Interaction. [HTML]. *Topics in Cognitive Science*. PMID: 39587986

Kalra, S., Saroj, J., & Chhabra, A. (2025). Data Protection and Encryption in Cloud Network Security: Security and Privacy in Cloud Network Security. Convergence of Cybersecurity and .... DOI: [HTML]DOI: 10.4018/979-8-3693-6859-6.ch017

Kelly, C., Karthikesalingam, A., Suleyman, M., Corrado, G. S., & King, D. (2019). Key challenges for delivering clinical impact with artificial intelligence. In Medicine, B. M. C. (Ed.), *Issue 1). BioMed Central* (Vol. 17)., DOI: 10.1186/s12916-019-1426-2

Keshta, I. & Odeh, A. (2021). Security and privacy of electronic health records: Concerns and challenges. Egyptian Informatics Journal. https://doi.org/ sciencedirect.comDOI: 10.1016/j.eij.2020.07.003

Khasawneh, M. A. S. (2023). The Potential of Ai in Facilitating Cross-Cultural Communication Through Translation. [namibian-studies.com]. *Journal ofNamibian Studies: History Politics Culture*, *37*, 107–130.

Khatiwada, P., Yang, B., Lin, J. C., & Blobel, B. (2024). Patient-Generated Health Data (PGHD): Understanding, Requirements, Challenges, and Existing Techniques for Data Security and Privacy. Journal of Personalized Medicine, 14(3), 282. https://doi.org/ mdpi.comDOI: 10.3390/jpm14030282

Komljenovic, J. (2022). The future of value in digitalised higher education: why data privacy should not be our biggest concern. Higher Education. https://doi.org/springer.comDOI: 10.1007/s10734-020-00639-7

Kuddus, K. (2022). *Artificial intelligence in language learning: Practices and prospects*. Advanced Analytics and Deep Learning Models. [HTML], DOI: 10.1002/9781119792437.ch1

Kulkarni, S., & Girish, G. N. (2024). *Navigating the Abyss–Illuminating Data Leakage Threats, Mitigations, and Future Horizons*. Cloud Security. [HTML], DOI: 10.1201/9781003455448-3

Landa Oregi, X. (2023). MLOps data ingestion pipeline for reciprocal benefit between customer and provider. aalto.fi

Leikas, J., Johri, A., Latvanen, M., Wessberg, N., & Hahto, A. (2022). Governing ethical AI transformation: a case study of AuroraAI. Frontiers in Artificial Intelligence, 5, 836557. https://doi.org/frontiersin.orgDOI: 10.3389/frai.2022.836557

Liang, Y. (2023). Balancing: The Effects of AI Tools in Educational Context. In Frontiers in Humanities and Social Sciences (Vol. 3, Issue 8, p. 7). https://doi.org/ DOI: 10.54691/fhss.v3i8.5531

Liyanage, U. P., & Ranaweera, N. D. (2023). Ethical considerations and potential risks in the deployment of large language models in diverse societal contexts. [vectoral.org]. *Journal of Computational Social Dynamics*, *8*(11), 15–25.

Lorè, F., Basile, P., Appice, A., de Gemmis, M., Malerba, D., & Semeraro, G. (2023). An AI framework to support decisions on GDPR compliance. Journal of Intelligent Information Systems, 61(2), 541-568. https://doi.org/springer.comDOI: 10.1007/s10844-023-00782-4

Lu, Q., Zhu, L., Whittle, J., & Xu, X. (2023). Responsible AI: Best Practices for Creating Trustworthy AI Systems. [HTML]

Malyuga, E. N. (2024). The language of corporate communication: Functional, pragmatic and cultural dimensions. [HTML]

Manning, L., Brewer, S., Craigon, P. J., Frey, J., Gutierrez, A., Jacobs, N., ... & Pearson, S. (2022). Artificial intelligence and ethics within the food sector: Developing a common language for technology adoption across the supply chain. Trends in Food Science & Technology, 125, 33-42. https://doi.org/ sciencedirect.comDOI: 10.1016/j.tifs.2022.04.025

Marinucci, L., Mazzuca, C., & Gangemi, A. (2023). Exposing implicit biases and stereotypes in human and artificial intelligence: state of the art and challenges with a focus on gender. AI & SOCIETY. https://doi.org/ springer.comDOI: 10.1007/s00146-022-01474-3

Matulewska, A., & Wagner, A. (2021). The multiplicity of third space of communication in law. International Journal for the Semiotics of Law-Revue internationale de Sémiotique juridique, 34(5), 1225-1243. https://doi.org/springer.comDOI: 10.1007/s11196-021-09855-5

Mengesha, Z., Heldreth, C., Lahav, M., Sublewski, J., & Tuennerman, E. (2021). "I don't think these devices are very culturally sensitive."—Impact of automated speech recognition errors on African Americans. Frontiers in Artificial Intelligence, 4, 725911. https://doi.org/frontiersin.orgDOI: 10.3389/frai.2021.725911

Meszaros, J., & Ho, C. (2021). AI research and data protection: Can the same rules apply for commercial and academic research under the GDPR? [HTML]. *Computer Law & Security Review*, *41*, 105532. Advance online publication. DOI: 10.1016/j.clsr.2021.105532

Mitchell, M. (2021). Abstraction and analogy-making in artificial intelligence. [PDF]. *Annals of the New York Academy of Sciences*, *1505*(1), 79–101. DOI: 10.1111/nyas.14619 PMID: 34173249

Mökander, J., Schuett, J., Kirk, H. R., & Floridi, L. (2023). Auditing large language models: a three-layered approach. AI and Ethics. https://doi.org/ springer.comDOI: 10.1007/s43681-023-00289-2

Moneus, A. M. & Sahari, Y. (2024). Artificial intelligence and human translation: A contrastive study based on legal texts. Heliyon. https://doi.org/cell.comDOI: 10.1016/j.heliyon.2024.e28106

Mor Barak, M. E., Luria, G., & Brimhall, K. C. (2022). What leaders say versus what they do: Inclusive leadership, policy-practice decoupling, and the anomaly of climate for inclusion. [HTML]. *Group & Organization Management*, *47*(4), 840–871. DOI: 10.1177/10596011211005916

Mughal, U. A., Seemab, S., Zaigham, M. S., Bhatti, A., & Khan, H. (2024). THE INTERSECTION OF LINGUISTICS AND ARTIFICIAL INTELLIGENCE: A CORPUS-BASED STUDY OF IDIOM TRANSLATION. [JALT]. *Journal of Applied Linguistics and TESOL*, *7*(4), 1453–1460. jalt.com.pk

Muldoon, J., Davis, P. E., Bendickson, J. S., McDowell, W. C., & Liguori, E. W. (2022). Paved with good intentions: Moral disengagement and social entrepreneurship. Journal of Innovation & Knowledge, 7(4), 100237. https://doi.org/ sciencedirect.comDOI: 10.1016/j.jik.2022.100237

Nadji, B. (2024). Data Security, Integrity, and Protection. [HTML]. *Data*, 59–83. Advance online publication. DOI: 10.1007/978-3-031-61117-9_4

Nagappa, A. N., & Naik, V. (2022). Patients: Gaps in Knowledge, Medication Errors, and Their Impact on Outcomes, Quality of Life, and Cost of Treatments. In Perspectives in Pharmacy Practice: Trends in Pharmaceutical Care (pp. 39-57). Singapore: Springer Singapore. https://doi.org/ [HTML]DOI: 10.1007/978-981-16-9213-0_4

Nanayakkara, N. D. G. T., Nanayakkara, G. A. S. Y., Karunanayaka, K. M. C. M., Kumara, C. P. T. K., & Karunanayake, N. (2024). Smart Cities, Secure Data: Navigating the Evolving Landscape of Data Protection Challenges. In Data Protection: The Wake of AI and Machine Learning (pp. 251-285). Cham: Springer Nature Switzerland. https://doi.org/ [HTML]DOI: 10.1007/978-3-031-76473-8_11

Naveen, P. & Trojovský, P. (2024). Overview and challenges of machine translation for contextually appropriate translations. Iscience. https://doi.org/cell.comDOI: 10.1016/j.isci.2024.110878

Nemani, P., Joel, Y. D., Vijay, P., & Liza, F. F. (2024). Gender bias in transformers: A comprehensive review of detection and mitigation strategies. Natural Language Processing Journal, 6, 100047. https://doi.org/sciencedirect.comDOI: 10.1016/j.nlp.2023.100047

Pandey, N. K., Kumar, K., Saini, G., & Mishra, A. K. (2023). Security issues and challenges in cloud of things-based applications for industrial automation. Annals of Operations Research. https://doi.org/springer.comDOI: 10.1007/s10479-023-05285-7

Park, P. S., Goldstein, S., O'Gara, A., Chen, M., & Hendrycks, D. (2024). AI deception: A survey of examples, risks, and potential solutions. Patterns. https://doi.org/cell.comDOI: 10.1016/j.patter.2024.100988

Patsakis, C. & Lykousas, N. (2023). Man vs the machine in the struggle for effective text anonymisation in the age of large language models. Scientific Reports. https://doi.org/nature.comDOI: 10.1038/s41598-023-42977-3

Petro anu, D. M., Pîrjan, A., & Tăbu că, A. (2023). Tracing the Influence of Large Language Models across the Most Impactful Scientific Works. Electronics. https://doi.org/mdpi.comDOI: 10.3390/electronics12244957

Pym, A. & Hao, Y. (2024). How to Augment Language Skills: Generative AI and Machine Translation in Language Learning and Translator Training. [HTML]

Ray, P. P. (2023). ChatGPT: A comprehensive review on background, applications, key challenges, bias, ethics, limitations and future scope. Internet of Things and Cyber-Physical Systems. https://doi.org/sciencedirect.comDOI: 10.1016/j.iotcps.2023.04.003

Saeed, M. M. A., Saeed, R. A., & Ahmed, Z. E. (2024). Data Security and Privacy in the Age of AI and Digital Twins. In Digital Twin Technology and AI Implementations in Future-Focused Businesses (pp. 99-124). IGI Global. DOI: [HTML]DOI: 10.4018/979-8-3693-1818-8.ch008

Samantray, K., İZGİ, F. D., Ocampo, M. B., Dehghan, M., Mohammadpour, S., Siriphaprapagon, Y., ... & Babu, S. D. (2024). The Power of Words in AI-Driven World: Exploring the Interplay of Language, Culture, and Communication. SKETSAMEDIA. [HTML]

Santos, O., & Radanliev, P. (2024). *Beyond the Algorithm: AI.* Security, Privacy, and Ethics. [HTML]

Sarker, I. H. (2021). Machine learning: Algorithms, real-world applications and research directions. SN computer science. https://doi.org/ springer.comDOI: 10.1007/s42979-021-00592-x

Sarker, I. H. (2022). AI-based modeling: techniques, applications and research issues towards automation, intelligent and smart systems. SN Computer Science. https://doi.org/ springer.comDOI: 10.1007/s42979-022-01043-x

Schmitt, M., & Koutroumpis, P. (2025). Cyber Shadows: Neutralizing Security Threats with AI and Targeted Policy Measures. In IEEE Transactions on Artificial Intelligence (p. 1). Institute of Electrical and Electronics Engineers. https://doi.org/ DOI: 10.1109/TAI.2025.3527398

Sharma, S., Rawal, R., & Shah, D. (2023). Addressing the challenges of AI-based telemedicine: Best practices and lessons learned [Review of Addressing the challenges of AI-based telemedicine: Best practices and lessons learned]. Journal of Education and Health Promotion, 12(1). Medknow. https://doi.org/DOI: 10.4103/jehp.jehp_402_23

Sinclair-Palm, J., & Chokly, K. (2023). 'It'sa giant faux pas': Exploring young trans people's beliefs about deadnaming and the term deadname. [HTML]. *Journal of LGBT Youth*, *20*(2), 370–389. Advance online publication. DOI: 10.1080/19361653.2022.2076182

Siregar, I. (2023). The Role of Language in a Dynamic Situation of Globalization. Britain International of Linguistics Arts and Education (BIoLAE) Journal, 5(1), 49-59. https://doi.org/biarjournal.comDOI: 10.33258/biolae.v5i1.868

Sun, Y., Sheng, D., Zhou, Z., & Wu, Y. (2024). AI hallucination: towards a comprehensive classification of distorted information in artificial intelligence-generated content. Humanities and Social Sciences Communications, 11(1), 1-14. https://doi.org/nature.comDOI: 10.1057/s41599-024-03811-x

Swiatek, L., Vujnovic, M., Galloway, C., & Kruckeberg, D. (2023). Artificial intelligence, strategic communicators and activism. [HTML]

Tian, X. (2024). Personalized translator training in the era of digital intelligence: Opportunities, challenges, and prospects. Heliyon. https://doi.org/ cell.comDOI: 10.1016/j.heliyon.2024.e39354

Timmons, A. C., Duong, J. B., Simo Fiallo, N., Lee, T., Vo, H. P. Q., Ahle, M. W., ... & Chaspari, T. (2023). A call to action on assessing and mitigating bias in artificial intelligence applications for mental health. Perspectives on Psychological Science, 18(5), 1062-1096. https://doi.org/sagepub.comDOI: 10.1177/17456916221134490

Tiribelli, S., Pansoni, S., Frontoni, E., & Giovanola, B. (2024). Ethics of Artificial Intelligence for Cultural Heritage: Opportunities and Challenges. IEEE Transactions on Technology and Society. https://doi.org/ieee.orgDOI: 10.1109/TTS.2024.3432407

Tomalin, M., Byrne, B., Concannon, S., Saunders, D., & Ullmann, S. (2021). The practical ethics of bias reduction in machine translation: Why domain adaptation is better than data debiasing. Ethics and Information Technology, 1-15. https://doi.org/ springer.comDOI: 10.1007/s10676-021-09583-1

Van Giffen, B., Herhausen, D., & Fahse, T. (2022). Overcoming the pitfalls and perils of algorithms: A classification of machine learning biases and mitigation methods. Journal of Business Research. https://doi.org/sciencedirect.comDOI: 10.1016/j.jbusres.2022.01.076

Varela, D. T. (2024). Diplomacy in the Age of AI: Challenges and Opportunities. Journal of Artificial Intelligence General science (JAIGS) ISSN: 3006-4023, 2(1), 101-128. boulibrary.com

Vieira, L. N., O'Hagan, M., & O'Sullivan, C. (2021). Understanding the societal impacts of machine translation: a critical review of the literature on medical and legal use cases. Information, Communication & Society, 24(11), 1515-1532. https://doi.org/tandfonline.comDOI: 10.1080/1369118X.2020.1776370

Wang, C., Zhang, J., Lassi, N., & Zhang, X. (2022). Privacy protection in using artificial intelligence for healthcare: Chinese regulation in comparative perspective. Healthcare. https://doi.org/ mdpi.comDOI: 10.3390/healthcare10101878

Wang, S., & Luo, H. (2021). Exploring the meanings and grammatical functions of idioms in teaching Chinese as a second language. [HTML]. *International Journal of Applied Linguistics*, *31*(2), 283–300. Advance online publication. DOI: 10.1111/ijal.12334

Wang, Y. (2023). Artificial Intelligence technologies in college English translation teaching. Journal of psycholinguistic research. https://doi.org/springer.comDOI: 10.1007/s10936-023-09960-5

Weber-Lewerenz, B. (2021). … digital responsibility (CDR) in construction engineering—ethical guidelines for the application of digital transformation and artificial intelligence (AI) in user practice. SN Applied Sciences. https://doi.org/springer.comDOI: 10.1007/s42452-021-04776-1

Williamson, S. M. & Prybutok, V. (2024). Balancing privacy and progress: a review of privacy challenges, systemic oversight, and patient perceptions in AI-driven healthcare. Applied Sciences. https://doi.org/ mdpi.comDOI: 10.3390/app14020675

Woo, J. H., & Choi, H. (2021). Systematic Review for AI-based Language Learning Tools. In Journal of Digital Contents Society (Vol. 22, Issue 11, p. 1783). Digital Contents Society. https://doi.org/DOI: 10.9728/dcs.2021.22.11.1783

Xivuri, K. & Twinomurinzi, H. (2023). How AI developers can assure algorithmic fairness. Discover Artificial Intelligence. https://doi.org/springer.comDOI: 10.1007/s44163-023-00074-4

Yu, Y., Zhuang, Y., Zhang, J., Meng, Y., Ratner, A. J., Krishna, R., . . . Zhang, C. (2024). Large language model as attributed training data generator: A tale of diversity and bias. Advances in Neural Information Processing Systems, 36. neurips.cc

Zhai, C., Wibowo, S., & Li, L. D. (2024). Evaluating the AI dialogue System's intercultural, humorous, and empathetic dimensions in English language learning: A case study. Computers and Education: Artificial Intelligence. https://doi.org/sciencedirect.comDOI: 10.1016/j.caeai.2024.100262

Zhou, W. (2022). Diplomatic interpreting and risk analysis: A literary survey. International Journal of Translation and Interpretation Studies, 2(2), 19-31. DOI: al-kindipublisher.comDOI: 10.32996/ijtis

Zou, R., Chang, W., Gao, S., & Qin, S. (2022). Strategies for improving the quality of computer-assisted translation based on internet. In International Journal of Advanced Academic Studies (Vol. 4, Issue 4, p. 156). https://doi.org/DOI: 10.33545/27068919.2022.v4.i4c.890

Compilation of References

Abdedaim, K. (2023). Cultural implications of AI-powered language translation: In Proceedings of the 3rd International Conference on Translation and Technological Developments. Elwahrani Academy for Scientific Studies and Cultural Interaction. https://www.researchgate.net/publication/374700791

Abdelali, Z. A. I. D., & Bennoudi, H. (2023). AI vs. Human Translators: Navigating the Complex World of Religious Texts and Cultural Sensitivity. International Journal of Linguistics, Literature and Translation, 6(11), 173-182. DOI: al-kindipublisher.comDOI: 10.32996/ijllt

Abu-Rayyash, H. (2024). AI meets comedy: Viewers' reactions to GPT-4 generated humor translation. Ampersand. https://doi.org/ sciencedirect.comDOI: 10.1016/j.amper.2023.100162

Acosta, J. N., Falcone, G. J., Rajpurkar, P., & Topol, E. J. (2022). Multimodal biomedical AI. *Nature Medicine*, *28*(9), 1773–1784. DOI: 10.1038/s41591-022-01981-2 PMID: 36109635

Adiel, M. A. E., Elsadig, M. A., Altigani, A., Mohamed, Y. A., Ahmed, B. E. S., & Elhassan, S. M. O. (2023). Accuracy and problems of machine-based translation in contrast to human-based translation when rendering health awareness texts versus poetry texts. *Academic Journal of Interdisciplinary Studies*, *12*(4), 223–231. DOI: 10.36941/ajis-2023-0108

Agarwal, U., Gupta, R., & Saranya, G. (2024, May). Advancing Multilingual Communication NLP based Translational Speech to Speech Dialogue System for Indian Languages. In *2024 International Conference on Electronics, Computing, Communication and Control Technology (ICECCC)* (pp. 1-6). IEEE.

Ahammad, T., Rahman, M. M., & Islam, M. S. (2024). Advances in Statistical Machine Translation: Techniques and Applications. *Journal of Computational Linguistics*.

Ahmed, N., Saha, A. K., Al Noman, M. A., Jim, J. R., Mridha, M. F., & Kabir, M. M. (2024). Deep learning-based natural language processing in human–agent interaction: Applications, advancements, and challenges. *Natural Language Processing Journal*, *9*, 100112. DOI: 10.1016/j.nlp.2024.100112

Ai, J. (2020). [Popular evolution of female writing in network literature]. *Writing*, (4), 61–65. DOI: 10.19867/j.cnki.writing.2020.04.007

Aini, R. P., Yuliati, Y., Febriyanto, B., & Safira, R. F. (2024, November). Meretas Paradigma Baru: Artificial Intelligence (AI) Dalam Pembelajaran IPA Di Sekolah Dasar. In *Prosiding Seminar Nasional Pendidikan* (Vol. 6, pp. 91-104).

Al Saadi, A., & Awashreh, R. (2024). Enhancing the performance of translation graduates through training: A proposed practical model. In N. Mansour & L. M. Bujosa Vadell (Eds.), Finance and law in the metaverse world (pp. 295–308). Contributions to Finance and Accounting. Springer. DOI: 10.1007/978-3-031-67547-8_19

Al Sharairi, R. (2025). Review paper on the evolving role of human translators in the age of AI. *Pakistan Journal of Life and Social Sciences*, *23*(1), 2672–2679. DOI: 10.57239/PJLSS-2025-23.1.00210

Albaroudi, E., Mansouri, T., & Alameer, A. (2024). A comprehensive review of AI techniques for addressing algorithmic bias in job hiring. *AI*, *5*(1), 383–404. DOI: 10.3390/ai5010019

Albir, A. H., & Molina, L. (2002). Translation techniques revisited: A dynamic and Functionalist approach: A dynamic and functionalist approach. *Meta: Journal Des Traducteurs = Translators'. Journal*, *47*(4), 498–512. https://dialnet.unirioja.es/servlet/articulo?codigo=2809718

Albulescu, C. T., Tiwari, A. K., & Kyophilavong, P. (2021). Nonlinearities and chaos: A new analysis of CEE stock markets. *Mathematics*, *9*(7), 707. DOI: 10.3390/math9070707

Aldelaa, A. S., & Malkawi, M. K. M. (2024). Investigating problems related to the translation of idiomatic expressions in the Arabic novels using neural machine translation. *Theory and Practice in Language Studies*, *14*(1), 71–78. DOI: 10.17507/tpls.1401.08

Alhaj, A. M. (2024). The impact of machine translation on the development of tourism translation from the perspectives of translators and experts in Saudi Arabia. *Theory and Practice in Language Studies*, *14*(4), 1274–1283. DOI: 10.17507/tpls.1404.35

Alharazi, A. F. A., Alhebshi, S. H. S., & Taleb, N. R. M. (2024). Leveraging AI-Powered Neural Machine Translation to Bridge the Gap: Translating Arabic Islamic Terminology into English. *Pakistan Journal of Life and Social Sciences*, *22*(2), 7150–7164. DOI: 10.57239/PJLSS-2024-22.2.00541

Alharbi, W. (2024). Future Translators' Linguistic and Non-linguistic Competencies and Skills in The Age of Neural Machine Translation and Artificial Intelligence: A Content Analysis. *International Journal of Linguistics. Literature and Translation*, *7*(4), 124–143. DOI: 10.32996/ijllt.2024.7.4.16

Alhitmi, H. K., Mardiah, A., Al-Sulaiti, K. I., & Abbas, J. (2024). Data security and privacy concerns of AI-driven marketing in the context of economics and business field: an exploration into possible solutions. Cogent Business & Management, 11(1), 2393743. https://doi.org/ tandfonline.comDOI: 10.1080/23311975.2024.2393743

Ali, K., Ambreen, S., Begum, R., & Sadiq, S., ul Haq, T., & Sahar, N. (2023). Exploring Translation Strategies For Idiomatic Expressions: A Study Of Sadat Hassan Manto's Short Stories "Khol Do" And "License". *Journal of Positive School Psychology*, *7*(6), 708–715.

Ali, N. (2023). Translating cultural identity: Skopos theory in the translation of Abdullah Al Faisal's Revolution of Doubts. *International Journal of English Literature and Social Sciences*, *8*(5), 1–9. DOI: 10.22161/ijels.85.26

Al-Kaabi, M. H., AlQbailat, N. M., Badah, A., Ismail, I. A., & Hicham, K. B. (2024). Examining the Cultural Connotations in Human and Machine Translations: A Corpus Study of Naguib Mahfouz's Zuqāq al-Midaqq. *Journal of Language Teaching and Research*, *15*(3), 707–718. DOI: 10.17507/jltr.1503.03

Alkaeed, M., Qayyum, A., & Qadir, J. (2024). Privacy preservation in Artificial Intelligence and Extended Reality (AI-XR) metaverses: A survey. [PDF]. *Journal of Network and Computer Applications*, *231*, 103989. DOI: 10.1016/j.jnca.2024.103989

Alkanaani, M. (2024). Navigating ethics in AI-driven translation for a human-centric future. *Academia Open*, *9*(2), 13. DOI: 10.21070/acopen.9.2024.9407

Al-kfairy, M., Mustafa, D., Kshetri, N., Insiew, M., & Alfandi, O. (2024). Ethical challenges and solutions of generative AI: An interdisciplinary perspective. Informatics. https://doi.org/ mdpi.comDOI: 10.3390/informatics11030058

Alkhawaja, L. (2024). Unveiling the new frontier: ChatGPT-3 powered translation for Arabic-English language pairs. *Theory and Practice in Language Studies*, *14*(2), 347–357. DOI: 10.17507/tpls.1402.05

Alkhouri, K. I. (2024). The role of artificial intelligence in the study of the psychology of religion. Religions. https://doi.org/mdpi.comDOI: 10.3390/rel15030290

Almaaytah, S. A., & Alzobidy, S. A. (2023). Challenges in Rendering Arabic text to English using Machine Translation: A Systematic Literature Review. *IEEE Access : Practical Innovations, Open Solutions*, *11*, 94772–94779. DOI: 10.1109/ACCESS.2023.3309642

Almaktary, H. (2025). Reflections on Translating Poetry through ChatGPT: Insights from Arabic, English, and French. *Journal of English Studies in Arabia Felix*, *4*(1), 1–12. DOI: 10.56540/jesaf.v4i1.108

Alowedi, N. A., & Al-Ahdal, A. A. M. H. (2023). Artificial Intelligence based Arabic-to-English machine versus human translation of poetry: An analytical study of outcomes. *Journal of Namibian Studies: History Politics Culture*, *33*, 1523–1538.

Alqudsi, A., Omar, N., & Shaker, K. (2014). Arabic machine translation: A survey. *Artificial Intelligence Review*, *42*(4), 549–572. DOI: 10.1007/s10462-012-9351-1

Al-Romany, T. A. H., & Kadhim, M. J. (2024). Artificial intelligence impact on human translation: Legal texts as a case study. *International Journal of Linguistics Literature & Translation*, *7*(5), 89–95. DOI: 10.32996/ijllt.2024.7.5.11

Alsaadi, A., & Awashreh, R. (2025). Practical university training impact on job performance of translation graduates in Oman. *Forum for Linguistic Studies*, *7*(2), 786–796. DOI: 10.30564/fls.v7i2.8306

Alsajri, A., Salman, H. A., & Steiti, A. (2024). Generative Models in Natural Language Processing: A Comparative Study of ChatGPT and Gemini. *Deleted Journal*, *2024*, 134–145. DOI: 10.58496/BJAI/2024/015

AlSaleem, B. I. (2024). Evaluating the Role of Machine Translation in Enhancing the Quality of Scientific Publishing in Arabic: A Comparative Study with Human Translation.

Alsulaimani, B., & Islam, A. (2022). Impact of 4IR technology and its impact on the current deployment. *International Journal of Computer Science and Information Technologies*, *14*(4), 53–67. DOI: 10.5121/ijcsit.2022.14405

Alwakeel, A. M. (2021). An overview of fog computing and edge computing security and privacy issues. Sensors. https://doi.org/mdpi.comDOI: 10.3390/s21248226

Al-Wasy, B. Q., Alkodimi, K., & Alqahtani, O. O. A. (2024). Human-AI collaboration in translation and back translation of literary texts. *The Journal of Social Studies*, *30*(2), 2024. DOI: 10.20428/jss.v30i2.2404

Amaro, V., & Pires, M. J. (2024). Found in translation, lost in education: Artificial intelligence's impacts on translation tertiary education in Macao. *Asian Education and Development Studies*, *13*(4), 269–281. DOI: 10.1108/AEDS-01-2024-0012

Amini, M., Ravindran, L., & Lee, K.-F. (2024). Implications of using AI in translation studies: Trends, challenges, and future direction. *Asian Journal of Research in Education and Social Sciences*, *6*(1), 740–754.

Amini, M., Ravindran, L., & Lee, K.-F. (2024). Implications of using AI in translation studies: Trends, challenges, and future directions. *Asian Journal of Research in Education and Social Sciences*, *6*(1), 740–754. DOI: 10.55057/ajress.2024.6.1.67

Anderson, C., Vandenberg, B., Hauser, C., Johansson, A., & Galloway, N. (2024). Semantic coherence dynamics in large language models through layered syntax-aware memory retention mechanism. *authorea*.com DOI: 10.22541/au.173016320.04754825/v1

Angel, N. A., Ravindran, D., Vincent, P. D. R., Srinivasan, K., & Hu, Y. C. (2021). Recent advances in evolving computing paradigms: Cloud, edge, and fog technologies. Sensors, 22(1), 196. https://doi.org/ mdpi.comDOI: 10.3390/s22010196

Angermeyer, P. S. (2021). Beyond translation equivalence: Advocating pragmatic equality before the law. Journal of Pragmatics. https://doi.org/ sciencedirect.comDOI: 10.1016/j.pragma.2020.12.022

Arachchige, I. A. N., Suraweera, S., & Herath, D. (2022). Transformer-based Language models for the Identification of Idiomatic Expressions. In *Proceedings of the International Conference EUROPHRAS* 2022 (short papers, posters and MUMTTT workshop contributions) (ss. 119-127). Incoma Ltd. Shoumen, Bulgaria. https://doi.org/DOI: 10.26615/978-954-452-080-9_015

Arnold, D., Balkan, L., Meijer, S., Humphreys, R. L., & Sadler, L. (1994). *Machine translation: An introductory guide.*

Arsad, A. Z., Sebastian, G., Hannan, M. A., Ker, P. J., Rahman, M. S. A., Mansor, M., & Lipu, M. S. H. (2021). Solid state switching control methods: A bibliometric analysis for future directions. *Electronics (Basel)*, *10*(16), 1944. DOI: 10.3390/electronics10161944

Ashraf, M. (2024). Innovations and challenges in neural machine translation: A review. [IJSR]. *International Journal of Science and Research (Raipur, India)*, *13*(10), 656–662. DOI: 10.21275/SR241008113336

Aslanyan, A. (2021). DANCING ON ROPES: Translators and the Balance of History. [HTML]

Asrifan, A., Rusmayadi, R., Hasmawaty, H., Nirwana, N., Sivaraja, S., & Dewi, A. C. (2025). Synergizing Human and Machine: Innovations in Knowledge Discovery and Management. In AI and Green Technology Applications in Society (pp. 249-282). IGI Global Scientific Publishing. DOI: [HTML]DOI: 10.4018/979-8-3693-9879-1.ch010

Asscher, O. (2023). The position of machine translation in translation studies a definitional perspective. *Translation Spaces*, *12*(1), 1–20. DOI: 10.1075/ts.22035.ass

Awashreh, R. (2024). Be Aware: Navigating Challenges in AI-Driven Higher Education. *The International Journal of Interdisciplinary Educational Studies*, *20*(1), 203–218. DOI: 10.18848/2327-011X/CGP/v20i01/203-218

Awashreh, R. (2024b). Omani private universities: Debates between progress in human development but weak education quality. *The International Journal of Educational Organization and Leadership*, *32*(1), 1–15. DOI: 10.18848/2329-1656/CGP/v32i01/1-15

Awashreh, R. (2025). AI in higher education: AI ethics, quality assurance, and academic integrity. In *Optimizing leadership and governance in higher education* (pp. 203–232). IGI Global., DOI: 10.4018/979-8-3693-3534-5.ch006

Awashreh, R., & AlGhunaimi, H. (2024). Navigating burnout in the public sector: Strategies for enhancing employee well-being and organizational performance. *Evolutionary Studies in Imaginative Culture*, *211*, 211–225. https://esiculture.com/index.php/esiculture/article/view/1855. DOI: 10.70082/esiculture.vi.1855

Awashreh, R., & Ramachandran, B. (2025). A study on ethical implementation of AI in collegiate studies using fuzzy implication. *Pakistan Journal of Life and Social Sciences*, *23*(1), 3998–4013. DOI: 10.57239/PJLSS-2025-23.1.00317

Aziza, S. (2024). Artificial Intelligence in Translation: Benefits and Drawbacks. International Journal of Scientific Trends. scientifictrends.org

Azizan, N., Smith, R., Cooper, V., & Abu Bakar, N. (2018). Qualitative Content Analysis: A Case Study of a Malaysian Government Education Website. *Malaysian Journal of Science Health & Technology*, *1*(1). Advance online publication. DOI: 10.33102/mjosht.v1i1.14

BaHammam, A. S. (2023). Balancing innovation and integrity: The role of AI in research and scientific writing. *Nature and Science of Sleep*, •••, 1153–1156.

Bahdanau, D., Cho, K., & Bengio, Y. (2014). Neural machine translation by jointly learning to align and translate. *arXiv preprint arXiv:1409.0473*. https://arxiv.org/abs/1409.0473

Bahdanau, D., Cho, K., & Bengio, Y. (2016). Neural machine translation by jointly learning to align and translate. *arXiv preprint arXiv:1409.0473.*

Bahdanau, D., Cho, K., & Bengio, Y. (2016). Neural machine translation by jointly learning to align and translate. *Arxiv.Org*. https://www.proquest.com/publiccontent/docview/2079082715?pq-origsite=primo&accountid=10134

Bahdanau, D., Cho, K., & Bengio, Y. (2015). Neural Machine Translation by Jointly Learning to Align and Translate. *Proceedings of the 3rd International Conference on Learning Representations (ICLR 2015).*

Bahroun, Z., Anane, C., Ahmed, V., & Zacca, A. (2023). Transforming education: A comprehensive review of generative artificial intelligence in educational settings through bibliometric and content analysis. *Sustainability (Basel), 15*(17), 12983. DOI: 10.3390/su151712983

Baigorri-Jalón, J., Fernández-Sánchez, M. M., & Payàs, G. (2021, November). Historical developments in conference interpreting: An overview. In *The Routledge handbook of conference interpreting* (pp. 9–18). Routledge. [HTML], DOI: 10.4324/9780429297878-3

Bai, W. (2024). Advancements and challenges in AI-driven creative translation: A comprehensive analysis. *Applied and Computational Engineering, 82*(1), 82–87. DOI: 10.54254/2755-2721/82/20240937

Bajčić, M., & Golenko, D. (2024). Applying large language models in legal translation: The state-of-the-art. [JLL]. *International Journal of Language & Law, 13*, 171–196. DOI: 10.14762/jll.2024.171

Baker, M. (1992). *In other words: A coursebook on translation.* Routledge.

Baker, M. (1992). *Other Words: A Coursebook on Translation.* Routledge.

Baker, M. (2011). *In Other Words: A Coursebook on Translation* (2nd ed.). Routledge. DOI: 10.4324/9780203832929

Balasubramaniam, N., Kauppinen, M., Rannisto, A., Hiekkanen, K., & Kujala, S. (2023). Transparency and explainability of AI systems: From ethical guidelines to requirements. Information and Software Technology, 159, 107197. https://doi.org/sciencedirect.comDOI: 10.1016/j.infsof.2023.107197

Bañeres, D., Rodríguez, M. E., Guerrero-Roldán, A. E., & Karadeniz, A. (2020). An early warning system to detect at-risk students in online higher education. *Applied Sciences (Basel, Switzerland), 10*(13), 4427. DOI: 10.3390/app10134427

Barbosa, A., Whiting, S., Simmonds, P., Scotini Moreno, R., Mendes, R., & Breda, J. (2020). Physical activity and academic achievement: An umbrella review. *International Journal of Environmental Research and Public Health, 17*(16), 5972. DOI: 10.3390/ijerph17165972 PMID: 32824593

Barman, S. (2024). Digital diplomacy: The influence of digital platforms on global diplomacy and foreign policy. VIDYA - A Journal of Gujarat University, 3(1), 61-75. DOI: 10.47413/vidya.v3i1.304

Barrault, L., Chung, Y. A., Meglioli, M. C., Dale, D., Dong, N., Duquenne, P. A., . . . Wang, S. (2023). SeamlessM4T-Massively Multilingual & Multimodal Machine Translation. https://arxiv.org/pdf/2308.11596

Barriga, N. A., & Besoaín, F. (2020). Artificial intelligence and mobile programming courses for a video game development program in Chile. *Computing in Science & Engineering, 22*(4), 17–25. DOI: 10.1109/MCSE.2020.2986758

Basak, S., Agrawal, H., Jena, S., Gite, S., Bachute, M., Pradhan, B., & Assiri, M. (2022). Challenges and limitations in speech recognition technology: A critical review of speech signal processing algorithms, tools and systems. *Computer Modeling in Engineering & Sciences, 135*(2), 1–37. DOI: 10.32604/cmes.2022.021755

Bates, D. W., Levine, D., Syrowatka, A., Kuznetsova, M., Craig, K. J. T., Rui, A., ... & Rhee, K. (2021). The potential of artificial intelligence to improve patient safety: a scoping review. NPJ digital medicine, 4(1), 54. https://doi.org/nature.comDOI: 10.1038/s41746-021-00423-6

Baziotis, C., Mathur, P., & Hasler, E. (2022). Automatic evaluation and analysis of idioms in neural machine translation. arXiv preprint arXiv:2210.04545.

Bécue, A., Praça, I., & Gama, J. (2021). Artificial intelligence, cyber-threats and Industry 4.0: Challenges and opportunities. [HTML]. *Artificial Intelligence Review, 54*(5), 3849–3886. Advance online publication. DOI: 10.1007/s10462-020-09942-2

Bekouche, M. F. (2024, November). Integrating artificial intelligence in translation: Analyzing technologies, ethical implications, and the future of human-AI collaboration. DOI: 10.13140/RG.2.2.28826.66242

Belenguer, L. (2022). AI bias: exploring discriminatory algorithmic decision-making models and the application of possible machine-centric solutions adapted from the pharmaceutical …. AI and Ethics. https://doi.org/ springer.comDOI: 10.1007/s43681-022-00138-8

Belinkov, Y., & Glass, J. (2019). Analysis methods in neural language processing: A survey. *Transactions of the Association for Computational Linguistics*, *7*, 49–72. DOI: 10.1162/tacl_a_00254

Bella, G., Byambadorj, E., Chandrashekar, Y., Batsuren, K., Cheema, D. A., & Giunchiglia, F. (2022). Language diversity: Visible to humans, exploitable by machines. arXiv preprint arXiv:2203.04723.

Bella, G., Helm, P., Koch, G., & Giunchiglia, F. (2024, June). Tackling Language Modelling Bias in Support of Linguistic Diversity. In The 2024 ACM Conference on Fairness, Accountability, and Transparency (pp. 562-572). hal.science DOI: 10.1145/3630106.3658925

Ben Sada, A., Naouri, A., Khelloufi, A., Dhelim, S., & Ning, H. (2023). A context-aware edge computing framework for smart internet of things. Future Internet. https://doi.org/mdpi.comDOI: 10.3390/fi15050154

Bender, E. M., Gebru, T., McMillan-Major, A., & Shmitchell, S. (2021). On the dangers of stochastic parrots: Can language models Be too big? . *Proceedings of the 2021 ACM Conference on Fairness, Accountability, and Transparency*, 610–623. DOI: 10.1145/3442188.3445922

Benmansour, M., & Hdouch, Y. (2023). The role of the latest technologies in the translation industry. Emirati Journal of Education and Literatures, 1(2), 31–36. https://www.emiratesscholar.com/system/publish/061223101243907.pdf

Berman, R. C., & Tyyskä, V. (2011). A critical reflection on the use of translators/interpreters in a qualitative cross-language research project. *International Journal of Qualitative Methods*, *10*(2), 178–190. DOI: 10.1177/160940691101000206

Bernardini, S. (Ed.). (2020). *Language service provision in the 21st century: challenges, opportunities and educational perspectives for translation studies*. Bologna: Bologna University Press (BUP).

Betal, A. K. (2023). Enhancing second language acquisition through artificial intelligence (AI): Current insights and future directions. *Journal for Research Scholars and Professionals of English Language Teaching*, *7*(39). Advance online publication. DOI: 10.54850/jrspelt.7.39.003

BeTranslated. (2023). Machine Translation with Natural Language Processing.

Bhadauria, A. S., Shukla, M., Kumar, P., & Dwivedi, N. (2023, November). Attention-Based Neural Machine Translation for Multilingual Communication. In International Conference on Trends in Computational and Cognitive Engineering (pp. 129-142). Singapore: Springer Nature Singapore. https://doi.org/ [HTML]DOI: 10.1007/978-981-97-1923-5_10

Bhadauria, A. S., Shukla, M., Kumar, P., & Dwivedi, N. (2023). Attention-based neural machine translation for multilingual communication. *International Conference on Trends in Computational and Cognitive Engineering*, 129–142.

Bhargava, C., & Sharma, P. K. (2021). *Artificial intelligence: Fundamentals and Applications*. CRC Press. DOI: 10.1201/9781003095910

Bharti, T., Ojha, S. C., & Tiwari, A. K. (2022). Interplay of workplace sustainability, sustainable work performance, optimism, and resilience: The moderating role of green creativity in luxury hotels. *Sustainability (Basel)*, *14*(22), 15097. DOI: 10.3390/su142215097

Bianchi, F., Fornaciari, T., Hovy, D., & Nozza, D. (2023). Gender and age bias in commercial machine translation. In Moniz, H., & Parra Escartín, C. (Eds.), *Towards Responsible Machine Translation: Ethical and Legal Considerations in Machine Translation* (pp. 159–184). Springer International Publishing., DOI: 10.1007/978-3-031-14689-3_9

Biswas, P., Neogi, S. G., Arockiam, D., & Mitra, A. (2024, March). The Importance of Multi-Lingual Sentiment Analysis in Digital Marketing. In 2024 11th International Conference on Reliability, Infocom Technologies and Optimization (Trends and Future Directions)(ICRITO) (pp. 1-8). IEEE. https://doi.org/ [HTML]DOI: 10.1109/ICRITO61523.2024.10522115

Bogina, V., Hartman, A., Kuflik, T., & Shulner-Tal, A. (2022). Educating software and AI stakeholders about algorithmic fairness, accountability, transparency and ethics. International Journal of Artificial Intelligence in Education, 1-26. https://doi.org/springer.comDOI: 10.1007/s40593-021-00248-0

Bojar, O., Chatterjee, R., Federmann, C., Graham, Y., Haddow, B., Huck, M., & Zampieri, M. (2016). *Proceedings of the First Conference on Machine Translation (WMT)*. Berlin: Association for Computational Linguistics.

Bo, L. (2023). *Ethical issues for literary translation in the era of artificial intelligence*. Babel-Revue Internationale De La Traduction-International Journal of Translation., DOI: 10.1075/babel.00334.li

Boulanger, A. (2024). The pros and cons of machine translation and AI in legal translation. McGill University, School of Continuing Studies. https://www.mcgill.ca/continuingstudies/article/pros-and-cons-machine-translation-and-ai-legal-translation

Boulanger, A. M. (2024). The use of machine translation and AI in medical translation: Pros and cons. *Medical Writing*, *33*(1), 62–65. DOI: 10.56012/fcbh4324

Bowker, L. (2020). Machine Translation and the Future of Language Professions. pp. 262-278. In Koskinen, K., & Pokorn, N.K. (Eds.). (2020). *The Routledge Handbook of Translation and Ethics*. Routledge. DOI: 10.4324/9781003127970

Bowker, L., & Fisher, D. (2010). Computer-aided translation. In Y. Gambier & L. Van Doorslaer (Eds.), *Handbook of Translation Studies* (Vol. 1, pp. 60–65). John Benjamins Publishing Company. DOI: 10.1075/hts.1.comp2

Bowker, L. (2023). *De-mystifying translation: Introducing Translation to Non-translators*. Taylor & Francis. DOI: 10.4324/9781003217718

Briva-Iglesias, V. (2024). Fostering human-centered, augmented machine translation: Analysing interactive post-editing (Doctoral dissertation, Dublin City University). Advisor: S.

Brown, P. F., Cocke, J., Pietra, S. A. D., Della Pietra, V. J., Jelinek, F., Lafferty, J. D., Mercer, R. L., & Roossin, P. S. (1990). A statistical approach to machine translation. *Computational Linguistics - Association for Computational Linguistics, 16*(2), 79–85.

Brown, P. F., Della Pietra, S. A., Della Pietra, V. J., & Mercer, R. L. (1993). The mathematics of statistical machine translation: Parameter estimation. *Computational Linguistics*, *19*(2), 263–311.

Brown, S., & Vacca, F. (2022). Cultural sustainability in fashion: reflections on craft and sustainable development models. Sustainability: Science. *Practice and Policy*, *18*(1), 590–600.

Brown, T. B., Mann, B., Ryder, N., Subbiah, M., Kaplan, J., Dhariwal, P., & Amodei, D. (2020). Language models are few-shot learners. *arXiv*. Retrieved from https://arxiv.org/abs/2005.14165

Buch, A., Eagleman, D., & Grosenick, L. (2022). Engineering diplomacy: How AI and human augmentation could remake the art of foreign relations. *Perspective*, *2*, 25.

Buden, B., Nowotny, S., Simon, S., Bery, A., & Cronin, M. (2009). Cultural translation: An introduction to the problem, and Responses. *Translation Studies*, 2(2), 196–219. DOI: 10.1080/14781700902937730

Buhler, H. (1979). Supersentential semantics and translation. *Meta, 24*(4), 451–458. DOI: 10.7202/002177ar

Burazer, L. (2013). Examining the Differences in Assessing Quality of Translations and Acceptability of Texts. *ELOPE, 10*(2), 127–137. DOI: 10.4312/elope.10.2.127-137

Cai, Z., Haslett, D. A., Duan, X., Wang, S., & Pickering, M. J. (2023). Does ChatGPT resemble humans in language use? *arXiv Preprint.*https://doi.org//arXiv.2303.08014 .DOI: 10.48550

California School Boards Association. (2023).AI has arrived: Task force will guide how artificial intelligence can be used in schools (Publication). Retrieved from https://publications.csba.org.) *Lardieri*, A. (2023, January 4).

Calvo-Ferrer, J. R. (2024). Can you tell the difference? A study of human vs machine-translated subtitles. *Perspectives-Studies in Translation Theory and Practice, 32*(6), 1115–1132. DOI: 10.1080/0907676X.2023.2268149

Campino, J. (2024). Unleashing the transformers: NLP models detect AI writing in education. In Journal of Computers in Education. Springer Science+Business Media. https://doi.org/DOI: 10.1007/s40692-024-00325-y

Carvalho, G., Cabral, B., Pereira, V., & Bernardino, J. (2021). Edge computing: Current trends, research challenges and future directions. [HTML]. *Computing, 103*(5), 993–1023. Advance online publication. DOI: 10.1007/s00607-020-00896-5

Castelló-Sirvent, F., Roger-Monzó, V., & Gouveia-Rodrigues, R. (2024). Quo Vadis, University? A Roadmap for AI and Ethics in Higher Education. *Electronic Journal of e-Learning, 22*(6), 35–51. DOI: 10.34190/ejel.22.6.3267

Castilho, S., Gaspari, F., Moorkens, J., & Way, A. (2018). A comparative quality evaluation of PBSMT and NMT using professional translators. *Machine Translation, 32*(1-2), 97–110.

Cellina, M., Cè, M., Irmici, G., Ascenti, V., Caloro, E., Bianchi, L., Pellegrino, G., D'Amico, N., Papa, S., & Carrafiello, G. (2022). Artificial intelligence in emergency radiology: Where are we going? *Diagnostics (Basel), 12*(12), 3223. DOI: 10.3390/diagnostics12123223 PMID: 36553230

Čepienė, A., & Vaitiekienė, N. (2019). Studentų profesinės praktikos organizavimo proceso kolegijoje analizė. *Mokslo Taikomieji Tyrimai Lietuvos Kolegijose*, (14), 53-62. Retrieved from https://ojs.kaunokolegija.lt/index.php/mttlk/article/view/256

Chaima, H. (2024). *Prospecting the future of translator amid AI and machine practices and outputs* [PhD Thesis, Université Kasdi Merbah-Ouargla]. https://dspace.univ-ouargla.dz/jspui/handle/123456789/37029

Chan, S.-W. (Ed.). (2016). *The Routledge Encyclopedia of the Chinese Language*. Routledge., DOI: 10.4324/9781315675541

Chen, M. (2021). Accounting Data Encryption Processing Based on Data Encryption Standard Algorithm. Complexity. https://doi.org/wiley.comDOI: 10.1155/2023/9856582

Chen, M. (2024). Trust, understanding, and machine translation: the task of translation and the responsibility of the translator. AI & SOCIETY. https://doi.org/ springer.comDOI: 10.1007/s00146-023-01681-6

Chen, X. (2009). [The Grammar, Rhetoric, and Role-play of Chinese Idioms]. *Showwe Information Co., Ltd.*

Chen, L. (2009). On literal translation of English idioms. *English Language Teaching, 2*(2). Advance online publication. DOI: 10.5539/elt.v2n2p164

Chen, L. (2020). Application of Explanational Translation approach to English idioms. *Theory and Practice in Language Studies, 10*(11), 1462. DOI: 10.17507/tpls.1011.17

Chen, P., Wu, L., & Wang, L. (2023). AI fairness in data management and analytics: A review on challenges, methodologies, and applications. *Applied Sciences (Basel, Switzerland), 13*(18), 10258. DOI: 10.3390/app131810258

Chen, Q., Wen, Y., Zhang, X., & Zhu, Z. (2022). Evolutionary overview of terrace research based on bibliometric analysis in web of science from 1991 to 2020. *International Journal of Environmental Research and Public Health, 19*(13), 7796. DOI: 10.3390/ijerph19137796 PMID: 35805456

Chen, S., Chen, Y., Yuan, F., & Chang, X. (2020). Establishment of herbal prescription vector space model based on word co-occurrence. *The Journal of Supercomputing, 76*(5), 3590–3601. DOI: 10.1007/s11227-018-2559-3

Cheong, H. I., Lyons, A., Houghton, R., & Majumdar, A. (2023). Secondary qualitative research methodology using online data within the context of social sciences. *International Journal of Qualitative Methods, 22*, 16094069231180160. DOI: 10.1177/16094069231180160

Chetouani, M., Dignum, V., Lukowicz, P., & Sierra, C. (2023). Lecture notes in computer science: Vol. 13500. *Human-centered artificial intelligence: Advanced lectures*. Springer., DOI: 10.1007/978-3-031-24349-3

Chia, Z. L., Ptaszynski, M., Karpinska, M., Eronen, J., & Masui, F. (2024). Initial exploration into sarcasm and irony through machine translation. *Natural Language Processing Journal*, *9*, 100106. DOI: 10.1016/j.nlp.2024.100106

Chiu, T. K., & Chai, C. S. (2020). Sustainable curriculum planning for artificial intelligence education: A self-determination theory perspective. *Sustainability (Basel)*, *12*(14), 5568. DOI: 10.3390/su12145568

Choi, S. R. & Lee, M. (2023). Transformer architecture and attention mechanisms in genome data analysis: a comprehensive review. Biology. https://doi.org/mdpi .comDOI: 10.3390/biology12071033

Chowdhury, A., & Hussan, M. (2023). A review-based study on different Text-to-Speech technologies. *arXiv*. Retrieved from https://arxiv.org/abs/2312.11563

Chuanmao, T. & Juntao, D. (2024). Translating the Future: Exploring the Impact of Technology and AI on Modern Translation Studies. [HTML]

Coleman, J., Krishnamachari, B., Rosales, R., & Iskarous, K. (2024). LLM-Assisted Rule-Based Machine Translation for Low/No-Resource Languages. *Proceedings of the 4th Workshop on Natural Language Processing for Indigenous Languages of the Americas (AmericasNLP 2024)*, 67-87. DOI: 10.18653/v1/2024.americasnlp-1.9

Costa-Jussa, M. R., & Fonollosa, J. A. (2015). Latest trends in hybrid machine translation and its applications. *Computer Speech & Language*, *32*(1), 3–10. DOI: 10.1016/j.csl.2014.11.001

Costa-jussà, M. R., & Rapp, R. (2016). *Hybrid approaches to machine translation*. Springer. DOI: 10.1007/978-3-319-21311-8

Creswell, J. W., & Guetterman, T. C. (2021). *Educational Research: Planning, Conducting, and Evaluating Quantitative and Qualitative Research* (6th ed.). Pearson.

Currie, G. M. (2023). Academic integrity and artificial intelligence: Is ChatGPT hype, hero or heresy? [HTML]. *Seminars in Nuclear Medicine*, *53*(5), 719–730. Advance online publication. DOI: 10.1053/j.semnuclmed.2023.04.008 PMID: 37225599

Curto, G., Jojoa Acosta, M. F., Comim, F., & Garcia-Zapirain, B. (2024). Are AI systems biased against the poor? A machine learning analysis using Word2Vec and GloVe embeddings. AI & society. https://doi.org/ springer.comDOI: 10.1007/s00146-022-01494-z

Dabre, R., Chu, C., & Kunchukuttan, A. (2020). A survey of multilingual neural machine translation. *ACM Computing Surveys*, *53*(5), 1–38. DOI: 10.1145/3406095

Dai, Y., Chai, C. S., Lin, P. Y., Jong, M. S. Y., Guo, Y., & Qin, J. (2020). Promoting students' well-being by developing their readiness for the artificial intelligence age. *Sustainability (Basel)*, *12*(16), 6597. DOI: 10.3390/su12166597

Dalayli, F. (2023). *Use of NLP Techniques in Translation by ChatGPT: Case Study*. ACL Anthology.

Daramola, G. O., Adewumi, A., Jacks, B. S., & Ajala, O. A. (2024). Navigating complexities: a review of communication barriers in multinational energy projects. International Journal of Applied Research in Social Sciences, 6(4), 685-697. DOI: fepbl.comDOI: 10.51594/ijarss.v6i4.1062

Davenport, T., & Kalakota, R. (2019). The potential for artificial intelligence in healthcare. *Future Healthcare Journal*, *6*(2), 94–98. DOI: 10.7861/futurehosp.6-2-94 PMID: 31363513

de León, C. M. (2019). Functionalism. In Baker, M., & Saldanha, G. (Eds.), *Routledge encyclopedia of translation studies* (3rd ed., pp. 199–203). Routledge. DOI: 10.4324/9781315678627-43

De Silva, D. I., & Gallage, I. S. (2024, November). The Role of Syntax and Semantics in Rule-Based Translation: A Comprehensive Review. In 2024 International Conference on Information and Communication Technology for Development for Africa (ICT4DA) (pp. 229-234). IEEE. https://doi.org/ [HTML]DOI: 10.1109/ICT4DA62874.2024.10777198

Dec, G., Stadnicka, D., Paśko, Ł., Mądziel, M., Figliè, R., Mazzei, D., Tyrovolas, M., Stylios, C., Navarro, J., & Solé-Beteta, X. (2022). Role of academics in transferring knowledge and skills on artificial intelligence, internet of things and edge computing. *Sensors (Basel)*, *22*(7), 2496. DOI: 10.3390/s22072496 PMID: 35408110

Del Mondo, G., Peng, P., Gensel, J., Claramunt, C., & Lu, F. (2021). Leveraging spatio-temporal graphs and knowledge graphs: Perspectives in the field of maritime transportation. *ISPRS International Journal of Geo-Information*, *10*(8), 541. DOI: 10.3390/ijgi10080541

Dengel, A., Gehrlein, R., Fernes, D., Görlich, S., Maurer, J., Pham, H. H., Großmann, G., & Eisermann, N. D. (2023). Qualitative research methods for large language models: Conducting semi-structured interviews with ChatGPT and BARD on computer science education. *Informatics (MDPI)*, *10*(4), 78. DOI: 10.3390/informatics10040078

Deng, L., & Abdullah, M. R. (2024). Category shifts in the Chinese–English translation of animal idioms in Journey to the West. *Journal of Language Teaching and Research, 15*(3), 953–959. DOI: 10.17507/jltr.1503.29

Devarajan, L. (2024). Innovations in Cloud Storage: Leveraging Generative AI for Enhanced Data Management. Generative AI and Implications for Ethics, Security, and Data Management, 322-349. DOI: [HTML]DOI: 10.4018/979-8-3693-8557-9.ch011

Devlin, J., Chang, M. W., Lee, K., & Toutanova, K. (2019). BERT: Pre-training of deep bidirectional transformers for language understanding. *Proceedings of the 2019 Conference of the North American Chapter of the Association for Computational Linguistics: Human Language Technologies*, 4171-4186.

Dewayanti, D., & Putu, S. (2024). The impact of contextual understanding on neural machine translation accuracy: A case study of Indonesian cultural idioms in English translation. *Englisia: Journal of Language. Education and Humanities, 12*(1), 223–223. DOI: 10.22373/ej.v12i1.24433

Díaz-Rodríguez, N., Del Ser, J., Coeckelbergh, M., de Prado, M. L., Herrera-Viedma, E., & Herrera, F. (2023). Connecting the dots in trustworthy Artificial Intelligence: From AI principles, ethics, and key requirements to responsible AI systems and regulation. Information Fusion, 99, 101896. https://doi.org/ sciencedirect.comDOI: 10.1016/j.inffus.2023.101896

Ding, L. (2024). Assessing and Mitigating Social Bias in Text and Natural Language Processing Systems. ualberta.ca

Dobreva, M., Rukavina, T., Stamou, V., Vidaki, A. N., & Zacharopoulou, L. (2023, July). A Multimodal Installation Exploring Gender Bias in Artificial Intelligence. In International Conference on Human-Computer Interaction (pp. 27-46). Cham: Springer Nature Switzerland. https://doi.org/ [HTML]DOI: 10.1007/978-3-031-35681-0_2

Dobrovol'skij, D. & Piirainen, E. (2021). Figurative language: Cross-cultural and cross-linguistic perspectives. [HTML]

Docomo, N. T. T. (2025). TTS system for Japanese navigation. *NTT Docomo*. Retrieved from https://nttdocomo.com

Doherty, S. (2016). The impact of translation technologies on the process and product of translation. [The University of New South Wales, Australia.]. *International Journal of Communication, 10*, 947–969.

Dolfing, H. (2024,). Case study 20: The $4 billion AI failure of IBM Watson for Oncology. Henricodolfing. https://www.henricodolfing.com/2024/12/case-study -ibm- watson-for-oncology-failure.html

Dong, J. (2023). Transfer learning-based neural machine translation for low-resource languages. *ACM Transactions on Asian and Low-Resource Language Information Processing, 3618111*, 3618111. Advance online publication. DOI: 10.1145/3618111

Dong, S., Wang, P., & Abbas, K. (2021). A survey on deep learning and its applications. [HTML]. *Computer Science Review, 40*, 100379. Advance online publication. DOI: 10.1016/j.cosrev.2021.100379

Doshi, A. V. (2024). The Loss in AI Translation. *ResearchGate*. https://www.researchgate.net/publication/383037053_The_Loss_in_AI_Translation

Doudou, W., & Faizi, H. (2024). *Enhancing Poetry Translation via ChatGPT 3.5: A Comparative Contrastive Study on Translated versions Qabbani's Poem Belqees & Fortune Teller by Kevin Moore* [MA Dissertation, Kasdi Merbah Ouargla University]. https://dspace.univ-ouargla.dz/jspui/bitstream/123456789/36859/1/Enhancing%20 Poetry%20Translation%20Via%20ChatGPT%203.5.pdf

Drugan, J., & Tipton, R. (2017). Translation, ethics and social responsibility. *The translator, 23*(2), 119-125. https://doi.org/.DOI: 10.1080/13556509.2017.1327008

Duan, H., Cui, W. W., & Gao, Y. D. (2014). Cultural Metaphor and translation Strategies in English and Chinese animal idioms. *Journal of Language Teaching and Research, 5*(6). Advance online publication. DOI: 10.4304/jltr.5.6.1292-1300

Du, X. (2012). A brief introduction of Skopos theory. *Theory and Practice in Language Studies, 2*(10), 2189–2193. DOI: 10.4304/tpls.2.10.2189-2193

Dwivedi, R. K., Nand, P., & Pal, O. (2025). Hybrid NMT model and comparison with existing machine translation approaches. *Multidisciplinary Science Journal, 7*(4), 2025146–2025146. DOI: 10.31893/multiscience.2025146

Dwivedi, Y. K., Kshetri, N., Hughes, L., Slade, E. L., Jeyaraj, A., Kar, A. K., Baabdullah, A. M., Koohang, A., Raghavan, V., Ahuja, M., Albanna, H., Albashrawi, M. A., Al-Busaidi, A. S., Balakrishnan, J., Barlette, Y., Basu, S., Bose, I., Brooks, L., Buhalis, D., & Wright, R. (2023). "So what if ChatGPT wrote it?" Multidisciplinary perspectives on opportunities, challenges and implications of generative conversational AI for research, practice and policy. *International Journal of Information Management, 71*, 102642. Advance online publication. DOI: 10.1016/j.ijinfomgt.2023.102642

Elendu, C., Amaechi, D. C., Okatta, A. U., Amaechi, E. C., Elendu, T. C., Ezeh, C. P., & Elendu, I. D. (2024). The impact of simulation-based training in medical education: A review. Medicine, 103(27), e38813. *DOI:*lww.comDOI: 10.1097/MD.0000000000038813

El-Meniawy, N., Rizk, M. R., Ahmed, M. A., & Saleh, M. (2022). An Authentication Protocol for the Medical Internet of Things. *Symmetry*, *14*(7), 1483. DOI: 10.3390/sym14071483

Enqvist, L. (2023). 'Human oversight' in the EU artificial intelligence act: What, when and by whom? *Law, Innovation and Technology*, *15*(2), 508–535. DOI: 10.1080/17579961.2023.2245683

Erdil, D. C., White, L., Foster, D., Adams, J., Arguelles Cruz, A. J., Hainey, B., & Stott, L. (2019, July). Toward developing a cloud computing model curriculum. In *Proceedings of the 2019 ACM Conference on Innovation and Technology in Computer Science Education* (pp. 255-256). DOI: 10.1145/3304221.3325536

Ernst, C., Schröter, J., & Sudmann, A. (2019). AI and the imagination to overcome difference. Spheres: Journal for Digital Culture. Retrieved from https://mediarep.org/bitstream/handle/doc/14423/spheres_5_0301_Ernst_ea_AI-Imagination-Difference.pdf

Eszenyi, R., Bednarova-Gibova, K., & Robin, E. (2023). Artificial intelligence, machine translation & cyborg translators: A clash of utopian and dystopian visions. Orbis Linguarum, 21(2). DOI: 10.37708/ezs.swu.bg.v21i2.13

European Commision. (n. d.). EMT members 2024-29. Retrieved from: https://commission.europa.eu/education/skills-and-qualifications/develop-your-language-skills/european-masters-translation-emt/emt-members-2024-29_en

European Commission. (2018). Artificial Intelligence for Europe. Retrieved from: https://eur-lex.europa.eu/legal-content/EN/TXT/HTML/?uri=CELEX:52018DC0237

European Commission. (2022a). Ethical guidelines on the use of artificial intelligence (AI) and data in teaching and learning for educators. Retrieved from: https://op.europa.eu/en/publication-detail/-/publication/d81a0d54-5348-11ed-92ed-01aa75ed71a1/language-en

European Commission. (2022b). European Master's in Translation Competence Framework 2022. Retrieved from: chrome-extension://efaidnbmnnnibpcajpcglclefindmkaj/https://commission.europa.eu/system/files/2022-11/emt_competence_fwk_2022_en.pdf

European Commission. (2024). European Master's in Translation Competence Annual Report 2023. Retrieved from: chrome-extension://efaidnbmnnnibpcajpcglclefindmkaj/https://commission.europa.eu/document/download/b0884886-305d-49f8-b2ba-a9a9ddcd66e5_en?filename=EMT_Annual_Report_2023.pdf

European Parliament. (2022). Digital Decade Policy Programme 2030. Retrieved from: https://commission.europa.eu/strategy-and-policy/priorities-2019-2024/europe-fit-digital-age/europes-digital-decade-digital-targets-2030_en

Fadhel, M. A., Duhaim, A. M., Albahri, A. S., Al-Qaysi, Z. T., Aktham, M. A., Chyad, M. A., ... & Gu, Y. (2024). Navigating the metaverse: unraveling the impact of artificial intelligence—a comprehensive review and gap analysis. Artificial Intelligence Review, 57(10), 264. https://doi.org/ springer.comDOI: 10.1007/s10462-024-10881-5

Fan, P., Gong, H., & Gong, X. (2023). The application of ChatGPT in translation teaching: Changes, challenges, and responses. *International Journal of Education and Humanities*, *11*(2), 49–52. DOI: 10.54097/ijeh.v11i2.13530

Fan, X., & Zhong, X. (2022). Artificial intelligence-based creative thinking skill analysis model using human–computer interaction in art design teaching. *Computers & Electrical Engineering*, *100*, 107957. DOI: 10.1016/j.compeleceng.2022.107957

Farahmand, F. (2021). Integrating cybersecurity and artificial intelligence research in engineering and computer science education. *IEEE Security and Privacy*, *19*(6), 104–110. DOI: 10.1109/MSEC.2021.3103460

Farghal, M., & Haider, A. S. (2024). Translating classical Arabic verse: Human translation vs. AI large language models (Gemini and ChatGPT). *Cogent Social Sciences*, *10*(1), 2410998. Advance online publication. DOI: 10.1080/23311886.2024.2410998

Farghaly, A., & Shaalan, K. (2009). Arabic natural language processing: Challenges and solutions. [TALIP]. *ACM Transactions on Asian Language Information Processing*, *8*(4), 1–22. DOI: 10.1145/1644879.1644881

Farhad, M. A. (2024). Consumer data protection laws and their impact on business models in the tech industry. [HTML]. *Telecommunications Policy*, *48*(9), 102836. Advance online publication. DOI: 10.1016/j.telpol.2024.102836

Fernández, C., Vicente, M. A., & Martínez-Rach, M. O. (2020). Implementation of a face recognition system as experimental practices in an artificial intelligence and pattern recognition course. *Computer Applications in Engineering Education*, *28*(3), 497–511. DOI: 10.1002/cae.22218

Ferrara, E. (2023). Fairness and bias in artificial intelligence: A brief survey of sources, impacts, and mitigation strategies. Sci. https://doi.org/mdpi.comDOI: 10.3390/sci6010003

Floranti, A. D., & Mubarok, Y. (2020). Indonesia–English translation of idiomatic expressions in the novel This Earth of Mankind. *Buletin Al-Turas*, *26*(2), 207–220. DOI: 10.15408/bat.v26i2.13834

FlowGent AI. (2023). *What is a Rules-based Machine Translation*. RBMT.

Fontes, C., Hohma, E., Corrigan, C. C., & Lütge, C. (2022). AI-powered public surveillance systems: why we (might) need them and how we want them. Technology in Society. https://doi.org/ sciencedirect.comDOI: 10.1016/j.techsoc.2022.102137

Gahoi, A. (2023). *Using domain knowledge to improve machine translation in Indian languages* [PhD Thesis, International Institute of Information Technology Hyderabad].

Gala, D., & Makaryus, A. N. (2023). The utility of language models in cardiology: a narrative review of the benefits and concerns of ChatGPT-4. International Journal of Environmental Research and Public Health, 20(15), 6438. https://doi.org/mdpi .comDOI: 10.3390/ijerph20156438

Gala, D., Behl, H., Shah, M., & Makaryus, A. N. (2024). The role of artificial intelligence in improving patient outcomes and future of healthcare delivery in cardiology: a narrative review of the literature. Healthcare. https://doi.org/mdpi .comDOI: 10.3390/healthcare12040481

Galderisi, S., Appelbaum, P. S., Gill, N., Gooding, P., Herrman, H., Melillo, A., Myrick, K., Pathare, S., Savage, M., Szmukler, G., & Torous, J. (2024). Ethical challenges in contemporary psychiatry: An overview and an appraisal of possible strategies and research needs. [wiley.com]. *World Psychiatry; Official Journal of the World Psychiatric Association (WPA)*, *23*(3), 364–386. DOI: 10.1002/wps.21230 PMID: 39279422

Gallegos, I. O., Rossi, R. A., Barrow, J., Tanjim, M. M., Kim, S., Dernoncourt, F., Yu, T., Zhang, R., & Ahmed, N. K. (2024). Bias and fairness in large language models: A survey. *Computational Linguistics*, *50*(3), 1097–1179. DOI: 10.1162/ coli_a_00524

Gambier, Y. (2016). Translations| Rapid and Radical Changes in Translation and Translation Studies. *International Journal of Communication*, *10*, 887–906. https:// ijoc.org/index.php/ijoc/article/view/3824

Gams, M., & Kolenik, T. (2021). Relations between electronics, artificial intelligence and information society through information society rules. *Electronics (Basel), 10*(4), 514. DOI: 10.3390/electronics10040514

Gao, Y., Wang, R., & Hou, F. (2023). Unleashing the power of ChatGPT for translation: An empirical study. *Arxiv Preprint Arxiv:2304.02182*. https://arxiv.org/pdf/2304.02182v1/1000

Gao, Y., & Zhou, G. (2024). Revealing the translator's style: A corpus-based study of English translations of Mencius. *PLoS One*, *19*(7), e0305894. Advance online publication. DOI: 10.1371/journal.pone.0305894 PMID: 39012898

Garcia Valencia, O. A., Suppadungsuk, S., Thongprayoon, C., Miao, J., Tangpanithandee, S., Craici, I. M., & Cheungpasitporn, W. (2023). Ethical implications of chatbot utilization in nephrology. *Journal of Personalized Medicine*, *13*(9), 1363. DOI: 10.3390/jpm13091363 PMID: 37763131

Gaspari, F. (2024). The History of Translation Technologies. In *The Routledge Handbook of the History of Translation Studies* (pp. 324–338). Routledge. [HTML], DOI: 10.4324/9781032690056-22

Gemini - chat to supercharge your ideas. (n.d.). Gemini. https://gemini.google.com/app?utm_source=google&utm_medium=cpc&utm_campaign=2024enIN_gemfeb&gad_source=1&gclid=Cj0KCQjwzby1BhCQARIsAJ_0t5PGHpF7rjUJug9QyXooWyoepqcoaVfpBOh9oMbRx-bQr-QhZylAMi4aAlloEALw_wcB

Geng, F., & Hu, J. (2023). New direction of artificial intelligence-assisted post-translation editing: A case study of ChatGPT-based translation. *Chinese Foreign Language*, *3*, 41–47.

Ghiurău, D. & Popescu, D. E. (2024). Distinguishing Reality from AI: Approaches for Detecting Synthetic Content. Computers. https://doi.org/mdpi.comDOI: 10.3390/computers14010001

Ghosh, S., & Caliskan, A. (2023). ChatGPT perpetuates gender bias in machine translation and ignores non-gendered pronouns: Findings across Bengali and five other low-resource languages. *arXiv Preprint*.https://doi.org//arXiv.2305.10510 .DOI: 10.1145/3600211.3604672

Ghosh, S., Ness, S., & Salunkhe, S. (2024). The role of AI enabled chatbots in omnichannel customer service. *Journal of Engineering Research and Reports*, *26*(6), 327–345. DOI: 10.9734/jerr/2024/v26i61184

Ghozali, N. I. M., Mansor, N. S., Awang, H., & Yusof, S. M. (2024). Automated translation tools for mualaf: Artificial intelligence solutions for accessing islamic texts and resources across languages. *International Journal of Islamic Theology & Civilization*, *2*(3), 60–64. DOI: 10.5281/zenodo.13943174

González-Gonzalo, C., Thee, E. F., Klaver, C. C., Lee, A. Y., Schlingemann, R. O., Tufail, A., ... & Sánchez, C. I. (2022). Trustworthy AI: closing the gap between development and integration of AI systems in ophthalmic practice. Progress in retinal and eye research, 90, 101034. https://doi.org/sciencedirect.comDOI: 10.1016/j.preteyeres.2021.101034

Gorzeń-Mitka, I., Bilska, B., Tomaszewska, M., & Kołożyn-Krajewska, D. (2020). Mapping the structure of food waste management research: A co-keyword analysis. *International Journal of Environmental Research and Public Health*, *17*(13), 4798. DOI: 10.3390/ijerph17134798 PMID: 32635284

Gough, J. (2024). Individual variations in information behaviour of professional translators: towards a classification of translation-oriented research styles. Translation studies. https://doi.org/ tandfonline.comDOI: 10.1080/14781700.2023.2231933

Green, S., Heer, J., & Manning, C. D. (2013). The efficacy of human post-editing for language translation. *Proceedings of the Sigchi Conference on Human Factors in Computing Systems*, 439–448. DOI: 10.1145/2470654.2470718

Grey, A., & Severin, A. A. (2022). Building towards best practice for governments' public communications in languages other than English: A case study of New South Wales, Australia. [HTML]. *Griffith Law Review*, *31*(1), 25–56. Advance online publication. DOI: 10.1080/10383441.2022.2031526

Grossman Liu, L., Grossman, R. H., Mitchell, E. G., Weng, C., Natarajan, K., Hripcsak, G., & Vawdrey, D. K. (2021). A deep database of medical abbreviations and acronyms for natural language processing. Scientific Data, 8(1), 149. https://doi.org/nature.comDOI: 10.1038/s41597-021-00929-4

Groves, M., & Mundt, K. (2015).Friend or foe? Google Translate in language for academic purposes, *English for Specific Purposes*, Volume 37, p. 112-121, ISSN 0889-4906, https://doi.org/DOI: 10.1016/j.esp.2014.09.001

Gruetzemacher, R. & Whittlestone, J. (2022). The transformative potential of artificial intelligence. Futures. https://doi.org/sciencedirect.comDOI: 10.1016/j.futures.2021.102884

Guerberof, A. (2009). Productivity and quality in MT post-editing. *Beyond Translation Memories: New Tools for Translators Workshop.* https://aclanthology.org/2009.mtsummit-btm.7.pdf

Guerberof-Arenas, A., & Toral, A. (2022). Creativity in translation: Machine translation as a constraint for literary texts. *Translation Spaces, 11*(2), 184–212. DOI: 10.1075/ts.21025.gue

Guo, S. (2022). Internet of things task migration algorithm under edge computing in the design of english translation theory and teaching practice courses. Computational Intelligence and Neuroscience. https://doi.org/wiley.comDOI: 10.1155/2022/9538917

Gupta, R. (2020). Microsoft Translator: Integrating translation with business platforms. *Journal of Business Language Solutions*, 15(2), 45-59. **checked**

Gupta, B. B., Gaurav, A., Arya, V., Alhalabi, W., Alsalman, D., & Vijayakumar, P. (2024). Enhancing user prompt confidentiality in Large Language Models through advanced differential encryption. [HTML]. *Computers & Electrical Engineering, 116*, 109215. DOI: 10.1016/j.compeleceng.2024.109215

Gupta, R., Srivastava, D., Sahu, M., Tiwari, S., Ambasta, R. K., & Kumar, P. (2021). Artificial intelligence to deep learning: Machine intelligence approach for drug discovery. *Molecular Diversity, 25*(3), 1315–1360. DOI: 10.1007/s11030-021-10217-3 PMID: 33844136

Gutierrez, R.Jr. (2024). *Unifying linguistic landscapes: The potential of AI and nanotechnology in facilitating real-time translation.* Artificial Intelligence in the Age of Nanotechnology. [HTML], DOI: 10.4018/979-8-3693-0368-9.ch005

Habash, N., & Sadat, F. (2006, June). Arabic preprocessing schemes for statistical machine translation. In *Proceedings of the human language technology conference of the naacl, companion volume: Short papers* (pp. 49-52). DOI: 10.3115/1614049.1614062

Hackett, S., Janssen, J., Beach, P., Perreault, M., Beelen, J., & Van Tartwijk, J. (2023). The effectiveness of Collaborative Online International Learning (COIL) on intercultural competence development in higher education. International Journal of Educational Technology in Higher Education, 20(1), 5. https://doi.org/ springer.comDOI: 10.1186/s41239-022-00373-3

Hading, E., Rustan, D. R. H. P., & Ruing, F. H. (2024). EFL Students' Perceptions on the Integration of AI in Fostering Critical Thinking Skills. *Global English Insights Journal, 2*(1), 1–10. DOI: 10.61220/glens.v2i1.466

Hadley, J. L., Taivalkoski-Shilov, K., Teixeira, C. S., & Toral, A. (2022). *Using technologies for creative-text translation.* Taylor & Francis. DOI: 10.4324/9781003094159

Haleem, A., Javaid, M., Qadri, M. A., Singh, R. P., & Suman, R. (2022). Artificial intelligence (AI) applications for marketing: A literature-based study. International Journal of Intelligent Networks, 3, 119-132. https://doi.org/ sciencedirect.comDOI: 10.1016/j.ijin.2022.08.005

Halliday Michael, A. K., & Hasan, R. (1976). *Cohesion in English*. Longman.

Hamamoto, R., Suvarna, K., Yamada, M., Kobayashi, K., Shinkai, N., Miyake, M., Takahashi, M., Jinnai, S., Shimoyama, R., Sakai, A., Takasawa, K., Bolatkan, A., Shozu, K., Dozen, A., Machino, H., Takahashi, S., Asada, K., Komatsu, M., Sese, J., & Kaneko, S. (2020). Application of artificial intelligence technology in oncology: Towards the establishment of precision medicine. *Cancers (Basel)*, *12*(12), 3532. DOI: 10.3390/cancers12123532 PMID: 33256107

Hamed, H. M. (2023). Exploring translation approaches for popularized scientific texts: Human- machine collaboration in the Arabic context. *Migration Letters : An International Journal of Migration Studies*, *20*(S11), 1301–1318. https://www .migrationletters.com

Hamood, M. I. (2024). The translation of English food idioms into Arabic through ChatGPT: Problems and solutions. *Midad Al-Adab Refereed Journal, 1*(Special issue of the Translation Department Conference), 55–76.

Han, L., Gladkoff, S., Erofeev, G., Sorokina, I., Galiano, B., & Nenadic, G. (2024). Neural machine translation of clinical text: an empirical investigation into multilingual pre-trained language models and transfer-learning. Frontiers in Digital Health, 6, 1211564. https://doi.org/frontiersin.orgDOI: 10.3389/fdgth.2024.1211564

Han, S., Wang, M., Zhang, J., Li, D., & Duan, J. (2024). A Review of Large Language Models: Fundamental Architectures, Key Technological Evolutions, Interdisciplinary Technologies Integration, Optimization and .... Electronics. https://doi.org/ mdpi. comDOI: 10.3390/electronics13245040

Hannun, A., Case, C., Casper, J., Catanzaro, B., Diamos, G., Elsen, E., & Prenger, R. (2024). Deep Speech: Scaling up end-to-end speech recognition. *arXiv*. Retrieved from https://arxiv.org/abs/1412.5567

Hansen, J. P. B. & Svennevig, J. (2021). Creating space for interpreting within extended turns at talk. Journal of Pragmatics. https://doi.org/sciencedirect.comDOI: 10.1016/j.pragma.2021.06.009

Hao, Y., & Pym, A. (2023). Where Do Translation Students Go? A Study of the Employment and Mobility of Master Graduates. *The Interpreter and Translator Trainer*, *17*(2), 211–229. DOI: 10.1080/1750399X.2022.2084595

Hardmeier, C. (2012). Discourse in statistical machine translation. A survey and a case study. *Discours. Revue De Linguistique, Psycholinguistique Et Informatique. a Journal of Linguistics, Psycholinguistics and Computational Linguistics, 11*. https://journals.openedition.org/discours/8726

Hardmeier, C. (2012). Discourse in Statistical Machine Translation: A Survey and a Case Study. *Discours, 11*(11), 1–23. DOI: 10.4000/discours.8726

Hartmann, K. V., Primc, N., & Rubeis, G. (2023). Lost in translation? Conceptions of privacy and independence in the technical development of AI-based AAL. *Medicine, Health Care, and Philosophy, 26*(1), 99–110.

Hartono, R. (2020). *Translation techniques & methods*. LPPM UNNES Press.

Hasal, M., Nowaková, J., Ahmed Saghair, K., Abdulla, H., Snášel, V., & Ogiela, L. (2021). Chatbots: Security, privacy, data protection, and social aspects. Concurrency and Computation: Practice and Experience, 33(19), e6426. DOI: wiley.comDOI: 10.1002/cpe.6426

Hasan, M. (2002). Partition narratives. *Social Scientist (New Delhi), 30*(7/8), 24. DOI: 10.2307/3518150

Hatano, K. (2024). The characteristics of Face-to-Face communication using consecutive speech machine translation technology. *Journal of Business Communication & Technology*, 44–53. https://doi.org/DOI: 10.56632/bct.2024.3104

Hatim, B. (1984). A text typological approach to syllabus design in translator training. *The Incorporated Linguist, 22*(3), 146–149.

Hatim, B. (2001). *Teaching and researching translation*. Longman.

Hatim, B., & Mason, I. (1990). *Discourse and the translator*. Longman.

Hatim, B., & Mason, I. (1997). *The Translator as Communicator*. Routledge.

Hatim, B., & Munday, J. (2004). *Translation: An advanced resource book*. Routledge. DOI: 10.4324/9780203501887

Heath, M., Hvass, A. M. F., & Wejse, C. M. (2023). Interpreter services and effect on healthcare - a systematic review of the impact of different types of interpreters on patient outcome. *Journal of Migration and Health, 7*, 100162. DOI: 10.1016/j.jmh.2023.100162 PMID: 36816444

Hedderich, D. M., Keicher, M., Wiestler, B., Gruber, M. J., Burwinkel, H., Hinterwimmer, F., & Navab, N. (2021, September). AI for doctors—A course to educate medical professionals in artificial intelligence for medical imaging. []. MDPI.]. *Health Care, 9*(10), 1278. PMID: 34682958

Heredia-Negron, F., Alamo-Rodriguez, N., Oyola-Velazquez, L., Nieves, B., Carrasquillo, K., Hochheiser, H., Fristensky, B., Daluz-Santana, I., Fernandez-Repollet, E., & Roche-Lima, A. (2023). Evaluation of AIML+ HDR—A Course to Enhance Data Science Workforce Capacity for Hispanic Biomedical Researchers. *International Journal of Environmental Research and Public Health, 20*(3), 2726. DOI: 10.3390/ijerph20032726 PMID: 36768092

Hersh, M., Leporini, B., & Buzzi, M. (2023). A comparative study of disabled people's experiences with the video conferencing tools Zoom, MS Teams, Google Meet and Skype. Behaviour & Information Technology, 1-20. https://doi.org/ tandfonline.comDOI: 10.1080/0144929X.2023.2286533

Hidalgo-Ternero, C. M. (2020). Google translate vs. DeepL: Analysing neural machine translation performance under the challenge of phraseological variation. *Monti. Monographs in Translation and Interpreting*, 154–177. DOI: 10.6035/MonTI.2020.ne6.5

Hine, E., & Floridi, L. (2023). The Blueprint for an AI Bill of Rights: In Search of Enaction, at Risk of Inaction. In Minds and Machines (Vol. 33, Issue 2, p. 285). Springer Science+Business Media. https://doi.org/DOI: 10.1007/s11023-023-09625-1

Hinton, G., Deng, L., Yu, D., Dahl, G. E., Mohamed, A. r., Jaitly, N., . . . Kingsbury, B. (2023). Deep neural networks for acoustic modeling in speech recognition: The shared views of four research groups. *IEEE Signal Processing Magazine*. Retrieved from https://ieeexplore.ieee.org/document/6296526

Hoang, T., Suh, J., & Sabharwal, M. (2022). Beyond a numbers game? Impact of diversity and inclusion on the perception of organizational justice. [HTML]. *Public Administration Review, 82*(3), 537–555. Advance online publication. DOI: 10.1111/puar.13463

Hochreiter, S., & Schmidhuber, J. (1997). Long short-term memory. *Neural Computation*. Retrieved from https://www.mitpressjournals.org/doi/abs/10.1162/neco.1997.9.8.1735

Holmes, W., & Miao, F. (2023). *Guidance for generative AI in education and research*. UNESCO Publishing. Retrieved from: https://unesdoc.unesco.org/ark:/48223/pf0000386693

Horváth, I. (2022). AI in interpreting: Ethical considerations. *Across Languages and Cultures*, *23*(1), 1–13. DOI: 10.1556/084.2022.00108

House, J. (1977). *A model for translation quality assessment.* Gunter Narr Verlag.

House, J. (1997). *Translation quality assessment: A model revisited.* Gunter Narr Verlag.

Hu, K., & Li, X. (2023). The creativity and limitations of AI neural machine translation: A corpus-based study of DeepL's English-to-Chinese translation of Shakespeare's plays. *Babel. Revue Internationale de La Traduction / International Journal ofTranslation, 69*(4), 546–563. https://doi.org/DOI: 10.1075/babel.00331.hu

Huang, X. (2021). Aims for cultivating students' key competencies based on artificial intelligence education in China. *Education and Information Technologies*, *26*(5), 5127–5147. DOI: 10.1007/s10639-021-10530-2

Huang, X., & Qiao, C. (2024). Enhancing computational thinking skills through artificial intelligence education at a STEAM high school. *Science & Education*, *33*(2), 383–403. DOI: 10.1007/s11191-022-00392-6

Hubscher-Davidson, S., & Devaux, J. (2021). Teaching translation and interpreting in virtual environments. *The Journal of Specialised Translation*, *36*, 184–192.

Hu, K., & Li, X. (2023). Development of Translation Research in the Context of Large Language Modeling: Problems and Prospects. *China Translation*, (6), 65–74.

Hutchins, J. (2001). Machine translation and human translation: In competition or in complementation. *International Journal of Translation*, *13*(1–2), 5–20.

Hutchins, J., & Somers, H. L. (1992). *An introduction to machine translation.* Academic Press.

Hwang, G. J., & Tu, Y. F. (2021). Roles and research trends of artificial intelligence in mathematics education: A bibliometric mapping analysis and systematic review. *Mathematics*, *9*(6), 584. DOI: 10.3390/math9060584

Hyman, Larry, M. (2014). How to Study a Tone Language, with Exemplification from Oku (Grassfields Bantu, Cameroon). *Language Documentation and Conservation*, *8*(3), 525–562.

IBM. (2020). IBM Watson Health recognizes top-performing U.S. hospitals and health systems. https://newsroom.ibm.com/2020-06-30-IBM-Watson-Health-Recognizes-Top-Performing-U-S-Hospitals-and-Health-Systems

IBM. (2023). *What is NLP*. Natural Language Processing.

IBM. (2024). Getting ready for artificial general intelligence with examples. https://www.ibm.com/think/topics/artificial-general-intelligence-examples

Ibn Khaldūn, A. (2010). *Muqaddimah Ibn Khaldūn* (1st ed.). Dār Ibn al-Jawziy.

Idami, Z., Wati, S., & Balqis, R. (2022). An Analysis of Students' Difficulties in Translating Idiomatic Expressions: What and Why? *ACITYA Journal of Teaching & Education*, *4*(1), 175–188. DOI: 10.30650/ajte.v4i1.3208

iFlytek. (2025). iFlytek TTS system for Mandarin Chinese. *iFlytek*. Retrieved from https://iflytek.com

Ilkka, T. (2018). The impact of artificial intelligence on learning, teaching, and education. *European Union*.

International Organization for Standardization. (2015). *Translation services – Requirements for translation services* (ISO Standard No. 17100:2015). https://www.iso.org/obp/ui/en/#iso:std:iso:17100:ed-1:v1:en

International Organization for Standardization. (2017). *Translation services – Post-editing of machine translation output – Requirements* (ISO Standard No. 18587:2017). https://www.iso.org/obp/ui/en/#iso:std:iso:18587:ed-1:v1:en

International Organization for Standardization. (2024). *Translation projects – General guidance* (ISO Standard No. 11669:2024). https://www.iso.org/obp/ui/en/#iso:std:iso:11669:ed-1:v1:en

Jain, P., Bhirud, N., Tatale, S., Kale, A., Bhale, M., Hajare, A., & Jain, N. K. (2023). Real-Time Interactive AR for Cognitive Learning. In *AI, IoT, Big Data and Cloud Computing for Industry 4.0* (pp. 219–239). Springer International Publishing. [HTML], DOI: 10.1007/978-3-031-29713-7_12

Jelsch, M., Roggo, Y., Kleinebudde, P., & Krumme, M. (2021). Model predictive control in pharmaceutical continuous manufacturing: A review from a user's perspective. [HTML]. *European Journal of Pharmaceutics and Biopharmaceutics*, *159*, 137–142. DOI: 10.1016/j.ejpb.2021.01.003 PMID: 33429008

Jia, F. (2023). Promoting the international dissemination of Chinese culture through international Chinese language education: A case study of Chinese-English idiomatic equivalence. [*Contemporary Social Sciences*], 2023(6). https://doi.org/DOI: 10.19873/j.cnki.2096-0212.2023.06.007

Jia, Y., & Weiss, R. (2019, May 15). *Introducing Translatotron: An End-to-End Speech-to-Speech Translation Model*. https://research.google/blog/introducing-translatotron-an-end-to-end-speech-to-speech-translation-model/

Jiang, L., Jiang, Y., & Han, L. (2024). The potential of ChatGPT in translation evaluation: A case study of the Chinese-Portuguese machine translation. *Cadernos de Tradução (Florianópolis)*, *44*(1), e98613. DOI: 10.5007/2175-7968.2024.e98613

Jiang, T., Sun, Z., Fu, S., & Lv, Y. (2024). Human-AI interaction research agenda: A user- centered perspective. *Data and Information Management*, *8*(4), 100078. DOI: 10.1016/j.dim.2024.100078

Jia, Y., Carl, M., & Wang, X. (2019). Post-editing neural machine translation versus phrase-based machine translation for English–Chinese. *Machine Translation*, *33*(1-2), 9–29. DOI: 10.1007/s10590-019-09229-6

Jiménez-Crespo, M. A. (2020). The "technological turn" in translation studies: Are we there yet? A transversal cross-disciplinary approach. *Translation Spaces*, *9*(2), 314–341. DOI: 10.1075/ts.19012.jim

Jim, J. R., Talukder, M. A. R., Malakar, P., Kabir, M. M., Nur, K., & Mridha, M. F. (2024). Recent advancements and challenges of NLP-based sentiment analysis: A state-of-the-art review. *Natural Language Processing Journal*, *6*, 100059. DOI: 10.1016/j.nlp.2024.100059

Jobin, A., Ienca, M., & Vayena, E. (2019). The global landscape of AI ethics guidelines. *Nature Machine Intelligence*, *1*(9), 389–399. DOI: 10.1038/s42256-019-0088-2

Johnson, M., Schuster, M., Le, Q. V., Krikun, M., Wu, Y., Chen, Z., Thorat, N., Viégas, F., Wattenberg, M., Corrado, G., Hughes, M., & Dean, J. (2017). Google's multilingual neural machine translation system: Enabling zero-shot translation. *Transactions of the Association for Computational Linguistics*, *5*, 339–351. DOI: 10.1162/tacl_a_00065

Jurafsky, D., & Martin, J. H. (2023). Speech and language processing. *Pearson*. Retrieved from https://web.stanford.edu/~jurafsky/slp3/

Kaduskar, V. P., Mhetre, H. V., Khatavkar, S. M., Chougule, P. A., Patil, M. V., Moje, R. J., & Naik, N. (2024). Navigating the Frontier of Generative AI Integration in Healthcare: Adoption, Governance, and Legal Compliance. In AI Healthcare Applications and Security, Ethical, and Legal Considerations (pp. 261-289). IGI Global. DOI: [HTML]DOI: 10.4018/979-8-3693-7452-8.ch016

Kallens, P. C., & Christiansen, M. H. (2024). Distributional Semantics: Meaning Through Culture and Interaction. [HTML]. *Topics in Cognitive Science*. PMID: 39587986

Kalra, S., Saroj, J., & Chhabra, A. (2025). Data Protection and Encryption in Cloud Network Security: Security and Privacy in Cloud Network Security. Convergence of Cybersecurity and .... DOI: [HTML]DOI: 10.4018/979-8-3693-6859-6.ch017

Kampakis, S. (2024). An introduction to AI. In The Decision Maker's Handbook to Data Science: AI and Data Science for Non-Technical Executives, Managers, and Founders (pp. 91-102). Berkeley, CA: Apress. https://doi.org/ [HTML]DOI: 10.1007/979-8-8688-0279-9_8

Kang, H., & Yang, Y. (2022). A study on English translation of Chinese four-characteridioms: Strategies and problems. *Linguistics and Culture Review*, *6*(1), 200–213. DOI: 10.21744/lingcure.v6n1.2185

Kanglang, L., & Afzaal, M. (2021). Artificial Intelligence (AI) and Translation Teaching: A Critical Perspective on the Transformation of Education. *International Journal of Educational Sciences*, *33*(1-3). Advance online publication. DOI: 10.31901/24566322.2021/33.1-3.1159

Karalis, V. D. (2024). The integration of artificial intelligence into clinical practice. *Applied Biosciences*, *3*(1), 14–44. DOI: 10.3390/applbiosci3010002

Kasirzadeh, A. & Gabriel, I. (2023). In conversation with artificial intelligence: aligning language models with human values. Philosophy & Technology. https://doi.org/springer.comDOI: 10.1007/s13347-023-00606-x

Kasperė, R., Horbačauskienė, J., Liubinienė, V., Motiejūnienė, J., Patašienė, I., & Patašius, M. (2024). *Machine translation and society: The case of Lithuania*. Kaunas University of Technology Press., DOI: 10.5755/e01.9786090218808

Katkov, S., Liotta, A., & Vietti, A. (2025). ASR systems under acoustic challenges: A multilingual study. In *AIxIA 2024 – Advances in Artificial Intelligence* (pp. 200–213). Springer., Retrieved from https://link.springer.com/chapter/10.1007/978-3-031-80607-0_16 DOI: 10.1007/978-3-031-80607-0_16

Kayed, M. M. A. (2023). The Challenges Facing Translation Students in Translating Sports Idiomatic Expressions from Arabic into English. *International Journal of Arabic-English Studies*. https://doi.org/DOI: 10.33806/ijaes.v24i1.568

Kelly, C., Karthikesalingam, A., Suleyman, M., Corrado, G. S., & King, D. (2019). Key challenges for delivering clinical impact with artificial intelligence. In Medicine, B. M. C. (Ed.), *Issue 1). BioMed Central* (Vol. 17)., DOI: 10.1186/s12916-019-1426-2

Kenny, D. (Ed.). (2024). Machine translation for everyone: Empowering users in the age of artificial intelligence (Translation and Multilingual Natural Language Processing 18). https://library.oapen.org/bitstream/id/2bf04510-1edf-4f35-be06-662f1632ae8e/external_content.pdf

Kenny, D. (2018). Machine translation. In Rawling, P., & Wilson, P. (Eds.), *The Routledge Handbook of Translation and Philosophy* (pp. 428–445). Routledge. DOI: 10.4324/9781315678481-27

Kenny, D. (2022). *Machine translation for everyone: Empowering users in the age of artificial intelligence*. Language Science Press.

Keshta, I. & Odeh, A. (2021). Security and privacy of electronic health records: Concerns and challenges. Egyptian Informatics Journal. https://doi.org/ sciencedirect.comDOI: 10.1016/j.eij.2020.07.003

Khasawneh, M. A. S. (2023). The potential of AI in facilitating cross-cultural communication through translation. King Khalid University. https://orcid.org/0000-0002-1390-3765

Khasawneh, M. A. S. (2023). The Potential of Ai in Facilitating Cross-Cultural Communication Through Translation. [namibian-studies.com]. *Journal of Namibian Studies: History Politics Culture*, *37*, 107–130.

Khatiwada, P., Yang, B., Lin, J. C., & Blobel, B. (2024). Patient-Generated Health Data (PGHD): Understanding, Requirements, Challenges, and Existing Techniques for Data Security and Privacy. Journal of Personalized Medicine, 14(3), 282. https:// doi.org/ mdpi.comDOI: 10.3390/jpm14030282

Khoshafah, F. (2023). ChatGPT for Arabic-English translation: Evaluating the accuracy. *Research Square*. https://doi.org/DOI: 10.21203/rs.3.rs-2814154/v2

Khurana, D., Koli, A., Khatter, K., & Singh, S. (2023). Natural language processing: state of the art, current trends and challenges. Multimedia tools and applications. https://doi.org/springer.comDOI: 10.1007/s11042-022-13428-4

Khurana, D., Koli, A., Khatter, K., & Singh, S. (2023). Natural language processing: State of the art, current trends, and challenges. *Journal of Artificial Intelligence Research*, *56*(1), 1–42. PMID: 35855771

Ki, D., & Carpuat, M. (2024). Guiding large language models to post-edit machine translation with error annotations. *arXiv Preprint, arXiv:2404.07851*. https://arxiv.org/abs/2404.07851 DOI: 10.18653/v1/2024.findings-naacl.265

Kimera, R., Kim, Y.-S., & Choi, H. (2024). Advancing AI with integrity: Ethical challenges and solutions in neural machine translation. https://arxiv.org/pdf/2404.01070

Kim, H. (2022). Cultural nuances in Asian languages and translation tools: A focus on Papago. *Asian Language Studies, 14*(1), 102–118.

Kim, Y. J. (2024). *The future of translation*. Jane Company.

Kishore, K. S., & Shaik, R. (2024). *Evaluating Telugu Proficiency in Large Language Models_ A Comparative Analysis of ChatGPT and Gemini*. https://www.semanticscholar.org/paper/Evaluating-Telugu-Proficiency-in-Large-Language-A-Kishore-Shaik/a0dc190626901a6e06db47a0fbe802b5226bb4a2

Kizi, T. G. A., & Saporbayevich, A. O. (2024). Pragmatic Strategies in Artistic Translation: Balancing Creativity and Cultural Adaptation. *International Journal of Language Learning and Applied Linguistics, 3*(3), 51–57. DOI: 10.51699/ijllal.v3i3.77

Knowles, R., & Koehn, P. (2018a). Context and copying in neural machine translation. *2018 Conference on Empirical Methods in Natural Language Processing*, 3034–3041. https://www.research.ed.ac.uk/en/publications/context-and-copying-in-neural-machine-translation

Knowles, R., & Koehn, P. (2018b). Lightweight word-level confidence estimation for neural interactive translation prediction. *Workshop on Translation Quality Estimation and Automatic Post-Editing*, 35–40. https://www.research.ed.ac.uk/en/publications/lightweight-word-level-confidence-estimation-for-neural-interacti

Knowles, L. (2016). *Artificial Intelligence and Language: Bridging the Cultural Gap*. University of Massachusetts Press.

Knowles, R., Sanchez-Torron, M., & Koehn, P. (2019). A user study of neural interactive translation prediction. *Machine Translation, 33*(1–2), 135–154. DOI: 10.1007/s10590-019-09235-8

Koehn, P. (2020). *Neural MT*. Cambridge University Press.

Koehn, P. (2010). *Statistical machine translation*. Cambridge University Press.

Koehn, P. (2020). *Neural machine translation*. University Press. DOI: 10.1017/9781108608480

Koehn, P., & Knowles, R. (2017). Six challenges for neural machine translation. *Proceedings of the First Workshop on Neural Machine Translation*, 28-39. DOI: 10.18653/v1/W17-3204

Koh, S. (2023). An analysis of ChatGPT's language translation based on the Korean film Minari. *Journal of English Teaching through Movies and Media, 24*(4), 1–14. https://doi.org/DOI: 10.16875/stem.2023.24.4.1

Komljenovic, J. (2022). The future of value in digitalised higher education: why data privacy should not be our biggest concern. Higher Education. https://doi.org/springer.comDOI: 10.1007/s10734-020-00639-7

Kong, Y. (2014). The study of English and Chinese Numerical Idioms and their translation. *Journal of Language Teaching and Research, 5*(2). Advance online publication. DOI: 10.4304/jltr.5.2.446-451

Koponen, M. (2012). Comparing human perceptions of post-editing effort with post-editing operations. *Proceedings of the Seventh Workshop on Statistical Machine Translation*, 181–190. https://aclanthology.org/W12-3123.pdf

Koponen, M., Mossop, B., & Robert, S. I., & Scocchera, G. (Eds.). (2020). *Translation Revision and Post-editing: Industry Practices and Cognitive Processes*. Routledge. DOI: 10.4324/9781003096962

Koponen, M. (2016). Is machine translation post-editing worth the effort? A survey of research into post-editing and effort. *The Journal of Specialised Translation, 25*(2), 131–148.

Kopp, S. & Krämer, N. (2021). Revisiting human-agent communication: The importance of joint co-construction and understanding mental states. Frontiers in Psychology. https://doi.org/ frontiersin.orgDOI: 10.3389/fpsyg.2021.580955

Köprülü, S. G. (2023). Comprehensibility in translation of medical texts. *RumeliDe Dil ve Edebiyat Arastirmalari Dergisi*, (35), 1487–1504.

Krishnankutty, R., Bharti, T., & Mishra, N. (2022). Herding behaviour and capital structure decision in BSE listed Indian firms. *International Journal of Managerial and Financial Accounting, 14*(2), 118–137. DOI: 10.1504/IJMFA.2022.122226

Krueger, F. A. (2023, June). *I built the world's largest translated Cuneiform corpus using AI*. https://praeclarum.org/2023/06/09/cuneiform.html

Kruger, R. (2022). Some translation studies informed suggestions for further balancing methodologies for machine translation quality evaluation. *Translation Spaces, 11*(2), 213–233. DOI: 10.1075/ts.21026.kru

Kuddus, K. (2022). *Artificial intelligence in language learning: Practices and prospects*. Advanced Analytics and Deep Learning Models. [HTML], DOI: 10.1002/9781119792437.ch1

Kulkarni, S., & Girish, G. N. (2024). *Navigating the Abyss–Illuminating Data Leakage Threats, Mitigations, and Future Horizons*. Cloud Security. [HTML], DOI: 10.1201/9781003455448-3

Kumar, C. R. (2022). Higher Level Abstraction of Deep Architecture. In Prediction and Analysis for Knowledge Representation and Machine Learning (pp. 143-161). Chapman and Hall/CRC. [HTML]

Kumar, Y., Koul, A., & Singh, C. (2023). A deep learning approach in text-to-speech systems: A systematic review and recent research perspective. *Multimedia Tools and Applications*. Retrieved from https://link.springer.com/article/10.1007/s11042-022-13943-4

Kumar, M. G. V., N, V., Čepová, L., Raja, M. A. M., Balaram, A., & Elangovan, M. (2023). Evaluation of the quality of practical teaching of agricultural higher vocational courses based on BP neural network. *Applied Sciences (Basel, Switzerland)*, *13*(2), 1180. DOI: 10.3390/app13021180

Kuzior, A., & Sira, M. (2022). A bibliometric analysis of blockchain technology research using VOSviewer. *Sustainability (Basel)*, *14*(13), 8206. DOI: 10.3390/su14138206

Lagoudaki, E. (2006). Translation memories survey 2006: User's perceptions around TM usage. *Proceedings of Translating and the Computer 28*. https://aclanthology.org/2006.tc-1.2.pdf

Lagoudaki, E. (2008). The value of machine translation for the professional translator. *Proceedings of the 8th Conference of the Association for Machine Translation in the Americas: Student Research Workshop*, 262–269. https://aclanthology.org/2008.amta-srw.4/

Lample, G., Conneau, A., Ranzato, M., Denoyer, L., & Jégou, H. (2019). Unsupervised Machine Translation Using Monolingual Corpora Only. *International Journal of Machine Learning*, *38*(1), 141–164.

Landa Oregi, X. (2023). MLOps data ingestion pipeline for reciprocal benefit between customer and provider. aalto.fi

Language Science Press. (2023). Translation and Multilingual Natural Language Processing.

Lankford, S., Afli, H., & Way, A. (2023). adaptNMT: an open-source, language-agnostic development environment for neural machine translation. Language Resources and Evaluation. https://doi.org/ springer.comDOI: 10.1007/s10579-023-09671-2

Larson, M. A. (1984). *Meaning-Based Translation.* University Press.

Latief, A. D., Jarin, A., Yaniasih, Y., Afra, D. I. N., Nurfadhilah, E., Pebiana, S., Hidayati, N. N., & Fajri, R. (2024). Latest research in data augmentation for low resource language text translation: A review. *2024 International Conference on Computer, Control, Informatics and Its Applications (IC3INA)*, 185–190. https://ieeexplore.ieee.org/abstract/document/10732042/

Laupichler, M. C., Hadizadeh, D. R., Wintergerst, M. W., Von Der Emde, L., Paech, D., Dick, E. A., & Raupach, T. (2022). Effect of a flipped classroom course to foster medical students' AI literacy with a focus on medical imaging: A single group pre-and post-test study. *BMC Medical Education*, *22*(1), 803. DOI: 10.1186/s12909-022-03866-x PMID: 36397110

Lauriola, I., Lavelli, A., & Aiolli, F. (2022). An introduction to deep learning in natural language processing: Models, techniques, and tools. [HTML]. *Neurocomputing*, *470*, 443–456. Advance online publication. DOI: 10.1016/j.neucom.2021.05.103

Lau, Y. L., Chee, S. P., Chua, R. H. H., Yong, Z. H., Yong, I. K., Tan, J. C., Yong, H. W., & Bakar, A. L. A. (2024). The datasets of human and AI translation. *Journal of Open Humanities Data*, *10*(45), 1–10. DOI: 10.5334/johd.212

Laviosa, S. (2021). Corpus-based translation studies: Theory, findings, applications. *Cambridge Scholars Publishing*. Retrieved from https://www.cambridgescholars.com/resources/pdfs/978-1-5275-7244-7-sample.pdf

Lavrenteva, E. & Orland-Barak, L. (2023). Conceptual-analytical framework for exploring culture in EFL coursebooks: Analysis of teaching materials from a multimodal perspective. Social Sciences & Humanities Open. https://doi.org/ science-direct.comDOI: 10.1016/j.ssaho.2023.100441

Learn Chinese Words: wáng yáng b láo. (2023, November 8). ChineseLearning. https://www.chineselearning.com/chinese-words/learn-chinese-words-wang-yang-bu-lao

LeCun, Y., Bengio, Y., & Hinton, G. (2015). Deep learning. *nature, 521*(7553), 436-444.

Lee, S.-M. (2023). The effectiveness of machine translation in foreign language education: A systematic review and meta-analysis. *Computer Assisted Language Learning*, *36*(1–2), 103–125. DOI: 10.1080/09588221.2021.1901745

Lee, T. (2024). Artificial intelligence and posthumanist translation: ChatGPT versus the translator. *Applied Linguistics Review*, *15*(6), 2351–2372. DOI: 10.1515/applirev-2023-0122

Leikas, J., Johri, A., Latvanen, M., Wessberg, N., & Hahto, A. (2022). Governing ethical AI transformation: a case study of AuroraAI. Frontiers in Artificial Intelligence, 5, 836557. https://doi.org/frontiersin.orgDOI: 10.3389/frai.2022.836557

Li, T. (2024, August). Exploring failures and possible remedies in AI and human translation of English idioms. DOI: 10.62051/199nqb23

Liang, Y. (2023). Balancing: The Effects of AI Tools in Educational Context. In Frontiers in Humanities and Social Sciences (Vol. 3, Issue 8, p. 7). https://doi.org/ DOI: 10.54691/fhss.v3i8.5531

Liang, Y., Meng, F., Chen, Y., Xu, J., & Zhou, J. (2021). Modeling bilingual conversational characteristics for neural chat translation. arXiv preprint arXiv:2107.11164.

Liang, C., Ghassemiazghandi, M., & Jamal, M. (2024). Post-editing challenges in Chinese-to-English neural machine translation of movie subtitles. *Social Sciences & Humanities Open*, *10*, 100949. DOI: 10.1016/j.ssaho.2024.100949

Liang, X., Haiping, L., Liu, J., & Lin, L. (2021). Reform of English interactive teaching mode based on cloud computing artificial intelligence–a practice analysis. *Journal of Intelligent & Fuzzy Systems*, *40*(2), 3617–3629. DOI: 10.3233/JIFS-189397

Lim, W. M. (2024). What is qualitative research? An overview and guidelines. Australasian Marketing Journal. DOI: sagepub.comDOI: 10.1177/14413582241264619

Lin, J., Zhao, Y., Huang, W., Liu, C., & Pu, H. (2021). Domain knowledge graph-based research progress of knowledge representation. *Neural Computing & Applications*, *33*(2), 681–690. DOI: 10.1007/s00521-020-05057-5

Lis, A., Sudolska, A., Pietryka, I., & Kozakiewicz, A. (2020). Cloud computing and energy efficiency: Mapping the thematic structure of research. *Energies*, *13*(16), 4117. DOI: 10.3390/en13164117

Liu, S., Liu, G., Zhu, B., Luo, Y., Wu, L., & Wang, R. (2024). Balancing innovation and privacy: Data security strategies in natural language processing applications. *arXiv preprint arXiv:2410.08553*. DOI: 10.1109/ICMLCA63499.2024.10754062

Liu, D. (2012). Translation and Culture: Translating Idioms between English and Chinese from a Cultural Perspective. *Theory and Practice in Language Studies*, *2*(11). Advance online publication. DOI: 10.4304/tpls.2.11.2357-2362

Liu, J. (2019). A comparative study on Chinese and English Animals Idioms and translation Strategies. *Theory and Practice in Language Studies*, *9*(2), 231. DOI: 10.17507/tpls.0902.14

Liu, J. (2024). ChatGPT: Perspectives from human–computer interaction and psychology. *Frontiers in Artificial Intelligence*, *7*, 1418869. Advance online publication. DOI: 10.3389/frai.2024.1418869 PMID: 38957452

Liu, Y., Ott, M., Goyal, N., Du, J., Joshi, M., Chen, D., & Stoyanov, V. (2019). RoBERTa: A robustly optimized BERT pretraining approach. *arXiv*. Retrieved from https://arxiv.org/abs/1907.11692

Liu, Z., Yang, Z., Xiao, C., Zhang, K., & Osmani, M. (2021). An investigation into art therapy aided health and well-being research: A 75-year bibliometric analysis. *International Journal of Environmental Research and Public Health*, *19*(1), 232. DOI: 10.3390/ijerph19010232 PMID: 35010491

Liyanage, U. P., & Ranaweera, N. D. (2023). Ethical considerations and potential risks in the deployment of large language models in diverse societal contexts. [vectoral.org]. *Journal of Computational Social Dynamics*, *8*(11), 15–25.

Lopez, A. (2008). Statistical machine translation. *ACM Computing Surveys*, *40*(3), 1–49. DOI: 10.1145/1380584.1380586

Lorè, F., Basile, P., Appice, A., de Gemmis, M., Malerba, D., & Semeraro, G. (2023). An AI framework to support decisions on GDPR compliance. Journal of Intelligent Information Systems, 61(2), 541-568. https://doi.org/springer.comDOI: 10.1007/s10844-023-00782-4

Low, D. S., Liew, C. J., & Ng, R. W. (2022). Endangered languages: A sociocognitive approach to language death, identity loss, and preservation in the age of artificial intelligence. *Journal of Language and Social Psychology*, *41*(1), 45–60. DOI: 10.1177/0261927X21100001

Lu, Q., Zhu, L., Whittle, J., & Xu, X. (2023). Responsible AI: Best Practices for Creating Trustworthy AI Systems. [HTML]

Luo, L. (2021). Architectures of neuronal circuits. Science. https://doi.org/science.orgDOI: 10.1126/science.abg7285

Luo, J., Cherry, C., & Foster, G. (2024). To diverge or not to diverge: A morphosyntactic perspective on machine translation vs human translation. *Transactions of the Association for Computational Linguistics*, *12*, 355–371. DOI: 10.1162/tacl_a_00645

Lyons, S. (2020). A review of Thai–English machine translation. *Machine Translation*, *34*(2-3), 197–230. DOI: 10.1007/s10590-020-09248-8

M Crisostomo, M., P Bernarte, R., & C Ambag, S. (2022). Cross-Cultural Translation Studies in the Context of Artificial Intelligence: Challenges and Response. European Online Journal of Natural and Social Sciences: Proceedings, 11(4 (s)), pp-187.

Ma, J. (2022). [Online Women's Literature from Social Generational Perspective: Spiritual World and Discourse Expression]. *Journal of Shenzhen University (Humanities & Social Sciences), 39*(6)

Maciel, T. (2024). Strategies for Professors on How to Mitigate the Negative Effects of ChatGPT in Higher Education.

Macken, L. (2024). Machine translation meets large language models: Evaluating ChatGPT's ability to automatically post-edit literary texts. *Proceedings of the 1st Workshop on Creative-Text Translation and Technology*, 65–81.

Madugu, U., & Ibrahim, F. (2025). Six Questions for Every Content Analysis: Revisiting the Stemler's Overview. *International Journal of Research and Innovation in Social Science, VIII*(XII), 2788–2794. DOI: 10.47772/IJRISS.2024.8120233

Maeda, Y., Caskurlu, S., Kenney, R. H., Kozan, K., & Richardson, J. C. (2022). Moving qualitative synthesis research forward in education: A methodological systematic review. *Educational Research Review, 35*, 100424. DOI: 10.1016/j.edurev.2021.100424

Magee, L., Arora, V., & Munn, L. (2023). Structured like a language model: Analysing AI as an automated subject. Big Data & Society. DOI: sagepub.comDOI: 10.1177/20539517231210273

Mahale, A., Desmukh, A.S., Mahajan, R., Vidyadharan, A., Hegde, V.S., & Vijayaraghavan, K. (2023). Data Validation using Sentence Transformers. 1504-1508. DOI: 10.1109/ICOEI56765.2023.10125780

Mair, V. (2023, June). *AI for Akkadian*. https://languagelog.ldc.upenn.edu/nll/?p=59411

Malyuga, E. N. (2024). The language of corporate communication: Functional, pragmatic and cultural dimensions. [HTML]

Manning, L., Brewer, S., Craigon, P. J., Frey, J., Gutierrez, A., Jacobs, N., ... & Pearson, S. (2022). Artificial intelligence and ethics within the food sector: Developing a common language for technology adoption across the supply chain. Trends in Food Science & Technology, 125, 33-42. https://doi.org/ sciencedirect.comDOI: 10.1016/j.tifs.2022.04.025

Mao, C., & Chang, D. (2023). Review of cross-device interaction for facilitating digital transformation in smart home context: A user-centric perspective. [HTML]. *Advanced Engineering Informatics*, *57*, 102087. Advance online publication. DOI: 10.1016/j.aei.2023.102087

Marie, B., Foster, G., & Kuhn, R. (2021). Improving SMT for Low-Resource Languages. *Journal of Machine Translation*, *35*(2), 123–145.

Marie, B., Fujita, A., & Rubino, R. (2021). Scientific Credibility of Machine Translation Research: A Meta-Evaluation of 769 Papers. *Proceedings of the 59th Annual Meeting of the Association for Computational Linguistics and the 11th International Joint Conference on Natural Language Processing(*Volume 1*: Long Papers)*, 7297-7306. DOI: 10.18653/v1/2021.acl-long.566

Marinucci, L., Mazzuca, C., & Gangemi, A. (2023). Exposing implicit biases and stereotypes in human and artificial intelligence: state of the art and challenges with a focus on gender. AI & SOCIETY. https://doi.org/ springer.comDOI: 10.1007/s00146-022-01474-3

Marzuki, , Widiati, U., Rusdin, D., Darwin, , & Indrawati, I. (2023). The impact of AI writing tools on the content and organization of students' writing: EFL teachers' perspective. *Cogent Education*, *10*(2), 2236469. Advance online publication. DOI: 10.1080/2331186X.2023.2236469

Matricciani, E. (2023). Readability across Time and Languages: The Case of Matthew's Gospel Translations. *AppliedMath*, *3*(2), 497–509. DOI: 10.3390/appliedmath3020026

Matulewska, A., & Wagner, A. (2021). The multiplicity of third space of communication in law. International Journal for the Semiotics of Law-Revue internationale de Sémiotique juridique, 34(5), 1225-1243. https://doi.org/springer.comDOI: 10.1007/s11196-021-09855-5

Mazur, O., & Thimmesch, A. B. (2024, May 28). *Beyond ChatGPT: Transforming Government with Augmented LLMs.* https://papers.ssrn.com/sol3/papers.cfm?abstract_id=4846472

Mehandru, N., Robertson, S., & Salehi, N. (2022). Reliable and Safe Use of Machine Translation in Medical Settings. *FAccT '22: 2022 ACM Conference on Fairness, Accountability, and Transparency*, Seoul, Republic of Korea. https://doi.org/DOI: 10.1145/3531146.3533244

Mehawesh, M. I. (2023). Human Translation vs. Machine Translation in the Naguib Mahfouz's Novel Palace Walk: A Case Study. *Mutah Journal of Humanities and Social Sciences, 38*(2). Advance online publication. DOI: 10.35682/mjhsc.v38i2.631

Memarian, B., & Doleck, T. (2023). Fairness, Accountability, Transparency, and Ethics (FATE) in Artificial Intelligence (AI) and higher education: A systematic review,Computers and Education. *Artificial Intelligence, 5*, 100152. Advance online publication. DOI: 10.1016/j.caeai.2023.100152

Memon, A., Kilby, J., Breñosa, J., Espinosa, J. C. M., & Ashraf, I. (2022). Analysis and implementation of human mobility behavior using similarity analysis based on co-occurrence matrix. *Sensors (Basel), 22*(24), 9898. DOI: 10.3390/s22249898 PMID: 36560266

Mendez, C., Gazzola, M., Clement-Wilz, L., Bachtler, J. F., Charamboulos, A., Djouvas, C., Mendez, F., & Triga, V. (2024). The European Union's approach to multilingualism in its own communications policy. ResearchGate. https://www.researchgate.net/publication/365777293

Mengesha, Z., Heldreth, C., Lahav, M., Sublewski, J., & Tuennerman, E. (2021). "I don't think these devices are very culturally sensitive."—Impact of automated speech recognition errors on African Americans. Frontiers in Artificial Intelligence, 4, 725911. https://doi.org/frontiersin.orgDOI: 10.3389/frai.2021.725911

Mensah, G. B. (2023). Artificial intelligence and ethics: A comprehensive review of bias mitigation, transparency, and accountability in AI systems. DOI: 10.13140/RG.2.2.23381.19685/1

Meszaros, J., & Ho, C. (2021). AI research and data protection: Can the same rules apply for commercial and academic research under the GDPR? [HTML]. *Computer Law & Security Review, 41*, 105532. Advance online publication. DOI: 10.1016/j.clsr.2021.105532

Mhlongo, S., Mbatha, K., Ramatsetse, B., & Dlamini, R. (2023). Challenges, opportunities, and prospects of adopting and using smart digital technologies in learning environments: An iterative review. Heliyon. https://doi.org/ cell.comDOI: 10.1016/j.heliyon.2023.e16348

Miller, S., Bobrow, R., Ingria, R., & Schwartz, R. (1994, June). Hidden understanding models of natural language. In *32nd Annual Meeting of the Association for Computational Linguistics* (pp. 25-32). DOI: 10.3115/981732.981736

Mirzayev, E. (2024). Machine translation vs. human translation: A comparative analysis. *Journal of Foreign Language Teaching and Applied Linguistics, 10*(1), 31–38.

Mishra, S. K. (2024). Translation Strategies and challenges for translating Maithili Idioms and Proverbs into English. *RESEARCH REVIEW International Journal of Multidisciplinary*, *9*(4), 79–88.

Mishra, S., & Manda, J. (2024). Improving real-time analytics through the Internet of Things and data processing at the network edge. [scienceacadpress.com]. *Journal of AI-Assisted Scientific Discovery*, *4*(1), 184–206.

Mitchell, M. (2021). Abstraction and analogy-making in artificial intelligence. [PDF]. *Annals of the New York Academy of Sciences*, *1505*(1), 79–101. DOI: 10.1111/nyas.14619 PMID: 34173249

Mohamed, Y. A., Khanan, A., Bashir, M., Mohamed, A. H. H. M., Adiel, M. A. E., & Elsadig, M. A. (2024a). The Impact of Artificial Intelligence on Language Translation: A Review. *IEEE Access, 12*, 25553–25579. IEEE Access. DOI: 10.1109/ACCESS.2024.3366802

Mohammed, T. A. (2023). Translating Islamic media discourse from Arabic into English: An analysis of translation process. In N. Bakrim (Ed.), *Translatology, Translation and Interpretation-Toward a New Scientific Endeavor*. IntechOpen. https://www.intechopen.com/chapters/1172609

Mohammed, T. A. S. (2011). *A taxonomy of problems in Arabic-English translation: A systematic functional grammar approach* [PhD thesis]. University of the Western Cape.

Mohammed, A. (2022). Linguistic and Cultural Problems in Translation and Solutions. *Govarî Qeła*, *7*(2). Advance online publication. DOI: 10.25212/lfu.qzj.7.2.37

Mohammed, S. Y., Khalaf, A. S., & Aljanabi, M. (2024). Challenges and opportunities in translation studies: The evolving role. In Mansour, N., & Bujosa Vadell, L. M. (Eds.), *Sustainability and Financial Services in the Digital Age* (pp. 107–117). Springer., DOI: 10.1007/978-3-031-67511-9_7

Mohan, G. (2023). *Vekariya., L., Natrayan., Amit, Barve* (Vol. K). G., Satish., Harshal, Patil. AI-Powered Chatbot for Bridging Language Barriers with Translation., DOI: 10.1109/ICIMIA60377.2023.10426216

Mökander, J., Schuett, J., Kirk, H. R., & Floridi, L. (2023). Auditing large language models: a three-layered approach. AI and Ethics. https://doi.org/ springer.comDOI: 10.1007/s43681-023-00289-2

Molina, L., & Hurtado Albir, A. (2002). Translation techniques revisited: A dynamic and functionalist approach. *Meta*, *47*(4), 498–512. DOI: 10.7202/008033ar

Moneus, A. M., & Sahari, Y. (2024). Artificial intelligence and human translation: A contrastive study based on legal texts. *Heliyon, 10*(6), e28106. Advance online publication. DOI: 10.1016/j.heliyon.2024.e28106 PMID: 38524597

Moorkens, J., & O'Brien, S. (2017). Assessing user interface needs of post-editors of machine translation. In *Human Issues in Translation Technology* (pp. 127–148). Routledge., https://www.taylorfrancis.com/chapters/edit/10.4324/9781315648934-17/assessing-user-interface-needs-post-editors-machine-translation-joss-moorkens-sharon-brien

Mor Barak, M. E., Luria, G., & Brimhall, K. C. (2022). What leaders say versus what they do: Inclusive leadership, policy-practice decoupling, and the anomaly of climate for inclusion. [HTML]. *Group & Organization Management, 47*(4), 840–871. DOI: 10.1177/10596011211005916

Mosqueira-Rey, E., Hernández-Pereira, E., Alonso-Ríos, D., Bobes-Bascarán, J., & Fernández-Leal, Á. (2023). Human-in-the-loop machine learning: A state of the art. *Artificial Intelligence Review, 56*(4), 3005–3054. DOI: 10.1007/s10462-022-10246-w

Mossop, B. (2014). *Revising and editing for translators.* Routledge. DOI: 10.4324/9781315767130

Mounadil, T. (2023). Strategies for translating idioms and proverbs from English into Arabic. British Journal of Translation, Linguistics and Literature, 3(2), 02-09.

Muftah, M. (2024). Machine vs human translation: A new reality or a threat to professional Arabic–English translators. *PSU Research Review, 8*(2), 484–497. DOI: 10.1108/PRR-02-2022-0024

Mufti, A. R. (2004). Towards a lyric history of India. *Boundary 2, 31*(2), 245–274. DOI: 10.1215/01903659-31-2-245

Mughal, U. A., Seemab, S., Zaigham, M. S., Bhatti, A., & Khan, H. (2024). THE INTERSECTION OF LINGUISTICS AND ARTIFICIAL INTELLIGENCE: A CORPUS-BASED STUDY OF IDIOM TRANSLATION. [JALT]. *Journal of Applied Linguistics and TESOL, 7*(4), 1453–1460. jalt.com.pk

Muldoon, J., Davis, P. E., Bendickson, J. S., McDowell, W. C., & Liguori, E. W. (2022). Paved with good intentions: Moral disengagement and social entrepreneurship. Journal of Innovation & Knowledge, 7(4), 100237. https://doi.org/ sciencedirect.comDOI: 10.1016/j.jik.2022.100237

Mulgund, P., Mulgund, B. P., Sharman, R., & Singh, R. (2021). The implications of the California Consumer Privacy Act (CCPA) on healthcare organizations: Lessons learned from early compliance experiences. [HTML]. *Health Policy and Technology, 10*(3), 100543. DOI: 10.1016/j.hlpt.2021.100543

Muñoz-Basols, J., Neville, C., Lafford, B. A., & Godev, C. (2023). Potentialities of applied translation for language learning in the era of artificial intelligence. Hispania, 106(2). Johns Hopkins University Press. https://muse.jhu.edu/article/899427

Muñoz-Basols, J., Neville, C., Lafford, B. A., & Godev, C. (2023). Potentialities of Applied Translation for Language Learning in the Era of Artificial Intelligence. *Hispania, 106*(2), 171–194. DOI: 10.1353/hpn.2023.a899427

Mykolas Romeris University. (2024). Generatyvinio dirbtinio intelekto įrankių naudojimo Mykolo Romerio universiteto studijų procese tvarka. Retrieved from: chrome-extension://efaidnbmnnnibpcajpcglclefindmkaj/https://www.mruni.eu/wp-content/uploads/2024/04/GDI-irankiu-naudojimo-MRU-studijose-tvarka_viesinimui.pdf

Nababan, M., Nuraeni, A., & Sumardiono. (2012). Pengembangan Model Penilaian Kualitas Terjemahan. Kajian Linguistik dan Sastra, 24(1), 39-57.

Nadji, B. (2024). Data Security, Integrity, and Protection. [HTML]. *Data*, 59–83. Advance online publication. DOI: 10.1007/978-3-031-61117-9_4

Nagappa, A. N., & Naik, V. (2022). Patients: Gaps in Knowledge, Medication Errors, and Their Impact on Outcomes, Quality of Life, and Cost of Treatments. In Perspectives in Pharmacy Practice: Trends in Pharmaceutical Care (pp. 39-57). Singapore: Springer Singapore. https://doi.org/ [HTML]DOI: 10.1007/978-981-16-9213-0_4

Naithani, K., & Raiwani, Y. P. (2023). Realization of natural language processing and machine learning approaches for text-based sentiment analysis. [HTML]. *Expert Systems: International Journal of Knowledge Engineering and Neural Networks, 40*(5), e13114. Advance online publication. DOI: 10.1111/exsy.13114

Nanayakkara, N. D. G. T., Nanayakkara, G. A. S. Y., Karunanayaka, K. M. C. M., Kumara, C. P. T. K., & Karunanayake, N. (2024). Smart Cities, Secure Data: Navigating the Evolving Landscape of Data Protection Challenges. In Data Protection: The Wake of AI and Machine Learning (pp. 251-285). Cham: Springer Nature Switzerland. https://doi.org/ [HTML]DOI: 10.1007/978-3-031-76473-8_11

Naveen, P., & Trojovský, P. (2024). Overview and challenges of machine translation for contextually appropriate translations. *iScience, 27*(10), 110878. DOI: 10.1016/j.isci.2024.110878 PMID: 39391737

Nemani, P., Joel, Y. D., Vijay, P., & Liza, F. F. (2024). Gender bias in transformers: A comprehensive review of detection and mitigation strategies. Natural Language Processing Journal, 6, 100047. https://doi.org/sciencedirect.comDOI: 10.1016/j.nlp.2023.100047

Newell, R., George, S., Patel, M., Dawe, H., Roelas, M., Wedmore, F., & Morris, M. (2022). Improving the quality of translation for patients with language barriers. *European Journal of Public Health, 32*(Supplement_3), ckac129.639. Advance online publication. DOI: 10.1093/eurpub/ckac129.639

Newmark, P. (1988). *A textbook of translation* (Vol. 66). Prentice hall.

Ngwenya, S., & Boshoff, N. (2022). Different manifestations of 'context': Examples from a bibliometric study of research in Zimbabwe in Southern Africa. *Scientometrics, 127*(7), 3911–3933. DOI: 10.1007/s11192-022-04435-1

Nida, E. A. (1993). *Language, culture, and translating*. Shanghai Foreign Language Education Press. https://ci.nii.ac.jp/ncid/BA71847354

Nida, E. A., & Taber, C. R. (1969). *The theory and practice of translation*. Brill.

Nor, A. K. M., Pedapati, S. R., Muhammad, M., & Leiva, V. (2021). Overview of explainable artificial intelligence for prognostic and health management of industrial assets based on preferred reporting items for systematic reviews and meta-analyses. *Sensors (Basel), 21*(23), 8020. DOI: 10.3390/s21238020 PMID: 34884024

Nord, C. (2005). *Text analysis in translation: Theory, methodology, and didactic application of a model for translation-oriented text analysis*. Routledge.

O'Brien, S. (2007). An empirical investigation of temporal and technical post-editing effort. *Translation and Interpreting Studies, 2*(1), 83–136. DOI: 10.1075/tis.2.1.03ob

O'Brien, S., & Ehrensberger-Dow, M. (2020). MT literacy—A cognitive view. *Translation. Cognition & Behavior, 3*(2), 145–164. DOI: 10.1075/tcb.00038.obr

O'Hagan, M. (2016). Massively Open Translation: Unpacking the relationship between technology and translation in the 21st century. *International Journal of Communication, 10*, 929–946. https://ijoc.org/index.php/ijoc/article/view/3507/1572

Obeidat, M. M., & Jaradat, M. A. (2024). Artificial intelligence accuracy in translating resistance literature from Arabic into English: Google Translate and ChatGPT as a model. *Research Journal in Advanced Humanities, 5*(2), 45–62.

O'Brien, S. (2024). Human-Centered augmented translation: against antagonistic dualisms. Perspectives. https://doi.org/tandfonline.comDOI: 10.1080/0907676X.2023.2247423

Och, F. J., & Ney, H. (2000). Statistical machine translation. In *5th EAMT Workshop: Harvesting Existing Resources*.

Och, F. J., & Ney, H. (2003). A systematic comparison of various statistical alignment models. *Computational Linguistics*, *29*(1), 19–51. DOI: 10.1162/089120103321337421

Och, F. J., & Ney, H. (2004). The alignment template approach to statistical machine translation. *Computational Linguistics*, *30*(4), 417–449. DOI: 10.1162/0891201042544884

Ofosu-Asare, Y. (2024). Cognitive imperialism in artificial intelligence: counteracting bias with indigenous epistemologies. AI & society. https://doi.org/ springer.comDOI: 10.1007/s00146-024-02065-0

Oku, K., Samayamantri, L. S., Singhal, S., & Steffi, R. (2024). Decoding AI Decisions on Depth Map Analysis for Enhanced Interpretability. In Advancing Intelligent Networks Through Distributed Optimization (pp. 143-164). IGI Global. DOI: [HTML]DOI: 10.4018/979-8-3693-3739-4.ch008

Omar, L. I., & Salih, A. A. (2024). Systematic review of English/Arabic machine translation postediting: Implications for AI application in translation research and pedagogy. *Informatics (MDPI)*, *11*(2), 23. DOI: 10.3390/informatics11020023

Ometov, A., Molua, O. L., Komarov, M., & Nurmi, J. (2022). A survey of security in cloud, edge, and fog computing. Sensors. https://doi.org/mdpi.comDOI: 10.3390/s22030927

Öncü, M. H., & Kutlu, Y. (2024). Performance comparison of known AI translation tools. *Tethys Env. Sci*, *1*(3), 117–126. DOI: 10.5281/zenodo.13269233

OpenGenus. (2023). *Key Terms/ Topics in Natural Language Processing*. NLP.

Pan, L., Sun, D., Zou, Y., Cao, Y., Zhang, J., & Li, F. (2023). Psycho-linguistic and educational challenges in Teaching Chinese (Mandarin) Language: voices from None-Chinese teachers of Mandarin language. BMC psychology. https://doi.org/springer.comDOI: 10.1186/s40359-023-01432-8

Pandey, N. K., Kumar, K., Saini, G., & Mishra, A. K. (2023). Security issues and challenges in cloud of things-based applications for industrial automation. Annals of Operations Research. https://doi.org/springer.comDOI: 10.1007/s10479-023-05285-7

Pantelimon, F. V., Bologa, R., Toma, A., & Posedaru, B. S. (2021). The evolution of AI-driven educational systems during the COVID-19 pandemic. *Sustainability (Basel)*, *13*(23), 13501. DOI: 10.3390/su132313501

Papatsimouli, M., Sarigiannidis, P., & Fragulis, G. F. (2023). A survey of advancements in real-time sign language translators: integration with IoT technology. Technologies. https://doi.org/ mdpi.comDOI: 10.3390/technologies11040083

Park, C. S. Y., Kim, M. G., & Han, H. W. (2024). Transforming nursing practice through cutting-edge AI in healthcare: Opportunities, challenges, and ethical implications. Contemporary Nurse. https://doi.org/ tandfonline.comDOI: 10.1080/10376178.2024.2424787

Park, P. S., Goldstein, S., O'Gara, A., Chen, M., & Hendrycks, D. (2024). AI deception: A survey of examples, risks, and potential solutions. Patterns. https://doi .org/cell.comDOI: 10.1016/j.patter.2024.100988

Park, S. C. (2018). The Fourth Industrial Revolution and implications for innovative cluster policies. *AI & Society*, *33*(3), 433–445. DOI: 10.1007/s00146-017-0777-5

Parthasarathi, A., Banu, A., & Joshi, A. (2023, December). Comprehensive Survey of Audio-to-Text Conversion. In International Symposium on Intelligent Informatics (pp. 129-145). Singapore: Springer Nature Singapore. https://doi.org/ [HTML]DOI: 10.1007/978-981-97-2147-4_10

Parthasarathi, A., Banu, A., & Joshi, A. (2025). Comprehensive Survey of Audio-to-Text. In Intelligent Informatics: Proceedings of Eighth International Symposium on Intelligent Informatics (ISI 2023) (Vol. 389, p. 129). Springer Nature. [HTML]

Paśko, Ł., Mądziel, M., Stadnicka, D., Dec, G., Carreras-Coch, A., Solé-Beteta, X., Pappa, L., Stylios, C., Mazzei, D., & Atzeni, D. (2022). Plan and develop advanced knowledge and skills for future industrial employees in the field of artificial intelligence, internet of things and edge computing. *Sustainability (Basel)*, *14*(6), 3312. DOI: 10.3390/su14063312

Patsakis, C. & Lykousas, N. (2023). Man vs the machine in the struggle for effective text anonymisation in the age of large language models. Scientific Reports. https:// doi.org/nature.comDOI: 10.1038/s41598-023-42977-3

Paul, B. (2023). Advancements and Perspectives in Machine Translation: A Comprehensive Review. *1st International Conference on Recent Innovations in Computing, Science & Technology*, 6 Pages. DOI: 10.2139/ssrn.4562254

Pavone, A. & Plebe, A. (2021). How neurons in deep models relate with neurons in the brain. Algorithms. https://doi.org/mdpi.comDOI: 10.3390/a14090272

Peng, Z., Bawden, R., & Yvon, F. (2024). *Handling very long contexts in neural machine translation: A survey* [PhD Thesis, Projet ANR MaTOS]. https://inria.hal .science/hal-04652584

Peng, K., Ding, L., Zhong, Q., Shen, L., Liu, X., Zhang, M., Ouyang, Y., & Tao, D. (2023). Towards making the most of ChatGPT for machine translation. *Findings of the Association for Computational Linguistics: EMNLP, 2023*, 5622–5633. DOI: 10.18653/v1/2023.findings-emnlp.373

Penguin Random House. (2020, February 23). Subh-e-Azadi (B. Farooqui, Trans.). *Penguin Random House India*. https://www.penguin.co.in/subh-e-azadi-an-anguished-evocation-of-the-pain-of-partition/

Pestov, I. (2018). A History of Machine Translation from the Cold War to Deep Learning. Freecodecamp.org. 12 Maret 2018. https://www.freecodecamp.org/news/a-history-of-machine-translation-from-the-cold-war-to-deep-learning-f1d335ce8b5/

Petro anu, D. M., Pîrjan, A., & Tăbu că, A. (2023). Tracing the Influence of Large Language Models across the Most Impactful Scientific Works. Electronics. https://doi.org/mdpi.comDOI: 10.3390/electronics12244957

Plitt, M., & Masselot, F. (2010). A productivity test of statistical machine translation post-editing in a typical localisation context. *Prague Bull. Math. Linguistics*, *93*(1), 7–16. DOI: 10.2478/v10108-010-0010-x

Pöchhacker, F. (2022). Interpreters and interpreting: shifting the balance?. The Translator. https://doi.org/ tandfonline.comDOI: 10.1080/13556509.2022.2133393

Postigo, M. L. (2024). ChatGPT and MT-systems: Advantages and limitations when translating english to spanish and portuguese. *Lengua Y Habla*, *28*, 369–390.

Povedano-Montero, F. J., Weinreb, R. N., Raga-Martínez, I., Romero, A., & López-Muñoz, F. (2020). Detection of neurological and ophthalmological pathologies with Optical Coherence Tomography using retinal thickness measurements: A bibliometric study. *Applied Sciences (Basel, Switzerland)*, *10*(16), 5477. DOI: 10.3390/app10165477

Prabhakaran, V., Qadri, R., & Hutchinson, B. (2022). Cultural incongruencies in artificial intelligence. arXiv preprint arXiv:2211.13069.

Pradeep, P., Krishnamoorthy, S., Pathinarupothi, R. K., & Vasilakos, A. V. (2021). Leveraging context-awareness for Internet of Things ecosystem: Representation, organization, and management of context. [HTML]. *Computer Communications*, *177*, 33–50. DOI: 10.1016/j.comcom.2021.06.004

PrimeGroupUSA. (2023). Advantages and limitations of Text-to-Speech technology. *PrimeGroupUSA*. Retrieved from https://primegroupusa.com

Pym, A. & Hao, Y. (2024). How to Augment Language Skills: Generative AI and Machine Translation in Language Learning and Translator Training. [HTML]

Pym, A. (2013). Translation skill-sets in a machine-translation age. *Meta*, *58*(3), 487–503. DOI: 10.7202/1025047ar

Pym, A. (2014). *Exploring translation theories* (2nd ed.). Routledge.

Rabiner, L. R. (2023). A tutorial on hidden Markov models and selected applications in speech recognition. *Proceedings of the IEEE*. Retrieved from https://ieeexplore.ieee.org/document/18626

Ragni, V., & Vieira, L. N. (2022). What has changed with neural machine translation? A critical review of human factors. *Perspectives-Studies in Translation Theory and Practice*, *30*(1), 137–158. DOI: 10.1080/0907676X.2021.1889005

Rahali, A. & Akhloufi, M. A. (2023). End-to-end transformer-based models in textual-based NLP. AI. https://doi.org/ mdpi.comDOI: 10.3390/ai4010004

Rahim, N. R. (2024). Google and legal translation: The case study of contracts. *Arab World English Journal for Translation & Literary Studies*, *8*(2), 196–210. DOI: 10.24093/awejtls/vol8no2.14

Ranathunga, S., Lee, E.-S. A., Prifti Skenduli, M., Shekhar, R., Alam, M., & Kaur, R. (2023). Neural machine translation for low-resource languages: A survey. *ACM Computing Surveys*, *55*(11), 1–37. DOI: 10.1145/3567592

Rane, N., Choudhary, S., & Rane, J. (2024). Gemini Versus ChatGPT: Applications, Performance, Architecture, Capabilities, and Implementation. SSRN *Electronic Journal*. DOI: 10.2139/ssrn.4723687

Rao, P., McGee, L. M., & Seideman, C. A. (2024). A comparative assessment of ChatGPT vs. Google Translate for the translation of patient instructions. *Journal of Medical Artificial Intelligence*, *7*, 11. DOI: 10.21037/jmai-24-24

Rauf, S. A., & Yvon, F. (2020). *Document level contexts for neural machine translation* [PhD Thesis, LIMSI-CNRS]. https://hal.science/hal-03687190/document

Ray, P. P. (2023). ChatGPT: A comprehensive review on background, applications, key challenges, bias, ethics, limitations and future scope. Internet of Things and Cyber-Physical Systems. https://doi.org/sciencedirect.comDOI: 10.1016/j.iotcps.2023.04.003

Rebolledo Font de la Vall, R., & Gonzalez Araya, F. (2023). Exploring the benefits and challenges of AI-language learning tools. *The International Journal of Social Sciences and Humanities Invention, 10*(01), 7569–7576. DOI: 10.18535/ijsshi/v10i01.02

Rehfeldt, R. A., Tyndall, I., & Belisle, J. (2021). Music as a cultural inheritance system: a contextual-behavioral model of symbolism, meaning, and the value of music. Behavior and Social Issues. https://doi.org/springer.comDOI: 10.1007/s42822-021-00084-w

Reiss, K. (2000). Type, kind and individuality of text: Decision making in translation. In Venuti, L. (Ed.), *The Translation Studies Reader* (pp. 168–179). Routledge.

Renuka, O., RadhaKrishnan, N., Priya, B. S., Jhansy, A., & Ezekiel, S. (2025). Data Privacy and Protection: Legal and Ethical Challenges. Emerging Threats and Countermeasures in Cybersecurity, 433-465. https://doi.org/ [HTML]DOI: 10.1002/9781394230600.ch19

Resende, N., & Hadley, J. (2024). The Translator's Canvas: Using LLMs to enhance Poetry translation. In *Proceedings of the 16th Conference of the Association for Machine Translation in the Americas* (Vol. 1). https://aclanthology.org/2024.amta-research.16.pdf

Ribeiro, A. P. D., Almeida, R. F., Medonca, J. G. A., & Leal, S. C. (2018). Oral health and its effect on the academic performance of children and adolescents. *Pediatric Dentistry, 40*(1), 12–17. PMID: 29482676

Rivera-Trigueros, I. (2022). Machine translation systems and quality assessment: A systematic review. *Language Resources and Evaluation, 56*(2), 593–619. DOI: 10.1007/s10579-021-09537-5

Rojo, J. J. L. (2018). Aspects of human translation: The current situation and an emerging trend. *Hermeneus: Revista De La Facultad De Traducción E Interpretación De Soria, 20*, 257–294.

Rosenthal, F. (1958). *The Muqaddimah: An Introduction to History*. Princeton University Press.

Rosset, C., Cheng, J., Saleh, M., & Dolan, B. (2020). Turing-NLG: A 17-billion-parameter language model by Microsoft. *Microsoft Research Blog*. Retrieved from [https://www.microsoft.com/en-us/research/blog/turing-nlg-a-17-billion-parameter-language-model-by-microsoft/](https://www.microsoft.com/en-us/research)

Rothwell, A., Moorkens, J., Fernández-Parra, M., Drugan, J., & Austermuehl, F. (2023). *Translation Tools and Technologies*. Routledge., DOI: 10.4324/9781003160793-1

Saeed, M. M. A., Saeed, R. A., & Ahmed, Z. E. (2024). Data Security and Privacy in the Age of AI and Digital Twins. In Digital Twin Technology and AI Implementations in Future-Focused Businesses (pp. 99-124). IGI Global. DOI: [HTML]DOI: 10.4018/979-8-3693-1818-8.ch008

Sahari, Y., Al-Kadi, A. M. T., & Ali, J. K. M. (2023). A cross sectional study of ChatGPT in translation: Magnitude of use, attitudes, and uncertainties. *Journal of Psycholinguistic Research*, *52*(6), 2937–2954. DOI: 10.1007/s10936-023-10031-y PMID: 37934302

Sakshi, T. M., Tyagi, P., & Jain, V. (2024). Emerging trends in hybrid information systems modeling in artificial intelligence. [HTML]. *Hybrid Information Systems: Non-Linear Optimization Strategies with Artificial Intelligence*, *115*, 115–152. Advance online publication. DOI: 10.1515/9783111331133-007

Salam, Z. A. A., & Kadir, R. A. (2017). A Study of Context Influences in Arabic-English Language Translation Technologies. *Jurnal Teknologi Maklumat dan Multimedia Asia-Pasifik, 6*(2), 43-52.

Salas-Pilco, S. Z., Xiao, K., & Oshima, J. (2022). Artificial intelligence and new technologies in inclusive education for minority students: A systematic review. *Sustainability (Basel)*, *14*(20), 13572. DOI: 10.3390/su142013572

Salinas, M.-J. V., & Burbat, R. (2023). Google translate and DeepL: Breaking taboos in translator training. Observational study and analysis. *Ibérica (New York, N.Y.)*, *45*(45), 243–266. DOI: 10.17398/2340-2784.45.243

Sam, A. K., & Olbrich, P. (2023). The need for AI ethics in higher education. In *AI ethics in higher education: Insights from Africa and beyond* (pp. 3–10). Springer International Publishing. DOI: 10.1007/978-3-031-23035-6_1

Samantray, K., İZGİ, F. D., Ocampo, M. B., Dehghan, M., Mohammadpour, S., Siriphaprapagon, Y., ... & Babu, S. D. (2024). The Power of Words in AI-Driven World: Exploring the Interplay of Language, Culture, and Communication. SKET-SAMEDIA.

Samantray, K., İZGİ, F. D., Ocampo, M. B., Dehghan, M., Mohammadpour, S., Siriphaprapagon, Y., ... & Babu, S. D. (2024). The Power of Words in AI-Driven World: Exploring the Interplay of Language, Culture, and Communication. SKET-SAMEDIA. [HTML]

Sanesi, M. (2024). Enhancing translation pedagogy through culture-specific terms. Педагогика. Вопросы теории и практики, 9(4), 287-294.

Santos, O., & Radanliev, P. (2024). *Beyond the Algorithm: AI.* Security, Privacy, and Ethics. [HTML]

Sarker, I. H. (2021). Deep learning: a comprehensive overview on techniques, taxonomy, applications and research directions. SN computer science. https://doi.org/ springer.comDOI: 10.1007/s42979-021-00815-1

Sarker, I. H. (2021). Machine learning: Algorithms, real-world applications and research directions. SN computer science. https://doi.org/ springer.comDOI: 10.1007/ s42979-021-00592-x

Sarker, I. H. (2022). AI-based modeling: techniques, applications and research issues towards automation, intelligent and smart systems. SN Computer Science. https:// doi.org/ springer.comDOI: 10.1007/s42979-022-01043-x

Savoldi, B., Gaido, M., Bentivogli, L., Negri, M., & Turchi, M. (2021). Gender bias in machine translation. *Proceedings of the 2021 Conference on Empirical Methods in Natural Language Processing (EMNLP 2021).*

Sayers, D., Sousa-Silva, R., Höhn, S., Ahmedi, L., Allkivi-Metsoja, K., Anastasiou, D., Beňuš, Š., Bowker, L., Bytyçi, E., Catala, A., Çepani, A., Chacón-Beltrán, R., Dadi, S., Dalipi, F., Despotovic, V., Doczekalska, A., Drude, S., Fort, K., Fuchs, R., . . . Yayilgan, S. Y. (2021, May 19). *The Dawn of the Human-Machine Era: A forecast of new and emerging language technologies.* https://hal.science/hal-03230287/

Scannell, C., Lambkin, K., O'Brien, E., Nolan, P., Holloway, P., Ryan, P., . . . Delmar, J. (2023). TRANSLATE: Providing Standardised National Climate Services for Ireland (No. EMS2023-296). Copernicus Meetings.

Schmitt, M., & Koutroumpis, P. (2025). Cyber Shadows: Neutralizing Security Threats with AI and Targeted Policy Measures. In IEEE Transactions on Artificial Intelligence (p. 1). Institute of Electrical and Electronics Engineers. https://doi.org/ DOI: 10.1109/TAI.2025.3527398

Schwartz, R., Vassilev, A., Greene, K., Perine, L., Burt, A., & Hall, P. (2021). Towards a standard for identifying and managing bias in artificial intelligence (NIST Special Publication 1270). National Institute of Standards and Technology. DOI: 10.6028/NIST.SP.1270

Scorpo, A. L. (2023). *Beyond Epistolary Standards? The Language of Entreaty in Political and Diplomatic Communications from Thirteenth-Century Iberia.* The Medieval Globe. [HTML]

Sebo, P., & de Lucia, S. (2024). Performance of machine translators in translating french medical research abstracts to english: A comparative study of DeepL, google translate, and CUBBITT. *PLoS One*, *19*(2), e0297183. DOI: 10.1371/journal.pone.0297183 PMID: 38300946

Seneff, S. (1992). TINA: A natural language system for spoken language applications. *Computational Linguistics*, *18*(1), 61–86.

Shaalan, K., Siddiqui, S., Alkhatib, M., & Abdel Monem, A. (2018). Challenges in Arabic natural language processing. In Computational linguistics, speech and image processing for Arabic language (pp. 59-83). DOI: 10.1142/9789813229396_0003

Shahmerdanova, R. (2025). Artificial Intelligence in Translation: Challenges and Opportunities. *Acta Globalis Humanitatis et Linguarum*, *2*(1), 62–70. DOI: 10.69760/aghel.02500108

Shaik, R. (2025). Enhancing text generation in joint Nlg/Nlu learning through curriculum learning, semi-supervised training, and advanced optimization techniques. *Multimedia Tools and Applications*. Advance online publication. DOI: 10.1007/s11042-025-20665-w

Shaip. (2024). ASR (Automatic Speech Recognition) - Definition, use cases, example. *Shaip*. Retrieved from https://www.shaip.com/blog/automatic-speech-recognitiona-complete-overview/

Shao, Z., Zhao, R., Yuan, S., Ding, M., & Wang, Y. (2022). Tracing the evolution of AI in the past decade and forecasting the emerging trends. Expert Systems with Applications, 209, 118221. https://doi.org/sciencedirect.comDOI: 10.1016/j.eswa.2022.118221

Sharahil, F. B., Lin, D. T. A., & Abbaspour, B. N. (2022). TRANSLATING IDIOMATIC EXPRESSIONS IN LITERARY PROSE: THE CASE OF HARPER LEE'S TO KILL A MOCKINGBIRD. *Deleted Journal*, *19*(2). Advance online publication. DOI: 10.17576/ebangi.2022.1902.14

Sharma, I., & Aggarwal, A. (2024). Revolutionizing Creative Tourism: Integrating AI in Marketing for Immersive Travel Experiences. Innovative Technologies for Increasing Service Productivity, 179-197. DOI: [HTML]DOI: 10.4018/979-8-3693-2019-8.ch011

Sharma, S., Rawal, R., & Shah, D. (2023). Addressing the challenges of AI-based telemedicine: Best practices and lessons learned [Review of Addressing the challenges of AI-based telemedicine: Best practices and lessons learned]. Journal of Education and Health Promotion, 12(1). Medknow. https://doi.org/DOI: 10.4103/jehp.jehp_402_23

Shava, G. N., Hleza, S., Tlou, F., Shonhiwa, S., & Mathonsi, E. (2021). Qualitative Content Analysis, Utility, Usability and Processes in Educational Research. *International Journal of Research and Innovation in Social Science*, *5*(07), 553–558.

Shi, Z. (2021). Brain-like intelligence. In Intelligence Science (pp. 537-593). DOI: 10.1016/B978-0-323-85380-4.00014-2

Shokoohifar, M. (2024). *Artificial Intelligence-Assisted Translation: A Study of Cognitive Load and Time Through EEG* [PhD Thesis, Allameh Tabataba'i University].

Shumba, A. T., Montanaro, T., Sergi, I., Fachechi, L., De Vittorio, M., & Patrono, L. (2022). Leveraging IoT-aware technologies and AI techniques for real-time critical healthcare applications. Sensors, 22(19), 7675. https://doi.org/mdpi.comDOI: 10.3390/s22197675

Silalahi, R. (2009). *Dampak teknik, metode, dan ideologi penerjemahan pada kualitas terjemahan teks medical surgical nursing dalam Bahasa Indonesia (The Impact of the Translation Techniques, Methods, and Ideologies on the Quality of the Translated Text Medical-Surgical Nursing in Bahasa Indonesia)*. Tesis Kedoktoran, Universitas Sumatera Utara.

Silu, P. (2024). *Issues in Machine Translation with reference to the Story "Thakur ka kuan" by Munshi Premchand*. International Journal For Multidisciplinary Research., DOI: 10.36948/ijfmr.2024.v06i05.28130

Simon Says, A. I. (2023). What is ASR? How does it work? Our in-depth 2023 guide. *Simon Says AI*. Retrieved from https://www.simonsaysai.com/blog/automatic-speech-recognition

Sinclair-Palm, J., & Chokly, K. (2023). 'It'sa giant faux pas': Exploring young trans people's beliefs about deadnaming and the term deadname. [HTML]. *Journal of LGBT Youth*, *20*(2), 370–389. Advance online publication. DOI: 10.1080/19361653.2022.2076182

Sindhu, B., Prathamesh, R. P., & Sameera, M. B., & KumaraSwamy, S. (2024, May). The evolution of large language model: Models, applications and challenges. In *2024 International Conference on Current Trends in Advanced Computing (ICCTAC)* (pp. 1-8). IEEE. https://doi.org/ [HTML]DOI: 10.1109/ICCTAC61556.2024.10581180

Singh, A. P., Saxena, R., & Saxena, S. (2024). The human touch in the age of artificial intelligence: A literature review on the interplay of emotional intelligence and AI. *Asian Journal of Current Research, 9*(4), 36–50. DOI: 10.56557/ajocr/2024/v9i48860

Sin-wai, C. (2023). THE DEVELOPMENT OF TRANSLATION TECHNOLOGY 1967-2023. Routledge Encyclopedia of Translation Technology. [HTML]

Sipayung, K. T., Pasaribu, A. N., & Sinaga, N. T. (2024). Common Problems and Overt Errors in Translating Idioms in The Film Maleficent. *Eurasian Journal of Applied Linguistics, 9*(2), 23–31. DOI: 10.32601/ejal.10203

Siregar, I. (2023). The Role of Language in a Dynamic Situation of Globalization. Britain International of Linguistics Arts and Education (BIoLAE) Journal, 5(1), 49-59. https://doi.org/biarjournal.comDOI: 10.33258/biolae.v5i1.868

Siu, S. C. (2023). *ChatGPT and GPT-4 for professional translators: Exploring the potential of large language models in translation*. Preprint., DOI: 10.2139/ssrn.4448091

Siu, S. C. (2024). Revolutionising translation with AI: Unravelling neural machine translation and generative pre-trained large language models. In Peng, Y., Huang, H., & Li, D. (Eds.), *New Advances in Translation Technology*. Springer., DOI: 10.1007/978-981-97-2958-6_3

Sjahrony, K., & Ahmad, M. (2013). Penterjemahan Frasa Al-Idafah Arab-Melayu Menggunakan Google Translate (*Translating Phrases of Al-Idafah of Arab-Malay Using Google Translate*). *Islāmiyyāt: International Journal of Islamic Studies, 35*(2), 101–108.

Skadiņa, I., Vasi jevs, A., Pinnis, M., Bērziņš, A., Aranberri, N., Bogaert, J. V. D., . . . Way, A. (2023). Deep Dive Machine Translation. In European Language Equality: A Strategic Agenda for Digital Language Equality (pp. 263-287). Cham: Springer International Publishing. https://doi.org/ springer.comDOI: 10.1007/978-3-031-28819-7_40

Skaria, S., Kumar, A., & Singh, R. (2024). AR-enhanced interpretation in tourism: A case study. *Journal of Tourism Studies, 12*(2), 145–160.

Škobo, M., & Petričević, V. (2023). Navigating the Challenges and Opportunities of Literary Translation in the Age of AI: Striking a Balance Between Human Expertise and Machine Power. *Društvene i Humanističke Studije, 8*(2(23)). *Article, 2*(23). Advance online publication. DOI: 10.51558/2490-3647.2023.8.2.317

Slator (2024). *Language AI Briefing August 2024*.https://slator.com/language-ai-briefing-august-2024/

Smith, E. (2008). Pitfalls and promises: The use of secondary data analysis in educational research. *British Journal of Educational Studies*, *56*(3), 323–339. DOI: 10.1111/j.1467-8527.2008.00405.x

Sobti, P., & Kumar, D. (2022). Partition as Memory: Construing Women Narratives. *Journal of Positive School Psychology*, *6*(9), 731–738.

Son, J. & Kim, B. (2023). Translation performance from the user's perspective of large language models and neural machine translation systems. Information. https://doi.org/mdpi.comDOI: 10.3390/info14100574

Song, B. (2024). What is translation cultural studies in the context of new technology? *Foreign Languages*, *47*(1), 11–14.

Song, Z. (2024). A Comparative Study of Two Translated Versions of Walden in Chinese from the Perspective of the Translator's Subjectivity. *Journal of Social Sciences and Humanities*, *6*(8), 122–127. DOI: 10.53469/jssh.2024.06(08).24

Southwell, R., Pugh, S., Perkoff, E. M., Clevenger, C., Bush, J. B., Lieber, R., . . . D'Mello, S. (2024). Challenges and feasibility of automatic speech recognition for modeling student collaborative discourse in classrooms. *Institute of Cognitive Science, University of Colorado Boulder*. Retrieved from [https://www.colorado.edu/research/ai-institute/sites/default/files/attached-files/challengesfeasibility.pdf](https://www.colorado.edu/research/ai-institute/sites

Soysal, F. (2023). Enhancing translation studies with artificial intelligence (AI): Challenges, opportunities, and proposals. *Karamanoğlu Mehmetbey University International Journal of Philology and Translation Studies*, *5*(2), 177–191. DOI: 10.55036/ufced.1402649

SpringerLink. (2023). Sign Language Statistical. *Machine Translation.*

Sreelekha, M. (2017). Comparing RBMT and SMT for English-Indian Language Translation. *Journal of Computational Linguistics*, *23*(4), 567–589.

Stahlberg, F. (2020). Neural machine translation: A review. *Journal of Artificial Intelligence Research*, *69*, 343–418. DOI: 10.1613/jair.1.12007

Stein, D. (2018). Machine translation: Past, present and future. In Rehm, G., Stein, D., Sasaki, F., & Witt, A. (Eds.), *Language technologies for a multilingual Europe. (Translation and Multilingual Natural Language Processing 5).* Language Science Press., DOI: 10.5281/zenodo.1291947

Sulubacak, U., Caglayan, O., Grönroos, S.-A., Rouhe, A., Elliott, D., Specia, L., & Tiedemann, J. (2020). Multimodal machine translation through visuals and speech. *Machine Translation, 34*(2–3), 97–147. DOI: 10.1007/s10590-020-09250-0

Sun, S. (2025). Corpora and Assessment of Translator Expertise. In The Routledge Handbook of Corpus Translation Studies (pp. 582-599). Routledge. https://doi.org/ [HTML]DOI: 10.4324/9781003184454

Sun, X., Li, T., Wang, P., Shang, L., Niu, M., Meng, X., & Shao, H. (2022). Nanomaterials and Advances in Tumor Immune-Related Therapy: A Bibliometric Analysis. *Journal of Biomedical Nanotechnology, 18*(9), 2154-2170.0

Sun, Y., Sheng, D., Zhou, Z., & Wu, Y. (2024). AI hallucination: towards a comprehensive classification of distorted information in artificial intelligence-generated content. Humanities and Social Sciences Communications, 11(1), 1-14. https://doi.org/nature.comDOI: 10.1057/s41599-024-03811-x

Sutskever, I., Vinyals, O., & Le, Q. V. (2014). Sequence to Sequence Learning with Neural Networks. *Advances in Neural Information Processing Systems, 27*, 3104–3112.

Swargiary, K. (2024). *Sacred codes: Artificial intelligence and the creation of religious texts*. ERA.

Swiatek, L., Vujnovic, M., Galloway, C., & Kruckeberg, D. (2023). Artificial intelligence, strategic communicators and activism. [HTML]

Sze Ming, L., & Sin-Wai, C. (Eds.). (2024). *Applying Technology to Language and Translation*. Routledge., DOI: 10.4324/9781003399261

Taghian, M. A. (2024). Assessing the Accuracy Criteria of AI Tools-aided Translation: A Case Study of Two-word Prophetic Hadiths. *CDELT Occasional Papers in the Development of English Education, 87*(1), 217–262. DOI: 10.21608/opde.2024.384369

Tao, G. (2023). A Study on Error Feature Analysis and Error Correction in English Translation Through Machine Translatio. [lithuanian Academy of Sciences]. *Informatica (Vilnius), 47*(8). Advance online publication. DOI: 10.31449/inf.v47i8.4862

Tatineni, S. (2019). Ethical considerations in AI and data science: Bias, fairness, and accountability. *International Journal of Information Technology and Management Information Systems, 10*(1), 11–20. https://iaeme.com/Home/issue/IJITMIS?Volume=10&Issue=1

Tavares, C., Oliveira, L., Duarte, P., & Moreira da Silva, M. (2023). Artificial intelligence: A blessing or a threat for language service providers in Portugal. *Informatics (MDPI), 10*(4), 81. DOI: 10.3390/informatics10040081

Taye, M. M. (2023). Understanding of machine learning with deep learning: architectures, workflow, applications and future directions. Computers. https://doi.org/mdpi.comDOI: 10.3390/computers12050091

Taylor, A. (2025, February 5). How real-world businesses are transforming with AI – with 50 new stories. Microsoft Blog. https://blogs.microsoft.com/blog/2025/02/05/https-blogs-microsoft-com-blog-2024-11-12-how-real-world-businesses-are-transforming-with-ai/

Technologies, O. (2023). What is Hybrid. *Machine Translation.*

Tedre, M., Toivonen, T., Kahila, J., Vartiainen, H., Valtonen, T., Jormanainen, I., & Pears, A. (2021). Teaching machine learning in K–12 classroom: Pedagogical and technological trajectories for artificial intelligence education. *IEEE Access : Practical Innovations, Open Solutions*, *9*, 110558–110572. DOI: 10.1109/ACCESS.2021.3097962

Tekwa, K. (2023). *Machine translation and foreign language learning*. Springer., DOI: 10.1007/978-981-99-8602-6

Theodorakopoulos, L., Theodoropoulou, A., & Stamatiou, Y. (2024). A state-of-the-art review in big data management engineering: Real-life case studies, challenges, and future research directions. Eng. https://doi.org/ mdpi.comDOI: 10.3390/eng5030068

Thompson, O. (2024). Advancements in Natural Language Processing: AI's Impact on Language Translation and Interpretation. *International Journal of Sustainable Development in Computing Science.*

Tian, X. (2024). Personalized translator training in the era of digital intelligence: Opportunities, challenges, and prospects. Heliyon. https://doi.org/ cell.comDOI: 10.1016/j.heliyon.2024.e39354

Timmons, A. C., Duong, J. B., Simo Fiallo, N., Lee, T., Vo, H. P. Q., Ahle, M. W., ... & Chaspari, T. (2023). A call to action on assessing and mitigating bias in artificial intelligence applications for mental health. Perspectives on Psychological Science, 18(5), 1062-1096. https://doi.org/sagepub.comDOI: 10.1177/17456916221134490

Tipà, I. & Moratto, R. Chinese interpreting in Italy: An overview. The Routledge Handbook of Chinese Interpreting. [HTML]

Tiribelli, S., Pansoni, S., Frontoni, E., & Giovanola, B. (2024). Ethics of Artificial Intelligence for Cultural Heritage: Opportunities and Challenges. IEEE Transactions on Technology and Society. https://doi.org/ieee.orgDOI: 10.1109/TTS.2024.3432407

Tiwari, A. K., Abakah, E. J. A., Gil-Alana, L. A., & Abakah, M. K. (2021). Inflation co-movement dynamics: A cross-country investigation using a continuous wavelet approach. *Journal of Risk and Financial Management*, *14*(12), 613. DOI: 10.3390/jrfm14120613

Toivonen, T., Jormanainen, I., Kahila, J., Tedre, M., Valtonen, T., & Vartiainen, H. (2020, July). Co-designing machine learning apps in K–12 with primary school children. In *2020 IEEE 20th International Conference on Advanced Learning Technologies (ICALT)* (pp. 308-310). IEEE. DOI: 10.1109/ICALT49669.2020.00099

Tomalin, M., Byrne, B., Concannon, S., Saunders, D., & Ullmann, S. (2021). The practical ethics of bias reduction in machine translation: Why domain adaptation is better than data debiasing. Ethics and Information Technology, 1-15. https://doi.org/ springer.comDOI: 10.1007/s10676-021-09583-1

Tomenchuk, M., & Popovych, K. (2024). *Large language models and machine translation*. https://dspace.uzhnu.edu.ua/jspui/handle/lib/68269

Toral, A., & Way, A. (2018). What level of quality can neural machine translation attain on literary text?. *Translation quality assessment: From principles to practice*, 263-287.

Torregrosa, D., Pasricha, N., Masoud, M., Chakravarthi, B. R., Alonso, J., & Casas, N. (2019). Leveraging rule-based machine translation knowledge for under-resourced neural machine translation models. In *Proceedings of Machine Translation Summit XVII: Translator, Project and User Tracks* (pp. 125-133). European Association for Machine Translation.

Touretzky, D., Gardner-McCune, C., Martin, F., & Seehorn, D. (2019, July). Envisioning AI for K-12: What should every child know about AI? *Proceedings of the AAAI Conference on Artificial Intelligence*, *33*(01), 9795–9799. DOI: 10.1609/aaai.v33i01.33019795

Turchi, M., Negri, M., Farajian, M., & Federico, M. (2017). Continuous learning from human post-edits for neural machine translation. *The Prague Bulletin of Mathematical Linguistics*, *108*(1), 233–244. DOI: 10.1515/pralin-2017-0023

Udupa, P. (2022). Application of artificial intelligence for university information system. *Engineering Applications of Artificial Intelligence*, *114*, 105038. DOI: 10.1016/j.engappai.2022.105038

UK Government. (2024). Generative AI framework for HMG. https://www.gov.uk/government/publications/generative-ai-framework-for-hmg/generative-ai-framework-for-hmg-html

University of Latvia. (2024). Guidelines for the use of artificial intelligence in the University of Ltavia. Retrieved from: chrome-extension://efaidnbmnnnibpcajpcglclefindmkaj/https://www.lu.lv/fileadmin/user_upload/LU.LV/www.lu.lv/Studijas/Guidelines_for_the_use_of_AI_in_the_UL_11.04.2024.v.0.1.pdf

University of Tartu. (2024). University of Tartu guidelines for using AI applications for teaching and studies. Retrieved from: https://ut.ee/en/node/151731

Urlaub, P., & Dessein, E. (2022). Machine translation and foreign language education. *Frontiers in Artificial Intelligence*, *5*, 936111. DOI: 10.3389/frai.2022.936111 PMID: 35937139

Valizadeh, M., & Vazifehkhah, A. E. (2021). Applied strategies in translating idiomatic expressions: Cultural-bound analysis in Brida novel by Paulo Coelho. *RumeliDe Dil ve Edebiyat Arastirmalari Dergisi*, *23*(23), 1058–1066. DOI: 10.29000/rumelide.950001

Van Giffen, B., Herhausen, D., & Fahse, T. (2022). Overcoming the pitfalls and perils of algorithms: A classification of machine learning biases and mitigation methods. Journal of Business Research. https://doi.org/sciencedirect.comDOI: 10.1016/j.jbusres.2022.01.076

Varela, D. T. (2024). Diplomacy in the Age of AI: Challenges and Opportunities. Journal of Artificial Intelligence General science (JAIGS) ISSN: 3006-4023, 2(1), 101-128. boulibrary.com

Varsha, P. S. (2023). How can we manage biases in artificial intelligence systems–A systematic literature review. International Journal of Information Management Data Insights, 3(1), 100165. https://doi.org/sciencedirect.comDOI: 10.1016/j.jjimei.2023.100165

Vasheghani Farahani, M., & Dastjerdi, H. V. (2021). Corpora and translation studies: Implications and applications. *Journal of Language and Translation.* Retrieved from https://www.researchgate.net/publication/361950371*Corpora*and*Translation*-Studies*Implications*and_Applications

Vaswani, A., Shazeer, N., Parmar, N., Uszkoreit, J., Jones, L., Gomez, A. N., Kaiser, Ł., & Polosukhin, I. (2017). Attention is all you need. *Advances in Neural Information Processing Systems, 30.* https://proceedings.neurips.cc/paper/2017/hash/3f5ee243547dee91fbd053c1c4a845aa-Abstract.html

Vaswani, A., Shazeer, N., Parmar, N., Uszkoreit, J., Jones, L., Gomez, A. N., Kaiser, Ł., & Polosukhin, I. (2017). Attention is all you need. In *Advances in Neural Information Processing Systems* (pp. 5998-6008). https://arxiv.org/abs/1706.03762

Vaswani, A., Bengio, S., Brevdo, E., Chollet, F., Gomez, A., Gouws, S., & Uszkoreit, J. (2018, March). Tensor2Tensor for Neural Machine Translation. In *Proceedings of the 13th Conference of the Association for Machine Translation in the Americas,* pp. 193-199.

Vaswani, A., Shazeer, N., Parmar, N., Uszkoreit, J., Jones, L., Gomez, A. N., Kaiser, Ł., & Polosukhin, I. (2017). Attention is all you need. *Advances in Neural Information Processing Systems, 30*, 5998–6008.

Vaughn, F. C. (2023). Viability of a career in the interpretation and translation industry with the advancements of artificial intelligence. Retrieved from: chrome-extension://efaidnbmnnnibpcajpcglclefindmkaj/https://www.theseus.fi/bitstream/handle/10024/806809/Vaughn_Fernando.pdf?sequence=2

Véstias, M. P., Duarte, R. P., de Sousa, J. T., & Neto, H. C. (2020). Moving deep learning to the edge. *Algorithms, 13*(5), 125. DOI: 10.3390/a13050125

Vida, K., Simon, J., & Lauscher, A. (2023). Values, ethics, morals? On the use of moral concepts in NLP research. *Findings of the Association for Computational Linguistics: EMNLP, 2023*, 5534–5554. DOI: 10.18653/v1/2023.findings-emnlp.368

Vieira, L. N. (2020). Machine translation in the news: A framing analysis of the written press. *Translation Spaces, 9*(1), 98–122. DOI: 10.1075/ts.00023.nun

Vieira, L. N., O'Hagan, M., & O'Sullivan, C. (2021). Understanding the societal impacts of machine translation: A critical review of the literature on medical and legal use cases. *Information Communication and Society, 24*(11), 1515–1532. DOI: 10.1080/1369118X.2020.1776370

Vieira, L. N., O'Sullivan, C., Zhang, X., & O'Hagan, M. (2022). Machine translation in society: Insights from UK users. *Language Resources and Evaluation*. Advance online publication. DOI: 10.1007/s10579-022-09589-1

Vilnius University. (2024). Dirbtinio intelekto naudojimo Vilniaus universitete gairės. Retrieved from: chrome-extension://efaidnbmnnnibpcajpcglclefindmkaj/https://www.vu.lt/site_files/SPN-54_2024_priedas.pdf

Voita, E., Serdyukov, P., Sennrich, R., & Titov, I. (2019). Context-aware neural machine translation learns anaphora resolution. *Proceedings of the 57th Annual Meeting of the Association for Computational Linguistics*, 1264-1274.

Von, V. (2008). *Towards an integrated translation approach: Proposal of a dynamic translation model (DTM)* [PhD dissertation]. der Universität Hamburg.

Wagner, G., Lukyanenko, R., & Paré, G. (2022). Artificial intelligence and the conduct of literature reviews. *Journal of Information Technology*, *37*(2), 209–226. DOI: 10.1177/02683962211048201

Wang, C., Zhang, J., Lassi, N., & Zhang, X. (2022). Privacy protection in using artificial intelligence for healthcare: Chinese regulation in comparative perspective. Healthcare. https://doi.org/ mdpi.comDOI: 10.3390/healthcare10101878

Wang, D. (2017, April,22).World Book Day: China's online fantasy novels earn fans abroad. *CGTN*.https://news.cgtn.com/news/3d456a4d33557a4d/index.html

Wang, H., Wu, H., He, Z., Huang, L., & Church, K. W. (2022). Progress in machine translation. Engineering. https://doi.org/sciencedirect.comDOI: 10.1016/j.eng.2021.03.023

Wang, L. (2023). Applying automated machine translation to educational video courses. *Education and Information Technologies*, *29*(9), 10377–10390. DOI: 10.1007/s10639-023-12219-0

Wang, L., & Wang, S. (2013). A Study of Idiom Translation Strategies between English and Chinese. *Theory and Practice in Language Studies*, *3*(9). Advance online publication. DOI: 10.4304/tpls.3.9.1691-1697

Wang, N., & Li, M. (2024). Teachers' perceptions of the risks and benefits of AI in higher education: A case study of ERNIE Bot. *Innovations in Education and Teaching International*, •••, 1–13. DOI: 10.1080/14703297.2024.2432429

Wang, S., & Luo, H. (2021). Exploring the meanings and grammatical functions of idioms in teaching Chinese as a second language. [HTML]. *International Journal of Applied Linguistics*, *31*(2), 283–300. Advance online publication. DOI: 10.1111/ijal.12334

Wang, Y. (2023). Artificial Intelligence Technologies in College English Translation Teaching. *Journal of Psycholinguistic Research*, *52*(5), 1525–1544. DOI: 10.1007/s10936-023-09960-5 PMID: 37100967

Wang, Y. (2024). The impact of technology on human translators and translation quality: A study on machine translation and computer-assisted translation tools. *English Linguistics Research*, *13*(1), 19. DOI: 10.5430/elr.v13n1p19

Wang, Y. (2024). Translating Four-Character Structures in Chinese Literary Works on Traditional Architecture—A Case Analysis of Canal Towns South of the Yangtze and Folk Houses South of the Yangtze. *Theory and Practice in Language Studies, 14*(10), 3221–3229. DOI: 10.17507/tpls.1410.25

Wang, Y. H., & Lin, G. Y. (2023). Exploring AI-healthcare innovation: Natural language processing-based patents analysis for technology-driven roadmapping. [HTML]. *Kybernetes, 52*(4), 1173–1189. Advance online publication. DOI: 10.1108/K-03-2021-0170

Wan, X., Zhang, Y., & Liu, J. (2022). Challenges and Solutions in Neural Machine Translation for Short Texts. *Computational Linguistics, 48*(2), 321–342. DOI: 10.1162/coli_a_00435

Way With Words. (2024). What is the future of AI translation? The future of AI in language translation and interpretation explained. https://waywithwords.net/resource/future-ai-translation-and-interpretation/

Weber-Lewerenz, B. (2021). … digital responsibility (CDR) in construction engineering—ethical guidelines for the application of digital transformation and artificial intelligence (AI) in user practice. SN Applied Sciences. https://doi.org/springer.comDOI: 10.1007/s42452-021-04776-1

Weerasekara, S., Lu, Z., Ozek, B., Isaacs, J., & Kamarthi, S. (2022). Trends in adopting industry 4.0 for asset life cycle management for sustainability: A keyword co-occurrence network review and analysis. *Sustainability (Basel), 14*(19), 12233. DOI: 10.3390/su141912233

Wei, X. (2024). The Use of Large Language Models for Translating Buddhist Texts from Classical Chinese to Modern English: An Analysis and Evaluation with ChatGPT 4, ERNIE Bot 4, and Gemini Advanced. *Religions, 15*(12), 1559. DOI: 10.3390/rel15121559

Wilkens, K. (2020). DeepL's role in revolutionizing the translation industry. *Translation Journal.* https://translationjournal.net/DeepL_revolution_translation

Williamson, S. M. & Prybutok, V. (2024). Balancing privacy and progress: a review of privacy challenges, systemic oversight, and patient perceptions in AI-driven healthcare. Applied Sciences. https://doi.org/ mdpi.comDOI: 10.3390/app14020675

Wireless World, R. F. (2023). Text-to-Speech technology in language learning. *RF Wireless World.* Retrieved from https://rfwirelessworld.com

Woo, J. H., & Choi, H. (2021). Systematic Review for AI-based Language Learning Tools. In Journal of Digital Contents Society (Vol. 22, Issue 11, p. 1783). Digital Contents Society. https://doi.org/DOI: 10.9728/dcs.2021.22.11.1783

Wu, Y., Schuster, M., Chen, Z., Le, Q. V., Norouzi, M., Macherey, W., . . . Dean, J. (2016). Google's neural machine translation system: Bridging the gap between human and machine translation. *arXiv preprint arXiv:1609.08144*. https://arxiv.org/abs/1609.08144

Wu, Y., Schuster, M., Chen, Z., Le, Q. V., Norouzi, M., Macherey, W., Krikun, M., Cao, Y., Gao, Q., Macherey, K., Klingner, J., Shah, A., Johnson, M., & Liu, X. Łukasz Kaiser, Gouws, S., Kato, Y., Kudo, T., Kazawa, H., … & Dean, J. (2016). Google's neural machine translation system: Bridging the gap between human and machine translation. *arXiv preprint arXiv:1609.08144.*

Wu, Y., Schuster, M., Chen, Z., Le, Q. V., Norouzi, M., Macherey, W., Krikun, M., Cao, Y., Gao, Q., Macherey, K., Klingner, J., Shah, A., Johnson, M., Liu, X., Kaiser, Ł., Gouws, S., Kato, Y., Kudo, T., Kazawa, H., . . . Dean, J. (2016). *Google's neural machine translation system: Bridging the gap between human and machine translation* (No. arXiv:1609.08144). arXiv. http://arxiv.org/abs/1609.08144

Wu, D., Wang, M., & Li, X. (2022). Automatic Scoring for Translations Based on Language Models. *Computational Intelligence and Neuroscience*, *2022*, 1–10. DOI: 10.1155/2022/2171206 PMID: 35800703

Wu, M. X., & Chen, H. J. (2023). Ethical issues of machine translation in the age of artificial intelligence. *Waiguoyu*, *7*(4), 80–89.

Wu, X., Xiao, L., Sun, Y., Zhang, J., Ma, T., & He, L. (2022). A survey of human-in-the-loop for machine learning. *Future Generation Computer Systems*, *135*, 364–381. DOI: 10.1016/j.future.2022.05.014

Wu, Y., & Gu, Y. q. (2019). : [Chinese Internet literature in the English-speaking world: Web-based writing, translation and dissemination]. *Comparative Literature in China*, (03), 66–79.

Wu, Y., Nouri, J., Li, X., Weegar, R., Afzaal, M., & Zia, A. (2021). Catching Group Criteria Semantic Information When Forming Collaborative Learning Groups. In *Technology-Enhanced Learning for a Free, Safe, and Sustainable World: 16th European Conference on Technology Enhanced Learning, EC-TEL 2021, Bolzano, Italy, September 20-24, 2021* [Springer International Publishing.]. *Proceedings*, *16*, 16–27.

Xiang, C. (2024). Study on the effectiveness of ChatGPT in translating forestry sci-tech texts. *International Journal of Linguistics. Literature & Translation*, *7*(9), 88–94. DOI: 10.32996/ijllt.2024.7.9.11

Xiao, L. (2023). The Use of Translation Strategy and Translation Methods in Tourism Texts under the Guidance of Peter Newmark's Translation Theory: A Case Study of Everglades National Park, Florida. *Educalitra: English Education, Linguistics, and Literature Journal*, *2*(2), 52–63.

Xie, T., Rong, Y., Zhang, P., & Liu, L. (2024). Towards controllable speech synthesis in the era of large language models: A survey. *arXiv*. Retrieved from https://arxiv.org/abs/2412.06602

Xinfei, L. (2024). A study on film subtitle translation from the perspective of skopos theory: A casestudy of kung fu panda. *Lecture Notes on Language and Literature*, *7*(1), 168–176.

Xing, Z., Zhao, S., Guo, W., Guo, X., Wang, S., Li, M., Wang, Y., & He, H. (2023). Analyzing point cloud of coal mining process in much dust environment based on dynamic graph convolution neural network. *Environmental Science and Pollution Research International*, *30*(2), 4044–4061. DOI: 10.1007/s11356-022-22490-2 PMID: 35963970

Xing, Z., Zhao, S., Guo, W., Guo, X., Wang, Y., Bai, Y., Zhu, S., & He, H. (2022). Identifying balls feature in a large-scale laser point cloud of a coal mining environment by a multiscale dynamic graph convolution neural network. *ACS Omega*, *7*(6), 4892–4907. DOI: 10.1021/acsomega.1c05473 PMID: 35187309

Xivuri, K. & Twinomurinzi, H. (2023). How AI developers can assure algorithmic fairness. Discover Artificial Intelligence. https://doi.org/springer.comDOI: 10.1007/s44163-023-00074-4

Xu, X., & Cai, H. (2021). Ontology and rule-based natural language processing approach for interpreting textual regulations on underground utility infrastructure. [HTML]. *Advanced Engineering Informatics*, *48*, 101288. Advance online publication. DOI: 10.1016/j.aei.2021.101288

Xu, Y., Zheng, X., Li, Y., Ye, X., Cheng, H., Wang, H., & Lyu, J. (2023). Exploring patient medication adherence and data mining methods in clinical big data: A contemporary review. *Journal of Evidence-Based Medicine*, *16*(3), 342–375. Advance online publication. DOI: 10.1111/jebm.12548 PMID: 37718729

Yang, Y. (2021, March,12). Chinese web novels and their TV spinoffs find welcoming audience abroad. *CGTN*.https://news.cgtn.com/news/2021-03-12/Chinese-web-novels-and-their-TV-spinoffs-find-audience-abroad-YzzUghnsB2/index.html

Yang, C. (2010). Cultural differences on Chinese and English idioms of diet and the translation. *English Language Teaching*, *3*(1). Advance online publication. DOI: 10.5539/elt.v3n1p148

Yang, H., & Kyun, S. (2022). The current research trend of artificial intelligence in language learning: A systematic empirical literature review from an activity theory perspective. *Australasian Journal of Educational Technology*, •••, 180–210. DOI: 10.14742/ajet.7492

Yao, S., & Wan, X. (2020). Multimodal transformer for multimodal machine translation. *Proceedings of the 58th Annual Meeting of the Association for Computational Linguistics*, 4346–4350. https://aclanthology.org/2020.acl-main.400/

Yazdi, M., Zarei, E., Adumene, S., & Beheshti, A. (2024). Navigating the power of artificial intelligence in risk management: A comparative analysis. *Safety (Basel, Switzerland)*, *10*(2), 42. DOI: 10.3390/safety10020042

Yermilov, O., Raheja, V., & Chernodub, A. (2023). Privacy- and utility-preserving NLP with anonymized data: A case study of pseudonymization. *Proceedings of the 3rd Workshop on Trustworthy Natural Language Processing (TrustNLP 2023)*. DOI: 10.18653/v1/2023.trustnlp-1.20

Yu, Y., Zhuang, Y., Zhang, J., Meng, Y., Ratner, A. J., Krishna, R., . . . Zhang, C. (2024). Large language model as attributed training data generator: A tale of diversity and bias. Advances in Neural Information Processing Systems, 36. neurips.cc

Yu, J., & Liu, K. (2024). Reshaping Translation Studies: Paradigm Shifts and Future Directions in the Age of AI Technology. *Waiguoyu*, *47*(4), 72–81.

Yulianto, A., & Supriatnaningsih, R. (2021). Google translate vs. DeepL: A quantitative evaluation of close-language pair translation (french to english). *Ajelp: Asian Journal of English Language and Pedagogy*, *9*(2), 2. Advance online publication. DOI: 10.37134/ajelp.vol9.2.9.2021

Yun, H. (2021). A Study of Idiom Translation in Bonsall's The Red Chamber Dream. *Contemporary Social Science*, *2021*(6), 114–123. DOI: 10.19873/j.cnki.2096-0212.2021.06.008

Zafar, A. (2024). Balancing the scale: navigating ethical and practical challenges of artificial intelligence (AI) integration in legal practices. Discover Artificial Intelligence. https://doi.org/ springer.comDOI: 10.1007/s44163-024-00121-8

Zaghlool, Z. D. M., & Khasawneh, M. A. S. (2024). Aligning translation curricula with technological advancements; Insights from artificial intelligence researchers and language educators. *Studies in Media and Communication*, *12*(1), 58–70. DOI: 10.11114/smc.v12i1.6378

Zalasiewicz, J., Waters, C. N., Ellis, E. C., Head, M. J., Vidas, D., Steffen, W., ... & Zinke, J. (2021). The Anthropocene: Comparing its meaning in geology (chronostratigraphy) with conceptual approaches arising in other disciplines. https://doi.org/ wiley.comDOI: 10.1029/2020EF001896

Zayed, M. H. T., & Nuirat, W. (2024). Human touch in AI translation: Strategies employed by professional translators in post-editing Arabic-English AI generated translations of media texts. *Educational Administration: Theory And Practice*, *30*(4), 2055–2062. DOI: 10.53555/kuey.v30i4.1804

Zhai, C., Wibowo, S., & Li, L. D. (2024). Evaluating the AI dialogue System's intercultural, humorous, and empathetic dimensions in English language learning: A case study. Computers and Education: Artificial Intelligence. https://doi.org/ sciencedirect.comDOI: 10.1016/j.caeai.2024.100262

Zhang, Y., Zhou, D., Hooi, B., Wang, K., & Feng, J. (2023). Expanding small-scale datasets with guided imagination. Advances in neural information processing systems, 36, 76558-76618. neurips.cc

Zhang, Q., & Wang, J. (2010). Application of Functional Equivalence Theory in English translation of Chinese idioms. *Journal of Language Teaching and Research*, *1*(6). Advance online publication. DOI: 10.4304/jltr.1.6.880-888

Zhang, S., Liu, Y., Xiong, D., Zhang, P., & Chen, B. (2021). Domain-aware self-attention for multi-domain neural machine translation. *Interspeech*, *2047–2051*, 2047–2051. Advance online publication. DOI: 10.21437/Interspeech.2021-1477

Zhang, W., & Xia, Y. (2024). A deep semantic learning framework based on cultural features for English machine translation: Taking tea culture as an example. *Pakistan Journal of Agricultural Sciences*, *61*(3), 971–981. DOI: 10.21162/PAKJAS/24.327

Zhao, A. P., Li, S., Cao, Z., Hu, P. J. H., Wang, J., Xiang, Y., ... & Lu, X. (2024). AI for science: predicting infectious diseases. Journal of Safety Science and Resilience. https://doi.org/sciencedirect.comDOI: 10.1016/j.jnlssr.2024.02.002

Zhao, D. (2024). The impact of AI-enhanced natural language processing tools on writing proficiency: An analysis of language precision, content summarization, and creative writing.... [HTML]. *Education and Information Technologies*. Advance online publication. DOI: 10.1007/s10639-024-13145-5

Zhao, X., & Jin, X. (2022). A comparative study of text genres in English-Chinese translation effects based on deep learning LSTM. *Journal of Chinese Linguistics, 50*(3), 287–304. DOI: 10.1177/00754242221100001 PMID: 35693269

Zhou, W. (2022). Diplomatic interpreting and risk analysis: A literary survey. International Journal of Translation and Interpretation Studies, 2(2), 19-31. DOI: al-kindipublisher.comDOI: 10.32996/ijtis

Zhu, G. (2022, January). Fast translation method of complex English sentences based on artificial intelligence technology. In 2022 14th International Conference on Measuring Technology and Mechatronics Automation (ICMTMA) (pp. 638-642). IEEE.

Zingoni, A., Taborri, J., Panetti, V., Bonechi, S., Aparicio-Martínez, P., Pinzi, S., & Calabrò, G. (2021). Investigating issues and needs of dyslexic students at university: Proof of concept of an artificial intelligence and virtual reality-based supporting platform and preliminary results. *Applied Sciences (Basel, Switzerland), 11*(10), 4624. DOI: 10.3390/app11104624

Zong, J. H. (2024). —— [Internet Fantasy Fiction External Communication Status and Path Exploration-- Take "Fighting To Break The Sky" as an Example]. *ETR, 2*(10), 41–43. DOI: 10.61369/ETR.7403

Zou, R., Chang, W., Gao, S., & Qin, S. (2022). Strategies for improving the quality of computer-assisted translation based on internet. In International Journal of Advanced Academic Studies (Vol. 4, Issue 4, p. 156). https://doi.org/DOI: 10.33545/27068919.2022.v4.i4c.890

Zuo, C. (2024). The Influence of Literary Translation in Drama and Film Works. *Scientific and social research*, 6(6):66-72. DOI: 10.26689/ssr.v6i6.7172

- . (n.d.). Rekhta. https://www.rekhta.org/nazms/subh-e-aazaadii-august-47-ye-daag-daag-ujaalaa-ye-shab-gaziida-sahar-faiz-ahmad-faiz-nazms?lang=hi

About The Contributors

Mohammed H. Alaqad is an Associate Professor of Translation at Israa University, Gaza, and a Postdoctoral Research Fellow at the Hashim Sani Centre for Palestine Studies, University of Malaya. He is a highly experienced conference interpreter with over 15 years of professional practice, specializing in translation, interpreting studies, and applied linguistics. With more than a decade of academic experience, Dr. Alaqad has presented at over 50 international conferences and has an extensive publication record in his fields of expertise. He serves on the editorial boards of several peer-reviewed journals and is the founder and CEO of the Asian Federation of Translators and Interpreters (AFTI), based in Malaysia. His current research interests include applied linguistics, translation and interpreting studies, educational technology, and Palestine studies.

***

Ahmed Aboeisheh is Assistant Professor of Human Resources Management, teaching courses in HR and management for undergraduate and postgraduate studies. He is the Coordinator of postgraduate programs and the author of several research papers and articles.

Mohammad Ali Abdellah Al-Saggaf is an Assistant Professor at the Department of English Language & Literature, Xiamen University Malaysia. He earned his Ph.D. in English Language Studies (Linguistics) from Universiti Kebangsaan Malaysia (UKM). With over 13 years of experience in teaching and research, Dr. Al-Saggaf has served as an EFL/ESL senior lecturer, researcher, and curriculum developer in Yemen and Malaysia. Dr. Al-Saggaf has published and presented research papers on topics such as Applied & Sociolinguistics, Cognitive and Corpus Linguistics, TESL, and Education in several prestigious journals, including the International Journal of Linguistics and Translation Studies, Pedagogical Research, and TESOL and Technology Studies. He is a certified trainer and expert in Outcome Based Education (OBE) and has extensive experience in supervising final year projects and theses, teaching Research Methodologies, and mentoring young researchers. He is a member of several professional organizations, including the Malaysian Association of Applied Linguistics (MAAL), the Malaysian English Language Teachers Association (MELTA), and the Asian Federation of Translators and Interpreters (AFTI). Dr. Al-Saggaf is also actively involved in various academic and professional activities, such as organizing conferences, training workshops, and serving on editorial boards. ORCID: 0000-0001-7401-0509

Amin Amirdabbaghian is a Senior Lecturer in Translation and Interpreting Studies at the Faculty of Languages and Linguistics, Univeriti Malaya. His main areas of research interest include socio-ideological aspects of translation, literary translation and audiovisual translation.

Andi Asrifan is an accomplished educator and academic leader with a Doctorate in Education, specializing in English Language Education from Universitas Negeri Makassar. With a strong academic foundation, he holds a Master's degree in the same field and a Bachelor's degree in Secondary Education. His dissertation focused on developing bilingual educational materials, reflecting his commitment to enhancing language education. Dr. Asrifan has extensive experience in various educational roles, including serving as the Head of the International Affairs Office at Politeknik Negeri Nunukan and as the Head of the Institute for Student Development and Alumni at Universitas Muhammadiyah Sidenreng Rappang. He is also an active member of several professional organizations, including the Linguistics Society of Indonesia and TEFLIN. In addition to his administrative roles, Dr. Asrifan is a passionate advocate for educational innovation and has participated in numerous international conferences and webinars, sharing his insights on language teaching and curriculum development. His dedication to professional development is evident through his participation in various training programs.

Raed Awashreh is an Assistant Professor of Management at A'Sharqiyah University in Ibra, Oman. He brings over 20 years of combined academic and industry experience, teaching undergraduate and postgraduate courses. Dr. Awashreh has authored 50 articles, several chapters, and 3 books spanning topics such as, human resources, governance, public policy, strategy, leadership, and management. In addition to his academic role, Dr. Awashreh serves as a consultant in business, management, governance, HR, and organizational development, working closely with government, private, and non-governmental sectors. He earned his degrees in

Public Administration and Management from Flinders University, Australia, and Monterey, USA.

Priyanka Bisht is a doctoral candidate in the Department of English and Cultural Studies at Christ University, Delhi NCR, specializing in Partition Literature, Migration Studies, Violence Studies and Trauma Theory. Her research interests extend beyond traditional literary analysis to encompass the emerging fields of Artificial Intelligence (AI) and Virtual Reality (VR). Bisht is particularly interested in exploring the intersection of these technologies with literature, history, and pedagogy. She has also published extensively in these fields.

Rui Fan is a lecturer at Guangdong University of Education and a research assistant at the Halliday Center for Intelligent Applications of Language Studies of City University of Hong Kong. Her research interests are corpus linguistics, cross-cultural studies in translation, and discourse analysis. Her translation work on knowledge transmission across East and Chinese cultures in late 19th century was published in 2024.

Mahi M. Hkikmat, M.Si., is a prominent academic and expert in the field of communication, with a special focus on media law, political communication, and the ethics of mass media. He holds a Doctorate in Communication and has an extensive background in journalism, having served in roles such as a provincial commissioner for both the Information Commission and the Indonesian Broadcasting Commission (KPI). His work covers various aspects of media ethics, including the laws governing mass media, broadcast media, and new media platforms. Dr. Hkikmat has published several influential books and articles, including topics on journalism ethics and political communication. He is affiliated with Universitas Islam Negeri Sunan Gunung Djati Bandung, where he contributes to the academic field through both teaching and research. His correlation in this call for book chapter is his expertise in writing texts related to Communication.

Jolita Horbačauskienė is a Professor at the Faculty of Social Sciences, Arts and Humanities, and the Principal Investigator of the Educational Studies research group at KTU. She teaches a range of subjects related to methodologies and research methods in education. Jolita is experienced in planning, designing, development, delivery, and improvement in teaching and learning activities at all levels of education.

Syazwan Naim Ibrahim is a lecturer at Department of Arabic Language and Middle Eastern Languages, Faculty of Languages and Linguistics, Universiti Malaya, Malaysia. He attained his bachelor's degree in Arabic Language and Linguistics from Cadi Ayyad University, Morocco, in 2019 and was awarded the Best Student title. Subsequently, he pursued a Master of Arts (Linguistics) at Universiti Malaya focusing on the pragmatics of implicature in the Quran. He is currently a Doctor of Philosophy (PhD) candidate at Universiti Sains Malaysia, specialising in interpreting studies. His research explores how interpreters manage (im)politeness in Arabic-English simultaneous interpreting, examining shifts in (im)politeness strategies under cognitive constraints. Grounded in pragmatics and interpreting studies theories, his work sheds light on the interplay between linguistic (im)politeness, cross-cultural mediation, and the real-time cognitive demands of interpreting. He has taught many undergraduate level courses and is always interested in developing Arabic language mastery among students, especially in writing and speaking skills. He welcomes insights most notably from language service providers and other stakeholders in the translation and interpreting industry, to conduct research projects related to translation and interpreting ethics and practices, translator and interpreter training, as well as discourse in translation and interpreting. Furthermore, he is a certified translator at the Institut Terjemahan & Buku Malaysia/Malaysian Institute of Translation & Books (ITBM) and has done a great deal of translating, editing, and proofreading of theses, books, and articles.

Tawffeek A. S. Mohammed is an Associate Professor of Applied Linguistics and Translation Studies in the Department of Foreign Languages, Faculty of Arts and Humanities, at the University of the Western Cape, South Africa. His research interests span a broad interdisciplinary spectrum situated at the nexus of linguistics, language pedagogy, media studies, critical discourse analysis (CDA), translation and interpreting studies, computer-aided translation technology, computer-assisted language learning (CALL), and mobile-assisted language learning (MALL). His research focuses specifically on areas such as computer-assisted language learning, computer-assisted translation, computer-assisted interpreting, localization, corpus linguistics and digital humanities, especially in response to emerging trends and developments in the language and translation industries. He is the recipient of several academic distinctions, most notably the Mellon Professoriate Award for the 2024–2025 academic year.

Jyoti Prakash Pujari is an Assistant Professor from the Department of English and Cultural Studies, Christ University, Delhi NCR Campus, India. His research interests involve intellectual history, postcolonial studies, and unusual women of the Raj. His Ph.D. was on colonial encounters of the English Memsahibs in an Indian setting and setting up their own literary canon. He is a former JNMF scholar and currently teaches American and World Literature.

Milda Ratkevičienė has a long experience in higher education, both as a practitioner and as a researcher. Currently, Milda Ratkevičienė works as an Assistant Professor at Kaunas University of Technology. She has more than ten years of experience in study programs quality assurance. She is working on topics of bi-and multilingual disciplinary literacies across educational levels addressing developmental trajectories of learner groups, focusing on the transition across educational levels (primary-secondary-tertiary education); research-oriented teachers' education and support pre-and in-service teachers in the teaching/learning process.

Andang Saehu, M.Pd., CHS, is a distinguished expert in translation, interpreting, language assessment, and education. He is a tenured lecturer at UIN Sunan Gunung Djati Bandung, where he currently heads the English Literature program in the Faculty of Adab and Humanities. In addition to his academic leadership, Dr. Andang serves as a Chairperson for the AUN-QA assessment of the English Literature department. He is also an assessor for the National Professional Certification Board (BNSP) and earned his certification in Humanities Studies from the International Board of Standards in 2021. His research, accessible on Google Scholar, reflects his broad expertise. He has authored two notable books: Interpreting: Teori dan Praktik (2019) and Penerjemahan Karya Sastra: Teori dan Praktik (2022), solidifying his reputation in the field of translation and interpreting.

Yue Zhang is an Assistant Professor in Department of English Language Education, The Education University of Hong Kong. She earned her M.Phil. and Ph.D. in Applied English Linguistics at The Chinese University of Hong Kong. Her research interests include informal digital learning of English, L2 motivation, identity, and investment, language teacher education, and critical inquiries and pedagogy. She has published in Computer Assisted Language Learning, TESOL Quarterly, ReCALL, Language Awareness, System, and Journal of Multilingual and Multicultural Development.

Index

A

B

C

D

E

F

G

Q

R

S

T

www.ingramcontent.com/pod-product-compliance
Lightning Source LLC
LaVergne TN
LVHW080609300926
849162LV00005B/1099
* 9 7 9 8 3 3 7 3 0 0 6 0 3 *